MAJOR MODERN ESSAYISTS

edited by

Gilbert H. Muller

The City University of New York
LaGuardia

A BLAIR PRESS BOOK

PRENTICE HALL, Englewood Cliffs, NJ 07632

Library of Congress Cataloging-in-Publication Data

Major modern essayists / [compiled by] Gilbert H. Muller.
    p.   cm.
   ISBN 0-13-546854-X
   1. English essays--20th century. 2. American essays--20th
century.   I. Muller, Gilbert H.
PR1367.M345 1991
824'.9108--dc20   90-35410
                                                      CIP

Editorial/production supervision and interior design: Jan Stephan
Cover design: Maureen Eide
Prepress buyer: Herb Klein
Manufacturing buyer: Dave Dickey
Photo Editor: Lorinda Morris-Nantz
Photo Research: Sonia Meyer and Barbara Schultz

Cover Art:
Painting, French, 20th Century
Laurencin, Marie   1883–1956
GROUP OF ARTISTS   1908
Oil on canvas; 25½"×31⅞" (64.8×81 cm.)
The Baltimore Museum of Art:
The Cone Collection, formed by Dr. Claribel Cone and Miss Etta Cone of
   Baltimore, Maryland
BMA 1950.215

Acknowledgements appear on pages 467–469, which constitute a continuation of
the copyright page.

Blair Press
160 Gould Street
Needham Heights, MA 02194-2310

 © 1991 by Prentice-Hall, Inc.
A Division of Simon & Schuster
Englewood Cliffs, New Jersey 07632

Printed in the United States of America
10 9 8 7 6 5 4 3 2 1

ISBN 0-13-546854-X

Prentice-Hall International (UK) Limited, *London*
Prentice-Hall of Australia Pty. Limited, *Sydney*
Prentice-Hall Canada Inc., *Toronto*
Prentice-Hall Hispanoamericana, S.A., *Mexico*
Prentice-Hall of India Private Limited, *New Delhi*
Prentice-Hall of Japan, Inc., *Tokyo*
Simon & Schuster Asia Pte. Ltd., *Singapore*
Editora Prentice-Hall do Brasil, Ltda., *Rio de Janeiro*

Again
for
Laleh

Preface

Major Modern Essayists provides composition instructors with in-depth introductions to twenty of this century's most distinctive writers of nonfiction prose in the English language. The collection, featuring ten women and ten men, is arranged chronologically from Virginia Woolf to Annie Dillard; it is balanced, diversified, and culturally rich, with authors drawn from several points on our global compass—Great Britain, the United States, Canada, Denmark, Africa—and from several backgrounds. Their work offers students outstanding models for the reciprocal activities of critical reading, thinking, and writing.

By limiting the collection to a small number of outstanding writers, I have been able to provide three to five complete prose models by each. The value of offering multiple essays by major writers lies in the enhanced opportunity for students to perceive authors working in a variety of voices, rhetorical modes, and prose forms. E. B. White, who occupies a notable part of the landscape in this anthology, spoke of the contemporary essayist as a quick-change artist—a "philosopher, scold, jester, raconteur, pundit, devil's advocate, enthusiast." Great essayists are chameleons, and students can profit from seeing them in their full range of guises.

An added value for students intensively studying major essayists lies in the illustration it provides them of how authorial visions and styles evolve in response to cultural contexts—and how these visions interconnect. Great essays are not mere expressions of individual sensibility, even when the personal voices behind them are most exquisite. A moth, a turtle, the sea, and the wind that blows: For the writers in this collection, these things radiate outward into the

diverse social landscape of the twentieth century. That landscape can be daunting, as when Orwell writes about a hanging in Burma, Baldwin about his
childhood in Harlem, Kingston about conflicts in her Chinese-American family,
or Selzer about AIDS in Haiti. Nevertheless, the visions of these authors tend
to be affirmative. In their essays, they celebrate life even as they stand in
opposition to those forces that threaten our human estate.

Major Modern Essayists is based on the assumption that writing does not
exist in a formal or aesthetic vacuum—a fact that all students in college must
recognize if they are to become competent writers. Essays possessing high
standards of excellence should be understood both on their own terms and in
relation to each other and to the public pressures of the age. Typically, they
reflect what Virginia Woolf termed "some fierce attachment to an idea." Being
passionately committed to an idea is not a bad starting point for college writers,
and indeed Woolf's message serves as a rationale for the selections in this text.

The essayists in this collection range over so many subjects and so much
terrain that *Major Modern Essayists* can serve as a cross-disciplinary,
multicultural reader. Included are essays on education, ecology, history, politics,
sociology, geography, anthropology, literature, writing, film, philosophy,
religion, medicine, and more. Students should find compelling such lucid, powerful essays as those by Stephen Jay Gould on women's brains or Joan Didion
on morality, even as the content of these essays introduces them to those
disciplines that define their academic lives. The relevance and readability of
the essays in this anthology liberate students so that they can discover their
own best compositional subjects across cultures and various fields of knowledge.

Major Modern Essayists also liberates teachers, who can use the collection as they please, with utmost flexibility. Its progressive, pluralistic ethos is,
I would like to think, clear and shared by the professoriate. This collection
permits teachers to focus on first-rate prose by modern figures—and to develop
their own pedagogical approaches. The format enables teachers to develop
rhetorical, topical, thematic, and genre-based pedagogies common to so many
college readers. An alternate thematic table of contents and a rhetorical index
facilitate these varied approaches to the teaching of writing.

To help situate students in the convergence of critical reading, thinking,
and writing activities, a consistent apparatus has been established. Substantial
introductions appear for each essayist and are designed to place the writers in
their cultural and rhetorical contexts. All essays are followed by four categories
of questions: "Purpose and Meaning," "Language and Style," "Strategy and
Structure," "Thinking and Writing." These questions reflect current issues and
trends in composition theory; they promote thoughtful reading, creative and
logical dialogue, and lucid writing.

All anthologists, as E. B. White reminds us, compile collections largely
to please themselves. In this preface I have confessed to such idiosyncracies,
but I hope that I have also made clear my attempt to please you and your

students. Many of your favorite essayists and essays are here, complemented by a few lesser-known but equally outstanding examples. Ultimately *Major Modern Essayists* is sufficiently varied that you may not want to step into the text the same way twice. It offers manifold ways to share with students twenty authors and seventy essays that are worth reading, discussing, and writing about.

Acknowledgements

Major Modern Essayists evolved with rare serendipity, and I should like to acknowledge those individuals who made the project such a delight. I owe thanks first of all to my friend and agent John Wright, who recommended an editor who would be perfect for this anthology. That person was Nancy Perry, Publisher of Blair Press. I am greatly indebted to her. To Phil Miller, Editor-in-Chief at Prentice Hall; Kate Morgan, Development Editor; and Jan Stephan in the Editorial Production Department, I am indebted for encouragement and advice. Leslie Arndt, Assistant Editor at Blair Press, has been an avid fan of this text and a contributor to its final form. A distinguished group of reviewers helped to mold the anthology, and I trust that they will detect their influence on it as I express my appreciation for their fine advice: Paul T. Bryant, Radford University; Susanna Defever, St. Clair County Community College; David Espey, University of Pennsylvania; Phyllis Frus, Vanderbilt University; Elizabeth Larsen, West Chester University; Martha K. Minter, University of Nevada—Reno; Robert G. Noreen, California State University, Northridge; and Charles I. Schuster, University of Wisconsin—Milwaukee.

Finally I want to thank my assistants Danielle Hickney, Parisa Muller, and Alan Gerstle for their research, typing, and generous aid.

Gilbert H. Muller

Contents

VIRGINIA WOOLF   1

   Professions for Women   *4*
   The Death of the Moth   *9*
   Middlebrow   *12*

ISAK DINESEN   19

   The Oxen   *22*
   Some African Birds   *24*
   Old Knudsen   *28*

E. B. WHITE   35

   Farewell, My Lovely!   *38*
   Once More to the Lake   *44*
   Education   *50*
   The Ring of Time   *54*
   The Sea and the Wind That Blows   *61*

GEORGE ORWELL   67

A Hanging   69
Shooting an Elephant   73
Politics and the English Language   80
"The Moon under Water"   91
Why I Write   95

BARBARA TUCHMAN   103

The Historian as Artist   105
On Our Birthday—America as Idea   110
Humanity's Better Moments   113

LEWIS THOMAS   129

Computers   131
The Iks   134
Notes on Punctuation   137
*Late Night Thoughts on Listening
    to Mahler's Ninth Symphony   141*

DORIS LESSING   145

Being Prohibited   147
My Father   151
A Deep Darkness: A Review of Out of Africa
    by Karen Blixen   158

JAMES BALDWIN   165

Autobiographical Notes   168
*Fifth Avenue, Uptown: A Letter
    from Harlem   173*
*The Discovery of What It Means
    to Be an American   181*
*If Black English Isn't a Language,
    Then Tell Me, What Is?   187*

RUSSELL BAKER   191

The Flag   193
Growing Up   198
Let Them Play Guitars   205

RICHARD SELZER   209

Lessons from the Art   211
Bald!   218
A Mask on the Face of Death   222
The Pen and the Scalpel   233

MARTIN LUTHER KING, JR.   239

I Have a Dream   242
Letter from Birmingham City Jail   246
Where Do We Go from Here: Chaos or
*   Community?   260*

EDWARD HOAGLAND   267

The Courage of Turtles   269
Violence, Violence   275
What I Think, What I Am   278

JOAN DIDION   283

Marrying Absurd   285
On Self-Respect   288
On Morality   293
Why I Write   298
Miami   304

JOYCE CAROL OATES   309

The Profane Art   311
On Boxing   315
"State-of-the-Art Car": The Ferrari
*   Testarossa   318*

MARGARET ATWOOD   325

Travels Back   327
Great Unexpectations   332
Adrienne Rich: Poems, Selected and New   336

MAXINE HONG KINGSTON   341

No Name Woman   343
High School Reunion   353
The Wild Man of the Green Swamp   357

STEPHEN JAY GOULD   361

Women's Brains   363
A Biological Homage to Mickey Mouse   369
Evolution as Fact and Theory   379

RICHARD RODRIGUEZ   387

Complexion   389
Across the Borders of History   394
Children of a Marriage   410

ALICE WALKER   415

In Search of Our Mothers' Gardens   417
Am I Blue?   426
Father   431

ANNIE DILLARD   439

Untying the Knot   441
An American Childhood   445
Singing with the Fundamentalists   452
Push It   462

Acknowledgements   467

Rhetorical Index   470

Alternate Thematic
Contents

CHILDHOOD AND FAMILY

E. B. WHITE   *Once More to the Lake*   44

E. B. WHITE   *Education*   50

DORIS LESSING   *My Father*   151

JAMES BALDWIN   *Autobiographical Notes*   168

RUSSELL BAKER   *Growing Up*   198

JOAN DIDION   *Marrying Absurd*   285

MAXINE HONG KINGSTON   *No Name Woman*   343

RICHARD RODRIGUEZ   *Complexion*   389

ALICE WALKER   *Father*   431

ANNIE DILLARD   *An American Childhood*   445

CULTURE AND SOCIETY

VIRGINIA WOOLF   *Professions for Women*   4

VIRGINIA WOOLF   *Middlebrow*   12

ISAK DINESEN   *Old Knudsen*   28

E. B. WHITE   *Education*   50

E. B. WHITE   *The Ring of Time*   54

GEORGE ORWELL   *A Hanging*   69

GEORGE ORWELL   *Shooting an Elephant*   73

GEORGE ORWELL   *"The Moon under Water"*   91

LEWIS THOMAS   *Computers*   *131*

LEWIS THOMAS   *The Iks*   *134*

JAMES BALDWIN   *Fifth Avenue, Uptown: A Letter from Harlem*   *173*

JAMES BALDWIN   *The Discovery of What It Means to Be an American*   *181*

RUSSELL BAKER   *The Flag*   *193*

RICHARD SELZER   *A Mask on the Face of Death*   *222*

EDWARD HOAGLAND   *Violence, Violence*   *275*

JOAN DIDION   *Marrying Absurd*   *285*

JOAN DIDION   *On Morality*   *293*

JOYCE CAROL OATES   *On Boxing*   *315*

JOYCE CAROL OATES   *"State-of-the-Art Car": The Ferrari Testarossa*   *318*

MAXINE HONG KINGSTON   *No Name Woman*   *343*

MAXINE HONG KINGSTON   *The Wild Man of the Green Swamp*   *357*

RICHARD RODRIGUEZ   *Complexion*   *389*

RICHARD RODRIGUEZ   *Across the Borders of History*   *394*

RICHARD RODRIGUEZ   *Children of Marriage*   *410*

ALICE WALKER   *In Search of Our Mothers' Gardens*   *417*

ETHICS AND RELIGION

VIRGINIA WOOLF   *The Death of the Moth*   *9*

GEORGE ORWELL   *A Hanging*   *69*

GEORGE ORWELL   *Shooting an Elephant*   *73*

LEWIS THOMAS   *The Iks*   *134*

RICHARD SELZER   *Lessons from the Art*   *211*

RICHARD SELZER   *A Mask on the Face of Death*   *222*

MARTIN LUTHER KING, JR.   *I Have a Dream*   *242*

MARTIN LUTHER KING, JR.   *Letter from Birmingham City Jail*   *246*

MARTIN LUTHER KING, JR.   *Where Do We Go from Here: Chaos or Community?*   *260*

JOAN DIDION   *On Self-Respect*   *288*

JOAN DIDION   *On Morality*   *293*

JOYCE CAROL OATES   *The Profane Art*   *311*

ANNIE DILLARD   *Untying the Knot*   *441*

ANNIE DILLARD   *Singing with the Fundamentalists*   *452*

HISTORY AND POLITICS

VIRGINIA WOOLF   *Middlebrow*   12

GEORGE ORWELL   *A Hanging*   69

GEORGE ORWELL   *Shooting an Elephant*   73

GEORGE ORWELL   *Politics and the English Language*   80

BARBARA TUCHMAN   *The Historian as Artist*   105

BARBARA TUCHMAN   *On Our Birthday—America as Idea*   110

BARBARA TUCHMAN   *Humanity's Better Moments*   113

LEWIS THOMAS   *The Iks*   134

LEWIS THOMAS   *Late Night Thoughts on Listening to Mahler's Ninth Symphony*   141

DORIS LESSING   *Being Prohibited*   147

JAMES BALDWIN   *Fifth Avenue, Uptown: A Letter from Harlem*   173

JAMES BALDWIN   *The Discovery of What It Means to Be an American*   181

JAMES BALDWIN   *If Black English Isn't a Language, Then Tell Me, What Is?*   187

MARTIN LUTHER KING, JR.   *I Have a Dream*   242

MARTIN LUTHER KING, JR.   *Letter from Birmingham City Jail*   246

MARTIN LUTHER KING, JR.   *Where Do We Go from Here: Chaos or Community?*   260

JOAN DIDION   *Miami*   304

JOYCE CAROL OATES   *The Profane Art*   311

STEPHEN JAY GOULD   *Evolution as Fact and Theory*   379

RICHARD RODRIGUEZ   *Across the Borders of History*   394

RICHARD RODRIGUEZ   *Children of Marriage*   410

HUMOR AND SATIRE

VIRGINIA WOOLF   *Middlebrow*   12

E. B. WHITE   *Farewell, My Lovely!*   38

E. B. WHITE   *Education*   50

GEORGE ORWELL   *Politics and the English Language*   80

LEWIS THOMAS   *Notes on Punctuation*   137

RUSSELL BAKER   *The Flag*   193

RUSSELL BAKER   *Growing Up*   198

RUSSELL BAKER   *Let Them Play Guitars*   205

RICHARD SELZER   *Bald!*   218

JOAN DIDION   *Marrying Absurd   285*

JOYCE CAROL OATES   *"State-of-the-Art Car": The Ferrari Testarossa   318*

MARGARET ATWOOD   *Great Unexpectations   332*

MAXINE HONG KINGSTON   *High School Reunion   353*

STEPHEN JAY GOULD   *Women's Brains   363*

STEPHEN JAY GOULD   *A Biological Homage to Mickey Mouse   369*

ANNIE DILLARD   *An American Childhood   445*

ANNIE DILLARD   *Singing with the Fundamentalists   452*

LANGUAGE AND LITERATURE

VIRGINIA WOOLF   *Professions for Women   4*

E. B. WHITE   *The Ring of Time   54*

GEORGE ORWELL   *Politics and the English Language   80*

GEORGE ORWELL   *Why I Write   95*

BARBARA TUCHMAN   *The Historian as Artist   105*

LEWIS THOMAS   *Notes on Punctuation   137*

DORIS LESSING   *A Deep Darkness: A Review of Out of Africa by Karen Blixen   158*

JAMES BALDWIN   *Autobiographical Notes   168*

JAMES BALDWIN   *If Black English Isn't a Language, Then Tell Me, What Is?   187*

RUSSELL BAKER   *Let Them Play Guitars   205*

RICHARD SELZER   *The Pen and the Scalpel   233*

EDWARD HOAGLAND   *What I Think, What I Am   278*

JOAN DIDION   *Why I Write   298*

JOYCE CAROL OATES   *The Profane Art   311*

MARGARET ATWOOD   *Travels Back   327*

MARGARET ATWOOD   *Great Unexpectations   332*

MARGARET ATWOOD   *Adrienne Rich: Poems, Selected and New   336*

ANNIE DILLARD   *An American Childhood   445*

ANNIE DILLARD   *Push It   462*

LEISURE AND SPORT

E. B. WHITE   *Farewell, My Lovely!   38*

E. B. WHITE   *The Ring of Time   54*

E. B. WHITE   *The Sea and the Wind That Blows   61*

GEORGE ORWELL   *"The Moon under Water"*   *91*

LEWIS THOMAS   *Late Night Thoughts on Listening to Mahler's Ninth Symphony*   *141*

EDWARD HOAGLAND   *Violence, Violence*   *275*

JOYCE CAROL OATES   *On Boxing*   *315*

JOYCE CAROL OATES   *"State-of-the-Art Car": The Ferrari Testarossa*   *318*

MAXINE HONG KINGSTON   *High School Reunion*   *353*

ALICE WALKER   *Am I Blue?*   *426*

THE MINORITY EXPERIENCE

GEORGE ORWELL   *A Hanging*   *69*

GEORGE ORWELL   *Shooting an Elephant*   *73*

DORIS LESSING   *Being Prohibited*   *147*

JAMES BALDWIN   *Autobiographical Notes*   *168*

JAMES BALDWIN   *Fifth Avenue, Uptown: A Letter from Harlem*   *173*

JAMES BALDWIN   *The Discovery of What It Means to Be an American*   *181*

JAMES BALDWIN   *If Black English Isn't a Language, Then Tell Me, What Is?*   *187*

RICHARD SELZER   *A Mask on the Face of Death*   *222*

MARTIN LUTHER KING, JR.   *I Have a Dream*   *242*

MARTIN LUTHER KING, JR.   *Letter from Birmingham City Jail*   *246*

JOAN DIDION   *Miami*   *304*

MAXINE HONG KINGSTON   *No Name Woman*   *343*

MAXINE HONG KINGSTON   *The Wild Man of the Green Swamp*   *357*

RICHARD RODRIGUEZ   *Complexion*   *389*

RICHARD RODRIGUEZ   *Across the Borders of History*   *394*

RICHARD RODRIGUEZ   *Children of a Marriage*   *410*

ALICE WALKER   *In Search of Our Mothers' Gardens*   *417*

ALICE WALKER   *Am I Blue?*   *426*

ALICE WALKER   *Father*   *431*

THE NATURAL WORLD

VIRGINIA WOOLF   *The Death of the Moth*   *9*

ISAK DINESEN   *The Oxen*   *22*

ISAK DINESEN   *Some African Birds*   *24*

E. B. WHITE   *Once More to the Lake*   44
E. B. WHITE   *The Sea and the Wind That Blows*   61
LEWIS THOMAS   *The Iks*   134
EDWARD HOAGLAND   *The Courage of Turtles*   269
ANNIE DILLARD   *Untying the Knot*   441

PERSONAL IDENTITY

VIRGINIA WOOLF   *Professions for Women*   4
VIRGINIA WOOLF   *Middlebrow*   12
ISAK DINESEN   *Old Knudsen*   28
E. B. WHITE   *Once More to the Lake*   44
E. B. WHITE   *The Sea and the Wind That Blows*   61
GEORGE ORWELL   *Why I Write*   95
DORIS LESSING   *Being Prohibited*   147
JAMES BALDWIN   *Autobiographical Notes*   168
JAMES BALDWIN   *The Discovery of What It Means to Be an American*   181
RUSSELL BAKER   *Growing Up*   198
RICHARD SELZER   *Bald!*   218
RICHARD SELZER   *The Pen and the Scalpel*   233
EDWARD HOAGLAND   *What I Think, What I Am*   278
JOAN DIDION   *Why I Write*   278
JOAN DIDION   *On Self-Respect*   288
MARGARET ATWOOD   *Travels Back*   327
MARGARET ATWOOD   *Great Unexpectations*   332
MAXINE HONG KINGSTON   *No Name Woman*   343
MAXINE HONG KINGSTON   *High School Reunion*   353
RICHARD RODRIGUEZ   *Complexion*   389
ALICE WALKER   *Father*   431
ANNIE DILLARD   *An American Childhood*   445
ANNIE DILLARD   *Singing with the Fundamentalists*   452

SCIENCE AND TECHNOLOGY

E. B. WHITE   *Farewell, My Lovely!*   38
LEWIS THOMAS   *Computers*   131
RICHARD SELZER   *Lessons from the Art*   211

RICHARD SELZER   *A Mask on the Face of Death*   222

RICHARD SELZER   *The Pen and the Scalpel*   233

RICHARD SELZER   *Bald!*   218

JOYCE CAROL OATES   *"State-of-the-Art Car": The Ferrari Testarossa*   318

STEPHEN JAY GOULD   *Women's Brains*   363

STEPHEN JAY GOULD   *A Biological Homage to Mickey Mouse*   369

STEPHEN JAY GOULD   *Evolution as Fact and Theory*   379

WOMEN'S EXPERIENCES

VIRGINIA WOOLF   *Professions for Women*   4

DORIS LESSING   *Being Prohibited*   147

DORIS LESSING   *My Father*   151

DORIS LESSING   *A Deep Darkness: A Review of* Out of Africa *by Karen Blixen*   158

RUSSELL BAKER   *The Flag*   193

RUSSELL BAKER   *Growing Up*   198

JOAN DIDION   *Marrying Absurd*   285

JOAN DIDION   *On Self-Respect*   288

JOAN DIDION   *On Morality*   293

JOAN DIDION   *Why I Write*   298

MARGARET ATWOOD   *Travels Back*   327

MARGARET ATWOOD   *Great Unexpectations*   332

MARGARET ATWOOD   *Adrienne Rich: Poems, Selected and New*   336

MAXINE HONG KINGSTON   *No Name Woman*   343

MAXINE HONG KINGSTON   *High School Reunion*   353

STEPHEN JAY GOULD   *Women's Brains*   363

ALICE WALKER   *In Search of Our Mothers' Gardens*   417

ALICE WALKER   *Am I Blue?*   426

ALICE WALKER   *Father*   431

VIRGINIA WOOLF

"Human nature changed in or about December 1910," Virginia Woolf once observed in attempting to define the modern sensibility. She was alluding to the Post-Impressionist Exhibition organized by art critic Roger Fry—an exhibition of modernist art by Manet, Gauguin, Cezanne, and Van Gogh that had been greeted with howls of contempt by the English public. Nevertheless, Woolf along with other artists and writers understood that new forms and techniques were needed to capture modern reality.

Virginia Stephen Woolf, born in London on January 25, 1882, is one of the modern era's most esteemed novelists and essayists. She was the daughter of the celebrated critic, philosopher, and biographer Leslie Stephen. The Stephen house pulsed with the conversation and conviviality of such distinguished guests as Robert Louis Stevenson, Oliver Wendell Holmes, Thomas Hardy, and John Ruskin. Lively and sociable, educated largely at home in her father's enormous library, Woolf grew up, as the critic David Daiches remarked, taking culture for granted. She took pride in being a member of the intellectual elite, but as her essay "Middlebrow" demonstrates, she could be witty and good-humored in her examination of the importance of intelligence as an index of culture.

Woolf's mother, Julia, died in 1895, precipitating the child's first nervous breakdown at the age of thirteen. Her father's death in 1904 led to a second breakdown and a suicide attempt. After Sir Leslie's death, Virginia settled with her sister and two brothers in Bloomsbury, where, with an independent income, she turned to writing. In Leonard Woolf, whom she married in 1912 after a friendship of eight years, she found a source of stability within the liberating but volatile environment of the Bloomsbury group of artists, writers, and intellectuals that consisted of E. M. Forster, John Maynard Keynes, T. S. Eliot, and others.

Woolf began her career as an essayist, becoming a reviewer for *The Times Literary Supplement* and publishing criticism in English and American journals. With the founding of the Hogarth Press by the Woolfs in 1917, Virginia Woolf became, in T. S. Eliot's words, "the centre . . . of literary life in London." Possessed of daring imagination, wide erudition, and extraordinary stylistic gifts, Woolf published several novels— *Mrs. Dolloway* (1925), *To the Lighthouse* (1927), *Orlando* (1928), and *The Waves* (1931). Yet even as Woolf established herself as a pioneer of modern experimental fiction and one of England's foremost novelists, she also secured her reputation as a major modern essayist.

Woolf's essays, collected in *The Common Reader* (1925, 1932), *The Death of the Moth* (1942), *the Moment* (1947), *The Captain's Death-Bed* (1950), *Granite and Rainbow* (1958), and the four-volume *Collected Essays* (1967), are noted for their range, vitality, and insight. "Whether you are writing a review or a love letter," Woolf stated, "the great thing is to be confronted with a very vivid idea of your subject." Woolf can be opinionated, resistant, truculent—as in the fine, self-acknowledged "Victorian tea table manner" that characterizes "Middlebrow." At the same time, the evocative and highly poetic intimacy of "The Death of the Moth" and brilliant feminist radicalism of "Professions for Women" suggest the vast range of her literary powers.

"Have I the power of conveying the true reality?" Virginia Woolf asked. "Or do I write essays about myself?" Woolf speaks to readers in a smooth, conversational, suggestive voice. She reveals herself but also sums up an entire era's social and political turmoil between the two world wars. Her many essays and two books on women's liberation—*A Room of One's Own* (1928) and *Three Guineas* (1938)—make her a decidedly contemporary figure, but they should be seen against a broader attempt to defend culture and intellectual freedom. Ultimately the ravages of World War II pressed too many horrors, as Woolf admitted, on her eyes and on her fragile psyche. The Woolfs' London home was bombed, their library destroyed. In Sussex on the morning of March 28, 1941, Virginia Woolf arose, wrote a tender note to her husband—"so perfectly good"—and then walked down to the River Ouse where, leaving her cane on the bank, she walked into the water and drowned herself.

Professions for Women

When your secretary invited me to come here, she told me that your
Society is concerned with the employment of women and she suggested that
I might tell you something about my own professional experiences. It is true
I am a woman; it is true I am employed; but what professional experiences have
I had? It is difficult to say. My profession is literature; and in that profession
there are fewer experiences for women than in any other, with the exception
of the stage—fewer, I mean, that are peculiar to women. For the road was cut
many years ago—by Fanny Burney, by Aphra Behn, by Harriet Martineau,
by Jane Austen, by George Eliot—many famous women, and many more
unknown and forgotten, have been before me, making the path smooth, and
regulating my steps. Thus, when I came to write, there were very few material
obstacles in my way. Writing was a reputable and harmless occupation. The
family peace was not broken by the scratching of a pen. No demand was made
upon the family purse. For ten and sixpence one can buy paper enough to write
all the plays of Shakespeare—if one has a mind that way. Pianos and models,
Paris, Vienna, and Berlin, masters and mistresses, are not needed by a writer.
The cheapness of writing paper is, of course, the reason why women have succeeded as writers before they have succeeded in the other professions.

But to tell you my story—it is a simple one. You have only got to figure
to yourselves a girl in a bedroom with a pen in her hand. She had only to move
that pen from left to right—from ten o'clock to one. Then it occurred to her
to do what is simple and cheap enough after all—to slip a few of those pages
into an envelope, fix a penny stamp in the corner, and drop the envelope into
the red box at the corner. It was thus that I became a journalist; and my effort
was rewarded on the first day of the following month—a very glorious day
it was for me—by a letter from an editor containing a cheque for one pound
ten shillings and sixpence. But to show you how little I deserve to be called
a professional woman, how little I know of the struggles and difficulties of such
lives, I have to admit that instead of spending that sum upon bread and butter,
rent, shoes and stockings, or butcher's bills, I went out and bought a cat—a
beautiful cat, a Persian cat, which very soon involved me in bitter disputes with
my neighbors.

What could be easier than to write articles and to buy Persian cats with
the profits? But wait a moment. Articles have to be about something. Mine,
I seem to remember, was about a novel by a famous man. And while I was
writing this review, I discovered that if I were going to review books I should

need to do battle with a certain phantom. And the phantom was a woman, and when I came to know her better I called her after the heroine of a famous poem. The Angel in the House. It was she who used to come between me and my paper when I was writing reviews. It was she who bothered me and wasted my time and so tormented me that at last I killed her. You who come of a younger and happier generation may not have heard of her—you may not know what I mean by The Angel in the House. I will describe her as shortly as I can. She was intensely sympathetic. She was immensely charming. She was utterly unselfish. She excelled in the difficult arts of family life. She sacrificed herself daily. If there was chicken, she took the leg; if there was a draught she sat in it—in short she was so consititued that she never had a mind or a wish of her own, but preferred to sympathize always with the minds and wishes of others. Above all—I need not say it—she was pure. Her purity was supposed to be her chief beauty—her blushes, her great grace. In those days—the last of Queen Victoria—every house had its Angel. And when I came to write I encountered her with the very first words. The shadow of her wings fell on my page; I heard the rustling of her skirts in the room. Directly, that is to say, I took my pen in my hand to review that novel by a famous man, she slipped behind me and whispered: "My dear, you are a young woman. You are writing about a book that has been written by a man. Be sympathetic; be tender; flatter; deceive; use all the arts and wiles of our sex. Never let anybody guess that you have a mind of your own. Above all, be pure." And she made as if to guide my pen. I now record the one act for which I take some credit to myself, though the credit rightly belongs to some excellent ancestors of mine who left me a certain sum of money—shall we say five hundred pounds a year?—so that it was not necessary for me to depend solely on charm for my living. I turned upon her and caught her by the throat. I did my best to kill her. My excuse if I were to be had up at a court of law, would be that I acted in self-defence. Had I not killed her she would have killed me. She would have plucked the heart out of my writing. For as I found directly I put pen to paper, you cannot review even a novel without having a mind of your own, without expressing what you think to be the truth about human relations, morality, sex. And all these questions, according to the Angel of the House cannot be dealt with freely and openly by women; they must charm, they must conciliate, they must—to put it bluntly—tell lies if they are to succeed. Thus, whenever I felt the shadow of her wing or the radiance of her halo upon my page, I took up the inkpot and flung it at her. She died hard. Her fictitious nature was of great assistance to her. It is far harder to kill a phantom than a reality. She was always creeping back when I thought I had despatched her. Though I flatter myself that I killed her in the end, the struggle was severe; it took much time that had better have been spent upon learning Greek grammar; or in roaming the world in search of adventures. But it was a real experience; it was an experience that was bound to befall all women writers at that time. Killing the Angel in the House was part of the occupation of a woman writer.

But to continue my story. The Angel was dead; what then remained? You may say that what remained was a simple and common object—a young woman in a bedroom with an inkpot. In other words, now that she had rid herself of falsehood, that young woman had only to be herself. Ah, but what is "herself?" I mean, what is a woman? I assure you, I do not know. I do not believe that you know. I do not believe that anybody can know until she has expressed herself in all the arts and professions open to human skill. That indeed is one of the reasons why I have come here—out of respect for you, who are in process of showing us by your experiments what a woman is, who are in process of providing us, by your failures and successes, with that extremely important piece of information.

But to continue the story of my professional experiences. I made one pound ten and six by my first review; and I bought a Persian cat with the proceeds. Then I grew ambitious. A Persian cat is all very well, I said; but a Persian cat is not enough. I must have a motor-car. And it was thus that I became a novelist—for it is a very strange thing that people will give you a motor-car if you will tell them a story. It is a still stranger thing that there is nothing so delightful in the world as telling stories. It is far pleasanter than writing reviews of famous novels. And yet, if I am to obey your secretary and tell you my professional experiences as a novelist, I must tell you about a very strange experience that befell me as a novelist. And to understand it you must try first to imagine a novelist's state of mind. I hope I am not giving away professional secrets if I say that a novelist's chief desire is to be as unconscious as possible. He has to induce in himself a state of perpetual lethargy. He wants life to proceed with the utmost quiet and regularity. He wants to see the same faces, to read the same books, to do the same things day after day, month after month, while he is writing, so that nothing may break the illusion in which he is living—so that nothing may disturb or disquiet the mysterious nosings about, feelings round, darts, dashes, and sudden discoveries of that very shy and illusive spirit, the imagination. I suspect that this state is the same both for men and women. Be that as it may, I want you to imagine me writing a novel in a state of trance. I want you to figure to yourselves a girl sitting with a pen in her hand, which for minutes, and indeed for hours, she never dips into the inkpot. The image that comes to my mind when I think of this girl is the image of a fisherman lying sunk in dreams on the verge of a deep lake with a rod held out over the water. She was letting her imagination sweep unchecked round every rock and cranny of the world that lies submerged in the depths of our unconscious being. Now came the experience that I believe to be far commoner with women writers than with men. The line raced through the girl's fingers. Her imagination had rushed away. It had sought the pools, the depths, the dark places where the largest fish slumber. And then there was a smash. There was an explosion. There was foam and confusion. The imagination had dashed itself against something hard. The girl was roused from her dream. She was indeed in a state of the most acute and difficult distress. To speak without figure, she had thought of something, something about the body, about the passion, which it was unfitting for her as a woman to say. Men, her reason told her, would be shocked. The consciousness of what men will say of a woman who speaks the truth about her passions had roused her from her artist's state of unconsciousness. She could write no more. The trance was over. Her imagination could work no longer. This I believe to be a very common experience with women writers—they are impeded by the extreme conventionality of the other sex. For though men sensibly allow themselves great freedom in these respects, I doubt that they realize or can control the extreme severity with which they condemn such freedom in women.

These then were two very genuine experiences of my own. These were   6 two of the adventures of my professional life. The first—killing the Angel in the House—I think I solved. She died. But the second, telling the truth about my own experiences as a body, I do not think I solved. I doubt that any woman has solved it yet. The obstacles against her are still immensely powerful—and yet they are very difficult to define. Outwardly, what is simpler than to write books? Outwardly, what obstacles are there for a woman rather than for a man? Inwardly, I think, the case is very different; she has still many ghosts to fight, many prejudices to overcome. Indeed it will be a long time still, I think, before a woman can sit down to write a book without finding a phantom to be slain, a rock to be dashed against. And if this is so in literature, the freest of all professions for women, how is it in the new professions which you are now for the first time entering?

Those are the questions that I should like, had I time, to ask you. And   7 indeed, if I have laid stress upon these professional experiences of mine, it is because I believe that they are, though in different forms, yours also. Even when the path is nominally open—when there is nothing to prevent a woman from being a doctor, a lawyer, a civil servant—there are many phantoms and obstacles, as I believe, looming in her way. To discuss and define them is I think of great value and importance; for thus only can the labour be shared, the difficulties be solved. But besides this, it is necessary also to discuss the ends and the aims for which we are fighting, for which we are doing battle with these formidable obstacles. Those aims cannot be taken for granted; they must be perpetually questioned and examined. The whole position, as I see it—here in this hall surrounded by women practising for the first time in history I know not how many different professions—is one of extraordinary interest and importance. You have won rooms of your own in the house hitherto exclusively owned by men. You are able, though not without great labour and effort, to pay the rent. You are earning your five hundred pounds a year. But this freedom is only a beginning; the room is your own, but it is still bare. It has to be furnished; it has to be decorated; it has to be shared. How are you going to furnish it, how are you going to decorate it? With whom are you going to share it, and upon what terms? These, I think are questions of the utmost importance and interest. For the first time in history you are able to ask them; for the first time you are able to decide for yourselves what the answers should be. Willingly would I stay and discuss those questions and answers—but not tonight. My time is up; and I must cease.

1931

Purpose and Meaning

1. What expectations does the title of this essay create for the reader? Do you think the title is an accurate reflection of the essay's thesis? Can you think of a better one?

2. Who is Woolf's immediate audience? Is the tone of the essay appropriate for its readers? Explain.

3. By mentioning the list of women writers in the first paragraph, what assumptions has Woolf made about her audience's educational and cultural background?

Language and Style

1. Why is the "Angel in the House" an appropriate way for Woolf to describe an adversary that got in the way of her writing? How does this extended image strengthen the thesis of the essay?

2. Woolf writes of struggling to overcome obstacles created by a male-dominated society. Yet she uses the pronouns *he* (paragraph 5) to describe novelists in general. Does the pronoun, as it is used here, indicate gender? What does this usage indicate about the author's assumptions about language? What can we infer about the essay's historical and cultural context from the use of this pronoun? Why might contemporary women writers choose a different one?

3. Is the word *room* (paragraph 7) used figuratively, literally, or in both ways? Explain.

Strategy and Structure

1. In paragraph 1, Woolf describes the physical requirements and the act of writing in straightforward terms. Is this description important for the overall thesis of the essay, or is it extraneous? How does the description affect the structure of the essay? How does it prepare the audience for what is to follow?

2. In paragraph 6, Woolf poses some questions for her audience. What is her purpose in doing this? How does it change the writer–audience relationship? How does it prepare readers for the concluding paragraph?

Thinking and Writing

1. Have women today overcome the second of the "adventures" Woolf describes in paragraph 6? Write an essay arguing for or against the thesis that a contemporary woman today is free to express "her own experiences as a body."

2. What professions other than writing possess a strong, inner, psychological dimension as well as an external, concrete one? Write an essay that describes a field of endeavor that requires both dimensions.

3. Think of an audience (for instance, fellow students, children, a college graduating class), and draw upon your experiences to tailor a speech that imparts a lesson to that particular audience. For example, what would you say about college life at your institution to a group of prospective students to encourage them to enroll at your institution?

The Death of the Moth

Moths that fly by day are not properly to be called moths; they do not excite that pleasant sense of dark autumn nights and ivy-blossom which the commonest yellow underwing asleep in the shadow of the curtain never fails to rouse in us. They are hybrid creatures, neither gay like butterflies nor sombre like their own species. Nevertheless the present specimen, with his narrow hay-coloured wings, fringed with a tassel of the same colour, seemed to be content with life. It was a pleasant morning, mid-September, mild, benignant, yet with a keener breath than that of the summer months. The plough was already scoring the field opposite the window, and where the share had been, the earth was pressed flat and gleamed with moisture. Such vigour came rolling in from the fields and the down beyond that it was difficult to keep the eyes strictly turned upon the book. The rooks too were keeping one of their annual festivities; soaring round the tree-tops until it looked as if a vast net with thousands of black knots in it has been cast up into the air; which, after a few moments sank slowly down upon the trees until every twig seemed to have a knot at the end of it. Then, suddenly, the net would be thrown into the air again in a wider circle this time, with the utmost clamour and vociferation, as thought to be thrown into the air and settle slowly down upon the tree-tops were a tremendously exciting experience.

The same energy which inspired the rooks, the ploughmen, the horses, and even, it seemed, the lean bare-backed downs, sent the moth fluttering from side to side of his square of the window-pane. One could not help watching him. One was, indeed, conscious of a queer feeling of pity for him. The possibilities of pleasure seemed that morning so enormous and so various that to have only a moth's part in life, and a day moth's at that, appeared a hard fate, and his zest in enjoying his meagre opportunities to the full, pathetic. He flew vigorously to one corner of his compartment, and, after waiting there a second, flew across to the other. What remained for him but to fly to a third corner and then to a fourth? That was all he could do, in spite of the size of the downs, the width of the sky, the far-off smoke of houses, and the romantic voice, now and then, of a steamer out at sea. What he could do he did. Watching him, it seemed as if a fibre, very thin but pure, of the enormous energy of the world had been thrust into his frail and diminutive body. As often as he crossed the pane, I could fancy that a thread of vital light became visible. He was little or nothing but life.

Yet, because he was so small, and so simple a form of the energy that was rolling in at the open window and driving its way through so many narrow and intricate corridors in my own brain and in those of other human beings, there was something marvelous as well as pathetic about him. It was as if someone had taken a tiny bead of pure life and decking it as lightly as possible with down and feathers, had set it dancing and zigzagging to show us the true nature of life. Thus displayed one could not get over the strangeness of it. One is apt to forget all about life, seeing it humped and bossed and garnished and cumbered so that it has to move with the greatest circumspection and dignity. Again, the thought of all that life might have been had he been born in any other shape caused one to view his simple activities with a kind of pity.

After a time, tired by his dancing apparently, he settled on the window ledge in the sun, and the queer spectacle being at an end, I forgot about him. Then, looking up, my eye was caught by him. He was trying to resume his dancing, but seemed either so stiff or so awkward that he could only flutter to the bottom of the window-pane; and when he tried to fly across it he failed. Being intent on other matters I watched these futile attempts for a time without thinking, unconsciously waiting for him to resume his flight, as one waits for a machine, that has stopped momentarily, to start again without considering the reason for its failure. After perhaps a seventh attempt he slipped from the wooden ledge and fell, fluttering his wings, on to his back on the window-sill. The helplessness of his attitude roused me. It flashed upon me that he was in difficulties; he could no longer raise himself; his legs struggled vainly. But, as I stretched out a pencil, meaning to help him to right himself, it came over me that the failure and awkwardness were the approach of death. I laid the pencil down again.

The legs agitated themselves once more. I looked as if for the enemy against which he struggled. I looked out of doors. What had happened there? Presumably it was midday, and work in the fields had stopped. Stillness and quiet had replaced the previous animation. The birds had taken themselves off to feed in the brooks. The horses stood still. Yet the power was there all the same, massed outside indifferent, impersonal, not attending to anything in particular. Somehow it was opposed to the little hay-coloured moth. It was useless to try to do anything. One could only watch the extraordinary efforts made by those tiny legs against an oncoming doom which could, had it chosen, have submerged an entire city, not merely a city, but masses of human beings; nothing, I knew, had any chance against death. Nevertheless after a pause of exhaustion the legs fluttered again. It was superb this last protest, and so frantic that he succeeded at last in righting himself. One's sympathies, of course, were all on the side of life. Also, when there was nobody to care or to know, this gigantic of such magnitude, to retain what no one else valued or desired to keep, moved one strangely. Again, somehow, one saw life, a pure bead. I lifted the pencil again, useless though I knew it to be. But even as I did so, the unmistakable tokens of death showed themselves. The body relaxed, and instantly grew stiff. The struggle was over. The insignificant little creature now knew death. As I looked at the dead moth, this minute wayside triumph of so great a force over so mean an antagonist filled me with wonder. Just as life had been strange a few minutes before, so death was now as strange. The moth having righted himself now lay most decently and uncomplainingly composed. O yes, he seemed to say, death is stronger than I am.

1942

Purpose and Meaning

1. What was your first response to the title of this essay? How did your response change after you read the essay?

2. What is Woolf's thesis in this essay? Does the tone of the essay suggest a death scene? Does the author maintain an emotional attitude, a rational attitude, or a combination toward the subject matter? How does this attitude affect the reader's understanding of death?

3. What religious or spiritual overtones does Woolf use in handling the subject matter? How do these overtones relate to the thesis of the essay?

Language and Style

1. The author uses the pronoun *one* to describe her own observations and reflections about the scene. What does her word choice suggest about her point of view? How does her use of *one* affect our own attitude toward the writer and her subject?

2. Locate and discuss places in the essay where Woolf combines literal and figurative descriptions.

3. Personification is the description of something nonhuman in human terms. Locate examples of this technique in the essay. For each example, explain what Woolf gains by using personification.

4. Woolf makes several references to abstract concepts such as "pure life," "energy," and "power." Why are these appropriate words for what she is describing? Give examples of other abstractions in the essay.

Strategy and Structure

1. The opening paragraph of this essay is quite long. Why did Woolf give so much attention to the scene outside the window?

2. The moth undergoes a dramatic change during the essay. What changes happen to it from paragraph to paragraph? Similarly, the author seems to undergo a change in her relationship to the moth. Explore the author's change by studying each paragraph individually. Is the change emotional, spiritual, or religious?

3. In the final paragraph of the previous essay ("Professions for Women"), Woolf asserts that a woman needs a room in which to flourish and achieve. How does "The Death of the Moth" demonstrate the relationship between having one's own space and the opportunity to be creative?

Thinking and Writing

1. For Woolf, an apparently insignificant event became an occasion for a meditative essay on life, death, nature, and human development. Select a seemingly insignificant event in your own life and describe it in a way that makes the reader understand that the episode was actually quite important.

2. Do you know of any events or objects that seem to embody principles of life itself? Select a specific object or event (for example, a storm, a bridge, a painting) and compare it to a principle (disorder, structure, harmony).

Middlebrow

TO THE EDITOR OF THE "NEW STATESMAN"

Sir,

Will you allow me to draw your attention to the fact that in a review of   1
a book by me (October) your reviewer omitted to use the word Highbrow? The review, save for that omission, gave me so much pleasure that I am driven to ask you, at the risk of appearing unduly egotistical, whether your reviewer, a man of obvious intelligence, intended to deny my claim to that title? I say "claim," for surely I may claim that title when a great critic, who is also a great novelist, a rare and enviable combination, always calls me a highbrow when he condescends to notice my work in a great newspaper; and further, always finds space to inform not only myself, who know it already, but the whole British Empire, who hang on his words, that I live in Bloomsbury? Is your critic unaware of that fact too? Or does he, for all his intelligence, maintain that it is necessary in reviewing a book to add the postal address of the writer?

His answer to these questions, though of real value to me, is of no possible   2 interest to the public at large. Of that I am well aware. But since larger issues are involved, since the Battle of the Brows troubles, I am told, the evening air, since the finest minds of our age have lately been engaged in debating, not without that passion which befits a noble cause, what a highbrow is and what a lowbrow, which is better and which is worse, may I take this opportunity to express my opinion and at the same time draw attention to certain aspects of the question which seem to me to have been unfortunately overlooked?

Now there can be no two opinions as to what a highbrow is. He is the man or woman of thoroughbred intelligence who rides his mind at a gallop across country in pursuit of an idea. That is why I have always been so proud to be called highbrow. That is why, if I could be more of a highbrow I would. I honour and respect highbrows. Some of my relations have been highbrows; and some, but by no means all, of my friends. To be a highbrow, a complete and representative highbrow, a highbrow like Shakespeare, Dickens, Byron, Shelley, Keats, Charlotte Brontë, Scott, Jane Austen, Flaubert, Hardy, or Henry James—to name a few highbrows from the same profession chosen at random—is of course beyond the wildest dreams of my imagination. And, though I would cheerfully lay myself down in the dust and kiss the print of their feet, no person of sense will deny that this passionate preoccupation of theirs—riding across country in pursuit of ideas—often leads to disaster. Undoubtedly, they come fearful croppers. Take Shelley—what a mess he made of his life! And Byron, getting into bed with first one woman and then with another and dying in the mud at Missolonghi. Look at Keats, loving poetry and Fanny Brawne so intemperately that he pined and died of consumption at the age of twenty-six. Charlotte Brontë again—I have been assured on good authority that Charlotte Brontë was, with the possible exception of Emily, the worst governess in the British Isles. Then there was Scott—he went bankrupt, and left, together with a few magnificant novels, one house, Abbotsford, which is perhaps the ugliest in the whole Empire. But surely these instances are enough—I need not further labour the point that highbrows, for some reason or another, are wholly incapable of dealing successfully with what is called real life. That is why, and here I come to a point that is often surprisingly ignored, they honour so wholeheartedly and depend so completely upon those who are called lowbrows. By a lowbrow is meant of course a man or a woman of thoroughbred vitality who rides his body in pursuit of a living at a gallop across life. That is why I honour and respect lowbrows—and I have never known a highbrow who did not. In so far as I am a highbrow (and my imperfections in that line are well known to me) I love lowbrows; I study them; I always sit next the conductor in an omnibus and try to get him to tell me what it is like—being a conductor. In whatever company I am I always try to know what it is like—being a conductor, being a woman with ten children and thirty-five shillings a week, being a stockbroker, being an admiral, being a bank clerk, being a dressmaker, being a duchess, being a miner, being a cook, being a prostitute. All that lowbrows do is of surpassing interest and wonder to me, because, in so far as I am a highbrow, I cannot do things myself.

This brings me to another point which is also surprisingly overlooked.   4
Lowbrows need highbrows and honour them just as much as highbrows need
lowbrows and honour them. This too is not a matter that requires much
demonstration. You have only to stroll along the Strand on a wet winter's night
and watch the crowds lining up to get into the movies. These lowbrows are
waiting, after the day's work, in the rain, sometimes for hours, to get into the
cheap seats and sit in hot theatres in order to see what their lives look like. Since
they are lowbrows, engaged magnificently and adventurously in riding full tilt
from one end of life to the other in pursuit of a living, they cannot see themselves
doing it. Yet nothing interests them more. Nothing matters to them more. It
is one of the prime necessities of life to them—to be shown what life looks like.
And the highbrows, of course, are the only people who can show them. Since
they are the only people who do not do things, they are the only people who
can see things being done. This is so—and so it is I am certain; nevertheless
we are told—the air buzzes with it by night, the Press booms with it by day,
the very donkeys in the fields do nothing but bray it, the very curs in the streets
do nothing but bark it—"Highbrows hate lowbrows! Lowbrows hate
highbrows!"—when highbrows need lowbrows, when lowbrows need
highbrows, when they cannot exist apart, when one is the complement and other
side of the other! How has such a lie come into existence. Who has set this
malicious gossip afloat?

There can be no doubt about that either. It is the doing of the middlebrows.   5
They are the people, I confess, that I seldom regard with entire cordiality. They
are the go-betweens; they are the busybodies who run from one to the other
with their tittle tattle and make all the mischief—the middlebrows, I repeat.
But what, you may ask, is a middlebrow? And that, to tell the truth, is no easy
question to answer. They are neither one thing nor the other. They are not
highbrows, whose brows are high; nor lowbrows, whose brows are low. Their
brows are betwixt and between. They do not live in Bloomsbury which is on
high ground; nor in Chelsea which is on low ground. Since they must live
somewhere presumably, they live perhaps in South Kensington, which is betwixt
and between. The middlebrow is the man, or woman, of middlebred intelligence
who ambles and saunters now on this side of the hedge, now on that, in pursuit
of no single object, neither art itself nor life itself, but both mixed in-
distinguishably, and rather nastily, with money, fame, power, or prestige. The
middlebrow curries favour with both sides equally. He goes to the lowbrows
and tells them that while he is not quite one of them, he is almost their friend.
Next moment he rings up the highbrows and asks them with equal geniality
whether he may not come to tea. Now there are highbrows—I myself have
known duchesses who were highbrows, also charwomen, and they have both
told me with that vigour of language which so often unites the aristocracy with
the working classes, that they would rather sit in the coal cellar, together, than
in the drawingroom with middlebrows and pour out tea. I have myself been
asked—but may I, for the sake of brevity, cast this scene which is only partly
fictitious, into the form of fiction?—I myself, then, have been asked to come

and "see" them—how strange a passion theirs is for being "seen"! They ring me up, therefore, at about eleven in the morning, and ask me to come to tea. I go to my wardrobe and consider, rather lugubriously, what is the right thing to wear? We highbrows may be smart, or we may be shabby; but we never have the right thing to wear. I proceed to ask next: What is the right thing to say? Which is the right knife to use? What is the right book to praise? All these are things I do not know for myself. We highbrows read what we like and do what we like and praise what we like. We also know what we dislike—for example, thin bread and butter tea. The difficulty of eating thin bread and butter in white kid gloves has always seemed to me one of life's more insuperable problems. Then I dislike bound volumes of the classics behind plate glass. Then I distrust people who call both Shakespeare and Wordsworth equally "Bill"—it is a habit moreover that leads to confusion. And in the matter of clothes, I like people either to dress very well; or to dress very badly; I dislike the correct thing in clothes. Then there is the question of games. Being a highbrow I do not play them. But I love watching people play who have a passion for games. These middlebrows pat balls about; they poke their bats and muff their catches at cricket. And when poor Middlebrow mounts on horseback and that animal breaks into a canter, to me there is no sadder sight in all Rotten Row. To put it in a nutshell (in order to get on with the story) that tea party was not wholly a success, nor altogether a failure; for Middlebrow, who writes, following me to the door, clapped me briskly on the back, and said, "I'm sending you my book!" (Or did he call it "stuff"?) And his book comes—sure enough, though called, so symbolically, *Keepaway*, it comes. And I read a page here, and I read a page there (I am breakfasting, as usual, in bed). And it is not well written; nor is it badly written. It is not proper, nor is it improper—in short it is betwixt and between. Now if there is any sort of book for which I have, perhaps, an imperfect sympathy, it is the betwixt and between. And so, though I suffer from the gout of a morning—but if one's ancestors for two or three centuries have tumbled into bed dead drunk one has deserved a touch of that malady—I rise. I dress. I proceed weakly to the window. I take that book in my swollen right hand and toss it gently over the hedge into the field. The hungry sheep—did I remember to say that this part of the story takes place in the country?—the hungry sheep look up but are not fed.

But to have done with fiction and its tendency to lapse into poetry—I will now report a perfectly prosaic conversation in words of one syllable. I often ask my friends the lowbrows, over our muffins and honey, why it is that while we, the highbrows, never buy a middlebrow book, or go to a middlebrow lecture, or read, unless we are paid for doing so, a middlebrow review, they, on the contrary, take these middlebrow activities so seriously? Why, I ask (not of course on the wireless), are you so damnably modest? Do you think that a description of your lives, as they are, is too sordid and too mean to be beautiful? Is that why you prefer the middlebrow version of what they have the impudence to call real humanity?—this mixture of geniality and sentiment stuck together with a sticky slime of calves-foot jelly? The truth, if you would only believe it, is much more beautiful than any lie. Then again, I continue, how can you let the middlebrows teach *you* how to write?—you, who write so beautifully when you write naturally, that I would give both my hands to write as you do—for which reason I never attempt it, but do my best to learn the art of writing as a highbrow should. And again, I press on, brandishing a muffin on the point of a teaspoon, how dare the middlebrows teach *you* how to read—Shakespeare, for instance? All you have to do is to read him. The Cambridge edition is both good and cheap. If you find *Hamlet* difficult, ask him to tea. He is a highbrow. Ask Ophelia to meet him. She is a lowbrow. Talk to them, as you talk to me, and you will know more about Shakespeare than all the middlebrows in the world can teach you—I do not think, by the way, from certain phrases, that Shakespeare liked middlebrows, or Pope either.

To all this the lowbrows reply—but I cannot imitate their style of 7 talking—that they consider themselves to be common people without education. It is very kind of the middlebrows to try to teach them culture. And after all, the lowbrows continue, middlebrows, like other people, have to make money. There must be money in teaching and in writing books about Shakespeare. We all have to earn our livings nowadays, my friends the lowbrows remind me. I quite agree. Even those of us whose Aunts came a cropper riding in India and left them an annual income of four hundred and fifty pounds, now reduced, thanks to the war and other luxuries, to little more than two hundred odd, even we have to do that. And we do it, too, by writing about anybody who seems amusing—enough has been written about Shakespeare—Shakespeare hardly pays. We highbrows, I agree, have to earn our livings; but when we have earned enough to live on, then we live. When the middlebrows, on the contrary, have earned enough to live on, they go on earning enough to buy— what are the things that middlebrows always buy? Queen Anne furniture (faked, but none the less expensive); first editions of dead writers—always the worst; pictures, or reproductions from pictures, by dead painters; houses in what is called "the Georgian style"—but never anything new, never a picture by a living painter, or a chair by a living carpenter, or books by living writers, for to buy living art requires living taste. And, as that kind of art and that kind of taste are what middlebrows call "highbrow", "Bloomsbury", poor middlebrow spends vast sums on sham antiques, and has to keep as it scribbling away, year in, year out, while we highbrows ring each other up, and are off for a day's jaunt into the country. That is the worst of course of living in a set—one likes being with one's friends.

Have I then made my point clear, sir, that the true battle in my opinion 8 lies not between highbrow and lowbrow, but between highbrows and lowbrows joined together in blood brotherhood against the bloodless and pernicious pest who comes between? If the B.B.C. stood for anything but the Betwixt and Between Company they would use their control of the air not to stir strife between brothers, but to broadcast the fact that highbrows and lowbrows must band together to exterminate a pest which is the bane of all thinking and living.

It may be, to quote from your advertisement columns, that "terrifically sensitive" lady novelists over-estimate the dampness and dinginess of this fungoid growth. But all I can say is that when, lapsing into that stream which people call, so oddly, consciousness, and gathering wool from the sheep that have been mentioned above, I ramble round my garden in the suburbs, middlebrows seem to me to be everywhere. "What's that?" I cry. "Middlebrow on the cabbages? Middlebrow infecting that poor old sheep? And what about the moon?" I look up and, behold, the moon is under eclipse. "Middlebrow at it again!" I exclaim. "Middlebrow obscuring, dulling, tarnishing and coarsening even the silver edge of Heaven's own scythe." (I "draw near to poetry," see advt.) And then my thoughts, as Freud assures us thoughts will do, rush (Middlebrow's saunter and simper, out of respect for the Censor) to sex, and I ask of the sea-gulls who are crying on desolate sea sands and of the farm hands who are coming home rather drunk to their wives, what will become of us, men and women, if Middlebrow has his way with us, and there is only a middle sex but no husbands or wives? The next remark I address with the utmost humility to the Prime Minister. "What, sir," I demand, "will be the fate of the British Empire and of our Dominions Across the Seas if Middlebrows prevail? Will you not, sir, read a pronouncement of an authoritative nature from Broadcasting House?"

Such are the thoughts, such are the fancies that visit "cultured invalidish [9] ladies with private means" (see advt.) when they stroll in their suburban gardens and look at the cabbages and at the red brick villas that have been built by middlebrows so that middlebrows may look at the view. Such are the thoughts "at once gay and tragic and deeply feminine" (see advt.) of one who has not yet "been driven out of Bloomsbury" (advt. again), a place where lowbrows and highbrows live happily together on equal terms and priests are not, nor priestesses, and, to be quite frank, the adjective "priestly" is neither often heard nor held in high esteem. Such are the thoughts of one who will stay in Bloomsbury until the Duke of Bedford, rightly concerned for the respectability of his squares, raises the rent so high that Bloomsbury is safe for middlebrows to live in. Then she will leave.

May I conclude, as I began, by thanking your receiver for his courteous [10] and interesting review, but may I tell him that though he did not, for reasons best known to himself, call me a highbrow, there is no name in the world that I prefer? I ask nothing better than that all reviewers, for ever, and everywhere, should call me a highbrow. I will do my best to oblige them. If they like to add Bloomsbury WCI, that is the correct postal address, and my telephone number is in the Directory. But if your reviewer, or any other reviewer, dares hint that I live in South Kensington, I will sue him for libel. If any human being, man, woman, dog, cat, or half-crushed worm dares call me "middlebrow" I will take my pen and stab him, dead.

Yours, etc.
VIRGINIA WOOLF

1942

Purpose and Meaning

1. In what way is this essay a standard letter? In what ways is it much more than that?

2. What allusions in the essay reveal the author's cultural and social milieu? How do these references affect your ability to comprehend the meaning of the essay?

3. The thesis of an essay often can be found in the introduction or the conclusion. Is this true of "Middlebrow"? Explain.

4. Do you think Woolf truly wrote this letter because a reviewer forgot to refer to her as a "highbrow"? If not, what do you think her purpose was?

Language and Style

1. What specific phrases in paragraph 1 are ironic? Find other instances of irony in the essay. What serious issues about culture does Woolf address despite her ironic tone?

2. Woolf defines *highbrow* and *lowbrow* in paragraph 3 and *middlebrow* in paragraph 5. Look up these words in a dictionary. In what way are Woolf's definitions more appropriate to the style and tone of the essay than the dictionary's?

3. Paragraph 1 contains an extremely long sentence with a complex syntax. It begins with "I say 'claim', for surely . . . ." Study this sentence and others that are lengthy. In what ways do these sentences display Woolf's mastery of writing?

Strategy and Structure

1. Where does Woolf's introduction end? How does the introduction prepare us for what is to follow?

2. Study paragraphs 3 and 5. How does Woolf make her long paragraphs successful?

3. Analyze Woolf's use of classification, contrast, and definition to structure this essay.

Thinking and Writing

1. Define highbrow, lowbrow, and middlebrow society today. What professions are representative of each class? What type of education does each class strive for? What leisure activities does each enjoy? Give examples to support these observations.

2. Write an essay entitled "In Defense of the Middlebrow." Use specific illustrations, examples, and anecdotes to support your position.

3. Prepare an essay in which you take a position on the current controversy over "cultural literacy." Is a culturally literate person a highbrow? Base your observations on Woolf's essay and on your own experience.

ISAK DINESEN

Isak Dinesen, the pen name of Baroness Karen Blixen of Rungstedlund, was born in Denmark in 1885. A storyteller and essayist of classic simplicity and impressionistic originality, Dinesen spent the years from 1914 to 1931 in British East Africa managing a coffee plantation for a time with her husband, Baron Bror Blixen, whom she divorced in 1921. From her African experiences, Dinesen derived the material for the memoirs of her years in Kenya, *Out of Africa* (1937). "When you have caught the rhythm of Africa," she wrote, "you find it the same in all of her music."

Dinesen's extraordinary life and adventures turn constantly upon the African continent. Her narratives and vignettes in *Out of Africa*—represented here by "The Oxen," "Some African Birds," and "Old Knudsen"—are, as she admitted, variations on the same theme of her love for Africa. That theme is not entirely simple, for it circles ambiguously around an Africa that had fallen from Edenic grace. The fate of Dinesen's heroic oxen, the beautiful but rigid classification of her African birds, the forlorn but legendary fate of Knudsen—all invite symbolic interpretations of liberation and loss.

After losing her farm, Blixen returned to Denmark at the age of forty-six, and it was only then, writing in English under the pseudonym Dinesen, that she began to create her deceptively simple myths about Africa. She considered her pen name a mask, and she used it clearly to probe a personal identity rooted in an acute sense of departure and loss. Her father, a military officer, committed suicide when Dinesen was ten. In 1904, following a privileged but unhappy childhood, she was sent abroad to study at Oxford and later in Paris. Her marriage to the unfaithful Blixen foundered after she contracted a serious case of syphilis from him—a disease that caused her years of pain and illness right up to her death in 1962. Her affair with Denys Finch-Hatton—gracefully recreated in Sidney Pollack's 1986 film version of *Out of Africa*—ended with his death in an airplane crash. After his death, Dinesen lost her farm because of poor climate, fire, and debt. Thus her major works—*Seven Gothic Tales* (1934), *Out of Africa*, *Winter's Tales* (1942), *Anecdotes of Destiny* (1958), and *Shadows on the Grass* (1960)—are governed by a search for the heroic and the romantic in what Dinesen once called in a conversation with her brother, "the deadly boring twentieth century."

Only Dinesen's memories of Africa offered her this heroic perspective. At the start of *Out of Africa*, she positions her narrative in terms of paradise gained and then lost:

> I had a farm in Africa, at the foot of the Ngong Hills. The Equator runs across the highlands, a hundred miles to the North, and the farm lay at the altitude of over six thousand feet. In the day-time you felt that you had got high up, near to the sun, but the early mornings and evenings were limpid and restful, and the nights were cold.

Here she writes with a painter's eye for detail. Her physical descriptions have a stylistic simplicity not unlike that of Ernest Hemingway. In fact, on receiving the Nobel Prize for Literature in 1951, Hemingway apologized for the award, saying that it should have gone to "that beautiful Isak Dinesen," who had been nominated twice. The imagery of liberation and exhilaration merges with a sense of loss signaled by the initial verb in the past tense, "I had a farm in Africa. . . ."

The contemporary British writer Margaret Drabble has referred to Dinesen as "witch, sybil, lion hunter, coffee planter, aristocrat and despot, a paradox in herself and a creator of paradoxes." These were her several masks. The truth behind the masks is that, for Isak Dinesen, Africa was a "great and unexpected happiness, a liberation." In the clean, precise perfection of her narrative and in the imaginative sympathy that she brings to all her subjects, Isak Dinesen works her own brand of magic in recreating lost things.

The Oxen

Saturday afternoon was a blessed time on the farm. First of all, there would now be no mail in till Monday afternoon, so that no distressing business letters could reach us till then, and this fact in itself seemed to close the whole place in, as within an enceinte. Secondly, everybody was looking forward to the day of Sunday, when they would rest or play all the day, and the Squatters could work on their own land. The thought of the oxen on Saturday pleased me more than all other things. I used to walk down to their paddock at six o'clock, when they were coming in after the day's work and a few hours' grazing. To-morrow, I thought, they would do nothing but graze all day.

We had one hundred and thirty-two oxen on the farm, which meant eight working teams and a few spare oxen. Now in the golden dust of the sunset they came wandering home across the plain in a long row, walking sedately, as they did all things; while I sat sedately on the fence of the paddock, smoking a cigarette of peace, and watching them. Here came Nyose, Ngufu and Faru, with Msungu,—which means a white man. The drivers also often give to their teams the proper names of white men, and Delamere is a common name in an ox. Here came old Malinda, the big yellow ox that I liked best of the lot; his skin was strangely marked with shadowy figures, like starfishes, from which pattern perhaps he had his name, for Malinda means a skirt.

As in civilized countries all people have a chronic bad conscience towards the slums, and feel uncomfortable when they think of them, so in Africa you have got a bad conscience, and feel a pang, when you think of the oxen. But towards the oxen on the farm, I felt as, I suppose, a king will be feeling towards his slums: "You are I, and I am you."

The oxen in Africa have carried the heavy load of the advance of European civilization. Wherever new land has been broken they have broken it, panting and pulling kneedeep in the soil before the ploughs, the long whips in the air over them. Where a road has been made they have made it; and they have trudged the iron and tools through the land, to the yelling and shouting of the drivers, by tracks in the dust and the long grass of the plains, before there ever were any roads. They have been inspanned before daybreak, and have sweated up and down the long hills, and across dungas and river-beds, through the burning hours of the day. The whips have marked their sides, and you will often see oxen that have had an eye, or both of them, taken away by the long cutting whip-lashes. The wagon-oxen of many Indian and white contractors worked every day, all their lives through, and did not know of the Sabbath.

It is a strange thing that we have done to the oxen. The bull is in a constant ⁵ stage of fury, rolling his eyes, shoveling up the earth, upset by everything that gets within his range of vision—still he has got a life of his own, fire comes from his nostrils, and new life from his loins; his days are filled with his vital cravings and satisfactions. All of that we have taken away from the oxen, and in reward we have claimed their existence for ourselves. The oxen walk along within our own daily life, pulling hard all the time, creatures without a life, things made for our use. They have moist, limpid, violet eyes, soft muzzles, silky ears, they are patient and dull in all their ways; sometimes they look as if they were thinking about things.

There was in my time a law against bringing a waggon or cart on the roads ⁶ without a brake, and the waggon-drivers were supposed to put on the brakes down all the long hills of the country. But the law was not kept; half the waggons and carts on the roads had no brakes to them, and on the others the brakes were but rarely put on. This made downhill work terribly hard on the oxen. They had to hold the loaded waggons up with their bodies, they laid their heads back under the labour until their horns touched the hump on their backs; their sides went like a pair of bellows. I have many times seen the carts of the firewood merchants which came along the Ngong Road, going into Nairobi the one after the other, like a long caterpillar, gain speed down the hill in the Forest Reserve, the oxen violently zig-zagging down in front of them. I have also seen the oxen stumble and fall under the weight of the cart, at the bottom of the hill.

The oxen thought: "Such is life, and the conditions of the world. They ⁷ are hard, hard. It has all to be borne,—there is nothing for it. It is a terribly difficult thing to get the carts down the hill, it is a matter of life and death. It cannot be helped."

If the fat Indians of Nairobi, who owned the carts, could have brought ⁸ themselves to pay two Rupees and have the brakes put in order, or if the slow young Native driver on the top of the loaded cart, had had it in him to get off and put on the brake, if it was there, then it could have been helped, and the oxen could have walked quietly down the hill. But the oxen did not know, and went on, day after day, in their heroic and desperate struggle, with the conditions of life.

1938

Purpose and Meaning

1. Dinesen is a careful and accurate observer of life in Africa. But her ultimate purpose seems to go far beyond description. State the main thesis of the essay in one sentence. Can you think of additional themes?

2. Although Dinesen does not mention her origins, we can infer from the essay that she is not a native African. What references does she make that give us clues to her social and cultural background?

3. In paragraph 3, Dinesen says that she feels toward the oxen as "a king will be feeling towards his slums: 'You are I, and I am you.' " What does she mean?

Language and Style

1. What elements in the essay determine its tone?

2. Contrast the tone of this essay with the things that are described, particularly the descriptions of the oxen's burdens (paragraphs 4 through 6). What does this contrast imply about the author's attitude toward the oxen's sufferings?

3. Is Dinesen a careful observer? How specific is she in her descriptions of the physical details of her surroundings? Cite examples in the text. Note any general images that might have been made more specific.

Strategy and Structure

1. Paragraphs 1 and 2 do not prepare us for later descriptions of the oxen's plight. How does this contribute to the strength of the images of their suffering? What would have been the difference in effect if the author had started the essay immediately with these later descriptions?

2. Reread paragraphs 3 and 4. How does the author structure her reflections and descriptions into an organized whole?

3. Paragraph 7 is intended to describe what the oxen think. Why has the author included this paragraph in the essay? Is it a good authorial device?

Thinking and Writing

1. This essay was originally from the author's notebook. Keep your own notebook for a week, selecting a different population in your community (for example, shop owners, police officers, children, teachers) for each day. Choose one group and write an essay describing their behavior.

2. Dinesen seems to consider the plight of the oxen an inescapable fact of life. Choose a writing topic inspired by an ongoing injustice you have personally observed (for example, the homeless, impoverished living conditions, inequity). Argue for or against the injustice as something necessary.

Some African Birds

Just at the beginning of the long rains, in the last week of March, or the first week of April, I have head the nightingale in the woods of Africa. Not the full song: a few notes only, — the opening bars of the concerto, a rehearsal, suddenly stopped and again begun. It was as if, in the solitude of the dripping woods, some one was, in a tree, tuning a small cello. It was, however, the same melody, and the same abundance and sweetness, as were soon to fill the forests of Europe, from Sicily to Elsinore.

We had the black and white storks in Africa, the birds that build their nests upon the thatched village roofs of Northern Europe. They look less imposing in Africa than they do there, for here they had such tall and ponderous birds as the Marabout and the Secretary Bird to be compared to. The storks have got other habits in Africa than in Europe, where they live as in married couples and are symbols of domestic happiness. Here they are seen together in big flights, as in clubs. They are called locust-birds in Africa, and follow along when the locusts come upon the land, living high on them. They fly over the plains, too, where there is a grass-fire on, circling just in front of the advancing line of small leaping flames, high up in the scintillating rainbow-coloured air, and the grey smoke, on watch for the mice and snakes that run from the fire. The storks have a gay time in Africa. But their real life is not here, and when the winds of spring bring back thoughts of mating and nesting, their hearts are turned towards the North, they remember old times and places and fly off, two and two, and are shortly after wading in the cold bogs of their birth-places.

Out on the plains, in the beginning of the rains, where the vast stretches of burnt grass begin to show fresh green sprouting, there are many hundred plovers. The plains always have a maritime air, the open horizon recalls the Sea and the long Sea-sands, the wandering wind is the same, the charred grass has a saline smell, and when the grass is long it runs in waves all over the land. When the white carnation flowers on the plains you remember the chopping white-specked waves all round you as you are tacking up the Sund. Out on the plains the plovers likewise take on the appearance of Sea-birds, and behave like Sea-birds on a beach, legging it, on the closing grass, as fast as they can for a short time, and then rising before your horse with high shrill shrieks, so that the light sky is all alive with wings and birds' voices.

The Crested Cranes, which come on to the newly rolled and planted maize-land, to steal the maize out of the ground, make up for the robbery by being birds of good omen, announcing the rain; and also by dancing to us. When the tall birds are together in large numbers, it is a fine sight to see them spread their wings and dance. There is much style in the dance, and a little affectation, for why, when they can fly, do they jump up and down as if they were held on to the earth by magnetism? The whole ballet has a sacred look, like some ritual dance; perhaps the cranes are making an attempt to join Heaven and earth like the winged angels walking up and down Jacob's Ladder. With their delicate pale grey colouring, the little black velvet skull-cap and the fan-shaped crown, the cranes have all the air of light, spirited frescoes. When, after the dance, they lift and go away, to keep up the sacred tone of the show they give out, by the wings or the voice, a clear ringing note, as if a group of church bells had taken to the wing and were sailing off. You can hear them a long way away, even after the birds themselves have become invisible in the sky: a chime from the clouds.

The Greater Hornbill was another visitor to the farm, and came there to eat the fruits of the Cape-Chestnut tree. They are very strange birds. It is an adventure or an experience to meet them, not altogether pleasant, for they look exceedingly knowing. One morning before sunrise I was woken up by a loud jabbering outside the house, and when I walked out on the terrace I saw forty-one Hornbills sitting in the trees on the lawn. There they looked less like birds than like some fantastic articles of finery set on the trees here and there by a child. Black they all were, with the sweet, noble black of Africa, deep darkness absorbed through an age, like old soot, that makes you feel that for elegance, vigour and vivacity, no colour rivals black. All the Hornbills were talking together in the merriest mood, but with choice deportment, like a party of inheritors after a funeral. The morning air was as clear as crystal, the sombre party was bathing in freshness and purity, and, behind the trees and the birds, the sun came up, a dull red ball. You wonder what sort of a day you are to get after such an early morning.

The Flamingos are the most delicately coloured of all the African birds, pink and red like a flying twig of an Oleander bush. They have incredibly long legs and bizarre and recherché curves of their necks and bodies, as if from some exquisite traditional prudery they were making all attitudes and movements in life as difficult as possible.

I once travelled from Port Said to Marseilles in a French boat that had on board a consignment of a hundred and fifty Flamingoes, which were going to the *Jardin D'Acclimatation* in Marseilles. They were kept in large dirty cases with canvas sides, ten in each, standing up close to one another. The keeper, who was taking the birds over, told me that he was counting on losing twenty per cent of them on a trip. They were not made for that sort of life, in rough weather they lost their balance, their legs broke, and the other birds in the cage trampled on them. At night when the wind was high in the Mediterranean and the ship came down in the waves with a thump, at each wave I heard, in the dark, the Flamingoes shriek. Every morning, I saw the keeper taking out one or two dead birds, and throwing them overboard. The noble wader of the Nile, the sister of the lotus, which floats over the landscape like a stray cloud of sunset, had become a slack cluster of pink and red feathers with a pair of long, thin sticks attached to it. The dead birds floated on the water for a short time, knocking up and down in the wake of the ship before they sank.

1938

Purpose and Meaning

1. Does Dinesen seem to have an audience in mind for this excerpt from her notebooks, or are these private musings? What evidence can you find to support your view?

2. The final paragraph includes a description of the pathetic and needless death of some flamingoes. Yet Dinesen describes the event in poetic terms. Does the author's use of poetic terms say anything about the times she lived in? About her own attitude toward animals?

3. What assumptions does the author make about the knowledge a reader should have to appreciate her references? What other references in the essay require special knowledge? Is Dinesen being presumptuous in not explaining or defining these for the reader?

Language and Style

1. Where does the author use personification? How does the use of this device affect your image of the birds? Compare Dinesen's use of personification with Woolf's in "The Death of the Moth."

2. Paragraph 3 contains much analogy. What specific comparisons does the author make? What is the overall comparison?

3. Cite examples from this essay that evoke the five senses. How does Dinesen's use of several senses to describe something contribute to the clarity of what is being described?

4. Compare one of the descriptive passages in this essay with the description of the oxen in the previous essay. What elements of style or tone suggest that both were written by the same author?

5. Note the abundant use of commas in the opening paragraph. What is the effect of dividing these sentences into such short phrases? Is there a relationship between the rhythm created by the punctuation and the subject matter?

Strategy and Structure

1. Does this essay have a discernible beginning, middle, and end, or does it seem to be an arbitrary section of writing? Explain.

2. Each of the first six paragraphs describes a particular species of bird. How does this organizational structure enhance the coherence of the essay?

3. How does Dinesen use classification in this essay? Is her classification scheme complete? Why, or why not?

Thinking and Writing

1. The birds in this essay are described denotatively as well as connotatively. List some of these denotative and connotative descriptions. Before you begin writing, select a specific person, animal, or object, and draw up two lists: one describing your choice objectively and the other subjectively. Use each list as the basis for a brief descriptive essay.

2. Do you consider yourself an expert at discerning differences among people in the same "class"? Prove it by writing an essay describing different types of teachers, students, parents, politicians, and so forth. For the purposes of your essay, try to think of at least three or four types. Try to avoid producing stereotypes by citing specific examples.

Old Knudsen

Sometimes visitors from Europe drifted into the farm like wrecked timber   1
into still waters, turned and rotated, till in the end they were washed out again, or dissolved and sank.

Old Knudsen, the Dane, had come to the farm, sick and blind, and stayed   2
there for the time it took him to die, a lonely animal. He walked along the roads all bent over his misery; for long periods he was without speech, for he had no strength left over from the hard task of carrying it, or, when he spoke, his voice, like the voice of the wolf or hyena, was in itself a wail.

But when he recovered breath, and for a little while was without pain,   3
then sparks flew from the dying rife once more. He would then come to me and explain how he had got to fight with a morbid melancholic disposition in himself, and absurd tendency to see things black. It must be outreasoned, for the outward circumstances they were not amiss, they were, the devil take him, not to be despised. Only pessimism, pessimism,—that was a bad vice!

It was Knudsen who advised me to burn charcoal and sell it to the Indians   4
of Nairobi, at a time when we were, on the farm, more than usually hard up. There were thousands of Rupees in it, he assured me. And it could not fail under the aegis of Old Knudsen, for he had, at one time of his tumultuous career, been to the utmost North of Sweden, and there had learned the craft at his finger's end. He took upon himself to instruct the Natives in the art. While we were thus working together in the wood I talked much with Knudsen.

Charcoal-burning is a pleasant job. There is undoubtedly something in-   5
toxicating about it, and it is known that charcoal-burners see things in a different light from other people; they are given to poetry and taradiddle, and wood-demons come and keep them company. Charcoal is a beautiful thing to turn out, when your kiln is burnt and opened up, and the contents spread on the ground. Smooth as silk, matter defecated, freed of weight and made imperishable, the dark experienced little mummy of the wood.

The mise-en-scène of the art of charcoal-buring is in itself as lovely as possi-   6
ble. As we were cutting down the undergrowth only,—for charcoal cannot be made from thick timber,—we were still working under the crowns of the tall

trees. In this stillness and shade of the African forest, the cut wood smelt like gooseberries; and the piercing, fresh, rank, sour smell of the burning kiln was as bracing as a sea breeze. The whole place had a theatrical atmosphere which, under the Equator, where there are no theatres, was of infinite charm. The thin blue whirls of smoke from the kilns arose at regular distances, and the dark kilns themselves looked like tents on the stage; the place was a smugglers' or soldiers' camp in a romantic Opera. The dark figures of the Natives moved noiselessly amongst them. Where the underwoods have been cleared away in an African forest you will always get a great number of butterflies, which seem to like to cluster on the stubs. It was all mysterious and innocent. In the surroundings, the small crooked form of Old Knudsen fitted in wonderfully well, flickering about, red-topped, agile, now that he had got a favourite job to attend to, sneering and encouraging, like a Puck grown old and blind and very malicious. He was conscientious about his work and surprisingly patient with his Native pupils. We did not always agree. In Paris, where as a girl I went to a painting school, I had learnt that olive-wood will make the best charcoal, but Knudsen explained that olive had no knots in it, and, seven thousand devils in Hell, every one knew that the heart of things was in their knots.

A particular circumstance there in the wood soothed Knudsen's hot temper. [7] The African trees have a delicate foliage, mostly digitate, so that when you have cleared away the dense undergrowth, so to say hollowing out the forest, the light is like the light in a beechwood in May at home, when the leaves are just unfolded, or hardly unfolded yet. I drew Knudsen's attention to the likeness, and the idea pleased him, for all the time of the charcoal-burning he kept up and developed a fantasy; we were on a Whitsunday picnic in Denmark. An old hollow tree he christened Lottenburg, after a place of amusement near Copenhagen. When I had a few bottles of Danish beer hidden in the depths of Lottenburg, and invited him to a drink there, he condescended to think it a good joke.

When we had all our kilns lighted we sat down and talked of life. I learned [8] much about Knudsen's past life, and the strange adventures that had fallen to him wherever he had wandered. You had, in these conversations, to talk of Old Knudsen himself, the one righteous man,—or you would sink into that black pessimism against which he was warning you. He had experienced many things: shipwrecks, plague, fishes of unknown colouring, drinking-spouts, waterspouts, three contemporaneous suns in the sky, false friends, black villainy, short successes, and showers of gold that instantly dried up again. One strong feeling ran through his Odyssey: the abomination of the law, and all its works, and all its doings. He was a born rebel, he saw a comrade in every outlaw. A heroic deed meant to him in itself an act of defiance against the law. He liked to talk of kings and royal families, jugglers, dwarfs and lunatics, for them he took to be outside the law,—and also of any crime, revolution, trick, and prank, that flew in the face of the law. But for the good citizen he had a deep contempt, and law-abidingness in any man was to him the sign of a slavish mind. He did not even respect, or believe in, the law of gravitation, which I learnt

while we were felling trees together: he saw no reason why it should not be—
by unprejudiced, enterprising people—changed into the exact reverse.

Knudsen was eager to imprint on my mind the names of people he had
known, preferably of swindlers and scoundrels. But he never in his narrations
mentioned the name of a woman. It was as if time had swept his mind both
of Elsinore's sweet girls, and of the merciless women of the harbourtowns of
the world. All the same, when I was talking with him I felt in his life the constant presence of an unknown woman I cannot say who she may have been:
wife, mother, school-dame or wife of his first employee,—in my thoughts I called
her Madam Knudsen. I imagined her short because he was so short himself.
She was the woman who ruins the pleasure of man, and therein is always right.
She was the wife of the curtain-lectures, and the housewife of the big cleaning-
days, she stopped all enterprises, she washed the faces of boys, and snatched
away the man's glass of gin from the table before him, she was law and order
embodied. In her claim of absolute power she had some likeness to the female
deity of the Somali women, but Madam Knudsen did not dream of enslaving
by love, she ruled by reasoning and righteousness. Knudsen must have met her
at a young age, when his mind was soft enough to receive an ineffaceable impression. He had fled from her to the Sea, for the Sea she loathes, and there
she does not come, but ashore again in Africa he had not escaped her, she was
still with him. In his wild heart, under his white-red hair, he feared her more
than he feared any man, and suspected all women of being in reality Madam
Knudsen in disguise.

Our charcoal-burning in the end was no financial success. From time to   10
time it would happen that one of our kilns caught fire, and there was our profit
gone up in smoke. Knudsen himself was much concerned about our failure,
and speculated hard upon it, at last he declared that nobody in the world could
burn charcoal if they did not have a fair supply of snow at hand.

Knudsen also helped me to make a pond on the farm. The farm-road in   11
one place ran through a wide cup of grassy ground, there was a spring here
and I thought out the plan of building a dam below it and turning the place
into a lake. You are always short of water in Africa, it would be a great gain
to the cattle to be able to drink in the field, and save themselves the long journey
down to the river. This idea of a dam occupied all the farm day and night, and
was much discussed; in the end, when it was finished, it was to all of us a majestic achievement. It was two hundred feet long. Old Knudsen took a great
interest in it, and taught Pooran Singh to fabricate a dam-scoop. We had trouble with the dam when it was built, because it would not hold water when,
after a long dry period, the big rains began; it gave way in a number of places
and was half washed away more than once. It was Knudsen who struck upon
the scheme of strengthening the earthwork by driving the farm oxen and the
Squatters' stock across the dam whenever they came to the pond to drink. Every
goat and sheep had to contribute to the great work and stamp the structure.
He had some big bloody fights with the little herdboys down here, for Knudsen

insisted that the cattle should walk over slowly, but the wild young Totos wanted them galloping across, tails in the air. In the end, when I had sided with Knudsen and he had got the better of the Totos, the long file of cattle, sedately marching along the narrow bank looked against the sky like Noah's procession of animals going into the ark; and Old Knudsen himself, counting them, his stick under his arm, looked like the boatbuilder Noah, content in the thought that everybody but himself was soon to drown.

In the course of time, I got a vast expanse of water here, seven feet deep [12] in places; the road went through the pond, it was very pretty. Later on we even built two more dams lower down and in this way obtained a row of ponds, like pearls upon a string. The pond now became the heart of the farm. It was always much alive, with a ring of cattle and children round it, and in the hot season, when water-holes dried up in the plains and the hills, the birds came to the farm: herons, ibis, kingfishers, quail, and a dozen varieties of geese and duck. In the evening, when the first stars sprang out in the sky, I used to go and sit by the pond, and then the birds came home. Swimming birds have a purposeful flight, unlike that of other birds: they are on a journey, going from one place to another,—and what perspective is there not in the roading wild swimmers! The duck concluded their orbit over the glass-clear sky, to swoop noiselessly into the dark water like so many arrow-heads let off backwards by a heavenly archer. I once shot a crocodile in the pond, it was a strange thing, for he must have wandered twelve miles from the Athi river to get there. How did he know that there would be water now, where it had never been before?

When the first pond was finished, Knudsen communicated to me the plan [13] of putting fish into it. We had in Africa a kind of perch, which was good to eat, and we dwelt much upon the idea of rich fishing on the farm. It was not, however, an easy thing to get them, the Game-Department had set out perch in ponds but would let nobody fish there yet. But Knudsen confided to me his knowlege of a pond of which no one else in the world knew, where we could get as many fish as we wanted. We would drive there, he explained, draw a net through the pond, and take the fish back in the car in tins and vats in which they would keep alive on the way if we remembered to put water-weeds in with the water. He was so keen on his scheme that he trembled while developing it to me; with his own hands he made one of his inimitable fishing-nets for it. But as the time for the expedition drew near it took on a more and more mysterious aspect. It should be undertaken, he held, on a full moon night, about midnight. At first we had meant to take three boys with us, then he reduced the number to two and to one, and kept asking whether he was absolutely trustworthy? In the end he declared that it would be better that he and I should be by ourselves. I thought this a bad plan, for we would not be able to carry the tins into the car, but Knudsen insisted that it would be by far the best, and added that we ought to tell no one of it.

I had friends in the Game-Department, and I could not help it. I had to [14] ask him: "Knudsen, to whom do these fish that we are going to catch, really belong?" Not a word answered Knudsen. He spat, a regular old sailor's spit, — stretched out his foot in the old patched shoe and rubbed out the spitting on the ground, turned on his heel and walked off deadly slowly. He drew his head down between his shoulders as he went, now he could no longer see at all, but was fumbling before him with his stick, he was once more a beaten man, a homeless fugitive in a low, cold world. And as if in his gesture he had pronounced a spell I stood upon the spot where he had left me, victorious, in Madam Knudsen's slippers.

The fishing project was never again approached between Knudsen and me. Only some time after his death did I, with the assistance of the Game Department, set perch into the pond. They thrived there, and added their silent, cool, mute, restive life to the other life of the pond. In the middle of the day one could, on passing the pond, see them standing near the surface, like fish made out of dark glass in the dim sunny water. My Toto Tumbo was sent to the pond with a primitive fishing-rod and drew up a perch of two pounds whenever an unexpected guest arrived at the house.

When I had found old Knudsen dead on the farm-road, I sent a runner to the Police of Nairobi and reported his death. I had meant to bury him on the farm, but late at night two police officers came out in a car to fetch him, and brought a coffin with them. In the meantime a thunderstorm had broken out, and we had had three inches of rain, for this was just at the beginning of the long rainy season. We drove down to his house through torrents and sheets of water, as we carried Knudsen out to the car the thunder rolled over our heads like cannons, and the flashes of lightning stood on all sides thick as ears in a cornfield. The car had no chains to it and could hardly keep on the road, it swung from one side of it to another. Old Knudsen would have like it, he would have been satisfied with his Exit from the farm.

Afterwards I had a disagreement with the Nairobi Municipality over his funeral arrangements, it developed into a heated argument and I had to go into town about it more than once. It was a legacy left to me by Knudsen, a last tilt, by proxy, at the face of the law. Thus I was no longer Madam Knudsen, but a brother.

1938

Purpose and Meaning

1. The author mentions in the first paragraph that visitors from Europe came to her farm. Why do you suppose, of all these visitors, she chose to write about Old Knudsen?

2. The author mentions in paragraph 5 that "charcoal burners see things in a different light from other people." What is it about this activity that might determine a person's outlook and behavior? How does Old Knudsen display the effects of working as a charcoal burner? Use examples from the essay to support your response.

3. In paragraph 8, the author mentions that Knudsen felt an "abomination of the law." What guided Knudsen? Cite examples in the essay to support your view. What is Dinesen's attitude about Knudsen's disdain for "law-abidingness"?

4. Does Dinesen see the change in her relationship to Knudsen as positive or negative? Even though Knudsen is now dead, does he seem to have any power over the author? Explain.

Language and Style

1. *Simile* refers to a comparison of two things by using the words *like* or *as*. For example, in paragraph 2, Dinesen mentions that Knudsen's voice was "like the voice of the wolf. . . ." In fact, paragraph 1 is one long, extended simile. What does Dinesen achieve by using this literary device?

2. What instances of figurative language can you find in the essay? How do they affect the style of the writing?

3. What stylistic devices does the author use to evoke Madame Knudsen in paragraph 9? Is she a real person? How does the author's depiction of her affect the mood of the essay? What is the mood?

Strategy and Structure

1. Paragraph 4 begins with a rather lengthy description of charcoal burning in the African forest. What function does this long description serve in the essay? Does the author effectively combine her imaginative musings and description of real life? Why does Dinesen include this description in an essay that focuses on a character study?

2. What narrative devices does Dinesen employ to unify this selection? What main episodes does she develop?

3. Although this essay describes the author's relationship to another person, it contains no direct quotations or dialogue. How does this absence of spoken langauge establish the tone of the essay?

4. Both the final paragraph of this essay and that of "Some African Birds" present dramatic reversals. Compare the two conclusions. How do these conclusions function in terms of the overall meanings of the essays? Are they interesting rhetorical strategies? If so, what makes them interesting?

Thinking and Writing

1. Although Dinesen cannot read Old Knudsen's mind, she can observe what seems to motivate his behavior. Select someone you know well whose actions are motivated by a particular philosophy of life, and write about that person's inner and outer selves.

2. Write a character sketch that includes both psychological and behavioral aspects—only this time, use yourself as the model. Write the essay in the third person, as though you are observing yourself from afar.

3. For a larger project, study the works of Dinesen, and explore how her cultural, social, and personal background helped shape her attitude toward her life in Africa and her writing about it.

E. B. WHITE

Perhaps the most distinguished American essayist of our time, Elwyn Brooks White was born in Mount Vernon, New York, on July 11, 1899. The youngest of six children, White, from an early age, treated life in the twentieth century as a wondrous, joyful adventure. "I was a skinny kid but hard," he stated, a latter-day Huck Finn preoccupied by questions of "life, love, war, girls." He was also a child writer, publishing his first work at the age of ten in *The Ladies' Home Journal.*

From Mount Vernon High School to Cornell University; from his half-century at *The New Yorker* to his half-century of marriage to Katharine Angell White; from his apartment in New York City to his farm in North Brooklin, Maine, E. B. White molded the American essay to suit his witty, open-minded, democratic vision of the national experience. He specialized, as he stated in a letter to his brother Stanley Hart White, in "the small things of the day, the trivial matters of the heart, the inconsequential but near things of this living." Although White could, in his own words, sound off at times, notably against "progress" and bureaucracy, his typical posture is that of a writer enamored of the discrete particulars of this world. He attends to detail—a treasured camp in "Once More to the Lake," an old car in "Farewell, My Lovely!" a country schoolhouse in "Education," a circus in the South in "The Ring of Time," a sailor's delights in "The Sea and the Wind That Blows." White doesn't let an essay out of his hands until he has captured in it a certain sharp, vibrant physicality of the world. His conversational manner and easy prose style are actually precise, formal instruments with which he measures the wondrous pulse of humanity and earth.

White's mature vision and style emerged during his years as an editor and writer for *The New Yorker,* which he joined as a part-timer in 1927, when the magazine was in its infancy. From 1927 to 1938, White worked at *The New Yorker* in a variety of capacities, writing satirical sketches, essays, poems, editorials, reviews, cartoon captions, and newsbreaks. Many of his contributions appeared anonymously in the magazine's delightful "Talk of the Town" section. White shaped the "New Yorker style"—witty and wise, above all graceful and urbane—more than any other contributor. In 1929, White published two books, *The Lady Is Cold* and, with his friend James Thurber, *Is Sex Necessary?* That same year, he married Katharine S. Angell, the fiction editor of *The New Yorker.*

In early 1938, the Whites left New York to live on a saltwater farm at Allen Cove on the Maine coast, and for years they divided their time between city and country. While continuing to contribute to *The New Yorker,* White also handled a column for *Harper's* that resulted in *One Man's Meat* (1942). With the publication of *Stuart Little* (1945), *Charlotte's Web* (1952), and *The Trumpet of the Swan* (1972), White achieved fame as a writer of books for children. With his former teacher, William Strunk, Jr., he developed *The Elements of Style* (1959), a concise, lucid guide to writing. His collected *Letters* (1976), *Essays* (1977), and *Poems and Sketches* (1981) are monuments to his career.

When White received the Gold Medal for Essays and Criticism from the National Institute of Arts and Letters in 1960, the presenter, Marchette Chute, captured his achievement. "Of all the gifts he has given us," she stated, "the best gift is himself. He has permitted us to meet a man who is both cheerful and wise, the owner of an uncommon sense that is lit by laughter. When he writes of large subjects he does not make them larger and windier than they are, and when he writes of small things they are never insignificant. He is, in fact, a civilized human being—an order of man that has always been distinguished for its rarity." White received many other awards, including honorary degrees from Harvard and Yale and, from John F. Kennedy in 1963, the first Presidential Medal of Freedom.

White's beloved wife Katharine died in 1977. "She seemed beautiful to me the first time I saw her," he wrote in a letter, "and she seemed beautiful when I gave her the small kiss that was goodbye." White had once observed in a *New Yorker* column that we live in a changed world, but in his own life he opted for the old values and loyalties, for reverence and celebration, and above all, for humor—for humor, as he once observed, "is a handy tool on the writer's workbench." E. B. White died in 1985.

Farewell, My Lovely !

(An aging male kisses an old flame good-bye, circa 1936)*

I see by the new Sears Roebuck catalogue that it is still possible to buy   1
an axle for a 1909 Model T Ford, but I am not deceived. The great days have
faded, the end is in sight. Only one page in the current catalogue is devoted
to parts and accessories for the Model T; yet everyone remembers springtimes
when the Ford gadget section was larger than men's clothing, almost as large
as household furnishings. The last Model T was built in 1927, and the car is
fading from what scholars call the American scene—which is an understatement, because to a few million people who grew up with it, the old Ford practically *was* the American scene.

It was the miracle God had wrought. And it was patently the sort of thing   2
that could only happen once. Mechanically uncanny, it was like nothing that
had ever come to the world before. Flourishing industries rose and fell with
it. As a vehicle, it was hard-working, commonplace, heroic, and it often seemed
to transmit those qualities to the persons who rode in it. My own generation
identifies it with Youth, with its gaudy, irretrievable excitements; before it fades
into the mist, I would like to pay it the tribute of the sigh that is not a sob, .
and set down random entries in a shape somewhat less cumbersome than a Sears
Roebuck catalogue.

The Model T was distinguished from all other makes of cars by the fact   3
that its transmission was of a type known as planetary—which was half
metaphysics, half sheer friction. Engineers accepted the word "planetary" in
its epicyclic sense, but I was always conscious that it also meant "wandering,"
"erratic." Because of the peculiar nature of this planetary element, there was
always, in Model T, a certain dull rapport between engine and wheels, and even
when the car was in a state known as neutral, it trembled with a deep imperative
and tended to inch forward. There was never a moment when the bands were
not faintly egging the machine on. In this respect it was like a horse, rolling
the bit on its tongue, and country people brought to it the same technique they
used with draft animals.

---

*This piece originally appeared in *The New Yorker* over the pseudonym Lee
Strout White. It was suggested by a manuscript submitted by Richard L. Strout, of
The Christian Science Monitor, and Mr. Strout, an amiable collaborator, has kindly
allowed me to include it in this collection. The piece was published as a little book
in 1936 by G. P. Putnam's Sons under the title "Farewell to Model T."

Its most remarkable quality was its rate of acceleration. In its palmy days   4
the Model T could take off faster than anything on the road. The reason was
simple. To get under way, you simply hooked the third finger of the right hand
around a lever on the steering column, pulled down hard, and shoved your
left foot forcibly against the low-speed pedal. These were simple, positive
motions; the car responded by lunging forward with a roar. After a few seconds
of this turmoil, you took your toe off the pedal, eased up a mite on the throttle,
and the car, possessed of only two forward speeds, catapulted directly into high
with a series of ugly jerks and was off on its glorious errand. The abruptness
of this departure was never equaled in other cars of the period. The human
leg was (and still is) incapable of letting in a clutch with anything like the forthright abandon that used to send Model T on its way. Letting in a clutch is a
negative, hesitant motion, depending on delicate nervous control; pushing down
the Ford pedal was a simple, country motion—an expansive act, which came
as natural as kicking an old door to make it budge.

The driver of the old Model T was a man enthroned. The car, with top   5
up, stood seven feet high. The driver sat on top of the gas tank, brooding it
with his own body. When he wanted gasoline, he alighted, along with everything
else in the front seat; the seat was pulled off, the metal cap unscrewed, and
a wooden stick thrust down to sound the liquid in the well. There were always
a couple of these sounding sticks kicking around in the ratty sub-cushion regions
of a flivver. Refueling was more of a social function then, because the driver
had to unbend, whether he wanted to or not. Directly in front of the driver
was the windshield—high, uncompromisingly erect. Nobody talked about air
resistance, and the four cylinders pushed the car through the atmosphere with
a simple disregard of physical law.

There was this about a Model T: the purchaser never regarded his pur-   6
chase as a complete, finished product. When you bought a Ford, you figured
you had a start—a vibrant, spirited framework to which could be screwed an
almost limitless assortment of decorative and functional hardware. Driving away
from the agency, hugging the new wheel between your knees, you were already
full of creative worry. A Ford was born naked as a baby, and a flourishing
industry grew up out of correcting its rare deficiencies and combatting its
fascinating diseases. Those were the great days of lily-painting. I have been
looking at some old Sears Roebuck catalogues, and they bring everything back
so clear.

First you bought a Ruby Safety Reflector for the rear, so that your posterior   7
would glow in another's car's brilliance. Then you invested thirty-nine cents
in some radiator Moto Wings, a popular ornament which gave the Pegasus touch
to the machine and did something godlike to the owner. For nine cents you
bought a fanbelt guide to keep the belt from slipping off the pulley.

You bought a radiator compound to stop leaks. This was as much a part   8
of everybody's equipment as aspirin tablets are of a medicine cabinet. You bought
special oil to prevent chattering, a clamp-on dash light, a patching outfit, a tool
box which you bolted to the running board, a sun visor, a steering-column brace

to keep the column rigid, and a set of emergency containers for gas, oil, and water—three thin, disc-like cans which reposed in a case on the running board during long, important journeys—red for gas, gray for water, green for oil. It was only a beginning. After the car was about a year old, steps were taken to check the alarming disintegration. (Model T was full of tumors, but they were benign.) A set of anti-rattlers (ninety-eight cents) was a popular panacea. You hooked them on to the gas and spark rods, to the brake pull rod, and to the steering-rod connections. Hood silencers, of black rubber, were applied to the fluttering hood. Shock-absorbers and snubbers gave "complete relaxation." Some people bought rubber pedal pads, to fit over the standard metal pedals. (I didn't like these, I remember.) Persons of a suspicious or pugnacious turn of mind bought a rear-view mirror; but most Model T owners weren't worried by what was coming from behind because they would soon enough see it out in front. They rode in a state of cheerful catalepsy. Quite a large mutinous clique among Ford owners went over to a foot accelerator (you could buy one and screw it to the floor board), but there was a certain madness in these people, because the Model T, just as she stood, had a choice of three foot pedals to push, and there were plenty of moments when both feet were occupied in the routine performance of duty and when the only way to speed up the engine was with the hand throttle.

Gadget bred gadget. Owners not only bought ready-made gadgets, they 9 invented gadgets to meet special needs. I myself drove my car directly from the agency to the blacksmith's, and had the smith affix two enormous iron brackets to the port running board to support an army trunk.

People who owned closed models builded along different lines: they bought 10 ball grip handles for opening doors, window antirattlers, and deluxe flower vases of the cut-glass antisplash type. People with delicate sensibilities garnished their car with a device called the Donna Lee Automobile Disseminator—a porous vase guaranteed, according to Sears, to fill the car with a "faint clean odor of lavender." The gap between open cars and closed cars was not as great then as it is now: for $11.95, Sears Roebuck converted your touring car into a sedan and you went forth renewed. One agreeable quality of the old Fords was that they had no bumpers, and their fenders softened and wilted with the years and permitted the driver to squeeze in and out of tight places.

Tires were 30×3½, cost about $12, and punctured readily. Everybody 11 carried a Jiffy patching set, with a nutmeg grater to roughen the tube before the goo was spread on. Everybody was capable of putting on a patch, expected to have to, and did have to.

During my association with Model T's, self-starters were not a prevalent 12 accessory. They were expensive and under suspicion. Your car came equipped with a serviceable crank, and the first thing you learned was how to Get Results. It was a special trick, and until you learned it (usually from another Ford owner, but sometimes by a period of appalling experimentation) you might as well have been winding up an awning. The trick was to leave the ignition switch off, proceed to the animal's head, pull the choke (which was a little wire protruding through the radiator) and give the crank two or three nonchalant upward lifts. Then, whistling as though thinking about something else, you would saunter back to the driver's cabin, turn the ignition on, return to the crank, and this time, catching it on the down stroke, give it a quick spin with plenty of that. If this procedure was followed, the engine almost always responded—first with a few scattered explosions, then with a tumultuous gunfire, which you checked by racing around to the driver's seat and retarding the throttle. Often, if the emergency brake hadn't been pulled all the way back, the car advanced on you the instant the first explosion occurred and you would hold it back by leaning your weight against it. I can still feel my old Ford nuzzling me at the curb, as though looking for an apple in my pocket.

In zero weather, ordinary cranking became an impossibility, except for giants. The oil thickened, and it became necessary to jack up the rear wheels, which, for some planetary reason, eased the throw.   13

The lore and legend that governed the Ford were boundless. Owners had   14 their own theories about everything; they discussed mutual problems in that wise, infinitely resourceful way old women discuss rheumatism. Exact knowledge was pretty scarce, and often proved less effective than superstition. Dropping a camphor ball into the gas tank was a popular expedient; it seemed to have a tonic effect on both man and machine. There wasn't much to base exact knowledge on. The Ford driver flew blind. He didn't know the temperature of his engine, the speed of his car, the amount of his fuel, or the pressure of his oil (the old Ford lubricated itself by what was amiably described as the "splash system"). A speedometer cost money and was an extra, like a windshield wiper. The dashboard of the early models was bare save for an ignition key; later models, grown effete, boasted an ammeter which pulsated alarmingly with the throbbing of the car. Under the dash was a box of coils, with vibrators which you adjusted, or thought you adjusted. Whatever the driver learned of his motor, he learned not through instruments but through sudden developments. I remember that the timer was one of the vital organs about which there was ample doctrine. When everything else had been checked, you "had a look" at the timer. It was an extravagantly odd little device, simple in construction, mysterious in function. It contained a roller, held by a spring, and there were four contact points on the inside of the case against which, many people believed, the roller rolled. I have had a timer apart on a sick Ford many times. But I never really knew what I was up to—I was just showing off before God. There were almost as many schools of thought as there were timers. Some people, when things went wrong, just clenched their teeth and gave the timer a smart crack with a wrench. Other people opened it up and blew on it. There was a school that held that the timer needed large amounts of oil; they fixed it by frequent baptism. And there was a school that was positive it was meant to run dry as a bone; these people were continually taking it off and wiping it. I remember once spitting into a timer; not in anger, but in a spirit of research. You see, the Model T driver moved in the realm of metaphysics. He believed his car could be hexed.

One reason the Ford anatomy was never reduced to an exact science was that, having "fixed" it, the owner couldn't honestly claim that the treatment had brought about the cure. There were too many authenticated cases of Fords fixing themselves—restored naturally to health after a short rest. Farmers soon discovered this, and it fitted nicely with their draft-horse philosophy: "Let 'er cool off and she'll snap into it again."

A Ford owner had Number One Bearing constantly in mind. This bearing, being at the front end of the motor, was the one that always burned out, because the oil didn't reach it when the car was climbing hills. (That's what I was always told, anyway.) The oil used to recede and leave Number One dry as a clam flat; you had to watch that bearing like a hawk. It was like a weak heart—you could hear it start knocking, and that was when you stopped to let her cool off. Try as you would to keep the oil supply right, in the end Number One always went out. "Number One Bearing burned out on me and I had to have her replaced," you would say, wisely; and your companions always had a lot to tell about how to protect and pamper Number One to keep her alive.

Sprinkled not too liberally among the millions of amateur witch doctors who drove Fords and applied their own abominable cures were the heaven-sent mechanics who could really make the car talk. These professionals turned up in undreamed-of spots. One time, on the banks of the Columbia River in Washington, I heard the rear end go out of my Model T when I was trying to whip it up a steep incline onto the deck of a ferry. Something snapped; the car slid backward into the mud. It seemed to me like the end of the trail. But the captain of the ferry, observing the withered remnant, spoke up.

"What's got her?" he asked.

"I guess it's the rear end," I replied, listlessly. The captain leaned over the rail and stared. Then I saw that there was a hunger in his eyes that set him off from other men.

"Tell you what," he said, carelessly, trying to cover up his eagerness, "Let's pull the son of a bitch up onto the boat, and I'll help you fix her while we're going back and forth on the river."

We did just this. All that day I plied between the towns of Pasco and Kennewick, while the skipper (who had once worked in a Ford garage) directed the amazing work of resetting the bones of my car.

Springtime in the heyday of the Model T was a delirious season. Owning a car was still a major excitement, roads were still wonderful and bad. The Fords were obviously conceived in madness: any car which was capable of going from forward into reverse without any perceptible mechanical hiatus was bound to be a mighty challenging thing to the human imagination. Boys used to veer them off the highway into a level pasture and run wild with them, as though they were cutting up with a girl. Most everybody used the reverse pedal quite as much as the regular foot brake—it distributed the wear over the bands and wore them all down evenly. That was the big trick, to wear all the bands down evenly, so that the final chattering would be total and the whole unit scream for renewal.

The days were golden, the nights were dim and strange. I still recall with 23 trembling those loud, nocturnal crises when you drew up to a signpost and raced the engine so the lights would be bright enough to read destinations by. I have never been really planetary since. I suppose it's time to say good-bye. Farewell, my lovely!

1936

Purpose and Meaning

1. According to White, what is the underlying property of the Model T that makes it so appealing? Why does he describe its mechanics in glowing terms?

2. In paragraph 1, White refers to the "great days" in American history. What is the significance of the word *great*? What era is he referring to? What was life like then, particularly in the realm of technology? Note the reference to the time the essay was written (1936). What were the historical and social contexts of that era?

3. White uses considerable hyperbole in the first three paragraphs. He says the Model T "practically *was* the American scene"; "It was the miracle God had wrought"; its transmission was "half metaphysics." How do these observations help determine the tone of the essay?

Language and Style

1. White's descriptions suggest that the Model T had a life of its own. (For example, in paragraph 14, White refers to the auto's "vital organs.") Specifically, where and how does the author use personification to transmit this impression?

2. We easily recognize humor in TV and film comedies and in jokes comedians tell. What stylistic elements make this essay humorous? In reading the essay, how long did it take until you became aware of its comic tone? What specific elements made you aware of this tone?

Strategy and Structure

1. How does White employ process analysis to organize large segments of this essay?

2. Why does White divide the essay into three sections?

3. How does White structure paragraph 14 so that it is an effective unit of writing? How does the opening sentence of the paragraph contribute to its unity?

4. Study the opening sentences of each paragraph. Which of these serve as the topic for the rest of the paragraph? Is this strategy an effective means of structuring an essay? Explain.

Thinking and Writing

1. Discuss the concept of nostalgia in class. What makes an object or era nostalgic? Consider some of the nostalgic interests people have in society today: old movies, out-of-fashion clothes, antique TV's and radios, the Fifties. Select one of these or something else nostalgic of your own choosing and describe what makes it so. Making a list of its properties may be an effective means of brainstorming the subject.

2. Examine the work of a contemporary writer of humor (for example, Russell Baker's essays in this book). Write an essay evaluating what makes the writing funny.

3. Interview one of your parents or someone from your parent's generation about his or her childhood or youth. Focus on those things, people, or events that are recalled with nostalgia. Ask what role these things played in the person's life. Then write an account of your findings.

Once More to the Lake

One summer, along about 1904, my father rented a camp on a lake in   1
Maine and took us all there for the month of August. We all got ringworm from some kittens and had to rub Pond's Extract on our arms and legs night and morning, and my father rolled over in a canoe with all his clothes on; but outside of that the vacation was a success and from then on none of us ever thought there was any place in the world like that lake in Maine. We returned summer after summer—always on August 1 for one month. I have since become a salt-water man, but sometimes in summer there are days when the restlessness of the tides and the fearful cold of the sea water and the incessant wind that blows across the afternoon and into the evening make me wish for the placidity of a lake in the woods. A few weeks ago this feeling got so strong I bought myself a couple of bass hooks and a spinner and returned to the lake where we used to go, for a week's fishing and to revisit old haunts.

I took along my son, who had never had any fresh water up his nose and   2
who had seen lily pads only from train windows. On the journey over to the lake I began to wonder what it would be like. I wondered how time would have

marred this unique, this holy spot—the coves and streams, the hills that the sun set behind, the camps and the paths behind the camps. I was sure that the tarred road would have found it out, and I wondered in what other ways it would be desolated. It is strange how much you can remember about places like that once you allow your mind to return into the grooves that lead back. You remember one thing, and that suddenly reminds you of another thing. I guess I remembered clearest of all the early mornings, when the lake was cool and motionless, remembered how the bedroom smelled of the lumber it was made of and of the wet woods whose scent entered through the screen. The partitions in the camp were thin and did not extend clear to the top of the rooms, and as I was always the first up I would dress softly so as not to wake the others, and sneak out into the sweet outdoors and start out in the canoe, keeping close along the shore in the long shadows of the pines. I remembered being very careful never to rub by paddle against the gunwale for fear of disturbing the stillness of the cathedral.

The lake had never been what you would call a wild lake. There were 3 cottages sprinkled around the shores, and it was in farming country although the shores of the lake were quite heavily wooded. Some of the cottages were owned by nearby farmers, and you would live at the shore and eat your meals at the farmhouse. That's what our family did. But although it wasn't wild, it was a fairly large and undisturbed lake and there were places in it that, to a child at least, seemed infinitely remote and primeval.

I was right about the tar; it led to within half a mile of the shore. But 4 when I got back there, with my boy, and we settled into a camp near a farm-house and into the kind of summertime I had known, I could tell that it was going to be pretty much the same as it had been before—I knew it, lying in bed the first morning, smelling the bedroom and hearing the boy sneak quietly out and go off along the shore in a boat. I began to sustain the illusion that he was I, and therefore, by simple transposition, that I was my father. This sensation persisted, kept cropping up all the time we were there. It was not an entirely new feeling, but in this setting it grew much stronger. I seemed to be living a dual existence. I would be in the middle of some simple act. I would be picking up a bait box or laying down a table fork, or I would be saying something, and suddenly it would be not I but my father who was saying the words or making the gesture. It gave me a creepy sensation.

We went fishing the first morning. I felt the same damp moss covering 5 the worms in the bait can, and saw the dragonfly alight on the tip of my rod as it hovered a few inches from the surface of the water. It was the arrival of this fly that convinced me beyond any doubt that everything was as it always had been, that the years were a mirage and that there had been no years. The small waves were the same, chucking the rowboat under the chin as we fished at anchor, and the boat was the same boat, the same color green and the ribs broken in the same places, and under the floorboards the same fresh-water leav-ings and débris—the dead helgramite, the wisps of moss, the rusty discarded fishhook, the dried blood from yesterday's catch. We stared silently at the tips of our rods, at the dragonflies that came and went. I lowered the tip of mine into the water, tentatively, pensively dislodging the fly, which darted two feet away, poised, darted two feet back, and came to rest again a little farther up the rod. There had been no years between the ducking of this dragonfly and the other one—the one that was part of memory. I looked at the boy, who was silently watching his fly, and it was my hands that held his rod, my eyes watching. I felt dizzy and didn't know which rod I was at the end of.

We caught two bass, hauling them in briskly as though they were mackerel,   6 pulling them over the side of the boat in a businesslike manner without any landing net, and stunning them with a blow on the back of the head. When we got back for a swim before lunch, the lake was exactly where we had left it, the same number of inches from the dock, and there was only the merest suggestion of a breeze. This seemed an utterly enchanted sea, this lake you could leave to its own devices for a few hours and come back to, and find that it had not stirred, this constant and trustworthy body of water. In the shallows, the dark, water-soaked sticks and twigs, smooth and old, were undulating in clusters on the bottom against the clean ribbed sand, and the track of the mussel was plain. A school of minnows swam by, each minnow with its small individual shadow, doubling the attendance, so clear and sharp in the sunlight. Some of the other campers were in swimming, along the shore, one of them with a cake of soap, and the water felt thin and clear and unsubstantial. Over the years there had been this person with the cake of soap, this cultist, and here he was. There had been no years.

Up to the farmhouse to dinner through the teeming, dusty field, the road   7 under our sneakers was only a two-track road. The middle track was missing, the one with the marks of the hooves and the splotches of dried, flaky manure. There had always been three tracks to choose from in choosing which track to walk in; now the choice was narrowed down to two. For a moment I missed terribly the middle alternative. But the way led past the tennis court, and something about the way it lay there in the sun reassured me; the tape had loosened along the backline, the alleys were green with plantains and other weeds, and the net (installed in June and removed in September) sagged in the dry noon, and the whole place steamed with midday heat and hunger and emptiness. There was a choice of pie for dessert, and one was blueberry and one was apple, and the waitresses were the same country girls, there having been no passage of time, only the illusion of it as in a dropped curtain—the waitresses were still fifteen; their hair had been washed, that was the only difference— they had been to the movies and seen the pretty girls with the clean hair.

Summertime, oh, summertime, pattern of life indelible, the fadeproof lake,   8 the woods unshatterable, the pasture with the sweetfern and the juniper forever and ever, summer without end; this was the background, and the life along the shore was the design, the cottagers with their innocent and tranquil design, their tiny docks with the flagpole and the American flag floating against the white clouds in the blue sky, the little paths over the roots of the trees leading from camp to camp and the paths leading back to the outhouses and the can of lime for sprinkling, and at the souvenir counters at the store the miniature birch-bark canoes and the postcards that showed things looking a little better than they looked. This was the American family at play, escaping the city heat, wondering whether the newcomers in the camp at the head of the cove were "common" or "nice," wondering whether it was true that the people who drove up for Sunday dinner at the farmhouse were turned away because there wasn't enough chicken.

It seemed to me, as I kept remembering all this, that those times and those summers had been infinitely precious and worth saving. There had been jollity and peace and goodness. The arriving (at the beginning of August) had been so big a business in itself, at the railway station the farm wagon drawn up, the first smell of the pine-laden air, the first glimpse of the smiling farmer, and the great importance of the trunks and your father's enormous authority in such matters, and the feel of the wagon under you for the long ten-mile haul, and at the top of the last long hill catching the first view of the lake after eleven months of not seeing this cherished body of water. The shouts and cries of the other campers when they saw you, and the trunks to be unpacked, to give up their rich burden. (Arriving was less exciting nowadays, when you sneaked up in your car and parked it under a tree near the camp and took out the bags and in five minutes it was all over, no fuss, no loud wonderful fuss about trunks.) 9

Peace and goodness and jollity. The only thing that was wrong now, really, 10 was the sound of the place, an unfamiliar nervous sound of the outboard motors. This was the note that jarred, the one thing that would sometimes break the illusion and set the years moving. In those other summertimes all motors were inboard; and when they were at a little distance, the noise they made was a sedative, an ingredient of summer sleep. They were one-cylinder and two-cylinder engines, and some were make-and-break and some were jump-spark, but they all made a sleepy sound across the lake. The one-lungers throbbed and fluttered, and the twin-cylinder ones purred and purred, and that was a quiet sound, too. But now the campers all had outboards. In the daytime, in the hot mornings, these motors made a petulant, irritable sound; at night, in the still evening when the afterglow lit the water, they whined about one's ears like mosquitoes. My boy loved our rented outboard, and his great desire was to achieve single-handed mastery over it, and authority, and he soon learned the trick of choking it a little (but not too much), and the adjustment of the needle valve. Watching him I would remember the things you could do with the old one-cylinder engine with the heavy flywheel, how you could have it eating out of your hand if you got really close to it spiritually. Motorboats in those days didn't have clutches, and you would make a landing by shutting off the motor at the proper time and coasting in with a dead rudder. But there was a way of reversing them, if you learned the trick, by cutting the switch and putting it on again exactly on the final dying revolution of the flywheel, so that it would kick back against compression and begin reversing. Approaching dock in a strong following breeze, it was difficult to slow up sufficiently by the ordinary coasting method, and if a boy felt he had complete mastery over his motor, he was tempted to keep it running beyond its time and then reverse it a few feet from the dock. It took a cool nerve, because if you threw the switch a twentieth of a second too soon you would catch the flywheel when it still had speed enough to go up past center, and the boat would leap ahead, charging bull-fashion at the dock.

We had a good week at the camp. The bass were biting well and the sun shone endlessly, day after day. We would be tired at night and lie down in the accumulated heat of the little bedrooms after the long hot day and the breeze would stir almost imperceptibly outside and the smell of the swamp drift in through the rusty screens. Sleep would come easily and in the morning the red squirrel would be on the roof, tapping out his gay routine. I kept remembering everything, lying in bed in the mornings—the small steamboat that had a long rounded stern like the lip of a Ubangi, and how quietly she ran on the moonlight sails, when the older boys played their mandolins and the girls sang and we ate doughnuts dipped in sugar, and how sweet the music was on the water in the shining night, and what it had felt like to think about girls then. After breakfast we would go up to the store and the things were in the same place— the minnows in a bottle, the plugs and spinners disarranged and pawed over by the youngsters from the boys' camp, the Fig Newtons and the Beeman's gum. Outside, the road was tarred and cars stood in front of the store. Inside, all was just as it had always been, except there was more Coca-Cola and not so much Moxie and root beer and birch beer and sarsaparilla. We would walk out with the bottle of pop apiece and sometimes the pop would backfire up our noses and hurt. We explored the streams, quietly, where the turtles slid off the sunny logs and dug their way into the soft bottom; and we lay on the town wharf and fed worms to the tame bass. Everywhere we went I had trouble making out which was I, the one walking at my side, the one walking in my pants.

One afternoon while we were there at that lake a thunderstorm came up. It was like the revival of an old melodrama that I had seen long ago with childish awe. The second-act climax of the drama of the electrical disturbance over a lake in America had not changed in any important respect. This was the big scene, still the big scene. The whole thing was so familiar, the first feeling of oppression and heat and a general air around the camp of not wanting to go very far away. In midafternoon (it was all the same) a curious darkening of the sky, and a lull in everything that had made life tick; and then the way the boats suddenly swung the other way at their moorings with the coming of a breeze out of the new quarter, and the premonitory rumble. Then the kettle drum, then the snare, then the bass drum and cymbals, then crackling light against the dark, and the gods grinning and licking their chops in the hills. Afterward the calm, the rain steadily rustling in the calm lake, the return of light and hope and spirits, and the campers running out in joy and relief to go swimming in the rain, their bright cries perpetuating the deathless joke about how they were getting simply drenched, and the children screaming with delight at the new sensation of bathing in the rain, and the joke about getting drenched linking the generations in a strong indestructible chain. And the comedian who waded in carrying an umbrella.

When the others went swimming, my son said he was going in, too. He 13 pulled his dripping trunks from the line where they had hung all through the shower and wrung them out. Languidly, and with no thought of going in, I watched him, his hard little body, skinny and bare, saw him wince slightly as he pulled up around his vitals the small, soggy, icy garment. As he buckled the swollen belt, suddenly my groin felt the chill of death.

1941

Purpose and Meaning

1. White's son is silent throughout the essay, yet his presence is essential to its thesis. How does the son affect the author's perspective during his trip? In what way would White's experience have been different had he gone alone?

2. Not much seems to have changed at the lake since White visited it as a boy. Does White endow this fact with any significance, or is it simply a neutral observation? Elaborate.

3. The lake elicits poignant memories for White. What is the purpose of his recording these memories? Why is it significant that he is writing down his observations and reflections so meticulously? What might White's response have been to the question, "Why bother writing about this experience?"

Language and Style

1. What is the effect of describing nature specifically and concretely yet in a way that strongly evokes the senses? Find some especially vivid sensory details.

2. In paragraph 2, White calls the lake "this holy spot." Locate other examples of this elevated diction. How do they affect the tone of the essay? What is the overall effect when White combines this "high" diction with more colloquial language? Find examples of this juxtaposition.

3. Repetition is a device often used for literary effect. Notice the use of the word *same* in paragraph 5. How does its repetition contribute to the tone of the paragraph?

4. White is describing a common scene of American life, a visit to the countryside. But his writing style is anything but typical. Paragraph 8, for example, begins with a ten-line sentence that contains unusual syntax. Read the sentence aloud to sense the rhythm of it. How does this and other long sentences contribute to the essay's mood?

Strategy and Structure

1. The author seems to write about nature with great facility, yet his essay is actually very carefully constructed. Which paragraphs constitute the introduction, body, and conclusion? How do they connect? What theme is introduced in paragraph 12?

2. Locate instances of comparison and contrast in this essay. Why does White mix comparison and description?

3. How does White develop the lake as a symbol?

4. What is the significance of the last sentence of the essay? How does it contribute to the overall organization of the piece?

Thinking and Writing

1. Explore the function and effect of figurative language—allusion, analogy, simile, personification, metaphor—in "Once More to the Lake."

2. How are the generations linked in White's essay? Review all the passages in the work that describe this linkage. Write a brief analysis of each reference the author makes to generations.

3. Write an essay on one memorable place that you have revisited. As in White's essay, try to capture the original feeling and the newer one.

Education

I have an increasing admiration for the teacher in the country school where 1
we have a third-grade scholar in attendance. She not only undertakes to instruct her charges in all the subjects of the first three grades, but she manages to function quietly and effectively as a guardian of their health, their clothes, their habits, their mothers, and their snowball engagements. She has been doing this sort of Augean task for twenty years, and is both kind and wise. She cooks for the children on the stove that heats the room, and she can cool their passions or warm their soup with equal competence. She conceives their costumes, cleans up their messes, and shares their confidences. My boy already regards his teacher as his great friend, and I think tells her a great deal more than he tells me.

The shift from city school to country school was something we worried 2
about quietly all last summer. I have always rather favored public school over

private school, if only because in public school you meet a greater variety of children. This bias of mine, I suspect, is partly an attempt to justify my own past (I never knew anything but public schools) and partly an involuntary defense against getting kicked in the shins by a young ceramist on his way to the kiln. My wife was unacquainted with public schools, never having been exposed (in her early life) to anything more public than the washroom of Miss Winsor's. Regardless of our backgrounds, we both knew that the change in schools was something that concerned not us but the scholar himself. We hoped it would work out all right. In New York our son went to a medium-priced private institution with semi-progressive ideas of education and modern plumbing. He learned fast, kept well, and we were satisfied. It was an electric, colorful, regimented existence with moments of pleasurable pause and giddy incident. The day the Christmas angel fainted and had to be carried out by one of the Wise Men was educational in the highest sense of the term. Our scholar gave imitations of it around the house for weeks afterward, and I doubt if it ever goes completely out of his mind.

His days were rich in formal experience. Wearing overalls and an old 3 sweater (the accepted uniform of the private seminary), he sallied forth at morn accompanied by a nurse or a parent and walked (or was pulled) two blocks to a corner where the school bus made a flag stop. This flashy vehicle was as punctual as death: seeing us waiting at the cold curb, it would sweep to a halt, open its mouth, suck the boy in, and spring away with an angry growl. It was a good deal like a train picking up a bag of mail. At school the scholar was worked on for six or seven hours by half a dozen teachers and a nurse, and was revived on orange juice in mid-morning. In a cinder court he played games supervised by an athletic instructor, and in a cafeteria he ate lunch worked out by a dietitian. He soon learned to read with gratifying facility and discernment and to make Indian weapons of a semi-deadly nature. Whenever one of his classmates fell low of a fever the news was put on the wires and there were breathless phone calls to physicians, discussing periods of incubation and allied magic.

In the country all one can say is that the situation is different and somehow 4 more casual. Dressed in corduroys, sweatshirts, and short rubber boots, and carrying a tin dinner-pail, our scholar departs at crack of dawn for the village school, two and a half miles down the road, next to the cemetery. When the road is open and the car will start, he makes the journey by motor, courtesy of his old man. When the snow is deep or the motor is dead or both, he makes it on the hoof. In the afternoons he walks or hitches all or part of the way home in fair weather, gets transported in foul. The schoolhouse is a two-room frame building, bungalow type, shingles stained a burnt brown with weather-resistant stain. It has a chemical toilet in the basement and two teachers above stairs. One takes the first three grades, the other the fourth, fifth, and sixth. They have little or no time for individual instruction, and no time at all for the esoteric. They teach what they know themselves, just as fast and as hard as they can manage. The pupils sit still at their desks in class, and do their milling around outdoors during recess.

There is no supervised play. They play cops and robbers (only they call ⁵ it "Jail") and throw things at one another—snowballs in winter, rose hips in fall. It seems to satisfy them. They also construct darts, pinwheels, and "pick-up sticks" (jackstraws), and the school itself does a brisk trade in penny candy, which is for sale right in the classroom and which contains "surprises." The most highly prized surprise is a fake cigarette, made of cardboard, fiendishly lifelike.

The memory of how apprehensive we were at the beginning is still strong. ⁶ The boy was nervous about the change too. The tension, on that first fair morning in September when we drove him to school, almost blew the windows out of the sedan. And when later we picked him up on the road, wandering along with his little blue lunch-pail, and got his laconic report "All right" in answer to our inquiry about how the day had gone, our relief was vast. Now, after almost a year of it, the only difference we can discover in the two school experiences is that in the country he sleeps better at night—and *that* probably is more the air than the education. When grilled on the subject of school-in-country *vs.* school-in-city, he replied that the chief difference is that the day seems to go so much quicker in the country. "Just like lightning," he reported.

1939

Purpose and Meaning

1. To what does the title specifically refer: White's child's education; White's own education; education in a general sense? What clues in the story lead you to this conclusion?

2. How do the diverse roles that White's son's teacher performs compare with the functions of contemporary teachers? What activities described in paragraph 1 and in other paragraphs "date" the essay?

3. Why does White favor public schools?

4. Although the author does not mention his economic or social status directly, what clues does he provide that indicate his background? Does he implicitly assume that the reader is of the same background as he? What evidence is there in the essay for your answer?

Language and Style

1. In paragraph 2, White mentions that "the day the Christmas angel fainted and had to be carried out by one of the Wise Men was educational in the highest

sense of the term." What does he mean by "educational"? Does this experience fulfill the requirements of your own definition of "educational"?

2. Today, discussions of education are often heated and argumentative. What contributes to the calm, even-tempered tone of this essay? Is it the difference in attitude toward education then and now? Is it a question of style? Explain your answer.

3. Some of White's sentences are lengthy without being confusing. Consider the following from paragraph 3: "Wearing overalls and an old sweater (the accepted uniform of the private seminary), he sallied forth at morn accompanied by a nurse or a parent and walked (or was pulled) two blocks to a corner where the school bus made a flag stop." Does this sentence demonstrate "good" writing? If so, why? If not, why not? Find other lengthy sentences in the essay and analyze them for clarity. Note how phrases relate to the basic subject-verb pattern of the sentence.

4. Consider the syntax and vocabulary in the following sentence from paragraph 2 and discuss how they are characteristic of White's prose style: "It was an electric, colorful, regimented existence with moments of pleasurable pause and giddy incident."

Strategy and Structure

1. The opening focuses on a teacher. However, she is not mentioned again in the essay. Why does White introduce the essay's subject matter in this way? Is it confusing or is it effective?

2. How does White employ comparison and contrast to advance his argument? What, specifically, is compared, and what contrasted?

3. What does the response in the last sentence "Just like lightning. . . ." reveal about the son's educational development? Why do you suppose White ended the essay with it?

Thinking and Writing

1. Imagine that the last paragraph of White's essay has been destroyed. Write your own conclusion to the essay, imitating the style of the author. Compare it to the original. How are they similar or different in terms of tone, syntax, vocabulary, and voice?

2. Write an essay describing one type of informal education that children receive today that differs from the type White's son received. For example, what type of education does one receive from television, from the city streets, from video games?

3. Write an essay comparing urban, suburban, and rural education in America today. Draw conclusions about the superiority of one to the others.

The Ring of Time

After the lions had returned to their cages, creeping angrily through the   1
chutes, a little bunch of us drifted away and into an open doorway nearby,
where we stood for a while in semidarkness, watching a big brown circus horse
go harumphing around the practice ring. His trainer was a woman of about
forty, and the two of them, horse and woman, seemed caught up in one of those
desultory treadmills of afternoon from which there is no apparent escape. The
day was hot, and we kibitzers were grateful to be briefly out of the sun's glare.
The long rein, or tape, by which the woman guided her charge counterclockwise
in his dull career formed the radius of their private circle, of which she was
the revolving center; and she, too, stepped a tiny circumference of her own,
in order to accommodate the horse and allow him his maximum scope. She
had on a short-skirted costume and a conical straw hat. Her legs were bare and
she wore high heels, which probed deep into the loose tanbark and kept her
ankles in a state of constant turmoil. The great size and meekness of the horse,
the repetitious exercise, the heat of the afternoon, all exerted a hypnotic charm
that invited boredom; we spectators were experiencing a languor—we neither
expected relief nor felt entitled to any. We had paid a dollar to get into the
grounds, to be sure, but we had got our dollar's worth a few minutes before,
when the lion trainer's whiplash had got caught around a toe of one of the lions.
What more did we want for a dollar?

Behind me I heard someone say, "Excuse me, please," in a low voice. She   2
was halfway into the building when I turned and saw her—a girl of sixteen or
seventeen, politely threading her way through us onlookers who blocked the
entrance. As she emerged in front of us, I saw that she was barefoot, her dirty
little feet fighting the uneven ground. In most respects she was like any of two
or three dozen showgirls you encounter if you wander about the winter quarters
of Mr. John Ringling North's circus, in Sarasota—cleverly proportioned, deeply
browned by the sun, dusty, eager, and almost naked. But her grave face and
the naturalness of her manner gave her a sort of quick distinction and brought
a new note into the gloomy octagonal building where we had all cast our lot
for a few moments. As soon as she had squeezed through the crowd, she spoke
a word or two to the older woman, whom I took to be her mother, stepped
to the ring, and waited while the horse coasted to a stop in front of her. She
gave the animal a couple of affectionate swipes on his enormous neck and then
swung herself aboard. The horse immediately resumed his rocking canter, the
woman goading him on, chanting something that sounded like "Hop! Hop!"

In attempting to recapture this mild spectacle, I am merely acting as record-   3
ing secretary for one of the oldest of societies—the society of those who, at one
time or another, have surrendered, without even a show of resistance, to the
bedazzlement of a circus rider. As a writing man, or secretary, I have always
felt charged with the safekeeping of all unexpected items of worldly or unwordly
enchantment, as though I might be held personally responsible if even a small
one were to be lost. But it is not easy to communicate anything of this nature.
The circus comes as close to being the world in microcosm as anything I know;
in a way, it puts all the rest of show business in the shade. Its magic is universal
and complex. Out of its wild disorder comes order; from its rank smell rises
the good aroma of courage and daring; out of its preliminary shabbiness comes
the final splendor. And buried in the familiar boasts of its advance agents lies
the modesty of most of its people. For me the circus is at its best before it has
been put together. It is at its best at certain moments when it comes to a point,
as through a burning glass, in the activity and destiny of a single performer
out of so many. One ring is always bigger than three. One rider, one aerialist,
is always greater than six. In short, a man has to catch the circus unawares
to experience its full impact and share its gaudy dream.

The ten-minute ride the girl took achieved—as far as I was concerned,   4
who wasn't looking for it, and quite unbeknownst to her, who wasn't even striving for it—the thing that is sought by performers everywhere, on whatever stage,
whether struggling in the tidal currents of Shakespeare or bucking the difficult
motion of a horse. I somehow got the idea she was just cadging a ride, improving a shining ten minutes in the diligent way all serious artists seize free moments
to hone the blade of their talent and keep themselves in trim. Her brief tour
included only elementary postures and tricks, perhaps because they were all
she was capable of, perhaps because her warmup at this hour was unscheduled
and the ring was not rigged for a real practice session. She swung herself off
and on the horse several times, gripping his mane. She did a few knee-stands—or
whatever they are called—dropping to her knees and quickly bouncing back
upon her feet again. Most of the time she simply rode in a standing position,
well aft on the beast, her hands hanging easily at her sides, her head erect, her
straw-colored ponytail lightly brushing her shoulders, the blood of exertion
showing faintly through the tan of her skin. Twice she managed a one-foot
stance—a sort of ballet pose, with arms outstretched. At one point the neck
strap of her bathing suit broke and she went twice around the ring in the classic
attitude of a woman making minor repairs to a garment. The fact that she was
standing on the back of a moving horse while doing this invested the matter
with a clownish significance that perfectly fitted the spirit of the circus—jocund,
yet charming. She just rolled the strap into a neat ball and stowed it inside her
bodice while the horse rocked and rolled beneath her in dutiful innocence. The
bathing suit proved as self-reliant as its owner and stood up well enough without
benefit of strap.

The richness of the scene was in its plainness, its natural condition—of horse, of ring, of girl, even to the girl's bare feet that gripped the bare back of her proud and ridiculous mount. The enchantment grew not out of anything that happened or was performed but out of something that seemed to go round and around and around with the girl, attending her, a steady gleam in the shape of a circle—a ring of ambition, of happiness, of youth. (And the positive pleasures of equilibrium under difficulties.) In a week or two, all would be changed, all (or almost all) lost: the girl would wear makeup, the horse would wear gold, the ring would be painted, the bark would be clean for the feet of the horse, the girls' feet would be clean for the slippers that she'd wear. All, all would be lost.

As I watched with the others, our jaws adroop, our eyes alight, I became painfully conscious of the element of time. Everything in the hideous old building seemed to take the shape of a circle, conforming to the course of the horse. The rider's gaze, as she peered straight ahead, seemed to be circular, as though bent by force of circumstance; then time itself began running in circles, and so the beginning was where the end was, and the two were the same, and one thing ran into the next and time went round and around and got nowhere. The girl wasn't so young that she did not know the delicious satisfaction of having a perfectly behaved body and the fun of using it to do a trick most people can't do, but she was too young to know that time does not really move in a circle at all. I thought: "She will never be as beautiful as this again"—a thought that made me acutely unhappy—and in a flash my mind (which is too much of a busybody to suit me) had projected her twenty-five years ahead, and she was now in the center of the ring, on foot, wearing a conical hat and high-heeled shoes, the image of the older woman, holding the long rein, caught in the tread-mill of an afternoon long in the future. "She is at that enviable moment in life [I thought] when she believes she can go once around the ring, make one complete circuit, and at the end be exactly the same age as at the start." Everything in her movements, her expression, told you that for her the ring of time was perfectly formed, changeless, predictable, without beginning or end, like the ring in which she was traveling at this moment with the horse that wallowed under her. And then I slipped back into my trance, and time was circular again—time, pausing quietly with the rest of us, so as not to disturb the balance of a performer.

Her ride ended as casually as it had begun. The older woman stopped the horse, and the girl slid to the ground. As she walked toward us to leave, there was a quick, small burst of applause. She smiled broadly, in surprise and pleasure; then her face suddenly regained its gravity and she disappeared through the door.

It has been ambitious and plucky of me to attempt to describe what is indescribable, and I have failed, as I knew I would. But I have discharged my duty to my society; and besides, a writer, like an acrobat, must occasionally try a stunt that is too much for him. At any rate, it is worth reporting that long before the circus comes to town, its most notable performances have already been given. Under the bright lights of the finished show, a performer need only reflect the electric candle power that is directed upon him; but in the dark and dirty old training rings and in the makeshift cages, whatever light is generated, whatever excitement, whatever beauty, must come from original sources— from internal fires of professional hunger and delight, from the exuberance and gravity of youth. It is the difference between planetary light and the combustion of stars.

The South is the land of the sustained sibilant. Everywhere, for the appreciative visitor, the letter "s" insinuates itself in the scene: in the sound of sea and sand, in the singing shell, in the heat of sun and sky, in the sultriness of the gentle hours, in the siesta, in the stir of birds and insects. In contrast to the softness of its music, the South is also cruel and hard and prickly. A little striped lizard, flattened along the sharp green bayonet of a yucca, wears in its tiny face and watchful eye the pure look of death and violence. And all over the place, hidden at the bottom of their small sandy craters, the ant lions lie in wait for the ant that will stumble into their trap. (There are three kinds of lions in this region: the lions of the circus, the ant lions, and the Lions of the Tampa Lions Club, who roared their approval of segregation at a meeting the other day—all except one, a Lion named Monty Gurwit, who declined to roar and thereby got his picture in the paper.)

The day starts on a note of despair: the sorrowing dove, alone on its telephone wire, mourns the loss of night, weeps at the bright perils of the unfolding day. But soon the mockingbird wakes and begins an early rehearsal, setting the dove down by force of character, running through a few slick imitations, and trying a couple of original numbers into the bargain. The redbird takes it from there. Despair gives way to good humor. The Southern dawn is a pale affair, usually, quite different from our northern daybreak. It is a triumph of gradualism; night turns to day imperceptibly, softly, with no theatrics. It is subtle and undisturbing. As a first light seeps in through the blinds I lie in bed half awake, despairing with the dove, sounding the A for the brothers Alsop. All seems lost, all seems sorrowful. Then a mullet jumps in the bayou outside the bedroom window. It falls back into the water with a smart smack. I have asked several people why the mullet incessantly jump and I have received a variety of answers. Some say the mullet jump to shake off a parasite that annoys them. Some say they jump for the love of jumping—as the girl on the horse seemed to ride for the love of riding (although she, too, like all artists, may have been shaking off some parasite that fastens itself to the creative spirit and can be got rid of only by fifty turns around a ring while standing on a horse).

In Florida at this time of year, the sun does not take command of the day until a couple of hours after it has appeared in the east. It seems to carry no authority at first. The sun and the lizard keep the same schedule; they bide their time until the morning has advanced a good long way before they come fully forth and strike. The cold lizard waits astride his warming leaf for the perfect moment; the cold sun waits in his nest of clouds for the crucial time.

On many days, the dampness of the air pervades all life, all living. Matches refuse to strike. The towel, hung to dry, grows wetter by the hour. The newspaper, with its headlines about integration, wilts in your hand and falls limply into the coffee and the egg. Envelopes seal themselves. Postage stamps mate with one another as shamelessly as grasshoppers. But most of the time the days are models of beauty and wonder and comfort, with the kind sea stroking the back of the warm sand. At evening there are great flights of birds over the sea, where the light lingers; the gulls, the pelicans, the terns, the herons stay aloft for half an hour after land birds have gone to roost. They hold their ancient formations, wheel and fish over the Pass, enjoying the last of day like children playing outdoors after suppertime.

To a beachcomber from the North, which is my present status, the race problem has no pertinence, no immediacy. Here in Florida I am a guest in two houses—the house of the sun, the house of the State of Florida. As a guest, I mind my manners and do not criticize the customs of my hosts. It gives me a queer feeling, though, to be at the center of the greatest social crisis of my time and see hardly a sign of it. Yet the very absence of signs seems to increase one's awareness. Colored people do not come to the public beach to bathe, because they would not be made welcome there; and they don't fritter away their time visiting the circus, because they have other things to do. A few of them turn up at the ballpark, where they occupy a separate but equal section of the left-field bleachers and watch Negro players on the visiting Braves team using the same bases as the white players, instead of separate (but equal) bases. I have had only two small encounters with "color." A colored woman named Viola, who had been a friend of my wife's sister years ago, showed up one day with some laundry of ours that she had consented to do for us, and with the bundle she brought a bunch of nasturtiums, as a sort of natural accompaniment to the delivery of clean clothes. The flowers seemed a very acceptable thing and I was touched by them. We asked Viola about her daughter, and she said she was at Kentucky State College, studying voice.

The other encounter was when I was explaining to our cook, who is from Finland, the mysteries of bus travel in the American Southland. I showed her the bus stop, armed her with a timetable, and then, as a matter of duty, mentioned the customs of the Romans. "When you get on the bus," I said, "I think you'd better sit in one of the front seats—the seats in back are for colored people." A look of great weariness came into her face, as it does when we use too many dishes, and she replied, "Oh, I know—isn't it silly!"

Her remark, coming as it did all the way from Finland and landing on this sandbar with a plunk, impressed me. The Supreme Court said nothing about silliness, but I suspect it may play more of a role than one might suppose. People are, if anything, more touchy about being thought silly than they are about being thought unjust. I note that one of the arguments in the recent manifesto of Southern Congressmen in support of the doctrine of "separate but equal" was that it had been founded on "common sense." The sense that is common to one generation is uncommon to the next. Probably the first slave ship, with Negroes lying in chains on its decks, seemed commonsensical to the owners who operated it and to the planters who patronized it. But such a vessel would not be in the realm of common sense today. The only sense that is common, in the long run, is the sense of change—and we all instinctively avoid it, and object to the passage of time, and would rather have none of it.

The Supreme Court decision is like the Southern sun, laggard in its early stages, biding its time. It has been the law in Florida for two years now, and the years have been like the hours of the morning before the sun has gathered its strength. I think the decision is as incontrovertible and warming as the sun, and, like the sun, will eventually take charge.   16

But there is certainly a great temptation in Florida to duck the passage of time. Lying in warm comfort by the sea, you receive gratefully the gift of the sun, the gift of the South. This is true seduction. The day is a circle—morning, afternoon, and night. After a few days I was clearly enjoying the same delusion as the girl on the horse—that I could ride clear around the ring of day, guarded by wind and sun and sea and sand, and be not a moment older.   17

P.S. (April 1962).   When I first laid eyes on Fiddler Bayou, it was wild land, populated chiefly by the little crabs that gave it its name, visited by wading birds and by an occasional fisherman. Today, houses ring the bayou, and part of the mangrove shore has been bulkheaded with a concrete wall. Green lawns stretch from patio to water's edge, and sprinklers make rainbows in the light. But despite man's encroachment, Nature manages to hold her own and assert her authority: high tides and high winds in the gulf sometimes send the sea crashing across the sand barrier, depositing its wrack on lawns and ringing everyone's front door bell. The birds and the crabs accommodate themselves quite readily to the changes that have taken place; every day brings herons to hunt around among the roots of the mangroves, and I have discovered that I can approach to within about eight feet of a Little Blue Heron simply by entering the water and swimming slowly toward him. Apparently he has decided that when I'm in the water, I am without guile—possibly even desirable, like a fish.   18

The Ringling circus has quit Sarasota and gone elsewhere for its hibernation. A few circus families still own homes in the town, and every spring the students at the high school put on a circus, to let off steam, work off physical requirements, and provide a promotional spectacle for Sarasota. At the drugstore you can buy a postcard showing the bed John Ringling slept in. Time has not stood still for anybody but the dead, and even the dead must be able to hear the acceleration of little sports cars and know that things have changed.   19

From the all-wise *New York Times*, which has the animal kingdom ever in mind, I have learned that one of the creatures most acutely aware of the passing   20 of time is the fiddler crab himself. Tiny spots on his body enlarge during daytime hours, giving him the same color as the mudbank he explores and thus protecting him from his enemies. At night the spots shrink, his color fades, and he is almost invisible in the light of the moon. These changes are synchronized with the tides, so that each day they occur at a different hour. A scientist who experimented with the crabs to learn more about the phenomenon discovered that even when they are removed from their natural environment and held in confinement, the rhythm of their bodily change continues uninterrupted, and they mark the passage of time in their laboratory prison, faithful to the tides in their fashion.

1956

Purpose and Meaning

1. How does the title of the essay provide a clue to its thesis? How does the "ring" of time connect with the circus? What is White's purpose in establishing this connection? To whom is he writing, and why?

2. In paragraph 6, the author says he "became painfully conscious of the element of time." What is the significance of the word *painfully* in this paragraph? Are there other places in the essay that suggest this particular perception?

3. Consider the first sentence of paragraph 5: "The richness of the scene was in its plainness. . . ." Isn't this self-contradictory? How does the rest of the paragraph support this opening observation?

4. Paragraph 13 mentions the idea of a "separate but equal" racial doctrine. How do the author's observations on the issue relate to his reflections on "time"?

Language and Style

1. The author describes at length the young acrobat's practice session on her horse. Yet in paragraph 8, he states, "It has been ambitious and plucky of me to attempt to describe what is indescribable, and I have failed." Reread the sections of the essay pertaining to the acrobat. How successful is White in describing her practice session? Why does he say it is "indescribable"? Has he really failed to describe the event? In what sections of the essay do you find his description most successful?

2. In paragraph 9, the author not only states that the letter *s* somehow is appropriate for the South, but actually uses many words in the paragraph that begin with *s*. What is the effect of this technique?

3. How many suggestions of circularity or images of rings can you find in the essay? How do these images contribute to the organization of the essay as a whole?

Strategy and Structure

1. This essay appears to be divided into two sections (excluding the postscript). Where do these sections begin and end? Why does the author divide them in this way? What is the focus of each and how is each one related to all the others?

2. The essay begins with an image of lions and ends with a description of crabs. What is the purpose for this organizational strategy?

3. What is the point of the postscript (written six years after the main text)?

Thinking and Writing

1. The author claims that there is "a great temptation in Florida to duck the passage of time." Yet images of Florida in 1956 and today show it as anything but timeless or unaffected by change. Select a place with great contrasts, then write an essay comparing and contrasting two aspects of this locale. Examples might be "The Two New Yorks," "The Two Californias," and so forth.

2. The last sentence of paragraph 8 says that the difference between a circus rehearsal and performance is like the difference between "planetary light and the combustion of stars." Develop an essay that investigates the differences between rehearsal and performance in an activity that you know well.

3. White claims he is acting as a "recording secretary" (paragraph 3) in his role as a writer. Write an essay evaluating White's role or function in "The Ring of Time" and his purpose. Does he record objectively, offer commentary, or does he do both?

The Sea and the Wind That Blows

Waking or sleeping, I dream of boats—usually of rather small boats under a slight press of sail. When I think how great a part of my life has been spent dreaming the hours away and how much of this total dream life has concerned small craft, I wonder about the state of my health, for I am told that it is not a good sign to be always voyaging into unreality, driven by imaginary breezes.

I have noticed that most men, when they enter a barber shop and must wait their turn, drop into a chair and pick up a magazine. I simply sit down and pick up the thread of my sea wandering, which began more than fifty years ago and is not quite ended. There is hardly a waiting room in the East that has not served as my cockpit, whether I was waiting to board a train or to see a dentist. And I am usually still trimming sheets when the train starts or the drill begins to whine.

If a man must be obsessed by something, I suppose a boat is as good as anything, perhaps a bit better than most. A small sailing craft is not only beautiful, it is seductive and full of strange promise and the hint of trouble. If it happens to be an auxiliary cruising boat, it is without question the most compact and ingenious arrangement for living ever devised by the restless mind of man—a home that is stable without being stationary, shaped less like a box than like a fish or a bird or a girl, and in which the homeowner can remove his daily affairs as far from shore as he has the nerve to take them, close-hauled or running free—parlor, bedroom, and bath, suspended and alive. 3

Men who ache all over for tidiness and compactness in their lives often find relief for their pain in the cabin of a thirty-foot sailboat at anchor in a sheltered cove. Here the sprawling panoply of The Home is compressed in orderly miniature and liquid delirium, suspended between the bottom of the sea and the top of the sky, ready to move on in the morning by the miracle of canvas and the witchcraft of rope. It is small wonder that men hold boats in the secret place of their mind almost from the cradle to the grave. 4

Along with my dream of boats has gone the ownership of boats, a long succession of them upon the surface of the sea, many of them makeshift and crank. Since childhood I have managed to have some sort of sailing craft and to raise a sail in fear. Now, in my seventies, I still own a boat, still raise my sail in fear in answer to the summons of the unforgiving sea. Why does the sea attract me in the way it does? Whence comes this compulsion to hoist a sail, actually or in dream? My first encounter with the sea was a case of hate at first sight. I was taken, at the age of four, to a bathing beach in New Rochelle. Everything about the experience frightened and repelled me: the taste of salt in my mouth, the foul chill of the wooden bathhouse, the littered sand, the stench of the tide flats. I came away hating and fearing the sea. Later, I found that what I had feared and hated, I now feared and loved. 5

I returned to the sea of necessity, because it would support a boat; and although I knew little of boats, I could not get them out of my thoughts. I became a pelagic boy. The sea became my unspoken challenge: the wind, the tide, the fog, the ledge, the bell, the gull that cried help, the never-ending threat and bluff of weather. Once having permitted the wind to enter the belly of my sail, I was not able to quit the helm; it was as though I had seized hold of a high-tension wire and could not let go. 6

I liked to sail alone. The sea was the same as a girl to me—I did not want anyone else along. Lacking instruction, I invented ways of getting things done, and usually ended by doing them in a rather queer fashion, and so did not learn to sail properly, and still cannot sail well, although I have been at it all my life. I was twenty before I discovered that charts existed; all my navigating up to that time was done with the wariness and the ignorance of the early explorers. 7

I was thirty before I learned to hang a coiled halyard on its cleat as it should be done. Until then I simply coiled it down on deck and dumped the coil. I was always in trouble and always returned, seeking more trouble. Sailing became a compulsion: there lay the boat, swinging to her mooring, there blew the wind; I had no choice but to go. My earliest boats were so small that when the wind failed, or when I failed, I could switch to manual control—I could paddle or row home. But then I graduated to boats that only the wind was strong enough to move. When I first dropped off my mooring in such a boat, I was an hour getting up the nerve to cast off the pennant. Even now, with a thousand little voyages notched in my belt, I still feel a memorial chill on casting off, as the gulls jeer and the empty mainsail claps.

Of late years, I have noticed that my sailing has increasingly become a ⁸ compulsive activity rather than a simple source of pleasure. There lies the boat, there blows the morning breeze—it is a point of honor, now, to go. I am like an alcoholic who cannot put his bottle out of his life. With me, I cannot not sail. Yet I know well enough that I have lost touch with the wind and, in fact, do not like the wind anymore. It jiggles me up, the wind does, and what I really love are windless days, when all is peace. There is a great question in my mind whether a man who is against wind should longer try to sail a boat. But this is an intellectual response—the old yearning is still in me, belonging to the past, to youth, and so I am torn between past and present, a common disease of later life.

When does a man quit the sea? How dizzy, how bumbling must he be? ⁹ Does he quit while he's ahead, or wait till he makes some major mistake, like falling overboard or being flattened by an accidental jibe? This past winter I spent hours arguing the question with myself. Finally, deciding that I had come to the end of the road, I wrote a note to the boatyard, putting my boat up for sale. I said I was "coming off the water." But as I typed the sentence, I doubted that I meant a word of it.

If no buyer turns up, I know what will happen: I will instruct the yard ¹⁰ to put her in again—"just till somebody comes along." And then there will be the old uneasiness, the old uncertainty, as the mild southeast breeze ruffles the cove, a gentle, steady, morning breeze, bringing the taint of the distant wet world, the smell that takes a man back to the very beginning of time, linking him to all that has gone before. There will lie the sloop, there will blow the wind, once more I will get under way. And as I reach across to the red nun off the Torry Islands, dodging the trap buoys and toggles, the shags gathered on the ledge will note my passage. "There goes the old boy again," they will say. "One more rounding of his little Horn, one more conquest of his Roaring Forties." And with the tiller in my hand, I'll feel again the wind imparting life to a boat, will smell again the old menace, the one that imparts life to me: the cruel beauty of the salt world, the barnacle's tiny knives, the sharp spine of the urchin, the stinger of the sun jelly, the claw of the crab.

1977

Purpose and Meaning

1. White claims the sea was something he "feared and loved" (paragraph 5). How can you explain this seeming contradiction? In what way does it relate to the thesis of the essay? Where else in the essay does White reveal this attitude?
2. Does the author have in mind a general or specialized audience for this essay? How do you know?
3. The author doesn't claim to be an expert sailor, yet he is obsessed by sailing. How does his *lack* of expertise contribute to his enjoyment?
4. In paragraph 8, White claims to be "torn between past and present." What is the significance of this conflict? How has his appreciation of sailing changed with age? What, if anything, does it reveal about the general effects of aging? What is the author's ultimate purpose in writing this essay?

Language and Style

1. The author uses special terms peculiar to sailing. With how many of these were you already familiar? Be sure to consult a dictionary for the meaning of any unfamiliar terms. How did your comprehension of the essay change after you learned the meaning of the words you did not know before?
2. In paragraph 3, the author compares the shape of a boat to "a fish or a bird or a girl." Does a sailboat truly resemble these? What is the sense of these comparisons? What does this use of analogy add to the essay?
3. Although this essay is rather short, it is full of images, ideas, and reflections. Note, for example, this sentence from paragraph 3: "A small sailing craft is not only beautiful, it is seductive and full of strange promise and the hint of trouble." How does the *structure* of the sentence allow for all these ideas? Are there other sentences in the essay that demonstrate the author's ability to convey considerable information in a small space?
4. What is the tone of the essay? How do the following sentences contribute to this tone? "The sea became my unspoken challenge: the wind, the tide, the fog, the ledge, the bell, the gull that cried help, the never-ending threat and bluff of weather" (paragraph 6); "Sailing became a compulsion: there lay the boat, swinging to her mooring, there blew the wind; I had no choice but to go" (paragraph 7). What do these and other sentences similarly structured reveal about White's mastery of writing?

Strategy and Structure

1. Does the first paragraph prepare you for what is to follow? If so, how? Why would the essay seem incomplete or less adequately structured if it started with paragraph 2?

2. Among other things, the essay describes White's changing attitude toward the sea. What are these changes? How does the paragraph sequence contribute to the ordering of this change? Where do the major transitions occur from one perspective to the next?

3. The final paragraph is written in the future tense. How does this contribute to the aspect of passing time in the essay? What is the paragraph's contribution to the essay's overall structure?

Thinking and Writing

1. Sailing seems to serve several functions for White: psychological, physical, emotional. Write a short essay summarizing how sailing satisfies these needs for the author.

2. The United States is often called an "addicted society." But is there such a thing as a "positive addiction"? White seems to suggest that there is. Think of an activity that *you* regularly perform, and write an essay explaining what positive value it has for you.

3. White admits to being a compulsive daydreamer. Does daydreaming serve important functions? Jot down reasons why daydreaming can be either constructive or destructive. Then, fashion your thoughts into an argumentative essay entitled "Daydreaming as a Constructive (or Destructive) Activity."

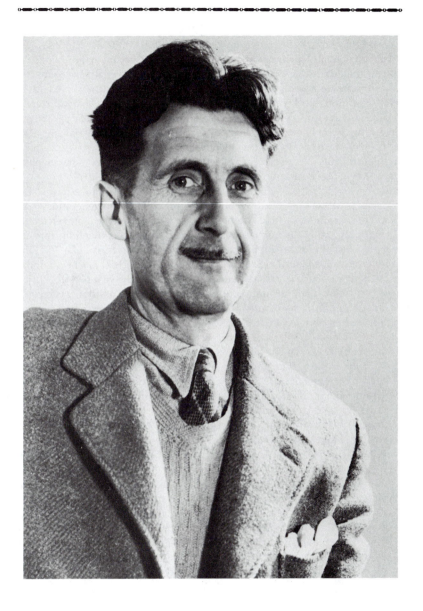

GEORGE ORWELL

George Orwell, the pen name of Eric Blair, was born in 1903 in Motihari, Bengal, India, the son of English parents. His father, a minor civil servant in the Opium Department of the Indian Customs Service, retired when his son was relatively young. Nevertheless, with considerable hardship, the family sent him to England for his education—a poor boy at fashionable British schools. Blair attended Eton on a scholarship, and then, on the advice of a tutor, accepted a position with the Indian Imperial Police in Burma. However, five years later, increasingly mistrustful of English imperialism, which he termed "a racket," Blair quit to become a writer. As George Orwell—the man who gave us such terms as "Newspeak," "Doublethink," and "Big Brother"—he demonstrated the ways in which we can transform "political writing into an art."

As a political writer, George Orwell was—in the words of the esteemed English essayist and fiction writer V. S. Pritchett—"the conscience of his generation." Orwell, a rather idiosyncratic socialist at odds with many of the ideological movements of the left of the 1930s and 1940s, came to his social and political convictions through experience. His disdain for British imperialism, seen in classic essays like "A Hanging" and "Shooting an Elephant," reflects the start of his intellectual journey in India and Burma in the 1920s. His early struggle to be a writer, an eight-year period of privation he spent as a dishwasher, a tramp, a tutor, and a bookshop assistant, is recorded in *Down and Out in Paris and London* (1935). His firsthand Depression-era reports on the English working class resulted in *The Road to Wigan Pier* (1937). Orwell's memorable *Homage to Catalonia* (1938), based on his participation in the Spanish Civil War, where as a volunteer in the Trotskyite People's Militia he was wounded severely in the neck, indicts both the political right and left for their rigid orthodoxies. His last books, the celebrated fable *Animal Farm* (1945) and the classic dystopian novel, *Nineteen Eighty-Four* (1950), published a year before his death from pulmonary tuberculosis, are towering attacks on totalitarianism and lust for power exhibited by big government.

Orwell's "sense of injustice," as he confessed in "Why I Write," was the stimulant for his writing. Lionel Trilling stated that Orwell "immediately put his mind to work the politics that he had experienced. He told the truth, and told it in an exemplary way, quietly, simply, with due warning to the readers that it was only one man's truth." Orwell himself, near the end of his life, acknowledged that he had a talent for facing unpleasant facts and powerfully conveying them to his audience. His essays, collected by his second wife, Sonia Orwell, in four volumes, *The Collected Essays, Journalism and Letters* (1968), are lucid reflections on an age that witnessed two world wars, the Great Depression, Stalinism and Fascism, and the emergence of the Cold War. Orwell illuminated these major events, exposing their terrors. For the imagination, as he observed, "like certain wild animals, will not breed in captivity."

A Hanging

It was in Burma, a sodden morning of the rains. A sickly light, like yellow   1
tinfoil, was slanting over the high walls into the jail yard. We were waiting outside the condemned cells, a row of sheds fronted with double bars, like small
animal cages. Each cell measured about ten feet by ten and was quite bare within
except for a plank bed and a pot for drinking water. In some of them brown
silent men were squatting at the inner bars, with their blankets draped round
them. These were the condemned men, due to be hanged within the next week
or two.

One prisoner had been brought out of his cell. He was a Hindu, a puny   2
wisp of a man, with a shaven head and vague liquid eyes. He had a thick,
sprouting moustache, absurdly too big for his body, rather like the moustache
of a comic man on the films. Six tall Indian warders were guarding him and
getting him ready for the gallows. Two of them stood by with rifles and fixed
bayonets, while the others handcuffed him, passed a chain through his handcuffs and fixed it to their belts, and lashed his arms tight to his sides. They
crowded very close about him, with their hands always on him in a careful,
caressing grip, as though all the while feeling him to make sure he was there.
It was like men handling a fish which is still alive and may jump back into the
water. But he stood quite unresisting, yielding his arms limply to the ropes,
as though he hardly noticed what was happening.

Eight o'clock struck and a bugle call, desolately thin in the wet air, floated   3
from the distant barracks. The superintendent of the jail, who was standing
apart from the rest of us, moodily prodding the gravel with his stick, raised
his head at the sound. He was an army doctor, with a grey toothbrush moustache
and a gruff voice. "For God's sake hurry up, Francis," he said irritably. "The
man ought to have been dead by this time. Aren't you ready yet?"

Francis, the head jailer, a fat Dravidian in a white drill suit and gold spec-   4
tacles, waved his black hand. "Yes sir, yes sir," he bubbled. "All iss satisfactorily
prepared. The hangman iss waiting. We shall proceed."

"Well, quick march, then. The prisoners can't get their breakfast till this   5
job's over."

We set out for the gallows. Two warders marched on either side of the   6
prisoner, with their rifles at the slope; two others marched close against him,
gripping him by arm and shoulder, as though at once pushing and supporting
him. The rest of us, magistrates and the like, followed behind. Suddenly, when
we had gone ten yards, the procession stopped short without any order or warning. A dreadful think had happened—a dog, come goodness knows whence,

had appeared in the yard. It came bounding among us with a loud volley of barks, and leapt round us wagging its whole body, wild with glee at finding so many human beings together. It was a large woolly dog, half Airedale, half pariah. For a moment it pranced round us, and then, before anyone could stop it, it had made a dash for the prisoner and, jumping up, tried to lick his face. Everyone stood aghast, too taken aback even to grab at the dog.

"Who let that bloody brute in here?" said the superintendent angrily. "Catch it, someone!"

A warder, detached from the escort, charged clumsily after the dog, but it danced and gambolled just out of his reach, taking everything as part of the game. A young Eurasian jailer picked up a handful of gravel and tried to stone the dog away, but it dodged the stones and cames after us again. Its yaps echoed from the jail walls. The prisoner, in the grasp of the two warders, looked on incuriously, as though this was another formality of the hanging. It was several minutes before someone managed to catch the dog. Then we put my handkerchief through its collar and moved off once more, with the dog still straining and whimpering.

It was about forty yards to the gallows. I watched the bare brown back of the prisoner marching in front of me. He walked clumsily with his bound arms, but quite steadily, with that bobbing gait of the Indian who never straightens his knees. At each step his muscles slid neatly into place, the lock of hair on his scalp danced up and down, his feet printed themselves on the wet gravel. And once, in spite of the men who gripped him by each shoulder, he stepped slightly aside to avoid a puddle on the path.

It is curious, but till that moment I had never realized what it means to destroy a healthy, conscious man. When I saw the prisoner step aside to avoid the puddle I saw the mystery, the unspeakable wrongness, of cutting a life short when it is in full tide. This man was not dying, he was alive just as we are alive. All the organs of his body were working—bowels digesting food, skin renewing itself, nails growing, tissues forming—all toiling away in solemn foolery. His nails would still be growing when he stood on the drop, when he was falling through the air with a tenth-of-a-second to live. His eyes saw the yellow gravel and the grey walls, and his brain still remembered, foresaw, reasoned—reasoned even about puddles. He and we were a party of men walking together, seeing, hearing, feeling, understanding the same world; and in two minutes, with a sudden snap, one of us would be gone—one mind less, one world less.

The gallows stood in a small yard, separate from the main grounds of the prison, and overgrown with tall prickly weeds. It was a brick erection like three sides of a shed, with planking on top, and above that two beams and a crossbar with the rope dangling. The hangman, a grey-haired convict in the white uniform of the prison, was waiting beside his machine. He greeted us with a servile crouch as we entered. At a word from Francis the two warders, gripping the prisoner more closely than ever, half led half pushed him to the gallows and helped him clumsily up the ladder. Then the hangman climbed up and fixed the rope round the prisoner's neck.

We stood waiting, five yards away. The warders had formed in a rough 12
circle round the gallows. And then, when the noose was fixed, the prisoner began
crying out to his god. It was a high, reiterated cry of "Ram! Ram! Ram! Ram!"
not urgent and fearful like a prayer or cry for help, but steady, rhythmical,
almost like the tolling of a bell. The dog answered the sound with a whine.
The hangman, still standing on the gallows, produced a small cotton bag like
a flour bag and drew it down over the prisoner's face. But the sound, muffled
by the cloth, still persisted, over and over again: "Ram! Ram! Ram! Ram! Ram!"

The hangman climbed down and stood ready, holding the lever. Minutes 13
seemed to pass. The steady, muffled crying from the prisoner went on and on.
"Ram! Ram! Ram!" never faltering for an instant. The superintendent, his head
on his chest, was slowly poking the ground with his stick; perhaps he was
counting the cries, allowing the prisoner a fixed number—fifty, perhaps, or a
hundred. Everyone had changed color. The Indians had gone grey like bad
coffee, and one or two of the bayonets were wavering. We looked at the lashed,
hooded man on the drop, and listened to his cries—each cry another second
of life; the same thought was in all our minds: oh, kill him quickly, get it over,
stop that abominable noise!

Suddenly the superintendent made up his mind. Throwing up his head 14
he made a swift motion with his stick. "Chalo!" he shouted almost fiercely.

There was a clanking noise, and then dead silence. The prisoner had 15
vanished, and the rope was twisting on itself. I let go of the dog, and it galloped
immediately to the back of the gallows; but when it got there it stopped short,
barked, and then retreated into a corner of the yard, where it stood among the
weeds, looking timorously out at us. We went round the gallows to inspect
the prisoner's body. He was dangling with his toes pointed straight downwards,
very slowly revolving, as dead as a stone.

The superintendent reached out with his stick and poked the bare brown 16
body; it oscillated slightly. "*He's* all right," said the superintendent. He backed
out from under the gallows, and blew out a deep breath. The moody look had
gone out of his face quite suddenly. He glanced at his wrist-watch. "Eight minutes
past eight. Well, that's all for this morning, thank God."

The warders unfixed bayonets and marched away. The dog, sobered and 17
conscious of having misbehaved itself, slipped after them. We walked out of
the gallows yard, past the condemned cells with their waiting prisoners, into
the big central yard of the prison. The convicts, under the command of warders
armed with lathis, were already receiving their breakfast. They squatted in long
rows, each man holding a tin panikin, while two warders with buckets marched
round ladling out rice; it seemed quite a homely, jolly scene, after the hanging.
An enormous relief had come upon us now that the job was done. One felt
an impulse to sing, to break into a run, to snigger. All at once everyone began
chattering gaily.

The Eurasian boy walking beside me nodded towards the way we had 18
come, with a knowing smile: "Do you know, sir, our friend [he meant the dead
man] when he heard his appeal had been dismissed, he pissed on the floor of

his cell. From fright. Kindly take one of my cigarettes, sir. Do you not admire my new silver case, sir? From the boxwalah, two rupees eight annas. Classy European style."

Several people laughed—at what, nobody seemed certain.

Francis was walking by the superintendent, talking garrulously: "Well, sir, all hass passed off with the utmost satisfactoriness. It was all finished— flick! like that. It iss not always so—oah, no! I have known cases where the doctor wass obliged to go beneath the gallows and pull the prissoner's legs to ensure decease. Most disagreeable!"

"Wriggling about, eh? That's bad," said the superintendent.

"Ach, sir, it iss worse when they become refractory! One man, I recall, clung to the bars of hiss cage when we went to take him out. You will scarcely credit, sir, that it took six warders to dislodge him, three pulling at each leg. We reasoned with him. 'My dear fellow,' we said, 'think of all the pain and trouble you are causing to us!' But no, he would not listen! Ach, he wass very troublesome!"

I found that I was laughing quite loudly. Everyone was laughing. Even the superintendent grinned in a tolerant way. "You'd better all come out and have a drink," he said quite genially. "I've got a bottle of whiskey in the car. We could do with it."

We went through the big double gates of the prison into the road. "Pull-ing at his legs!" exclaimed a Burmese magistrate suddenly, and burst into a loud chuckling. We all began laughing again. At that moment Francis' anecdote seemed extraordinarily funny. We all had a drink together, native and Euro-pean alike, quite amicably. The dead man was a hundred yards away.

1931

Purpose and Meaning

1. By this narrative account, Orwell intends to persuade. What is his persuasive purpose and what evidence in the text supports this purpose?

2. Orwell never mentions the condemned man's crime. Explain why this omission was intentional. How does the omission illuminate the essay's theme?

3. Does Orwell approach his subject matter emotionally, objectively, analytically, or in a combination of any of these? How does the essay's brief title suggest the author's tone? What is ironic about such a terse title?

4. Orwell describes the dog at some length. Why does he devote so much of the essay to the animal? Why are the soldiers and officials so disturbed by its behavior?

Language and Style

1. Analyze Orwell's use of the first-person point of view. Is Orwell a participant in or observer of the action?

2. Orwell uses adjectives such as *sodden, sickly, limply,* and adverbs such as

desolately and *moodily* in paragraphs 1 through 3. How do these descriptive words contribute to the mood of the narrative? What is this mood? How else is description used in latter paragraphs to maintain this mood?

3. Compare Orwell's writing style to White's. How do their sentence structures compare in terms of syntax, figurative language, and length? Do you prefer one style to the other? If so, why?

Strategy and Structure

1. How does Orwell frame his narrative in this essay? How does he handle action, setting, and time?

2. Orwell intersperses his story with bits of dialogue. How does the dialogue contribute to the overall effect? What effect does the description of the prisoner's prayer have on the reader?

3. Paragraph 10, a moral reflection upon the hanging, temporarily breaks up the narrative flow of the story. Is this an effective rhetorical strategy? Should Orwell have placed the paragraph at the conclusion of the essay instead? Justify your answer.

4. Is the last part of the essay—after the prisoner has been hanged—anticlimactic? What is Orwell's purpose in including this section? Why has Orwell written so much dialogue into the last five paragraphs? Is the content of what the speakers are saying significant, or is it something else?

Thinking and Writing

1. Orwell was, among other things, a journalist. Does this piece of writing remind you more of a newspaper article or an essay? Discuss in class the differences between the two. Try describing one incident in two ways: the first, in purely objective terms; the second, as a means to advance a theme or thesis.

2. We learn much about the inner feelings of the people in this essay from what they say. Analyze the dialogue in "A Hanging" and what it reveals about the characters.

3. Write a narrative account that reveals your own attitude toward capital punishment.

4. Write an essay comparing "A Hanging" and White's "The Ring of Time." Attempt to explain how each essay arrives at a political statement about the human condition.

Shooting an Elephant

In Moulmein, in Lower Burma, I was hated by large numbers of people— 1
the only time in my life that I have been important enough for this to happen to me. I was sub-divisional police officer of the town, and in an aimless, petty kind of way anti-European feeling was very bitter. No one had the guts to raise

a riot, but if a European woman went through the bazaars alone somebody would probably spit betel juice over her dress. As a police officer I was an obvious target and was baited whenever it seemed safe to do so. When a nimble Burman tripped me up on the football field and the referee (another Burman) looked the other way, the crowd yelled with hideous laughter. This happened more than once. In the end the sneering yellow faces of young men that met me everywhere, the insults hooted after me when I was at a safe distance, got badly, on my nerves. The young Buddhist priests were the worst of all. There were several thousands of them in the town and none of them seemed to have anything to do except stand on street corners and jeer at Europeans.

All this was perplexing and upsetting. For at that time I had already made up my mind that imperialism was an evil thing and the sooner I chucked up my job and got out of it the better. Theoretically—and secretly, of course—I was all for the Burmese and all against their oppressors, the British. As for the job I was doing, I hated it more bitterly than I can perhaps make clear. In a job like that you see the dirty work of Empire at close quarters. The wretched prisoners huddling in the stinking cages of the lock-ups, the grey, cowed faces of the long-term convicts, the scarred buttocks of the men who had been flogged with bamboos—all these oppressed me with an intolerable sense of guilt. But I could get nothing into perspective. I was young and ill-educated and I had had to think out my problems in the utter silence that is imposed on every Englishman in the East. I did not even know that the British Empire is dying, still less did I know that it is a great deal better than the younger empires that are going to supplant it. All I knew was that I was stuck between my hatred of the empire I served and my rage against the evil-spirited little beasts who tried to make my job impossible. With one part of my mind I thought of the British Raj as an unbreakable tyranny, as something clamped down, *in saecula saeculorum*, upon the will of prostrate peoples; with another part I thought that the greatest joy in the world would be to drive a bayonet into a Buddhist priest's guts. Feelings like these are the normal by-products of imperialism; ask any Anglo-Indian official, if you can catch him off duty.

One day something happened which in a roundabout way was enlightening. It was a tiny incident in itself, but it gave me a better glimpse than I had had before of the real nature of imperialism—the real motives for which despotic governments act. Early one morning the sub-inspector at a police station the other end of the town rang me up on the phone and said that an elephant was ravaging the bazaar. Would I please come and do something about it? I did not know what I could do, but I wanted to see what was happening and I got on to a pony and started out. I took my rifle, an old ·44 Winchester and much too small to kill an elephant, but I thought the noise might be useful *in terrorem*. Various Burmans stopped me on the way and told me about the elephant's doings. It was not, of course, a wild elephant, but a tame one which had gone "must." It had been chained up as tame elephants always are when their attack of "must" is due, but on the previous night it had broken its chain and escaped.

Its mahout, the only person who could manage it when it was in that state, had set out in pursuit, but he had taken the wrong direction and was now twelve hours' journey away, and in the morning the elephant had suddenly reappeared in the town. The Burmese population had no weapons and were quite helpless against it. It had already destroyed somebody's bamboo hut, killed a cow and raided some fruit-stalls and devoured the stock; also it had met the municipal rubbish van, and, when the driver jumped out and took to his heels, had turned the van over and inflicted violence upon it.

The Burmese sub-inspector and some Indian constables were waiting for   4
me in the quarter where the elephant had been seen. It was a very poor quarter, a labyrinth of squalid bamboo huts, thatched with palm-leaf, winding all over a steep hillside. I remember that it was a cloudy stuffy morning at the beginning of the rains. We began questioning the people as to where the elephant had gone, and, as usual, failed to get any definite information. That is invariably the case in the East; a story always sounds clear enough at a distance, but the nearer you get to the scene of events the vaguer it becomes. Some of the people said that the elephant had gone in one direction, some said that he had gone in another, some professed not even to have heard of any elephant. I had almost made up my mind that the whole story was a pack of lies, when we heard yells a little distance away. There was a loud, scandalised cry of "Go away, child! Go away this instant!" and an old woman with a switch in her hand came round the corner of a hut, violently shooing away a crowd of naked children. Some more women followed, clicking their tongues and exclaiming; evidently there was something there that the children ought not to have seen. I rounded the hut and saw a man's dead body sprawling in the mud. He was an Indian, a black Dravidian coolie, almost naked, and he could not have been dead many minutes. The people said that the elephant had come suddenly upon him round the corner of the hut, caught him with its trunk, put its foot on his back and ground him into the earth. This was the rainy season and the ground was soft, and his face had scored a trench a foot deep and a couple of yards long. He was lying on his belly with arms crucified and head sharply twisted to one side. His face was coated with mud, the eyes wide open, the teeth bared and grinning with an expression of unendurable agony. (Never tell me, by the way, that the dead look peaceful. Most of the corpses I have seen looked devilish.) The friction of the great beast's foot had stripped the skin from his back as neatly as one skins a rabbit. As soon as I saw the dead man I sent an orderly to a friend's house nearby to borrow an elephant rifle. I had already sent back the pony, not wanting it to go mad with fright and throw me if it smelled the elephant.

The orderly came back in a few minutes with a rifle and five cartridges,   5
and meanwhile some Burmans had arrived and told us that the elephant was in the paddy fields below, only a few hundred yards away. As I started forward practically the whole population of the quarter flocked out of their houses and followed me. They had seen the rifle and were all shouting excitedly that I was going to shoot the elephant. They had not shown much interest in the

elephant when he was merely ravaging their homes, but it was different now that he was going to be shot. It was a bit of fun to them, as it would be to an English crowd; besides, they wanted the meat. It made me vaguely uneasy. I had no intention of shooting the elephant—I had merely sent for the rifle to defend myself if necessary—and it is always unnerving to have a crowd following you. I marched down the hill, looking and feeling a fool, with the rifle over my shoulder and an evergrowing army of people jostling at my heels. At the bottom, when you got away from the huts, there was a metalled road and beyond that a miry waste of paddy fields a thousand yards across, not yet ploughed but soggy from the first rains and dotted with coarse grass. The elephant was standing eighty yards from the road, his left side towards us. He took not the slightest notice of the crowd's approach. He was tearing up bunches of grass, beating them against his knees to clean them and stuffing them into his mouth.

I had halted on the road. As soon as I saw the elephant I knew with perfect certainty that I ought not to shoot him. It is a serious matter to shoot a working elephant—it is comparable to destroying a huge and costly piece of machinery— and obviously one ought not to do it if it can possibly be avoided. And at that distance, peacefully eating, the elephant looked no more dangerous than a cow. I thought then and I think now what his attack of "must" was already passing off; in which case he would merely wander harmlessly about until the mahout came back and caught him. Moreover, I did not in the least want to shoot him. I decided that I would watch him for a little while to make sure that he did not turn savage again, and then go home.

But at that moment I glanced round at the crowd that had followed me. It was an immense crowd, two thousand at the least and growing every minute. It blocked the road for a long distance on either side. I looked at the sea of yellow faces above the garish clothes—faces all happy and excited over this bit of fun, all certain that the elephant was going to be shot. They were watching me as they would watch a conjuror about to perform a trick. They did not like me, but with the magical rifle in my hands I was momentarily worth watching. And suddenly I realised that I should have to shoot the elephant after all. The people expected it of me and I had got to do it; I could feel their two thousand wills pressing me forward, irresistibly. And it was at this moment, as I stood there with the rifle in my hands, that I first grasped the hollowness, the futility of the white man's dominion in the East. Here was I, the white man with his gun, standing in front of the unarmed native crowd—seemingly the leading actor of the piece; but in reality I was only an absurd puppet pushed to and fro by the will of those yellow faces behind. I perceived in this moment that when the white man turns tyrant it is his own freedom that he destroys. He becomes a sort of hollow, posing dummy, the conventionalised figure of a sahib. For it is the condition of his rule that he shall spend his life in trying to impress the "natives" and so in every crisis he has got to do what the "natives" expect of him. He wears a mask, and his face grows to fit it. I had got to shoot the elephant. I had committed myself to doing it when I sent for the rifle. A sahib has got to act like a sahib; he has got to appear resolute, to know his own mind and do definite things. To come all that way, rifle in hand, with two thousand people marching at my heels, and then to trail feebly away, having done nothing—no that was impossible. The crowd would laugh at me. And my whole life, every white man's life in the East, was one long struggle not to be laughed at.

But I did not want to shoot the elephant. I watched him beating his bunch   8
of grass against his knees, with that preoccupied grandmotherly air that elephants have. It seemed to me that it would be murder to shoot him. At that age I was not squeamish about killing animals, but I had never shot an elephant and never wanted to. (Somehow it always seems worse to kill a *large* animal.) Besides, there was the beast's owner to be considered. Alive, the elephant was worth at least a hundred pounds; dead, he would only be worth the value of his tusks— five pounds, possibly. But I had got to act quickly. I turned to some experienced-looking Burmans who had been there when we arrived, and asked them how the elephant had been behaving. They all said the same thing: he took no notice of you if you left him alone, but he might charge if you went too close to him.

It was perfectly clear to me what I ought to do. I ought to walk up to   9
within, say, twenty-five yards of the elephant and test his behaviour. If he charged I could shoot, if he took no notice of me it would be safe to leave him until the mahout came back. But also I knew that I was going to do no such thing. I was a poor shot with a rifle and the ground was soft mud into which one would sink at every step. If the elephant charged and I missed him, I should have about as much chance as a toad under a steam-roller. But even then I was not thinking particularly of my own skin, only the watchful yellow faces behind. For at that moment, with the crowd watching me, I was not afraid in the ordinary sense, as I would have been if I had been alone. A white man mustn't be frightened in front of "natives"; and so, in general, he isn't frightened. The sole thought in my mind was that if anything went wrong those two thousand Burmans would see me pursued, caught, trampled on and reduced to a grinning corpse like that Indian up the hill. And if that happened it was quite probable that some of them would laugh. That would never do. There was only one alternative. I shoved the cartridges into the magazine and lay down on the road to get a better aim.

The crowd grew very still, and a deep, low, happy sigh, of people who   10
see the theatre curtain go up at last, breathed from innumerable throats. They were going to have their bit of fun after all. The rifle was a beautiful German thing with cross-hair sights. I did not then know that in shooting an elephant one should shoot to cut an imaginary bar running from ear-hole to ear-hole. I ought therefore, as the elephant was sideways on, to have aimed straight at his ear-hole; actually I aimed several inches in front of this, thinking the brain would be further forward.

When I pulled the trigger I did not hear the bang or feel the kick—one   11
never does when a shot goes home—but I heard the devilish roar of glee that

went up from the crowd. In that instant, in too short a time, one would have thought, even for the bullet to get there, a mysterious, terrible change had come over the elephant. He neither stirred nor fell, but every line of his body had altered. He looked suddenly stricken, shrunken, immensely old, as though the frightful impact of the bullet had paralysed him without knocking him down. At last, after what seemed a long time—it might have been five seconds, I dare say—he sagged flabbily to his knees. His mouth slobbered. An enormous senility seemed to have settled upon him. One could have imagined him thousands of years old. I fired again into the same spot. At the second shot he did not collapse but climbed with desperate slowness to his feet and stood weakly upright, with legs sagging and head drooping. I fired a third time. That was the shot that did for him. You could see the agony of it jolt his whole body and knock the last remnant of strength from his legs. But in falling he seemed for a moment to rise, for as his hindlegs collapsed beneath him he seemed to tower upwards like a huge rock toppling, his trunk reaching skyward like a tree. He trumpeted, for the first and only time. And then down he came, his belly towards me, with a crash that seemed to shake the ground even where I lay.

I got up. The Burmans were already racing past me across the mud. It was obvious that the elephant would never rise again, but he was not dead. He was breathing very rhythmically with long rattling gasps, his great mound of a side painfully rising and falling. His mouth was wide open—I could see far down into caverns of pale pink throat. I waited a long time for him to die, but his breathing did not weaken. Finally I fired my two remaining shots into the spot where I thought his heart must be. The thick blood welled out of him like red velvet, but still he did not die. His body did not even jerk when the shots hit him, the tortured breathing continued without a pause. He was dying, very slowly and in great agony, but in some world remote from me where not even a bullet could damage him further. I felt that I had got to put an end to that dreadful noise. It seemed dreadful to see the great beast lying there, powerless to move and yet powerless to die, and not even to be able to finish him. I sent back for my small rifle and poured shot after shot into his heart and down his throat. They seemed to make no impression. The tortured gasps continued as steadily as the ticking of a clock.

In the end I could not stand it any longer and went away. I heard later that it took him half an hour to die. Burmans were arriving with dahs and baskets even before I left, and I was told they had stripped his body almost to the bones by the afternoon.

Afterwards, of course, there were endless discussions about the shooting of the elephant. The owner was furious, but he was only an Indian and could do nothing. Besides, legally I had done the right thing, for a mad elephant has to be killed, like a mad dog, if its owner fails to control it. Among the Europeans opinion was divided. The older men said I was right, the younger men said it was a damn shame to shoot an elephant for killing a coolie, because an elephant was worth more than any damn Coringhee coolie. And afterwards I was very glad that the coolie had been killed; it put me legally in the right and it gave me a sufficient pretext for shooting the elephant. I often wondered whether any of the others grasped that I had done it solely to avoid looking a fool.

1936

Purpose and Meaning

1. Orwell quite clearly states the thesis of this essay. What sentence reveals it?

2. Why do the Burmese hate Orwell? What is Orwell's attitude toward those who hate him?

3. In paragraph 2, Orwell refers to the British Empire and "the younger empires that are going to supplant it." To what historical context is he referring? What other specific allusions in the essay suggest the period in which the action occurs?

4. What relevance does this essay have beyhond the historical period in which it was written?

Language and Style

1. The killing of the elephant is described in great detail (paragraph 11). Why does Orwell devote so much attention to the act? How does it compare to the execution of the condemned man in "A Hanging"?

2. Orwell describes the Burmese as "evil-spirited little beasts" in paragraph 2. What other *dehumanizing* terms does Orwell use to characterize them? In paragraph 7, he feels "two thousand wills pressing me forward." How does this description *depersonalize* the crowd? Where else are the Burmese portrayed in this manner? What type of relationship does this portrayal set up between Orwell and the colonized?

3. Orwell's style in this essay is a complex mixture of slang, Latinisms, imagery, metaphors, and similes. Locate examples of each and explain their overall effect.

Strategy and Structure

1. The first two paragraphs are a general reflection on Orwell's experience in Burma and on his attitudes toward imperialism. Paragraph 3 begins the narrative. What is the purpose and effect of this organizational strategy?

2. At the beginning of paragraph 10, Orwell states that the crowd behaved like "people who see the theatre curtain go up at last." How do the preceding paragraphs prepare us for this culminating moment?

3. Identify when Orwell uses irony and paradox in this essay.

4. How does the concluding paragraph capture the main conflcts in this narrative?

Thinking and Writing

1. Has an incident in your life ever served to illustrate a general principle about the world you live in? Develop a personal narrative that presents such a relationship. Pay careful attention to how you integrate the specific details of the event with your general insights.

2. Orwell's social, political, and cultural perspective toward the Burmese greatly influences the way he describes them. In an essay, discuss how the *status* of an individual affects the *attitude* of that individual toward others.

3. Orwell claims that he was "only an absurd puppet pushed to and fro" and that at the time he was "young and ill-educated" and had "to think out [his] problems in...utter silence." Consider Orwell's role in the narrative. Did he have a choice in whether to kill the elephant or not? Develop an argumentative essay advancing your point of view.

Politics and the English Language

Most people who bother with the matter at all would admit that the English language is in a bad way, but it is generally assumed that we cannot by conscious action do anything about it. Our civilization is decadent and our language—so the argument runs—must inevitably share in the general collapse. It follows that any struggle against the abuse of language is a sentimental archaism, like preferring candles to electric light or hansom cabs to aeroplanes. Underneath this lies the half-conscious belief that language is a natural growth and not an instrument which we shape for our own purposes.

Now, it is clear that the decline of a language must ultimately have political and economic causes: it is not due simply to the bad influence of this or that individual writer. But an effect can become a cause, reinforcing the original cause and producing the same effect in an intensified form, and so on indefinitely. A man may take to drink because he feels himself to be a failure, and then fail all the more completely because he drinks. It is rather the same thing that is happening to the English language. It becomes ugly and inaccurate because our thoughts are foolish, but the slovenliness of our language makes it easier for us to have foolish thoughts. The point is that the process is reversible. Modern English, especially written English, is full of bad habits which spread by imitation and which can be avoided if one is willing to take the necessary trouble. If one gets rid of these habits one can thing more clearly, and to think clearly is a necessary first step towards political regeneration: so that the fight against bad English is not frivolous and is not the exclusive concern of professional writers. I will come back to this presently, and I hope that by that time the meaning of what I have said here will have become clearer. Meanwhile, here are five specimens of the English language as it is now habitually written.

These five passages have not been picked out because they are especially bad—I could have quoted far worse if I had chosen—but because they illustrate various of the mental vices from which we now suffer. They are a little below the average, but are fairly representative samples. I number them so that I can refer back to them when necessary: 3

> (1) I am not, indeed, sure whether it is not true to say that the Milton who once seemed not unlike a seventeenth-century Shelley had not become, out of an experience every more bitter in each year, more alien [*sic*] to the founder of that Jesuit sect which nothing could induce him to tolerate.
>
> > Professor Harold Laski
> > (Essay in *Freedom of Expression*).

> (2) Above all, we cannot play ducks and drakes with a native battery of idioms which prescribes such egregious collocations of vocables as the Basic *put up with* for *tolerate* or *put at a loss* for *bewilder*.
>
> > Professor Lancelot Hogben (*Interglossa*).

> (3) On the one side we have the free personality: by definition it is not neurotic, for it has neither conflict nor dream. Its desires, such as they are, are transparent, for they are just what institutional approval keeps in the forefront of consciousness; another institutional pattern would alter their number and intensity; there is little in them that is natural, irreducible, or culturally dangerous. But on the other side, the social bond itself is nothing but the mutual reflection of these self-secure integrities. Recall the definition of love. Is not this the very picture of a small academic? Where is there a place in this hall of mirrors for either personality or fraternity?
>
> > Essay on psychology in *Politics* (New York).

> (4) All the "best people" from the gentlemen's clubs, and all the frantic fascist captains, united in common hatred of Socialism and bestial horror of the rising tide of the mass revolutionary movement, have turned to acts of provocation, to foul incendiarism, to medieval legends of poisoned wells, to legalize their own destruction of proletarian organizations, and rouse the agitated petty-bourgeoisie to chauvinistic fervor on behalf of the fight against the revolutionary way out of the crisis.
>
> > Communist pamphlet.

(5) If a new spirit is to be infused into this old country, there is one thorny and contentious reform which must be tackled, and that is the humanization and galvanization of the B.B.C. Timidity here will bespeak canker and atrophy of the soul. The heart of Britain may be sound and of strong beat, for instance, but the British lion's roar at present is like that of Bottom in Shakespeare's *Midsummer Night's Dream*—as gentle as any sucking dove. A virile new Britain cannot continue indefinitely to be traduced in the eyes or rather ears, of the world by the effete languors of Langham Place, brazenly masquerading as "standard English." When the Voice of Britain is heard at nine o'clock, better far and infinitely less ludicrous to hear aitches honestly dropped than the present priggish, inflated, inhibited, school-ma'amish arch braying of blameless bashful mewing maidens!

Letter in *Tribune*

Each of these passages has faults of its own, but, quite apart from avoidable ⁴ ugliness, two qualities are common to all of them. The first is staleness of imagery; the other is lack of precision. The writer either has a meaning and cannot express it, or he inadvertently says something else, or he is almost indifferent as to whether his words mean anything or not. This mixture of vagueness and sheer incompetence is the most marked characteristic of modern English prose, and especially of any kind of political writing. As soon as certain topics are raised, the concrete melts into the abstract and no one seems able to think of turns of speech that are not hackneyed: prose consists less and less of *words* chosen for the sake of their meaning, and more and more of *phrases* tacked together like the sections of a prefabricated hen-house. I list below, with notes and examples, various of the tricks by means of which the work of prose-construction is habitually dodged:

Dying metaphors. A newly invented metaphor assists thought by evok- ⁵ ing a visual image, while on the other hand a metaphor which is technically "dead" (e.g. *iron resolution*) has in effect reverted to being an ordinary word and can generally be used without loss of vividness. But in between these two classes there is a huge dump of worn-out metaphors which have lost all evocative power and are merely used because they save people the trouble of inventing phrases for themselves. Examples are: *Ring the changes on, take up the cudgels for, toe the line, ride roughshod over, stand shoulder to shoulder with, play into the hands of, no axe to grind, grist to the mill, fishing in troubled waters, on the order of the day, Achilles' heel, swan song, hotbed.* Many of these are used without knowledge of their meaning (what is a "rift," for instance?), and incompatible metaphors are frequently mixed, a sure sign that the writer is not interested in what he is saying. Some metaphors now current have been twisted out of their original meaning without those who use them even being aware of the fact. For example, *toe the line* is sometimes written *tow the line.* Another example is the *hammer and the anvil*, now always used with the implication that the anvil gets the worst of it. In real life it is always the anvil that breaks the hammer, never the other way about: a writer who stopped to think what he was saying would be aware of this, and would avoid perverting the original phrase.

Operators or verbal false limbs. These save the trouble of picking out appropriate verbs and nouns, and at the same time pad each sentence with extra syllables which give it an appearance of symmetry. Characteristic phrases are *render inoperative, militate against, make contact with, be subjected to, give rise to, give grounds for, have the effect of, play a leading part (role) in, make itself felt, take effect, exhibit a tendency to, serve the purpose of, etc., etc.* The keynote is the elimination of simple verbs. Instead of being a single word, such as *break, stop, spoil, mend, kill,* a verb becomes a *phrase,* made up of a noun or adjective tacked on to some general-purposes verb such as *prove, serve, form, play, render.* In addition, the passive voice is wherever possible used in preference to the active, and noun constructions are used instead of gerunds (*by examination of* instead of *by examining*). The range of verbs is further cut down by means of the *-ize* and *de-* formations, and the banal statements are given an appearance of profundity by means of the *not un-* formation. Simple conjunctions and prepositions are replaced by such phrases as *with respect to, having regard to, the fact that, by dint of, in view of, in the interests of, on the hypothesis that;* and the ends of sentences are saved by anticlimax by such resounding common-places as *greatly to be desired, cannot be left out of account, a development to be expected in the near future, deserving of serious consideration, brought to a satisfactory conclusion,* and so on and so forth.

Pretentious diction. Words like *phenomenon, element, individual* (as noun), *objective, categorical, effective, virtual, basic, primary, promote, constitute, exhibit, exploit, utilize, eliminate, liquidate,* are used to dress up simple statement and give an air of scientific impartiality to biased judgments. Adjectives like *epoch-making, epic, historic, unforgettable, triumphant, age-old, inevitable, inexorable, veritable,* are used to dignify the sordid processes of international politics, while writing that aims at glorifying war usually takes on an archaic color, its characteristic words being: *realm, throne, chariot, mailed fist, trident, sword, shield, buckler, banner, jackboot, clarion.* Foreign words and expressions such as *cul de sac, ancien régime, deus ex machina, mutatis mutandis, status quo, gleichschaltung, weltanschauung,* are used to give an air of culture and elegance. Except for the useful abbreviations *i.e., e.g.,* and *etc.,* there is no real need for any of the hundreds of foreign phrases now current in English. Bad writers, and expecially scientific, political and sociological writers, are nearly always haunted by the notion that Latin or Greek words are grander than Saxon ones, and unnecessary words like *expedite, ameliorate, predict, extraneous, deracinated, clandestine, subaqueous* and hundreds of others constantly gain ground from their Anglo-Saxon opposite numbers.* The jargon peculiar to Marxist writing (*hyena, hangman, cannibal, petty bourgeois, these gentry, lacquey, flunkey, mad dog, White Guard,* etc.) consists largely of words and phrases translated from Russian, German or French; but the normal way of coining a new word is to use a Latin or Greek root with the appropriate affix and, where necessary, the size formation. It is often easier to make up words of this kind (*deregionalize, impermissible, extramarital, nonfragmentary* and so forth) than to think up the English words that will cover one's meaning. The result, in general, is an increase in slovenliness and vagueness.

Meaningless words. In certain kinds of writing, particularly in art criticism and literary criticism, it is normal to come across long passages which are almost completely lacking in meaning.† Words like *romantic, plastic, values, human, dead, sentimental, natural, vitality,* as used in art criticism, are strictly meaningless, in the sense that they not only do not point to any discoverable object, but are hardly ever expected to do so by the reader. When one critic writes, "The outstanding feature of Mr. X's work is its living quality," while another writes, "The immediately striking thing about Mr. X's work is its peculiar deadness," the reader accepts this as a simple difference of opinion. If words like *black* and *white* were involved, instead of the jargon words *dead* and *living,* he would see at once that language was being used in an improper way. Many political words are similarly abused. The word *Fascism* has now no meaning except in so far as it signifies "something not desirable." The words *democracy, socialism, freedom, patriotic, realistic, justice,* have each of them several different meanings which cannot be reconciled with one another. In the case of a word like *democracy,* not only is there no agreed definition, but the attempt to make one is resisted from all sides. It is almost universally felt that when we call a country democratic we are praising it: consequently the defenders of every kind of régime claim that it is a democracy, and fear that they might have to stop using the word if it were tied down to any one meaning. Words of this kind are often used in a consciously dishonest way. That is, the person who uses them has his own private definition, but allows his hearer to think he means something quite different. Statements like *Marshal Pétain was a true*

*An interesting illustration of this is the way in which the English flower names which were in use till very recently are being ousted by Greek ones, *snapdragon* becoming *antirrhinum, forget-me-not* becoming *myosotis,* etc. It is hard to see any practical reason for this change of fashion: it is probably due to an instinctive turning-away from the more homely word and a vague feeling that the Greek word is scientific.

†Example: "Comfort's catholicity of perception and image, strangely Whitmanesque in range, almost the exact opposite in aesthetic compulsion, continues to evoke that trembling atmospheric accumulative hinting at a cruel, an inexorably serene timelessness. . . . Wrey Gardiner scores by aiming at simple bull's-eyes with precision. Only they are not so simple, and through this contented sadness runs more than the surface bitter-sweet of resignation." (*Poetry Quarterly.*)

patriot, The Soviet Press is the freest in the world, The Catholic Church is opposed to persecution, are almost always made with intent to deceive. Other words used in variable meanings, in most cases more or less dishonestly, are: *class, totalitarian, science, progressive, reactionary, bourgeois, equality.*

Now that I have made this catalogue of swindles and perversions, let me   9
give another example of the kind of writing that they lead to. This time it must of its nature be an imaginary one. I am going to translate a passage of good English into modern English of the worst sort. Here is a well-known verse from *Ecclesiastes:*

"I returned and saw under the sun, that the race is not to the swift, nor   10
the battle to the strong, neither yet bread to the wise, nor yet riches to men of understanding, nor yet favour to men of skill; but time and chance happeneth to them all."

Here it is in modern English: 11

"Objective considerations of contemporary phenomena compels the con-   12
clusion that success or failure in competitive activities exhibits no tendency to be commensurate with innate capacity, but that a considerable element of the unpredictable must invariably be taken into account."

This is a parody, but not a very gross one. Exhibit (3), above, for instance,   13
contains several patches of the same kind of English. It will be seen that I have not made a full translation. The beginning and ending of the sentence follow the original meaning fairly closely, but in the middle the concrete illustrations— race, battle, bread—dissolve into the vague phrase "success or failure in competitive activities." This had to be so, because no modern writer of the kind I am discussing—no one capable of using phrases like "objective consideration of contemporary phenomena"—would ever tabulate his thoughts in that precise and detailed way. The whole tendency of modern prose is away from concreteness. Now analyse these two sentences a little more closely. The first contains forty-nine words but only sixty syllables, and all its words are those of everyday life. The second contains thirty-eight words of ninety syllables: eighteen of its words are from Latin roots, and one from Greek. The first sentence contains six vivid images, and only one phrase ("time and chance") that could be called vague. The second contains not a single fresh, arresting phrase, and in spite of its ninety syllables it gives only a shortened version of the meaning contained in the first. Yet without a doubt it is the second kind of sentence that is gaining ground in modern English. I do not want to exaggerate. This kind of writing is not yet universal, and outcrops of simplicity will occur here and there in the worst-written page. Still, if you or I were told to write a few lines on the uncertainty of human fortunes, we should probably come much nearer to my imaginary sentence than to the one from *Ecclesiastes.*

As I have tried to show, modern writing at its worst does not consist of   14
picking out words for the sake of their meaning and inventing images in order to make the meaning clearer. It consists in gumming together long strips of words

which have already been set in order by someone else, and making the results presentable by sheer humbug. The attraction of this way of writing is that it is easy. It is easier—even quicker, once you have the habit—to say *In my opinion it is not an unjustifiable assumption that* than to say *I think*. If you use ready-made phrases, you not only don't have to hunt about for words; you also don't have to bother with the rhythms of your sentences, since these phrases are generally so arranged as to be more or less euphonious. When you are composing in a hurry—when you are dictating to a stenographer, for instance, or making a public speech—it is natural to fall into a pretentious, Latinized style. Tags like *a consideration which we should do well to bear in mind* or *a conclusion to which all of us would readily assent* will save many a sentence from coming down with a bump. By using stale metaphors, similes and idioms, you save much mental effort, at the cost of leaving your meaning vague, not only for your reader but for yourself. This is the significance of mixed metaphors. The sole aim of a metaphor is to call up a visual image. When these images clash— as in *The Fascist octopus has sung its swan song, the jackboot is thrown into the melting pot*—it can be taken as certain that the writer is not seeing a mental image of the objects he is naming; in other words he is not really thinking. Look again at the examples I gave at the beginning of this essay. Professor Laski (1) uses five negatives in fifty-three words. One of these is superfluous, making nonsense of the whole passage, and in addition there is the slip *alien* for akin, making further nonsense, and several avoidable pieces of clumsiness which increase the general vagueness. Professor Hogben (2) plays ducks and drakes with a battery which is able to write prescriptions, and, while disapproving of the everyday phrase *put up with,* is unwilling to look *egregious* up in the dictionary and see what it means; (3), if one takes an uncharitable attitude towards it, is simply meaningless: probably one could work out its intended meaning by reading the whole of the article in which it occurs. In (4), the writer knows more or less what he wants to say, but an accumulation of stale phrases chokes him like tea leaves blocking a sink. In (5), words and meaning have almost parted company. People who write in this manner usually have a general emotional meaning—they dislike one thing and want to express solidarity with another— but they are not interested in the detail of what they are saying. A scrupulous writer, in every sentence that he writes, will ask himself at least four questions, thus: What am I trying to say? What words will express it? What image or idiom will make it clearer? Is this image fresh enough to have an effect? And he will probably ask himself two more: Could I put it more shortly? Have I said anything that is avoidably ugly? But you are not obliged to go to all this trouble. You can shirk it by simply throwing your mind open and letting the ready-made phrases come crowding in. They will construct your sentences for you—even think your thoughts for you, to a certain extent—and at need they will perform the important service of partially concealing your meaning even from yourself. It is at this point that the special connection between politics and the debasement of language becomes clear.

In our time it is broadly true that political writing is bad writing. Where it is not true, it will generally be found that the writer is some kind of rebel, expressing his private opinions and not a "party line." Orthodoxy, of whatever color, seems to demand a lifeless, imitative style. The political dialects to be found in pamphlets, leading articles, manifestos, White Papers and the speeches of under-secretaries do, of course, vary from party to party, but they are all alike in that one almost never finds in them a fresh, vivid, home-made turn of speech. When one watches some tired hack on the platform mechanically repeating the familiar phrases—*bestial atrocities, iron heel, bloodstained tyranny, free peoples of the world, stand shoulder to shoulder*—one often has a curious feeling that one is not watching a live human being but some kind of dummy: a feeling which suddenly becomes stronger at moments when the light catches the speaker's spectacles and turns them into blank discs which seem to have no eyes behind them. And this is not altogether fanciful. A speaker who uses that kind of phraseology has gone some distance towards turning himself into a machine. The appropriate noises are coming out of his larynx, but his brain is not involved as it would be if he were choosing his words for himself. If the speech he is making is one that he is accustomed to make over and over again, he may be almost unconscious of what he is saying, as one is when one utters the responses in church. And this reduced state of consciousness, if not indispensable, is at any rate favorable to political conformity.

In our time, political speech and writing are largely the defence of the ⟨16⟩ indefensible. Things like the continuance of British rule in India, the Russian purges and deportation, the dropping of the atom bombs on Japan, can indeed be defended, but only by arguments which are too brutal for most people to face, and which do not square with the professed aims of political parties. Thus political language has to consist largely of euphemism, question-begging and sheer cloudy vagueness. Defenceless villages are bombarded from the air, the inhabitants driven out into the countryside, the cattle machine-gunned, the huts set on fire with incendiary bullets: this is called *pacification*. Millions of peasants are robbed of their farms and sent trudging along the roads with no more than they can carry: this is called *transfer of population* or *rectification of frontiers*. People are imprisoned for years without trial, or shot in the back of the neck or sent to die of scurvy in Arctic lumber camps: this is called *elimination of unreliable elements*. Such phraseology is needed if one wants to name things without calling up mental pictures of them. Consider for instance some comfortable English professor defending Russian totalitarianism. He cannot say outright, "I believe in killing off your opponents when you can get good results by doing so." Probably, therefore, he will say something like this:

"While freely conceding that the Soviet régime exhibits certain features ⟨17⟩ which the humanitarian may be inclined to deplore, we must, I think, agree that a certain curtailment of the right to political opposition is an unavoidable concomitant of transitional periods, and that the rigors which the Russian people have been called upon to undergo have been amply justified in the sphere of concrete achievement."

The inflated style is itself a kind of euphemism. A mass of Latin words ⟨18⟩

falls upon the facts like soft snow, blurring the outlines and covering up all the details. The great enemy of clear language is insincerity. When there is a gap between one's real and one's declared aims, one turns as it were instinctively to long words and exhausted idioms, like a cuttlefish squirting out ink. In our age there is no such thing as "keeping out of politics." All issues are political issues, and politics itself is a mass of lies, evasions, folly, hatred and schizophrenia. When the general atmosphere is bad, language must suffer. I should expect to find—this is a guess which I have not sufficient knowledge to verify—that the German, Russian and Italian languages have all deteriorated in the last ten or fifteen years, as a result of dictatorship.

But if thought corrupts language, language can also corrupt thought. A bad usage can spread by tradition and imitation, even among people who should and do know better. The debased language that I have been discussing is in some ways very convenient. Phrases like *a not unjustifiable assumption, leaves much to be desired, would serve no good purpose, a consideration which we should do well to bear in mind*, are a continuous temptation, a packet of aspirins always at one's elbow. Look back through this essay, and for certain you will find that I have again and again committed the very faults I am protesting against. By this morning's post I have received a pamphlet dealing with conditions in Germany. The author tells me that he "felt impelled" to write it. I open it at random, and here is almost the first sentence that I see: "[The Allies] have an opportunity not only of achieving a radical transformation of Germany's social and political structure in such a way as to avoid a nationalistic reaction in Germany itself, but at the same time of laying the foundations of a co-operative and unified Europe." You see, he "feels impelled" to write—feels, presumably, that he has something new to say—and yet his words, like cavalry horses answering the bugle, group themselves automatically into the familiar dreary pattern. This invasion of one's mind by ready-made phrases (*lay the foundations, achieve a radical transformation*) can only be prevented if one is constantly on guard against them, and every such phrase anaesthetizes a portion of one's brain.

I said earlier that the decadence of our language is probably curable. Those who deny this would argue, if they produced an argument at all, that language merely reflects existing social conditions, and that we cannot influence its development by any direct tinkering with words and constructions. So far as the general tone or spirit of a language goes, this may be true, but it is not true in detail. Silly words and expressions have often disappeared, not through any evolutionary process but owing to the conscious action of a minority. Two recent examples were *explore every avenue* and *leave no stone unturned*, which were killed by the jeers of a few journalists. There is a long list of flyblown metaphors which could similarly be got rid of if enough people would interest themselves in the job; and it should also be possible to laugh the *not un-* formation out of existence,* to reduce the amount of Latin and Greek in the average sentence,

---

*One can cure oneself of the *non un-* formation by memorizing this sentence: *A not unblack dog was chasing a not unsmall rabbit across a not ungreen field.*

to drive out foreign phrases and strayed scientific words, and, in general, to make pretentiousness unfashionable. But all these are minor points. The defence of the English language implies more than this, and perhaps it is best to start by saying what is does *not* imply.

To begin with it has nothing to do with archaism, with the salvaging of   21 obsolete words and turns of speech, or with the setting up of a "standard English" which must never be departed from. On the contrary, it is especially concerned with the scrapping of every word or idiom which has outworn its usefulness. It has nothing to do with correct grammar and syntax, which are of no importance so long as one makes one's meaning clear, or with the avoidance of Americanisms, or with having what is called a "good prose style." On the other hand it is not concerned with fake simplicity and the attempt to make written English colloquial. Nor does it even imply in every case preferring the Saxon word to the Latin one, though it does imply using the fewest and shortest words that will cover one's meaning. What is above all needed is to let the meaning choose the word, and not the other way about. In prose, the worst thing one can do with words is to surrender to them. When you think of a concrete object, you think wordlessly, and then, if you want to describe the thing you have been visualizing you probably hunt about till you find the exact words that seem to fit it. when you think of something abstract you are more inclined to use words from the start, and unless you make a conscious effort to prevent it, the existing dialect will come rushing in and do the job for you, at the expense of blurring or even changing your meaning. Probably it is better to put off using words as long as possible and get one's meaning as clear as one can through pictures or sensations. Afterwards one can choose—not simply *accept*—the phrases that will best cover the meaning, and then switch round and decide what impression one's words are likely to make on another person. This last effort of the mind cuts out all stale or mixed images, all prefabricated phrases, needless repetitons, and humbug and vagueness generally. But one can often be in doubt about the effect of a word or a phrase, and one needs rules that one can rely on when instinct fails. I think the following rules will cover most cases:

    i. Never use a metaphor, simile or other figure of speech which you are used to seeing in print.

    ii. Never use a long word where a short one will do.

    iii. If it is possible to cut a word out, always cut it out.

    iv. Never use the passive where you can use the active.

    v. Never use a foreign phrase, a scientific word or a jargon word if you can think of an everyday English equivalent.

    vi. Break any of these rules sooner than say anything outright barbarous.

These rules sound elementary, and so they are, but they demand a deep change of attitude in anyone who has grown used to writing in the style now fashionable.

One could keep all of them and still write bad English, but one could not write the kind of stuff that I quoted in those five specimens at the beginning of this article.

I have not here been considering the literary use of language, but merely 2 language as an instrument for expressing and not for concealing or preventing thought. Stuart Chase and others have come near to claiming that all abstract words are meaningless, and have used this as a pretext for advocating a kind of political quietism. Since you don't know what Fascism is, how can you struggle against Fascism? One need not swallow such absurdities as this, but one ought to recognize that the present political chaos is connected with the decay of language, and that one can probably bring about some improvement by starting at the verbal end. If you simplify your English, you are freed from the worst follies of orthodoxy. You cannot speak any of the necessary dialects, and when you make a stupid remark its stupidity will be obvious, even to yourself. Political language—and with variations this is true of all political parties, from Conservatives to Anarchists—is designed to make lies sound truthful and murder respectable, and to give an appearance of solidity to pure wind. One cannot change this all in a moment, but one can at least change one's own habits, and from time to time one can even, if one jeers loudly enough, send some worn-out and useless phrase—some *jackboot, Achilles' heel, hotbed, melting pot, acid test, veritable inferno* or other lump of verbal refuse—into the dustbin where it belongs.

1946

Purpose and Meaning

1. In what sense is the word *politics* used in the title? What is the significance of this word in terms of the thesis of the essay?

2. What is the historical and political context of this essay? What conditions in Orwell's time contributed to using English "in a bad way"?

3. According to Orwell, what is it about the nature of language that makes it so difficult to break bad writing habits and acquire good ones? Why, for example, does Orwell use the generic *he*?

Language and Style

1. Orwell discusses four major attributes of poor writing: dying metaphors, operators, pretentious diction, and meaningless words. Is Orwell's own writing in this essay free of these devices? Choose any of Orwell's other essays in this book, and apply his own standards to it.

2. Orwell claims that good English has "nothing to do with correct grammar and syntax . . . as long as one makes one's meaning clear." Examine the syntax of the

following sentence from paragraph 2: "But an effect can become a cause, reinforcing the original cause and producing the same effect in an intensified form, and so on indefinitely." Using Orwell's criteria for good writing, can you call this a clear sentence? Are Orwell's grammar and syntax clear throughout the essay? Justify your response.

3. Orwell provides us with a writing lesson in this essay. What is his tone as a teacher? How did you arrive at your opinion?

Strategy and Structure

1. Study the first two paragraphs. How well do they establish Orwell's basic argument? What specific rhetorical devices does Orwell use to introduce his subject?

2. Orwell uses an abundance of examples for every point he tries to demonstrate about bad writing. Does he need so many to get his point across? Would fewer examples make the essay clearer and more concise? What effect was Orwell trying to create on the reader by including such an extensive catalogue?

3. Orwell interrupts the serious tone of his essay with an example of a passage he "translated" from the Bible. What is the purpose of this example? Why is the passage a good device for maintaining the reader's interest? Do you agree that it is not a "very gross" parody? Explain your answer.

4. Explain the importance of definition and hypothetical reasoning in the structure of this essay.

Thinking and Writing

1. Using Orwell's four categories of bad writing, write an argumentative essay using examples from contemporary politics and media to demonstrate that English remains a dangerously bankrupt language.

2. Try your hand at writing a parody of poor writing. Select a paragraph from this essay or any of the other essays by Orwell in this book, and create a specimen of bad prose. Afterwards, study the results. What makes the writing unclear, pretentious, or meaningless?

3. Write an extended definition of a "meaningless" term that is abused frequently or used hypocritically in the United States today. You might want to check the annual "Doublespeak" awards.

"The Moon under Water"

My favourite public house, "The Moon under Water," is only two minutes   1
from a bus stop, but it is on a side-street, and drunks and rowdies never seem
to find their way there, even on Saturday nights.

Its clientèle, though fairly large, consists mostly of "regulars" who ²
occupy the same chair every evening and go there for conversation as much
as for the beer.

If you are asked why you favour a particular public house, it would seem ³
natural to put the beer first, but the thing that most appeals to me about "The
Moon under Water" is what people call its "atmosphere."

To begin with, its whole artchitecture and fittings are uncompromisingly ⁴
Victorian. It has no glass-topped tables or other modern miseries, and, on the
other hand, no sham roof-beams, ingle-nooks or plastic panels masquerading
as oak. The grained woodwork, the ornamental mirrors behind the bar, the
cast-iron fireplaces, the florid ceiling stained dark yellow by tobacco-smoke,
the stuffed bull's head over the mantelpiece—everything has the solid comfortable ugliness of the nineteenth century.

In winter there is generally a good fire burning in at least two of the bars, ⁵
and the Victorian lay-out of the place gives one plenty of elbow-room. There
are a public bar, a saloon bar, a ladies' bar, a bottle-and-jug for those who are
too bashful to buy their supper beer publicly, and upstairs, a dining-room.

Games are only played in the public, so that in the other bars you can ⁶
walk about without constantly ducking to avoid flying darts.

In "The Moon under Water" it is always quiet enough to talk. The house ⁷
possesses neither a radio nor a piano, and even on Christmas Eve and such
occasions the singing that happens is of a decorous kind.

The barmaids know most of their customers by name, and take a per- ⁸
sonal interest in everyone. They are all middle-aged women—two of them have
their hair dyed in quite surprising shades—and they call everyone "dear,"
irrespective of age or sex. ("Dear," not "Ducky": pubs where the barmaid calls
you "Ducky" always have a disagreeable raffish atmosphere.)

Unlike most pubs, "The Moon under Water" sells tobacco as well as ⁹
cigarettes, and it also sells aspirins and stamps, and is obliging about letting
you use the telephone.

You cannot get dinner at "The Moon under Water," but there is always 1
the snack counter where you can get liver-sausage sandwiches, mussels (a
specialty of the house), cheese, pickles and those large biscuits with caraway
seeds in them which only seem to exist in public houses.

Upstairs, six days a week, you can get a good, solid lunch—for example, 1
a cut off the joint, two vegetables and boiled jam roll—for about three shillings.

The special pleasure of this lunch is that you can have draught stout with 1.
it. I doubt whether as many as ten per cent of London pubs serve draught stout,
but "The Moon under Water" is one of them. It is a soft, creamy sort of stout,
and it goes better in a pewter pot.

They are particular about their drinking vessels at "The Moon under 1
Water" and never, for example, make the mistake of serving a pint of beer in
a handleless glass. Apart from glass and pewter mugs, they have some of those

pleasant strawberry-pink china ones which are now seldom seen in London. China mugs went out about thirty years ago, because most people like their drink to be transparent, but in my opinion beer tastes better out of china.

The great surprise of "The Moon under Water" is its garden. You go through a narrow passage leading out of the saloon, and find yourself in a fairly large garden with plane trees under which there are little green tables with iron chairs round them. Up at one end of the garden there are swings and a chute for the children. 14

On summer evenings there are family parties, and you sit under the plane trees having beer or draught cider to the tune of delighted squeals from children going down the chute. The prams with the younger children are parked near the gate. 15

Many as are the virtues of "The Moon under Water" I think that the garden is its best feature, because it allows whole families to go there instead of Mum having to stay at home and mind the baby while Dad goes out alone. 16

And though, strictly speaking, they are only allowed in the garden, the children tend to seep into the pub and even to fetch drinks for their parents. This, I believe, is against the law, but it is a law that deserves to be broken, for it is the puritanical nonsense of excluding children—and therefore to some extent, women—from pubs that has turned these places into mere boozing-shops instead of the family gathering-places that they ought to be. 17

"The Moon under Water" is my ideal of what a pub should be—at any rate, in the London area. (The qualities one expects of a country pub are slightly different.) 18

But now is the time to reveal something which the discerning and disillusioned reader will probably have guessed already. There is no such place as "The Moon under Water". 19

That is to say, there may well be a pub of that name, but I don't know of it, nor do I know any pub with just that combination of qualities. 20

I know pubs where the beer is good but you can't get meals, others where you can get meals but which are noisy and crowded, and others which are quiet but where the beer is generally sour. As for gardens, offhand I can only think of three London pubs that possess them. 21

But, to be fair, I do know of a few pubs that almost come up to "The Moon under Water". I have mentioned above ten qualities that the perfect pub should have, and I know one pub that has eight of them. Even there, however, there is no draught stout and no china mugs. 22

And if anyone knows of a pub that has draught stout, open fires, cheap meals, a garden, motherly barmaids and no radio, I should be glad to hear of it, even though its name were something as prosaic as "The Red Lion" or "The Railway Arms". 23

1946

Purpose and Meaning

1. Orwell describes many of the attributes that make "The Moon under Water" his favorite pub. What is its *overall* appeal to him?

2. Why does the author wait until the end of the essay to reveal that the pub he is describing is only a fantasy? How does this revelation contribute to the effectiveness of the writing?

3. What assumptions does Orwell make about his audience in this essay?

Language and Style

1. What terms does Orwell use that "date" the essay? What terms help indicate that the pub is British and not American?

2. What is the tone of this essay? Why is it appropriate for the subject matter? What attitude does Orwell seem to have toward the patrons of the pub?

3. What special details does Orwell employ to create a certain Victorian charm for his pub?

4. Orwell uses the second person "you" quite often in the essay. How does this choice help determine the relationship between the author and the reader? Between the reader and what is being described?

Strategy and Structure

1. This essay is composed of many short paragraphs no longer than two or three sentences each. Why might have Orwell adopted this approach? How does he maintain coherence despite the brevity of his paragraphs?

2. How does Orwell order the features of his ideal pub? What dominant impression emerges from this presentation of details?

3. Considering the general tone of the essay, Orwell makes a rather strong and abrupt pronouncement in paragraph 17. Does this pronouncement break up the continuity of the essay, or is the interruption justified?

4. Should we take the final paragraph seriously? Does Orwell truly expect a reader to respond to his request? How does the ending help maintain the implied relationship between the author and his audience?

Thinking and Writing

1. What constitutes the "atmosphere" of a place? Is it its people? Its decor? Its activities? Select two restaurants, two bars, two discotheques, or two libraries. Compare and contrast them in as many ways as you can.

2. To experiment on just how a particular audience affects one's writing style, write a brief essay describing a place for an audience of your peers. What assumptions do you have in common with your intended audience? Which of these assumptions would be foreign to a different audience?

3. "The Moon under Water" describes an ideal pub. In an essay of your own, describe your ideal of a type of place. Be as specific as possible. After all, only you know all its nuances.

Why I Write

From a very early age, perhaps the age of five or six, I knew that when   1
I grew up I should be a writer. Between the ages of about seventeen and twenty-four I tried to abandon this idea, but I did so with the consciousness that I was outraging my true nature and that sooner or later I should have to settle down and write books.

I was the middle child of three, but there was a gap of five years on either   2
side, and I barely saw my father before I was eight. For this and other reasons I was somewhat lonely, and I soon developed disagreeable mannerisms which made me unpopular throughout my schooldays. I had the lonely child's habit of making up stories and holding conversations with imaginary persons, and I think from the very start my literary ambitions were mixed up with the feeling of being isolated and undervalued. I knew that I had a facility with words and a power of facing unpleasant facts, and I felt that this created a sort of private world in which I could get my own back for my failure in everyday life. Nevertheless the volume of serious—i.e. seriously intended—writing which I produced all through my childhood and boyhood would not amount to half a dozen pages. I wrote my first poem at the age of four or five, my mother taking it down to dictation. I cannot remember anything about it except that it was about a tiger and the tiger had "chair-like teeth"—a good enough phrase, but I fancy the poem was a plagiarism of Blake's "Tiger, Tiger." At eleven, when the war of 1914–18 broke out, I wrote a patriotic poem which was printed in the local newspaper, as was another, two years later, on the death of Kitchener. From time to time, when I was a bit older, I wrote bad and usually unfinished "nature poems" in the Georgian style. I also, about twice, attempted a short story which was a ghastly failure. That was the total of the would-be serious work that I actually set down on paper during all those years.

However, throughout this time I did in a sense engage in literary activities.   3
To begin with there was the made-to-order stuff which I produced quickly, easily

and without much pleasure to myself. Apart from school work, I wrote *vers d'occasion*, semicomic poems which I could turn out at what now seems to me astonishing speed—at fourteen I wrote a whole rhyming play, in imitation of Aristophanes, in about a week—and helped to edit school magazines, both printed and in manuscript. These magazines were the most pitiful burlesque stuff that you could imagine, and I took far less trouble with them than I now would with the cheapest journalism. But side by side with all this, for fifteen years or more, I was carrying out a literary exercise of a quite different kind: this was the making up of a continuous "story" about myself, a sort of diary existing only in the mind. I believe this is a common habit of children and adolescents. As a very small child I used to imagine that I was, say, Robin Hood, and picture myself as the hero of thrilling adventures, but quite soon my "story" ceased to be narcissistic in a crude way and became more and more a mere description of what I was doing and the things I saw. For minutes at a time this kind of thing would be running through my head: "He pushed the door open and entered the room. A yellow beam of sunlight, filtering through the muslin curtains, slanted on to the table, where a matchbox, half open, lay beside the inkpot. With his right hand in his pocket he moved across to the window. Down in the street a tortoise-shell cat was chasing a dead leaf," etc. etc. This habit continued till I was about twenty-five, right through my non-literary years. Although I had to search, and did search, for the right words, I seemed to be making this descriptive effort almost against my will, under a kind of compulsion from outside. The "story" must, I suppose, have reflected the styles of the various writers I admired at different ages, but so far as I remember it always had the same meticulous descriptive quality.

When I was about sixteen I suddenly discovered the joy of mere words,   4
i.e. the sounds and associations of words. The lines from *Paradise Lost*,

> So hee with difficulty and labour hard
> Moved on: with difficulty and labour hee,

which do not now seem to be so very wonderful, sent shivers down my backbone; and the spelling "hee" for "he" was an added pleasure. As for the need to describe things, I knew all about it already. So it is clear what kind of books I wanted to write, in so far as I could be said to want to write books at that time. I wanted to write enormous naturalistic novels with unhappy endings, full of detailed descriptions and arresting similes, and also full of purple passages in which words were used partly for the sake of their sound. And in fact my first completed novel, *Burmese Days*, which I wrote when I was thirty but projected much earlier, is rather that kind of book.

I give all this background information because I do not think one can assess   5
a writer's motives without knowing something of his early development. His subject matter will be determined by the age he lives in—at least this is true in tumultuous, revolutionary ages like our own—but before he ever begins to

write he will have acquired an emotional attitude from which he will never completely escape. It is his job, no doubt, to discipline his temperament and avoid getting stuck at some immature stage, or in some perverse mood: but if he escapes from his early influences altogether, he will have killed his impulse to write. Putting aside the need to earn a living, I think there are four great motives for writing, at any rate for writing prose. They exist in different degrees in every writer, and in any one writer the proportions will vary from time to time, according to the atmosphere in which he is living. They are:

1. Sheer egoism. Desire to seem clever, to be talked about, to be 6
remembered after death, to get your own back on grown-ups who snubbed you in childhood, etc. etc. It is humbug to pretend that this is not a motive, and a strong one. Writers share this characteristic with scientists, artists, politicians, lawyers, soldiers, successful businessmen—in short, with the whole top crust of humanity. The great mass of human beings are not acutely selfish. After the age of about thirty they abandon individual ambition—in many cases, indeed, they almost abandon the sense of being individuals at all—and live chiefly for others, or are simply smothered under drudgery. But there is also the minority of gifted, wilful people who are determined to live their own lives to the end, and writers belong in this class. Serious writers, I should say, are on the whole more vain and self-centered than journalists, though less interested in money.

2. Aesthetic enthusiasm. Perception of beauty in the external world, or, 7
on the other hand, in words and their right arrangement. Pleasure in the impact of one sound on another, in the firmness of good prose or the rhythm of a good story. Desire to share an experience which one feels is valuable and ought not to be missed. The aesthetic motive is very feeble in a lot of writers, but even a pamphleteer or a writer of textbooks will have pet words and phrases which appeal to him for non-utilitarian reasons; or he may feel strongly about typography, width of margins, etc. Above the level of a railway guide, no book is quite free from aesthetic considerations.

3. Historical impulse. Desire to see things as they are, to find out true 8
facts and store them up for the use of posterity.

4. Political purpose—using the word "political" in the widest possible 9
sense. Desire to push the world in a certain direction, to alter other people's idea of the kind of society that they should strive after. Once again, no book is genuinely free from political bias. The opinion that art should have nothing to do with politics is itself a political attitude.

It can be seen how these various impulses must war against one another, 10
and how they must fluctuate from person to person and from time to time. By nature—taking your "nature" to be the state you have attained when you are first adult—I am a person in whom the first three motives would outweigh the fourth. In a peaceful age I might have written ornate or merely descriptive books, and might have remained almost unaware of my political loyalties. As it is I have been forced into becoming a sort of pamphleteer. First I spent five years in an unsuitable profession (the Indian Imperial Police, in Burma), and then

I underwent poverty and the sense of failure. This increased my natural hatred of authority and made me for the first time fully aware of the existence of the working classes, and the job in Burma had given me some understanding of the nature of imperialism: but these experiences were not enough to give me an accurate political orientation. Then came Hitler, the Spanish civil war, etc. By the end of 1935 I had still failed to reach a firm decision. I remember a little poem that I wrote at that date, expressing my dilemma:

> A happy vicar I might have been
> Two hundred years ago,
> To preach upon eternal doom
> And watch my walnuts grow;
>
> But born, alas, in an evil time,
> I missed that pleasant haven,
> For the hair has grown on my upper lip
> And the clergy are all clean-shaven.
>
> And later still the times were good,
> We were so easy to please,
> We rocked our troubled thoughts to sleep
> On the bosoms of the trees.
>
> All ignorant we dared to own
> The joys we now dissemble;
> The greenfinch on the apple bough
> Could make my enemies tremble.
>
> But girls' bellies and apricots,
> Roach in a shaded stream,
> Horses, ducks in flight at dawn,
> All these are a dream.
>
> It is forbidden to dream again;
> We maim our joys or hide them;
> Horses are made of chromium steel
> And little fat men shall ride them.
>
> I am the worm who never turned,
> The eunuch without a harem;
> Between the priest and the commissar
> I walk like Eugene Aram;
>
> And the commissar is telling my fortune
> While the radio plays,
> But the priest has promised an Austin Seven,
> For Duggie always pays.

> I dreamed I dwelt in marble halls,
> And woke to find it true;
> I wasn't born for an age like this;
> Was Smith? Was Jones? Were you?

The Spanish war and other events in 1936–37 turned the scale and thereafter I knew where I stood. Every line of serious work that I have written since 1936 has been written, directly or indirectly, *against* totalitarianism and *for* democratic Socialism, as I understand it. It seems to me nonsense, in a period like our own, to think that one can avoid writing of such subjects. Everyone writes of them in one guise or another. It is simply a question of which side one takes and what approach one follows. And the more one is conscious of one's political bias, the more chance one has of acting politically without sacrificing one's aesthetic and intellectual integrity.

What I have most wanted to do throughout the past ten years is to make 11 political writing into an art. My starting point is always a feeling of partisanship, a sense of injustice. When I set down to write a book, I do not say to myself, "I am going to produce a work of art." I write it because there is some lie that I want to expose, some fact to which I want to draw attention, and my initial concern is to get a hearing. But I could not do the work of writing a book, or even a long magazine article, if it were not also an aesthetic experience. Anyone who cares to examine my work will see that even when it is downright propaganda it contains much that a full-time politician would consider irrelevant. I am not able, and I do not want, completely to abandon the world-view that I acquired in childhood. So long as I remain alive and well I shall continue to feel strongly about prose style, to love the surface of the earth, and to take pleasure in solid objects and scraps of useless information. It is no use trying to suppress that side of myself. The job is to reconcile my ingrained likes and dislikes with the essentially public, non-individual activities that this age forces on all of us.

It is not easy. It raises problems of construction and of language, and it 12 raises in a new way the problem of truthfulness. Let me give just one example of the cruder kind of difficulty that arises. My book about the Spanish civil war, *Homage to Catalonia*, is, of course, a frankly political book, but in the main it is written with a certain detachment and regard for form. I did try very hard in it to tell the whole truth without violating my literary instincts. But among other things it contains a long chapter, full of newspaper quotations and the like, defending the Trotskyists who were accused of plotting with Franco. Clearly such a chapter, which after a year or two would lose its interest for any ordinary reader, must ruin the book. A critic whom I respect read me a lecture about it. "Why did you put in all that stuff?" he said. "You've turned what might have been a good book into journalism." What he said was true, but I could not have done otherwise. I happened to know, what very few people in England had been allowed to know, that innocent men were being falsely accused. If I had not been angry about that I should never have written the book.

In one form or another this problem comes up again. The problem of language is subtler and would take too long to discuss. I will only say that of late years I have tried to write less picturesquely and more exactly. In any case I find that by the time you have perfected any style of writing, you have always outgrown it. *Animal Farm* was the first book in which I tried, with full consciousness of what I was doing, to fuse political purpose and artistic purpose into one whole. I have not written a novel for seven years, but I hope to write another fairly soon. It is bound to be a failure, every book is a failure, but I know with some clarity what kind of book I want to write.

Looking back through the last page or two, I see that I have made it appear as though my motives in writing were wholly public-spirited. I don't want to leave that as the final impression. All writers are vain, selfish and lazy, and at the very bottom of their motives there lies a mystery. Writing a book is a horrible, exhausting struggle, like a long bout of some painful illness. One would never undertake such a thing if one were not driven on by some demon whom one can neither resist nor understand. For all one knows that demon is simply the same instinct that makes a baby squall for attention. And yet it is also true that one can write nothing readable unless one constantly struggles to efface one's own personality. Good prose is like a window pane. I cannot say with certainty which of my motives are the strongest, but I know which of them deserve to be followed. And looking back through my work, I see that it is invariably where I lacked a political purpose that I wrote lifeless books and was betrayed into purple passages, sentences without meaning, decorative adjectives and humbug generally.

1946

Purpose and Meaning

1. In the final paragraph, Orwell states that no one would write a book "if one were not driven on by some demon." Tracing Orwell's autobiographical sketch from the beginning, find those "demons" that seem to have driven him to write?

2. Examine the four motives that Orwell lists as to why a writer writes. How do these motives correspond to Orwell's own experience as a developing writer?

3. In paragraph 5, the author states "no book is genuinely free from political bias" and "that art should have nothing to do with politics is itself a political attitude." How do you reconcile this seeming contradiction? If Orwell is correct, in what way are any one of the authors in this anthology "political writers"?

4. In paragraph 10, Orwell says "every book is a failure." What did he mean by "failure"? If this statement is true, why would Orwell—or anyone for that matter—write?

Language and Style

1. Orwell states in the final paragraph that "one can write nothing readable unless

one constantly struggles to efface one's personality." What can you say about the tone, diction, or mood in "A Hanging" or "Shooting an Elephant" that provides evidence of this effacement?

2. In paragraph 3, Orwell quotes a passage he wrote during his youth. How does it compare to his writing as an adult? What makes Orwell's "adult" writing more "mature?"

3. The author makes quite a few references to other authors, writing genres, particular works of writing (including his own), and historical events. How does this knowledge add to our appreciation of the essay?

Strategy and Structure

1. Orwell enumerates the main motives for writing. How does listing them by number affect Orwell's authority? Would the impact or effect have differed if he had not numbered them?

2. Why do you think Orwell has inserted the poem in the essay? Why couldn't the sentiments in the poem have been expressed as succinctly in prose? How does the poem affect the unity of the essay? What does the poem contribute to the essay?

3. Does Orwell's conclusion summarize or add to the information he has already provided? How does the emphasis Orwell places in the final sentence create a strong ending? How does this emphasis help iterate the theme of the essay?

Thinking and Writing

1. Has any experience or experiences in your own life influenced your choice of major or your choice of a present or future career? Write an essay exploring this relationship.

2. Follow up on Orwell's assertion that the social and political climate of the times influenced the type of writer he became. Conduct research on Orwell and his times. Then write an extended essay exploring this influence of events on Orwell's literary career.

3. To what specific type of writing is Orwell referring in this essay? Does the *function* of writing affect one's motivation for writing? Consider such forms of writing as instruction manuals, textbooks, newspaper articles, and college research papers. How do their functions influence the motivation behind the writing of them? Select a particular type of writing and compose an essay enumerating the motives an author would have for writing it.

BARBARA TUCHMAN

Barbara Tuchman was one of the preeminent historians of our era, but she herself preferred to be acknowledged as "a writer whose subject is history." She was born in 1912 in New York City, the daughter of Maurice Wertheim, a prominent banker and philanthropist; and Alma Morganthau Wertheim, a sister of Henry Morganthau, Jr., who later became Secretary of Treasury under President Franklin D. Roosevelt. Tuchman received a B.A. from Radcliffe College in 1933 with a concentration in history and literature. In the tradition of her family, she began her career in public service, working for an international organization overseas.

"Paying jobs did not hang on trees," Tuchman observed in describing her entry into the Depression-era job market. Consequently, she took an unpaid research position in Tokyo and Peking with the American Council of the Institute of Pacific Relations. Shortly after she returned to the United States in 1935, her father purchased *The Nation*; and in 1937, Tuchman was assigned as correspondent in Valencia and Madrid. Like Orwell, the twenty-four-year-old writer gained her first experience as a journalist covering the Spanish Civil War. "It was a somber, exciting, believing time," Tuchman wrote in the preface to a collection of her essays, *Practicing History* (1981), "with heroes, hopes and illusions." Tuchman came home to the United States on the eve of Munich and the outbreak of World War II; on June 18, 1940, the day Hitler entered Paris, she married a New York physician, Dr. Lester Tuchman.

While raising three daughters, Barbara Tuchman wrote eleven books and numerous essays. She lived outside the boundaries of academic life. She never took a doctoral degree, explaining that doing so would have "stifled" her writing capacity. It is clear from "The Historian as Artist" that Tuchman appropriates the creative process—the imaginative art of the novelist and poet—for the historian. She exercises "the artist's privilege of selection" in arranging the facts and evidence of history in a dynamic way. For as she once told an audience, "The writer's object is—or should be—to hold the reader's attention."

Tuchman, however, is no facile popularizer of history, but is noted for her prodigious research. Before she wrote her fourth book, the Pulitzer Prize–winning *Guns of August* (1962), she rented a Renault and toured the battlefields of World War I, the one war that for her represented the "chasm between our world and a world that died forever." Her second Pulitzer came with *Stilwell and the American Experience in China* (1971), where again relentless research (started twenty years earlier when she covered Stilwell's campaign in Burma) combines with vivid style and accessible narration to create a lucid account of complex matters. Yet for Tuchman, writing did not come easily. "It means," she said, "rearrangement, revision, adding, cutting, rewriting. But it brings a sense of excitement, almost of rapture. . . it is an act of creation."

As in her bicentennial salute, "On Our Birthday—America as Idea," and in "Humanity's Better Moments," Tuchman as historian tries to balance our human follies and misgovernment against our promise. Described by English historian A. L. Rowse as "the most successful practicing historian in the United States. . .and the best," she is capable of focusing on one historical example or on countless historical examples to vividly recount "the past." As a historian of rare craft and ability, Barbara Tuchman, who died in 1989, shows how human conduct is "a steady stream running through endless fields of changing circumstances."

The Historian as Artist

I would like to share some good news with you. I recently came back   1
from skiing at Aspen, where on one occasion I shared the double-chair ski-lift
with an advertising man from Chicago. He told me he was in charge of all copy
for his firm in all media: TV, radio, *and* the printed word. On the strength of
this he assured me—and I quote—that "Writing is coming back. *Books* are
coming back." I cannot tell you how pleased I was, and I knew you would be too.

Now that we know that the future is safe for writing, I want to talk about   2
a particular kind of writer—the Historian—not just as historian but as artist;
that is, as a creative writer on the same level as the poet or novelist. What follows
will sound less immodest if you will take the word "artist" in the way I think
of it, not as a form of praise but as a category, like clerk or laborer or actor.

Why is it generally assumed that in writing, the creative process is the   3
exclusive property of poets and novelists? I would like to suggest that the thought
applied by the historian to his subject matter can be no less creative than the
imagination applied by the novelist to his. And when it comes to writing as
an art, is Gibbon necessarily less of an artist in words than, let us say, Dickens?
Or Winston Churchill less so than William Faulkner or Sinclair Lewis?

George Macaulay Trevelyan, the late professor of modern history at Cam-   4
bridge and the great champion of literary as opposed to scientific history, said
in a famous essay on his muse that ideally history should be the exposition of
facts about the past, "in their full emotional and intellectual value to a wide
public by the difficult art of literature." Notice "wide public." Trevelyan always
stressed writing for the general reader as opposed to writing just for fellow
scholars because he knew that when you write for the public you have to be
clear and you have to be *interesting* and these are the two criteria which make
for good writing. He had no patience with the idea that only imaginative writing
is literature. Novels, he pointed out, if they are bad enough, are *not* literature,
while even pamphlets, if they are good enough, and he cites those of Milton,
Swift, and Burke, are.

The "difficult art of literature" is well said. Trevelyan was a dirt farmer   5
in that field and he knew. I may as well admit now that I have always *felt* like
an artist when I work on a book but I did not think I ought to say so until someone else said it first (it's like waiting to be proposed to). Now that an occasional
reviewer here and there has made the observation, I feel I can talk about it.
I see no reason why the word should always be confined to writers of fiction
and poetry while the rest of us are lumped together under that despicable term

"Nonfiction"—as if we were some sort of remainder. I do not feel like a Non-something; I feel quite specific. I wish I could think of a name in place of "Non-fiction." In the hope of finding an antonym I looked up "Fiction" in Webster and found it defined as opposed to "Fact, Truth and Reality." I thought for a while of adopting FTR, standing for Fact, Truth, and Reality, as my new term, but it is awkward to use. "Writers of Reality" is the nearest I can come to what I want, but I cannot very well call us "Realtors" because that has been pre-empted—although as a matter of fact I would like to. "Real Estate," when you come to think of it, is a very fine phrase and it is exactly the sphere that writers of nonfiction deal in: the real estate of man, of human conduct. I wish we could get it back from the dealers in land. Then the categories could be poets, novelists, and realtors.

I should add that I do not entirely go along with Webster's statement that fiction is what is distinct from fact, truth, and reality because good fiction (as opposed to junk), even if it has nothing to do with fact, is usually *founded* on reality and *perceives* truth—often more truly than some historians. It is exactly this quality of perceiving truth, extracting it from irrelevant surroundings and conveying it to the reader or the viewer of a picture, which distinguishes the artist. What the artist has is an *extra* vision and an *inner* vision plus the ability to express it. He supplies a view or an understanding that the viewer or reader would not have gained without the aid of the artist's creative vision. This is what Monet does in one of those shimmering rivers reflecting poplars, or El Greco in the stormy sky over Toledo, or Jane Austen compressing a whole society into Mr. and Mrs. Bennet, Lady Catherine, and Mr. Darcy. We realtors, at least those of us who aspire to write literature, do the same thing. Lytton Strachey perceived a truth about Queen Victoria and the Eminent Victorians, and the style and form which he created to portray what he saw have changed the whole approach to biography since his time. Rachel Carson perceived truth about the seashore or the silent spring, Thoreau about Walden Pond, De Tocqueville and James Bryce about America, Gibbon about Rome, Karl Marx about Capital, Caryle about the French Revolution. Their work is based on study, observation, and accumulation of fact, but does anyone suppose that these realtors did not make use of their imagination? Certainly they did; that is what gave them their extra vision.

Trevelyan wrote that the best historian was he who combined knowledge of the evidence with "the largest intellect, the warmest human sympathy and the highest imaginative powers." The last two qualities are no different than those necessary to a great novelist. They are a necessary part of the historian's equipment because they are what enable him to *understand* the evidence he has accumulated. Imagination stretches the available facts—extrapolates from them, so to speak, thus often supplying an otherwise missing answer to the "Why" of what happened. Sympathy is essential to the understanding of motive. Without sympathy and imagination the historian can copy figures from a tax roll forever—or count them by computer as they do nowadays—but he will never know or be able to portray the people who paid the taxes.

When I say that I felt like an artist, I mean that I constantly found myself   8
perceiving a historical truth (at least, what I believe to be truth) by seizing upon
a suggestion; then, after careful gathering of the evidence, conveying it in turn
to the reader, not by piling up a list of all the facts I have collected, which is
the way of the Ph.D., but by exercising the artist's privilege of selection.

Actually the idea for *The Proud Tower* evolved in that way from a number   9
of such perceptions. The initial impulse was a line I quoted in *The Guns of August*
from Belgian Socialist poet Emile Verhaeren. After a lifetime as a pacifist
dedicated to the social and humanitarian ideas which were then believed to erase
national lines, he found himself filled with hatred of the German invader and
disillusioned in all he had formerly believed in. And yet, as he wrote, "Since
it seems to me that in this state of hatred my conscience becomes diminished,
I dedicate these pages, with emotion, to the man I used to be."

I was deeply moved by this. His confession seemed to me so poignant,   10
so evocative of a time and mood, that it decided me to try to retrieve that
vanished era. It led to the last chapter in *The Proud Tower* on the Socialists,
to Jaurès as the authentic Socialist, to his prophetic lines, "I summon the living,
I mourn the dead," and to his assassination as the perfect and dramatically right
ending for the book, both chronologically and symbolically.

Then there was Lord Ribblesdale. I owe this to *American Heritage*, which   11
back in October 1961 published a piece on Sargent and Whistler with a handsome reproduction of the Ribblesdale portrait. In Sargent's painting Ribblesdale
stared out upon the world, as I later wrote in *The Proud Tower*, "in an attitude
of such natural arrogance, elegance and self-confidence as no man of a later
day would ever achieve." Here too was a vanished era which came together
in my mind with Verhaeren's line, "the man I used to be"—like two globules
of mercury making a single mass. From that came the idea for the book. Ribblesdale, of course, was the suggestion that ultimately became the opening chapter
on the Patricians. This is the reward of the artist's eye: It always leads you to
the right thing.

As I see it, there are three parts to the creative process: first, the extra   12
vision with which the artist perceives a truth and conveys it by suggestion.
Second, medium of expression: language for writers, paint for painters, clay
or stone for sculptors, sound expressed in musical notes for composers. Third,
design or structure.

When it comes to language, nothing is more satisfying than to write a   13
good sentence. It is no fun to write lumpishly, dully, in prose the reader must
plod through like wet sand. But it is a pleasure to achieve, if one can, a clear
running prose that is simple yet full of surprises. This does not just happen.
It requires skill, hard work, a good ear, and continued practice, as much as
it takes Heifetz to play the violin. The goals, as I have said, are clarity, interest,
and aesthetic pleasure. On the first of these I would like to quote Macaulay,
a great historian and great writer, who once wrote to a friend, "How little the
all important art of making meaning pellucid is studied now! Hardly any popular
writer except myself thinks of it."

As to structure, my own form is narrative, which is not every historian's,
I may say—indeed, it is rather looked down on now by the advanced academics,
but I don't mind because no one could possibly persuade me that telling a story
is not the most desirable thing a writer can do. Narrative history is neither as
simple nor as straightforward as it might seem. It requires arrangement, composition, planning just like a painting—Rembrandt's "Night Watch," for example. He did not fit in all those figures with certain ones in the foreground
and others in back and the light falling on them just so, without much trial and
error and innumerable preliminary sketches. It is the same with writing history.
Although the finished result may look to the reader natural and inevitable, as
if the author had only to follow the sequence of events, it is not that easy.
Sometimes, to catch attention, the crucial event and the causative circumstances
have to be reversed in order—the event first and the cause afterwards, as in
The Zimmermann Telegram. One must juggle with time.

In *The Proud Tower*, for instance, the two English chapters were originally
conceived as one. I divided them and placed them well apart in order to give
a feeling of progression, of forward chronological movement to the book. The
story of the Anarchists with their ideas and deeds set in counterpoint to each
other was a problem in arrangement. The middle section of the Hague chapter
on the Paris Exposition of 1900 was originally planned as a separate short center-
piece, marking the turn of the century, until I saw it as a bridge linking the two
Hague Conferences, where it now seems to belong.

Structure is chiefly a problem of selection, an agonizing business because
there is always more material than one can use or fit into a story. The problem
is how and what to select out of all that happened without, by the very process
of selection, giving an over- or under-emphasis which violates truth. One cannot put in everything: The result would be a shapeless mass. The job is to achieve
a narrative line without straying from the essential facts or leaving out any essential facts and without twisting the material to suit one's convenience. To do
so is a temptation, but if you do it with history you invariably get tripped up
by later events. I have been tempted once or twice and I know.

The most difficult task of selection I had was in the Dreyfus chapter. To
try to skip over the facts about the *bordereau* and the handwriting and the
forgeries—all the elements of the Case as distinct from the Affair—in order to
focus instead on what happened to France and yet at the same time give the
reader enough background information to enable him to understand what was
going on, nearly drove me to despair. My writing slowed down to a trickle
until one dreadful day when I went to my study at nine and stayed there all
day in a blank coma until five, when I emerged without having written a single
word. Anyone who is a writer will know how frightening that was. You feel
you have come to the end of your powers; you will not finish the book; you
may never write again.

There are other problems of structure peculiar to writing history: how
to explain background and yet keep the story moving; how to create suspense

and sustain interest in a narrative of which the outcome (like who won the war) is, to put it mildly, known. If anyone thinks this does not take creative writing, I can only say, try it.

Mr. Capote's *In Cold Blood*, for example, which deals with real life as does mine, is notable for conscious design. One can see him planning, arranging, composing his material until he achieves his perfectly balanced structure. That is art, although the hand is too obtrusive and the design too contrived to qualify as history. His method of investigation, moreover, is hardly so new as he thinks. He is merely applying to contemporary material what historians have been doing for years. Herodotus started it more than two thousand years ago, walking all over Asia Minor asking questions. Francis Parkman went to live among the Indians: hunted, traveled, and ate with them so that his pages would be steeped in understanding; E. A. Freeman, before he wrote *The Norman Conquest*, visited every spot the Conqueror had set foot on. New to these techniques, Mr. Capote is perhaps naively impressed by them. He uses them in a deliberate effort to raise what might be called "creative" journalism to the level of literature. A great company from Herodotus to Trevelyan have been doing the same with history for quite some time.

1966

Purpose and Meaning

1. According to Tuchman, what are the chief qualities of a historian that make him or her an artist? What value judgments does Tuchman make concerning the artist-historian and the traditional historian?

2. In paragraph 2, Tuchman would like us to consider the word *artist* as a category, "like clerk or laborer or actor." How does her use of the word determine the way she presents her argument? Does her argument *require* that she define the artist in this way? What is the basis for your view?

Language and Style

1. Define the tone of this essay. How does the language of the introductory paragraph set the essay's tone? What type of relationship does it establish between the reader and writer? Is the tone that is established in the opening paragraph maintained as the essay progresses?

2. Paragraph 6 (as well as elsewhere) contains specific references to painting, literature, biography, philosophy, and history. With how many of these allusions were you already familiar? How essential is it for you to be familiar with these references to appreciate Tuchman's argument? What assumptions is she making about her audience? How do you respond to allusions you are not familiar with?

3. Tuchman mixes colloquial and relatively formal diction in this essay. Locate examples of this juxtaposition. What is the effect?

4. In paragraph 5, Tuchman considers changing the name of "nonfiction" writers to "realtors." Considering the tone in which she presents this argument, are we to take her seriously? Do you agree that the word used to signify something often determines our perception of the thing signified? Why or why not?

Strategy and Structure

1. Tuchman uses a variety of devices to support her argument, including examples, appeals to authority, definitions, and analogies. Find examples of each device. How effective are these devices in advancing Tuchman's thesis? Are any of the devices more effective than others?

2. Tuchman concludes her essay with a critique of another contemporary writer. What gives this conclusion its rhetorical strength? How does she use the critique to further advance her argument? In general, is it a good idea to add extra supporting points in the conclusion to a persuasive essay? Why is it a good idea here?

3. In paragraph 16, the author states that "structure is chiefly a problem of selection." Has Tuchman done a good job of selecting specific examples and references for her essay? Is her structure "clear" and "interesting" as she claims that writing for the general public should be (paragraph 4)?

Thinking and Writing

1. Extending Tuchman's view that we define artists too narrowly, can you think of a type of work that could be considered artistic that is not usually thought to be artistic? Using Tuchman's definition of the term *artist*, argue for the extension of the term to another profession.

2. Review "Politics and the English Language" by George Orwell. Write an essay comparing and contrasting Orwell's view of good writing with Tuchman's.

3. To explore Tuchman's statement that "structure is a problem of selection," choose a partner in class, and together, select an object or a person both of you know. Write a descriptive essay (ideally with some historical slant), and compare it with your partner's. What guided your choice of what to include? How did it differ from your partner's? Discuss with him or her the different choices in your essays.

On Our Birthday—America as Idea

The United States is a nation consciously conceived, not one that evolved   1
slowly out of an ancient past. It was a planned idea of democracy, of liberty
of conscience and pursuit of happiness. It was the promise of equality of

opportunity and individual freedom within a just social order, as opposed to the restrictions and repressions of the Old World. In contrast to the militarism of Europe, it would renounce standing armies and "sheathe the desolating sword of war." It was an experiment in Utopia to test the thesis that, given freedom, independence, and local self-government, people, in Kossuth's words, "will in due time ripen into all the excellence and all the dignity of humanity." It was a new life for the oppressed, it was enlightenment, it was optimism.

Regardless of hypocrisy and corruption, of greed, chicanery, brutality, and all the other bad habits man carries with him whether in the New World or Old, the founding idea of the United States remained, on the whole, dominant through the first hundred years. With reservations, it was believed in by Americans, by visitors who came to aid our Revolution or later to observe our progress, by immigrants who came by the hundreds of thousands to escape an intolerable situation in their native lands. **2**

The idea shaped our politics, our institutions, and to some extent our national character, but it was never the only influence at work. Material circumstances exerted an opposing force. The open frontier, the hardships of homesteading from scratch, the wealth of natural resources, the whole vast challenge of a continent waiting to be exploited, combined to produce a prevailing materialism and an American drive bent as much, if not more, on money, property, and power than was true of the Old World from which we had fled. The human resources we drew upon were significant: Every wave of immigration brought here those people who had the extra energy, gumption, or restlessness to uproot themselves and cross an unknown ocean to seek a better life. Two other factors entered the shaping process—the shadow of slavery and the destruction of the native Indian. **3**

At its Centennial the United States was a material success. Through its second century the idea and the success have struggled in continuing conflict. The Statue of Liberty, erected in 1886, still symbolized the promise to those "yearning to breathe free." Hope, to them, as seen by a foreign visitor, was "domiciled in America as the Pope is in Rome." But slowly in the struggle the idea lost ground, and at a turning point around 1900, with American acceptance of a rather half-hearted imperialism, it lost dominance. Increasingly invaded since then by self-doubt and disillusion, it survives in the disenchantment of today, battered and crippled but not vanquished. **4**

What has happened to the United States in the twentieth century is not a peculiarly American phenomenon but a part of the experience of the West. In the Middle Ages plague, wars, and social violence were seen as God's punishment upon man for his sins. If the concept of God can be taken as man's conscience, the same explanation may be applicable today. Our sins in the twentieth century—greed, violence, inhumanity—have been profound, with the result that the pride and self-confidence of the nineteenth century have turned to dismay and self-disgust. **5**

In the United States we have a society pervaded from top to bottom by contempt for the law. Government—including the agencies of law **6** enforcement—business, labor, students, the military, the poor no less than the rich, outdo each other in breaking the rules and violating the ethics that society has established for its protection. The average citizen, trying to hold a footing in standards of morality and conduct he once believed in, is daily knocked over by incoming waves of venality, vulgarity, irresponsibility, ignorance, ugliness, and trash in all senses of the word. Our government collaborates abroad with the worst enemies of humanity and liberty. It wastes our substance on useless proliferation of military hardware that can never buy security no matter how high the pile. It learns no lessons, employs no wisdom, and corrupts all who succumb to Potomac fever.

Yet the idea does not die. Americans are not passive under their faults.   7
We expose them and combat them. Somewhere every day some group is fighting a public abuse—openly and, on the whole, notwithstanding the FBI, with confidence in the First Amendment. The U.S. has slid a long way from the original idea. Nevertheless, somewhere between Gulag Archipelago and the featherbed of cradle-to-the-grave welfare, it still offers a greater opportunity for social happiness—that is to say, for well-being combined with individual freedom and initiative—than is likely elsewhere. The ideal society for which mankind has been striving through the ages will remain forever beyond our grasp. But if the great question, whether it is still possible to reconcile democracy with social order and individual liberty, is to find a positive answer, it will be here.

1976

Purpose and Meaning

1. This essay was published in the July 12, 1976, *Newsweek* magazine. What historic occasion does it focus on? What cultural assumptions does Tuchman make about her readers?

2. Tuchman declares at the start of paragraph 6: "In the United States we have a society pervaded from top to bottom by contempt for the law." Is this the characteristic message of her essay? Explain.

3. What does Tuchman mean by her subtitle, "America as Idea"? What were the major social, cultural, and historical influences that molded this "idea"?

Language and Style

1. How clear and interesting is Tuchman's style—the style she subscribes to in "The Historian as Artist"? Cite specific examples from the essay to support your view.

2. Tuchman employs a variety of parallel sentence strategies in this essay. Locate instances of parallelism in paragraphs 1 and 2, and discuss the stylistic effect.

3. Is there a discernible bias to Tuchman's writing? Is she reporting the facts of

history, or is there some personal attitude that comes across that gives us a clue to her emotional ties to the subject? Is she writing as an "artist" or as a "nonfiction writer" (see "The Historian as Artist")?

Strategy and Structure

1. Tuchman's first paragraph is, in many ways, a model introduction. How is it composed? What echoes and intimations does it provide? Does it contain Tuchman's thesis, or does it just hint at it?

2. How does Tuchman use the introductory sentences of her paragraphs to keep the paragraphs coherent? Select any three paragraphs and study their structure as well as their organizational relationship to the paragraphs that precede and follow them.

3. Why might this essay be considered an extended definition?

4. Where does Tuchman use comparative devices? What is the point of the central comparison?

5. How does the concluding paragraph reflect and expand the meaning and content of Tuchman's first paragraph? Does it logically follow from the entire essay?

Thinking and Writing

1. Write your own extended definition of America as an "idea." Base your definition on specific historical information as well as on personal opinion.

2. Argue for or against Tuchman's proposition: "The ideal society for which mankind has been striving through the ages will remain forever beyond our grasp."

Humanity's Better Moments

For a change from prevailing pessimism, I should like to recall some of the positive and even admirable capacities of the human race. We hear very little of them lately. Ours is not a time of self-esteem or self-confidence—as was, for instance, the nineteenth century, when self-esteem may be seen oozing from its portraits. Victorians, especially the men, pictured themselves as erect, noble, and splendidly handsome. Our self-image looks more like Woody Allen or a character from Samuel Beckett. Amid a mass of worldwide troubles and a poor record for the twentieth century, we see our species—with cause—as functioning very badly, as blunders when not knaves, as violent, ignoble, corrupt, inept, incapable of mastering the forces that threaten us, weakly subject to our worst instincts; in short, decadent.

The catalogue is familiar and valid, but it is growing tiresome. A study of history reminds one that mankind has its ups and downs and during the ups has accomplished many brave and beautiful things, exerted stupendous endeavors, explored and conquered oceans and wilderness, achieved marvels of beauty in the creative arts and marvels of science and social progress; has loved liberty with a passion that throughout history has led men to fight and die for it over and over again; has pursued knowledge, exercised reason, enjoyed laughter and pleasures, played games with zest, shown courage, heroism, altruism, honor, and decency; experienced love; known comfort, contentment, and occasionally happiness. All these qualities have been part of human experience, and if they have not had as important notice as the negatives nor exerted as wide and persistent an influence as the evils we do, they nevertheless deserve attention, for they are currently all but forgotten.

Among the great endeavors, we have in our own time carried men to the moon and brought them back safely—surely one of the most remarkable achievements in history. Some may disapprove of the effort as unproductive, too costly, and a wrong choice of priorities in relation to greater needs, all of which may be true but does not, as I see it, diminish the achievement. If you look carefully, all positives have a negative underside—sometimes more, sometimes less—and not all admirable endeavors have admirable motives. Some have sad consequences. Although most signs presently point from bad to worse, human capacities are probably what they have always been. If primitive man could discover how to transform grain into bread, and reeds growing by the riverbank into baskets; if his successors could invent the wheel, harness the insubstantial air to turn a millstone, transform sheep's wool, flax, and worms' cocoons into fabric—we, I imagine, will find a way to manage the energy problem.

Consider how the Dutch accomplished the miracle of making land out of sea. By progressive enclosure of the Zuider Zee over the last sixty years, they have added half a million acres to their country, enlarging its area by eight percent and providing homes, farms, and towns for close to a quarter of a million people. The will to do the impossible, the spirit of can-do that overtakes our species now and then, was never more manifest than in this earth-altering act by the smallest of the major European nations.

A low-lying, windswept, waterlogged land, partly below sea level, pitted with marshes, rivers, lakes, and inlets, sliding all along its outer edge into the stormy North Sea with only fragile sand dunes as nature's barrier against the waves, Holland, in spite of physical disadvantages, has made itself into one of the most densely populated, orderly, prosperous, and, at one stage of its history, dominant nations of the West. For centuries, ever since the first inhabitants, fleeing enemy tribes, settled in the bogs where no one cared to bother them, the Dutch struggled against water and learned how to live with it: building on mounds, constructing and reconstructing seawalls of clay mixed with straw, carrying mud in an endless train of baskets, laying willow mattresses weighted with stones, repairing each spring the winter's damage, draining marshes, channeling streams, building ramps to their attics to save the cattle in times of flood, gaining dike-enclosed land from the waves in one place and losing as much to the revengeful ocean somewhere else, progressively developing methods to cope with their eternal antagonist.

The Zuider Zee was a tidal gulf penetrating eighty miles into the land over an area ten to thirty miles wide. The plan to close off the sea by a dam across the entire mouth of the gulf had long been contemplated but never adopted, for fear of the cost, until a massive flood in 1916, which left saltwater standing on all the farmlands north of Amsterdam, forced the issue. The act for enclosure was passed unanimously by both houses of Parliament in 1918. As large in ambition as the country was small, the plan called for a twenty-mile dike from shore to shore, rising twenty feet above sea level, wide enough at the top to carry an auto road and housing for the hydraulic works, and as much as six hundred feet wide on the sea bottom. The first cartload of gravel was dumped in 1920.

The dike was but part of the task. The inland sea it formed had to be drained of its saltwater and transformed from salt to fresh by the inflow from lower branches of the Rhine. Four polders, or areas rising from the shallows, would be lifted by the draining process from under water into the open air. Secondary dikes, pumping stations, sluices, drainage ditches to control the inflow, as well as locks and inland ports for navigation, had to be built, the polder lands restored to fertility, trees planted, roads, bridges, and rural and urban housing constructed, the whole scheduled for completion in sixty years.

The best-laid plans of engineers met errors and hazards. During construction, gravel that had been painstakingly dumped within sunken frameworks would be washed away in a night by heavy currents or a capricious storm. Means proved vulnerable, methods sometimes unworkable. Yet slowly the dike advanced from each shore toward the center. As the gap narrowed, the pressure of the tidal current rushing through increased daily in force, carrying away material at the base, undermining the structure, and threatening to prevent a final closing. In the last days a herd of floating derricks, dredges, barges, and every piece of available equipment was mustered at the spot, and fill was desperately poured in before the next return of the tide, due in twelve hours. At this point, gale winds were reported moving in. The check dam to protect the last gap showed signs of giving way; operations were hurriedly moved thirty yards inward. Suspense was now extreme. Roaring and foaming with sand, the tide threw itself upon the narrowing passage; the machines closed in, filled the last space in the dike, and it held. Men stood that day in 1932 where the North Sea's waves had held dominion for seven hundred years.

As the dry land appeared, the first comers to take possession were the birds. Gradually, decade by decade, crops, homes, and civilization followed, and unhappily, too, man's destructive intervention. In World War II the retreating Germans blew up a section of the dike, completely flooding the western polder, but by the end of the year the Dutch had pumped it dry, resowed the fields in the spring, and over the next seven years restored the polder's farms and villages. Weather, however, is never conquered. The disastrous floods of 1953 laid most of coastal Holland under water. The Dutch dried themselves out and, while the work at Zuider Zee continued, applied its lessons elsewhere and lent their hydraulic skills to other countries. Today the *Afsluitdijk*, or Zuider Zee road, is a normal thoroughfare. To drive across it between the sullen ocean on one side and new land on the other is for that moment to feel optimism for the human race.

Great endeavor requires vision and some kind of compelling impulse, not necessarily practical as in the case of the Dutch, but sometimes less definable, more exalted, as in the case of the Gothic cathedrals of the Middle Ages. The architectural explosion that produced this multitude of soaring vaults—arched, ribbed, pierced with jeweled light, studded with thousands of figures of the stone-carvers' art—represents in size, splendor, and numbers one of the great, permanent artistic achievements of human hands. What accounts for it? Not religious fervor alone but the zeal of a dynamic age, a desire to outdo, an ambition for the biggest and the best. Only the general will, shared by nobles, merchants, guilds, artisans, and commoners, could command the resources and labor to sustain so great an undertaking. Each group contributed donations, especially the magnates of commerce, who felt relieved thereby from the guilt of money-making. Voluntary work programs involved all classes. "Who has ever seen or heard tell in times past," wrote an observer, "that powerful princes of the world, that men brought up in honors and wealth, that nobles—men and women—have bent their haughty necks to the harness of carts and, like beasts of burden, have dragged to the abode of Christ these wagons loaded with wines, grains, oil, stones, timber and all that is necessary for the construction of the church?"

Abbot Suger, whose renovation of St.-Denis is considered the start of Gothic architecture, embodied the spirit of the builders. Determined to create the most splendid basilica in Christendom, he supervised every aspect of the work from fund-raising to decoration, and caused his name to be inscribed for immortality on keystones and capitals. He lay awake worrying, as he tells us, where to find trees large enough for the beams, and went personally with his carpenters to the forest to question the woodcutters under oath. When they swore that nothing of the kind he wanted could be found in the area, he insisted on searching for them himself and, after nine hours of scrambling through thorns and thickets, succeeded in locating and marking twelve trees of the necessary size.

Mainly the compelling impulse lay in the towns, where, in those years, economic and political strengths and wealth were accumulating. Amiens, the thriving capital of Picardy, decided to build the largest church in France, "higher than all the saints, higher than all the kings." For the necessary space, the hospital and bishop's palace had to be relocated and the city walls moved back. At the same time Beauvais, a neighbor town, raised a vault over the crossing of transept and nave to an unprecedented height of 158 feet, the apogee of architects' daring in its day. It proved too daring, for the height of the columns and spread of the supports caused the vault to collapse after twelve years. Repaired with undaunted purpose, it was defiantly topped by a spire rising 492 feet above ground, the tallest in France. Beauvais, having used up its resources, never built the nave, leaving a structure foreshortened but glorious. The interior is a fantasy of soaring space, to enter is to stand dazed in wonder, breathless in admiration.

The higher and lighter grew the buildings and the slenderer the columns,   13
the more new expedients and techniques had to be devised to hold them up. Buttresses flew like angels' wings against the exteriors. This was a period of innovation and audacity, and a limitless spirit of excelsior. In a single century, from 1170 to 1270, six hundred cathedrals and major churches were built in France alone. In England in that period, the cathedral of Salisbury, with the tallest spire in the country, was completed in thirty-eight years. The spire of Freiburg in Germany was constructed entirely of filigree in stone as if spun by some supernatural spider. In the St.-Chapelle in Paris the fifteen miraculous windows swallow the walls; they have become the whole.

Embellishment was integral to the construction. Reins is populated by five   14
thousand statues of saints, prophets, kings and cardinals, bishops, knights, ladies, craftsmen and commoners, devils, animals and birds. Every type of leaf known in northern France is said to appear in the decoration. In carving, stained glass, and sculpture the cathedrals displayed the art of medieval hands, and the marvel of these buildings is permanent even when they no longer play a central role in everyday life. Rodin said he could feel the beauty and presence of Reims even at night when he could not see it. "Its power," he wrote, "transcends the senses so that the eye sees what it sees not."

Explanations for the extraordinary burst that produced the cathedrals are   15
several. Art historians will tell you that it was the invention of the ribbed vault. Religious historians will say it was the product of an age of faith which believed that with God's favor anything was possible; in fact it was not a period of untroubled faith, but of heresies and Inquisition. Rather, one can only say that conditions were right. Social order under monarchy and the towns was replacing the anarchy of the barons, so that existence was no longer merely a struggle to stay alive but allowed a surplus of goods and energies and greater opportunity for mutual effort. Banking and commerce were producing capital, roads were making possible wheeled transport, universities nourishing ideas and communication. It was one of history's high tides, an age of vigor, confidence, and forces converging to quicken the blood.

Even when the historical tide is low, a particular group of doers may   16
emerge in exploits that inspire awe. Shrouded in the mists of the eighth century, long before the cathedrals, Viking seamanship was a wonder of daring,

stamina, and skill. Pushing relentlessly outward in open boats, the Vikings sailed south, around Spain to North Africa and Arabia, north to the top of the world, west across uncharted seas to American coasts. They hauled their boats overland from the Baltic to make their way down Russian rivers to the Black Sea. Why? We do not know what engine drove them, only that it was part of the human endowment.

What of the founding of our own country, America? We take the *Mayflower* for granted—yet think of the boldness, the enterprise, the determined independence, the sheer grit it took to leave the known and set out across the sea for the unknown where no houses or food, no stores, no cleared land, no crops or livestock, none of the equipment or settlement of organized living awaited.

Equally bold was the enterprise of the French in the northern forests of the American continent, who throughout the seventeenth century explored and opened the land from the St. Lawrence to the Mississippi, from the Great Lakes to the Gulf of Mexico. They came not for liberty like the Pilgrims, but for gain and dominion, whether in spiritual empire for the Jesuits or in land, glory, and riches for the agents of the King; and rarely in history have men willingly embraced such hardship, such daunting adventure, and persisted with such tenacity and endurance. They met hunger, exhaustion, frostbite, capture and torture by Indians, wounds and disease, dangerous rapids, swarms of insects, long portages, bitter weather, and hardly ever did those who suffered the experience fail to return, re-enter the menacing but bountiful forest, and pit themselves once more against danger, pain, and death.

Above all others, the perserverance of La Salle in his search for the mouth of the Mississippi was unsurpassed. While preparing in Quebec, he mastered eight Indian languages. From then on he suffered accidents, betrayals, desertions, losses of men and provisions, fever and snow blindness, the hostility and intrigues of rivals who incited the Indians against him and plotted to ambush or poison him. He was truly pursued, as Francis Parkman wrote, by "a demon of havoc." Paddling through heavy waves in a storm over Lake Ontario, he waded through freezing surf to beach the canoes each night, and lost guns and baggage when a canoe was swamped and sank. To lay the foundations of a fort above Niagara, frozen ground had to be thawed by boiling water. When the fort was at last built, La Salle christened is Crèvecoeur—that is, Heartbreak. It earned the name when in his absence it was plundered and deserted by its half-starved mutinous garrison. Father on, a friendly Indian village, intended as a destination, was found laid waste by the Iroquois with only charred stakes stuck with skulls standing among the ashes, while wolves and buzzards prowled through the remains.

When at last, after four months' hazardous journey down the Great River, La Salle reached the sea, he formally took possession in the name of Louis XIV of all the country from the river's mouth to it source and of its tributaries—that is, of the vast basin of the Mississippi from the Rockies to the Appalachians—

and named it Louisiana. The validity of the claim, which seems so hollow to us (though successful in its own time), is not the point. What counts is the conquest of fearful adversity by one man's extraordinary exertions and inflexible will.

Happily, man has a capacity for pleasure too, and in contriving ways to   21
entertain and amuse himself has created brilliance and delight. Pageants, carnivals, festivals, fireworks, music, dancing and drama, parties and picnics, sports and games, the comic spirit and its gift of laughter—all the range of enjoyment from grand ceremonial to the quiet solitude of a day's fishing has helped to balance the world's infelicity.

The original Olympic Games held every fourth year in honor of Zeus was   22
the most celebrated festival of classic times, of such significance to the Greeks that they dated their history from the first games in 776 B.C. as we date ours from the birth of Christ. The crown of olive awarded to the winner in each contest was considered the crown of happiness. While the Romans took this to be a sign of the essential frivolity of the Greek character, the ancient games endured for twelve centuries, a longer span than the supremacy of Rome.

Homo ludens, man at play, is surely as significant a figure as man at war   23
or at work. In human activity the invention of the ball may be said to rank with the invention of the wheel. Imagine America without baseball, Europe without soccer, England without cricket, the Italians without bocci, China without Ping-Pong, and tennis for no one. Even stern John Calvin, the examplar of Puritan self-denial, was once discovered playing bowls on Sunday, and in 1611 an English supply ship arriving at Jamestown found the starving colonists suppressing their misery in the same game. Cornhuskings, logrollings, barnraisings, horseraces, and wrestling and boxing matches have engaged America as, somewhat more passively, the armchair watching of football and basketball does today.

Play was invented for diversion, exertion, and escape from routine cares.   24
In colonial New York, sleighing parties preceded by fiddlers on horseback drove out to country inns, where, according to a participant, "we danced, sang, romped, ate and drank and kicked away care from morning to night." John Audubon, present at a barbeque and dance on the Kentucky frontier, wrote, "Every countenance beamed with joy, every heart leaped with gladness...care and sorrow were flung to the winds."

Play has its underside, too, in the gladiatorial games, in cockfights and   25
prizefights, which arouse one of the least agreeable of human characteristics, pleasure in blood and brutality, but in relation to play as a whole, this is minor.

Much of our pleasure derives from eating and sex, two components which   26
have received an excess of attention in our time—allowing me to leave them aside as understood, except to note how closely they are allied. All those recipes, cuisines, exotic foods, and utensils of kitchen chic seem to proliferate in proportion to pornography, sex therapy, blue movies, and instructive tales for

children on pederasty and incest. Whether this twin increase signifies decadence or liberation is disputable. Let us move on to other ground.

To the carnival, for instance. Mardi Gras in all its forms is an excuse for letting go; for uninhibited fun before the abstinence of Lent; for dressing up, play-acting, cavorting in costumes and masks, constructing imaginative floats; for noise, pranks, jokes, battles of flowers and confetti, balls and banquets, singing and dancing, and fireworks. In the Belgian carnival of Gilles-Binche, originating in the sixteenth century in honor of Charles V's conquest of Peru, the dancers are spectacular in superlatively tall feather headdresses representing the Incas, and brilliant costumes trimmed with gold lace and tinkling bells. They wear wooden shoes to stamp out the rhythm of their dance and carry baskets of oranges symbolizing the treasures of Peru with which they pelt the onlookers. In the celebrated Palio of Siena at harvest time, a horse and rider from each neighborhood race madly around a sloping cobblestoned course in the public square, while the citizens shriek in passionate rivalry. Walpurgis Night on the eve of May Day is an excuse for bacchanalia in the guise of witches' revels; winter's festival at Christmas is celebrated by gift-giving. Humanity has invented infinite ways to enjoy itself.

No people have invented more ways than have the Chinese, perhaps to balance floods, famine, warlords, and other ills of fate. The clang of gongs, clashing of cymbals, and beating of drums sound through their long history. No month is without fairs and theatricals when streets are hung with fantasies of painted lanterns and crowded with "carriages that flow like water, horses like roaming dragons." Night skies are illumined by firecrackers—a Chinese invention—bursting in the form of peonies, flowerpots, fiery devils. The ways of pleasure are myriad. Music plays in the air through bamboo whistles of different pitch tied to the wings of circling pigeons. To skim a frozen lake in an ice sleigh with a group of friends on a day when the sun is warm is rapture, like "moving in a cup of jade." What more delightful than the ancient festival called "Half an Immortal," when everyone from palace officials to the common man took a ride on a swing? When high in the air, one felt like an Immortal; when back to earth once again, human—no more than to be for an instant a god.

In Europe's age of grandeur, princes devised pageants of dazzling splendor to express their magnificence, none more spectacular than the extravaganza of 1660 celebrating the marriage of Leopold I of Austria to the Infanta of Spain. As the climax to festivities lasting three months, an equestrian contest of the Four Elements was performed in the grand plaza, each element represented by a company of a thousand, gorgeously costumed. Water's company were dressed in blue and silver covered with fish scales and shells; Air's in gold brocade shaded in the colors of the rainbow; Earth's decorated with flowers; Fire's with curling flames. Neptune, surrounded by marine monsters and winds, rode in a car drawn by a huge whale spouting water. Earth's car contained a garden with Pan and shepherds, drawn by elephants with castles on their backs; Air rode a dragon escorted by thirty griffins; Fire was accompanied by Vulan, thirty Cyclopes, and a flame-spouting salamander. A rather irrelevant ship carrying the Argonauts to the Golden Fleece was added for extras. The contest was resolved when a star-studded globe, arched by an artificial rainbow representing Peace, rolled across the plaza and opened to display a Temple of Immortality from which emerged riders impersonating the fifteen previous Hapsburg emperors, ending with Leopold in person. Dressed as Glory, in silver lace and diamonds, and wearing his crown, he rode in a silver seashell drawn by eight white horses and carrying seven singers in jeweled robes, who serenaded the Infanta. Then followed the climactic equestrian ballet performed by four groups of eight cavaliers each, whose elaborate movements were marked by trumpet flourishes, kettledrums, and cannon salutes. In a grand finale a thousand rockets blazed from two artificial mountains named Parnassus and Aetna, and the sky was lit in triumph by the Hapsburg acrostic AEIOU standing for *Austria Est Imperare Omne Universo*, meaning, approximately, "Austria rules the world."

The motive may have been self-aggrandizement, but the results were 30 sumptuous and exciting; viewers were enthralled, performers proud, and the designer of the pageant was made a baron. It was a case of men and women engaged in the art of enjoyment, a function common to all times, although one would hardly know it from today's image of ourselves as wretched creatures forever agonizing over petty squalors of sex and drink as if we had no other recourse or destiny.

The greatest recourse, and mankind's most enduring achievement, is art. 31 At its best, it reveals the nobility that coexists in human nature along with flaws and evils, and the beauty and truth it can perceive. Whether in music or architecture, literature, painting or sculpture, art opens our eyes, ears, and feelings to something beyond ourselves, something we cannot experience without the artist's vision and the genius of his craft. The placing of Greek temples, like the Temple of Poseidon on the promontory at Sunion, outlined against the piercing blue of the Aegean Sea, Poseidon's home; the majesty of Michelangelo's sculptured figures in stone; Shakespeare's command of language and knowledge of the human soul; the intricate order of Bach, the enchantment of Mozart; the purity of Chinese monochrome pottery with its lovely names—celadon, oxblood, peach blossom, clair de lune; the exuberance of Tiepolo's ceilings where, without picture frames to limit movement, a whole world in exquisitely beautiful colors lives and moves in the sky; the prose and poetry of all the writers from Homer to Cervantes to Jane Austen and John Keats to Dostoevski and Chekhov—who made all these things? We—our species—did. The range is too vast and various to do justice to it in this space, but the random samples I have mentioned, and all the rest they suggest, are sufficient reason to honor mankind.

If we have (as I think) lost beauty and elegance in the modern world, we 32 have gained much, through science and technology and democratic pressures, in the material well-being of the masses. The change in the lives of, and society's attitude toward, the working class marks the great divide between the modern world and the old regime. From the French Revolution through the brutal labor wars of the nineteenth and twentieth centuries, the change was earned mainly by force against fierce and often vicious opposition. While this was a harsh process, it developed and activated a social conscience hardly operative before. Slavery, beggary, unaided misery, and want have, on the whole, been eliminated in the developed nations of the West. That much is a credit in the human record, even if the world is uglier as a result of adapting to mass values. History generally arranges these things so that gain is balanced by loss, perhaps in order not to make the gods jealous.

The material miracles wrought by science and technology—from the harnessing of steam and electricity to anesthesia, antisepsis, antibiotics, and woman's liberator, the washing machine, and all the labor-savers that go with it—are too well recognized in our culture to need my emphasis. Pasteur is as great a figure in the human record as Michelangelo or Mozart—probably, as far as the general welfare is concerned, greater. We are more aware of his kind of accomplishment than of those less tangible. Ask anyone to suggest the credits of mankind and the answer is likely to start with physical things. Yet the under-side of scientific progress is prominent and dark. The weaponry of war in its ever-widening capacity to kill is the deadly example, and who is prepared to state with confidence that the over-all effect of the automobile, airplane, telephone, television, and computer has been, on balance, beneficent? 33

Pursuit of knowledge for its own sake has been a more certain good. There was a springtime in the eighteenth century when, through knowledge and reason, everything seemed possible; when reason was expected to break through religious dogma like the sun breaking through fog, and man, armed with knowledge and reason, would be able at last to control his own fate and construct a good society. The theory that because this world exists it is the best of all possible worlds spread outward from Leibniz; the word "optimism" was used for the first time in 1737. 34

What a burst of intellectual energies shook these decades! In twenty years, 1735–55, Linnaeus named and classified all of known botany, Buffon system-atized natural History in thirty-six volumes, and an American, John Bartram, scoured the wilderness for plants to send to correspondents in Europe. Voltaire, Montesquieu, and Hume investigated the nature of man and the moral foundations of law and society. Benjamin Franklin demonstrated electricity from lightning. Dr. Johnson by himself compiled the first dictionary of the English language; Diderot and the Encyclopedists of France undertook to present the whole of knowledge in enlightened terms. The Chinese secret of making porcelain having been uncovered by Europeans, its manufacture flourished at Meissen and Dresden. Clearing for the Place de la Concorde, to be the most majestic in Europe, was begun in Paris. No less than 150 newspapers and journals cir-culated in England. The novel was exuberantly born in the work of Richardson and Fielding. Chardin, a supreme artist, portrayed humanity with a loving brush in his gentle domestic scenes. Hogarth, seeing another creature, exposed the 35 underside in all its ribaldry and squalor. It was an age of enthusiasm; at the first London performance of Handel's *Messiah* in 1743, George II was so carried away by the "Hallelujah Chorus" that he rose to his feet, causing the whole audience to stand with him, and thereby establishing a custom still sometimes followed by *Messiah* audiences. The man in whom the spirit of the age was to flower, Thomas Jefferson, was born.

If the twenty-year period is stretched by another ten, it includes the reverberating voice of Rousseau's *Social Contract*, Beccaria's ground-breaking study *Essay on Crimes and Punishment*, Gibbon's beginning of the *Decline and Fall*, and, despite the Lisbon earthquake and *Candide*, the admission of "optimism" into the dictionary of the Académie Française. [36]

Although the Enlightenment may have overestimated the power of reason to guide human conduct, it nevertheless opened to men and women a more humane view of their fellow passengers. Slowly the harshest habits gave way to reform—in treatment of the insane, reduction of death penalties, mitigation of the fierce laws against debtors and poachers, and in the passionately fought cause for abolition of the slave trade. [37]

The humanitarian movement was not charity, which always carries an overtone of being done in the donor's interest, but a more disinterested benevolence or altruism, motivated by conscience. It was personified in William Wilberforce, who in the later eighteenth century stirred the great rebellion of the English conscience against the trade in human beings. In America the immorality of slavery had long troubled the colonies. By 1789 slavery had been legally abolished by the New England states followed by New York, New Jersey, and Pennsylvania, but the southern states, as their price for joining the Union, insisted that the subject be excluded from the Constitution. [38]

In England, where the home economy did not depend on slave labor, Wilberforce had more scope. His influence could have carried him to the Prime Minister's seat if personal power had been his goal, but he channeled his life instead toward a goal for mankind. He instigated, energized, inspired a movement whose members held meetings, organized petitions, collected information on the horrors of the middle passage, showered pamphlets on the public, gathered Nonconformist middle-class sentiment into a swelling tide that, in Trevelyan's phrase, "melted the hard prudence of statesmen." Abolition of the slave trade under the British flag was won in 1807. The British Navy was used to enforce the ban by searches on the high seas and regular patrols of the African coast. When Portugal and Spain were persuaded to join in the prohibition, they were paid a compensation of £300,000 and £400,000 respectively by the British taxpayer. Violations and smuggling continued, convincing the abolitionists that, in order to stop the trade, slavery itself had to be abolished. Agitation resumed. By degrees over the next quarter-century, compensaton reduced the opposition of the West Indian slave-owners and their allies in England until emancipation of all slaves in the British Empire was enacted in 1833. The total cost to the British taxpayer was reckoned at £20 million. [39]

Through recent unpleasant experiences we have learned to expect ambi-   40
tion, greed, or corruption to reveal itself behind every public act, but, as we
have just seen, it is not invariably so. Human beings do possess better impulses,
and occasionally act upon them, even in the twentieth century. Occupied
Denmark, during World War II, outraged by Nazi orders for deportation of
its Jewish fellow citizens, summoned the courage of defiance and transformed
itself into a united underground railway to smuggle virtually all eight thousand
Danish Jews out to Sweden, and Sweden gave them shelter. Far away and unconnected, a village in southern France, Le Chambon-sur-Lignon, devoted itself
to rescuing Jews and other victims of the Nazis at the risk of the inhabitants'
own lives and freedom. "Saving lives became a hobby of the people of Le
Chambon," said one of them. The larger record of the time was admittedly
collaboration, passive or active. We cannot reckon on the better impulses
predominating in the world, only that they will always appear.

The strongest of these in history, summoner of the best in men, has been   41
zeal for liberty. Time after time, in some spot somewhere on the globe, people
have risen in what Swinburne called the "divine right of insurrection"—to overthrow despots, repel alien conquerors, achieve independence—and so it will
be until the day power ceases to corrupt, which, I think, is not a near expectation.

The ancient Jews rose three times against alien rulers, beginning with the   42
revolt of the Maccabees against the effort of Antiochus to outlaw observance
of the Jewish faith. Mattathias the priest and his five sons, assembling loyal
believers in the mountains, opened a guerrilla war which, after the father's death,
was to find a leader of military genius in his son Judah, called Maccabee or
the Hammer. Later honored in the Middle Ages as one of the Nine Worthies
of the world, he defeated his enemies, rededicated the temple, and re-established
the independence of Judea. In the next century the uprising of the Zealots against
Roman rule was fanatically and hopelessly pursued through famines, sieges,
the fall of Jerusalem and destruction of the temple until a last stand of fewer
than a thousand on the rock of Masada ended in group suicide in preference
to surrender. After sixty years as an occupied province, Judea rose yet again
under Simon Bar Kochba, who regained Jerusalem for a brief moment of Jewish
control but could not withstand the arms of Hadrian. The rebellion was crushed,
but the zeal for selfhood, smoldering in exile through eighteen centuries, was
to revive and regain its home in our time.

The phenomenon continues in our own day, in Algeria, in Vietnam,   43
although, seen at close quarters and more often than not manipulated by outsiders, contemporary movements seem less pure and heroic than those polished
by history's gloss—as, for instance, the Scots under William Wallace, the Swiss
against the Hapsburgs, the American colonies against the mother country.

I have always cherished the spirited rejoinder of one of the great colonial   44
landowners of New York who, on being advised not to risk his property by
signing the Declaration of Independence, replied, "Damn the property; give me
the pen!" On seeking confirmation for puroposes of this essay, I am deeply

chagrined to report that the saying appears to be apocryphal. Yet not its spirit, for the signers well knew they were risking their property, not to mention their heads, by putting their names to the Declaration.

Nor did they escape. Left vulnerable by Washington's defeat on Long Island, their estates were deliberately wrecked by the British, their homes ransacked and looted, books and papers burned, furniture smashed, livestock and stores destroyed, tenants and servants driven out, a thousand acres of Lewis Morris' timberland left in stumps. All were reduced to living by the charity of friends during the war. Philip Livingston died without ever seeing his home and lands again; the rich merchant William Floyd was permanently ruined. Other affluent men who signed had much to lose—Hancock of Massachusetts, who wrote his name large so that no one would mistake it, Lee of Virginia, Carroll of Baltimore. George Washington himself epitomized the spirit later in the war when he wrote to reproach his overseer at Mount Vernon for supplying provisions to a British landing party that had sailed up to the Potomac and threatened to burn the estate unless their demands were met. It would have been "less painful," he wrote, to have learned that, as a result of refusal, "they had burnt my House and laid my plantation in ruins." Economic self-interest, as this illustrates, is not always our guiding instinct.

So far I have considered qualities of the group rather than of the individual—except for art, which in most cases is a product of the single spirit. Happiness, too, is an individual matter. It springs up here or there, haphazard, random, without origin or explanation. It resists study, laughs at sociology, flourishes, vanishes, reappears somewhere else. Take Izaak Walton, author of *The Compleat Angler*, that guide to contentment as well as fishing, of which Charles Lamb said, "It would sweeten any man's temper at any time to read it." Though Walton lived in distracted times of revolution and regicide, though he adhered to the losing side in the English Civil War, though he lost in their infancy all seven children by his first wife and the eldest son of his second marriage, though he was twice a widower, his misfortunes could not sour an essentially buoyant nature. "He passed through turmoil," in the words of a biographer, "ever accompanied by content."

Walton's secret was friendship. Born to a yeoman family and apprenticed in youth as an ironmonger, he managed to gain an education and, through sweetness of disposition and a cheerful religious faith, became a friend on equal terms of various learned clergymen and poets whose lives he wrote and works he prefaced—among them John Donne, George Herbert, and Michael Drayton. Another companion, Charles Cotton, wrote of Izaak, "In him I have the happiness to know the worthiest man, and to enjoy the best and truest friend any man ever had."

The Compleat Angler, published when the author was sixty, glows in the sunshine of his character. In it are humor and piety, grave advice on the idiosyncrasies of fish and the niceties of landing them, delight in nature and in music. Walton saw five editions reprinted in his lifetime, while unnumerable later editions secured him immortality. The surviving son by his second wife became a clergyman; the surviving daughter married one and gave her father a home among grandchildren. He wrote his last work at eighty-five and died at ninety after being celebrated in verse by one of his circle as a "happy old man" whose life "showed how to compass true felicity." Let us think of him when we grumble.

Is anything to be learned from my survey? I raise the question only because most people want history to teach them lessons, which I believe it can do, although I am less sure we can use them when needed. I gathered these examples not to teach but merely to remind people in a despondent era that the good in mankind operates even if the bad secures more attention. I am aware that selecting out the better moments does not result in a realistic picture. Turn them over and there is likely to be a darker side, as when Project Apollo, our journey to the moon, was authorized because its glamour could obtain subsidies for rocket and missile development that otherwise might not have been forthcoming. That is the way things are.

Whole philosophies have evolved over the question whether the human species is predominately good or evil. I only know that it is mixed, that you cannot separate good from bad, that wisdom, courage, and benevolence exist alongside knavery, greed, and stupidity; heroism and fortitude alongside vainglory, cruelty, and corruption.

It is a paradox of our time in the West that never have so many people been so relatively well off and never has society been more troubled. Yet I suspect that humanity's virtues have not vanished, although the experiences of our century seem to suggest that they are in abeyance. A century that took shape in the disillusion which followed the enormous effort and hopes of World War I, that saw revolution in Russia congeal into the same tyranny it overthrew, saw a supposedly civilized nation revert under the Nazis into organized and unparalleled savagery, saw the craven appeasement by the democracies, is understandably marked by suspicion of human nature. A literary historian, Van Wyck Brooks, discussing the 1920s and '30s, spoke of "an eschatological despair of the world." Whereas Whitman and Emerson, he wrote, "had been impressed by the worth and good sense of the people, writers of the new time" were struck by their lusts, cupidity, and violence, and had come to dislike their fellow men. The same theme reappeared in a recent play in which a mother struggled against her two "pitilessly contemptuous" children. Her problem was that she wanted them to be happy and they did not want to be. They preferred to watch horrors on television. In essence this is our epoch. It insists upon the flaws and corruptions, without belief in valor or virtue or the possibility of happiness. It keeps turning to look back on Sodom and Gomorrah; it has no view of the Delectable Mountains.

We must keep a balance, and I know of no better prescription than a phrase from Condorcet's eulogy on the death of Benjamin Franklin: "He pardoned the present for the sake of the future."

1980

Purpose and Meaning

1. What is Tuchman's purpose in this essay? How does her purpose affect the tone of her writing?

2. What does the final quotation of the essay mean: "He pardoned the present for the sake of the future"? What is its relevance to this compendium of "Humanity's Better Moments"?

3. Can you add examples of other "better moments"? What principle governed Tuchman's choice of these?

Language and Style

1. What is the purpose of making references to Woody Allen and Samuel Beckett in the opening paragraph? Would you be likely to find such references in a history textbook? Does it make the author's diction seem less "professional"?

2. In paragraph 2, Tuchman states that human beings have "accomplished many brave and beautiful things." Is this an objective reporting of history, or is it a value judgment? How does this phrase affect the mood of the essay? What other examples can you find where Tuchman displays the same attitude toward her subject?

3. In paragraphs 6 through 9, the author describes the task of building a dike on the Zuider Zee. Is she clear in explaining what happened? Does the writing give you a precise step-by-step picture? What word choices does Tuchman make that enable her to describe this complex series of events in just three paragraphs?

Strategy and Structure

1. How do the first three paragraphs serve as the introduction for Tuchman's essay?

2. After paragraphs 20 and 30, there are double spaces separating the text. What is the purpose of these structural breaks? Would it have been better to divide the essay into three sections and label them? Why or why not?

3. Paragraphs 33 through 36 include a long list of accomplishments made during the Enlightenment. Considering that Tuchman spent several paragraphs describing selected achievements in history, why has she chosen to run through this roster so quickly? What function does this list serve in the overall organization of the essay?

4. In paragraph 45, Tuchman changes her focus from describing the successes of groups to describing the success of an individual. Why was this example saved for last? Why was it included at all? How does it affect your response to the overall organization of the essay?

Thinking and Writing

1. In paragraph 3, Tuchman states, "all positives have a negative underside." With a partner in class, select a topic that most people would view positively, then search for the negative side. Based on your discussion, write an essay reflecting Tuchman's point about "negative underside."

2. In paragraph 3, Tuchman argues that if primitive peoples could overcome problems of living, then "we . . . will find a way to manage the energy problem." Is it true that today's global problems can be solved as readily as those of our early ancestors? Write an essay arguing for or against this proposition.

3. Tuchman delivered this address in 1980. Is it important to recall "Humanity's Better Moments" today, or is it a futile effort, considering the current state of the world? Develop and write an argument advancing the view that it is either valuable or not valuable to recall the successes of history as a means of coping with the problems of the 1990s.

LEWIS THOMAS

No one surveys the vast spectrum of contemporary science, medicine, technology, and culture more eloquently than Dr. Lewis Thomas—since 1973 researcher, professor, director, and chancellor of the Memorial Sloan-Kettering Cancer Center in New York City. Born in 1913, in Flushing, New York, the son of a doctor, Thomas received his undergraduate education at Princeton University and his M.D. from Harvard. He wrote poetry at Princeton and published verse during the Depression. He also wrote more than 200 articles on pathology, his specialty, for professional medical journals. At the age of 57, after teaching at Johns Hopkins, Tulane, the University of Minnesota, and NYU, where he became dean of the medical school, he began his career as an essayist, writing a monthly column for the *New England Journal of Medicine*.

When Thomas, who at the time was dean of the Yale medical school, undertook his monthly column, "Notes of a Biology Watcher," he intended merely to offer 1,200-word reports on current topics of interest in medical and biological science. Yet his clarity, precision, wit, and graceful style, combined with a reverence for the worldly, human estate, soon earned him a broad, popular audience. For Thomas, writing is a labor of love. "We have language," he writes "and can find metaphors as skillfully and precisely as ribosomes make proteins." He wrestles playfully with language, as we see in "Notes on Punctuation," but turns it typically toward an affirmation of life.

Thomas collected twenty-nine of his columns in a book titled *The Lives of a Cell: Notes of a Biology Watcher* (1974). To his surprise, the book became a best-seller; clearly the reading public was intrigued by a scientist who could write engaging, persuasive prose about varied and complex topics. Whether comparing us with machines, as in "Computers," or disagreeing with anthropologists about an elusive Ugandan tribe in "The Iks," Thomas finds ways to celebrate humanity "embedded in nature." In 1975, Thomas received the National Book Award in Arts and Letters for his first essay collection. His subsequent essay collections include *The Medusa and the Snail* (1979) and *Late Night Thoughts on Listening to Mahler's Ninth Symphony* (1983). In *The Youngest Science* (1983), Thomas offers a memoir of his father's career as a doctor and his own decision to become one.

Thomas seems to astonish himself as much as he does his readers. "I get surprised by an idea that I hadn't anticipated getting, which is a little bit like being in a laboratory. Including, in fact, that the outcome in writing essays, like the outcome in a laboratory, often turns out to be a dud." This bemused, self-effacing, and analogical reflection scarcely obscures Thomas's prominence as the dean of American science writers—a group represented also in this collection by Richard Selzer and Stephen Jay Gould. Yet ultimately—as we sense in his essay "Late Night Thoughts on Listening to Mahler's Ninth Symphony"—Thomas seems closer to Annie Dillard, another writer in this anthology, in his meditative, philosophical explorations of first and last things. Whether somber or playful, he remains forever in awe of natural creation, offering in his essays a startling testament to the mysteries and marvels of life.

Computers

You can make computers that are almost human. In some respects they
are superhuman; they can beat most of us at chess, memorize whole telephone
books at a glance, compose music of a certain kind and write obscure poetry,
diagnose heart ailments, send personal invitations to vast parties, even go
transiently crazy. No one has yet programmed a computer to be of two minds
about a hard problem, or to burst out laughing, but that may come. Sooner
or later, there will be real human hardware, great whirring, clicking cabinets
intelligent enough to read magazines and vote, able to think rings around the
rest of us.

Well, maybe, but not for a while anyway. Before we begin organizing
sanctuaries and reservations for our software selves, lest we vanish like the
whales, here is a thought to relax with.

Even when technology succeeds in manufacturing a machine as big as
Texas to do everything we recognize as human, it will still be, at best, a single
individual. This amounts to nothing, practically speaking. To match what we
can do, there would have to be 3 billion of them with more coming down the
assembly line, and I doubt that anyone will put up the money, much less make
room. And even so, they would all have to be wired together, intricately and
delicately, as we are, communicating with each other, talking incessantly, listening. If they weren't *at* each other this way, all their waking hours, they wouldn't
be anything like human, after all. I think we're safe, for a long time ahead.

It is in our collective behavior that we are most mysterious. We won't
be able to construct machines like ourselves until we've understood this, and
we're not even close. All we know is the phenomenon: we spend our time sending messages to each other, talking and trying to listen at the same time, exchanging information. This seems to be our most urgent biological function;
it is what we do with our lives. By the time we reach the end, each of us has
taken in a staggering store, enough to exhaust any computer, much of it incomprehensible, and we generally manage to put out even more than we take
in. Information is our source of energy; we are driven by it. It has become a
tremendous enterprise, a kind of energy system on its own. All 3 billion of us
are being connected by telephones, radios, television sets, airplanes, satellites,
harangues on public-address systems, newspapers, magazines, leaflets dropped
from great heights, words got in edgewise. We are becoming a grid, a circuitry
around the earth. If we keep at it, we will become a computer to end all
computers, capable of fusing all the thoughts of the world into a syncytium.

131

Already, there are no closed, two-way conversations. Any word you speak this afternoon will radiate out in all directions, around town before tomorrow, out and around the world before Tuesday, accelerating to the speed of light, modulating as it goes, shaping new and unexpected messages, emerging at the end as an enormously funny Hungarian joke, a fluctuation in the money market, a poem, or simply a long pause in someone's conversation in Brazil.

We do a lot of collective thinking, probably more than any other social species, although it goes on in something like secrecy. We don't acknowledge the gift publicly, and we are not as celebrated as the insects, but we do it. Effortlessly, without giving it a moment's thought, we are capable of changing our language, music, manners, morals, entertainment, even the way we dress, all around the earth in a year's turning. We seem to do this by general agreement, without voting or even polling. We simply think our way along, pass information around, exchange codes disguised as art, change our minds, transform ourselves.

Computers cannot deal with such levels of improbability, and it is just as well. Otherwise, we might be tempted to take over the control of ourselves in order to make long-range plans, and that would surely be the end of us. It would mean that some group or other, marvelously intelligent and superbly informed, undoubtedly guided by a computer, would begin deciding what human society ought to be like, say, over the next five hundred years or so, and the rest of us would be persuaded, one way or another, to go along. The process of social evolution would then grind to a standstill, and we'd be stuck in today's rut for a millennium.

Much better we work our way out of it on our own, without governance. The future is too interesting and dangerous to be entrusted to any predictable, reliable agency. We need all the fallibility we can get. Most of all, we need to preserve the absolute unpredictability and total improbability of our connected minds. That way we can keep open all the options, as we have in the past.

It would be nice to have better ways of monitoring what we're up to so that we could recognize change while it is occurring, instead of waking up as we do now to the astonished realization that the whole century just past wasn't what we thought it was, at all. Maybe computers can be used to help in this, although I rather doubt it. You can make simulation models of cities, but what you learn is that they seem to be beyond the reach of intelligent analysis; if you try to use common sense to make predictions, things get more botched up than ever. This is interesting, since a city is the most concentrated aggregation of humans, all exerting whatever influence they can bring to bear. The city seems to have a life of its own. If we cannot understand how this works, we are not likely to get very far with human society at large.

Still, you'd think there would be some way in. Joined together, the great mass of human minds around the earth seems to behave like a coherent, living system. The trouble is that the flow of information is mostly one-way. We are all obsessed by the need to feed information in, as fast as we can, but we lack sensing mechanisms for getting anything much back. I will confess that I have no more sense of what goes on in the mind of mankind than I have for the mind of an ant. Come to think of it, this might be a good place to start.

1974

Purpose and Meaning

1. Is the title of this essay appropriate? What is the thesis of this essay? Is the essay really about computers? Explain. Why be concerned with such an issue in the 1990s?

2. What property or properties distinguish human beings from computers? Does Thomas believe that computers will one day become like human beings?

3. In paragraphs 4 and 10, Thomas emphasizes the importance of information. How does he define this elusive word?

Language and Style

1. Tuchman, in her essay "The Historian as Artist," claims that writing for the general public should be clear and interesting. Does Thomas's style fulfill these criteria? What makes this essay appropriate for the general public? What implicit social, educational, and cultural background does this general public have?

2. Notice Thomas's choice of pronouns. He uses *you* and *we* throughout. To whom do these words refer? How does his choice of pronouns influence the relationship between the writer and the reader? How does it affect the overall tone of the essay?

3. Paragraphs 4 and 5 have sentences that include a long series of items. Locate and analyze these two sentences. Do they seem to contribute to the unique voice of the writer? What other atypical syntax can you find in the essay?

Strategy and Structure

1. Thomas cites few specific names, dates, statistics, or events in this essay. How does the absence of this evidence determine the tone of his argument? Does Thomas's propensity toward writing in general terms affect the strength of his argument?

2. What points of contrast between computers and human beings does Lewis establish to structure his argument?

3. Thomas seems to alternate between familiar phrases like "burst out laughing" (paragraph 1) and unusual ones like "software selves" (paragraph 1). Can you find other examples of these two extremes? What rhetorical function might this strategy have on the essay as a whole?

4. Paragraph 5 is nearly all one sentence. Is this sentence too long? What relationship is there between the length and structure of this sentence and its content?

5. Thomas concludes the essay ironically. What does he suggest by this unusual ending? If the last sentence of the essay had been deleted, how would it have influenced the impact of the work?

Thinking and Writing

1. Argue for or against the proposition that technology ultimately will make much human behavior unnecessary or obsolete. Specify the behaviors.

2. In paragraph 8, Thomas states, "We need all the fallibility we can get." What does he mean by this? Develop and write an argument either supporting or rejecting this view.

3. How are computers and human beings similar to and different from one another? Brainstorm the idea by compiling two lists: one listing the attributes of human beings, the other of computers. Using these lists as a starting point, write an essay comparing and contrasting the two.

The Iks

The small tribe of Iks, formerly nomadic hunters and gatherers in the mountain valleys of northern Uganda, have become celebrities, literary symbols for the ultimate fate of disheartened, heartless mankind at large. Two disastrously conclusive things happened to them: the government decided to have a national park, so they were compelled by law to give up hunting in the valleys and become farmers on poor hillside soil, and then they were visited for two years by an anthropologist who detested them and wrote a book about them.

The message of the book is that the Iks have transformed themselves into an irreversibly disagreeable collection of unattached, brutish creatures, totally selfish and loveless, in response to the dismantling of their traditional culture. Moreover, this is what the rest of us are like in our inner selves, and we will all turn into Iks when the structure of our society comes all unhinged.

The argument rests, of course, on certain assumptions about the core of human beings, and is necessarily speculative. You have to agree in advance that man is fundamentally a bad lot, out for himself alone, displaying such graces as affection and compassion only as learned habits. If you take this view, the story of the Iks can be used to confirm it. These people seem to be living together, clustered in small, dense villages, but they are really solitary, unrelated individuals with no evident use for each other. They talk, but only to make ill-tempered demands and cold refusals. They share nothing. They never sing. They turn the children out to forage as soon as they can walk, and desert the elders to starve whenever they can, and the foraging children snatch food from the mouths of the helpless elders. It is a mean society.

They breed without love or even casual regard. They defecate on each   4
other's doorsteps. They watch their neighbors for signs of misfortune, and only then do they laugh. In the book they do a lot of laughing, having so much bad luck. Several times they even laughed at the anthropologist, who found this especially repellent (one senses, between the lines, that the scholar is not himself the world's luckiest man). Worse, they took him into the family, snatched his food, defecated on his doorstep, and hooted dislike at him. They gave him two bad years.

It is a depressing book. If, as he suggests, there is only Ikness at the center   5
of each of us, our sole hope for hanging on to the name of humanity will be in endlessly mending the structure of our society, and it is changing so quickly and completely that we may never find the threads in time. Meanwhile, left to ourselves alone, solitary, we will become the same joyless, zestless, untouching lone animals.

But this may be too narrow a view. For one thing, the Iks are extraor-   6
dinary. They are absolutely astonishing, in fact. The anthropologist has never seen people like them anywhere, nor have I. You'd think, if they were simply examples of the common essence of mankind, they'd seem more recognizable. Instead, they are bizarre, anomalous. I have known my share of peculiar, difficult, nervous, grabby people, but I've never encountered any genuinely, consistently detestable human beings in all my life. The Iks sound more like abnormalities, maladies.

I cannot accept it. I do not believe that the Iks are representative of isolated,   7
revealed man, unobscured by social habits. I believe their behavior is something extra, something laid on. This unremitting, compulsive repellence is a kind of complicated ritual. They must have learned to act this way; they copied it, somehow.

I have a theory, then. The Iks have gone crazy.   8

The solitary Ik, isolated in the ruins of an exploded culture, has built a   9
new defense for himself. If you live in an unworkable society you can make up one of your own, and this is what the Iks have done. Each Ik has become a group, a one-man tribe on its own, a constituency.

Now everything falls into place. This is why they do seem, after all, vaguely   10
familiar to all of us. We've seen them before. This is precisely the way groups of one size or another, ranging from committees to nations, behave. It is, of course, this aspect of humanity that has lagged behind the rest of evolution, and this is why the Ik seems so primitive. In his absolute selfishness, his incapacity to give anything away, no matter what, he is a successful committee.

When he stands at the door of his hut, shouting insults at his neighbors in a loud harangue, he is city addressing another city.

Cities have all the Ik characteristics. They defecate on doorsteps, in rivers and lakes, their own or anyone else's. They leave rubbish. They detest all neighboring cities, give nothing away. They even built institutions for deserting elders out of sight. 11

Nations are the most Iklike of all. No wonder the Iks seem familiar. For total greed, rapacity, heartlessness, and irresponsibility there is nothing to match a nation. Nations, by law, are solitary, self-centered, withdrawn into themselves. There is no such thing as affection between nations, and certainly no nation ever loved another. They bawl insults from their doorsteps, defecate into whole oceans, snatch all the food, survive by detestation, take joy in the bad luck of others, celebrate the death of others, live for the death of others. 12

That's it, and I shall stop worrying about the book. It does not signify that man is a sparse, inhuman thing at his center. He's all right. It only says what we've always known and never had enough time to worry about, that we haven't yet learned how to stay human when assembled in masses. The Ik, in his despair, is acting out this failure, and perhaps we should pay closer attention. Nations have themselves become too frightening to think about, but we might learn some things by watching these people. 13

1974

Purpose and Meaning

1. How important is it for the reader of this essay to have read the book about the Iks that Thomas is citing? Has Thomas summarized the main points of the book so that we can understand the gist of it?

2. In the conclusion, Thomas states that "we might learn some things by watching these people." What things is he referring to? How do the Iks differ from what the anthropologist seems to have inferred about them?

3. Thomas mentions in the introduction that the Iks have become "celebrities." What historical and cultural assumptions is he making about his audience by referring to the Iks in this way?

Language and Style

1. Paragraph 1 contains a long sentence with six different ideas. Identify each idea. Compare this sentence with the final sentence in paragraph 12. Is such density of meaning typical of Thomas's style?

2. In paragraph 4, Thomas repeats the word *they* in referring to the Iks. What is the purpose of the repetition? How does this repetition reveal Thomas's attitude toward the Iks?

3. In paragraph 5, the author coins a term "Ikness" and in paragraph 12, "Iklike." What tone do they establish? Could other words be substituted for them successfully? What would the effect be of these substitutions?

4. Paragraph 11 is an extended personification. Does Thomas make a good argument for comparing cities to humans?

Strategy and Structure

1. How does Thomas establish a pattern of refutation to advance his own argument in this essay?

2. At what point in the essay does Thomas begin comparing the Iks to other groups? How effective is this organization in advancing Thomas's thesis?

3. Paragraph 6 begins with the conjunction *but*. Is this an appropriate transition word to use between paragraphs? Why are many of the opening sentences of the paragraphs in this essay short and colloquial?

4. Paragraph 8 is one short sentence. Why does Thomas use such an odd structural device? How does this paragraph fit into the organizational scheme of the entire essay?

5. Notice the way Thomas begins his concluding sentence. Is it more effective than the typical phrases "in conclusion," or "to conclude" that are common to many student essays?

Thinking and Writing

1. In an essay, trace the process whereby Thomas comes to terms with the Iks and what they represent.

2. Thomas believes the Iks are crazy. Argue against this view by maintaining that they *do* represent humankind.

3. In both "The Iks" and "Computers," Thomas explains why neither group is human. Write an essay comparing the reasons he offers for the inhumanity of the Iks to the inhumanity of computers.

Notes on Punctuation

There are no precise rules about punctuation (Fowler lays out some general advice (as best he can under the complex circumstances of English prose (he points out, for example, that we possess only four stops (the comma, the semicolon, the colon and the period (the question mark and exclamation point are not, strictly speaking, stops; they are indicators of tone (oddly enough, the Greeks employed the semicolon for their question mark (it produces a strange sensation to read a Greek sentence which is a straightforward question: Why weepest thou; (instead of Why weepest thou? (and, of course, there are parentheses (which are surely a kind of puncutation making this whole matter much more complicated by having to count up the left-handed parentheses in order to be sure of closing with the right number (but if the parentheses were left out, with nothing to work with but the stops, we would have considerably more flexibility in the deploying of layers of meaning than if we tried to separate all the clauses by physical barriers (and in the latter case, while we might have more precision and exactitude for our meaning, we would lose the essential flavor of language, which is its wonderful ambiguity))))))))))) .

The commas are the most useful and usable of all the stops. It is highly important to put them in place as you go along. If you try to come back after doing a paragraph and stick them in the various spots that tempt you you will discover that they tend to swarm like minnows into all sorts of crevices whose existence you hadn't realized and before you know it the whole long sentence becomes immobilized and lashed up squirming in commas. Better to use them sparingly, and with affection, precisely when the need for each one arises, nicely, by itself.

I have grown fond of semicolons in recent years. The semicolon tells you that there is still some question about the preceding full sentence; something needs to be added; it reminds you sometimes of the Greek usage. It is almost always a greater pleasure to come across a semicolon than a period. The period tells you that that is that; if you didn't get all the meaning you wanted or expected, anyway you got all the writer intended to parcel out and now you have to move along. But with a semicolon there you get a pleasant little feeling of expectancy; there is more to come; read on; it will get clearer.

Colons are a lot less attractive, for several reasons: firstly, they give you the feeling of being rather ordered around, or at least having your nose pointed in a direction you might not be inclined to take if left to yourself, and, secondly, you suspect you're in for one of those sentences that will be labeling the points to be made: firstly, secondly and so forth, with the implication that you haven't sense enough to keep track of a sequence of notions without having them numbered. Also, many writers use this system loosely and incompletely, starting out with number one and number two as though counting off on their fingers but then going on and on without the succession of labels you've been led to expect, leaving you floundering about searching for the ninethly or seventeenthly that ought to be there but isn't.

Exclamation points are the most irritating of all. Look! they say, look at what I just said! How amazing is my thought! It is like being forced to watch someone else's small child jumping up and down crazily in the center of the living room shouting to attract attention. If a sentence really has something of importance to say, something quite remarkable, it doesn't need a mark to point it out. And if it is really, after all, a banal sentence needing more zing, the exclamation point simply emphasizes its banality!

Quotation marks should be used honestly and sparingly, when there is 6 a genuine quotation at hand, and it is necessary to be very rigorous about the words enclosed by the marks. If something is to be quoted, the *exact* words must be used. If part of it must be left out becuase of space limitations, it is good manners to insert three dots to indicate the omission, but it is unethical to do this if it means connecting two thoughts which the original author did not intend to have tied together. Above all, quotation marks should not be used for ideas that you'd like to disown, things in the air so to speak. Nor should they be put in place around clichés; if you want to use a cliché you must take full responsibility for it yourself and not try to fob it off on anon., or on society. The most objectionable misuse of quotation marks, but one which illustrates the dangers of misuse in ordinary prose, is seen in advertising, especially in advertisement for small restaurants, for example "just around the corner," or "a good place to eat." No single, identifiable, citable person ever really said, for the record, "just around the corner," much less "a good place to eat," least likely of all for restaurants of the type that use this type of prose.

The dash is a handy device, informal and essentially playful, telling you 7 that you're about to take off on a different tack but still in some way connected with the present course—only you have to remember that the dash is there, and either put a second dash at the end of the notion to let the reader know that he's back on course, or else end the sentence, as here, with a period.

The greatest danger in punctuation is for poetry. Here it is necessary to 8 be as economical and parsimonious with commas and periods as with the words themselves, and any marks that seem to carry their own subtle meanings, like dashes and little rows of periods, even semicolons and questions marks, should be left out altogether rather than inserted to clog up the thing with ambiguity. A single exclamation point in a poem, no matter what else the poem has to say, is enough to destroy the whole work.

The things I like best in T. S. Eliot's poetry, especially in the *Four Quartets*, 9 are the semicolons. You cannot hear them, but they are there, laying out the connections between the images and the ideas. Sometimes you get a glimpse of a semicolon coming, a few lines farther on, and it is like climbing a steep path through woods and seeing a wooden bench just at a bend in the road ahead, a place where you can expect to sit for a moment, catching your breath.

Commas can't do this sort of thing; they can only tell you how the dif- 10 ferent parts of a complicated thought are to be fitted together, but you can't sit, not even take a breath, just because of a comma,

1979

Purpose and Meaning

1. How is Thomas's approach to the subject of punctuation different from the standard textbook method? What level of competency does he assume on the

part of the reader for him or her to appreciate the tone and content of the essay?

2. Is Thomas's purpose to instruct, entertain, show off, or a combination of these? How does his approach demonstrate that he is an expert in the subject matter?

3. What does punctuation mean to Thomas? What does he value in punctuation?

Language and Style

1. What is the first indication that Thomas is approaching the subject in a humorous way? When did you first realize that nature of his approach?

2. Does Thomas give us a clue to his attitude about punctuation in the tone of the essay? Does his style imply that proper punctuation is something immutable? Something subject to change? Something to be feared? To be respected? To be experimented with?

3. In paragraph 2, Thomas states that without proper usage, commas "tend to swarm like minnows into all sorts of crevices." Where else does Thomas endow punctuation marks with animate qualities? What is there about prose writing that lends itself to depicting punctuation marks in this way?

Strategy and Structure

1. Study the first paragraph. Does Thomas's use of parentheses make sense? Are they used appropriately "in the deploying of layers of meaning"?

2. Thomas is using the same humorous approach in paragraphs 1 and 7. What is this strategy? What makes it funny?

3. While Thomas is being clever in his use of examples to illustrate his major points on punctuation, the essay's basic organization is quite conventional. How does Thomas create a coherent essay? How does each paragraph fit into the scheme? How do the topic sentences help give coherence to the paragraphs?

Thinking and Writing

1. Rewrite paragraph 1 without using any parentheses. Compare both versions. How do they differ in meaning and effect? Does the version without parentheses have the "wonderful ambiguity" Thomas suggests? Similarly, add commas in the long sentence in paragraph 2 that is devoid of them, and compare both versions.

2. Select one of Thomas's other essays in this book, and analyze his use of punctuation in several of its paragraphs. Does this essay reflect Thomas's advice on punctuation? Write an essay demonstrating that Thomas's use of punctuation conforms, or does not conform, to his personal views on it.

3. Argue for or against the proposition that English teachers are too strict and conventional in the way they teach punctuation. Use examples, illustrations, and personal experience.

0➤━●━0━●━0━●━0━●━0━●━0━●━0━●━0➤━0━●━0━●━0━●━0

Late Night Thoughts on Listening to Mahler's Ninth Symphony

I cannot listen to Mahler's Ninth Symphony with anything like the old 1
melancholy mixed with the high pleasure I used to take from this music. There
was a time, not long ago, when what I heard, especially in the final movement,
was an open acknowledgment of death and at the same time a quiet celebration
of the tranquillity connected to the process. I took this music as a metaphor
for reassurance, confirming my own strong hunch that the dying of every living creature, the most natural of all experiences, has to be a peaceful experience.
I rely on nature. The long passages on all the strings at the end, as close as music
can come to expressing silence itself, I used to hear as Mahler's ideas of leave-
taking at its best. But always, I have heard this music as a solitary, private
listener, thinking about death.

Now I hear it differently. I cannot listen to the last movement of the Mahler 2
Ninth without the door-smashing intrusion of a huge new thought: death
everywhere, the dying of everything, the end of humanity. The easy sadness
expressed with such gentleness and delicacy by that repeated phrase on faded
strings, over and over again, no longer comes to me as old, familiar news of
the cycle of living and dying. All through the last notes my mind swarms with
images of a world in which the thermonuclear bombs have begun to explode,
in New York and San Francisco, in Moscow and Leningrad, in Paris, in Paris,
in Paris. In Oxford and Cambridge, in Edinburgh. I cannot push away the
thought of a cloud of radioactivity drifting along the Engadin, from the Moloja
Pass to Ftan, killing off the part of the earth I love more than any other part.

I am old enough by this time to be used to the notion of dying, saddened 3
by the glimpse when it has occurred but only transiently knocked down, able
to regain my feet quickly at the thought of continuity, any day. I have acquired
and held in affection until very recently another sideline of an idea which serves
me well at dark times: the life of the earth is the same as the life of an organism:
the great round being possesses a mind: the mind contains an infinite number
of thoughts and memories: when I reach my time I may find myself still hanging around in some sort of midair, one of those small thoughts, drawn back
into the memory of the earth: in that peculiar sense I will be alive.

Now all that has changed. I cannot think that way anymore. Not while 4
those things are still in place, aimed everywhere, ready for launching.

This is a bad enough thing for the people in my generation. We can put up with it, I suppose, since we must. We are moving along anyway, like it or not. I can even set aside my private fancy about hanging around, in midair.

What I cannot imagine, what I cannot put up with, the thought that keeps grinding its way into my mind, making the Mahler into a hideous noise close to killing me, is what it would be like to be young. How do the young stand it? How can they keep their sanity? If I were very young, sixteen or seventeen years old, I think I would begin, perhaps very slowly and imperceptibly, to go crazy.

There is a short passage near the very end of the Mahler in which the almost vanishing violins, all engaged in a sustained backward glance, are edged aside for a few bars by the cellos. Those lower notes pick up fragments from the first movement, as though prepared to begin everything all over again, and then the cellos subside and disappear, like an exhalation. I used to hear this as a wonderful few seconds of encouragement: we'll be back, we're still here, keep going, keep going.

Now, with a pamphlet in front of me on a corner of my desk, published by the Congressional Office of Technology Assessment, entitled MX Basing, an analysis of all the alternative strategies for placement and protection of hundreds of these missiles, each capable of creating artificial suns to vaporize a hundred Hiroshimas, collectively capable of destroying the life of any continent, I cannot hear the same Mahler. Now, those cellos sound in my mind like the opening of all the hatches and the instant before ignition.

If I were sixteen or seventeen years old, I would not feel the cracking of my own brain, but I would know for sure that the whole world was coming unhinged. I can remember with some clarity what it was like to be sixteen. I had discovered the Brahms symphonies. I knew that there was something going on in the late Beethoven quartets that I would have to figure out, and I knew that there was plenty of time ahead for all the figuring I would ever have to do. I had never head of Mahler. I was in no hurry. I was a college sophomore and had decided that Wallace Stevens and I possessed a comprehensive understanding of everything needed for a life. The years stretched away forever ahead, forever. My great-great grandfather had come from Wales, leaving his signature in the family Bible on the same page that carried, a century later, my father's signature. It never crossed my mind to wonder aobut the twenty-first century; it was just there, given, somewhere in the sure distance.

The man on television, Sunday midday, middle-aged and solid, nice-looking chap, all the facts at his fingertips, more dependable looking than most high-school principals, is talking about civilian defense, his responsibility in Washington. It can make an enormous difference, he is saying. Instead of the outright death of eighty million American citizens in twenty minutes, he says, we can, by careful planning and practice, get that number down to only forty million, maye even twenty. The thing to do, he says is to evacuate the cities quickly and have everyone get under shelter in the countryside. That way we can recover, and meanwhile we will have retaliated, incinerating all of Soviet society, he says. What about the radioactive fallout? he is asked. Well, he says. Anyway, he says, if the Russians know they can only destroy forty million of us instead of eighty million, this will deter them. Of course, he adds, they have the capacity to kill all two hundred and twenty million of us if they were to try real hard, but they know we can do the same to them. If the figure is only forty million this will deter them, not worth the trouble, not worth the risk. Eighty million would be another matter, we should guard ourselves against losing that many all at once, he says.

If I were sixteen or seventeen years old and had to listen to that, or read 11 things like that, I would want to give up listening and reading. I would begin thinking up new kinds of sounds, different from any music heard before, and I would be twisting and turning to rid myself of human language.

1983

Purpose and Meaning

1. What is the thesis of this essay? Must one listen to Mahler's Ninth Symphony to fully understand the thesis? Could the thesis have been expressed without any reference to the music? Why, or why not?

2. Why has Thomas's experience of and response to the music changed? Why has Thomas's general attitude toward death changed? Does the author's tone suggest that a profound change has occurred in the world at large? If so, how?

3. Does Thomas treat his subject too seriously? Why, or why not? How might a general audience respond to the issue he discusses?

Language and Style

1. In paragraph 7, the author claims that the end of the symphony was "a wonderful few seconds of encouragement." In paragraph 4, he refers to missiles as "those things." How do these descriptions help communicate his attitude about his subject? What other word choices does he use that reveal his positive or negative attitudes?

2. As in other of Thomas's essays, the author seems to be experimenting with punctuation. Observe the use of colons in paragraph 3. How does Thomas integrate their use into the content and context of the paragraph? Refer to his paragraph on the colon in "Notes on Punctuation." Is he using them as he advocated they be used in that essay?

3. What is the irony behind Thomas's description of the "man on television" in paragraph 10? What is the irony behind what the man says?

4. What is Thomas's overall tone in the essay? Explain your view.

Strategy and Structure

1. The author describes the writing as "late night thoughts." Is there anything in the transitions in subject matter from paragraph to paragraph that resembles the nature of thought? How is the writing structured so that it provides a coherent progression of paragraphs?

2. There is a marked change in diction in paragraph 10: no figurative language, no metaphor, no reference to music. How is this alteration in style analogous to Thomas's altered attitude toward his musical appreciation and his reflections on death?

3. The conclusion suggests an even further evolution in the author's attitude. What is the effect of ending the essay on a tone more radical that what precedes it?

Thinking and Writing

1. From the perspective of someone younger than Thomas, argue for or against his assertion that the threat of a nuclear holocaust is far worse for the young than for the old.

2. Reread the essay's conclusion. It contains some provocative yet ambiguous ideas. What is Thomas suggesting in this paragraph? If you were to write from the perspective of a sixteen- or seventeen-year-old, what "new kinds of sounds" would you think up? How would you "rid [yourself] of human language"? Develop a descriptive essay in which you imaginatively address these challenges.

3. Does a piece of music or any other creative work provoke thoughts and ideas in you? Select a work of art that has personal meaning to you, and write an essay describing the reflections and musings it inspires in you.

DORIS LESSING

One of the most important, prolific, and radically experimental writers of our time, Doris Lessing was born in 1919 of British parents in Kermanshah, Persia, where her father was a bank clerk. She moved with her family to Southern Rhodesia when she was five years old, and in 1949 emigrated to England, where she lives today. The author of more than thirty books—novels, short stories, essays, reportage, poetry and plays—she is renowned for describing in such works as *The Golden Notebook* (1962) what poet Gwendolyn Brooks terms "the intricate terrors and glories of womanhood."

While relations between the sexes might be Lessing's best-known territory, she actually is—like Orwell—a crusader and a utopian, preoccupied in her fiction and non-fiction with questions of gender, race, ethnicity, and class. Like Orwell, the colonial experience—treated in both "My Father" and "Being Prohibited"—is central to her role as a writer and to her vision of a world destined to change, for she observes in the preface to *Collected African Stories* (1972), "white-dominated Africa cannot last very long." Indeed, from the publication of her first novel, *The Grass is Growing* (1950), Lessing's fiction has been governed by metaphors of the colonial experience. She is like Isak Dinesen, whom she praises in "A Deep Darkness," in acknowledging that Africa "was my air, my landscape, and above all, my sun," but she is also a refugee caught between an African openness that in reality is not hers and an innate English conservatism that her radical politics rebels against.

Isolated on her father's Southern Rhodesia farm, one hundred miles west of Mozambique, Lessing was largely self-educated, reading "the best—the classics of European and American literature." In 1938, she moved to Salisbury, working as a nursemaid and telephone operator. At nineteen, she married a civil servant, had two children, and divorced in 1943. Two years later she married Gottfried Lessing and had a second son, before the marriage ended in 1949. It was then that she left for England with the manuscript of her first novel.

Lessing's movement from the African world to the prototypical Western city, London, provided her with a rare perspective on the crisis in world culture, as well as a visionary desire to imagine better worlds. One novel cycle, *Children of Violence*, is mildly utopian. A second cycle of visionary novels, *Canopus in Argos; Archives*, underscore Lessing's assertion that "the petty fates of planets, let alone individuals, are only aspects of cosmic evolution expressed in the rivalries and interactions of great galactic Empires." The prophetic mode, which Joyce Carol Oates in the United States and Margaret Atwood in Canada also appropriate in their fiction, allows Lessing to locate commitment, heroism, and transcendence as universal possibilities for men and women today. "We are all of us," she writes, "directly or indirectly caught up in a whirlwind of change; and I believe that if an artist has once felt this, in himself . . . it is an end of despair, and the aridity of self-pity."

Lessing's essays, some collected in *A Small Personal Voice* (1974), reflect the same intelligence and passion—Joan Didion calls it "native power"—characteristic of her fiction. Her essays reflect once again the need for commitment, especially by writers who as "architects of the soul" must offer a hopeful vision of the world.

Being Prohibited

A large number of my friends are locked out of countries and unable to return; locked into countries and unable to get out; have been deported, prohibited, and banned. Among this select company I can now hold up my head. I am troubled, however, by secret doubts.

Before planning my trip to South Africa, it crossed my mind to wonder whether I should be allowed in; humility checked me. What have I, in fact, done to the Union government? In 1947 when I was on holiday, I worked for the *Guardian* in Cape Town for two months, as a typist. The *Guardian*, like the *Daily Worker* now, was in permanent financial crisis; and that brave band of people, the finance committee, sat in almost continuous session, wondering how to pay for the next issue and muttering enviously about Moscow gold. I wrote a lot of letters for this committee.

In 1949, on my way through to England, I undeniably consorted with people since named as Communists. Some were, some were not.

Of course, since I joined the Communist party in England I have made no secret of the fact; but the idea that M.I.5 would send warnings to South Africa of my approach seems to border on megalomania. This state of mind was ably described by a friend of mine who not only believed that the sword was mightier than the pen, but acted on it. An admirable person, he said that his chief handicap as an agitator was that at moments of crisis he could never really believe he was about to be arrested, because he was obviously right in his views and surely everyone must agree with him when it came to the point. My friend also used to say that the main fault of the Left was that we continually ascribe our own intelligence and high-mindedness to our opponents. Apropos, I remember that once, by a series of mischances, I spent an evening with the backroom boys of the Nationalist party. It was a salutary experience. I still find it hard to believe that such cynical oafs can keep a whole subcontinent in thrall.

Some weeks before leaving England this time, I was visited by two people, deported from South Africa, who told me I was mad to think I should be allowed in and that I was politically very naíve. Almost immediately afterwards, came another visitor, a political *émigré* of a superior kind who has for some years now been conducting a really epic fight with the Nationalists.

He said: "What's this I hear? What makes you think *you* are so dangerous that you won't be allowed in? You ought to be ashamed of yourself. You are on the official list of South African authors at South Africa House." It will be seen why I was in a confused state of mind when I left England.

I had worked out a really cunning plot to enter the Union: it depended

147

on an intimate knowledge of the habits of their immigration officials. This plot was received with amusement by my friends in Salisbury, who suggested I was suffering from a persecution complex. Not for one moment do I blame them for their attitude: the atmosphere of Southern Rhodesia, in contrast with the troubled territories north and south, is one of good humour. Everybody one meets says how efficient the C.I.D. is and that nothing one does ever escapes them; but it is rather as one speaks of a benevolent uncle. And I have it on the highest possible authority that the leaders of the Africans in that country are both "pleasant and sound." No, I have no doubt that if I lived again in Salisbury, within six months I should be talking about troublemakers and agitators with the best.

Lulled, therefore, into a state of innocence. I spent four days seeing old   8
friends and reviving the sundowner habit before actually flying south. In the aircraft there was plenty of time for reminiscence: that first time, for instance, that I entered the Union, in 1937. . . .

The border is Mafeking, a little dorp with nothing interesting about it   9
but its name. The train waits (or used to wait) interminably on the empty tracks, while immigration and customs officials made their leisurely way through the coaches, and pale gritty dust settled over everything. Looking out, one saw the long stretch of windows, with the two, three, or four white faces at each; then at the extreme end, the single coach for "natives" packed tight with black humans; and, in between, two or three Indians or Coloured people on sufferance in the European coaches.

Outside, on the scintillating dust by the tracks, a crowd of ragged black   10
children begged for *bonsellas*. One threw down sandwich crusts or bits of spoiled fruit and watched them dive and fight to retrieve them from the dirt.

I was sixteen. I was not, as one says, politically conscious; nor did I know   11
the score. I knew no more, in fact, than on which side my bread was buttered. But I already felt uneasy about being a member of the Herrenvolk. When the immigration official reached me, I had written on the form: *Nationality*, British, *Race*, European; and it was the first time in my life I had had to claim myself as a member of one race and disown the others. I remember distinctly that I had to suppress an impulse opposite *Race:* Human. Of course I *was* very young.

The immigration man had the sarcastic surliness which characterises the   12
Afrikaans official, and he looked suspiciously at my form for a long time before saying that I was in the wrong part of the train. I did not understand him. (I forgot to mention that where the form asked, Where were you born?, I had written, Persia.)

"Asiatics," said he, "have to go to the back of the train; and anyway you   13
are prohibited from entry unless you have documents proving you conform to the immigration quota for Asians."

"But," I said, "I am not an Asiatic."   14

The compartment had five other females in it; skirts were visibly being   15
drawn aside. To prove my bona fides I should, of course, have exclaimed with outraged indignation at any such idea.

"You were born in Persia?"   16

"Yes."   17

"Then you are an Asiatic. You know the penalties for filling in the form   18
wrongly?"

This particular little imbroglio involved my being taken off the train,   19
escorted to an office, and kept under watch while they telephoned Pretoria for
a ruling.

When next I entered the Union it was 1939. Sophistication had set in in   20
the interval, and it took me no more than five minutes to persuade the official
that one could be born in a country without being a citizen. The next two times
there was no trouble at all, although my political views had in the meantime
become nothing less than inflammatory: in a word, I had learned to disapprove
of the colour bar.

This time, two weeks ago, what happened was as follows: one gets off   21
the plane and sits for about fifteen minutes in a waiting room while they check
the plane list with a list, or lists, of their own. They called my name first, and
took me to an office which had two tables in it. At one sat a young man being
pleasant to the genuine South African citizens. At the one where they made
me sit was a man I could have sworn I had seen before. He proceeded to go
through my form item by item, as follows: "You *say*, Mrs. Lessing, that, etc. . . ."
From time to time he let out a disbelieving laugh and exchanged ironical looks
with a fellow official who was standing by. Sure enough, when he reached that
point on my form when he had to say: "You *claim* that you are British; you
say you were born in Persia," I merely said "Yes," and sat still while he gave
me a long, exasperated stare. Then he let out an angry exclamation in Afrikaans
and went next door to telephone Pretoria. Ten minutes later I was informed
I must leave at once. A plane was waiting and I must enter it immediately.

I did so with dignity. Since then I have been unable to make up my mind   22
whether I should have made a scene or not. I never have believed in the efficacy
of dignity.

On the plane I wanted to sit near the window but was made to sit by myself   23
and away from the window. I regretted infinitely that I had no accomplices
hidden in the long grass by the airstrip, but, alas, I had not thought of it
beforehand.

It was some time before it came home to me what an honour had been   24
paid me. But now I am uneasy about the whole thing: suppose that I owe these
attentions, not to my political views, but to the accident of my birthplace?

Mr. Donges was asked about the incident, but all he said was, "No   25
comment."*

1956

*T. E. Donges (1898–1968), South African Minister of the Interior (1948–58)
and Finance Minister (1958–66). Elected President of South Africa in 1968, he died
before being inaugurated.

Purpose and Meaning

1. What is Lessing's purpose in writing this essay?

2. What perplexes Lessing most about her concern over "being prohibited" from entering South Africa? How does she resolve her bewilderment by the end of the essay?

3. What is significant about Lessing's statement that she "should be talking about troublemakers and agitators with the best" had she lived again in Salisbury, Rhodesia?

Language and Style

1. One usually thinks of being prohibited from entering a country as a serious matter. Is Lessing's tone serious? If not, what is the chief characteristic of her tone? Upon what stylistic evidence do you base your view?

2. What references does Lessing make that assume specific knowledge of the political and social structure described in the essay? What effect would a reader's ignorance of some of the references have on an appreciation of the essay?

3. How does Lessing use imagery to assist us in understanding life in South Africa? Would the essay have been less effective if the imagery had been omitted? If so, why?

Strategy and Structure

1. How many times did Lessing attempt to visit South Africa? Is the essay structured in a linear, chronological fashion, or does it skip back and forth? Explain.

2. What is the function of dialogue in this narrative?

3. To which visit to South Africa does paragraph 21 refer? How does Lessing provide this information?

4. How does the final paragraph reinforce the main thesis of the essay? How does it add another dimension to the topic? Is the conclusion intentionally vague? Would it have been more effective for Lessing to include her interpretation of the South African official's remark?

Thinking and Writing

1. Compare conditions in South Africa today with those suggested by Lessing's essay.

2. Argue for or against the idea that there are times when a person (other than an escaped criminal) should be prohibited from entering a country, even for a brief visit.

3. Write a personal essay describing a time in your life when you defended an ethical or moral view that placed you at odds with group opinion.

0◆━0━0━◆━0━◆━0◆━0━0

My Father

We use our parents like recurring dreams, to be entered into when needed; they are always there for love or for hate; but it occurs to me that I was not always there for my father. I've written about him before, but novels, stories, don't have to be "true." Writing this article is difficult because it has to be "true." I knew him when his best years were over.

There are photographs of him. The largest is of an officer in the 1914–18 war. A new uniform—buttoned, badged, strapped, tabbed—confines a handsome, dark young man who holds himself stiffly to confront what he certainly thought of as his duty. His eyes are steady, serious, and responsible, and show no signs of what he became later. A photograph at sixteen is of a dark, introspective youth with the same intent eyes. But it is his mouth you notice—a heavily-jutting upper lip contradicts the rest of a regular face. His moustache was to hide it: "Had to do something—a damned fleshy mouth. Always made me uncomfortable, that mouth of mine."

Earlier a baby (eyes already alert) appears in a lace waterfall that cascades from the pillowy bosom of a fat, plain woman to her feet. It is the face of a head cook. "Lord, but my mother was a practical female—almost as bad as you!" as he used to say, or throw at my mother in moments of exasperation. Beside her stands, or droops, arms dangling, his father, the source of the dark, arresting eyes, but otherwise masked by a long beard.

The birth certificate says: Born 3rd August, 1886, Walton Villa, Creffield Road, S. Mary at the Wall, R.S.D. Name, Alfred Cook. Name and surname of Father: Alfred Cook Tayler. Name and maiden name of Mother: Caroline May Batley. Rank or Profession: Bank Clerk. Colchester, Essex.

They were very poor. Clothes and boots were a problem. They "made their own amusements." Books were mostly the Bible and *The Pilgrim's Progress*. Every Saturday night they bathed in a hip-bath in front of the kitchen fire. No servants. Church three times on Sundays. "Lord, when I think of those Sundays! I dreaded them all week, like a nightmare coming at you full tilt and no escape." But he rabbited with ferrets along the lanes and fields, bird-nested, stole fruit, picked nuts and mushrooms, paid visits to the blacksmith and the mill and rode a farmer's carthorse.

They ate economically, but when he got diabetes in his forties and sub- 6
sisted on lean meat and lettuce leaves, he remembered suet puddings, treacle
puddings, raisin and currant puddings, steak and kidney puddings, bread and
butter pudding, "batter cooked in the gravy with the meat," potato cake, plum
cake, butter cake, porridge with treacle, fruit tarts and pies, brawn, pig's trotters
and pig's cheek and home-smoked ham and sausages. And "lashings of fresh
butter and cream and eggs." He wondered if this diet had produced the diabetes,
but said it was worth it.

There was an elder brother described by my father as: "Too damned clever 7
by half. One of those quick, clever brains. Now I've always had a slow brain,
but I get there in the end, damn it!"

The brothers went to a local school and the elder did well, but my father 8
was beaten for being slow. They both became bank clerks in, I think, the
Westminster Bank, and one must have found it congenial, for he became a
manager, the "rich brother," who had cars and even a yacht. But my father
did not like it, though he was conscientious. For instance, he changed his writing,
letter by letter, because a senior criticised it. I never saw his unregenerate hand,
but the one he created was elegant, spiky, careful. Did this mean he created
a new personality for himself, hiding one he did not like, as he hid his "damned
fleshy mouth"? I don't know.

Nor do I know when he left home to live in Luton or why. He found family 9
life too narrow? A safe guess—he found everything too narrow. His mother
was too down-to-earth? He had to get away from his clever elder brother?

Being a young man in Luton was the best part of his life. It ended in 1914, 10
so he had a decade of happiness. His reminiscences of it were all of pleasure,
the delight of physical movement, of dancing in particular. All his girls were
"a beautiful dancer, light as a feather." He played billiards and ping-pong (both
for his country); he swam, boated, played cricket and football, went to picnics
and horse races, sang at musical evenings. One family of a mother and two
daughters treated him "like a son only better. I didn't know whether I was in
love with the mother or the daughters, but oh I did love going there; we had
such good times." He was engaged to one daughter, then, for a time, to the
other. An engagement was broken off because she was rude to a waiter. "I could
not marry a woman who allowed herself to insult someone who was defenceless."
He used to say to my wryly smiling mother: "Just as well I didn't marry either
of *them*; they would never have stuck it out the way you have, old girl."

Just before he died he told me he had dreamed he was standing in a kitchen 11
on a very high mountain holding X in his arms. "Ah, yes, that's what I've missed
in my life. Now don't you let yourself be cheated out of life by the old dears.
They take all the colour out of everything if you let them."

But in that decade—"I'd walk 10, 15 miles to a dance two or three times 12
a week and think nothing of it. Then I'd dance every dance and walk home
again over the fields. Sometimes it was moonlight, but I liked the snow best,
all crisp and fresh. I loved walking back and getting into my digs just as the

sun was rising. My little dog was so happy to see me, and I'd feed her, and make myself porridge and tea, then I'd wash and shave and go off to work."

The boy who was beaten at school, who went too much to church, who carried the fear of poverty all his life, but who nevertheless was filled with the memories of country pleasures; the young bank clerk who worked such long hours for so little money, but who danced, sang, played, flirted—this naturally vigorous, sensuous being was killed in 1914, 1915, 1916. I think the best of my father died in that war, that his spirit was crippled by it. The people I've met, particularly the women, who knew him young, speak of his high spirits, his energy, his enjoyment of life. Also of his kindness, his compassion and—a word that keeps recurring—his wisdom. "Even when he was just a boy he understood things that you'd think even an old man would find it easy to condemn." I do not think these people would have easily recognised the ill, irritable, abstracted, hypochondriac man I knew.

He "joined up" as an ordinary soldier out of a characteristically quirky scruple: it wasn't right to enjoy officers' privileges when the Tommies had such a bad time. But he could not stick the communal latrines, the obligatory drinking, the collective visits to brothels, the jokes about girls. So next time he was offered a commission he took it.

His childhood and young man's memories, kept fluid, were added to, grew, as living memories do. But his war memories were congealed in stories that he told again and again, with the same words and gestures, in stereotyped phrases. They were anonymous, general, as if they had come out of a communal war memoir. He met a German in no-man's-land, but both slowly lowered their rifles and smiled and walked away. The Tommies were the salt of the earth, the British fighting men the best in the world. He had never known such comradeship. A certain brutal officer was shot in a sortie by his men, but the other officers, recognising rough justice, said nothing. He had known men intimately who saw the Angels at Mons. He wished he could force all the generals on both sides into the trenches for just one day, to see what the common soldiers endured—*that* would have ended the war at once.

There was an undercurrent of memories, dreams, and emotions much deeper, more personal. This dark region in him, fate-ruled, where nothing was true but horror, was expressed inarticulately, in brief, bitter exclamations or phrases of rage, incredulity, betrayal. The men who went to fight in that war believed it when they said it was to end war. My father believed it. And he was never able to reconcile his belief in his country with his anger at the cynicism of its leaders. And the anger, the sense of betrayal, strengthened as he grew old and ill.

But in 1914 he was naive, the German atrocities in Belgium inflamed him, and he enlisted out of idealism, although he knew he would have a hard time. He knew because a fortuneteller told him. (He could be described as uncritically superstitious or as psychically gifted.) He would be in great danger twice, yet not die—he was being protected by a famous soldier who was his ancestor.

13

14

15

16

17

"And sure enough, later I heard from the Little Aunties that the church records showed we were descended the backstairs way from the Duke of Wellington, or was it Marlborough? Damn it, I forget. But one of them would be beside me all through the war, she said." (He was romantic, not only about this solicitous ghost, but also about being a descendant of the Huguenots, on the strength of the "e" in Tayler; and about "the wild blood" in his veins from a great uncle who, sent unjustly to prison for smuggling, came out of a ten-year sentence and earned it, very efficiently, along the coasts of Cornwall until he died.)

The luckiest thing that ever happened to my father, he said, was getting   18 his leg shatterd by shrapnel ten days before Passchendaele. His whole company was killed. He knew he was going to be wounded because of the fortuneteller, who had said he would know. "I did not understand what she meant, but both times in the trenches, first when my appendix burst and I nearly died, and then just before Passchendaele, I felt for some days as if a thick, black velvet pall was settled over me. I can't tell you what it was like. Oh, it was awful, awful, and the second time it was so bad I wrote to the old people and told them I was going to be killed."

His leg was cut off at mid-thigh, he was shell-shocked, he was very ill   19 for many months, with a prolonged depression afterwards. "You should always remember that sometimes people are all seething underneath. You don't know what terrible things people have to fight against. You should look at a person's eyes, that's how you tell....When I was like that, after I lost my leg, I went to a nice doctor man and said I was going mad, but he said, don't worry, everyone locks up things like that. You don't know—horrible, horrible, awful things. I was afraid of myself, of what I used to dream. I wasn't myself at all."

In the Royal Free Hospital was my mother, Sister McVeagh. He married   20 his nurse which, as they both said often enough (though in different tones of voice), was just as well. That was 1919. He could not face being a bank clerk in England, he said, not after the trenches. Besides, England was too narrow and conventional. Besides, the civilians did not know what the soldiers had suffered, they didn't want to know, and now it wasn't done even to remember "The Great Unmentionable." He went off to the Imperial Bank of Persia, in which country I was born.

The house was beautiful, with great stone-floored high-ceilinged rooms   21 whose windows showed ranges of snow-streaked mountains. The gardens were full of roses, jasmine, pomegranates, walnuts. Kermanshah he spoke of with liking, but soon they went to Teheran, populous with "Embassy people," and my gregarious mother created a lively social life about which he was irritable even in recollection.

Irritableness—that note was first struck here, about Persia. He did not   22 like, he said, "the graft and the corruption." But here it is time to try and describe something difficult—how a man's good qualities can also be his bad ones, or if not bad, a danger to him.

My father was honourable—he always knew exactly what that word 23
meant. He had integrity. His "one does not do that sort of thing," his "no, it
is *not* right," sounded throughout my childhood and were final for all of us.
I am sure it was true he wanted to leave Persia because of "the corruption."
But it was also because he was already unconsciously longing for something
freer, because as a bank official he could not let go into the dream-logged personality that was waiting for him. And later in Rhodesia, too, what was best
in him was also what prevented him from shaking away the shadows: it was
always in the name of honesty or decency that he refused to take this step or
that out of the slow decay of the family's fortunes.

In 1925 there was leave from Persia. That year in London there was an 24
Empire Exhibition, and on the Southern Rhodesian stand some very fine maize
cobs and a poster saying that fortunes could be made on maize at 25/-a bag.
So on an impulse, turning his back forever on England, washing his hands of
the corruption of the East, my father collected all his capital, £800, I think, while
my mother packed curtains from Liberty's, clothes from Harrods, visiting cards,
a piano, Persian rugs, a governess and two small children.

Soon, there was my father in a cigar-shaped house of thatch and mud 25
on the top of a kopje that overlooked in all directions a great system of mountains, rivers, valleys, while overhead the sky arched from horizon to empty
horizon. This was a couple of hundred miles south from the Zambesi, a hundred
or so west from Mozambique, in the district of Banket, so called because certain
of its reefs were of the same formation as those called *banket* on the Rand.
Lomagundi—gold country, tobacco country, maize country—wild, almost
empty. (The Africans had been turned off it into reserves.) Our neighbours were
four, five, seven miles off. In front of the house . . . no neighbours, nothing; no
farms, just wild bush with two rivers but no fences to the mountains seven miles
away. And beyond these mountains and bush again to the Portuguese border,
over which "our boys" used to escape when wanted by the police for pass or
other offences.

And then? There was bad luck. For instance, the price of maize dropped 26
from 25/- to 9/- a bag. The seasons were bad, prices bad, crops failed. This
was the sort of thing that made it impossible for him ever to "get off the farm,"
which, he agreed with my mother, was what he most wanted to do.

It was an absurd country, he said. A man could "own" a farm for years 27
that was totally mortgaged to the Government and run from the Land Bank,
meanwhile employing half-a-hundred Africans at 12/- a month and none of
them knew how to do a day's work. Why, two farm labourers from Europe
could do in a day what twenty of these ignorant black savages would take a
week to do. (Yet he was proud that he had a name as a just employer, that
he gave "a square deal.") Things got worse. A fortuneteller had told him that
her heart ached when she saw the misery ahead for my father: this was the
misery.

But it was my mother who suffered. After a period of neurotic illness, 28 which was a protest against her situation, she became brave and resourceful. But she never saw that her husband was not living in a real world, that he had made a captive of her common sense. We were always about to "get off the farm." A miracle would do it—a sweepstake, a goldmine, a legacy. And then? What a question! We would go to England where life would be normal with people coming in for musical evenings and nice supper parties at the Trocadero after a show. Poor woman, for the twenty years we were on the farm, she waited for when life would begin for her and for her children, for she never understood that what was a calamity for her was for them a blessing.

Meanwhile my father sank towards his death (at 61). Everything changed in him. He had been a dandy and fastidious, now he hated to change out of shabby khaki. He had been sociable, now he was misanthropic. His body's disorders—soon diabetes and all kinds of stomach ailments—dominated him. He was brave about his wooden leg, and even went down mine shafts and climbed trees with it, but he walked clumsily and it irked him badly. He greyed fast, and slept more in the day, but would be awake half the night pondering about. . . .

It could be gold divining. For ten years he experimented on private theories to do with the attractions and repulsions of metals. His whole soul went into it but his theories were wrong or he was *unlucky*—after all, if he had found a mine he would have had to leave the farm. It could be the relation between the minerals of the earth and of the moon; his decision to make infusions of all the plants on the farm and drink them himself in the interests of science; the criminal folly of the British Government in not realising that the Germans and the Russians were conspiring as Anti-Christ to . . . the inevitability of war because no one would listen to Churchill, but it would be all right because God (by then he was a British Israelite) had destined Britain to rule the world; a prophecy said 10 million dead would surround Jerusalem—how would the corpses be cleared away?; people who wished to abolish flogging should be flogged; the natives understood nothing but a good beating; hanging must not be abolished because the Old Testament said "an eye for an eye and a tooth for a tooth. . . ."

Yet, as this side of him darkened, so that it seemed all his thoughts were of violence, illness, war, still no one dared to make an unkind comment in his presence or to gossip. Criticism of people, particularly of women, made him more and more uncomfortable till at last he burst out with: "It's all very well, but no one has the right to say that about another person."

In Africa, when the sun goes down, the stars spring up, all of them in their expected places, glittering and moving. In the rainy season, the sky flashed and thundered. In the dry season, the great dark hollow of night was lit by veld fires: the mountains burned through September and October in chains of red fire. Every night my father took out his chair to watch the sky and the mountains, smoking, silent, a thin shabby fly-away figure under the stars. "Makes you think—there are so many worlds up there, wouldn't really matter if we did blow ourselves up—plenty more where we came from."

The Second World War, so long foreseen by him, was a bad time. His 33 son was in the Navy and in danger, and his daughter a sorrow to him. He became very ill. More and more often it was necessary to drive him into Salisbury with him in a coma, or in danger of one, on the back seat. My mother moved him into a pretty little suburban house in town near the hospitals, where he took to his bed and a couple of years later died. For the most part he was unconscious under drugs. When awake he talked obsessively (a tongue licking a nagging sore place) about "the old war." Or he remembered his youth. "I've been dreaming—Lord, to see those horses come lickety-split down the course with their necks stretched out and the sun on their coats and everyone shouting. . . .I've been dreaming how I walked along the river in the mist as the sun was rising. . . .Lord, lord, lord, what a time that was, what good times we all had then, before the old war."

1963

Purpose and Meaning

1. How clearly does the introductory paragraph express the purpose of the essay? In the first sentence, Lessing includes the phrase "use our parents." Is there anything that indicates how she is using her father at the time of the writing?

2. Why is the truth about her father so difficult for Lessing to write about, as she explains in paragraph 1? Does this difficulty reflect on Lessing's singular relationship to her father, on relationships between parents and children in general, or both?

Language and Style

1. Note how rich with information and uniquely structured the following two sentences are: "A new uniform—buttoned, badged, strapped, tabbed—confines a handsome, dark young man who holds himself stiffly to confront what he certainly thought of as his duty" (paragraph 2); "Beside her stands, or droops, arms dangling, his father, the source of the dark, arresting eyes, but otherwise masked by a long beard" (paragraph 3). What other sentences can you find in the essay that possess unusual syntax and density of description?

2. Lessing intersperses her descriptions with direct quotations from her father. How successful are they in helping us get a "picture" of the man?

3. Lessing's diction and tone as a writer contrast with the father's diction and tone as indicated by what he says. How does this difference contribute toward our understanding the relationship between the father and daughter? How does it affect our awareness of why Lessing has adopted her singular tone toward her father?

Strategy and Structure

1. Where does Lessing's introduction end and the body of the narrative begin?
2. What is the function of listing the information on the father's birth certificate (paragraph 4)? How does it prepare, or fail to prepare, the reader for what is to follow? Paragraph 6 also includes a listing. What purpose does it serve?
3. What strategies does Lessing use from fiction writing to structure her essay and develop her thesis?
4. What is the effect of the final quotation on the essay as a whole? Does it reinforce the tragic quality of the father's life? How does it reaffirm Lessing's statement in paragraph 13 that her father's "sensuous being was killed in 1914, 1915, 1916"? How do other quotes from her father contribute to making the final paragraph a culmination of his life after the war?

Thinking and Writing

1. After studying the examples you found as a response to question 1 under "Language and Style," write a short, descriptive essay of approximately 300 words describing someone you know. Include at least five or six sentences imitating the structure of the sentences you found.
2. Investigate the concept of "tragedy" in writing. Write an essay explaining how the life of Lessing's father can be viewed as tragic.
3. Lessing seems to suggest that her father became a different man after the war. Do you know someone who underwent a major change in personality because of a specific event or experience? Develop a comparison/contrast essay exploring the differences between your subject's former and later "selves."
4. One particular event in recent history that had a profound effect on the people who fought in it is the Vietnam War. Interview a Vietnam veteran, and develop an essay from your interview in which you discuss the changes in attitude, beliefs, and personality the interviewee experienced as a result of his or her participation in the war. Develop a series of significant questions that will elicit the appropriate information.

A Deep Darkness: A Review of
Out of Africa by Karen Blixen

Karen Blixen was a Dane and a baroness. She identified with sea adventurers. Also with the nobility, noble behaviour. By heredity, experience, temperament, she was an enemy of the commonplace, and it is not surprising she became a Kenyan coffee farmer—even now a hard thing for a young woman to be alone, and with little money. That was 1913 and she was twenty-eight. The farm was too high for good coffee, there were years of drought and locusts, finally the slump. She was bankrupt and went back to Denmark in 1931. *Out of Africa* is twenty years of her life; but it is only when you work things out that you find she must have been at such an age when she did this or thus—fifty, when she left Kenya—that you understand the book's special quality, of a tale much concentrated, like a myth.

Partly this is because of her feeling for the past, her own life being seen   2 as a small putting-forth from the root of her ancestry—which is how the Africans she lived among saw theirs—and partly because there is nothing in it of the grind of one day after another. It is all distillation; and happiness, pain, this or that bit of luck or misfortune, are parts of a pattern or plot. By the best of script writers, of course, if not Cervantes, then Conrad, whose view of people as items in a high drama she shares. The players on her stage are white, black, brown. On her farm lived the Kikuyu. The Masai were across the river. Her major-domo and friend was Farah, a Somali. She enjoyed the company of the Indian merchants from Nairobi and Mombasa. She quotes: "Noble found I ever the Native and insipid the Immigrant," complaining that while the natives, because of their long contact with raiding and trading Arabs and Indians, are cosmopolitan, the whites are provincial. Except, of course, for her small band of special friends.

Casually she allows to emerge the picture of a young woman living in   3 a house with doors opening onto a terrace, beyond which are lawns with great trees under which she sits to palaver with chiefs and commoners. Beyond these the river, plains, the Ngong hills. She was alone in Eden save for the deerhounds, and the bushbuck Lulu, for whom they would give up their places by the fire. Proud that her table was the best in the Colony, she gave dinner parties, danced, rode, shot. She hints it was a callous or careless young woman who was ground into maturity, but does not make much of either state, since growth is to be expected of people. Her guests were mostly men. Needing the company of women, she sat at sundown in the house of Farah, whose womenfolk were her especial friends. For her real life was not the social one, but with "her people"—particularly Farah; the boy Kamante, whom she saved from crippledom and whom she taught to be a great chef; the farm's women, and Chief Kinanjui the Kikuyu. All these understood so well where she belonged in heart that when she emerged from a time of personal crisis, or from writing, they spoke thus: "When you were away"; or "That tree fell down, my child died, while you were with the white people."

This being so feudal fitted her well for that epoch of younger sons living   4 on mortgages off vast farms, with innocently open-hearted Africans. But that ended with indiscriminate white immigration. Newcomers called "The Mayflower People" arrogant. She says they were blind.

Nine thousand feet up we felt safe and we laughed at the ambition of the new arrivals, the Missions, the business people and the Government itself, to make the Continent of Africa respectable.

She mentions a husband, once. What she wants to say about loving friend- 5 ship is in accounts of Berkely Cole and Denys Finch-Hatton who made her house their own. Berkely had his own farm, but preferred hers; whereas Denys never had a home, but, like Virginia Woolf's Orlando's lover, was always on safari. These two men kept her in wine, ordered her books and records from Europe, inspired Kamante with comparison from the great houses and restaurants of Europe. They were self-conscious, self-parodying dandies. Berkely Cole drank a bottle of champagne under her trees each morning at eleven, and complained, being given coarse and vulgar glass, since she did not want her good glass broken, "I know, my dear, but it is so sad." Thereafter they always used the best glass. He died, and peole dated an epoch from it: "While Berkely Cole was alive." He should have been a Cavalier; and Denys Finch-Hatton, really an Elizabethan, taught her Latin and Greek; taught himself to fly so that she might see Africa from the air, and, loving music, said he could have liked Beethoven if he were not so vulgar. One New Year they sat at a table made of a millstone brought from India by merchants, and saw the moon, Venus, Jupiter radiantly together. Once she was at tea when he descended from the sky in his Moth, saying she must come to see buffalo feeding in the hills. She protested her guests, but he promised to have her back in fifteen minutes, and she was, having seen buffalo, sky, and hills.

All this time she got poorer, and when he knew she must leave, Denys 6 refused to take her on a trip to the coast—and he had never refused before— and he crashed and was buried in the Ngong hills. On the plateau where his grave is, lions came to sit and gaze over plains where soon would creep the suburbs of Nairobi. As Denys said, refusing a house in such a suburb, when people felt he ought not to be always in a tent or in the air, "This continent of Africa has a terrible strong sense of sarcasm." To the end she fought for her farm, and fought, too, for "her people" against the ravages of the new creed: Teach the Native to want; and against white officialdom. For while the idea that a man has rights was not one she could hold, she could not stand that he should be hurt or insulted.

The plot of this drama isn't important. If it had been: she came to Africa, farmed successfully, pleased the respectable—it would have been the same. For the book is not "about" anything but Africa:

The sweet noble black of Africa, deep darkness absorbed through age, like old soot, that makes you feel that for elegance, vigour and vivacity, no colours rival black.

About what lies behind the words heard always when black men are first shocked by white, the epitaph, "White men are very clever, but they have no hearts." About the landscape: rivers, hills, plains, creatures. When she was back in

Denmark old servants wrote to her: "Honourable Lioness," as they had called Denys Finch-Hatton a lion, and knew that she thought of them and would soon be back with them. She did not have the money, though she dreamed of going back to start a school, or a hospital.

Instead she wrote a sequel, *Shadows on the Grass*, out of love and   7 homesickness, recalling Farah in particular, who, when at the end she was so poor she had no furniture in her house, put on all the magnificence of his best clothes to open doors onto empty rooms and to walk behind her as she went begging from office to office for "her" Kikuyu—the land had been bought to build villas on. No, she never saw that her 6,000 acres were not hers, and that it was not enough to call the Kikuyu squatters (similarly, masters, servants, lions, kings, chameleons) even if she did count herself a squatter with them.

In the postscript book are two photographs, one of a young beauty so   8 sure of herself she is in sloppy khaki trousers and a man's hat, the only elegance being a deerhound half her height. The other is of a crone which, when I first saw it, made me want to shout to her: How can you!—the way women do when they feel another is letting the side down. But now the decades have begun to tick past I understand the relish with which I am sure she juxtaposed the two. She and the jocose old Kikuyu women who had lived through to the other side of happiness and pain had the closest of silent understandings. She approved, before the Government forbade it, the Kikuyu way of putting out their dead to be cleaned to the bone by vultures and hyenas, death being one with life and neither more than a process. A noble one—of course, for everything is, and nothing without meaning; which is why she is on so many people's special shelf, to be taken down more and more often as an antidote to our eleventh hour of squalid destructiveness.

> The chief feature of the landscape, and of your life in it, was the air. Looking back on a sojourn in the African highlands, you are struck by your feeling of having lived for a time up in the air. The sky was rarely more than pale blue or violet, with a profusion of might, weightless, ever-changing clouds towering up and sailing on it, but it has a blue vigour in it, and at a short distance it painted the ranges of the hills and the woods a fresh deep blue. In the middle of the day the air was alive over the land, like a flame burning: it scintillated, waved, and shone like running water, mirrored and doubled all objects, and created great Fata Morgana. Up in this high air you breathed easily, drawing in a vital assurance and lightness of heart. In the highlands you woke up in a morning and thought: Here am I, where I ought to be.

1977

Purpose and Meaning

1. Lessing compares *Out of Africa* to a myth. What elements must a story have to constitute a myth? From information you derive from Lessing's description

of the book, from your own reading of the selections by Blixen (Dinesen), and from her discussion of Blixen's self-image and her outlook on life, explain what makes the book mythlike.

2. In referring to the book in paragraph 7, Lessing claims that "The plot of this drama isn't important." Since plot often *is* an essential ingredient in any story, what makes Blixen's story different?

3. What references does Lessing make in her review to indicate that she has more than a layperson's knowledge of Blixen's life? What references does she make that indicate that she read the book carefully before embarking on this review? What is Lessing's ultimate purpose in this book review?

Language and Style

1. In paragraph 8, Lessing claims that Blixen found "nothing without meaning." How do the excerpts from Blixen's writings reveal this outlook? How does Lessing use these excerpts to emphasize her own sense of style?

2. Review the use of the following terms: *major-domo* in paragraph 2; *palavar* in paragraph 3; *especial* in paragraph 3; and *Elizabethan* in paragraph 5. What other words or phrases can you find that help create the literary diction of the review? Does Lessing's diction suggest the implicit audience for the book?

3. In this essay, as in previous essays, many of Lessing's sentences display a unique syntax: "Proud that her table was the best in the Colony, she gave dinner parties, danced, rode, shot"; "Beyond these the river, plains, the Ngong Hills." How do these examples contribute to the literary tone of the review?

Strategy and Structure

1. This essay is called a book review, but Lessing spends much time describing Blixen's life in Africa without reference to the book. How successfully does she integrate this depiction of Blixen's life with a discussion of her literary work?

2. Although this is a review of the book *Out of Africa,* Lessing begins describing Blixen's second book in paragraph 8. Was the inclusion of this second book necessary? Explain.

3. Why does Lessing end her review with an extended quotation from the book?

Thinking and Writing

1. You may be accustomed to thinking of the purpose of a book or movie review as presenting either a positive or a negative evaluation (e.g., "thumbs up" or "thumbs down"). But Lessing does not make that sort of evaluation. Select an author from this anthology and write a review of his or her work. Before you

begin to write, list what aspects of the work you plan to review: meaning, style, biographical data, purpose, and so on. After you have compiled this list, fashion it into a review, using direct quotations where appropriate.

2. In paragraph 8, Lessing comments that *Out of Africa* is a popular book, that it is "to be taken down more and more often as an antidote to our eleventh hour of squalid destructiveness." Do you have a favorite book that you turn to for sustenance, relief, or pleasure when things get tough? Write a review of this particular book, focusing on what special significance and function the book holds for you.

3. For an extended project, read *Out of Africa.* Write your own review of the book. Before you begin, however, decide on which aspects of the book you will discuss: its quality, meaning, style, organization, revelation as autobiography, and so forth.

JAMES BALDWIN

Langston Hughes once referred to James Baldwin as "thought-provoking, tantalizing, irritating, abusing and amusing. And he uses words as the sea uses waves, to grow and beat, advance and retreat, rise and take a bow in disappearing." Indeed, Baldwin, who was born in Harlem in 1924, had many voices and a rhythmical, highly poetic prose style. Passionate, probing, controversial, Baldwin—as novelist, short story writer, dramatist and, above all, essayist—probed the American consciousness in more than fifteen books from the perspective of what he termed in *The Fire Next Time* (1963), our "racial nightmare."

Part of Baldwin's power and greatness is his willingness to candidly expose his own psychic consciousness within the dual dialects of race and sexuality, for he was an African American and a homosexual. Forced to react to multiple bigotries, Baldwin developed extraordinary methods, notably in his essays, for conveying the harrowing, personal pain of his situation, the implication of this pain for America's social fabric, and a transcendent faith that we cannot surrender to despair. As Baldwin asserts in the introduction to one of his essay collections, *Nobody Knows My Name* (1961), "One can only face in others what one can face in oneself. On this confrontation depends the measure of our wisdom and our compassion."

From childhood, raised in a fundamentalist Christian household with a stern and fanatical stepfather, Baldwin sensed his isolation and his calling as a writer. From 1924 to 1942, Baldwin lived in Harlem, attending Frederick Douglass Junior High School and DeWitt Clinton High School. In junior high, he studied under famed poet Countee Cullen and published material in the school newspaper. In "Autobiographical Notes" and "Fifth Avenue, Uptown," Baldwin offers autobiographical and sociological analyses of the nature of the Harlem ghetto that shaped his early life and threatened to entrap him.

Baldwin did break with the ghetto and also with his brief career as a young evangelical minister. Shortly after graduation, he left Harlem, going first to New Jersey and then to Greenwich Village, determined, as he once put it, to fight the devil in order to be a writer. For six years, aided by Saxton and Rosenwald fellowships for writers, he toiled with scant success. Then, in 1948, Baldwin sailed for Europe on a one-way ticket, beginning his adult years of transcendental voyaging in France, Switzerland, and Turkey, with one notable period from 1957 to 1965 back in the United States, where he became an eloquent crusader and lecturer for the civil rights movement. Baldwin's early years in Europe gave him a global perspective on racial and cultural issues as typified in "What It Means to Be an American," as well as an inspiring burst of creativity. During his first phase overseas, from 1948 to 1957, he published the novels *Go Tell It on the Mountain* (1953) and *Giovanni's Room* (1956) along with his magisterial collection of essays, *Notes of a Native Son* (1955). Subsequent works—the powerful essay *The Fire Next Time* (1963), the play *Blues for Mister Charley* (1964) and the novel *Another Country* (1967)—are among his most militant, filled with the apocalyptic overtones characteristic of the American 1960s. From the civil rights era to the end of his life in 1987, Baldwin's steady output was consciously political, treating such topics as the American criminal justice system in *If Beale Street Could Talk* (1974) and the Atlanta child murders in *Evidence of Things Not Seen* (1985).

Baldwin's essays have been collected in *The Price of the Ticket: Collected Nonfiction 1948–1985*, a testament to his towering reputation in the genre. Early in his career, he had declared that he wanted to be "an honest man and a good writer." With searing honesty and intense autobiographical introspection, his essays, owing much to the hellfire and brimstone oratory of his evangelical youth, move from emotion to logical abstraction. These essays seek what is good and honest in human nature. For life is a journey and each person must pay the price of the ticket. Moreover, as Baldwin declares on the last page of *The Price of the Ticket*, "We are a part of each other."

Autobiographical Notes

I was born in Harlem thirty-one years ago. I began plotting novels at about the time I learned to read. The story of my childhood is the usual bleak fantasy, and we can dismiss it with the restrained observation that I certainly would not consider living it again. In those days my mother was given to the exasperating and mysterious habit of having babies. As they were born, I took them over with one hand and held a book with the other. The children probably suffered, though they have since been kind enough to deny it, and in this way I read *Uncle Tom's Cabin* and *A Tale of Two Cities* over and over and over again; in this way, in fact, I read just about everything I could get my hands on—except the Bible, probably because it was the only book I was encouraged to read. I must also confess that I wrote—a great deal—and my first professional triumph, in any case, the first effort of mine to be seen in print, occurred at the age of twelve or thereabouts, when a short story I had written about the Spanish revolution won some sort of prize in an extremely short-lived church newspaper. I remember the story was censored by the lady editor, though I don't remember why, and I was outraged.

Also wrote plays, and songs, for one of which I received a letter of congratulations from Mayor La Guardia, and poetry, about which the less said, the better. My mother was delighted by all these goings-on, but my father wasn't; he wanted me to be a preacher. When I was fourteen I became a preacher, and when I was seventeen I stopped. Very shortly thereafter I left home. For God knows how long I struggled with the world of commerce and industry—I guess they would say they struggled with *me*—and when I was about twenty-one I had enough done of a novel to get a Saxton Fellowship. When I was twenty-two the fellowship was over, the novel turned out to be unsalable, and I started waiting on tables in a Village restaurant and writing book reviews—mostly, as it turned out, about the Negro problem, concerning which the color of my skin made me automatically an expert. Did another book, in company with photographer Theodore Pelatowski, about the storefront churches in Harlem. This book met exactly the same fate as my first—fellowship, but no sale. (It was a Rosenwald Fellowship.) By the time I was twenty-four I had decided to stop reviewing books about the Negro problem—which, by this time, was only slightly less horrible in print than it was in life—and I packed my bags and went to France, where I finished, God knows how, *Go Tell It on the Mountain*.

Any writer, I suppose, feels that the world into which he was born is nothing less than a conspiracy against the cultivation of his talent—which attitude certainly has a great deal to support it. On the other hand, it is only because

168

the world looks on his talent with such a frightening indifference that the artist is compelled to make his talent important. So that any writer, looking back over even so short a span of time as I am here forced to assess, finds that the things which hurt him and the things which helped him cannot be divorced from each other; he could be helped in a certain way only because he was hurt in a certain way; and his help is simply to be enabled to move from one conundrum to the next—one is tempted to say that he moves from one disaster to the next. When one begins looking for influences one finds them by the score. I haven't thought much about my own, not enough anyway; I hazard that the King James Bible, the rhetoric of the store-front church, something ironic and violent and perpetually understated in Negro speech—and something of Dickens' love for bravura—have something to do with me today; but I wouldn't stake my life on it. Likewise, innumerable people have helped me in many ways; but finally, I suppose, the most difficult (and most rewarding) thing in my life has been the fact that I was born a Negro and was forced, therefore, to effect some kind of truce with this reality. (Truce, by the way, is the best one can hope for.)

One of the difficulties about being a Negro writer (and this is not special 4 pleading, since I don't mean to suggest that he has it worse than anybody else) is that the Negro problem is written about so widely. The bookshelves groan under the weight of information, and everyone therefore considers himself informed. And this information, furthermore, operates usually (generally, popularly) to reinforce traditional attitudes. Of traditional attitudes there are only two—For or Against—and I, personally, find it difficult to say which attitude has caused me the most pain. I am speaking as a writer; from a social point of view I am perfectly aware that the change from ill-will to good-will, however motivated, however imperfect, however expressed, is better than no change at all.

But it is part of the business of the writer—as I see it—to examine attitudes, 5 to go beneath the surface, to tap the source. From this point of view the Negro problem is nearly inaccessible. It is not only written about so widely; it is written about so badly. It is quite possible to say that the price a Negro pays for becoming articulate is to find himself, at length, with nothing to be articulate about. ("You taught me language," says Caliban to Prospero, "and my profit on't is I know how to curse.") Consider: the tremendous social activity that this problem generates imposes on whites and Negroes alike the necessity of looking forward, of working to bring about a better day. This is fine, it keeps the waters troubled; it is all, indeed, that has made possible the Negro's progress. Nevertheless, social affairs are not generally speaking the writer's prime concern, whether they ought to be or not; it is absolutely necessary that he establish between himself and these affairs a distance which will allow, at least, for clarity, so that before he can look forward in any meaningful sense, he must first be allowed to take a long look back. In the context of the Negro problem neither whites nor blacks, for excellent reasons of their own, have the faintest desire to look back; but I think that the past is all that makes the present coherent, and further, that the past will remain horrible for exactly as long as we refuse to assess it honestly.

I know, in any case, that the most crucial time in my own development came when I was forced to recognize that I was a kind of bastard of the West; when I followed the line of my past I did not find myself in Europe but in Africa. And this meant that in some subtle way, in a really profound way, I brought to Shakespeare, Bach, Rembrandt, to the stones of Paris, to the cathedral at Chartres, and to the Empire State Building, a special attitude. These were not really my creations, they did not contain my history; I might search in them in vain forever for any reflection of myself. I was an interloper; this was not my heritage. At the same time I had no other heritage which I could possibly hope to use—I had certainly been unfitted for the jungle or the tribe. I would have to appropriate these white centuries. I would have to make them mine—I would have to accept my special attitude, my special place in this scheme— otherwise I would have no place in *any* scheme. What was the most difficult was the fact that I was forced to admit something I had always hidden from myself, which the American Negro has had to hide from himself as the price of his public progress; that I hated and feared white people. This did not mean that I loved black people; on the contrary, I despised them, possibly because they failed to produce Rembrandt. In effect, I hated and feared the world. And this meant, not only that I thus gave the world an altogether murderous power over me, but also that in such a self-destroying limbo I could never hope to write.

One writes out of one thing only—one's own experience. Everything depends on how relentlessly one forces from this experience the last drop, sweet or bitter, it can possibly give. This is the only real concern of the artist, to recreate out of the disorder of life that order which is art. The difficulty then, for me, of being a Negro writer was the fact that I was, in effect, prohibited from examining my own experience too closely by the tremendous demands and the very real dangers of my social situation.

I don't think the dilemma outlined above is uncommon. I do think, since writers work in the disastrously explicit medium of language, that it goes a little way towards explaining why, out of the enormous resources of Negro speech and life, and despite the example of Negro music, prose written by Negroes has been generally speaking so pallid and so harsh. I have not written about being a Negro at such length because I expect that to be my only subject, but only because it was the gate I had to unlock before I could hope to write about anything else. I don't think that the Negro problem in America can be even discussed coherently without bearing in mind its context; its context being the history, traditions, customs, the moral assumptions and preoccupations of the country; in short, the general social fabric. Appearances to the contrary, no one in America escapes its effects and everyone in America bears some responsibility for it. I believe this the more firmly because it is the overwhelming tendency to speak of this problem as though it were a thing apart. But in the work of Faulkner, in the general attitude and certain specific passages in Robert Penn Warren, and, most significantly, in the advent of Ralph Ellison, one sees the beginnings—at least—of a more genuinely penetrating search. Mr. Ellison, by the way, is the first Negro novelist I have ever read to utilize in language, and brilliantly, some of the ambiguity and irony of Negro life.

About my interests: I don't know if I have any, unless the morbid desire   9
to own a sixteen-millimeter camera and make experimental movies can be so classified. Otherwise, I love to eat and drink—it's my melancholy conviction that I've scarcely ever had enough to eat (this is because it's *impossible* to eat enough if you're worried about the next meal)—and I love to argue with people who do not disagree with me too profoundly, and I love to laugh. I do *not* like bohemia, or bohemians, I do not like people whose principal aim is pleasure, and I do not like people who are *earnest* about anything. I don't like people who like me because I'm a Negro; neither do I like people who find in the same accident grounds for contempt. I love America more than any other country in the world, and, exactly for this reason, I insist on the right to criticize her perpetually. I think all theories are suspect, that the finest principles may have to be modified, or may even be pulverized by the demands of life, and that one must find, therefore, one's own moral center and move through the world hoping that this center will guide one aright. I consider that I have many responsibilities, but none greater than this: to last, as Hemingway says, and get my work done.

I want to be an honest man and a good writer.   10

1963

Purpose and Meaning

1. What is Baldwin's main purpose here? Summarize the essay's thesis in a few sentences.

2. What special burden does Baldwin feel he carries as a result of having been born black? What was his strategy in coping with this burden? Baldwin also states that being born an African American was the "most rewarding thing in my life." Why does he feel this way?

3. Baldwin states "the price a Negro pays for becoming articulate is to find himself, at length, with nothing to be articulate about." What does this mean? How does Baldwin's own writing disprove the universality of this statement?

Language and Style

1. In paragraph 3, Baldwin states as one of his influences the "ironic and violent and perpetually understated in Negro speech." How can the following quota-

tions be placed into these categories: "The story of my childhood is the usual bleak fantasy" (paragraph 1); ". . . . poetry, about which the less said, the better" (paragraph 2); "I love to argue with people who do not disagree with me too profoundly" (paragraph 9). Can you find statements that have a similar tone?

2. Consider how these two sentences begin: "Also wrote plays, and songs. . ." (paragraph 2); "Did another book. . ." (paragraph 2). How do they contribute to the tone of the essay? Do they seem to have the quality of "notes" as expressed in the title?

3. How often does Baldwin make didactic statements? How do these affect the tone of the essay? Consider these two as examples: "One of the difficulties about being a Negro writer is that the Negro problem is written about so widely" (paragraph 4); and "One writes out of one thing only—one's own experience" (paragraph 7). Are these assertions (and others) based on fact, opinion, emotion, or a combination of these? Find other examples of didactic statements.

Strategy and Structure

1. This essay might be divided into three parts: Baldwin's description of his early years; his reflections on the role and struggles of the writer in general and the black writer in particular; and a concluding section that describes his interests. How do these sections complement one another? Do they give us a well-rounded picture of the author until the age of thirty-one? Are there any glaring omissions?

2. Examine the topic sentences of each paragraph. How do they contribute to structuring the array of ideas that Baldwin presents? How do they aid in the essay's coherence?

3. The concluding one-sentence paragraph is intentionally terse. How does it contribute to the organizational strength of the essay? Is it a good conclusion? Does it simply summarize, or does it add a new dimension to what has gone before it?

Thinking and Writing

1. In paragraph 9, Baldwin states, "I love America more than any other country in the world, and, exactly for this reason, I insist on the right to criticize it." Develop an essay in which you defend or criticize this proposition.

2. Write your own essay entitled "Autobiographical Notes." Include both facts of your life and reflections on what you have observed about life.

3. In paragraph 9, Baldwin states that "one must find. . . one's own moral center." What does Baldwin mean by this term? Develop an essay in which you present an extended definition of the term "moral center." What is it? How is it acquired? What is its purpose? What happens to a person who lacks one?

Fifth Avenue, Uptown

A letter from Harlem

There is a housing project standing now where the house in which we   1
grew up once stood, and one of those stunted city trees is snarling where our
doorway used to be. This is on the rehabilitated side of the avenue. The other
side of the avenue—for progress takes time—has not been rehabilitated yet and
it looks exactly as it looked in the days when we sat with our noses pressed
against the windowpane, longing to be allowed to go "across the street." The
grocery store which gave us credit is still there, and there can be no doubt that
it is still giving credit. The people in the project certainly need it—far more,
indeed, than they ever needed the project. The last time I passed by, the Jewish
proprietor was still standing among his shelves, looking sadder and heavier but
scarcely any older. Farther down the block stands the shoe-repair store in which
our shoes were repaired until reparation became impossible and in which, then,
we bought all our "new" ones. The Negro proprietor is still in the window, head
down, working at the leather.

These two, I imagine, could tell a long tale if they would (perhaps they   2
would be glad to if they could), having watched so many, for so long, struggling
in the fishhooks, the barbed wire, of this avenue.

The avenue is elsewhere the renowned and elegant Fifth. The area I am   3
describing, which, in today's gang parlance, would be called "the turf," is
bounded by Lenox Avenue on the west, the Harlem River on the east, 135th
Street on the north, and 130th Street on the south. We never lived beyond these
boundaries; this is where we grew up. Walking along 145th Street, for example,
familiar as it is, and similar, does not have the same impact because I do not
know any of the people on the block. But when I turn east on 131st Street and
Lenox Avenue, there is first a soda-pop joint, then a shoeshine "parlor," then
a grocery store, then a dry cleaners', then the houses. All along the street there
are people who watched me grow up, people who grew up with me, people
I watched grow up along with my brothers and sisters; and, sometimes in my
arms, sometimes underfoot, sometimes at my shoulder—or on it—their children,
a riot, a forest of children, who include my nieces and nephews.

When we reach the end of this long block, we find ourselves on wide,   4
filthy, hostile Fifth Avenue, facing that project which hangs over the avenue
like a monument to the folly, and the cowardice, of good intentions. All along

the block, for anyone who knows it, are immense human gaps, like craters. These gaps are not created merely by those who have moved away, inevitably into some other ghetto; or by those who have risen, almost always into a greater capacity for self-loathing and self-delusion; or yet by those who, by whatever means—the Second World War, the Korean war, a policeman's gun or billy, a gang war, a brawl, madness, an overdose of heroin, or, simply, unnatural exhaustion—are dead. I am talking about those who are left, and I am talking principally about the young. What are they doing? Well, some, a minority, are fanatical churchgoers, members of the more extreme of the Holy Roller sects. Many, many more are "moslems," by affiliation or sympathy, that is to say that they are united by nothing more—and nothing less—than a hatred of the white world and all its works. They are present, for example, at every Buy Black street-corner meeting—meetings in which the speaker urges his hearers to cease trading with white men and establish a separate economy. Neither the speaker nor his hearers can possibly do this, of course, since Negroes do not own General Motors or RCA or the A&P, nor indeed, do they own more than a wholly insufficient fraction of anything else in Harlem (those who *do* own anything are more interested in their profits than in their fellows). But these meetings nevertheless keep alive in the participators a certain pride of bitterness without which, however futile this bitterness may be, they could scarcely remain alive at all. Many have given up. They stay home and watch the TV screen, living on the earnings of their parents, cousins, brothers, or uncles, and only leave the house to go to the movies or to the nearest bar. "How're you making it?" one may ask, running into them along the block, or in the bar. "Oh, I'm TV-ing it"; with the saddest, sweetest, most shamefaced of smiles, and from a great distance. This distance one is compelled to respect; anyone who has traveled so far will not easily be dragged again into the world. There are further retreats, of course, than the TV screen or the bar. There are those who are simply sitting on their stoops, "stoned," animated for a moment only, and hideously, by the approach of someone who may lend them the money for a "fix." Or by the approach of someone from whom they can purchase it, one of the shrewd ones, on the way to prison or just coming out.

And the others, who have avoided all of these deaths, get up in the morning   5
and go downtown to meet "the man." They work in the white man's world all day and come home in the evening to this fetid block. They struggle to instill in their children some private sense of honor or dignity which will help the child to survive. This means, of course, that they must struggle, stolidly, incessantly, to keep this sense alive in themselves, in spite of the insults, the indifference, and the cruelty they are certain to encounter in their working day. They patiently browbeat the landlord into fixing the heat, the plaster, the plumbing; this demands prodigious patience; nor is patience usually enough. In trying to make their hovels habitable, they are perpetually throwing good money after bad. Such frustration, so long endured, is driving many strong, admirable men and women whose only crime is color to the very gates of paranoia.

One remembers them from another time—playing handball in the   6 playground, going to church, wondering if they were going to be promoted at school. One remembers them going off to war—gladly, to escape this block. One remembers their return. Perhaps one remembers their wedding day. And one sees where the girl is now—vainly looking for salvation from some other embittered, trussed, and struggling boy—and sees the all-but-abandoned children in the streets.

Now I am perfectly aware that there are other slums in which white men are fighting for their lives, and mainly losing. I know that blood is also flowing through those streets and that the human damage there is incalculable. People are continually pointing out to me the wretchedness of white people in order to console me for the wretchedness of blacks. But an itemized account of the American failure does not console me and it should not console anyone else. That hundreds of thousands of white people are living, in effect, no better than the "niggers" is not a fact to be regarded with complacency. The social and moral bankruptcy suggested by this fact is the bitterest, most terrifying kind.

The people, however, who believe that this democratic anguish has some consoling value are always pointing out that So-and-So, white, and So-and-So, black, rose from the slums into the big time. The existence—the public existence—of, say, Frank Sinatra and Sammy Davis, Jr., proves to them that America is still the land of opportunity and that inequalities vanish before the determined will. It proves nothing of the sort. The determined will is rare—at the moment, in this country, it is unspeakably rare—and the inequalities suffered by the many are in no way justified by the rise of a few. A few have always risen—in every country, every era, and in the teeth of regimes which can by no stretch of the imagination be thought of as free. Not all of these people, it is worth remembering, left the world better than they found it. The determined will is rare, but it is not invariably benevolent. Furthermore, the American equation of success with the big times reveals an awful disrespect for human life and human achievement. This equation has placed our cities among the most dangerous in the world and has placed our youth among the most empty and most bewildered. The situation of our youth is not mysterious. Children have never been very good at listening to their elders, but they have never failed to imitate them. They must, they have no other models. That is exactly what our children are doing. They are imitating our immorality, our disrespect for the pain of others.

All other slum dwellers, when the bank account permits it, can move out of the slum and vanish altogether from the eye of persecution. No Negro in this country has ever made that much money and it will be a long time before any Negro does. The Negroes in Harlem, who have no money, spend what they have on such gimcracks as they are sold. These include "wider" TV screens, more "faithful" hi-fi sets, more "powerful" cars, all of which, of course, are obsolete long before they are paid for. Anyone who has ever struggled with poverty knows how extremely expensive it is to be poor; and if one is a member of a captive population, economically speaking, one's feet have simply been placed on the treadmill forever. One is victimized, economically, in a thousand

ways—rent, for example, or car insurance. Go shopping one day in Harlem—
for anything—and compare Harlem prices and quality with those downtown.

The people who have managed to get off this block have only got as far   10
as a more respectable ghetto. This respectable ghetto does not even have the
advantages of the disreputable one—friends, neighbors, a familiar church, and
friendly tradesmen; and it is not, moreover, in the nature of any ghetto to remain respectable long. Every Sunday, people who have left the block take the
lonely ride back, dragging their increasingly discontented children with them.
They spend the day talking, not always with words, about the trouble they've
seen and the trouble—one must watch their eyes as they watch their children—
they are only too likely to see. For children do not like ghettos. It takes them
nearly no time to discover exactly why they are there.

The projects in Harlem are hated. They are hated almost as much as policemen,   11
and this is saying a great deal. And they are hated for the same reason: both
reveal, unbearably, the real attitude of the white world, no matter how many
liberal speeches are made, no matter how many lofty editorials are written,
no matter how many civil-rights commissions are set up.

The projects are hideous, of course, there being a law, apparently respected   12
throughout the world, that popular housing shall be as cheerless as a prison.
They are lumped all over Harlem, colorless, bleak, high, and revolting. The
wide windows look out on Harlem's invincible and indescribable squalor: the
Park Avenue railroad tracks, around which, about forty years ago, the present
dark community began; the unrehabilitated houses, bowed down, it would seem,
under the great weight of frustration and bitterness they contain; the dark, the
ominous schoolhouses from which the child may emerge maimed, blinded,
hooked, or enraged for life; and the churches, churches, block upon block of
churches, niched in the walls like cannon in the walls of a fortress. Even if the
administration of the projects were not so insanely humiliating (for example:
one must report raises in salary to the management, which will then eat up the
profit by raising one's rent; the management has the right to know who is staying in your apartment; the management can ask you to leave, at their discre-
tion), the projects would still be hated because they are an insult to the meanest
intelligence.

Harlem got its first private project, Riverton*—which is now, naturally,   13
a slum—about twelve years ago because at that time Negroes were not allowed

*The inhabitants of Riverton were much embittered by this description; they
have, apparently, forgotten how their project came into being; and have repeatedly
informed me that I cannot possibly be referring to Riverton, but to another housing
project which is directly across the street. It is quite clear, I think, that I have no interest
in accusing any individuals or families of the depredations herein described: but neither
can I deny the evidence of my own eyes. Nor do I blame anyone in Harlem for making
the best of a dreadful bargain. But anyone who lives in Harlem and imagines that he
has *not* struck this bargain, or that what he takes to be his status (in whose eyes?) pro-
tects him against the common pain, demoralization, and danger, is simply self-deluded.

to live in Stuyvesant Town. Harlem watched Riverton go up, therefore, in the most violent bitterness of spirit, and hated it long before the builders arrived. They began hating it at about the time people began moving out of their condemned houses to make room for this additional proof of how thoroughly the white world despised them. And they had scarcely moved in, naturally, before they began smashing windows, defacing walls, urinating in the elevators, and fornicating in the playgrounds. Liberals, both white and black, were appalled at the spectacle. I was appalled by the liberal innocence—or cynicism, which comes out in practice as much the same thing. Other people were delighted to be able to point to proof positive that nothing could be done to better the lot of the colored people. They were, and are, right in one respect: that nothing can be done as long as they are treated like colored people. The people in Harlem know they are living there because white people do not think they are good enough to live anywhere else. No amount of "improvement" can sweeten this fact. Whatever money is now being earmarked to improve this, or any other ghetto, might as well be burnt. A ghetto can be improved in one way only: out of existence.

Similarly, the only way to police a ghetto is to be oppressive. None of the Police Commissioner's men, even with the best will in the world, have any way of understanding the lives led by the people they swagger about in twos and threes controlling. Their very presence is an insult, and it would be, even if they spent their entire day feeding gumdrops to children. They represent the force of the white world, and that world's real intentions are, simply, for that world's criminal profit and ease, to keep the black man corraled up here, in his place. The badge, the gun in the holster, and the swinging club make vivid what will happen should his rebellion become overt. Rare, indeed, is the Harlem citizen, from the most circumspect church member to the most shiftless adolescent, who does not have a long tale to tell of police incompetence, injustice, or brutality. I myself have witnessed and endured it more than once. The businessmen and racketeers also have a story. And so do the prostitutes. (And this is not, perhaps, the place to discuss Harlem's very complex attitude toward black policemen, nor the reasons, according to Harlem, that they are nearly all downtown.) 14

It is hard, on the other hand, to blame the policeman, blank, good-natured, thoughtless, and insuperably innocent, for being such a perfect representative of the people he serves. He, too, believes in good intentions and is astounded and offended when they are not taken for the deed. He has never, himself, done anything for which to be hated—which of us has?—and yet he is facing, daily and nightly, people who would gladly see him dead, and he knows it. There is no way for him not to know it: there are few things under heaven more unnerving than the silent, accumulating contempt and hatred of a people. He moves through Harlem, therefore, like an occupying soldier in a bitterly hostile country; which is precisely what, and where, he is, and is the reason he walks in twos and threes. And he is not the only one who knows why he is always in company: the people who are watching him know why, too. Any street meeting, 15 sacred or secular, which he and his colleagues uneasily cover has as its explicit or implicit burden the cruelty and injustice of the white domination. And these days, of course, in terms increasingly vivid and jubilant, it speaks of the end of that domination. The white policeman standing on a Harlem street corner finds himself at the very center of the revolution now occurring in the world. He is not prepared for it—naturally, nobody is—and, what is possibly much more to the point, he is exposed, as few white people are, to the anguish of the black people around him. Even if he is gifted with the merest mustard grain of imagination, something must seep in. He cannot avoid observing that some of the children, in spite of their color, remind him of children he has known and loved, perhaps even of his own children. He knows that he certainly does not want *his* children living this way. He can retreat from his uneasiness in only one direction: into a callousness which very shortly becomes second nature. He becomes more callous, the population becomes more hostile, the situation grows more tense, and the police force is increased. One day, to everyone's astonishment, someone drops a match in the powder keg and everything blows up. Before the dust has settled or the blood congealed, editorials, speeches, and civil-rights commissions are loud in the land, demanding to know what happened. What happened is that Negroes want to be treated like men.

Negroes want to be treated like men: a perfectly straightforward state-   16
ment, containing only seven words. People who have mastered Kant, Hegel, Shakespeare, Marx, Freud, and the Bible find this statement utterly impenetrable. The idea seems to threaten profound, barely conscious assumptions. A kind of panic paralyzes their features, as though they found themselves trapped on the edge of a steep place. I once tried to describe to a very well-known American intellectual the conditions among Negroes in the South. My recital disturbed him and made him indignant; and he asked me in perfect innocence. "Why don't all the Negroes in the South move North?" I tried to explain what *has* happened, unfailingly, whenever a significant body of Negroes move North. They do not escape Jim Crow: they merely encounter another, not-less-deadly variety. They do not move to Chicago, they move to the South Side; they do not move to New York, they move to Harlem. The pressure within the ghetto causes the ghetto walls to expand, and this expansion is always violent. White people hold the line as long as they can, and in as many ways as they can, from verbal intimidation to physical violence. But inevitably the border which has divided the ghetto from the rest of the world falls into the hands of the ghetto. The white people fall back bitterly before the black horde; the landlords make a tidy profit by raising the rent, chopping up the rooms, and all but dispensing with the upkeep; and what has once been a neighborhood turns into a "turf." This is precisely what happened when the Puerto Ricans arrived in their thousands—and the bitterness thus caused is, as I write, being fought out all up and down those streets.

Northerners indulge in an extremely dangerous luxury. They seem to feel   17
that because they fought on the right side during the Civil War, and won, they

have earned the right merely to deplore what is going on in the South, without taking any responsibility for it; and that they can ignore what is happening in northern cities because what is happening in Little Rock or Birmingham is worse. Well, in the first place, it is not possible for anyone who has not endured both to know which is "worse." I know Negroes who prefer the South and white southerners, because "At least there, you haven't got to play any guessing games." The guessing games referred to have driven more than one Negro into the narcotics ward, the madhouse, or the river. I know another Negro, a man very dear to me, who says, with conviction and with truth, "The spirit of the South is the spirit of America." He was born in the North and did his military training in the South. He did not, as far as I can gather, find the South "worse"; he found it, if anything, all too familiar. In the second place, though, even if Birmingham *is* worse, no doubt Johannesburg, South Africa, beats it by several miles, and Buchenwald was one of the worst things that ever happened in the entire history of the world. The world has never lacked for horrifying examples; but I do not believe that these examples are meant to be used as justification for our own crimes. This perpetual justification empties the heart of all human feeling. The emptier our hearts become, the greater will be our crimes. Thirdly, the South is not merely an embarrassingly backward region, but a part of this country, and what happens there concerns every one of us.

As far as the color problem is concerned, there is but one great difference [18] between the southern white and the northerner: the southerner remembers, historically and in his own psyche, a kind of Eden in which he loved black people and they loved him. Historically, the flaming sword laid across this Eden is the Civil War. Personally, it is the southerner's sexual coming of age, when, without any warning, unbreakable taboos are set up between himself and his past. Everything, thereafter, is permitted him except the love he remembers and has never ceased to need. The resulting, indescribable torment affects every southern mind and is the basis of the southern hysteria.

None of this is true for the northerner. Negroes represent nothing to him [19] personally, except, perhaps, the dangers of carnality. He never sees Negroes. Southerners see them all the time. Northerners never think about them whereas southerners are never really thinking of anything else. Negroes are, therefore, ignored in the North and are under surveillance in the South, and suffer hideously in both places. Neither the southerner nor northerner is able to look on the Negro simply as a man. It seems to be indispensable to the national self-esteem that the Negro be considered either as a kind of ward (in which case we are told how many Negroes, comparatively, bought Cadillacs last year and how few, comparatively, were lynched), or as a victim (in which case we are promised that he will never vote in our assemblies or go to school with our kids). They are two sides of the same coin and the South will not change—*cannot* change—until the North changes. The country will not change until it reexamines itself and discovers what it really means by freedom. In the meantime, generations keep being born, bitterness is increased by incompetence, pride, and folly, and the world shrinks around us.

It is a terrible, an inexorable, law that one cannot deny the humanity of   20 another without diminishing one's own: in the face of one's victim, one sees oneself. Walk through the streets of Harlem and see what we, this nation, have become.

1960

Purpose and Meaning

1. What connotations are conveyed in the title? In what way does it implicate its intended audience? Why did Baldwin write a letter to people who lived only a short distance from him?

2. Whom is Baldwin addressing in this "letter"? What attitude toward black socie-ty does Baldwin presume his audience has?

3. In paragraph 10, Baldwin states, "The people who have managed to get off this block have only got as far as a more respectable ghetto." What does he mean? What additional information in the essay supports this observation?

Language and Style

1. Is the diction of the essay typical of most letters? Explain.

2. Baldwin often writes long, substantive sentences. Consider this one from paragraph 12: "The wide windows look out on Harlem's invincible and in-describable squalor: the Park Avenue railroad tracks, around which, about for-ty years ago, the present dark community began; the unrehabilitated houses, bowed down, it would seem, under the great weight of frustration and bitterness they contain; the dark, the ominous schoolhouses from which the child may emerge maimed, blinded, hooked, or enraged for life; and the churches, chur-ches, block upon block of churches, niched in the walls like cannon in the walls of a fortress." Study its syntax, vocabulary, and rhythm. Reading the sentence aloud may be helpful. What distinctive "voice" emerges in the writing? Locate other sentences in this essay that display the writer's voice.

3. Paragraph 2 is all one sentence. Would it have been easier to understand if Baldwin had divided it into several sentences? What was his purpose in writing one long sentence?

Strategy and Structure

1. Paragraph 8 offers an argument condemning the "American Dream." How does Baldwin support his argument? How persuasive is he?

2. Paragraph 11 marks a new section of the essay. How does paragraph 11 denote a new mood? If you were to give this second section a title, what would it be?

3. Is the progression of Baldwin's argument a result of explanation, emotion, description, or a combination of these? How effective is the final paragraph as a culmination of Baldwin's overall theme?

Thinking and Writing

1. In paragraph 9, Baldwin states, "All other slum dwellers, when the bank account permits it, can move out of the slum and vanish altogether from the eye of persecution. No Negro in this country has ever made that much money and it will be a long time before any Negro does." Has this situaiton changed since 1960, the year this essay was published? Argue for or against the proposition that Baldwin's statement is no longer true.

2. Follow Baldwin's suggestion in the final sentence of his essay. Walk through a poor neighborhood, and write an essay in which you analyze the "mood" and "health" of the area by observing its people, its physical features, and its activities. Contrast this to a walk through an upper-middle-class neighborhood. How do you assess "what America has become"?

3. Baldwin claims that many people find the phrase "Negroes want to be treated like men . . . utterly impenetrable." Taking Baldwin's own reasoning as a foundation, argue for or against this thesis.

The Discovery of What It Means to Be an American

"It is a complex fate to be an American," Henry James observed, and the principal discovery an American writer makes in Europe is just how complex this fate is. America's history, her aspirations, her peculiar triumphs, her even more peculiar defeats, and her position in the world—yesterday and today—are all so profoundly and stubbornly unique that the very word "America" remains a new, almost completely undefined and extremely controversial proper noun. No one in the world seems to know exactly what it describes, not even we motley millions who call ourselves Americans.

I left America because I doubted my ability to survive the fury of the color problem here. (Sometimes I still do.) I wanted to prevent myself from becoming *merely* a Negro; or, even, merely a Negro writer. I wanted to find out in what way the *specialness* of my experience could be made to connect me with other people instead of dividing me from them. (I was as isolated from Negroes as I was from whites, which is what happens when a Negro begins, at bottom, to believe what white people say about him.)

In my necessity to find the terms on which my experience could be related   3 to that of others, Negroes and whites, writers and non-writers, I proved, to my astonishment, to be as American as any Texas GI. And I found my experience was shared by every American writer I knew in Paris. Like me, they had been divorced from their origins, and it turned out to make very little difference that the origins of white Americans were European and mine were African—they were no more at home in Europe than I was.

The fact that I was the son of a slave and they were the sons of free men meant   4 less, by the time we confronted each other on European soil, than the fact that we were both searching for our separate identities. When we had found these, we seemed to be saying, why, then, we would no longer need to cling to the shame and bitterness which had divided us so long.

It became terribly clear in Europe, as it never had been here, that we knew   5 more about each other than any European ever could. And it also became clear that, no matter where our fathers had been born, or what they had endured, the fact of Europe had formed us both, was part of our identity and part of our inheritance.

I had been in Paris a couple of years before any of this became clear to   6 me. When it did, I, like many a writer before me upon the discovery that his props have all been knocked out from under him, suffered a species of breakdown and was carried off to the mountains of Switzerland. There, in that absolutely alabaster landscape, armed with two Bessie Smith records and a typewriter, I began to try to recreate the life that I had first known as a child and from which I had spent so many years in flight.

It was Bessie Smith, through her tone and her cadence, who helped me   7 to dig back to the way I myself must have spoken when I was a pickaninny, and to remember the things I had heard and seen and felt. I had buried them very deep. I had never listened to Bessie Smith in America (in the same way that, for years, I would not touch watermelon), but in Europe she helped to reconcile me to being a "nigger."

I do not think that I could have made this reconciliation here. Once I was able   8 to accept my role—as distinguished, I must say, from my "place"—in the extraordinary drama which is America, I was released from the illusion that I hated America.

The story of what can happen to an American Negro writer in Europe   9 simply illustrates, in some relief, what can happen to any American writer there.

It is not meant, of course, to imply that it happens to them all, for Europe can be very crippling, too; and, anyway, a writer, when he has made his first breakthrough, has simply won a crucial skirmish in a dangerous, unending, and unpredictable battle. Still, the breakthrough is important, and the point is that an American writer, in order to achieve it, very often has to leave this country.

The American writer, in Europe, is released, first of all, from the necessi-   10
ty of apologizing for himself. It is not until he *is* released from the habit of flexing his muscles and proving that he is just a "regular guy" that he realizes how crippling this habit has been. It is not necessary for him, there, to pretend to be something he is not, for the artist does not encounter in Europe the same suspicion he encounters here. Whatever the Europeans may actually think of artists, they have killed enough of them off by now to know that they are as real—and as persistent—as rain, snow, taxes, or businessmen.

Of course, the reason for Europe's comparative clarity concerning the dif-   11
ferent functions of men in society is that European society has always been divided into classes in a way that American society never has been. A European writer considers himself to be part of an old and honorable tradition—of intellectual activity, of letters—and his choice of a vocation does not cause him any uneasy wonder as to whether or not it will cost him all his friends. But this tradition does not exist in America.

On the contrary, we have a very deep-seated distrust of real intellectual   12
effort (probably because we suspect that it will destroy, as I hope it does, that myth of America to which we cling so desperately). An American writer fights his way to one of the lowest rungs on the American social ladder by means of pure bullheadedness and an indescribable series of odd jobs. He probably *has* been a "regular fellow" for much of his adult life, and it is not easy for him to step out of that lukewarm bath.

We must, however, consider a rather serious paradox: though American   13
society is more mobile than Europe's, it is easier to cut across social and occupational lines there than it is here. This has something to do, I think, with the problem of status in American life. Where everyone has status, it is also perfectly possible, after all, that no one has. It seems inevitable, in any case, that a man may become uneasy as to just what his status is.

But Europeans have lived with the idea of status for a long time. A man   14
can be as proud of being a good waiter as of being a good actor, and, in neither case, feel threatened. And this means that the actor and the waiter can have a freer and more genuinely friendly relationship in Europe than they are likely to have here. The waiter does not feel, with obscure resentment, that the actor has "made it," and the actor is not tormented by the fear that he may find himself, tomorrow, once again a waiter.

This lack of what may roughly be called social paranoia causes the   15
American writer in Europe to feel—almost certainly for the first time in his life—

that he can reach out to everyone, that he is accessible to everyone and open to everything. This is an extraordinary feeling. He feels, so to speak, his own weight, his own value.

It is as though he suddenly came out of a dark tunnel and found himself   16 beneath the open sky. And, in fact, in Paris, I began to see the sky for what seemed to be the first time. It was borne in on me—and it did not make me feel melancholy—that this sky had been there before I was born and would be there when I was dead. And it was up to me, therefore, to make of my brief opportunity the most that could be made.

I was born in New York, but have lived only in pockets of it. In Paris,   17 I lived in all parts of the city—on the Right Bank and the Left, among the bourgeoisie and among *les misérables,* and knew all kinds of people, from pimps and prostitutes in Pigalle to Egyptian bankers in Neuilly. This may sound extremely unprincipled or even obscurely immoral: I found it healthy. I love to talk to people, all kinds of people, and almost everyone, as I hope we still know, loves a man who loves to listen.

This perpetual dealing with people very different from myself caused a   18 shattering in me of preconceptions I scarcely knew I held. The writer is meeting in Europe people who are not American, whose sense of reality is entirely different from his own. They may love or hate or admire or fear or envy this country—they see it, in any case, from another point of view, and this forces the writer to reconsider many things he had always taken for granted. This reassessment, which can be very painful, is also very valuable.

This freedom, like all freedom, has its dangers and its responsibilities. One   19 day it begins to be borne in on the writer, and with great force, that he is living in Europe as an American. If he were living there as a European, he would be living on a different and far less attractive continent.

This crucial day may be the day on which an Algerian taxi-driver tells him how   20 it feels to be an Algerian in Paris. It may be the day on which he passes a café terrace and catches a glimpse of the tense, intelligent, and troubled face of Albert Camus. Or it may be the day on which someone asks him to explain Little Rock and he begins to feel that it would be simpler—and, corny as the words may sound, more honorable—to *go* to Little Rock than sit in Europe, on an American passport, trying to explain it.

This is a personal day, a terrible day, the day to which his entire sojourn   21 has been tending. It is the day he realizes that there are no untroubled countries in this fearfully troubled world; that if he has been preparing himself for anything in Europe, he has been preparing himself—for America. In short, the freedom that the American writer finds in Europe brings him, full circle, back to himself, with the responsibility for his development where it always was: in his own hands.

Even the most incorrigible maverick has to be born somewhere. He may   22
leave the group that produced him—he may be forced to—but nothing will
efface his origins, the marks of which he carries with him everywhere. I think
it is important to know this and even find it a matter for rejoicing, as the strongest
people do, regardless of their station. On this acceptance, literally, the life of
a writer depends.

The charge has often been made against American writers that they do   23
not describe society, and have no interest in it. They only describe individuals
in opposition to it, or isolated from it. Of course, what the American writer
is describing is his own situation. But what is *Anna Karenina* describing if not
the tragic fate of the isolated individual, at odds with her time and place?

The real difference is that Tolstoy was describing an old and dense society   24
in which everything seemed—to the people in it, though not to Tolstoy—to
be fixed forever. And the book is a masterpiece because Tolstoy was able to
fathom, and make us see, the hidden laws which really governed this society
and made Anna's doom inevitable.

American writers do not have a fixed society to describe. The only socie-   25
ty they know is one in which nothing is fixed and in which the individual must
fight for his identity. This is a rich confusion, indeed, and it creates for the
American writer unprecedented opportunities.

That the tensions of American life, as well as the possibilities, are tremen-   26
dous is certainly not even a question. But these are dealt with in contemporary
literature mainly compulsively; that is, the book is more likely to be a symptom of our tension than an examination of it. The time has come, God knows,
for us to examine ourselves, but we can do this only if we are willing to free
ourselves of the myth of America and try to find out what is really happening
here.

Every society is really governed by hidden laws, by unspoken but pro-   27
found assumptions on the part of the people, and ours is no exception. It is
up to the American writer to find out what these laws and assumptions are.
In a society much given to smashing taboos without thereby managing to be
liberated from them, it will be no easy matter.

It is no wonder, in the meantime, that the American writer keeps running   28
off to Europe. He needs sustenance for his journey and the best models he can
find. Europe has what we do not have yet, a sense of the mysterious and
inexorable limits of life, a sense, in a word, of tragedy. And we have what they
sorely need: a new sense of life's possibilities.

In this endeavor to wed the vision of the Old World with that of the New,   29
it is the writer, not the statesman, who is our strongest arm. Though we do
not wholly believe it yet, the interior life is a real life, and the intangible dreams
of people have a tangible effect on the world.

1959

Purpose and Meaning

1. Baldwin says that being an American is a "complex fate." What does he mean by this? What about Baldwin's own life makes his situation particularly complex? (You may find some additional clues in "Autobiographical Notes.")

2. According to Baldwin, what advantages does Europe have over the United States for American writers? How did Baldwin benefit from these advantages?

3. Why does Baldwin assert that it was an "illusion that [he] hated America" (paragraph 8)? How did living in Europe make him aware of this?

Language and Style

1. In paragraph 9, Baldwin uses the image of war to describe the writer's role in society. How apt is this metaphor for writers, particularly Baldwin?

2. Baldwin begins his essay with a quote by Henry James, an American writer known for his formal, complex style. To what extent are Baldwin's sentences complex? Locate examples from paragraphs 4 and 5. What effect do these and other long sentences have on our perception of Baldwin's tone? What would be the effect of breaking down these sentences into simpler ones?

3. Another formal element of Baldwin's style is his level of diction. How do the following phrases reflect this level: "absolutely alabaster landscape" (paragraph 6); "incorrigible maverick" (paragraph 22); "inexorable limits of life" (paragraph 28)?

Strategy and Structure

1. Baldwin has divided this essay into four sections that are neither numbered nor titled. What is the organizing idea in each section? Give each section a title.

2. As in "Autobiographical Notes," in this essay Baldwin combines his personal experience with reflections about the fate and role of the American writer. Does he organize these two elements in the same way as in the former essay (that is, reflection alternating with personal information), or is his strategy different in this essay?

3. Study the opening sentence of each paragraph in the first section. What function does each opening sentence serve in making the paragraphs coherent? Do the same for other sections of the essay. How essential to the organization of the essay is it to have a topic sentence for each paragraph?

Thinking and Writing

1. Do you believe that "it is a complex fate to be an American"? Using your own cultural and social background as a base, develop an argument supporting or refuting this statement.

2. The final sentence of the essay says, "the intangible dreams of people have a tangible effect on the world." Select a person in your life who was motivated by a "dream." How did that person realize his or her dream? What was the effect of the realized dream on others?

3. Compare Baldwin's description of the struggles of the black writer as presented in "Autobiographical Notes" and "The Discovery of What it Means to Be an American" with Woolf's description of the plight of the woman writer in "Professions for Women." What main points does each writer emphasize? Are their struggles similar?

If Black English Isn't a Language, Then Tell Me, What Is?

The argument concerning the use, or the status, or the reality, of black English is rooted in American history and has absolutely nothing to do with the question the argument supposes itself to be posing. The argument has nothing to do with language itself but with the role of language. Language, incontestably, reveals the speaker. Language, also, far more dubiously, is meant to define the other—and, in this case, the other is refusing to be defined by a language that has never been able to recognize him.

People evolve a language in order to describe and thus control their circumstances or in order not to be submerged by a situation that they cannot articulate. (And if they cannot articulate it, they are submerged.) A Frenchman living in Paris speaks a subtly and crucially different language from that of the man living in Marseilles; neither sounds very much like a man living in Quebec; and they would all have great difficulty in apprehending what the man from Guadeloupe, or Martinique, is saying, to say nothing of the man from Senegal—although the "common" language of all these areas is French. But each has paid, and is paying, a different price for this "common" language, in which, as it turns out, they are not saying, and cannot be saying, the same things: They each have very different realities to articulate, or control.

What joins all languages, and all men, is the necessity to confront life, in order, not inconceivably, to outwit death: The price for this is the acceptance, and achievement, of one's temporal identity. So that, for example, though it is not taught in the schools (and this has the potential of becoming a political issue) the south of France still clings to its ancient and musical Provençal, which resists being described as a "dialect." And much of the tension in the Basque countries, and in Wales, is due to the Basque and Welsh determination not to allow their languages to be destroyed. This determination also feeds the flames in Ireland for among the many indignities the Irish have been forced to undergo at English hands is the English contempt for their language.

It goes without saying, then, that language is also a political instrument, 4 means, and proof of power. It is the most vivid and crucial key to identity. It reveals the private identity, and connects one with, or divorces one from, the larger, public, or communal identity. There have been, and are, times and places, when to speak a certain language could be dangerous, even fatal. Or, one may speak the same language, but in such a way that one's antecedents are revealed, or (one hopes) hidden. This is true in France, and is absolutely true in England: The range (and reign) of accents on that damp little island make England coherent for the English and totally incomprehensible for everyone else. To open your mouth in England is (if I may use black English) to "put your business in the street." You have confessed your parents, your youth, your school, your salary, your self-esteem, and, alas, your future.

Now, I do not know what white Americans would sound like if there had 5 never been any black people in the United States, but they would not sound the way they sound. *Jazz*, for example, is a very specific sexual term, as in *jazz me, baby*, but white people purified it into the Jazz Age. *Sock it to me*, which means, roughly, the same thing, has been adopted by Nathaniel Hawthorne's descendants with no qualms or hesitations at all, along with *let it all hang out* and *right on! Beat to his socks*, which was once the black's most total and despairing image of poverty, was transformed into a thing called the Beat Generation, which phenomenon was, largely, composed of *uptight*, middle-class white people, imitating poverty, trying to *get down*, to get *with it*, doing their *thing*, doing their despairing best to be *funky*, which we, the blacks, never dreamed of doing—we were funky, baby, like *funk* was going out of style.

Now, no one can eat his cake, and have it, too, and it is late in the day 6 to attempt to penalize black people for having created a language that permits the nation its only glimpse of reality, a language without which the nation would be even more *whipped* than it is.

I say that the present skirmish is rooted in American history, and it is. 7 Black English is the creation of the black diaspora. Blacks came to the United States chained to each other, but from different tribes. Neither could speak the other's language. If two black people, at that bitter hour of the world's history, had been able to speak to each other, the institution of chattel slavery could never have lasted as long as it did. Subsequently, the slave was given, under the eye, and the gun, of his master, Congo Square, and the Bible—or, in other words, and under those conditions, the slave began the formation of the black church, and it is within this unprecedented tabernacle that black English began to be formed. This was not, merely, as in the European example, the adoption of a foreign tongue, but an alchemy that transformed ancient elements into a new language: *A language comes into existence by means of brutal necessity, and the rules of the language are dictated by what the language must convey.*

There was a moment, in time, and in this place, when my brother, or 8 my mother, or my father, or my sister, had to convey to me, for example, the danger in which I was standing from the white man standing just behind me, and to convey this with a speed and in a language, that the white man could not possibly understand, and that, indeed, he cannot understand, until today. He cannot afford to understand it. This understanding would reveal to him too much about himself and smash that mirror before which he has been frozen for so long.

Now, if this passion, this skill, this (to quote Toni Morrison) "sheer 9 intelligence," this incredible music, the mighty achievement of having brought a people utterly unknown to, or despised by "history"—to have brought this people to their present, troubled, troubling, and unassailable and unanswerable place—if this absolutely unprecedented journey does not indicate that black English is a language, I am curious to know what definition of languages is to be trusted.

A people at the center of the western world, and in the midst of so hostile 10 a population, has not endured and transcended by means of what is patronizingly called a "dialect." We, the blacks, are in trouble, certainly, but we are not inarticulate because we are not compelled to defend a morality that we know to be a lie.

The brutal truth is that the bulk of the white people in America never 11 had any interest in educating black people, except as this could serve white purposes. It is not the black child's language that is despised. It is his experience. A child cannot be taught by anyone who despises him, and a child cannot afford to be fooled. A child cannot be taught by anyone whose demand, essentially, is that the child repudiate his experience, and all that gives him sustenance, and enter a limbo in which he will no longer be black, and in which he knows that he can never become white. Black people have lost too many black children that way.

And, after all, finally, in a country with standards so untrustworthy, a 12 country that makes heroes of so many criminal mediocrities, a country unable to face why so many of the nonwhite are in prison, or on the needle, or standing, futureless, in the streets—it may very well be that both the child, and his elder, have concluded that they have nothing whatever to learn from the people of a country that has managed to learn so little.

1979

Purpose and Meaning

1. According to Baldwin, how should a language be defined?

2. Where in essay does Baldwin "prove" that Black English is a language? In your own words, restate the gist of his argument.

3. In paragraph 4, Baldwin says that "language is also a political instrument." What does this mean? How does he support this contention?

Language and Style

1. In paragraph 1, Baldwin refers to black Americans as "the other." In paragraph 5, Baldwin refers to white Americans as "Nathaniel Hawthorne's descendants." What is he suggesting in these descriptions?

2. Do the references Baldwin makes in paragraphs 3 to 5 concerning the importance of language to other societal groups strengthen his authority as a writer on the subject? Is there anything in Baldwin's tone that gives him his authority?

3. Baldwin states that "A language comes into existence by means of brutal necessity" (paragraph 7). Where does Baldwin refer to the brutality of America toward blacks?

4. Study paragraph 9, which is a single sentence. How many ideas does Baldwin present? How does he join these ideas together? How does the structure of this paragraph contribute to Baldwin's assertive voice?

Strategy and Structure

1. Observe the way Baldwin begins his paragraphs. What devices does he use to keep his argument moving? How do they serve in connecting one paragraph to the next?

2. In paragraph 5, approximately halfway through the essay, Baldwin presents several terms from Black English that have influenced standard English. How do his choice of examples and their placement contribute to the structure of the essay?

3. How does Baldwin culminate his argument in the concluding paragraph? What is the intended emotional effect on the audience? To leave them frustrated? Angry? Motivated? What is Baldwin suggesting about the future of Black English? What is Baldwin suggesting about the future of America?

Thinking and Writing

1. Examine your own speech. Write down any words or expressions you regularly use that originate from Black English. Write an essay explaining what function they serve in your vocabulary.

2. Develop an essay in which you argue for or against the proposition that every English speaking person should have a right to his or her own dialect.

3. Do you use a different "language" in different situations? For example, how does your vocabulary differ when you speak with your friends, teachers, parents, employers, and so on? Select two groups with whom you regularly come into contact, and write an essay comparing and contrasting your language choices when communicating with them.

4. Compare Baldwin's vision of the modern world and the artist's role in it with that of George Orwell.

RUSSELL BAKER

Russell Wayne Baker was born in Loudon County, Virginia, in 1925 into a large and extended family. He was, as he describes it, "well equipped with uncles"—twenty of them to be exact—along with a dozen aunts. His huge family prepared him to be a writer, "for it gives you a chance to learn a lot about humanity from close-up observation." As journalist, columnist, and most recently, memoir writer, Baker's prescient and amusing assessments of humanity have established him as the preeminent humorist of our time.

Baker's boyhood in the mountains of Virginia and then in the impoverished neighborhoods of northern New Jersey during the Great Depression is chronicled in his Pulitzer Prize–winning *Growing Up* (1982). After graduating from The Johns Hopkins University and serving in the Navy, he was hired by the *Baltimore Sun* as White House correspondent and subsequently, in 1954, by *The New York Times*. His funny, exciting, and spectacular career in journalism—from childhood newsboy to famed "Observer" columnist for the *Times* since 1962—is recorded in *The Good Times* (1989). In 1979, Baker won the George Polk Award for commentary and his first Pulitzer Prize for distinguished commentary. He lives today with his wife, Mimi, in Leesburg, Virginia.

Surrounded by an army of grown-ups in childhood, Baker learned to watch and listen, especially to the reminiscences and anecdotes of his relatives, many of whom would become the stuff of his articles and autobiographies. Yet the central figure, as we see in the chapter from *Growing Up* that appears here, was Baker's mother, Betty. "My mother," he writes in *The Good Times*, "dead now to this world but roaming free in my mind, wakes me some mornings before daybreak. 'If it's one thing I can't stand, it's a quitter.' I have heard her say that all my life." The times they experienced together are the impetus for his memoirs.

Just as *Growing Up* captured not only his life but the life of the Great Depression, Baker's columns reveal a bemused, irreverent writer doing battle with history and people. Through numerous collections—*All Things Considered* (1965), *So This Is Depravity* (1980), and *The Rescue of Miss Yaskell and Other Pipe Dreams* (1983), and others—Baker offers zany burlesques, brilliant parodies, gentle satires, and devastating critiques of his culture and his times. He takes on sacred cows, as in his timely assessment of patriotism in "The Flag." Or, as in "Let Them Play Guitars," he spoofs physical and intellectual culture. The critic Malcolm Cowley captured the essence of Baker's humor when he declared, "If it is possible to imagine such a thing, Russell Baker is a sunny Swift."

Russell Baker, like Mark Twain and James Thurber, is both likable and disarmingly funny. He captures the best and worst of times and of humanity. From gentle caricature to grotesque imaginings, he holds the humorist's mirror up to nature, a witty daredevil who would have us laugh at but never tolerate civilization's imperfections.

The Flag

At various times when young, I was prepared to crack skulls, kill and   1
die for Old Glory. I never wholly agreed with the LOVE IT OR LEAVE IT bumper
stickers, which held that everybody who didn't love the flag ought to be thrown
out of the country, but I wouldn't have minded seeing them beaten up. In fact,
I saw a man come very close to being beaten up at a baseball park one day
because he didn't stand when they raised the flag in the opening ceremonies,
and I joined the mob screaming for him to get to his feet like an American if
he didn't want lumps all over his noodle. He stood up, all right. I was then
thirteen and a Boy Scout, and I knew you never let the flag touch the ground,
or threw it out with the trash when it got dirty (you burned it), or put up with
disrespect for it at the baseball park.

At eighteen, I longed to die for it. When World War II ended in 1945 before   2
I could reach the combat zone, I moped for months about being deprived of
the chance to go down in flames under the guns of a Mitsubishi Zero. There
was never much doubt that I would go down in flames if given the opportunity,
for my competence as a pilot was such that I could barely remember to lower
the plane's landing gear before trying to set it down on a runway.

I had even visualized my death. It was splendid. Dead, I would be stand-   3
ing perhaps 4,000 feet up in the sky. (Everybody knew that heroes floated in
those days.) Erect and dashing, surrounded by beautiful cumulus clouds, I would
look just as good as ever, except for being slightly transparent. And I would
smile, devil-may-care, at the camera—oh, there would be cameras there—and
the American flag would unfurl behind me across 500 miles of glorious American
sky, and back behind the cumulus clouds the Marine Band would be playing
"The Stars and Stripes Forever," but not too fast.

Then I would look down at June Allyson and the kids, who had a gold   4
star in the window and brave smiles shining through their tears, and I would
given them a salute and one of those brave, wistful Errol Flynn grins, then turn
and mount to Paradise, becoming more transparent with each step so the
audience could get a great view of the flag waving over the heavenly pastures.

Okay, so it owes a lot to Louis B. Mayer in his rococo period. I couldn't   5
help that. At eighteen, a man's imagination is too busy with sex to have much
energy left for fancy embellishments of patriotic ecstasy. In the words of a
popular song of the period, there was a star-spangled banner waving somewhere
in The Great Beyond, and only Uncle Sam's brave heroes got to go there. I was
ready to make the trip.

All this was a long time ago, and, asinine though it now may seem, I con-   6
fess it here to illustrate the singularly masculine pleasures to be enjoyed in devoted
service to the Stars and Stripes. Not long ago I felt a twinge of the old fire when
I saw an unkempt lout on a ferryboat with a flag sewed in the crotch of his
jeans. Something in me wanted to throw him overboard, but I didn't since he
was a big muscular devil and the flag had already suffered so many worse indignities anyhow, having been pinned in politicians' lapels, pasted on cars to
promote gasoline sales and used to sanctify the professional sports industry as
the soul of patriotism even while the team owners were instructing their athletes
in how to dodge the draft.

For a moment, though, I felt some of the old masculine excitement kicked   7
up by the flag in the adrenal glands. It's a man's flag, all right. No doubt about
that. Oh, it may be a scoundrel's flag, too, and a drummer's flag, and a fraud's
flag, and a thief's flag. But first and foremost, it is a man's flag.

Except for decorating purposes—it looks marvelous on old New England   8
houses—I cannot see much in it to appeal to women. Its pleasures, in fact, seem
so exclusively masculine and its sanctity so unassailable by feminist iconoclasts
that it may prove to be America's only enduring, uncrushable male sex symbol.

Observe that in my patriotic death fantasy, the starring role is not June   9
Allyson's, but mine. As defender of the flag, I am able to leave a humdrum
job, put June and the kids with all their humdrum problems behind me, travel
the world with a great bunch of guys, do exciting things with powerful flying
machines, and, fetchingly uniformed, strut exotic saloons on my nights off.

In the end, I walk off with all the glory and the big scene.   10

And what does June get? Poor June. She gets to sit home with the kids   11
the rest of her life dusting my photograph and trying to pay the bills, with
occasional days off to visit the grave.

No wonder the male pulse pounds with pleasure when the Stars and Stripes   12
comes fluttering down the avenue with the band smashing out those great noises.
Where was Mr. Teddy Roosevelt when Teddy was carrying it up San Juan Hill?
What was Mrs. Lincoln doing when Abe was holding it aloft for the Union?
What was Martha up to while George Washington was carrying it across the
Delaware? Nothing, you may be sure, that was one-tenth as absorbing as what
their husbands were doing.

Consider some of the typical masculine activities associated with Old   13
Glory: Dressing up in medals. Whipping cowards, slackers and traitors within
an inch of their miserable lives. Conquering Mount Suribachi. Walking on the
moon. Rescuing the wagon train. Being surrounded by the whole German Army
and being asked to surrender and saying, "You can tell Schicklgruber my answer
is 'Nuts.' " In brief, having a wonderful time. With the boys.

Yes, surely the American flag is the ultimate male sex symbol. Men flaunt   14
it, wave it, punch noses for it, strut with it, fight for it, kill for it, die for it.

And women—? Well, when do you see a woman with the flag? Most   15
commonly when she is wearing black and has just received it, neatly folded,

from coffin of husband or son. Later, she may wear it to march in the Veterans Day parade, widows' division.

Male pleasures and woman's sorrow—it sounds like the old definition of 16 sex. Yet these are the immemorial connotations of the flag, and women, having shed the whalebone girdle and stamped out the stag bar, nevertheless accept it, ostensibly at least, with the same emotional devotion that men accord it.

There are good reasons, of course, why they may be reluctant to pursue 17 logic to its final step and say, "To hell with the flag, too." In the first place, it would almost certainly do them no good. Men hold all the political trumps in this matter. When little girls first toddle off to school, does anyone tell them the facts of life when they stand to salute the flag? Does anyone say, "You are now saluting the proud standard of the greatest men's club on earth?" You bet your chewing gum nobody tells them that. If anyone did, there would be a joint session of Congress presided over by the President of the United States to investigate the entire school system of the United States of America.

What little girls have drilled into them is that the flag stands for one nation 18 indivisible, with liberty and justice for all. A few years ago, the men of the Congress, responding to pressure from the American Legion (all men) and parsons (mostly all men), all of whom sensed perhaps that women were not as gullible as they used to be, revised the Pledge of Allegiance with words intimating that it would be ungodly not to respect the flag. The "one nation indivisible" became "one nation *under God*, indivisible," and another loophole for skeptics was sealed off. The women's movement may be brave, but it will not go far taking on national indivisibility, liberty, justice and God, all in one fight. If they tried it, a lot of us men would feel perfectly justified in raising lumps on their lovely noodles.

Philosophically speaking, the masculinity of the American flag is entirely appro- 19 priate. America, after all, is not a motherland—many places still are—but a fatherland, which is to say a vast nation-state of disparate people scattered over great distances, but held together by a belligerent,loyalty-to-the-death devotion to some highly abstract political ideas. Since these ideas are too complex to be easily grasped, statesmen have given us the flag and told us it sums up all these noble ideas that make us a country.

Fatherland being an aggressive kind of state, the ideas it embodies must 20 be defended, protected and propagated, often in blood. Since the flag is understood to represent these ideas, in a kind of tricolor shorthand, we emote, fight, bleed and rejoice in the name of the flag.

Before fatherland there was something that might be called motherland. 21 It still exists here and there. In the fifties, when Washington was looking for undiscovered Asiatic terrain to save from un-American ideologies, somebody stumbled into an area called Laos, a place so remote from American consciousness that few had ever heard its name pronounced. (For the longest time, Lyndon Johnson, then Democratic leader of the Senate, referred to it as "Low Ass.")

Federal inspectors sent to Laos returned with astounding information. Most of the people living there were utterly unaware that they were living in a country. Almost none of them knew the country they were living in was called Laos. All they knew was that they lived where they had been born and where their ancestors were buried.

What Washington had discovered, of course, was an old-fashioned motherland, a society where people's loyalties ran to the place of their birth. It was a Pentagon nightmare. Here were these people, perfectly happy with their home turf and their ancestors' graves, and they had to be put into shape to die for their country, and they didn't even know they had a country to die for. They didn't even have a flag to die for. And yet, they were content!

The point is that a country is only an idea and a fairly modern one at that. Life would still be going on if nobody had ever thought of it, and would probably be a good deal more restful. No flags. Not much in the way of armies. No sharing of exciting group emotions with millions of other people ready to do or die for national honor. And so forth. Very restful, and possibly very primitive, and almost surely very nasty on occasion, although possibly not as nasty as occasions often become when countries disagree.

I hear my colleagues in masculinity protesting, "What? No country? No flag? But there would be nothing noble to defend, to fight for, to die for, in the meantime having a hell of a good time doing all those fun male things in the name of!"

Women may protest, too. I imagine some feminists may object to the suggestion that fatherland's need for prideful, warlike and aggressive citizens to keep the flag flying leaves women pretty much out of things. Those who hold that sexual roles are a simple matter of social conditioning may contend that the flag can offer the same rollicking pleasures to both sexes once baby girls are trained as thoroughly as baby boys in being prideful, warlike and aggressive.

I think there may be something in this, having seen those harridans who gather outside freshly desegregated schools to wave the American flag and terrify children. The question is whether women really want to start conditioning girl babies for this hitherto largely masculine sort of behavior, or spend their energies trying to decondition it out of the American man.

In any case, I have no quarrel with these women. Living in a fatherland, they have tough problems, and if they want to join the boys in the flag sports, it's okay with me. The only thing is, if they are going to get a chance, too, to go up to Paradise with the Marine Band playing "The Stars and Stripes Forever" back behind the cumulus clouds, I don't want to be stuck with the role of sitting home dusting their photographs the rest of my life after the big scene is ended.

1980

Purpose and Meaning

1. Who and what is Baker satirizing in this essay? At what point does it become clear that "The Flag" is a satire?

2. Baker says that the flag is "the ultimate male sex symbol" (paragraph 14). What does the flag traditionally symbolize? What clue does Baker's description of the flag provide about an understanding of the theme of the essay?

3. What does Baker accomplish with humor in this essay that he could not otherwise achieve?

Language and Style

1. In paragraph 17, Baker states, "You bet your chewing gum nobody tells them that" and "there would be a joint session of Congress presided over by the President of the United States to investigate the entire school system of the United States of America." Whose tone and diction is Baker mimicking? Where else in the essay does he use a comparable tone and diction?

2. How does the repetition of the word *flag* in paragraph 7 contribute to the tone of the essay as a whole? What form of public speech is Baker imitating in this paragraph?

3. In the references to Laos in paragraphs 21 and 22, how does Baker's tone satirize a jingoist attitude? What is the effect of using diction such as "home turf" and "had to be put into shape" in this context?

4. In what way is Baker's definition of a "fatherland" in paragraph 19 to be taken seriously? In what respect should we take this section of the essay as well as the essay as a whole seriously? What are the feminist implications of the language Baker uses throughout the essay?

Strategy and Structure

1. How does the end of the first section of the essay contrast with the beginning of the second? What function does the break after paragraph 18 serve? How does the tone of the essay change in section two? What major issue is addressed in the second half?

2. How does Baker create an effective parody of a movie in paragraphs 3 through 5? What type of movie does the description suggest?

3. Why is paragraph 23 composed almost entirely of fragments? What is the effect of placing this paragraph between the paragraphs that precede and follow it?

Thinking and Writing

1. Write a humorous letter, using Baker's style, to the editor of a newspaper, either supporting or condemning Baker's point of view. Use examples, illustrations, and anecdotes to defend your position.

2. Select a controversial issue in the news, and defend the point of view you *disagree* with. Write your argument from the opposing viewpoint, using tone and diction that mock your own thesis. For example, if you are against hunting, defend

hunting. If you are against the nuclear arms race, defend the arms race. Be sure to include elements that make it clear you are using a satiric voice.

3. Do you have a private, grandiose fantasy—for example, winning an Olympic medal, winning the Nobel Prize, being the first human being on Mars? Write a narrative that describes your feat, the public's response to it, and your corresponding response to the public's adulation.

Growing Up

I began working in journalism when I was eight years old. It was my   1
mother's idea. She wanted me to "make something" of myself and, after a levelheaded appraisal of my strengths, decided I had better start young if I was to have any chance of keeping up with the competition.

The flaw in my character which she had already spotted was lack of   2
"gumption." My idea of a perfect afternoon was lying in front of the radio rereading my favorite Big Little Book, *Dick Tracy Meets Stooge Viller.* My mother despised inactivity. Seeing me having a good time in repose, she was powerless to hide her disgust. "You've got no more gumption than a bump on a log," she said. "Get out in the kitchen and help Doris do those dirty dishes."

My sister Doris, though two years younger than I, had enough gumption   3
for a dozen people. She positively enjoyed washing dishes, making beds, and cleaning the house. When she was only seven she could carry a piece of short-weighted cheese back to the A&P, threaten the manager with legal action, and come back triumphantly with the full quarter-pound we'd paid for and a few ounces extra thrown in for forgiveness. Doris could have made something of herself if she hadn't been a girl. Because of this defect, however, the best she could hope for was a career as a nurse or schoolteacher, the only work that capable females were considered up to in those days.

This must have saddened my mother, this twist of fate that had allocated   4
all the gumption to the daughter and left her with a son who was content with Dick Tracy and Stooge Viller. If disappointed, though, she wasted no energy on self-pity. She would make me make something of myself whether I wanted to or not. "The Lord helps those who help themselves," she said. That was the way her mind worked.

She was realistic about the difficulty. Having sized up the material the   5
Lord had given her to mold, she didn't overestimate what she could do with it. She didn't insist that I grow up to be President of the United States.

Fifty years ago parents still asked boys if they wanted to grow up to be   6
President, and asked it not jokingly but seriously. Many parents who were hardly
more than paupers still believed their sons could do it. Abraham Lincoln had
done it. We were only sixty-five years from Lincoln. Many a grandfather who
walked among us could remember Lincoln's time. Men of grandfatherly age
were the worst for asking if you wanted to grow up to be President. A surprising number of little boys said yes and meant it.

I was asked many times myself. No, I would say, I didn't want to grow   7
up to be President. My mother was present during one of these interrogations.
An elderly uncle, having posed the usual question and exposed my lack of interest
in the Presidency, asked, "Well, what *do* you want to be when you grow up?"

I loved to pick through trash piles and collect empty bottles, tin cans with   8
pretty labels, and discarded magazines. The most desirable job on earth sprang
instantly to mind. "I want to be a garbage man," I said.

My uncle smiled, but my mother had seen the first distressing evidence   9
of a bump budding on a log. "Have a little gumption, Russell," she said. Her
calling me Russell was a signal of unhappiness. When she approved of me I
was always "Buddy."

When I turned eight years old she decided that the job of starting me on   10
the road toward making something of myself could no longer be safely delayed.
"Buddy," she said one day, "I want you to come home right after school this
afternoon. Somebody's coming and I want you to meet him."

When I burst in that afternoon she was in conference in the parlor with   11
an executive of the Curtis Publishing Company. She introduced me. He bent
low from the waist and shook my hand. Was it true as my mother had told
him, he asked, that I longed for the opportunity to conquer the world of business?

My mother replied that I was blessed with a rare determination to make   12
something of myself.

"That's right," I whispered.   13

"But have you got the grit, the character, the never-say-quit spirit it takes   14
to succeed in business?"

My mother said I certainly did.   15

"That's right," I said.   16

He eyed me silently for a long pause, as though weighing whether I could   17
be trusted to keep his confidence, then spoke man-to-man. Before taking a crucial
step, he said, he wanted to advise me that working for the Curtis Publishing
Company placed enormous responsibility on a young man. It was one of the
great companies of America. Perhaps the greatest publishing house in the world.
I had heard, no doubt, of the *Saturday Evening Post?*

Heard of it? My mother said that everyone in our house had heard of   18
the *Saturday Post* and that I, in fact, read it with religious devotion.

Then doubtless, he said, we were also familiar with those two monthly   19
pillars of the magazine world, the *Ladies Home Journal* and the *Country
Gentleman.*

Indeed we were familiar with them, said my mother.   20

Representing the *Saturday Evening Post* was one of the weightiest honors   21
that could be bestowed in the world of business, he said. He was personally
proud of being a part of that great corporation.

My mother said he had every right to be.   22

Again he studied me as though debating whether I was worthy of a   23
knighthood. Finally: "Are you trustworthy?"

My mother said I was the soul of honesty.   24

"That's right," I said.   25

The caller smiled for the first time. He told me I was a lucky young man.   26
He admired my spunk. Too many young men thought life was all play. Those
young men would not go far in this world. Only a young man willing to work
and save and keep his face washed and his hair neatly combed could hope to
come out on top in a world such as ours. Did I truly and sincerely believe that
I was such a young man?

"He certainly does," said my mother.   27

"That's right," I said.   28

He said he had been so impressed by what he had seen of me that he was   29
going to make me a representative of the Curtis Publishing Company. On the
following Tuesday, he said, thirty freshly printed copies of the *Saturday Evening
Post* would be delivered at our door. I would place these magazines, still damp
with the ink of the presses, in a handsome canvas bag, sling it over my shoulder,
and set forth through the streets to bring the best in journalism, fiction, and
cartoons to the American public.

He had brought the canvas bag with him. He presented it with reverence   30
fit for a chasuble. He showed me how to drape the sling over my left shoulder
and across the chest so that the pouch lay easily accessible to my right hand,
allowing the best in journalism, fiction, and cartoons to be swiftly extracted
and sold to a citizenry whose happiness and security depended upon us soldiers
of the free press.

The following Tuesday I raced home from school, put the canvas bag   31
over my shoulder, dumped the magazines in, and, tilting to the left to balance
their weight on my right hip, embarked on the highway of journalism.

We lived in Belleville, New Jersey, a commuter town at the northern fringe   32
of Newark. It was 1932, the bleakest year of the Depression. My father had
died two years before, leaving us with a few pieces of Sears, Roebuck furniture
and not much else, and my mother had taken Doris and me to live with one
of her younger brothers. This was my Uncle Allen. Uncle Allen had made
something of himself by 1932. As salesman for a soft-drink bottler in Newark,
he had an income of $30 a week; wore pearl-gray spats, detachable collars, and
a three-piece suit; was happily married; and took in threadbare relatives.

With my load of magazines I headed toward Belleville Avenue. That's   33
where the people were. There were two filling stations at the intersection with
Union Avenue, as well as an A&P, a fruit stand, a bakery, a barber shop,

Zuccarelli's drugstore, and a diner shaped like a railroad car. For several hours I made myself highly visible, shifting position now and then from corner to corner, from shop window to shop window, to make sure everyone could see the heavy black lettering on the canvas bag that said THE SATURDAY EVENING POST. When the angle of the light indicated it was suppertime, I walked back to the house.

"How many did you sell, Buddy?" my mother asked. 34

"None." 35

"Where did you go?" 36

"The corner of Belleville and Union Avenues." 37

"What did you do?" 38

"Stood on the corner waiting for somebody to buy a *Saturday Evening Post.*" 39

"You just stood there?" 40

"Didn't sell a single one." 41

"For God's sake, Russell!" 42

Uncle Allen intervened. "I've been thinking about it for some time," he said, "and I've about decided to take the *Post* regularly. Put me down as a regular customer." I handed him a magazine and he paid me a nickel. It was the first nickel I earned. 43

Afterwards my mother instructed me in salesmanship. I would have to ring doorbells, address adults with charming self-confidence, and break down resistance with a sales talk pointing out that no one, no matter how poor, could afford to be without the *Saturday Evening Post* in the home. 44

I told my mother I'd changed my mind about wanting to succeed in the magazine business. 45

"If you think I'm going to raise a good-for-nothing," she replied, "you've got another thing coming." She told me to hit the streets with the canvas bag and start ringing doorbells the instant school was out next day. When I objected that I didn't feel any aptitude for salesmanship, she asked how I'd like to lend her my leather belt so she could whack some sense into me, I bowed to superior will and entered journalism with a heavy heart. 46

My mother and I had fought this battle almost as long as I could remember. It probably started even before memory began, when I was a country child in northern Virginia and my mother, dissatisfied with my father's plain workman's life, determined that I would not grow up like him and his people, with calluses on their hands, overalls on their backs, and fourth-grade educations in their heads. She had fancier ideas of life's possibilities. Introducing me to the *Saturday Evening Post,* she was trying to wean me as early as possible from my father's world where men left with their lunch pails at sunup, worked with their hands until the grime ate into the pores, and died with a few sticks of mail-order furniture as their legacy. In my mother's vision of the better life there were desks and white collars, well-pressed suits, evenings of reading and lively talk, and perhaps—if a man were very, very lucky and hit the jackpot, really made 47 something important of himself—perhaps there might be a fantastic salary of $5,000 a year to support a big house and a Buick with a rumble seat and a vacation in Atlantic City.

And so I set forth with my sack of magazines. I was afraid of the dogs that snarled behind the doors of potential buyers. I was timid about ringing the doorbells of strangers, relieved when no one came to the door, and scared when someone did. Despite my mother's instructions, I could not deliver an engaging sales pitch. When a door opened I simply asked, "Want to buy a *Saturday Evening Post*?" In Belleville few persons did. It was a town of 30,000 people, and most weeks I rang a fair majority of its doorbells. But I rarely sold my thirty copies. Some weeks I canvassed the entire town for six days and still had four or five unsold magazines on Monday evening; then I dreaded the coming of Tuesday morning, when a batch of thirty fresh *Saturday Evening Posts* was due at the front door.

"Better get out there and sell the rest of those magazines tonight," my mother would say.

I usually posted myself then at a busy intersection where a traffic light controlled commuter flow from Newark. When the light turned red I stood on the curb and shouted my sales pitch at the motorists.

"Want to buy a *Saturday Evening Post*?"

One rainy night when car windows were sealed against me I came back soaked and with not a single sale to report. My mother beckoned to Doris.

"Go back down there with Buddy and show him how to sell these magazines," she said.

Brimming with zest, Doris, who was then seven years old, returned with me to the corner. She took a magazine from the bag, and when the light turned red she strode to the nearest car and banged her small fist against the closed window. The driver, probably startled at what he took to be a midget assaulting his car, lowered the window to stare, and Doris thrust a *Saturday Evening Post* at him.

"You need this magazine," she piped, "and it only costs a nickel."

Her salesmanship was irresistible. Before the light changed half a dozen times she disposed of the entire batch. I didn't feel humiliated. To the contrary, I was so happy I decided to give her a treat. Leading her to the vegetable store on Belleville Avenue, I bought three apples, which cost a nickel, and gave her one.

"You shouldn't waste money," she said.

"Eat your apple." I bit into mine.

"You shouldn't eat before supper," she said. "It'll spoil your appetite."

Back at the house that evening, she dutifully reported me for wasting a nickel. Instead of a scolding, I was rewarded with a pat on the back for having the good sense to buy fruit instead of candy. My mother reached into her bottomless supply of maxims and told Doris, "An apple a day, keeps the doctor away."

By the time I was ten I had learned all my mother's maxims by heart.

Asking to stay up past normal bedtime, I knew that a refusal would be explained with, "Early to bed and early to rise, makes a man healthy, wealthy, and wise." If I whimpered about having to get up early in the morning, I could depend on her to say, "The early bird gets the worm."

The one I most despised was, "If at first you don't succeed, try, try again." 62 This was the battle cry with which she constantly sent me back into the hopeless struggle whenever I moaned that I had rung every doorbell in town and knew there wasn't a single potential buyer left in Belleville that week. After listening to my explanation, she handed me the canvas bag and said, "If at first you don't succeed. . ."

Three years in that job, which I would gladly have quit after the first day 63 except for her insistence, produced at least one valuable result. My mother finally concluded that I would never make something of myself by pursuing a life in business and started considering careers that demanded less competitive zeal.

One evening when I was eleven I brought home a short "composition" 64 on my summer vacation which the teacher had graded with an A. Reading it with her own schoolteacher's eye, my mother agreed that it was top-drawer seventh grade prose and complimented me. Nothing more was said about it immediately, but a new idea had taken life in her mind. Halfway through supper she suddenly interrupted the conversation.

"Buddy," she said, "maybe you could be a writer." 65

I clasped the idea to my heart. I had never met a writer, had shown no 66 previous urge to write, and hadn't a notion how to become a writer, but I loved stories and thought that making up stories must surely be almost as much fun as reading them. Best of all, though, and what really gladdened my heart, was the ease of the writer's life. Writers did not have to trudge through the town peddling from canvas bags, defending themselves against angry dogs, being rejected by surly strangers. Writers did not have to ring doorbells. So far as I could make out, what writers did couldn't even be classified as work.

I was enchanted. Writers didn't have to have any gumption at all. I did 67 not dare tell anybody for fear of being laughed at in the schoolyard, but secretly I decided that what I'd like to be when I grew up was a writer.

1982

Purpose and Meaning

1. How does the first paragraph alert us to Baker's general attitude and personality as a child? How does it set the tone for the rest of the essay?

2. What perceptions about childhood and growing up does Baker convey in this selection?

3. What does the attitude of Baker's mother toward her son reveal about the historical context of the essay? In what way would a contemporary parent treat his or her child differently if confronted with the same issues?

Language and Style

1. What terms and descriptions does Baker use in the essay that indicate that the year is 1932? What attitudes does he describe that appear dated? What sort of mood do these references create? Quaint? Idealistic? Naive? Bleak? Something else?

2. How does the tone of the essay indicate that Baker is looking back at the events after a long period of time?

3. In paragraph 23, Baker says the man from Curtis Publishing studied him "as though debating whether I was worthy . . ." and in paragraph 30, presented him with a canvas bag "with reverence fit for a chasuble." What makes these descriptions humorous? What other references are there to the *Saturday Evening Post* that create a comic image of the publishing representative?

Strategy and Structure

1. What is the effect, in paragraph 47, of describing serious matters? What is Baker's intent in including this portrait of his family? How seriously are we to take the depiction of his parents' struggles?

2. In paragraphs 11 through 27, what makes Baker's dialogue funny? How authentic does the dialogue sound? Where else does Baker use dialogue to humorous effect?

3. What is the effect of using the word *gumption* in the final paragraph? How does it contribute to the essay's sense of closure? What does the conclusion reveal about Baker's success? How do the results of Baker's early work selling newspapers make the title of the essay ironic?

Thinking and Writing

1. Select a word that describes an attitude, quality, or state of being, such as *ambition, fortitude,* or *determination.* Write a humorous, extended definition of the word using examples and illustrations.

2. Choose the same word as in the previous writing assignment, but use an anecdote from your own life that illustrates the word you are defining.

3. For a research project, select either a word that is no longer in common usage (perhaps a word used by your parents or grandparents), and trace its history. When was the word first used in the context you are describing? What function did the word serve? What was its meaning? When and why did it leave common usage? What word or words have replaced it?

4. It is common for parents to teach their children lessons. Did you ever fail to learn a lesson your parents tried to teach you? Describe a lesson you were supposed to learn, discuss why you refused to learn it, and justify either your parents' or your own perspective on the lesson.

Let Them Play Guitars

The literary world is stunned by recent evidence that Henry James used anabolic steroids. Not since the disclosure of Shoeless Joe Jackson's role in "fixing" the 1919 World Series has there been such an emotional blow to American youth.

Typical of those whose little hearts have been broken was 8-year-old Felix Crompetter. The other day in Columbus, Ohio, with tears running down his cheeks, he called a local TV station to report that he was standing before his treasured postcard reproduction of John Singer Sargent's portrait of Henry James and would sob "Say it ain't so, Henry" if they sent a camera crew around.

Suspecting Felix was trying to work his way up to an appearance with Geraldo Rivera, they declined. As the news director commented, "Television treasures its precious heritage from Henry James too much to let cunning little kids exploit the Master for their own gain."

Unfortunately for little Felix and all American kids who want just one great chemical-free American writer to look up to, it looks all too true about Henry James.

A computer analysis by researchers in organic writing shows that James's immense paragraphs, rippling with immense sentences that bulge with massive "which" clauses, could not have been written without steroids.

His earlier novels like "Roderick Hudson" and "The American" show only slight traces of steroidally created bulk, as though James at first took the chemical only once or twice, probably on a dare from some unscrupulous writing acquaintance he had met in London.

Following "Portrait of a Lady," however, the rapidly expanding weight and mass of James's prose leaves no doubt that he was taking heavier and heavier doses.

The authors of the James research paper, writing in the Journal of the American Medical Scandals Association, state that "the Henry James who wrote 'The Ambassadors' was so packed with steroids he could have held his own as a defensive lineman in the National Football League."

The researchers plan next to turn their attention to Theodore Dreiser. The mastodonic bulk of Dreiser's novels has baffled literary scientists for four generations.

How could the man bear the incredibly dreary toll of composing his books, each as ponderous as the Great Pyramid of Cheops? How could he stand writing sentence after sentence after sentence, not one of which could have been the slightest pleasure to compose? So asked the great critic, H. L. Mencken.

Can the answer be anabolic steroids? If so, what about Edith Wharton? Admittedly, her work was not as massive as Dreiser's and James's. Still, she was a suspiciously good writer, and there is little evidence of alcoholism to explain it.

Recent medico-literary studies now at the bookstore suggest that American writing rests very heavily on alcohol abuse. These books have left little doubt that we owe much of the glory of American literature to a bunch of drunks.

Those cited as probable or certain alcoholics in recent studies include Edgar Allan Poe, Herman Melville, Jack London and the usual Paris suspects led by Ernest Hemingway and F. Scott Fitzgerald.

As literary science labors to expand the list, good and clean-living people have naturally become alarmed about the effect on children who want to grow up and be writers.

The evidence is so overwhelming, how could bright, sensible, observant American children fail to see that to become great American writers they must take to whisky by the gallon?

This is why Henry James was so important. Literary scientists had nailed most of America's literary biggies as boozers, but not Henry James.

Nathaniel Hawthorne had given them trouble, too, but they had finally got a handle on Hawthorne. So maybe Hawthorne wasn't a drunk, but what about this shred of evidence that he might have been incestuous? It might be only a shred, but when it comes to incest, a shred is reason enough for clean-cut boys and girls to look elsewhere for role models.

And they could always look to Henry James. Not a breath of alcohol on him. Not the slightest suspicion of illegal substance use. Despite all those stories in which he empathized with little girls, the most zealous Freudians were strapped for hints that he went in for eerie sexual practices.

Henry James was the last great American writer an 8-year-old could look up to. And now—anabolic steroids. What next? Can we doubt periodic unannounced urine tests for every American kid who ever says, "I'd like to be a writer"?

1989

Purpose and Meaning

1. What type of news reporting is Baker satirizing? What comment is Baker making about this form of reporting? How does the reference to Geraldo Rivera reflect Baker's satiric purpose?

2. Baker makes several historical allusions in the essay. These include the title of the essay as well as the reference to Joe Jackson and to many of America's most famous writers and their works. Look up some of these allusions and assess whether your knowledge of them affects your appreciation of the essay.

3. This essay was written for the OP-ED section of *The New York Times*. What assumptions does Baker make about his audience? How do you know?

Language and Style

1. What is the common tone in these phrases: "The literary world is stunned" (paragraph 1); "an emotional blow to American youth" (paragraph 1); "unscrupulous writing acquaintance" (paragraph 6); "It looks all too true about Henry James" (paragraph 4) and "suspiciously good writer" (paragraph 11)? How do they reflect the overall tone of the essay? What tone is Baker satirizing?

2. In paragraphs 5 through 8, Baker makes some presumptions about James's writing. How scientifically sound are these presumptions? What attitude do they suggest Baker is assuming toward his subject?

3. In paragraph 16, the author states, "Literary scientists had nailed most of America's literary biggies as boozers, but not Henry James." Why has Baker "lowered" his diction in this sentence? What does it indicate about the narrator's attitude toward the literary "greats?"

Strategy and Structure

1. Baker cites scientific research in paragraphs 5, 8, 9, and 12 to support his case. How appropriately or inappropriately is this evidence used? How is the evidence intended to lend authority to his argument? In what type of journalism does one find such appeals to authority?

2. In paragraphs 5 through 8, what analogy is Baker drawing? How does he develop this analogy?

3. Beginning with paragraph 9, Baker broadens his accusations to include writers besides James. What is Baker's purpose in expanding his scope? How does it strengthen his argument? What fear, often exploited by the media, is he satirizing?

Thinking and Writing

1. Write a satiric essay in which you describe a scandalous discovery. What evidence do you have of the scandal? How will the scandal affect innocent and unsuspecting people? How can the negative effects of the scandal be reduced? How can such a thing be prevented in the future? Possible subjects are a television show, a new clothing style, or a new style of music.

2. What makes Russell Baker's writing humorous? For a research project, do background reading on the form and structure of humor writing. Then, using the three selections from Baker in this book, explain how Baker creates humor in his essays.

3. The media seem to thrive on exposing taboo subjects and revealing secrets about celebrities. Select a quirk about yourself and magnify it into a major threat to society—for example, drinking Coca-Cola for breakfast, watching horror movies, waiting until the last minute to study for an exam. Describe the depths of your depravity and the destructive way your habits influence your well-being.

RICHARD SELZER

Richard Selzer is a surgeon and a writer—an essayist who writes compassionately and often starkly about mortality and the transitory nature of life. Born in Troy, New York, in 1928, the son of a family practitioner, he was educated at Union College, Albany Medical College, and Yale. He practiced general surgery in New Haven from 1960 to the 1980s, and is on the faculty of the Yale School of Medicine. In recent years, as he admits in an essay in this collection, he has turned in the scalpel for the pen.

Selzer is in the great modern tradition of the physician-author that includes such major figures as Chekhov, William Carlos Williams, and his contemporary Lewis Thomas. His essays, collected in *Mortal Lessons* (1977), *Confessions of a Knife* (1979), *Letters to a Young Doctor* (1982), and *Taking the World in for Repairs* (1986), contain the pathos and subtle narrative force of a Chekhov story, as we witness in his memorable essay on AIDS, "A Mask on the Face of Death," which originally appeared in *Life* magazine. At the same time, in essays like "Lessons from the Art," Selzer imbues the surgeon's craft with the vivid coloring of a Williams poem. With Selzer, we can find ourselves—often uncomfortably—inside the patient, learning more about our fragile lives than we might care to imagine. Yet Selzer's compassion for the living and the dead, his precise technical gifts, and his bizarre sense of humor as he dissects the human condition make him one of the most daring and distinctive writers today.

Although he is no frequenter of churches—indeed, he calls himself an infidel— Selzer in his essays invites us to faith and to heroism. Selzer likens religious faith to "perfect pitch," and it is his own fine-tuning of the essayist's art that makes his work sparkle with literary magic. As a surgeon, he "has grown accustomed to primordial dramas, organic events involving flesh, blood, and violence." Yet it is precisely Selzer's intimacy with the stark realities of the operating room that compels him to erect an affirmative—almost sacred—vision of life. Whether interviewing prostitutes infected with the AIDS virus in Haiti, or offering sage, sardonic consolation in "Bald" to the legions who suffer from hair loss, Selzer finds ways to convey a sacred vision of life. Essayist Edward Hoagland, whose own work also appears in this collection, sees Selzer "reaching toward faith" in his passionate quest for ultimate moral truth.

Perhaps the loss of ritual in the act of surgery is what led Selzer, as he acknowledges in "The Pen and the Scalpel," to move gradually from one profession into another. Always fond of metaphor, Selzer has often likened surgery to varieties of faith and worship, yet ultimately he finds the surgeon-as-priest comparison to be somewhat specious, since surgery today is lacking in religious ecstasy. If ritual, as he once wrote, has receded from the act of surgery, then Selzer seems to find it in the craft of writing.

As a teacher of writing at Yale, recipient of the National Magazine Award for essays in 1975 and the American Medical Writers Award in 1984, and guest lecturer and fellow at numerous universities, Selzer in recent years has had the opportunity to serve as literary shaman. His lyrical voice invites us to insight and to vision.

Lessons from the Art

With trust the surgeon approaches the operating table. To be sure, he is 1
impeccably trained. He has stood here so many times before. The belly that
presents itself to him this morning, draped in green linen and painted with red
disinfectant, is little different from those countless others he has entered. It is
familiar terrain, to be managed. He watches it rise and fall in the regular rhythm
of anesthesia. Vulnerable, it returns his trust, asks but his excellence, his clever
ways. With a blend of arrogance and innocence the surgeon makes his incision, expecting a particular organ to be exactly where he knows it to be. He
has seen it there, in just that single place, over and again. He has aimed his
blade for that very spot, found the one artery he seeks, the one vein, captured
them in his hemostats, ligated them, and cut them safely; then on to the next,
and the one after that, until the sick organ falls free into his waiting hand—mined.

But this morning, as the surgeon parts the edges of the wound with his 2
retractor, he feels uncertain, for in that place where he *knows* the duct to be,
there is none. Only masses of scar curtained with blood vessels of unimagined
fragility. They seem to rupture even as he studies them, as though it is the
abrasion of the air that breaks them. Blood is shed into the well of the wound.
It puddles upon the banks of scar, concealing the way inward. The surgeon
sees this, and knows that the fierce wind of inflammation has swept this place,
burying the tubes and canals he seeks. It is an alien land. Now all is forestial,
swampy. The surgeon suctions away the blood, even as he does so, new red
trickles; his eyes are full of it; he cannot see. He advances his fingers into the
belly, feeling the walls of scar, running the tips gently over each eminence, into
each furrow, testing the roll of the land, probing for an opening, the smallest
indentation that will accept his pressure, and invite him to follow with his instruments. There is none. It is terra incognita. Hawk-eyed, he peers, waiting
for a sign, a slight change in color, that would declare the line of a tube mounding
from its sunken position. There is no mark, no trail left by some earlier explorer.

At last he takes up his scissors and forceps and begins to dissect, millimeter- 3
ing down and in. The slightest step to either side may be the bit of excess that
will set off avalanche or flood. And he is *alone.* No matter how many others
crowd about the mouth of the wound, no matter their admiration and encouragement, it is *he* that rappels this crevasse, dangles in this dreadful place, and he
is *afraid*—for he knows well the worth of this belly, that it is priceless and
irreplaceable.

"Socked in," he says aloud. His language is astronaut terse. The others 4
are silent. They know the danger, but they too have given him their reliance.
He speaks again.

"The common bile duct is bricked up in scar . . . the pancreas swollen about it . . . soup." His voice is scarcely more than the movement of his lips. The students and interns must strain to hear, as though the sound comes from a great distance. They envy him his daring, his dexterity. They do not know that he envies them their safe footing, their distance from the pit. [5]

The surgeon cuts. And all at once there leaps a mighty blood. As when from the hidden mountain ledge a pebble is dislodged, a pebble behind whose small slippage the whole of the avalanche is pulled. Now the belly is a vast working lake in which it seems both patient and surgeon will drown. He speaks. [6]

"Pump the blood in. Faster! Faster! Jesus! We are losing him." [7]

And he stands there with his hand sunk in the body of his patient, leaning with his weight upon the packing he has placed there to occlude the torn vessel, and he watches the transfusion of new blood leaving the bottles one after the other and entering the tubing. He knows it is not enough, that the shedding outraces the donation. [8]

At last the surgeon feels the force of the hemorrhage slacken beneath his hand, sees that the suction machine has cleared the field for him to see. He can begin once more to approach that place from which he was driven. Gently he teases the packing from the wound so as not to jar the bleeding alive. He squirts in saline to wash away the old stains. Gingerly he searches for the rent in the great vein. Then he hears. [9]

"I do not have a heartbeat." It is the man at the head of the table who speaks. "The cardiogram is flat," he says. Then, a moment later . . . "This man is dead." [10]

Now there is no more sorrowful man in the city, for this surgeon has discovered the surprise at the center of his work. It is death. [11]

The events of this abdomen have conspired to change him, for no man can travel back from such darkness and be the same as he was. [12]

As much from what happens *outside* the human body as within that place that for him has become the image of his mind, the surgeon learns. [13]

It is Korea. 1955. [14]

I am awakened by a hand on my chest, jostling. [15]

"Sir Doc! Sir Doc!" It is Jang, the Korean man who assists me. [16]

I open my eyes. Not gladly. To awaken here, in this place, in this time, is to invite despair. [17]

"Boy come. Gate. Very scared. His brother bad sick. Pain belly. You come?" [18]

O God, I think, let it not be appendicitis. I do not know how many more anesthesia-less operations I have left in me. Not many, I think. For I can no longer bear the gagged mouths, the trembling, frail bodies strapped to the table, round and round with the wide adhesive tape from neck to ankles, with a space at the abdomen for the incision. Nor the knuckles burning white as they clutch [19] the "courage stick" thrust into their hands at the last minute by a mamasan. Nor the eyes, slant and roving, enkindled with streaky lights. Something drags at my arms, tangles my fingers. They grow ponderous at the tips.

"Couldn't they bring him here?" [20]

"No, Sir Doc. Too very sick." [21]

It is midnight. I force myself to look at the boy who will guide us. He [22] is about ten years old, small, thin, and with a festoon of snot connecting one nostril to his upper lip. It gives a harelip effect.

We are four in the ambulance. Jang, Galloway the driver, the boy, and [23] myself. A skinny bare arm points up into the mountains where I know the road is narrow, winding. There are cliffs.

"We'll go up the stream bed," says Galloway. "It's still dry, and safer. [24] Far as we can, then tote in."

I make none of these decisons. The ambulance responds to the commands [25] of the boy like a huge trained beast. Who would have thought a child to have so much power in him? Soon we are in the dry gully of the stream. It is slow. Off in the distance there is a torch. It swings from side to side like the head of a parrot. A signal. We move on.

The first cool wind plays with the hair, blows the lips dry, brightens the [26] tops of cigarettes, then skips away. In a moment it returns. Its strength is up.

"Rain start today," says Jang. [27]

"Today?" [28]

"Now," says Galloway. A thrum hits the windshield, spreads to the roof, [29] and we are enveloped in rain. A flashlight floats morosely off to one side, ogling. There is shouting in Korean.

Now we are suckstepping through rice paddies, carrying the litter and [30] tarps. We arrive at the house.

A sliding paper door opens. It is like stepping into a snail shell. On the [31] floor mat lies a boy, he is a little smaller than the other. He wears only a loose-fitting cotton shirt out of which his head sticks like a fifth limb. His face is as tightly drawn as a fist. Flies preen there. His eyes rove in their fissures like a pendulum. I kneel. Heat rises from the skin in a palpable cloud. The ribbed bellows of the chest work above the swollen taut abdomen. Tight parts shine, I think. Knuckles and blisters and a belly full of pus. I lay my hand upon the abdomen. It helps me. I grow calm. Still, my fingers inform of the disease packaged there, swarming, lapping in untouched corners. For one moment, I long to leave it there, encased. To let it out, to cut it open, is to risk loosing it over the earth, an oceanic tide.

The abdomen is rigid, guarded. *Défense musculaire*, the French call it. [32] You could bounce a penny on it. The slight pressure of my hand causes pain, and the child raises one translucent hand to ward me off. *Peritonitis.* Fluttering at the open lips, a single bubble expands and contracts with each breath. A soul budding there.

Outside, the sound of the rain has risen. There is anger in it. We place 33 the boy on the litter, cover him with the tarpaulin. The door is slid open, twists of water skirl from the roof.

"Don't run," I say. "No jouncing." 34

The two men and the litter disappear like a melting capital H. I bow to 35 the family of the child. Their faces are limp, flaccid; the muscles, skin, lips, eyelids—everything still. I recognize it as woe. The mother hunkers by the pallet gazing at the door. Fine colonies of sweat, like seed pearls, show upon her nose; strapped to her back, an infant twists its head away from hers in sleep. The father stands by the door. His breath is rich with kimchi, he seems to be listening. I am relieved to thrust myself into the rain.

Once again we are in the ambulance. 36

"The bumps," I say. "They hurt him." I need not have said that. The others 37 knew.

There is no longer a stream bed. Where it had been, a river rushes. It has 38 many mouths. It is maniacal. In the morning the fields below will be flooded. We drive into the torrent because...there is nothing else to do. We hear his little grunts, the "hic" at the end of each breath, and we enter the river. In a minute the water is at the running board, sliding back and forth on the floor. We move out to the middle. It is deeper there. In the back of the vehicle, Jang hovers over the litter, bracing it with his body. All at once, I feel the impact of the wave, like the slap of a giant tail. We are silent as the ambulance goes over on its side. We are filling with water. I push with my boots against Galloway's body, and open the door. I climb out onto the side of the ambulance.

"Pass him out. Give him here." 39

The moaning white figure is held up. He is naked save for the shirt. I hold 40 him aloft. I am standing on the red cross. The others climb out. We huddle as the water screens the surface around where we stand. Then we are *in*. Rolling over and over, choking. I see the boy fly from my hands, watch him rise into the air, as in slow motion, his shirt-ends fluttering, the wind whipping the cloth. For an instant, he hangs there, his small bare arms raised, his fingers waving airily. Then he is a fish, streaking whitely, now ducking, now curving above. At last, he is a twig, turning lazily, harbored. When we reach him, he is on his back, the water rolling in and out of his mouth, his cracked head ribboning the water with blood.

All that night we walk, carrying the body in turns. The next day the father 41 arrives. We give him the body, and I listen as Jang tells him the story of the drowning. We do not look at each other.

A man of letters lies in the intensive care unit. A professor, used to words 42 and students. He has corrected the sentences of many. He understands punctuation. One day in his classroom he was speaking of Emily Dickinson when suddenly he grew pale, and a wonder sprang upon his face, as though he had just, for the first time, *seen* something, understood something that had eluded him all his life. It was the look of the Wound, the struck blow that makes no noise, but happens in the depths somewhere, unseen. His students could not have known that at that moment his stomach had perforated, that even as he spoke, its contents were issuing forth into his peritoneal cavity like a horde of marauding goblins. From the blackboard to the desk he reeled, fell across the top of it, and turning his face to one side, he vomited up his blood, great gouts and gobbets of it, as though having given his class the last of his spirit, he now offered them his fluid and cells.

In time, he was carried to the operating room, this man whom I had known, who had taught me poetry. I took him up, in my hands, and laid him open, and found from where he bled. I stitched it up, and bandaged him, and said later, "Now you are whole."   43

But it was not so, for he had begun to die. And I could not keep him from it, not with all my earnestness, so sure was his course. From surgery he was taken to the intensive care unit. His family, his students were stopped at the electronic door. They could not pass, for he had entered a new state of being, a strange antechamber where they may not go.   44

For three weeks he has dwelt in that House of Intensive Care, punctured by needles, wearing tubes of many calibers in all of his orifices, irrigated, dialyzed, insufflated, pumped, and drained . . . and feeling every prick and pressure the way a lover feels desire spring acutely to his skin.   45

In the room a woman moves. She is dressed in white. Lovingly she measures his hourly flow of urine. With hands familiar, she delivers oxygen to his nostrils and counts his pulse as though she were telling beads. Each bit of his decline she records with her heart full of grief, shaking her head. At last, she turns from her machinery to the simple touch of the flesh. Sighing, she strips back the sheet, and bathes his limbs.   46

The man of letters did not know this woman before. Preoccupied with dying, his is scarcely aware of her presence now. But this nurse is his wife in his new life of dying. They are close, these two, intimate, depending one upon the other, loving. It is a marriage, for although they own no shared past, they possess this awful, intense present, this matrimonial now, that binds them as strongly as any promise.   47

A man does not know whose hands will stroke from him the last bubbles of his life. That alone should make him kinder to strangers.   48

I stand by the bed where a young woman lies, her face postoperative, her mouth twisted in palsy, clownish. A tiny twig of the facial nerve, the one to the muscles of her mouth, has been severed. She will be thus from now on. The surgeon had followed with religious fervor the curve of her flesh; I promise you that. Nevertheless, to remove the tumor in her cheek, I had cut the little nerve.   49

Her young husband is in the room. He stands on the opposite side of the bed, and together they seem to dwell in the evening lamplight, isolated from   50 me, private. Who are they, I ask myself, he and this wry-mouth I have made, who gaze at and touch each other so generously, greedily? The young woman speaks.

"Will my mouth always be like this?" she asks. 51

"Yes," I say, "it will. It is because the nerve was cut." 52

She nods, and is silent. But the young man smiles. 53

"I like it," he says. "It is kind of cute." 54

All at once I *know* who he is. I understand, and I lower my gaze. One 55 is not bold in an encounter with a god. Unmindful, he bends to kiss her crooked mouth, and I so close I can see how he twists his own lips to accommodate to hers, to show her that their kiss still works. I remember that the gods appeared in ancient Greece as mortals, and I hold my breath and let the wonder in.

Far away from the operating room, the surgeon is taught that some deaths 56 are undeniable, that this does not deny their meaning. To *perceive* tragedy is to wring from it beauty and truth. It is a thing beyond mere competence and technique, or the handsomeness to precisely cut and stitch. Further, he learns that love can bloom in the stoniest desert, an intensive care unit, perhaps.

These are things of longest memory, and like memory, they cut. When 57 the patient becomes the surgeon, he goes straight for the soul.

I do not know when it was that I understood that it is precisely this hell 58 in which we wage our lives that offers us the energy, the possibility to care for each other. A surgeon does not slip from his mother's womb with compassion smeared upon him like the drippings of his birth. It is much later that it comes. No easy shaft of grace this, but the cumulative murmuring of the numberless wounds he has dressed, the incisions he has made, all the sores and ulcers and cavities he has touched in order to heal. In the beginning it is barely audible, a whisper, as from many mouths. Slowly it gathers, rises from the streaming flesh until, at last, it is a pure *calling*—an exclusive sound, like the cry of certain solitary birds—telling that out of the resonance between the sick man and the one who tends him there may spring that profound courtesy that the religious call Love.

1976

Purpose and Meaning

1. "Lessons from the Art" describes four wide-ranging medical cases. What are these cases and what is Selzer's purpose in separating them with simple double spacing? What is the central "lesson" that Selzer learns from his experiences?

2. In paragraph 56, Selzer says, "To *perceive* tragedy is to wring from it beauty and truth." What form of beauty does Selzer find in his cases? How does he depict the events he describes as beautiful? What does he mean by tragedy?

Language and Style

1. In paragraphs 2 and 3, Selzer uses figurative language to describe the patient: "the fierce wind of inflammation has swept this place"; "all is forestial, swampy,"; "It is terra incognita." What is the extended image he is using in these paragraphs? What image does he use to portray the role of the surgeon?

2. Selzer describes the sick Korean boy's disease as "swarming, lapping in untouched corners" and "to let it out is to risk loosing it over the earth, an oceanic tide" (paragraph 31). To what is Selzer comparing the disease? How does his description connect the boy's illness with the weather outside the hut? What fear does Selzer express in this paragraph that comes true in an unexpected way?

3. In the third section of the essay, Selzer refers to the intensive-care unit as the "House of Intensive Care." What does this suggest about the purpose and function of the intensive-care unit? How does the description of the nurse and her duties contribute to this purpose?

4. Selzer is as careful with the art of writing as with the art of surgery. Study the following sentences. How does their unique syntax contribute to the tone of the essay: "As much from what happens outside the human body as within that place that for him has become the image of his mind, the surgeon learns" (paragraph 13); "The surgeon had followed with religious fervor the curve of her flesh; I promise you that" (paragraph 49).

5. Read the following aloud. How does the sound of the words contribute to the poetic quality of this sentence? "I do not know when it was that I understood that it is precisely this hell in which we wage our lives that offers us the energy, the possibility to care for each other" (paragraph 58).

Strategy and Structure

1. The first and last sections are written in the third person *he,* while the middle sections are written in the first person. What is the purpose of this organizational strategy? How does the use of first or third person affect the tone of each section?

2. Section 1 begins with a terse, unexpected sentence. What effect is Selzer trying to achieve with this strategy? How does the sentence compare to the final one of section 1?

3. Section 4 is quite short. How does the *length* of this section correspond to what *occurs* in it?

Thinking and Writing

1. Select five to ten sentences from the essay that have a particularly interesting syntax, sound, or imagery. In an essay of your own, discuss these aspects of Selzer's style.

2. Reread and carefully study "Lessons from the Art." Then write an essay listing the small lessons and the overall lesson Selzer learned as a surgeon.

3. In the final paragraph, Selzer explains that the experiences of a surgeon accumulate into "a pure *calling*." What other professions resemble a religious mission in their intensity? Select any profession you wish and write an essay explaining why it transcends the category of "profession."

o◗━◖●◗◖●◗◖●◖o

Bald!

What plague is this that so thrives in the night a whole forest is notoriously   1
laid waste? It is a smoldering of the dark hours—infection! The bedroom air steams with pestilence. By dawn the rigor has passed, the fever broken, and cold gray light is witness to a rumpled pillow bestrewn with the Fallen and the Shed.

It is Baldness that rages thus.   2

O Scalp, Scalp, wilt thou not bleed, not scream from this murderous   3
depilation? Behold, thou art scythed and give no sign save a silence from nape to brow.

To the mirror. Oh, God. The comb trembles! A pass, tentative, light,   4
from occiput forward. Now you hold the comb aloft at the window, through which indifferent morning bestows light in whose lidless glare you see the carnage of the night. Desperate lips tell the mournful numbers. Twenty-eight! Twenty-eight corpselets hanging limp between the teeth. And even as you watch, twenty-nine and thirty, made airborne by some tardy gust, rock sinkward.

O wild punching of the air! O damn and damn!   5

Frantic fingers forage among the survivors. You search for tomahawk   6
wounds, fissures, all the lacerations and gougings of assault. There is nothing. All is smooth. All is still. Barren. A curse has come and passed, leaving no trace. Ah, lion unmaned, cock uncombed.

Your fingertips speculate back and forth upon the apex of your noggin.   7
It has an obscene feel. One is joyless playing with himself *here*. You incline your head forward; your eye strains: an impossible angle. A pinkness flashes into view, and the horror is confirmed. Pink!

A punishment, you think. One has gazed too long on low delights.   8

Hair today, gone tomorrow, you say, and give a soldierly little smile.   9
Yet you know that it is the joke and not the hair that is on you. Steady. You *will* look on the bright side. Good riddance, you say. Think of Absalom hanging by his hair from a tree. No such infringement for you. And what of Samson?

Oh, God, *Samson,* you say weakly, and read in the pattern of those hairs in the sink the clarion message of power failing.

But, come, come, worrier, won't you think of all the time to be saved? 10 At least half an hour a day of primping? And money? No haircuts, no combs, no brushes. No soap.

It is no use. You are shorn, forlorn. Delilahed. You lurch to the telephone 11 to sound the alarm: Dermatologist! Barber! Quack shop! There is no rescue, no Column of Light Brigade. You grow old. You get ugly. And you get it all figured out: you lose your hair, you lose your *mind.*

What is it, this snatching that pains worse than gout, hurts worse than 12 hernia? It is called by doctors alopecia—fox mange, that is, for it comes to elderly foxes even as it does to us. Nor is it news. In ancient Egypt Amenophis II, Rameses II, and even Nefertiti had it. Aristotle was bald, as was Julius Caesar. Let us learn:

Embedded in the deepest layer of the skin, the dermis, are nests of special- 13 ized cells: hair follicles. Here the bubbling of cell division is most intense, new cells forming along the periphery, crowding the older ones toward the center of the follicle. These flatten, attenuate, and turn into filaments of protein called *keratin.* It is this keratin, both the secretion of the follicle and that which it will become, that is the hair.

Lucky follicle. To have its destiny in its secretion. It is what the poet wants 14 but seldom gets.

Longer and longer grows the hair. On and on spins the follicle gnome, 15 its growth intermittent; for there are rest periods: the gnome nods, and the hair remains in these respites the same length.

The scalp of the young adult boasts between 100,000 and 150,000 of these 16 strands. Ninety percent grow while ten percent rest. At a hectic four tenths of a millimeter per day, the hair grows, accumulating unto itself its daily measure of keratin. Beard hair, if left intact, can reach a length of some thirty centimeters, that of the scalp, much longer. Just how long is still a matter of dispute among trichologists. George Catlin, artist, went West to draw Indians, and reported back to a breathless world that it was not uncommon among the Crow tribe for a warrior's hair to fall five feet, brushing his heels as he walked. Long Hair, chief of the Crows, possessed the bravest follicles of all. His unbound tresses not only reached the ground but trailed after him for several feet. Less heroic but more accessible to view were the seven legendary Sutherland Sisters, displayed from town to town by patent medicine men. The unslung manes of these ladies cascaded to the insteps of their high-button shoes.

Long hair has always been construed as prima facie evidence for virility 17 and power, while the bare scalp is a mark of degradation. Thus was the topknot taken in battle as a trophy of war—for he who possesses the hair of his slain enemy takes unto himself all the strength and courage of that foe. Not by Indians alone was such bushwhacking done, but by Scythians, Visigoths, and yes, Maccabees as well. And prisoners, novice soldiers, traitors, and adulteresses alike were shaved to announce their ignominy. Along came Christianity to change shame into humility by having its monks plow their manes into tonsures. Still, there is nothing to indicate that it made a single baldy feel one whit better.

Will you not be comforted by the knowledge that, balding, you lose not the possibility of hair? Will it help to learn that the follicles, for some reason as yet unknown, involute, close down only? That they bank the fires of their mitosis, but do not perish? On rare occasions they may be roused from their long sleep to thrive once more. One must cultivate such tiny hopes. They are all you have.   18

Numberless are the unguents and poultices, the stoups and butters with which desperate man has rubbed his pate. Eau de Portugal, d'Égypte, de Chine— all in vain. To no avail electricity, vibration, massage, frightening, and the wearing of all manner of strange devices including hog's bladder, which folk wisdom was whispered to me by an indebted witch whose instructions were to wear for seven days and seven nights a fresh porcine urinary bladder as a yarmulke or capulet.   19

Actually, the entire body is covered with hair, save for the palms and soles, most of it being of the vellus type, that fine fuzz that can be seen in a good light. These are like the hairs that we wore in our embryonic life. It is only here and there that creatures affect a more conspicuous display, for pur- poses of either sexual attraction or specific protection. The bristles of the warthog are, after all, a distant-early-warning system, an exteriorized hypersense that instructs of friend, foe, or food nearby. And the tail-tuft of cattle? Despite the biological cynicism that insists that the tuft was developed as a kind of evolu- tional fly whisk, anyone knows what a coy cow can do to a bull with a flick— now here, now there.   20

Why not revise your thinking, adopt a Grecian Urn mentality? Seen hair is nice, but that unseen is nicer still.   21

Nothing is known about the cause of baldness. At a seventeenth-century symposium called *De Capelli e Peli,* on the scalp and hair, air pollution (miasmi pestiferi) was blamed for it. That hair follicles transplanted from another part of the body to the scalp flourish would indicate that hair-fall owes not to any deficiency of the tissue, nor is any impairment of the circulation thus suspected of fault. What *is* known is that androgen, the male sex hormone, must be present for baldness to develop, thus reinforcing the folk wisdom that baldness and virility go hand in hand. The replacement or addition of androgen by inges- tion, injection, or smearing does nothing to delay or reverse the rate of balding. Only castration is effective. Thus did bald Aristotle gaze in envy at the flowing locks of the eunuchs of Athens. Nor is it known why, even as scalp hair is lost, otherwise hairless areas wax jungly. Witness the winglets of hair that sprout upon the shoulders of old men. Genes matter. As failed your father's, so fail yours. It is upon the reef of heredity that the fragile barque of beauty founders.   22

Why then this grieving over plait and lock? Does it comfort to learn baldness is the natural fate of the he-man? Come. With heart defiant, advance your naked pate proudly to the public eye. Hair is but a keepsake with sen- timental value. We mourn its loss as we would any memento that must be sur-   23 rendered to the earth. Therefore let your balditude be boldly proclaimed. Bald is beautiful!

There is comfort for man in the comradeship of the orangutan, the chimpanzee, the ouakari, and the stumptailed macaque, for they share in this unthatching. Nor has any of these beasts ever been observed to utter the least oath of shame or sorrow at such a falling out. Is not the dolphin bald? The whale? The dugong? What is clearly needed is a change of heart. The heart of a dugong is what you needs must have. In lieu of hair, it is the brain must be washed. ₂₄

All right then, try philosophy. Be persuaded that it is in our nudity lies our greatness. In our nakedness are we most admirable. Who needs feathers? Of what use plumage when a blush will do? Still unconsoled? Well, then, obtain by any means practical, the bladder of a hog... ₂₅

1976

Purpose and Meaning

1. What is Selzer's purpose in writing this essay? Is it to amuse, entertain, educate, inform?

2. This essay is, of course, about baldness. Is it about anything else? What inferences and implications about human behavior does Selzer draw from his topic?

3. In your own words, state the essay's thesis.

4. Does Selzer have both primary and secondary audiences for this essay? How do you know?

Language and Style

1. What type of style does Selzer adopt in the early paragraphs of this essay? Identify some of the components of this style.

2. Identify and explain the varieties of figurative language that Selzer employs. How does he use this language for comic effect?

3. Where does Selzer become more technical in his diction? Is this shift in language level justified? If so, in what way?

4. Selzer is fond of short, staccato sentences. Examine one or two paragraphs that reflect this syntactic pattern. What tone is established by such sentences?

Strategy and Structure

1. Consider the structure of this essay. What main divisions do you detect? Is there unity, for example, among paragraphs 1 through 12? How does Selzer unify the entire essay?

2. Selzer uses several rhetorical devices to give his essay a lighthearted tone. How and where does Selzer employ causal and process analysis, definition, and comparison and contrast to make the structure of the essay effective?

3. Complementing Selzer's fondness for short sentences is his penchant for brief paragraphs. What is the effect of such paragraphs? If they were combined, what would be lost or gained?

Thinking and Writing

1. Write an essay about any personal or health issue—for example, complexion or weight—that preoccupies people. Develop the comic implications of your topic. Try to use some of Selzer's specific comic devices to make your main point.

2. Write a self-help essay to an audience that needs practical advice on a problem or issue. If you prefer, make the essay humorous rather than serious.

3. Write a humorous essay titled "Bald is Beautiful!"

A Mask on the Face of Death

It is ten o'clock at night as we drive up to the Copacabana, a dilapidated brothel on the rue Dessalines in the red-light district of Port-au-Prince. My guide is a young Haitain, Jean-Bernard. Ten years before, J-B tells me, at the age of fourteen, "like every good Haitian boy" he had been brought here by his older cousins for his *rite de passage*. From the car to the entrance, we are accosted by a half dozen men and women for sex. We enter, go down a long hall that breaks upon a cavernous room with a stone floor. The cubicles of the prostitutes, I am told, are in an attached wing of the building. Save for a red-purple glow from small lights on the walls, the place is unlit. Dark shapes float by, each with a blindingly white stripe of teeth. Latin music is blaring. We take seats at the table farthest from the door. Just outside, there is the rhythmic lapping of the Caribbean Sea. About twenty men are seated at the tables or lean against the walls. Brightly dressed women, singly or in twos or threes, stroll about, now and then exchanging banter with the men. It is as though we have been deposited in act two of Bizet's *Carmen*. If this place isn't Lillas Pastia's tavern, what is it?

Within minutes, three light-skinned young women arrive at our table. They are very beautiful and young and lively. Let them be Carmen, Mercedes and Frasquita.

"I want the old one," says Frasquita, ruffling my hair. The women laugh   3
uproariously.

"Don't bother looking any further," says Mercedes. "We are the prettiest   4
ones."

"We only want to talk," I tell her.   5

"Aaah, aaah," she crows. "*Massissi.* You are *massissi.*" It is the contemp-   6
tuous Creole term for homosexual. If we want only to talk, we must be gay.
Mercedes and Carmen are slender, each weighing one hundred pounds or less.
Frasquita is tall and hefty. They are dressed for work: red taffeta, purple chiffon
and black sequins. Among them a thousand gold bracelets and earrings multiply
every speck of light. Their bare shoulders are like animated lamps gleaming
in the shadowy room. Since there is as yet no business, the women agree to
sit with us. J-B orders beer and cigarettes. We pay each woman $10.

"Where are you from?" I begin.   7

"We are Dominican."   8

"Do you miss your country?"   9

"Oh, yes, we do." Six eyes go muzzy with longing. "Our country is the   10
most beautiful in the world. No country is like the Dominican. And it doesn't
stink like this one."

"Then why don't you work there? Why come to Haiti?"   11

"Santo Domingo has too many whores. All beautiful, like us. All light-   12
skinned. The Haitian men like to sleep with light women."

"Why is that?"   13

"Because always, the whites have all the power and the money. The black   14
men can imagine they do, too, when they have us in bed."

Eleven o'clock. I looked around the room that is still sparsely peopled   15
with men.

"It isn't getting any busier," I say. Frasquita glances over her shoulder.   16
He eyes drill the darkness.

"It is still early," she says.   17

"Could it be that the men are afraid of getting sick?" Frasquita is offended.   18

"Sick! They do not get sick from us. We are healthy, strong. Every week   19
we go for a checkup. Besides, we know how to tell if we are getting sick."

"I mean sick with AIDS." The word sets off a hurricane of taffeta, chiffon   20
and gold jewelry. They are all gesticulation and fury. It is Carmen who speaks.

"AIDS!" Her lips curl about the syllable. "There is no such thing. It is   21
a false disease invented by the American government to take advantage of the
poor countries. The American President hates poor people, so now he makes
up AIDS to take away the little we have." The others nod vehemently.

"*Mira, mon cher.* Look, my dear," Carmen continues. "One day the police   22
came here. Believe me, they are worse than the *tonton macoutes* with their sub-
machine guns. They rounded up one hundred and five of us and they took our
blood. That was a year ago. None of us have died, you see? We are all still
here. *Mira,* we sleep with all the men and we are not sick."

"But aren't there some of you who have lost weight and have diarrhea?"   23
"One or two, maybe. But they don't eat. That is why they are weak."   24
"Only the men die," says Mercedes. "They stop eating, so they die. It is   25
hard to kill a woman."
"Do you eat well?"   26
"Oh, yes, don't worry, we do. We eat like poor people, but we eat." There   27
is a sudden scream from Frasquita. She points to a large rat that has emerged
from beneath the table.
"My God!" she exclaims. "It is big like a pig." They burst into laughter.   28
For a moment the women fall silent. There is only the restlessness of their many
bracelets. I give them each another $10.
"Are many of the men here bisexual?"   29
"Too many. They do it for money. Afterward, they come to us." Carmen   30
lights a cigarette and looks down at the small lace handkerchief she has been
folding and unfolding with immense precision on the table. All at once she turns
it over as though it were the ace of spades.
"*Mira, blanc*...look, white man," she says in a voice suddenly full of   31
foreboding. Her skin too seems to darken to coincide with the tone of her voice.
"*Mira*, soon many Dominican women will die in Haiti!"   32
"Die of what?"   33
She shrugs. "It is what they do to us."   34
"Carmen," I say, "if you knew that you had AIDS, that your blood was   35
bad, would you still sleep with men?" Abruptly, she throws back her head and
laughs. It is the same laughter with which Frasquita had greeted the rat at our
feet. She stands and the others follow.
"*Méchant!* You wicked man," she says. Then, with terrible solemnity,   36
"You don't know anything."
"But you are killing the Haitian men," I say.   37
"As for that," she says, "everyone is killing everyone else." All at once,   38
I want to know everything about these three—their childhood, their dreams,
what they do in the afternoon, what they eat for lunch.
"Don't leave," I say. "Stay a little more." Again, I reach for my wallet.   39
But they are gone, taking all the light in the room with them—Mercedes and
Carmen to sit at another table where three men have been waiting. Frasquita
is strolling about the room. Now and then, as if captured by the music, she
breaks into a few dance steps, snapping her fingers, singing to herself.
Midnight. And the Copacabana is filling up. Now it is like any other seedy   40
nightclub where men and women go hunting. We get up to leave. In the center
a couple are dancing a *méringue*. He is the most graceful dancer I have ever
watched; she, the most voluptuous. Together they seem to be riding the back
of the music as it gallops to a precisely sexual beat. Closer up, I see that the
man is short of breath, sweating. All at once, he collapses into a chair. The
woman bends over him, coaxing, teasing, but he is through. A young man with
a long polished stick blocks my way.

"I come with you?" he asks. "Very good time. You say yes? Ten dollars?   41
Five?"

I have been invited by Dr. Jean William Pape to attend the AIDS clinic   42
of which he is the director. Nothing from the outside of the low whitewashed
structure would suggest it as a medical facility. Inside, it is divided into many
small cubicles and a labyrinth of corridors. At nine A.M. the hallways are already
full of emaciated silent men and women, some sitting on the few benches, the
rest leaning against the walls. The only sounds are subdued moans of discom-
fort interspersed with coughs. How they eat us with their eyes as we pass.

The room where Pape and I work is perhaps ten feet by ten. It contains   43
a desk, two chairs and a narrow table that is covered with a sheet that will not
be changed during the day. The patients are called in one at a time, asked how
they feel and whether there is any change in their symptoms, then examined
on the table. If the patient is new to the clinic, he or she is questioned about
sexual activities.

A twenty-seven-year-old man whose given name is Miracle enters. He   44
is wobbly, panting, like a groggy boxer who has let down his arms and is waiting
for the last punch. He is neatly dressed and wears, despite the heat, a heavy
woolen cap. When he removes it, I see that his hair is thin, dull reddish and
straight. It is one of the signs of AIDS in Haiti, Pape tells me. The man's skin
is covered with a dry itchy rash. Throughout the interview and examination
he scratches himself slowly, absentmindedly. The rash is called prurigo. It is
another symptom of AIDS in Haiti. This man has had diarrhea for six months.
The laboratory reports that the diarrhea is due to an organism called cryp-
tosporidium, for which there is no treatment. The telltale rattling of the tuber-
culous moisture in his chest is audible without a stethoscope. He is like a leaky
cistern that bubbles and froths. And, clearly, exhausted.

"Where do you live?" I ask.   45

"Kenscoff." A village in the hills above Port-au-Prince.   46

"How did you come here today?"   47

"I came on the *tap-tap*." It is the name given to the small buses that swarm   48
the city, each one extravagantly decorated with religious slogans, icons, flowers,
animals, all painted in psychedelic colors. I have never seen a *tap-tap* that was
not covered with passengers as well, riding outside and hanging on. The vehicles
are little masterpieces of contagion, if not of AIDS then of the multitude of germs
which Haitian flesh is heir to. Miracle is given a prescription for a supply of
Sera, which is something like Gatorade, and told to return in a month.

"*Mangé kou bêf*," says the doctor in farewell. "Eat like an ox." What can   49
he mean? The man has no food or money to buy any. Even had he food, he
has not the appetite to eat or the ability to retain it. To each departing patient
the doctor will say the same words—"*Mangé kou bêf*." I see that it is his way
of offering a hopeful goodbye.

"Will he live until his next appointment?" I ask.   50

"No." Miracle leaves to catch the *tap-tap* for Kenscoff.   51

Next is a woman of twenty-six who enters holding her right hand to her   52
forehead in a kind of permanent salute. In fact, she is shielding her eye from
view. This is her third visit to the clinic. I see that she is still quite well nourished.

"Now, you'll see something beautiful, tremendous," the doctor says. Once   53
seated upon the table, she is told to lower her hand. When she does, I see that
her right eye and its eyelid are replaced by a hugh fungating ulcerated tumor,
a side product of her AIDS. As she turns her head, the cluster of lymph glands
in her neck to which the tumor has spread is thrown into relief. Two years ago
she received a blood transfusion at a time when the country's main blood bank
was grossly contaminated with AIDS. It has since been closed down. The only
blood available in Haiti is a small supply procured from the Red Cross.

"Can you give me medicine?" the woman wails.   54

"No."   55

"Can you cut it away?"   56

"No."   57

"Is there radiation therapy?" I ask.   58

"No."   59

"Chemotherapy?" The doctor looks at me in what some might call weary   60
amusement. I see that there is nothing to do. She has come here because there
is nowhere else to go.

"What will she do?"   61

"Tomorrow or the next day or the day after that she will climb up into   62
the mountains to seek relief from the *houngan*, the voodoo priest, just as her
slave ancestors did two hundred years ago."

Then comes a frail man in his thirties, with a strangely spiritualized face,   63
like a child's. Pus runs from one ear onto his cheek, where it has dried and caked.
He has trouble remembering, he tells us. In fact, he seems confused. It is from
toxoplasmosis of the brain, an effect of his AIDS. This man is bisexual. Two
years ago he engaged in oral sex with foreign men for money. As I palpate the
swollen glands of his neck, a mosquito flies between our faces. I swat at it, miss.
Just before coming to Haiti I had read that the AIDS virus had been isolated
from a certain mosquito. The doctor senses my thought.

"Not to worry," he says. "So far as we know there has never been a case   64
transmitted by insects."

"Yes," I say. "I see."   65

And so it goes until the last, the thirty-sixth AIDS patient has been seen.   66
At the end of the day I am invited to wash my hands before leaving. I go down
a long hall to a sink. I turn on the faucets but there is no water.

"But what about *you*?" I ask the doctor. "You are at great personal risk   67
here—the tuberculosis, the other infections, no water to wash . . ." He shrugs,
smiles faintly and lifts his hands palm upward.

We are driving up a serpiginous steep road into the barren mountains   68
above Port-au-Prince. Even in the bright sunshine the countryside has the

bloodless color of exhaustion and indifference. Our destination is the Baptist
Mission Hospital, where many cases of AIDS have been reported. Along the
road there are slow straggles of schoolchildren in blue uniforms who stretch
out their hands as we pass and call out, "Give me something." Already a crowd
of outpatients has gathered at the entrance to the mission compound. A tour
of the premises reveals that in contrast to the aridity outside the gates, this is
an enclave of productivity, lush with fruit trees and poinsettia.

The hospital is clean and smells of creosote. Of the forty beds less than   69
a third are occupied. In one male ward of twelve beds, there are two patients.
The chief physician tells us that last year he saw ten cases of AIDS each week.
Lately the number has decreased to four or five.

"Why is that?" we want to know.   70

"Because we do not admit them to the hospital, so they have learned not   71
to come here."

"Why don't you admit them?"   72

"Because we would have nothing but AIDS here then. So we send them   73
away."

"But I see that you have very few patients in bed."   74

"That is also true."   75

"Where do the AIDS patients go?"   76

"Some go to the clinic in Port-au-Prince or the general hospital in the city.   77
Others go home to die or to the voodoo priest."

"Do the people with AIDS know what they have before they come here?"   78

"Oh, yes, they know very well, and they know there is nothing to be done   79
for them."

Outside, the crowd of people is dispersing toward the gate. The clinic has   80
been canceled for the day. No one knows why. We are conducted to the office
of the reigning American pastor. He is a tall, handsome Midwesterner with an
ecclesiastical smile.

"It is voodoo that is the devil here." He warms to his subject. "It is a   81
demonic religion, a cancer on Haiti. Voodoo is worse than AIDS. And it is one
of the reasons for the epidemic. Did you know that in order for a man to become
a *houngan* he must perform anal sodomy on another man? No, of course you
didn't. And it doesn't stop there. The *houngans* tell the men that in order to
appease the spirits they too must do the same thing. So you have ritualized
homosexuality. That's what is spreading the AIDS." The pastor tells us of a
nun who witnessed two acts of sodomy in a provincial hospital where she came
upon a man sexually assaulting a houseboy and another man mounting a male
patient in his bed.

"Fornication," he says. "It is Sodom and Gomorrah all over again, so what   82
can you expect from these people?" Outside his office we are shown a cage of
terrified, cowering monkeys to whom he coos affectionately. It is clear that he
loves them. At the car, we shake hands.

"By the way," the pastor says, "what is your religion? Perhaps I am a   83
kinsman?"

"While I am in Haiti," I tell him, "it will be voodoo or it will be nothing   84
at all."

Abruptly, the smile breaks. It is as though a crack had suddenly appeared   85
in the face of an idol.

From the mission we go to the general hospital. In the heart of Port-au-   86
Prince, it is the exact antithesis of the immaculate facility we have just left—
filthy, crowded, hectic and staffed entirely by young interns and residents.
Though it is associated with a medical school, I do not see any members of
the faculty. We are shown around by Jocelyne, a young intern in a scrub suit.
Each bed in three large wards is occupied. On the floor about the beds, hunkered
in the posture of the innocent poor, are family members of the patients. In the
corridor that constitutes the emergency room, someone lies on a stretcher receiving an intravenous infusion. She is hardly more than a cadaver.

"Where are the doctors in charge?" I ask Jocelyne. She looks at me   87
questioningly.

"We are in charge."   88

"I mean your teachers, the faculty."   89

"They do not come here."   90

"What is wrong with that woman?"   91

"She has had diarrhea for three months. Now she is dehydrated." I ask   92
the woman to open her mouth. Her throat is covered with the white plaques
of thrush, a fungus infection associated with AIDS.

"How many AIDS patients do you see here?"   93

"Three or four a day. We send them home. Sometimes the families   94
abandon them, then we must admit them to the hospital. Every day, then, a
relative comes to see if the patient has died. They want to take the body. That
is important to them. But they know very well that AIDS is contagious and
they are afraid to keep them at home. Even so, once or twice a week the truck
comes to take away the bodies. Many are children. They are buried in mass
graves."

"Where do the wealthy patients go?"   95

"There is a private hospital called Canapé Vert. Or else they go to Miami.   96
Most of them, rich and poor, do not go to the hospital. Most are never
diagnosed."

"How do you know these people have AIDS?"   97

"We don't know sometimes. The blood test is inaccurate. There are many   98
false positives and false negatives. Fifteen percent of those with the disease have
negative blood tests. We go by their infections—tuberculosis, diarrhea, fungi,
herpes, skin rashes. It is not hard to tell."

"Do they know what they have?"   99

"Yes. They understand at once and they are prepared to die."   100

"Do the patients know how AIDS is transmitted?"   101

"They know, but they do not like to talk about it. It is taboo. Their   102 memories do not seem to reach back to the true origins of their disaster. It is understandable, is it not?"

"Whatever you write, don't hurt us any more than we have already been   103 hurt." It is a young Haitian journalist with whom I am drinking a rum punch. He means that any further linkage of AIDS and Haiti in the media would complete the economic destruction of the country. The damage was done early in the epidemic when the Centers for Disease Control in Atlanta added Haitians to the three other high-risk groups—hemophiliacs, intravenous drug users and homosexual and bisexual men. In fact, Haitians are no more susceptible to AIDS than anyone else. Although the CDC removed Haitians from special scrutiny in 1985, the lucrative tourism on which so much of the country's economy was based was crippled. Along with tourism went much of the foreign business investment. Worst of all was the injury to the national pride. Suddenly Haiti was indicated as the source of AIDS in the western hemisphere.

What caused the misunderstanding was the discovery of a large number   104 of Haitian men living in Miami with AIDS antibodies in their blood. They denied absolutely they were homosexuals. But the CDC investigators did not know that homosexuality is the strongest taboo in Haiti and that no man would ever admit to it. Bisexuality, however, is not uncommon. Many married men and heterosexually oriented males will occasionally seek out other men for sex. Further, many, if not most, Haitian men visit female prostitutes from time to time. It is not difficult to see that once the virus was set loose in Haiti, the spread would be swift through both genders.

Exactly how the virus of AIDS arrived is not known. Could it have been   105 brought home by the Cuban soldiers stationed in Angola and thence to Haiti, about fifty miles away? Could it have been passed on by the thousands of Haitians living in exile in Zaire, who later returned home or immigrated to the United States? Could it have come from the American and Canadian homosexual tourists, and, yes, even some U.S. diplomats who have traveled to the island to have sex with impoverished Haitian men all too willing to sell themselves to feed their families? Throughout the international gay community Haiti was known as a good place to go for sex.

On a private tip from an official at the Ministry of Tourism, J-B and I   106 drive to a town some fifty miles from Port-au-Prince. The hotel is owned by two Frenchmen who are out of the country, one of the staff tells us. He is a man of about thirty and clearly he is desperately ill. Tottering, short of breath, he shows us about the empty hotel. The furnishings are opulent and extreme— tiger skins on the wall, a live leopard in the garden, a bedroom containing a giant bathtub with gold faucets. Is it the heat of the day or the heat of my imagination that makes these walls echo with the painful cries of pederasty?

The hotel where we are staying is in Pétionville, the fashionable suburb   107 of Port-au-Prince. It is the height of the season but there are no tourists, only a dozen or so French and American businessmen. The swimming pool is used once or twice a day by a single person. Otherwise, the water remains undisturbed until dusk, when the fruit bats come down to drink in midswoop. The hotel keeper is an American. He is eager to set me straight on Haiti.

"What did and should attract foreign investment is a combination of reliable weather, an honest and friendly populace, low wages and multilingual managers."

"What spoiled it?"

"Political instability and a bad American press about AIDS." He pauses, then adds: "To which I hope you won't be contributing."

"What about just telling the truth?" I suggest.

"Look," he says, "there is no more danger of catching AIDS in Haiti than in New York or Santo Domingo. It is not where you are but what you do that counts." Agreeing, I ask if he had any idea that much of the tourism in Haiti during the past few decades was based on sex.

"No idea whatsoever. It was only recently that we discovered that that was the case."

"How is it that you hoteliers, restaurant owners and the Ministry of Tourism did not know what *tout* Haiti knew?"

"Look. All I know is that this is a middle-class, family-oriented hotel. We don't allow guests to bring women, or for that matter men, into their rooms. If they did, we'd ask them to leave immediately."

At five A.M. the next day the telephone rings in my room. A Creole-accented male voice.

"Is the lady still with you, sir?"

"There is no lady here."

"In your room, sir, the lady I allowed to go up with a package?"

"There is no lady here, I tell you."

At seven A.M. I stop at the front desk. The clerk is a young man.

"Was it you who called my room at five o'clock?"

"Sorry," he says with a smile. "It was a mistake, sir. I meant to ring the room next door to yours." Still smiling, he holds up his shushing finger.

Next to Dr. Pape, director of the AIDS clinic, Bernard Liautaud, a derma-tologist, is the most knowledgeable Haitian physician on the subject of the epidemic. Together, the two men have published a dozen articles on AIDS in international medical journals. In our meeting they present me with statistics:

There are more than one thousand documented cases of AIDS in Haiti, and as many as one hundred thousand carriers of the virus.

Eighty-seven percent of AIDS is now transmitted heterosexually. While it is true that the virus was introduced via the bisexual community, that route has decreased to 10 percent or less.

Sixty percent of the wives or husbands of AIDS patients tested positive for the [127] antibody.

Fifty percent of the prostitutes tested in the Port-au-Prince area are infected. [128]

Eighty percent of the men with AIDS have had contact with prostitutes. [129]

The projected number of active cases in four years is ten thousand. (Since my [130] last visit, the Haitian Medical Association broke its silence on the epidemic by warning that one million of the country's six million people could be carriers by 1992.)

The two doctors have more to tell. "The crossing over of the plague from [131] the homosexual to the heterosexual community will follow in the United States within two years. This, despite the hesitation to say so by those who fear to sow panic among your population. In Haiti, because bisexuality is more common, there was an early crossover into the general population. The trend, inevitably, is the same in the two countries."

"What is there to do, then?" [132]

"Only education, just as in America. But here the Haitians reject the use [133] of condoms. Only the men who are too sick to have sex are celibate."

"What is to be the end of it?" [134]

"When enough heterosexuals of the middle and upper classes die, perhaps [135] there will be the panic necessary for the people to change their sexual lifestyles."

This evening I leave Haiti. For two weeks I have fastened myself to this [136] lovely fragile land like an ear pressed to the ground. It is a country to break a traveler's heart. It occurs to me that I have not seen a single jogger. Such a public expenditure of energy while everywhere else strength is ebbing—it would be obscene. In my final hours, I go to the Cathédral of Sainte Trinité, the inner walls of which are covered with murals by Haiti's most renowned artists. Here are all the familiar Bible stories depicted in naïveté and piety, and all in such an exuberance of color as to tax the capacity of the retina to receive it, as though all the vitality of Haiti had been turned to paint and brushed upon these walls. How to explain its efflorescence at a time when all else is lassitude and inertia? Perhaps one day the plague will be rendered in poetry, music, painting, but not now. Not now.

1987

Purpose and Meaning

1. In the essay's title, to what does the word *mask* refer? What significance does "mask" have for the thesis of the essay?

2. What is Selzer's stance toward the AIDS epidemic in Haiti? Does he make any moral judgments? Is Selzer an objective observer? What seems to be his purpose for writing? How does his stance suggest a model for the reader?

Language and Style

1. Selzer uses images of light and dark to describe the prostitutes in the first section—for example, "Dark shapes float by, each with a blindingly white stripe of teeth" (paragraph 1); "Their bare shoulders are like animated lamps gleaming in the shadowy room" (paragraph 6); "They are gone, taking all the light in the room with them" (paragraph 39). What does this say about Selzer's attitude toward the women? What irony is there in these descriptions, considering the prostitutes' role in the transmission of AIDS?

2. Compare the descriptions of places and people with those in the preceding essay "Lessons from the Art." How is the earlier essay different from this one in diction and vocabulary?

3. In the concluding paragraph, Selzer states, "For two weeks I have fastened myself to this lovely fragile land like an ear pressed to the ground." How has the breadth of Selzer's investigation, the exactness of the recorded dialogue, and the clarity of his descriptions all contributed to the truth of this simile?

Strategy and Structure

1. The beginning of each of the eight sections of the essay establishes where Selzer is and whom he is with. How does this information contribute to the coherence of the essay? How does it help create transitions from one section to the next?

2. Does Selzer's recording of dialogue seem truthful? Why do you think he uses so much direct speech in this essay? How does it compare in quality and quantity to the dialogue in his previous essays in this collection? By what means does Selzer seem to recall the actual conversations he had? Did he tape record them? Or does he just have a good memory? Is he giving us the gist of the conversations instead of the actual words?

3. As in his previous two essays, Selzer composes this one as a series of vignettes centering on a common theme. How does this structural choice challenge the reader's comprehension? What critical talents must the reader possess to appreciate the full import of the essay?

Thinking and Writing

1. To enhance your skill at writing dialogue, keep a "dialogue journal" for a week, recording conversations you hear among schoolmates, friends, and relatives. After a week, rewrite the conversations so they have maximum effectiveness.

Then compare them to the dialogue in this essay. How does your dialogue differ from Selzer's in terms of dramatic effect, realism, and attention to detail?

2. How successful is the interview method in uncovering people's attitudes about a controversial subject? Select a site such as a school or place of business, and conduct four or five interviews about a particular issue. Use these interviews as the basis for an essay.

3. Study the means Selzer uses to investigate the AIDS phenomenon in Haiti. In an essay of your own, explain the various methods he used. Whom did he interview? What did he observe? What conclusions did he draw? What were his overall failings and accomplishments as a medical investigator?

0━0━0━0━0━0━0━0━0━0━0━0━0━0━0━0━0━0━0━0

The Pen and the Scalpel

I had been a general surgeon for 15 years when, at the age of 40, the psychic   1
energy for writing inexplicably appeared. It was an appearance that was to knock over my life. For 15 years I had studied, practiced and taught surgery at the Yale School of Medicine, all the while enjoying the usefulness and the *handsomeness* of the craft. For the next 16 years, until my recent retirement, I would practice both surgery and writing. But where to fit in the writing when all of my days and half of my nights were fully engaged? Certainly not evenings. In the evening, one visits with one's next-of-kin; in the evening one helps with homework; in the evening, if one is so inclined, one has a martini. Instead, I became the first adult in the state of Connecticut to go to bed in the evening. Having slept from 8:30 P.M. to 1 in the morning, I rose, went down to the kitchen, put on a pot of tea and wrote in longhand (a typewriter would disturb the household) until 3 o'clock. Then it was back upstairs and to sleep until 6 in the morning, when I began the day's doctoring. Plenty of sleep, only divided by two hours, when I was alone with my pen, and all the light in the world gathered upon a sheet of paper. In this way, I wrote three collections of stories, essays and memoirs.

Time was when in the professions—medicine and law—to patronize the   2
arts was respectable; to practice them was not. For a surgeon it was even more questionable. Who wants to know, after all, what a surgeon does in his spare time? When it became known how I was spending my wild nights, my colleagues at the hospital were distressed. "Come, come" they coaxed in (more or less) the words of the poet Richard Wilbur, "Forsake those roses of the mind, and tend the true, the moral flower." But because the subject of my writings was

my work as a doctor, the two seemed inseparable. The one fertilized the other. Why, I wondered, doesn't every surgeon write? A doctor walks in and out of a dozen short stories a day. It is irresistible to write them down. When, at last, the time came to make a choice between my two passions, it had already been made for me. Listen:

In the operating room, the patient must be anesthetized in order that he feel no pain. The surgeon too must be "anesthetized" in order to remain at some distance from the event: when he cuts the patient, his own flesh must not bleed. It is this seeming lack of feeling that gives the surgeon the image of someone who is out of touch with his humanity, a person wanting only to cut, to perform. I assure you that it is the image only. A measure of insulation against the laying open of the bodies of his fellow human beings is necessary for the well-being of both patient and doctor. In surgery, if nowhere else, dispassion is an attribute. But the surgeon-writer is not anesthetized. He remains awake; sees everything; censors nothing. It is his dual role to open and repair the body of his patient and to report back to the waiting world in the keenest language he can find. By becoming a writer, I had stripped off the protective carapace. It was time to go. A surgeon can unmake himself; a writer cannot.

A Faustian bargain, you say? Perhaps, but, truth to tell, New Haven had begun to seem rather like the Beast With a Thousand Gallbladders. And where is it graven in stone that, once having been ordained, a surgeon must remain at the operating table until the scalpel slips from his lifeless fingers? Nor had I any wish to become like the old lion whose claws are long since blunt but not the desire to use them. Still, one does not walk away from the workbench of one's life with a cheery wave of the hand. In the beginning, I felt a strange sense of dislocation. As though I were standing near a river whose banks were flowing while the stream itself stood still. Only now, after two years, have I ceased to have attacks of longing for the labor that so satisfied and uplifted my spirit. Then, too, there was the risk that by withdrawing from the hospital, with its rich cargo of patients and those who tend them, I would be punished as a writer, suffer from impotence of the pen. A writer turns his back upon his native land at his own peril. Besides, to begin the life of a writer at the age of 56 is to toil under the very dart of death. As did another doctor-writer, John Keats, I too "have fears that I may cease to be before my pen has gleaned my teeming brain."

In medicine, there is a procedure called transillumination. If, in a darkened room, a doctor holds a bright light against a hollow part of the body, he will see through the outer tissues to the structures within that cavity—arteries, veins, projecting shelves of bone. In such a ruby gloom he can distinguish among a hernia, a hydorcele of the scrotum and a tumor of the testicle. Or he can light up a sinus behind the brow. Unlike surgery, which opens the body to direct examination, transillumination gives an indirect vision, calling into play the simplest perceptions of the doctor. To write about a patient is like transillumination. You hold the lamp of language against his body and gaze through the covering layers at the truths within.

At first glance, it would appear that surgery and writing have little in com-   6
mon, but I think that is not so. For one thing, they are both sub-celestial arts;
as far as I know, the angels disdain to perform either one. In each of them you
hold a slender instrument that leaves a trail wherever it is applied. In one, there
is the shedding of blood; in the other it is ink that is spilled upon a page. In
one, the scalpel is restrained; in the other, the pen is given rein. The surgeon
sutures together the tissues of the body to make whole what is sick or injured;
the writer sews words into sentences to fashion a new version of human experience. A surgical operation is rather like a short story. You make the incision,
rummage around inside for a bit, then stitch up. It has a beginning, a middle
and an end. If I were to choose a medical specialist to write a novel, it would
be a psychiatrist. They tend to go on and on. And on.

Despite that I did not begin to write until the middle of my life, I think   7
I must always have been a writer. Like my father who was a general practitioner during the Depression in Troy, N.Y., and who wrote a novel. It was
all about a prostitute with a heart of gold (her name was Goldie!) and the doctor
who first saves her life, then falls in love with her. Mother read it and told him:
"Keep it away from the children."

Father's office was on the ground floor of an old brownstone, and we lived   8
upstairs. At night, after office hours, my brother Billy and I (we were 10 and
9 years old) would sneak downstairs to Father's darkened consultation room
and there, shamefaced, by the light of a candle stub, we would take down from
the shelves his medical textbooks. Our favorite was "The Textbook of Obstetrics
and Gynecology."

It was there that I first became aware of the rich language of medicine.   9
Some of the best words began with the letter C. *Carcinoma*, I read, and thought
it was that aria from "Rigoletto" that mother used to sing while she washed
and dried the dishes. *Cerebellum.* I said the word aloud, letting it drip off the
end of my tongue like melted chocolate. And I read *choledochojejunostomy*,
which later I was to learn as the name of an operation. All those syllables
marching off in my mind to that terminal *y*! If that was the way surgeons talked,
I thought, I would be one of them, and live forever in a state of mellifluous
rapture. I do not use these words in my writing, but I do try to use language
that evokes the sounds of the body—the *lub-dup, lub-dup* of the garrulous heart,
the gasp and wheeze of hard breathing, all the murmur and splash of anatomy
and physiology. And I have tried to make use of the poetic potential in scientific language. Here, from my diary, this specimen:

How gentle the countryside near Troy, with much farming everywhere.   10
Farming gives a sense of health to the land. It is replenishing to watch at dusk
as the herd of cattle flows like a giant amoeba toward the barn. First one cow
advances. She pauses. Another pseudopodium is thrust ahead, pulling the others
behind it until all of the cytoplasm, trailing milk, is inside the barn. All along
the banks of the Hudson River, oak, elm and locust trees have grown very tall.
The bark of the locust is thrown into deep folds coated with lichen and moss.
So old are these treees that, without the least wind, one will drop off a quite

large branch as if to shed a part of its burden. This letting-fall doesn't seem to do the tree any harm. It is more an anatomical relinquishment of a part so that the whole might remain healthy. Much as a diabetic will accept amputation of a gangrenous toe in order that he might once again walk on his foot. How clever of these locust trees to require no surgeon for their trimmage, only their own corporeal wisdom.

1988

Purpose and Meaning

1. Does the title of this essay prepare us for Selzer's purpose and approach to the subject? Would your expectations have been different if the title of the essay had been "Memories of a Surgeon-Writer"?

2. Selzer's essay appeared in *The New York Times Magazine*. In paragraph 1, Selzer describes what "one" normally does in the evening. What does this suggest about author-reader backgrounds? What other elements of the essay reveal the assumptions the author has made about readers' cultural, social, and economic background?

Language and Style

1. Like doctor-writer John Keats, Selzer is a bit of a poet. Discuss these instances of figurative language: "rich cargo of patients" (paragraph 4); "ruby gloom" (paragraph 5); "a writer sews words into sentences" (paragraph 6). Identify some of the poetic devices in the essay. How does the figurative language change from paragraph 3 to paragraph 6; from paragraph 8 to paragraph 10? Why do these shifts occur?

2. In paragraph 9, Selzer gives examples of several medical terms and talks about the "poetic potential in scientific language." What elements in his own writing are "poetic"?

3. Explain how the following sentences create a tone appropriate to Selzer's subject and audience: "Time was when in the professions—medicine and law—to patronize the arts was respectable; to practice them was not" (paragraph 2); "He remains awake; sees everything; censors nothing" (paragraph 3); "How gentle the countryside near Troy, with much farming everywhere" (paragraph 10).

Strategy and Structure

1. The opening paragraph of the essay contains biographical and factual information. Many of the following paragraphs are more general, addressing the nature of writing, surgery, and Selzer's emotional conflict in choosing between the two. Then the author reverts to specifics toward the end, finishing the essay with a

"specimen" from his diary. What effect does this organizational structure achieve? How does the structure contribute to Selzer's thesis?

2. One special rhetorical strategy in writing is analogy—finding similarities between two different things. Locate some of Selzer's analogies.

3. In the final paragraph, Selzer provides a journal in which he muses on the beauty and elegance of nature. How does this passage synthesize elements of the essay's form and content?

Thinking and Writing

1. Selzer expresses several doubts and fears concerning his decision to become a writer. How significant is "experience" for a writer? Argue for or against his decision to become a full-time writer.

2. Write an essay using analogy. The "signifier"—that is, the subject being used to describe another subject—may be a sport, an art or craft, or an occupation. The "signified"—that is, the subject being described—may be a topic such as love, life, marriage, or friendship.

3. Study Selzer's four essays in this section and conduct additional research on the author. Drawing on this material, write an essay on how Selzer's first profession influences his writing.

MARTIN LUTHER KING, JR.

Few people have had as profound an impact on contemporary affairs as Martin Luther King, Jr. Born in Atlanta, in 1929, the son of a Baptist minister, King himself became an ordained minister, a famous civil rights leader of the late 1950s and 1960s, and the recipient of the Nobel Peace Prize in 1964. As first president of the Southern Christian Leadership Council, the Reverend King was an inspired and inspirational spokesperson for nonviolence, integration, and international cooperation. As cochairperson of Clergy and Laymen Concerned about Vietnam, he opposed American military involvement in Indochina. "As a minister of God," he declared in 1966 before his congregation at Ebenezer Baptist Church in Atlanta, "I have a mission to work harder for peace and I plan to do just that." On the evening of April 4, 1968, while planning a poor people's march on Washington for that spring, King was assassinated on the balcony of his hotel in Memphis, Tennessee.

Dr. King's funeral in Atlanta was attended by more than 150,000 mourners, the largest private service ever held in the United States. His tombstone at the Martin Luther King Center for Nonviolence, close to his family home, bears the inscription "Free at last, free at last, Thank God Almighty, I'm free at last." These words, taken from a slave spiritual, are also the concluding lines of one of his historic speeches, "I Have a Dream," delivered at the Lincoln Memorial to more than 250,000 people who had gathered for the August 28, 1963, March on Washington. To that hushed crowd, King, in phrases echoing the Declaration of Independence, the patriotic hymn "My Country 'Tis of Thee," Lincoln's Emancipation Proclamation, and the Bible, called on Americans to realize the dilemma and promise of their nation—the dream to achieve freedom, equality, and justice for all.

King, however, was not simply a dreamer. Like Mahatma Gandhi, he was a philosopher of nonviolence—not as a passive way of life but as a militant and deeply subversive instrument of social and political change. Having read "Civil Disobedience" while at Morehouse College between 1944 and 1948, King came to share Thoreau's conviction that one cannot adjust to an evil system but instead must be willing to violate a polity's laws in order to reform the system. King's own "Letter from Birmingham City Jail," growing out of his arrest on Good Friday, April 12, 1963, was written in response to his own violation of an Alabama state court injunction prohibiting protest demonstrations. Written as an open letter to local white clergymen who had opposed King's protest movement, King's letter synthesizes the ideas that he had developed from his Morehouse days through the 1954 *Brown* vs. *Board of Education* decisions, the 1955 Montgomery boycott, the 1961 Freedom Rider sit-ins, and the 1962 admission of James Meredith to the University of Mississippi. Conciliatory in tone, King's letter sets forth his doctrine of nonviolent resistance as the best antidote to injustice. It is the manifesto of the American civil rights movement.

King, in his writings, is a systematic thinker. He had received his doctorate in systematic theology from Boston University School of Theology in 1955, and he could range easily and logically over issues as diverse as black power and nuclear disarmament. He was profoundly religious, attempting to find Christian answers to such contemporary predicaments as war, poverty, and racism. In his conclusion to *Where Do We Go From Here?* (1967), King reduces our predicament to a stark choice: "nonviolent coexistence or violent coannihilation." King's work, collected in *A Testament of Hope: The Essential Writings of Martin Luther King, Jr.* (1986), reveals to us the author's struggle to offer an ethic of love for our troubled situation. As James Baldwin said, Martin Luther King "succeeded in a way no Negro before him... managed to do, to carry the battle into the individual heart and make its resolution the province of the human will. He has made it a matter, on both sides of the racial fence, of self-examination."

I Have a Dream

I am happy to join with you today in what will go down in history as   1
the greatest demonstration for freedom in the history of our nation.

Fivescore years ago, a great American, in whose symbolic shadow we   2
stand today, signed the Emancipation Proclamation. This momentous decree
came as a great beacon light of hope to millions of Negro slaves who had been
seared in the flames of withering injustice. It came as a joyous daybreak to end
the long night of their captivity.

But one hundred years later, the Negro still is not free; one hundred years   3
later, the life of the Negro is still sadly crippled by the manacles of segregation
and the chains of discrimination; one hundred years later, the Negro lives on
a lonely island of poverty in the midst of a vast ocean of material prosperity;
one hundred years later, the Negro is still languished in the corners of American
society and finds himself in exile in his own land.

So we've come here today to dramatize a shameful condition. In a sense   4
we've come to our nation's capital to cash a check. When the architects of our
republic wrote the magnificent words of the Constitution and the Declaration
of Independence, they were signing a promissory note to which every American
was to fall heir. This note was the promise that all men, yes, black men as well
as white men, would be guaranteed the unalienable rights of life, liberty, and
the pursuit of happiness.

It is obvious today that America has defaulted on this promissory note   5
in so far as her citizens of color are concerned. Instead of honoring this sacred
obligation, America has given the Negro people a bad check; a check which
has come back marked "insufficient funds." We refuse to believe that there are
insufficient funds in the great vaults of opportunity of this nation. And so we've
come to cash this check, a check that will give us upon demand the riches of
freedom and the security of justice.

We have also come to this hallowed spot to remind America of the fierce   6
urgency of now. This is no time to engage in the luxury of cooling off or to
take the tranquilizing drug of gradualism. Now is the time to make real the
promises of democracy; now is the time to rise from the dark and desolate valley
of segregation to the sunlit path of racial justice; now is the time to lift our nation from the quicksands of racial injustice to the solid rock of brotherhood;
now is the time to make justice a reality for all God's children. It would be fatal
for the nation to overlook the urgency of the moment. This sweltering summer
of the Negro's legitimate discontent will not pass until there is an invigorating
autumn of freedom and equality.

Nineteen sixty-three is not an end, but a beginning. And those who hope 7
that the Negro needed to blow off steam and will now be content, will have
a rude awakening if the nation returns to business as usual.

There will be neither rest nor tranquility in America until the Negro is 8
granted his citizenship rights. The whirlwinds of revolt will continue to shake
the foundations of our nation until the bright day of justice emerges.

But there is something that I must say to my people who stand on the 9
warm threshold which leads into the palace of justice. In the process of gaining
our rightful place we must not be guilty of wrongful deeds.

Let us not seek to satisfy our thirst for freedom by drinking from the cup 10
of bitterness and hatred. We must forever conduct our struggle on the high plane
of dignity and discipline. We must not allow our creative protest to degenerate
into physical violence. Again and again we must rise to the majestic heights
of meeting physical force with soul force.

The marvelous new militancy which has engulfed the Negro community 11
must not lead us to a distrust of all white people, for many of our white brothers,
as evidenced by their presence here today, have come to realize that their destiny
is tied up with our destiny and they have come to realize that their freedom
is inextricably bound to our freedom. This offense we share mounted to storm
the battlements of injustice must be carried forth by a biracial army. We cannot
walk alone.

And as we walk, we must make the pledge that we shall always march 12
ahead. We cannot turn back. There are those who are asking the devotees of
civil rights, "When will you be satisfied?" We can never be satisfied as long
as the Negro is the victim of the unspeakable horrors of police brutality.

We can never be satisfied as long as our bodies, heavy with fatigue of 13
travel, cannot gain lodging in the motels of the highways and the hotels of the
cities. We cannot be satisfied as long as the Negro's basic mobility is from a
smaller ghetto to a larger one.

We can never be satisfied as long as our children are stripped of their 14
selfhood and robbed of their dignity by signs stating "for whites only." We cannot
be satisfied as long as a Negro in Mississippi cannot vote and a Negro in New
York believes he has nothing for which to vote. No, we are not satisfied, and
we will not be satisfied until justice rolls down like waters and righteousness
like a mighty stream.

I am not unmindful that some of you have come here out of excessive 15
trials and tribulation. Some of you have come fresh from narrow jail cells. Some
of you have come from areas where your quest for freedom left you battered
by the storms of persecution and staggered by the winds of police brutality.
You have been the veterans of creative suffering. Continue to work with the
faith that unearned suffering is redemptive.

Go back to Mississippi; go back to Alabama; go back to South Carolina; 16
go back to Georgia; go back to Louisiana; go back to the slums and ghettos
of the northern cities, knowing that somehow this situation can, and will be
changed. Let us not wallow in the valley of despair.

So I say to you, my friends, that even though we must face the difficulties   17
of today and tomorrow, I still have a dream. It is a dream deeply rooted in
the American dream that one day this nation will rise up and live out the true
meaning of its creed—we hold these truths to be self-evident, that all men are
created equal.

I have a dream that one day on the red hills of Georgia, sons of former   18
slaves and sons of former slave-owners will be able to sit down together at the
table of brotherhood.

I have a dream that one day, even the state of Mississippi, a state swelter-   19
ing with the heat of injustice, sweltering with the heat of oppression, will be
transformed into an oasis of freedom and justice.

I have a dream my four little children will one day live in a nation where   20
they will not be judged by the color of their skin but by the content of their
character. I have a dream today!

I have a dream that one day, down in Alabama, with its vicious racists,   21
with its governor having his lips dripping with the words of interposition and
nullification, that one day, right there in Alabama, little black boys and black
girls will be able to join hands with little white boys and white girls as sisters
and brothers. I have a dream today!

I have a dream that one day every valley shall be exalted, every hill and   22
mountain shall be made low, the rough places shall be made plain, and the
crooked places shall be made straight and the glory of the Lord will be revealed
and all flesh shall see it together.

This is our hope. This is the faith that I go back to the South with.   23

With this faith we will be able to hear out of the mountain of despair a   24
stone of hope. With this faith we will be able to transform the jangling discords
of our nation into a beautiful symphony of brotherhood.

With this faith we will be able to work together, to pray together, to   25
struggle together, to go to jail together, to stand up for freedom together, knowing that we will be free one day. This will be the day when all of God's children
will be able to sing with new meaning—"my country 'tis of thee; sweet land
of liberty; of thee I sing; land where my fathers died, land of the pilgrim's pride;
from every mountainside, let freedom ring"—and if America is to be a great
nation, this must become true.

So let freedom ring from the prodigious hilltops of New Hampshire.   26
Let freedom ring from the mighty mountains of New York.   27
Let freedom ring from the heightening Alleghenies of Pennsylvania.   28
Let freedom ring from the snow-capped Rockies of Colorado.   29
Let freedom ring from the curvaceous slopes of California.   30
But not only that.   31
Let freedom ring from Stone Mountain of Georgia.   32
Let freedom ring from Lookout Mountain of Tennessee.   33
Let freedom ring from every hill and molehill of Mississippi, from every   34
mountainside, let freedom ring.

And when we allow freedom to ring, when we let it ring from every village ³⁵ and hamlet, from every state and city, we will be able to speed up that day when all of God's children—black men and white men, Jews and Gentiles, Catholics and Protestants—will be able to join hands and to sing in the words of the old Negro spiritual, "Free at last, free at last; thank God Almighty, we are free at last."

1963

Purpose and Meaning

1. With what historical and social facts should one be familiar to best appreciate the significance of this speech? To what other famous historical speech is King referring in paragraph 2?

2. What facts about King's life and philosophy should a reader know in order to understand his thesis?

3. In paragraph 15, King uses the phrase "creative suffering." What does this mean? To what social and political action is he referring?

4. Does King offer any clues as to how his "dream" can be realized? Does the presence or absence of specific plans strengthen or weaken his theme?

Language and Style

1. Nearly every paragraph of the speech contains figurative language. Why does paragraph 2, for example, use the image of light? What extended metaphors can you find in other paragraphs? How do those images strengthen King's thesis?

2. In paragraphs 2, 4, 6, 17, 25, and 26, King makes references to specific historical and literary documents. What works are these references citing? What is the significance and intended effect of using them in the context of the speech?

3. "I Have a Dream" was originally a speech. What about its style indicates that it is spoken language rather than written language? What *type* of spoken language is it: everyday conversation, political speech, or something else?

Strategy and Structure

1. What transitions in the speech alter the content from that of reason to that of emotion? How does this pattern culminate naturally in the last line?

2. Review paragraph 16. What is the intended effect of repeating the phrase "go back"? Why does King call upon those present to "go back"? What are they to do when they go back?

3. Paragraphs 18 through 22 begin with the same words. What is the effect of this rhetorical strategy? What type of speech is this device reminiscent of?

4. Examine the repetition of the phrase "Let freedom ring" in the final section of the essay. What gives this repetition its rhetorical force? What connection is there between the *meaning* of these repeated phrases and the *form* of the repetition?

Thinking and Writing

1. Write an expository essay examining the use of figurative language in this speech. What images are used to describe which phenomena? What specific biblical references is King alluding to?

2. To understand the full significance of the style, diction, and tone of this speech, rewrite all or part of it, deleting all figurative language, any reference to other historical or literary sources, and all evidence of emotion. Compare your version with the original. How do the two differ in effect? (Review Orwell's rewriting of the Biblical passage quoted in "Politics and the English Language.")

3. For a research project, investigate the history of the sermon in American religious life. How are sermons structured? What literary influences do they have? What is their function? How does King's speech fit within this tradition?

4. Listen to a recording of this speech and analyze King's delivery. Then write an essay analyzing those elements of the delivery—pacing, intonation, emphasis, rhythm, etc.—that reinforce its meaning.

Letter from
Birmingham City Jail

My dear Fellow Clergymen,

While confined here in the Birmingham city jail, I came across your recent   1
statement calling our present activities "unwise and untimely." Seldom, if ever, do I pause to answer criticism of my work and ideas. If I sought to answer all of the criticisms that cross my desk, my secretaries would be engaged in little else in the course of the day, and I would have no time for constructive work. But since I feel that you are men of genuine good will and your criticisms are sincerely set forth, I would like to answer your statement in what I hope will be patient and reasonable terms.

I think I should give the reason for my being in Birmingham, since you   2
have been influenced by the argument of "outsiders coming in." I have the honor of serving as president of the Southern Christian Leadership Conference, an

organization operating in every southern state, with headquarters in Atlanta, Georgia. We have some eighty-five affiliate organizations all across the South— one being the Alabama Christian Movement for Human Rights. Whenever necessary and possible we share staff, educational and financial resources with our affiliates. Several months ago our local affiliate here in Birmingham invited us to be on call to engage in a nonviolent direct-action program if such were deemed necessary. We readily consented and when the hour came we lived up to our promises. So I am here, along with several members of my staff, because we were invited here. I am here because I have basic organizational ties here.

Beyond this, I am in Birmingham because injustice is here. Just as the eighth   3 century prophets left their little villages and carried their "thus saith the Lord" far beyond the boundaries of their hometowns; and just as the Apostle Paul left his little village of Tarsus and carried the gospel of Jesus Christ to practically every hamlet and city of the Graeco-Roman world, I too am compelled to carry the gospel of freedom beyond my particular hometown. Like Paul, I must constantly respond to the Macedonian call for aid.

Moreover, I am cognizant of the interrelatedness of all communities and   4 states. I cannot sit idly by in Atlanta and not be concerned about what happens in Birmingham. Injustice anywhere is a threat to justice everywhere. We are caught in an inescapable network of mutuality, tied in a single garment of destiny. Whatever affects one directly affects all indirectly. Never again can we afford to live with the narrow, provincial "outside agitator" idea. Anyone who lives in the United States can never be considered an outsider anywhere in this country.

You deplore the demonstrations that are presently taking place in Bir-   5 mingham. But I am sorry that your statement did not express a similar concern for the conditions that brought the demonstrations into being. I am sure that each of you would want to go beyond the superficial social analyst who looks merely at effects, and does not grapple with underlying causes. I would not hesitate to say that it is unfortunate that so-called demonstrations are taking place in Birmingham at this time, but I would say in more emphatic terms that it is even more unfortunate that the white power structure of this city left the Negro community with no other alternative.

In any nonviolent campaign there are four basic steps: (1) collection of   6 the facts to determine whether injustices are alive, (2) negotiation, (3) self-purification, and (4) direct action. We have gone through all of these steps in Birmingham. There can be no gainsaying of the fact that racial injustice engulfs this community.

Birmingham is probably the most thoroughly segregated city in the United   7 States. Its ugly record of police brutality is known in every section of this country. Its unjust treatment of Negroes in the courts is a notorious reality. There have been more unsolved bombings of Negro homes and churches in Birmingham than any city in this nation. These are the hard, brutal and unbelievable facts. On the basis of these conditions Negro leaders sought to negotiate with the city fathers. But the political leaders consistently refused to engage in good faith negotiation.

Then came the opportunity last September to talk with some of the leaders   8 of the economic community. In these negotiating sessions certain promises were made by the merchants—such as the promise to remove the humiliating racial signs from the stores. On the basis of these promises Rev. Shuttlesworth and the leaders of the Alabama Christian Movement for Human Rights agreed to call a moratorium on any type of demonstrations. As the weeks and months unfolded we realized that we were the victims of a broken promise. The signs remained. Like so many experiences of the past we were confronted with blasted hopes, and the dark shadow of a deep disappointment settled upon us. So we had no alternative except that of preparing for direct action, whereby we would present our very bodies as a means of laying our case before the conscience of the local and national community. We were not unmindful of the difficulties involved. So we decided to go through a process of self-purification. We started having workshops on nonviolence and repeatedly asked ourselves the questions, "Are you able to accept blows without retaliating?" "Are you able to endure the ordeals of jail?" We decided to set our direct-action program around the Easter season, realizing that with the exception of Christmas, this was the largest shopping period of the year. Knowing that a strong economic withdrawal program would be the by-product of direct action, we felt that this was the best time to bring pressure on the merchants for the needed changes. Then it occurred to us that the March election was ahead and so we speedily decided to postpone action until after election day. When we discovered that Mr. Connor was in the run-off, we decided again to postpone action so that the demonstrations could not be used to cloud the issues. At this time we agreed to begin our nonviolent witness the day after the run-off.

This reveals that we did not move irresponsibly into direct action. We   9 too wanted to see Mr. Connor defeated; so we went through postponement after postponement to aid in this community need. After this we felt that direct action could be delayed no longer.

You may well ask, "Why direct action? Why sit-ins, marches, etc.? Isn't   10 negotiation a better path?" You are exactly right in your call for negotiation. Indeed, this is the purpose of direct action. Nonviolent direct action seeks to create such a crisis and establish such creative tension that a community that has constantly refused to negotiate is forced to confront the issue. It seeks so to dramatize the issue that it can no longer be ignored. I just referred to the creation of tension as a part of the work of the nonviolent resister. This may sound rather shocking. But I must confess that I am not afraid of the word tension. I have earnestly worked and preached against violent tension, but there is a type of constructive nonviolent tension that is necessary for growth. Just as Socrates felt that it was necessary to create a tension in the mind so that individuals could rise from the bondage of myths and half-truths to the unfettered realm of creative analysis and objective appraisal, we must see the need of having nonviolent gadflies to create the kind of tension in society that will help men to rise from the dark depths of prejudice and racism to the majestic heights of understanding and brotherhood. So the purpose of the direct action is to create a situation so crisis-packed that it will inevitably open the door to negotiation. We, therefore, concur with you in your call for negotiation. Too long has our beloved Southland been bogged down in the tragic attempt to live in monologue rather than dialogue.

One of the basic points in your statement is that our acts are untimely. [11] Some have asked, "Why didn't you give the new administration time to act?" The only answer that I can give to this inquiry is that the new administration must be prodded about as much as the outgoing one before it acts. We will be sadly mistaken if we feel that the election of Mr. Boutwell will bring the millennium to Birmingham. While Mr. Boutwell is much more articulate and gentle than Mr. Connor, they are both segregationists, dedicated to the task of maintaining the status quo. The hope I see in Mr. Boutwell is that he will be reasonable enough to see the futility of massive resistance to desegregation. But he will not see this without pressure from the devotees of civil rights. My friends, I must say to you that we have not made a single gain in civil rights without determined legal and nonviolent pressure. History is the long and tragic story of the fact that privileged groups seldom give up their privileges voluntarily. Individuals may see the moral light and voluntarily give up their unjust posture; but as Reinhold Niebuhr has reminded us, groups are more immoral than individuals.

We know through painful experience that freedom is never voluntarily [12] given by the oppressor; it must be demanded by the oppressed. Frankly, I have never yet engaged in a direct action movement that was "well-timed," according to the timetable of those who have not suffered unduly from the disease of segregation. For years now I have heard the words "Wait!" It rings in the ear of every Negro with a piercing familiarity. This "Wait" has almost always meant "Never." It has been a tranquilizing thalidomide, relieving the emotional stress for a moment, only to give birth to an ill-formed infant of frustration. We must come to see with the distinguished jurist of yesterday that "justice too long delayed is justice denied." We have waited for more than 340 years for our constitutional and God-given rights. The nations of Asia and Africa are moving with jetlike speed toward the goal of political independence, and we still creep at horse and buggy pace toward the gaining of a cup of coffee at a lunch counter. I guess it is easy for those who have never felt the stinging darts of segregation to say, "Wait." But when you have seen vicious mobs lynch your mothers and fathers at will and drown your sisters and brothers at whim; when you have seen hate-filled policemen curse, kick, brutalize and even kill your black brothers and sisters with impunity; when you see the vast majority of your twenty million Negro brothers smothering in an airtight cage of poverty in the midst of an affluent society; when you suddenly find your tongue twisted and your speech stammering as you seek to explain to your six-year-old daughter why she can't go to the public amusement park that has just been advertised on television, and see tears welling up in her little eyes when she is told that Funtown is closed to colored children, and see the depressing clouds of inferiority begin to form in her little mental sky, and see her begin to distort her little personality by unconsciously developing a bitterness toward white people; when you have to concoct an answer for a five-year-old son asking in agonizing pathos: "Daddy, why do white people treat colored people so mean?"; when you take a cross-country drive and find it necessary to sleep night after night in the uncomfortable corners of your automobile because no motel will accept you; when you are humiliated day in and day out by nagging signs reading "white" and "colored"; when your first name becomes "nigger" and your middle name becomes "boy" (however old you are) and your last name becomes "John," and when your wife and mother are never given the respected title "Mrs."; when you are harried by day and haunted by night by the fact that you are a Negro, living constantly at tiptoe stance never quite knowing what to expect next, and plagued with inner fears and outer resentments; when you are forever fighting a degenerating sense of "nobodiness"; then you will understand why we find it difficult to wait. There comes a time when the cup of endurance runs over, and men are no longer willing to be plunged into an abyss of injustice where they experience the blackness of corroding despair. I hope, sirs, you can understand our legitimate and unavoidable impatience.

You express a great deal of anxiety over our willingness to break laws. 13 This is certainly a legitimate concern. Since we so diligently urge people to obey the Supreme Court's decision of 1954 outlawing segregation in the public schools, it is rather strange and paradoxical to find us consciously breaking laws. One may well ask, "How can you advocate breaking some laws and obeying others?" The answer is found in the fact that there are two types of laws: there are *just* and there are *unjust* laws. I would agree with Saint Augustine that "An unjust law is no law at all."

Now what is the difference between the two? How does one determine 14 when a law is just or unjust? A just law is a man-made code that squares with the moral law or the law of God. An unjust law is a code that is out of harmony with the moral law. To put it in the terms of Saint Thomas Aquinas, an unjust law is a human law that is not rooted in eternal and natural law. Any law that uplifts human personality is just. Any law that degrades human personality is unjust. All segregation statutes are unjust because segregation distorts the soul and damages the personality. It gives the segregator a false sense of superiority, and the segregated a false sense of inferiority. To use the words of Martin Buber, the great Jewish philosopher, segregation substitutes an "I-it" relationship for the "I-thou" relationship, and ends up relegating persons to the status of things. So segregation is not only politically, economically and sociologically unsound, but it is morally wrong and sinful. Paul Tillich has said that sin is separation. Isn't segregation an existential expression of man's tragic separation, an expression of his awful estrangement, his terrible sinfulness? So

I can urge men to disobey segregation ordinances because they are morally wrong.

Let us turn to a more concrete example of just and unjust laws. An unjust law is a code that a majority inflicts on a minority that is not binding on itself. This is difference made legal. On the other hand a just law is a code that a majority compels a minority to follow that it is willing to follow itself. This is sameness made legal.

Let me give another explanation. An unjust law is a code inflicted upon a minority which that minority had no part in enacting or creating because they did not have the unhampered right to vote. Who can say that the legislature of Alabama which set up the segregation laws was democratically elected? Throughout the state of Alabama all types of conniving methods are used to prevent Negroes from becoming registered voters and there are some counties without a single Negro registered to vote despite the fact that the Negro constitutes a majority of the population. Can any law set up in such a state be considered democratically structured?

These are just a few examples of unjust and just laws. There are some instances when a law is just on its face and unjust in its application. For instance, I was arrested Friday on a charge of parading without a permit. Now there is nothing wrong with an ordinance which requires a permit for a parade, but when the ordinance is used to preserve segregation and to deny citizens the First Amendment privilege of peaceful assembly and peaceful protest, then it becomes unjust.

I hope you can see the distinction I am trying to point out. In no sense do I advocate evading or defying the law as the rabid segregationist would do. This would lead to anarchy. One who breaks an unjust law must do it *openly*, *lovingly* (not hatefully as the white mothers did in New Orleans when they were seen on television screaming, "nigger, nigger, nigger"), and with a willingness to accept the penalty. I submit that an individual who breaks a law that conscience tells him is unjust, and willingly accepts the penalty by staying in jail to arouse the conscience of the community over its injustice, is in reality expressing the very highest respect for law.

Of course, there is nothing new about this kind of civil disobedience. It was seen sublimely in the refusal of Shadrach, Meshach and Abednego to obey the laws of Nebuchadnezzar because a higher moral law was involved. It was practiced superbly by the early Christians who were willing to face hungry lions and the excruciating pain of chopping blocks, before submitting to certain unjust laws of the Roman Empire. To a degree academic freedom is a reality today because Socrates practiced civil disobedience.

We can never forget that everything Hitler did in Germany was "legal" and everything the Hungarian freedom fighters did in Hungary was "illegal." It was "illegal" to aid and comfort a Jew in Hitler's Germany. But I am sure that if I had lived in Germany during that time I would have aided and comforted my Jewish brothers even though it was illegal. If I lived in a Communist country today where certain principles dear to the Christian faith are suppressed, I believe I would openly advocate disobeying these anti-religious laws. I must make two honest confessions to you, my Christian and Jewish brothers. First, I must confess that over the last few years I have been gravely disappointed with the white moderate. I have almost reached the regrettable conclusion that the Negro's great stumbling block in the stride toward freedom is not the White Citizen's Counciler or the Ku Klux Klanner, but the white moderate who is more devoted to "order" than to justice; who prefers a negative peace which is the absence of tension to a positive peace which is the presence of justice; who constantly says, "I agree with you in the goal you seek, but I can't agree with your methods of direct action"; who paternalistically feels that he can set the timetable for another man's freedom; who lives by the myth of time and who constantly advises the Negro to wait until a "more convenient season." Shallow understanding from people of good will is more frustrating than absolute misunderstanding from people of ill will. Lukewarm acceptance is much more bewildering than outright rejection.

I had hoped that the white moderate would understand that law and order 21 exist for the purpose of establishing justice, and that when they fail to do this they become dangerously structured dams that block the flow of social progress. I had hoped that the white moderate would understand that the present tension of the South is merely a necessary phase of the transition from an obnoxious negative peace, where the Negro passively accepted his unjust plight, to a substance-filled positive peace, where all men will respect the dignity and worth of human personality. Actually, we who engage in nonviolent direct action are not the creators of tension. We merely bring to the surface the hidden tension that is already alive. We bring it out in the open where it can be seen and dealt with. Like a boil that can never be cured as long as it is covered up but must be opened with all its pus-flowing ugliness to the natural medicines of air and light, injustice must likewise be exposed, with all of the tension its exposing creates, to the light of human conscience and the air of national opinion before it can be cured.

In your statement you asserted that our actions, even though peaceful, 22 must be condemned because they precipitate violence. But can this assertion be logically made? Isn't this like condemning the robbed man because his possession of money precipitated the evil act of robbery? Isn't this like condemning Socrates because his unswerving commitment to truth and his philosophical delvings precipitated the misguided popular mind to make him drink the hemlock? Isn't this like condemning Jesus because His unique God-consciousness and never-ceasing devotion to his will precipitated the evil act of crucifixion? We must come to see, as federal courts have consistently affirmed, that it is immoral to urge an individual to withdraw his efforts to gain his basic constitutional rights because the quest precipitates violence. Society must protect the robbed and punish the robber.

I had also hoped that the white moderate would reject the myth of time. 23

I received a letter this morning from a white brother in Texas which said: "All Christians know that the colored people will receive equal rights eventually, but it is possible that you are in too great of a religious hurry. It has taken Christianity almost two thousand years to accomplish what it has. The teachings of Christ take time to come to earth." All that is said here grows out of a tragic misconception of time. It is the strangely irrational notion that there is something in the very flow of time that will inevitably cure all ills. Actually time is neutral. It can be used either destructively or constructively. I am coming to feel that the people of ill will have used time much more effectively than the people of good will. We will have to repent in this generation not merely for the vitriolic words and actions of the bad people, but for the appalling silence of the good people. We must come to see that human progress never rolls in on wheels of inevitability. It comes through the tireless efforts and persistent work of men willing to be co-workers with God, and without this hard work time itself becomes an ally of the forces of social stagnation. We must use time creatively, and forever realize that the time is always ripe to do right. Now is the time to make real the promise of democracy, and transform our pending national elegy into a creative psalm of brotherhood. Now is the time to lift our national policy from the quicksand of racial injustice to the solid rock of human dignity.

You spoke of our activity in Birmingham as extreme. At first I was rather disappointed that fellow clergymen would see my nonviolent efforts as those of the extremist. I started thinking about the fact that I stand in the middle of two opposing forces in the Negro community. One is a force of complacency made up of Negroes who, as a result of long years of oppression, have been so completely drained of self-respect and a sense of "somebodiness" that they have adjusted to segregation, and, of a few Negroes in the middle class who, because of a degree of academic and economic security, and because at points they profit by segregation, have unconsciously become insensitive to the problems of the masses. The other force is one of bitterness and hatred, and comes perilously close to advocating violence. It is expressed in the various black nationalist groups that are springing up over the nation, the largest and best known being Elijah Muhammad's Muslim movement. This movement is nourished by the contemporary frustration over the continued existence of racial discrimination. It is made up of people who have lost faith in America, who have absolutely repudiated Christianity, and who have concluded that the white man is an incurable "devil." I have tried to stand between these two forces, saying that we need not follow the "do-nothingism" of the complacent or the hatred and despair of the black nationalist. There is the more excellent way of love and nonviolent protest. I'm grateful to God that, through the Negro church, the dimension of nonviolence entered our struggle. If this philosophy had not emerged, I am convinced that by now many streets of the South would be flowing with floods of blood. And I am further convinced that if our white brothers dismiss us as "rabble-rousers" and "outside agitators" those of us who are working through the channels of nonviolent direct action and refuse to support our nonviolent efforts, millions of Negroes, out of frustration and despair, will seek solace and security in black nationalist ideologies, a development that will lead inevitably to a frightening racial nightmare.

Oppressed people cannot remain oppressed forever. The urge for freedom 25 will eventually come. This is what happened to the American Negro. Something within has reminded him of his birthright of freedom; something without has reminded him that he can gain it. Consciously and unconsciously, he has been swept in by what the Germans call the *Zeitgeist,* and with his black brothers of Africa, and his brown and yellow brothers of Asia, South America and the Caribbean, he is moving with a sense of cosmic urgency toward the promised land of racial justice. Recognizing this vital urge that has engulfed the Negro community, one should readily understand public demonstrations. The Negro has many pent-up resentments and latent frustrations. He has to get them out. So let him march sometime; let him have his prayer pilgrimages to the city hall; understand why he must have sit-ins and freedom rides. If his repressed emotions do not come out in these nonviolent ways, they will come out in ominous expressions of violence. This is not a threat; it is a fact of history. So I have not said to my people "get rid of your discontent." But I have tried to say that this normal and healthy discontent can be channelized through the creative outlet of nonviolent direct action. Now this approach is being dismissed as extremist. I must admit that I was initially disappointed in being so categorized.

But as I continued to think about the matter I gradually gained a bit of 26 satisfaction from being considered an extremist. Was not Jesus an extremist in love—"Love your enemies, bless them that curse you, pray for them that despitefully use you." Was not Amos an extremist for justice—"Let justice roll down like waters and righteousness like a mighty stream." Was not Paul an extremist for the gospel of Jesus Christ—"I bear in my body the marks of the Lord Jesus." Was not Martin Luther an extremist—"Here I stand; I can do none other so help me God." Was not John Bunyan an extremist—"I will stay in jail to the end of my days before I make a butchery of my conscience." Was not Abraham Lincoln an extremist—"This nation cannot survive half slave and half free." Was not Thomas Jefferson an extremist—"We hold these truths to be self-evident, that all men are created equal." So the question is not whether we will be extremist but what kind of extremist will we be. Will we be extremists for hate or will we be extremists for love? Will we be extremists for the preservation of injustice—or will we be extremists for the cause of justice? In that dramatic scene on Calvary's hill, three men were crucified. We must not forget that all three were crucified for the same crime—the crime of extremism. Two were extremists for immorality, and thusly fell below their environment. The other, Jesus Christ, was an extremist for love, truth and goodness, and thereby rose above his environment. So, after all, maybe the South, the nation and the world are in dire need of creative extremists.

I had hoped that the white moderate would see this. Maybe I was too 27 optimistic. Maybe I expected too much. I guess I should have realized that few members of a race that has oppressed another race can understand or appreciate the deep groans and passionate yearnings of those that have been oppressed and still fewer have the vision to see that injustice must be rooted out by strong, persistent and determined action. I am thankful, however, that some of our white brothers have grasped the meaning of this social revolution and committed themselves to it. They are still all too small in quantity, but they are big in quality. Some like Ralph McGill, Lillian Smith, Harry Golden and James Dabbs have written about our struggle in eloquent, prophetic and understanding terms. Others have marched with us down nameless streets of the South. They have languished in filthy roach-infested jails, suffering the abuse and brutality of angry policemen who see them as "dirty nigger-lovers." They, unlike so many of their moderate brothers and sisters, have recognized the urgency of the moment and sensed the need for powerful "action" antidotes to combat the disease of segregation.

Let me rush on to mention my other disappointment. I have been so greatly [28] disappointed with the white church and its leadership. Of course, there are some notable exceptions. I am not unmindful of the fact that each of you has taken some significant stands on this issue. I commend you, Rev. Stallings, for your Christian stance on this past Sunday, in welcoming Negroes to your worship service on a non-segregated basis. I commend the Catholic leaders of this state for integrating Springhill College several years ago.

But despite these notable exceptions I must honestly reiterate that I have [29] been disappointed with the church. I do not say that as one of the negative critics who can always find something wrong with the church. I say it as a minister of the gospel, who loves the church; who was nurtured in its bosom; who has been sustained by its spiritual blessings and who will remain true to it as long as the cord of life shall lengthen.

I had the strange feeling when I was suddenly catapulted into the leader- [30] ship of the bus protest in Montgomery several years ago that we would have the support of the white church. I felt that the white ministers, priests and rabbis of the South would be some of our strongest allies. Instead, some have been outright opponents, refusing to understand the freedom movement and misrepresenting its leaders; all too many others have been more cautious than courageous and have remained silent behind the anesthetizing security of the stained-glass windows.

In spite of my shattered dreams of the past, I came to Birmingham with [31] the hope that the white religious leadership of this community would see the justice of our cause, and with deep moral concern, serve as the channel through which our just grievances would get to the power structure. I had hoped that each of you would understand. But again I have been disappointed. I have heard numerous religious leaders of the South call upon their worshippers to comply with a desegregation decision because it is the *law*, but I have longed to hear white ministers say, "Follow this decree because integration is morally *right* and the Negro is your brother." In the midst of blatant injustices inflicted upon the Negro, I have watched white churches stand on the sideline and merely mouth pious irrelevancies and sanctimonious trivialities. In the midst of a mighty struggle to rid our nation of racial and economic injustice, I have heard so many ministers say, "Those are social issues with which the gospel has no real concern," and I have watched so many churches commit themselves to a completely other-wordly religion which made a strange distinction between body and soul, the sacred and the secular.

So here we are moving toward the exit of the twentieth century with a religious community largely adjusted to the status quo, standing as a taillight behind other community agencies rather than a headlight leading men to higher levels of jutsice. 32

I have traveled the length and breadth of Alabama, Mississippi and all the other southern states. On sweltering summer days and crisp autumn mornings I have looked at her beautiful churches with their lofty spires pointing heavenward. I have beheld the impressive outlay of her massive religious education buildings. Over and over again I have found myself asking: "What kind of people worship here? Who is their God? Where were their voices when the lips of Governor Barnett dripped with words of interposition and nullification? Where were they when Governor Wallace gave the clarion call for defiance and hatred? Where were their voices of support when tired, bruised and weary Negro men and women decided to rise from the dark dungeons of complacency to the bright hills of creative protest?" 33

Yes, these questions are still in my mind. In deep disappointment, I have wept over the laxity of the church. But be assured that my tears have been tears of love. There can be no deep disappointment where there is not deep love. Yes, I love the church; I love her sacred walls. How could I do otherwise? I am in the rather unique position of being the son, the grandson and the great-grandson of preachers. Yes, I see the church as the body of Christ. But, oh! How we have blemished and scarred that body through social neglect and fear of being nonconformists. 34

There was a time when the church was very powerful. It was during that period when the early Christians rejoiced when they were deemed worthy to suffer for what they believed. In those days the church was not merely a ther-mometer that recorded the ideas and principles of popular opinion; it was a thermostat that transformed the mores of society. Wherever the early Christians entered a town the power structure got disturbed and immediately sought to convict them for being "disturbers of the peace" and "outside agitators." But they went on with the conviction that they were "a colony of heaven," and had to obey God rather than man. They were small in number but big in commitment. They were too God-intoxicated to be "astronomically intimidated." They brought an end to such ancient evils as infanticide and gladiatorial contest. 35

Things are different now. The contemporary church is often a weak, in-effectual voice with an uncertain sound. It is so often the arch-supporter of the status quo. Far from being disturbed by the presence of the church, the power 36 structure of the average community is consoled by the church's silent and often vocal sanction of things as they are.

But the judgment of God is upon the church as never before. If the church 37 of today does not recapture the sacrificial spirit of the early church, it will lose its authentic ring, forfeit the loyalty of millions, and be dismissed as an irrelevant social club with no meaning for the twentieth century. I am meeting young people every day whose disappointment with the church has risen to outright disgust.

Maybe again, I have been too optimistic. Is organized religion too inex- 38 tricably bound to the status quo to save our nation and the world? Maybe I must turn my faith to the inner spiritual church, the church within the church, as the true *ecclesia* and the hope of the world. But again I am thankful to God that some noble souls from the ranks of organized religion have broken loose from the paralyzing chains of conformity and joined us as active partners in the struggle for freedom. They have left their secure congregations and walked the streets of Albany, Georgia, with us. They have gone through the highways of the South on tortuous rides for freedom. Yes, they have gone to jail with us. Some have been kicked out of their churches, and lost support of their bishops and fellow ministers. But they have gone with the faith that right defeated is stronger than evil triumphant. These men have been the leaven in the lump of the race. Their witness has been the spiritual salt that has preserved the true meaning of the gospel in these troubled times. They have carved a tunnel of hope through the dark mountain of disappointment.

I hope the church as a whole will meet the challenge of this decisive hour. 39 But even if the church does not come to the aid of justice, I have no despair about the future. I have no fear about the outcome of our struggle in Birmingham, even if our motives are presently misunderstood. We will reach the goal of freedom in Birmingham and all over the nation, because the goal of America is freedom. Abused and scorned though we may be, our destiny is tied up with the destiny of America. Before the Pilgrims landed at Plymouth we were here. Before the pen of Jefferson etched across the pages of history the majestic words of the Declaration of Independence, we were here. For more than two centuries our foreparents labored in this country without wages; they made cotton king; and they built the homes of their masters in the midst of brutal injustice and shameful humiliation—and yet out of a bottomless vitality they continued to thrive and develop. If the inexpressible cruelties of slavery could not stop us, the opposition we now face will surely fail. We will win our freedom because the sacred heritage of our nation and the eternal will of God are embodied in our echoing demands.

I must close now. But before closing I am impelled to mention one other 40 point in your statement that troubled me profoundly. You warmly commended the Birmingham police force for keeping "order" and "preventing violence." I don't believe you would have so warmly commended the police force if you had seen its angry violent dogs literally biting six unarmed, nonviolent Negroes.

I don't believe you would so quickly commend the policemen if you would observe their ugly and inhuman treatment of Negroes here in the city jail; if you would watch them push and curse old Negro women and young Negro girls; if you would see them slap and kick old Negro men and young boys; if you will observe them, as they did on two occasions, refuse to give us food because we wanted to sing our grace together. I'm sorry that I can't join you in your praise for the police department.

It is true that they have been rather disciplined in their public handling of the demonstrators. In this sense they have been rather publicly "nonviolent." But for what purpose? To preserve the evil system of segregation. Over the last few years I have consistently preached that nonviolence demands that the means we use must be as pure as the ends we seek. So I have tried to make it clear that it is wrong to use immoral means to attain moral ends. But now I must affirm that it is just as wrong, or even more so, to use moral means to preserve immoral ends. Maybe Mr. Connor and his policemen have been rather publicly nonviolent, as Chief Pritchett was in Albany, Georgia, but they have used the moral means of nonviolence to maintain the immoral end of flagrant racial injustice. T. S. Eliot has said that there is no greater treason than to do the right deed for the wrong reason. 41

I wish you had commended the Negro sit-inners and demonstrators of Birmingham for their sublime courage, their willingness to suffer and their amazing discipline in the midst of the most inhuman provocation. One day the South will recognize its real heroes. They will be the James Merediths, courageously and with a majestic sense of purpose facing jeering and hostile mobs and the agonizing loneliness that characterizes the life of the pioneer. They will be old, oppressed, battered Negro women, symbolized in a seventy-two-year-old woman of Montgomery, Alabama, who rose up with a sense of dignity and with her people decided not to ride the segregated buses, and responded to one who inquired about her tiredness with ungrammatical profundity: "My feet is tired, but my soul is rested." They will be the young high school and college students, young ministers of the gospel and a host of their elders courageously and nonviolently sitting-in at lunch counters and willingly going to jail for conscience's sake. One day the South will know that when these disinherited children of God sat down at lunch counters they were in reality standing up for the best in the American dream and the most sacred values in our Judeo-Christian heritage, and thusly, carrying our whole nation back to those great wells of democracy which were dug deep by the Founding Fathers in the formulation of the Constitution and the Declaration of Independence. 42

Never before have I written a letter this long (or should I say a book?). I'm afraid that it is much too long to take your precious time. I can assure you that it would have been much shorter if I had been writing from a comfortable desk, but what else is there to do when you are alone for days in the dull monotony of a narrow jail cell other than write long letters, think strange thoughts, and pray long prayers? 43

If I have said anything in this letter that is an overstatement of the truth   44
and is indicative of an unreasonable impatience, I beg you to forgive me. If
I have said anything in this letter that is an understatement of the truth and
is indicative of my having a patience that makes me patient with anything less
than brotherhood, I beg God to forgive me.

I hope this letter finds you strong in the faith. I also hope that circumstances   45
will soon make it possible for me to meet each of you, not as an integrationist
or a civil rights leader, but as a fellow clergyman and a Christian brother. Let
us all hope that the dark clouds of racial prejudice will soon pass away and
the deep fog of misunderstanding will be lifted from our fear-drenched communities and in some not too distant tomorrow the radiant stars of love and
brotherhood will shine over our great nation with all of their scintillating beauty.

> Yours for the cause of Peace and Brotherhood,
> Martin Luther King, Jr.

1963

Purpose and Meaning

1. Outline the racial problems raised by King in this selection.

2. What additional purpose does King have in this letter beyond serving as a rebuttal
   to an open letter from clergy opposed to his nonviolent resistance? Who is King's
   intended audience besides the original eight clergy to whom it is addressed?

3. What is King's moral stance toward his imprisonment? How does his own imprisonment directly relate to the thesis of his essay?

Language and Style

1. How do King's references to specific organizations, individuals, and events modify
   the religious tone and diction of his essay? What makes a tone religious? How
   do the tone and diction of this letter compare with "I Have a Dream"? In what
   way does the *purpose* of the two works help determine their tone?

2. In paragraph 1, King says, "I would like to answer your statement in what I
   hope will be patient and reasonable terms." To what extent is King's voice "patient
   and reasonable"? Can you find any instances in the essay where he "loses his
   patience"?

3. In paragraph 12, King writes an extremely long sentence with many clauses
   separated by semicolons. What is his purpose in constructing this long sentence?
   What effect does the content have on the reader? Why would it have been less
   effective broken up into smaller sentences?

Strategy and Structure

1. How does King acknowledge his opposition at the beginning of his letter? At what point does he introduce the essential problem he plans to address?

2. In paragraphs 5, 10, 11, 13, and 21, King considers the criticisms of the clergy toward his policies and action and then proceeds to defend himself. How does King structure his defense? How successful is he in promoting his views?

3. In paragraphs 13 through 20, King defines the moral and legal concepts of law. What strategy does he use in advancing his argument? What forms of support does he offer? Does he maintain a strong argument throughout this rather long section of the letter?

4. King cites many theologians—both historical and modern—in his thesis, including Saint Augustine, Thomas Aquinas, and Martin Buber. Does the effectiveness of this strategy require the reader to be familiar with his references, or is the manner in which he uses them sufficient in lending authority to his argument? Explain.

Thinking and Writing

1. In this letter, King relies on many forms of support to advance his thesis. Carefully reread the letter, then write an expository essay in which you discuss King's thesis and the ways he defends it. For example, does he use examples, illustrations, statistics, facts, personal experience, logic, definition? Besides enumerating the ways he poses his argument, include specific examples of each.

2. Quoting Saint Augustine, King writes, "An unjust law is no law at all." What laws exist today either in the United States or elsewhere that are unjust? Select a law that you perceive as being unjust, and write an argumentative essay, defending your view. Use as many different types of support as you can.

3. Imagine that you have been unjustly imprisoned. Write an essay in the first person to your captors or those who may support your incarceration explaining why you consider your incarceration unfair.

Where Do We Go from Here: Chaos or Community?

The stability of the large world house which is ours will involve a revolution of values to accompany the scientific and freedom revolutions engulfing the earth. We must rapidly begin the shift from a "thing"-oriented society to a "person"-oriented society. When machines and computers, profit motives and property rights are considered more important than people, the giant triplets of racism, materialism and militarism are incapable of being conquered. A civilization can flounder as readily in the face of moral and spiritual bankruptcy as it can through financial bankruptcy.

This revolution of values must go beyond traditional capitalism and communism. We must honestly admit that capitalism has often left a gulf between superfluous wealth and abject poverty, has created conditions permitting necessities to be taken from the many to give luxuries to the few, and has encouraged smallhearted men to become cold and conscienceless so that, like Dives before Lazarus, they are unmoved by suffering, poverty-stricken humanity. The profit motive, when it is the sole basis of an economic system, encourages a cutthroat competition and selfish ambition that inspire men to be more I–centered than thou–centered. Equally, communism reduces men to a cog in the wheel of the state. The communist may object, saying that in Marxian theory the state is an "interim reality" that will "wither away" when the classless society emerges. True—in theory; but it is also true that, while the state lasts, it is an end in itself. Man is a means to that end. He has no inalienable rights. His only rights are derived from, and conferred by, the state. Under such a system the foundation of freedom runs dry. Restricted are man's liberties of press and assembly, his freedom to vote and his freedom to listen and to read.

Truth is found neither in traditional capitalism nor in classical communism. Each represents a partial truth. Capitalism fails to see the truth in collectivism. Communism fails to see the truth in individualism. Capitalism fails to realize that life is social. Communism fails to realize that life is personal. The good and just society is neither the thesis of capitalism nor the antithesis of communism, but a socially conscious democracy which reconciles the truths of individualism and collectivism.

We have seen some moves in this direction. The Soviet Union has gradually moved away from its rigid communism and begun to concern itself with consumer products, art and a general increase in benefits to the individual citizen. At the same time, through constant social reforms, we have seen many modifications in laissez-faire capitalism. The problems we now face must take us beyond slogans for their solution. In the final analysis, the right-wing slogans on "government control" and "creeping socialism" are as meaningless and adolescent as the Chinese Red Guard slogans against "bourgeois revisionism." An intelligent approach to the problems of poverty and racism will cause us to see that the words of the Psalmist—"The earth is the Lord's and the fullness thereof"—are still a judgment upon our use and abuse of the wealth and resources with which we have been endowed.

A true revolution of values will soon cause us to question the fairness and justice of many of our past and present policies. We are called to play the good samaritan on life's roadside; but that will be only an initial act. One day the whole Jericho road must be transformed so that men and women will not be beaten and robbed as they make their journey through life. True compassion is more than flinging a coin to a beggar; it understands that an edifice which produces beggars needs restructuring.

A true revolution of values will soon look uneasily on the glaring con-   6
trast of poverty and wealth. With righteous indignation, it will look at thousands of working people displaced from their jobs with reduced incomes as a result of automation while the profits of the employers remain intact, and say: "This is not just." It will look across the oceans and see individual capitalists of the West investing huge sums of money in Asia, Africa and South America, only to take the profits out with no concern for the social betterment of the countries, and say: "This is not just." It will look at our alliance with the landed gentry of Latin America and say: "This is not just." The Western arrogance of feeling that it has everything to teach others and nothing to learn from them is not just. A true revolution of values will lay hands on the world order and say of war: "This way of settling differences is not just." This business of burning human beings with napalm, of filling our nation's homes with orphans and widows, of injecting poisonous drugs of hate into the veins of peoples normally humane, of sending men home from dark and bloody battlefields physically handicapped and psychologically deranged, cannot be reconciled with wisdom, justice and love. A nation that continues year after year to spend more money on military defense than on programs of social uplift is approaching spiritual death.

America, the richest and most powerful nation in the world, can well lead   7
the way in this revolution of values. There is nothing to prevent us from paying adequate wages to schoolteachers, social workers and other servants of the public to insure that we have the best available personnel in these positions which are charged with the responsibility of guiding our future generations. There is nothing but a lack of social vision to prevent us from paying an adequate wage to every American citizen whether he be a hospital worker, laundry worker, maid or day laborer. There is nothing except shortsightedness to prevent us from guaranteeing an annual minimum—and *livable*—income for every American family. There is nothing, except a tragic death wish, to prevent us from reordering our priorities, so that the pursuit of peace will take precedence over the pursuit of war. There is nothing to keep us from remodeling a recalcitrant status quo with bruised hands until we have fashioned it into a brotherhood.

This kind of positive revolution of values is our best defense against com-   8
munism. War is not the answer. Communism will never be defeated by the use of atomic bombs or nuclear weapons. Let us not join those who shout war and who through their misguided passions urge the United States to relinquish its participation in the United Nations. These are days which demand wise restraint and calm reasonableness. We must not call everyone a Communist or an appeaser who advocates the seating of Red China in the United Nations, or who recognizes that hate and hysteria are not the final answers to the problems of these turbulent days. We must not engage in a negative anticommunism, but rather in a positive thrust for democracy, realizing that our greatest defense

against communism is to take offensive action in behalf of justice. We must with affirmative action seek to remove those conditions of poverty, insecurity and injustice which are the fertile soil in which the seed of communism grows and develops.

These are revolutionary times. All over the globe men are revolting against [9] old systems of exploitation and oppression, and out of the wombs of a frail world new systems of justice and equality are being born. The shirtless and barefoot people of the earth are rising up as never before. "The people who sat in darkness have seen a great light." We in the West must support these revolutions. It is a sad fact that, because of comfort, complacency, a morbid fear of communism and our proneness to adjust to injustice, the Western nations that initiated so much of the revolutionary spirit of the modern world have now become the arch antirevolutionaries. This has driven many to feel that only Marxism has the revolutionary spirit. Communism is a judgment on our failure to make democracy real and to follow through on the revolutions that we initiated. Our only hope today lies in our ability to recapture the revolutionary spirit and go out into a sometimes hostile world declaring eternal opposition to poverty, racism and militarism. With this powerful commitment we shall boldly challenge the status quo and unjust mores and thereby speed the day when "every valley shall be exalted, and every mountain and hill shall be made low: and the crooked shall be made straight and the rough places plain."

A genuine revolution of values means in the final analysis that our loyalties [10] must become ecumenical rather than sectional. Every nation must now develop an overriding loyalty to mankind as a whole in order to preserve the best in their individual societies.

This call for a world-wide fellowship that lifts neighborly concern beyond [11] one's tribe, race, class and nation is in reality a call for an all-embracing and unconditional love for all men. This often misunderstood and misinterpreted concept has now become an absolute necessity for the survival of man. When I speak of love, I am speaking of that force which all the great religions have seen as the supreme unifying principle of life. Love is the key that unlocks the door which leads to ultimate reality. This Hindu-Moslem-Christian-Jewish-Buddhist belief about ultimate reality is beautifully summed up in the First Epistle of Saint John:

> Let us love one another: for love is of God: and every one that loveth is born of God, and knoweth God. He that loveth not knoweth not God: for God is love. . . . If we love one another, God dwelleth in us, and his love is perfected in us.

Let us hope that this spirit will become the order of the day. We can no [12] longer afford to worship the God of hate or bow before the altar of retaliation. The oceans of history are made turbulent by the ever-rising tides of hate. History is cluttered with the wreckage of nations and individuals who pursued this self-defeating path of hate. As Arnold Toynbee once said in a speech: "Love is the

ultimate force that makes for the saving choice of life and good against the dam-
ning choice of death and evil. Therefore the first hope in our inventory must
be the hope that love is going to have the last word."

We are now faced with the fact that tomorrow is today. We are confronted   13
with the fierce urgency of *now*. In this unfolding conundrum of life and history
there is such a thing as being too late. Procrastination is still the thief of time.
Life often leaves us standing bare, naked and dejected with a lost opportunity.
The "tide in the affairs of men" does not remain at the flood; it ebbs. We may
cry out desperately for time to pause in her passage, but time is deaf to every
plea and rushes on. Over the bleached bones and jumbled residues of numerous
civilizations are written the pathetic words: "Too late." There is an invisible
book of life that faithfully records our vigilance or our neglect. "The moving
finger writes, and having writ moves on. . . ." We still have a choice today: nonviolent coexistence or violent coannihilation. This may well be mankind's last
chance to choose between chaos and community.

1967

Purpose and Meaning

1. In paragraph 9, King refers to "revolutionary times." Is the historical and social
   context of King's essay clear? Considering that this selection was published in
   1967, what events had conspired to make the times "revolutionary"?

2. King calls "racism, materialism and militarism" the "giant triplets." Why does
   he place these three things in the same category? How are they related?

Language and Style

1. In paragraphs 6 and 7, King repeats the key phrases "It will look" and "There
   is nothing." What does this repetition suggest about the writer's tone and diction? In what way does it resemble Biblical writing? How is this use of repetition
   similar to that in "I Have a Dream"?

2. How effective is the long quote from Saint John that follows paragraph 11? How
   does the Biblical diction resemble King's own diction in this essay and in "I Have
   a Dream"?

3. How does the use of such terms as "the large world house" (paragraph 1); "Jericho
   road" (paragraph 5); and "altar of retaliation" (paragraph 12) contribute to providing King with his unique voice?

Strategy and Structure

1. In paragraph 4, King criticizes the slogans of capitalism and communism. Yet
   he quotes from religious texts to support his argument. Are these Biblical

references the same as or different from slogans? How are they used in advancing his thesis? Through emotional appeal? Through appeal to authority? Through logic?

2. How does King structure his comparison between the systems of communism and capitalism in paragraphs 3 and 4? Does he alternate between the two or summarize each separately? Does he seem to favor one system over the other, or does he effectively neutralize the two?

3. What shift in tone occurs in the conclusion? King says we are faced with the "urgency of *now*." How does King organize his conclusion to create this sense of urgency?

Thinking and Writing

1. To explore the impact and effect of the Bible's influence on King's diction as well as the direct quotations he uses from the Bible, go through the essay, and replace Biblical language with everyday diction. Compare the differences in tone, mood, and authority.

2. Does King's argument still hold true today? Develop an argumentative essay drawing upon events of the recent past that support or refute the continued relevance of his thesis. Are racism, materialism, and militarism still the giant issues?

3. King argues without supporting his thesis with specific historical facts and statistics. He also provides no specific ways that would inspire the revolution in values he advances. Do these omissions contribute to or detract from his thesis? Write an essay defending or criticizing King's persuasive strategy in this essay.

EDWARD HOAGLAND

Edward Hoagland was born in New York City in 1932 and grew up in Fairfield County, Connecticut. Hoagland has spent his adult years alternating between a Manhattan residence and a rural New England home—in Hoagland's case, a small town in the countryside of northern Vermont. Within two years of his graduation from Harvard in 1954, Hoagland had published the first of several novels, *Cat Man*, a semidocumentary work based on Hoagland's fascination with the circus. Yet, having begun to write essays in 1967, he is better known as an essayist and travel writer. He is a frequent contributor to *Harper's*, the *Atlantic*, *The New York Times*, *Esquire*, *Life*, and other major publications. He is also the author of several essay collections. In 1981, a citation from the American Academy of Arts and Letters read: "His voice, like Montaigne's, sounds the sweet note of open and unabashed human curiosity and, like Thoreau's, the sharp note of man's independence."

"A personal essay," writes Hoagland in "What I Think, What I Am," "is like the human voice talking, its order the mind's natural flow, instead of a systematized outline of ideas." Hoagland's own personal, sagacious essays adhere to this concept. He is a self-described "happy" writer who takes visceral pleasure—as did White—in describing the minute particulars of the world and the things he loves, from city parades to country fairs. He is equally adept at invoking chokeberries and wild strawberries in blossom near his country home as he is a diner in Manhattan. In fact, Hoagland possesses one of the finest talents for describing city and country rhythms, as well as the men, women, and animals who exist on the rough edges of life. His essay, "The Courage of Turtles," a contemporary classic included in this collection, demonstrates the way Hoagland can take his own "human voice talking" into both vividly descriptive and engagingly philosophical realms as he depicts a beloved species trying to survive in a hostile environment.

Hoagland seems to see both the rural and urban scene as a delightful, occasionally harrowing, often primal wilderness that tests our capacity to survive. His essays focus on circuses, rodeos, tugboats, wolves and mountain lions, taxidermy, and city rats. Boxing is for Hoagland the penultimate primal scene and, as he demonstrates in "Violence, Violence," a sport that requires a second philosophical look before we dismiss it as utterly barbarian. Hoagland, more so than most contemporary essayists, is adept at finding meaning in both typical and atypical scenes—whether it is modern marriage or a remote and treacherous river—that embody "the prime of life."

Hoagland's musings on the contemporary scene possess a curious, quirky "old-fashioned masculinity." He writes about pain and loss eloquently, as in his sharp-eyed portrayal of the shrunken domain of the turtle or the ritualistic bloodletting of a boxing match. Nevertheless, he is fascinated constantly by nature's capacity for perfection, endurance, and survival. In his notable essay collections and travel writings—*The Courage of Turtles* (1971), *Walking the Dead Diamond River* (1973), *Red Wolves and Black Bears* (1976), *African Calliope* (1979), *The Edward Hoagland Reader* (1979), *The Tugman's Passage* (1982)—Edward Hoagland, as he describes it, "can shape and shave his memories as long as the purpose is served of elucidating a truthful point."

The Courage of Turtles

Turtles are a kind of bird with the governor turned low. With the same attitude of removal, they cock a glance at what is going on, as if they need only to fly away. Until recently they were also a case of virtue rewarded, at least in the town where I grew up, because, being humble creatures, there were plenty of them. Even when we still had a few bobcats in the woods the local snapping turtles, growing up to forty pounds, were the largest carnivores. You would see them through the amber water, as big as greeny wash basins at the bottom of the pond, until they faded into the inscrutable mud as if they hadn't existed at all.

When I was ten I went to Dr. Green's Pond, a two-acre pond across the road. When I was twelve I walked a mile or so to Taggart's Pond, which was lusher, had big water snakes and a waterfall; and shortly after that I was bicycling way up to the adverturesome vastness of Mud Pond, a lake-sized body of water in the reservoir system of a Connecticut city, possessed of cat-backed little islands and empty shacks and a forest of pines and hardwoods along the shore. Otters, foxes and mink left their prints on the bank; there were pike and perch. As I got older, the estates and forgotten back lots in town were parceled out and sold for nice prices, yet, though the woods had shrunk, it seemed that fewer people walked in the woods. The new residents didn't know how to find them. Eventually, exploring, they did find them, and it required some ingenuity and doubling around on my part to go for eight miles without meeting someone. I was grown by now, I lived in New York, and that's what I wanted on the occasional weekends when I came out.

Since Mud Pond contained drinking water I had felt confident nothing untoward would happen there. For a long while the developers stayed away, until the drought of the mid-1960s. This event, squeezing the edges in, convinced the local water company that the pond really wasn't a necessity as a catch basin, however; so they bulldozed a hole in the earthen dam, bulldozed the banks to fill in the bottom, and landscaped the flow of water that remained to wind like an English brook and provide a domestic view for the houses which were planned. Most of the painted turtles of Mud Pond, who had been inaccessible as they sunned on their rocks, wound up in boxes in boys' closets within a matter of days. Their footsteps in the dry leaves gave them away as they wandered forlornly. The snappers and the little musk turtles, neither of whom leave the water except once a year to lay their eggs, dug into the drying mud for another siege of hot weather, which they were accustomed to doing whenever the pond got low. But this time it was low for good; the mud baked over them and slowly entombed them. As for the ducks, I couldn't stroll in the woods and not feel guilty, because they were crouched beside every stagnant pothole, or were slinking between the bushes with their heads tucked into their shoulders so that I wouldn't see them. If they decided I had, they beat their way up through the screen of trees, striking their wings dangerously, and wheeled about with that headlong, magnificent velocity to locate another poor puddle.

I used to catch possums and black snakes as well as turtles, and I kept dogs and goats. Some summers I worked in a menagerie with the big personalities of the animal kingdom, like elephants and rhinoceroses. I was twenty before these enthusiasms began to wane, and it was then that I picked turtles as the particular animal I wanted to keep in touch with. I was allergic to fur, for one thing, and turtles need minimal care and not much in the way of quarters. They're personable beasts. They see the same colors we do and they seem to see just as well, as one discovers in trying to sneak up on them. In the laboratory they unravel the twists of a maze with the hot-blooded rapidity of a mammal. Though they can't run as fast as a rat, they improve on their errors just as quickly, pausing at each crossroads to look left and right. And they rock rhythmically in place, as we often do, although they are hatched from eggs, not the womb. (A common explanation psychologists give for our pleasure in rocking quietly is that it recapitulates our mother's heartbeat *in utero*.)

Snakes, by contrast, are dryly silent and priapic. They are smooth movers, legalistic, unblinking, and they afford the humor which the humorless do. But they make challenging captives; sometimes they don't eat for months on a point of order—if the light isn't right, for instance. Alligators are sticklers too. They're like war-horses, or German shepherds, and with their bar-shaped, vertical pupils adding emphasis, they have the *idée fixe* of eating, eating, even when they choose to refuse all food and stubbornly die. They delight in tossing a salamander up towards the sky and grabbing him in their long mouths as he comes down. They're so eager that they get the jitters, and they're too much of a proposition for a casual aquarium like mine. Frogs are depressingly defenseless: that moist, extensive back, with the bones almost sticking through. Hold a frog and you're holding its skeleton. Frogs' tasty legs are the staff of life to many animals— herons, raccoons, ribbon snakes—though they themselves are hard to feed. It's not an enviable role to be the staff of life, and after frogs you descend down the evolutionary ladder a big step to fish.

Turtles cough, burp, whistle, grunt and hiss, and produce social judgments. They put their heads together amicably enough, but then one drives the other back with the suddenness of two dogs who have been conversing in tones too low for an onlooker to hear. They pee in fear when they're first caught, but exercise both pluck and optimism in trying to escape, walking for hundreds of yards within the confines of their pen, carrying the weight of that cumbersome box on legs which are cruelly positioned for walking. They don't feel that the contest is unfair; they keep plugging, rolling like sailorly souls—a bobbing, infirm gait, a brave, sea-legged momentum—stopping occasionally to study the lay of the land. For me, anyway, they manage to contain the rest of the animal world. They can stretch out their necks like a giraffe, or loom underwater like an apocryphal hippo. They browse on lettuce thrown on the water like a cow moose which is partly submerged. They have a penguin's alertness, combined with a build like a Brontosaurus when they rise up on tiptoe. Then they hunch and ponderously lunge like a grizzly going forward.

Baby turtles in a turtle bowl are a puzzle in geometrics. They're as [7] decorative as pansy petals, but they are also self-directed building blocks, propping themselves on one another in different arrangements, before upending the tower. The timid individuals turn fearless, or vice versa. If one gets a bit arrogant he will push the others off the rock and afterwards climb down into the water and cling to the back of one of those he has bullied, tickling him with his hind feet until he bucks like a bronco. On the other hand, when this same milder-mannered fellow isn't exerting himself, he will stare right into the face of the sun for hours. What could be more lionlike? And he's at home in or out of the water and does lots of metaphysical tilting. He sinks and rises, with an infinity of levels to choose from; or, elongating himself, he climbs out on the land again to perambulate, sits boxed in his box, and finally slides back in the water, submerging into dreams.

I have five of these babies in a kidney-shaped bowl. The hatchling, who [8] is a painted turtle, is not as large as the top joint of my thumb. He eats chicken gladly. Other foods he will attempt to eat but not with sufficient perseverance to succeed because he's so little. The yellow-bellied terrapin is probably a yearling, and he eats salad voraciously, but no meat, fish or fowl. The Cumberland terrapin won't touch salad or chicken but eats fish and all of the meats except for bacon. The little snapper, with a black crenelated shell, feasts on any kind of meat, but rejects greens and fish. The fifth of the turtles is African. I acquired him only recently and don't know him well. A mottled brown, he unnerves the green turtles, dragging their food off to his lairs. He doesn't seem to want to be green—he bites the algae off his shell, hanging meanwhile at daring, steep, head-first angles.

The snapper was a Ferdinand until I provided him with deeper water. Now [9] he snaps at my pencil with his downturned and fearsome mouth, his swollen face like a napalm victim's. The Cumberland has an elliptical red mark on the side of his green-and-yellow head. He is benign by nature and ought to be as elegant as his scientific name (*Pseudemys scripta elegans*), except he has contracted a disease of the air bladder which has permanently inflated it; he floats high in the water at an undignified slant and can't go under. There may have been internal bleeding, too, because his carapace is stained along its ridge. Unfortunately, like flowers, baby turtles often die. Their mouths fill up with a white fungus and their lungs with pneumonia. Their organs clog up from the rust in the water, or diet troubles, and, like a dying man's, their eyes and heads become too prominent. Toward the end, the edge of the shell becomes flabby as felt and folds around them like a shroud.

While they live they're like puppies. Although they're vivacious, they 10 would be a bore to be with all the time, so I also have an adult wood turtle about six inches long. Her shell is the equal of any seashell for sculpturing, even a Cellini shell; it's like an old, dusty, richly engraved medallion dug out of a hillside. Her legs are salmon-orange bordered with black and protected by canted, heroic scales. Her plastron—the bottom shell—is splotched like a margay cat's coat, with black ocelli on a yellow background. It is convex to make room for the female organs inside, whereas a male's would be concave to help him fit tightly on top of her. Altogether, she exhibits every camouflage color on her limbs and shells. She has a turtleneck neck, a tail like an elephant's, wise old pachydermous hind legs and the face of a turkey—except that when I carry her she gazes at the passing ground with a hawk's eyes and mouth. Her feet fit to the fingers of my hand, one to each one, and she rides looking down. She can walk on the floor in perfect silence, but usually she lets her shell knock portentously, like a footstep, so that she resembles some grand, concise, slow-moving id. But if an earthworm is presented, she jerks swiftly ahead, poises above it and strikes like a mongoose, consuming it with wild vigor. Yet she will climb on my lap to eat bread or boiled eggs.

If put into a creek, she swims like a cutter, nosing forward to intercept 11 a strange turtle and smell him. She drifts with the current to go downstream, maneuvering behind a rock when she wants to take stock, or sinking to the nether levels, while bubbles float up. Getting out, choosing her path, she will proceed a distance and dig into a pile of humus, thrusting herself to the coolest layer at the bottom. The hole closes over her until it's as small as a mouse's hole. She's not as aquatic as a musk turtle, not quite as terrestrial as the box turtles in the same woods, but because of her versatility she's marvelous, she's everywhere. And though she breathes the way we breathe, with scarcely perceptible movements of her chest, sometimes instead she pumps her throat ruminatively, like a pipe smoker sucking and puffing. She waits and blinks, pumping her throat, turning her head, then sets off like a loping tiger in slow motion, hurdling the jungly lumber, the pea vine and twigs. She estimates angles so well that when she rides over the rocks, sliding down a drop-off with her rugged front legs extended, she has the grace of a rodeo mare.

But she's well off to be with me rather than at Mud Pond. The other turtles 12 have fled—those that aren't baked into the bottom. Creeping up the brooks to sad, constricted marshes, burdened as they are with that box on their backs, they're walking into a setup where all their enemies move thirty times faster than they. It's like the nightmare most of us have whimpered through, where we are weighted down disastrously while trying to flee; fleeing our home ground, we try to run.

I've seen turtles in still worse straits. On Broadway, in New York, there 13 is a penny arcade which used to sell baby terrapins that were scrawled with bon mots in enamel paint, such as KISS ME BABY. The manager turned out to be a wholesaler as well, and once I asked him whether he had any larger turtles to sell. He took me upstairs to a loft room devoted to the turtle business. There were desks for the paper work and a series of racks that held shallow tin bins atop one another, each with several hundred babies crawling around in it. He was a smudgy-complexioned, serious fellow and he did have a few adult terrapins, but I was going to school and wasn't actually planning to buy; I'd only wanted to see them. They were aquatic turtles, but here they went without water, presumably for weeks, lurching about in those dry bins like handicapped citizens, living on gumption. An easel where the artist worked stood in the middle of the floor. She had a palette and a clip attachment for fastening the babies in place. She wore a smock and a beret, and was homely, short and eccentric-looking, with funny black hair, like some of the ladies who show their paintings in Washington Square in May. She had a cold, she was smoking, and her hand wasn't very steady, although she worked quickly enough. The smile that she produced for me would have looked giddy if she had been happier, or drunk. Of course the turtles' doom was sealed when she painted them, because their bodies inside would continue to grow but their shells would not. Gradually, invisibly, they would be crushed. Around us their bellies—two thousand belly shells—rubbed on the bins with a mournful, momentous hiss.

Somehow there were so many of them I didn't rescue one. Years later, however, I was walking on First Avenue when I noticed a basket of living turtles in front of a fish store. They were as dry as a heap of old bones in the sun; nevertheless, they were creeping over one another gimpily, doing their best to escape. I looked and was touched to discover that they appeared to be wood turtles, my favorites, so I bought one. In my apartment I looked closer and realized that in fact this was a diamondback terrapin, which was bad news. Diamondbacks are tidewater turtles from brackish estuaries, and I had no sea water to keep him in. He spent his days thumping interminably against the baseboards, pushing for an opening through the wall. He drank thirstily but would not eat and had none of the hearty, accepting qualities of wood turtles. He was morose, paler in color, sleeker and more Oriental in the carved ridges and rings that formed his shell. Though I felt sorry for him, finally I found his unrelenting presence exasperating. I carried him, struggling in a paper bag, across town to the Morton Street Pier on the Hudson. It was August but gray and windy. He was very surprised when I tossed him in; for the first time in our association, I think, he was afraid. He looked afraid as he bobbed about on top of the water, looking up at me from ten feet below. Though we were both accustomed to his resistance and rigidity, seeing him still pitiful, I recognized that I must have done the wrong thing. At least the river was salty, but it was also bottomless; the waves were too rough for him, and the tide was coming in, bumping him against the pilings underneath the pier. Too late, I realized that he wouldn't be able to swim to a peaceful inlet in New Jersey, even if he could figure out which way to swim. But since, short of diving in after him, there was nothing I could do, I walked away.

14

1970

Purpose and Meaning

1. Why has Hoagland titled his essay, "The Courage of Turtles"? What makes them courageous?
2. What is the purpose of Hoagland's essay?
3. Who is the implied audience of the essay? Explain your answer.

Language and Style

1. Hoagland goes beyond objective physical description of animals to personify them. For example, in paragraph 5, he says snakes are "legalistic," alligators "get the jitters," and "frogs are depressingly defenseless." Find other examples of this technique. Are these appropriate descriptions of animals? What do these characterizations have in common?
2. In paragraph 8, Hoagland describes the uniqueness of each of his five pet turtles. What is his purpose in providing specific details of each one?
3. People often use an emotional tone in describing their pets. What tone does Hoagland use in describing turtles? Provide examples of this stylistic effect. Connect the tone of his essay with the thesis.

Strategy and Structure

1. How does Hoagland's early experience with turtles give us clues to his later attitude toward them? At what point does Hoagland portray the turtles as having "courage"?
2. In paragraph 13, Hoagland spends some time describing the turtle painter. What is his point in portraying her in such a detailed way? Does this interfere with the coherence of his theme, or is it a part of the theme?
3. Does Hoagland conclude the essay on a negative note? What is the significance of the last line? Does the essay end abruptly, or does it seem to come to a logical conclusion? Explain your view.

Thinking and Writing

1. Personification is the act of endowing something nonhuman with human qualities. Reread Hoagland's essay, noting his use of personification. What function does this type of description serve? What is its effect on the relationship between the observer and the observed? Write a brief essay on this topic.
2. Reread the essay, noting Hoagland's use of description. Observe an animal carefully on your own. How accurately can you describe its physical appearance? What attitudes does the animal seem to exude? How can the animal's behavior

be described through personification? In your descriptive essay, try to include at least five analogies. Title your essay with the trait you feel best characterizes your chosen animal.

3. Hoagland depicts the turtles as being continually exploited. Their natural habitats are destroyed; they are cruelly made into ornaments; pet baby turtles often die; Hoagland himself eventually carelessly dooms one of them. Argue for or against one of the following two propositions: (1) Undomesticated animals should never be kept in zoos; (2) undomesticated animals should never be kept as pets.

Violence, Violence

It is curious that with such a crushing, befuddling climate of general   1
violence as there is in New York we should still be paying money to go to the prizefights. The fight fan, as one used to picture him, was a kind of overweight frustrated homebody whose life was practically devoid of danger and drama. Middle-aged rather than young, a small businessman or a warehouse foreman, a nostalgic war veteran, he looked about and found the world torpid, so he came to St. Nicholas Arena to holler and twist on his folding chair, throw starts of punches, or did the same thing in front of the television set in a bar. But now this fellow has all the firepower of Vietnam on television, the racial-college riots, the hippies to hate, the burglaries in his building, the fear of being mugged when he is on the street. Going home from the prizefight, he runs a chance of being beaten up worse than the loser was. And boxing, which began as an all-out sport, has not been able to cinch its procedures tighter, the way pro football has, to make for a more modish, highstrung commotion and wilder deeds. It's the simplest pageant of all: two men fight, rest a minute, and fight some more. Like the mile run, it's traditionalist and finite, humble in its claims.

Baseball, which seemed the natural man's sport above all, has turned out   2
to be overly ceremonious and time-consuming for the 1960s, and even burlesque and the belly dancers of Eighth Avenue, forthright as we once supposed they were, have been eclipsed by still more elementary displays of the human physique. The entrepreneurs of boxing didn't at first suspect that their sport had any kick left except as a TV filler for the hinterlands, where the old modes prevail. The custom of weekly fights at St. Nick's or the old Garden had lapsed (since which, both buildings have gone *poof*). But then they tried a few cards at the National Maritime Union hiring hall, counting on the roughhouse seamen to provide a box-office backlog. When the shows sold out, they shifted them to the Felt Forum in the new Madison Square Garden and discovered that the

sport pays there as well. As a result, live boxing has become a feature of New York life again. The problem of the promoters is not to streamline the *Geist* to fit the sixties but to find fighters who fight, because unlike many other athletes, prizefighters do not really enjoy their sport very much, as a rule; they fight for the purse. All our Irish and Italian citizens have elevated themselves until they don't have to choose between simonizing cars for a living or the prize ring, and the Negroes and Spanish-speakers too are scrambling upward toward better livelihoods, if only in campier sports with lots of legwork, or the various ornate sports where if the team loses the coach loses his job. Boxing isn't like that, and we are bringing in hungry souls from Nigeria, the Philippines and the Bahamas to do the dirt. Pepole sometimes make the mistake of feeling sorry for boxers, however, and want to abolish the sport, when they should look instead at the man in the neighborhood car wash who *isn't* a fighter—doesn't fly to Seattle for a big card—but runs the steam hose and polishes fenders.

And is it dirt? I'm not one of those professional eyewitnesses who is willing to watch anything just on the grounds that it is happening. I live on Ambulance Alley and don't need to go to the Garden in order to see men in desperate straits. I go to admire a trial of skills, a contest of limited violence between unintimidated adversaries which, even when it does spill out of the ring after a bad decision and the crowd in its anger sways shoulder to shoulder, is very nineteenth-century, from the era of cart horses in the street. Every sport is a combat between its participants, but boxing is combat distilled, purer even than combat with weapons. When a referee steps in and stops a fight in which one man is receiving punishment without any hope of recouping, the crowd is not disappointed at seeing the punishment stopped; they are glad enough about that. If they are disappointed, it's because the drama is over, which was true as soon as the fight became one-sided. Boxing's appeal is its drama and grace, a blizzarding grace that amounts to an impromptu, exigent ballet, especially in the lighter and nimbler weights. Hands, arms, feet, legs, head, torso—more is done per moment than in fast ice hockey; and since there is more motion, the athletes in other sports cannot surpass a consummate boxer for grace.

Still, why this extra violence in such a violent time? Is it choreographed like a bullfight; is it like a fine tragedy which one goes to although one's own life is tangled enough? Of course it isn't these things at all. There is no program, no unity, no meaning as such unless a parable fortuitously develops, and the spectators are there for the combat. Writers of the Hemingway-Mailer axis have been fascinated by the combat, locating relevancies and identities in the prefight rituals, but they have not made claims for the sport as an art. Ten years ago, when we did not live alongside such an ocean of violence, some of us went to the fights perhaps as one keeps an aquarium. We realized most of the world was under water, but we were high and dry with Eisenhower, and knowing that life is salt and life is action, life is tears and life is water, we kept a fish tank to represent the four-fifths of the world which breathed with gills.

But nowadays we're flooded and swimming for dear life, no matter where we happen to live. That we nevertheless prefer our sports violent—the irreducible conciseness of boxing—is evidence of a relation to violence, a need and a curiosity, so basic that it cannot be sated. Though we do tire of the delirium in the streets, we are only tiring of the disorder. Make it concise, put ropes or white lines around it, and we will go, we will go, just as people on vacation go down to the roaring sea.

1970

Purpose and Meaning

1. There are a number of references to historical events, famous personalities, and place names in this essay. What assumptions is Hoagland making about his audience's historical, social, and cultural knowledge by making these allusions necessary to the appreciation of the essay?

2. According to Hoagland, what is the primary aspect of boxing that appeals to its fans? What characteristics of the time in which Hoagland is writing contribute to this special appreciation? Is Hoagland's own appreciation of boxing in keeping with the reactions he describes?

Language and Style

1. Hoagland makes several unusual adjective choices in his descriptions. How do the following contribute to his diction as a writer: "a *crushing, befuddling* climate" (paragraph 1); "found the world *torpid*" (paragraph 1); "only in *campier* sports" (paragraph 2); "a *blizzarding* grace" (paragraph 3)?

2. In paragraph 1, Hoagland describes the typical fight fan without describing any specific individual. What word choices does Hoagland use to portray the type without describing the individual?

3. In paragraphs 4 and 5, Hoagland uses images of water to describe viewing boxing. Follow the logic of his analogy. How does it strengthen his argument about boxing's appeal? How does it help give the essay its unique style?

Strategy and Structure

1. The title of the essay is "Violence, Violence." Why has Hoagland repeated the word? Are there *two* "violences" that he is describing? How can one interpret the title as serving as an organizing function for the thesis of the essay?

2. Paragraph 4 begins with a question. How effective is this strategy of using a question as a topic sentence? Does Hoagland eventually answer the question?

3. Consider the first sentence in the essay and the final two sentences. How do these sentences together help unify the essay? How do they contribute to making the essay a distinct unit?

Thinking and Writing

1. Is there such a thing as a typical sports fan? For example, what are the characteristics of a typical hockey fan? Write a descriptive essay explaining the attitudes, traits, background, and behavior of such a fan.

2. At the end of paragraph 2, Hoagland argues that we should feel sorrier for low-paid, unskilled workers than we should for boxers. Argue for or against the thesis that boxing is beneficial to society because it enables those with low incomes to raise their standard of living.

3. What makes sensational, violent TV shows so popular? Write an essay explaining the appeal of these shows.

4. Write a persuasive essay arguing for or against the thesis that boxing is a sport.

What I Think,
What I Am

Our loneliness makes us avoid column readers these days. The personalities in the San Francisco *Chronicle*, Chicago *Daily News*, New York *Post* constitute our neighbors now, some of them local characters but also the opinionated national stars. And movie reviewers thrive on our yearning for somebody emotional who is willing to pay attention to us and return week after week, year after year, through all the to-and-fro of other friends, to flatter us by pouring out his/her heart. They are essayists of a type, as Elizabeth Hardwick is, James Baldwin was.

We sometimes hear that essays are an old-fashioned form, that so-and-so is the "last essayist," but the facts of the marketplace argue quite otherwise. Essays of nearly any kind are so much easier than short stories for a writer to sell, so many more see print, it's strange that though two fine anthologies remain that publish the year's best stories, no comparable collection exists for essays. Such changes in the reading public's taste aren't always to the good, needless to say. The art of telling stories predated even cave painting, surely; and if we ever find ourselves living in caves again, it (with painting and drumming) will be the only art left, after movies, novels, photography, essays, biography, and all the rest have gone down the drain—the art to build from.

One has the sense with the short story as a form that while everything may have been done, nothing has been overdone; it has a permanence. Essays, if a comparison is to be made, although they go back four hundred years to

Montaigne, seem a mercurial, newfangled, sometimes hokey affair that has lent itself to many of the excesses of the age, from spurious autobiography to spurious hallucination, as well as to the shabby careerism of traditional journalism. It's a greased pig. Essays are associated with the way young writers fashion a name—on plain, crowded newsprint in hybrid vehicles like the *Village Voice, Rolling Stone,* the *New York Review of Books,* instead of the thick paper stock and thin readership of *Partisan Review.*

Essays, however, hang somewhere on a line between two sturdy poles: 4
this is what I think, and this is what I am. Autobiographies which aren't novels are generally extended essays, indeed. A personal essay is like the human voice talking, its order the mind's natural flow, instead of a systematized outline of ideas. Though more wayward or informal than an article or treatise, somewhere it contains a point which is its real center, even if the point couldn't be uttered in fewer words than the essayist has used. Essays don't usually boil down to a summary, as articles do, and the style of the writer has a "nap" to it, a combination of personality and originality and energetic loose ends that stand up like the nap on a piece of wool and can't be brushed flat. Essays belong to the animal kingdom, with a surface that generates sparks, like a coat of fur, compared with the flat, conventional cotton of the magazine article writer, who works in the vegetable kingdom, instead. But essays, on the other hand, may have fewer "levels" than fiction, because we are not supposed to argue much about their meaning. In the old distinction between teaching and storytelling, the essayist, however cleverly he camouflages his intentions, is a bit of a teacher or reformer, and an essay is intended to convey the same point to each of us.

This emphasis upon mind speaking to mind is what makes essays less   5
universal in their appeal than stories. They are addressed to an educated, perhaps a middle-class, reader, with certain presuppositions, a frame of reference, even a commitment to civility that is shared—not the grand and golden empathy inherent in every man or woman that a storyteller has a chance to tap.

Nevertheless, the artful "I" of an essay can be as chameleon as any nar-   6
rator in fiction; and essays do tell a story quite as often as a short story stakes a claim to a particular viewpoint. Mark Twain's piece called "Corn-pone Opinions," for example, which is about public opinion, begins with a vignette as vivid as any in *Huckleberry Finn.* Twain says that when he was a boy of fifteen, he used to hang out a back window and listen to the sermons preached by a neighbor's slave standing on top of a woodpile: "He imitated the pulpit style of the several clergymen of the village, and did it well and with fine passion and energy. To me he was a wonder. I believed he was the greatest orator in the United States and would some day be heard from. But it did not happen; in the distribution of rewards he was overlooked. . . . He interrupted his preaching now and then to saw a stick of wood, but the sawing was a pretense— he did it with his mouth, exactly imitating the sound the bucksaw makes in shrieking its way through the wood. But it served its purpose, it kept his master from coming out to see how the work was getting along."

A novel would go on and tell us what happened next in the life of the 7
slave—and we miss that. But the extraordinary flexibility of essays is what has
enabled them to ride out rough weather and hybridize into forms that suit the
times. And just as one of the first things a fiction writer learns is that he needn't
actually be writing fiction to write a short story—that he can tell his own history
or anybody else's as exactly as he remembers it and it will be "fiction" if it remains primarily a story—an essayist soon discovers that he doesn't have to tell
the whole truth and nothing but the truth; he can shape or shave his memories,
as long as the purpose is served of elucidating a truthful point. A personal essay
frequently is not autobiographical at all, but what it does keep in common with
autobiography is that, through its tone and tumbling progression, it conveys
the quality of the author's mind. Nothing gets in the way. Because essays are
directly concerned with the mind and the mind's idiosyncrasy, the very freedom
the mind possesses is bestowed on this branch of literature that does honor to
it, and the fascination of the mind is the fascination of the essay.

1976

Purpose and Meaning

1. According to Hoagland, what unique properties constitute an essay? What is
   the unique purpose of an essayist?

2. Consider the attributes Hoagland applies in defining the essay and the essayist.
   How does this particular essay fulfill Hoagland's own criteria for an essay?

Language and Style

1. Hoagland describes the essay form with some unusual images: "It's a greased
   pig" (paragraph 3); "the style of the writer has a 'nap' to it" (paragraph 4); "Essays
   belong to the animal kingdom" (paragraph 4). Do these examples of figurative
   language clarify or cloud Hoagland's definition? Explain. How does the use of
   these images exemplify Hoagland's idea of the form of an essay? What other
   examples of figurative language can be found in the essay?

2. Hoagland seems to enjoy using adjectives in an innovative fashion. What is the
   effect of the following on his style; "a *mercurial, newfangled,* sometimes *hokey*
   affair" (paragraph 3); "*shabby* careerism" (paragraph 3); "*tumbling* progression"
   (paragraph 7)? Try substituting more "usual" adjectives for these. What is their
   effect on the style?

3. Hoagland states that the essay assumes "a commitment to civility that is shared"
   between the writer and reader. In what way are Hoagland's diction and tone
   "civil"? Can you apply this "civility" to the other writers in this book? Are there
   any whom you would consider "uncivil"?

Strategy and Structure

1. In paragraph 4, Hoagland states: "A personal essay is like the human voice talk-ing," and in paragraph 7, he says that the essay "conveys the quality of the author's mind." Does this essay have either of these two characteristics? Or is it really a "systemized outline of ideas," the very thing Hoagland says it isn't?

2. What function does the extended example in paragraph 6 serve in the overall pattern of the essay? Why was or wasn't it necessary to include it?

3. Although Hoagland is himself an essayist, he never refers to his own experience as a writer. How does this strategy contribute to the focus of the essay?

Thinking and Writing

1. Writing has many literary forms: the novel, the short story, the poem, and some more familiar forms like the letter, the instruction manual, the newspaper report, and the advertisement. Select one of the latter types and write an expository essay explaining its form and function.

2. Write an essay arguing that the essay is indeed a highly disciplined mode of writing with a clear organization, structure, and coherence, and is *not* like "a human voice talking."

3. List all the criteria that Hoagland gives in describing the essay. Using this list as a guide, select one of the writers in this book, and write your own essay explaining how the works of the writer you have selected exemplify the essayist's art.

Photograph © 1990 by Jill Krementz

JOAN DIDION

In her essay "Why I Write," developed originally as an address to the faculty at the University of California at Berkeley, Joan Didion acknowledges that she took the title of her talk from an essay by George Orwell. Like Orwell, she functions, in her writing, as the conscience of her generation. Both authors attack received opinion and bankrupt ideology. Both are militant writers seeking to expose shoddy thinking and blatant lying with a style that is crisp, concrete, and clear. Both are superb at creating nonfiction of stupendous narrative and descriptive strength.

Didion was born in Sacramento, California, in 1934, educated in Sacramento schools and, from 1952 to 1956, at the University of California at Berkeley. The physical, psychological, and cultural landscape of California has been a dominant element in both her fiction and nonfiction. For example, in her first essay collection, *Slouching Towards Bethlehem* (1968), is a section subtitled "Lifestyles in the Golden Land." That section contains eight journalistic feature articles that treat the American West as an emblem for the national experience and the American character. As she indicates in "Marrying Absurd," "Las Vegas is the most extreme and allegorical of American settlements." Personal essays, such as "On Self-Respect" and "On Morality," also appear in Didion's classic first collection and continue the theme initiated by its Yeatsean title—that the center of contemporary civilization cannot hold. Nevertheless, Didion, with sophistication, perception, and ironic nuance, forces herself, as she declares in her preface, "to come to terms with disorder" and thereby assert her worth as a writer.

As a writer—and notably as an essayist—Joan Didion has few living peers. American poet and novelist James Dickey calls her "the finest woman prose stylist writing in English today." Precise and unsentimental, she has a talent—as did Orwell—for the minute, telling detail. The sharpness, for instance, of her portrayal of the Cuban presence in "Miami" and its uneasy coexistence with old-fashioned Southern culture demonstrates Didion's ability to capture both the grotesque and the apocalyptic contours of contemporary culture in a collage of memorable images. In *Slouching Towards Bethlehem; The White Album* (1979), her second essay collection; *Salvador* (1983); and *Miami* (1987), she offers unforgettable portraits of people and places caught in the absurdity and terror of the times.

Didion also engages in relentless self-scrutiny. Readers of her essays learn more than they might feel comfortable learning about her marriage to writer John Gregory Dunne, their drinking, her depression, her "migraine personality," and their daily lives in Brentwood Park, Los Angeles. Even readers of her novels—among them *Run River* (1963) and *Play It As It Lays* (1970), which was nominated for a National Book Award—will find in their characters images of the frail, diminutive, volatile author.

Didion's introspective impulse is a major literary strength, for it opens her to the feelings and attitudes of others. Dubbed by her California friends as "the Kafka of Brentwood Park," Joan Didion is a wise and often witty purveyor of the postures of contemporary alienation. For Didion, even the myth of the American Eden, the Golden Land, contains within it what she has termed "the unspeakable peril of the everyday," which she locates in the tension between the innocence and evil in the American grain.

Marrying Absurd

To be married in Las Vegas, Clark County, Nevada, a bride must swear
that she is eighteen or has parental permission and a bridegroom that he is
twenty-one or has parental permission. Someone must put up five dollars for
the license. (On Sundays and holidays, fifteen dollars. The Clark County Courthouse issues marriage licenses at any time of the day or night except between
noon and one in the afternoon, between eight and nine in the evening, and
between four and five in the morning.) Nothing else is required. The State of
Nevada, alone among these United States, demands neither a premarital blood
test nor a waiting period before or after the issuance of a marriage license. Driving
in across the Mojave from Los Angeles, one sees the signs way out on the desert,
looming up from that moonscape of rattlesnakes and mesquite, even before
the Las Vegas lights appear like a mirage on the horizon: "GETTING MARRIED?
Free License Information First Strip Exit." Perhaps the Las Vegas wedding
industry achieved its peak operational efficiency between 9:00 p.m. and midnight of August 26, 1965, an otherwise unremarkable Thursday which happened
to be, by Presidential order, the last day on which anyone could improve his
draft status merely by getting married. One hundred and seventy-one couples
were pronounced man and wife in the name of Clark County and the State
of Nevada that night, sixty-seven of them by a single justice of the peace,
Mr. James A. Brennan. Mr. Brennan did one wedding at the Dunes and the
other sixty-six in his office, and charged each couple eight dollars. One bride
lent her veil to six others. "I got it down from five to three minutes," Mr. Brennan
said later of his feat. "I could've married them *en masse*, but they're people,
not cattle. People expect more when they get married."

What people who get married in Las Vegas actually do expect—what,
in the largest sense, their "expectations" are—strikes one as a curious and self-
contradictory business. Las Vegas is the most extreme and allegorical of
American settlements, bizarre and beautiful in its venality and in its devotion
to immediate gratification, a place the tone of which is set by mobsters and
call girls and ladies' room attendants with amyl nitrite poppers in their uniform
pockets. Almost everyone notes that there is no "time" in Las Vegas, no night
and no day and no past and no future (no Las Vegas casino, however, has taken
the obliteration of the ordinary time sense quite so far as Harold's Club in Reno,
which for a while issued, at odd intervals in the day and night, mimeographed
"bulletins" carrying news from the world outside); neither is there any logical
sense of where one is. One is standing on a highway in the middle of a vast

hostile desert looking at an eighty-foot sign which blinks "STARDUST" or "CAESAR'S PALACE." Yes, but what does that explain? This geographical implausibility reinforces the sense that what happens there has no connection with "real" life; Nevada cities like Reno and Carson are ranch towns, Western towns, places behind which there is some historical imperative. But Las Vegas seems to exist only in the eye of the beholder. All of which makes it an extraordinarily stimulating and interesting place, but an odd one in which to want to wear a candlelight satin Priscilla of Boston wedding dress with Chantilly lace insets, tapered sleeves and a detachable modified train.

And yet the Las Vegas wedding business seems to appeal to precisely that   3 impulse. "Sincere and Dignified Since 1954," one wedding chapel advertises. There are nineteen such wedding chapels in Las Vegas, intensely competitive, each offering better, faster, and, by implication, more sincere services than the next: Our Photos Best Anywhere, Your Wedding on A Phonograph Record, Candlelight with Your Ceremony, Honeymoon Accommodations, Free Transportation from Your Motel to Courthouse to Chapel and Return to Motel, Religious or Civil Ceremonies, Dressing Rooms, Flowers, Rings, Announcements, Witnesses Available, and Ample Parking. All of these services, like most others in Las Vegas (sauna baths, payroll-check cashing, chinchilla coats for sale or rent) are offered twenty-four hours a day, seven days a week, presumably on the premise that marriage, like craps, is a game to be played when the table seems hot.

But what strikes one most about the Strip chapels, with their wishing wells   4 and stained-glass paper windows and their artificial bouvardia, is that so much of their business is by no means a matter of simple convenience, of late-night liaisons between show girls and baby Crosbys. Of course there is some of that. (One night about eleven o'clock in Las Vegas I watched a bride in an orange minidress and masses of flame-colored hair stumble from a Strip chapel on the arm of her bridegroom, who looked the part of the expendable nephew in movies like *Miami Syndicate*. "I gotta get the kids," the bride whimpered. "I gotta pick up the sitter, I gotta get to the midnight show." "What you gotta get," the bridegroom said, opening the door of a Cadillac Coupe de Ville and watching her crumple on the seat, "is sober.") But Las Vegas seems to offer something other than "convenience"; it is merchandising "niceness," the facsimile of proper ritual, to children who do not know how else to find it, how to make the arrangements, how to do it "right." All day and evening long on the Strip, one sees actual wedding parties, waiting under the harsh lights at a crosswalk, standing uneasily in the parking lot of the Frontier while the photographer hired by The Little Church of the West ("Wedding Place of the Stars") certifies the occasion, takes the picture: the bride in a veil and white satin pumps, the bridegroom usually in a white dinner jacket, and even an attendant or two, a sister or a best friend in hot-pink *peau de soie*, a flirtation veil, a carnation nosegay. "When I Fall in Love It Will Be Forever," the organist plays, and then a few bars of

Lohengrin. The mother cries; the stepfather, awkward in his role, invites the chapel hostess to join them for a drink at the Sands. The hostess declines with a professional smile; she has already transferred her interest to the group waiting outside. One bride out, another in, and again the sign goes up on the chapel door: "One moment please—Wedding."

I sat next to one such wedding party in a Strip restaurant the last time   5
I was in Las Vegas. The marriage had just taken place; the bride still wore her dress, the mother her corsage. A bored waiter poured out a few swallows of pink champagne ("on the house") for everyone but the bride, who was too young to be served. "You'll need something with more kick than that," the bride's father said with heavy jocularity to his new son-in-law; the ritual jokes about the wedding night had a certain Panglossian character, since the bride was clearly several months pregnant. Another round of pink champagne, this time not on the house, and the bride began to cry. "It was just as nice," she sobbed, "as I hoped and dreamed it would be."

1967

Purpose and Meaning

1. What makes getting married in Las Vegas absurd? What is Didion's purpose here? What assumptions do we have about marriage that make the Las Vegas practice seem absurd?

2. What is Didion's thesis? How effective is the title in suggesting the thesis? What alternative title could you give it that would summarize the author's thesis?

3. What does Didion mean in paragraph 2 when she says that "Las Vegas is the most extreme and allegorical of American settlements"?

Language and Style

1. Reread paragraph 2. Note the way in which Didion describes the "atmosphere" of Las Vegas. In what way do the syntax and length of her sentences help create a sense of this atmosphere? Study, in particular, the sentence that begins, "Almost everyone notes that there is no 'time' in Las Vegas...."

2. In paragraph 2, Didion states that what people expect in Las Vegas is "a curious and self-contradictory business." How are Mr. Brennan's comments in paragraph 1 about marriage a self-contradiction? Where else does Didion use irony to provide evidence of this self-contradiction?

3. In paragraphs 3 and 4, Didion is quite specific in her itemization, listing the many signs that advertise the marriage services in Las Vegas, car models, and song titles. How does this attention to detail contribute to the portrayal of merchandising that goes on in the city?

Strategy and Structure

1. Is Didion's theme made clear in the introduction? What is the effect of starting the essay as if we had jumped into it in the middle?

2. Paragraph 2 makes almost no reference to marriage. Is there little connection between it and paragraph 1? What function does paragraph 2 serve in the overall scheme of the essay?

3. Didion uses narration, description, and exposition in her essay. Which paragraphs coincide with which of these three forms? Does this blend of forms contribute to or detract from the impact of the essay?

4. The essay's conclusion describes a brief incident that Didion witnessed. How effective was it to conclude the essay this way? Why does the essay end with a direct quotation? Would it have been more effective to *summarize* the theme of the essay in the conclusion?

Thinking and Writing

1. Select a place that has special significance to you. Write an essay in which you reveal your attitude about this place in the way you present it. Try to avoid stating a specific thesis about the place, but instead allow the description and narration to convey your main meaning.

2. Compare your own image of Las Vegas or Atlantic City with that of Didion. What elements have shaped your image?

3. Select from among TV, theme parks, circuses, or shopping malls. Then write an expository essay explaining the techniques one of these places uses to manipulate or satisfy your expectations of it. What are your desires and expectations? What methods, techniques, props, and timing does the place use to influence us?

On Self-Respect

Once, in a dry season, I wrote in large letters across two pages of a notebook that innocence ends when one is stripped of the delusion that one likes oneself. Although now, some years later, I marvel that a mind on the outs with itself should have nonetheless made painstaking record of its every tremor, I recall with embarrassing clarity the flavor of those particular ashes. It was a matter of misplaced self-respect.

I had not been elected to Phi Beta Kappa. This failure could scarcely have   2
been more predictable or less ambiguous (I simply did not have the grades),
but I was unnerved by it; I had somehow thought myself a kind of academic
Raskolnikov, curiously exempt from the cause-effect relationships which
hampered others. Although even the humorless nineteen-year-old that I was
must have recognized that the situation lacked real tragic stature, the day that
I did not make Phi Beta Kappa nonetheless marked the end of something, and
innocence may well be the word for it. I lost the conviction that lights would
always turn green for me, the pleasant certainty that those rather passive virtues
which had won me approval as a child automatically guaranteed me not only
Phi Beta Kappa keys but happiness, honor, and the love of a good man; lost
a certain touching faith in the totem power of good manners, clean hair, and
proven competence on the Stanford-Binet scale. To such doubtful amulets had
my self-respect been pinned, and I faced myself that day with the nonplused
apprehension of someone who has come across a vampire and has no crucifix
at hand.

Although to be driven back upon oneself is an uneasy affair at best, rather   3
like trying to cross a border with borrowed credentials, it seems to me now
the one condition necessary to the beginnings of real self-respect. Most of our
platitudes notwithstanding, self-deception remains the most difficult deception.
The tricks that work on others count for nothing in that very well-lit back alley
where one keeps assignations with oneself: no winning smiles will do here, no
prettily drawn lists of good intentions. One shuffles flashily but in vain through
one's marked cards—the kindness done for the wrong reason, the apparent
triumph which involved no real effort, the seemingly heroic act into which one
had been shamed. The dismal fact is that self-respect has nothing to do with
the approval of others—who are, after all, deceived easily enough; has nothing
to do with reputation, which, as Rhett Butler told Scarlett O'Hara, is something
people with courage can do without.

To do without self-respect, on the other hand, is to be an unwilling   4
audience of one to an interminable documentary that details one's failings, both
real and imagined, with fresh footage spliced in for every screening. *There's
the glass you broke in anger, there's the hurt on X's face; watch now, this next
scene, the night Y came back from Houston, see how you muff this one.* To
live without self-respect is to lie awake some night, beyond the reach of warm
milk, phenobarbital, and the sleeping hand on the coverlet, counting up the
sins of commission and omission, the trusts betrayed, the promises subtly
broken, the gifts irrevocably wasted through sloth or cowardice or carelessness.
However long we postpone it, we eventually lie down alone in that notoriously
uncomfortable bed, the one we make ourselves. Whether or not we sleep in
it depends, of course, on whether or not we respect ourselves.

To protest that some fairly improbable people, some people who *could*   5
not possibly respect themselves, seem to sleep easily enough is to miss the point
entirely, as surely as those people miss it who think that self-respect has

necessarily to do with not having safety pins in one's underwear. There is a common superstition that "self-respect" is a kind of charm against snakes, something that keeps those who have it locked in some unblighted Eden, out of strange beds, ambivalent conversations, and trouble in general. It does not at all. It has nothing to do with the face of things, but concerns instead a separate peace, a private reconciliation. Although the careless, suicidal Julian English in *Appointment in Samarra* and the careless, incurably dishonest Jordan Baker in *The Great Gatsby* seem equally improbable candidates for self-respect, Jordan Baker had it, Julian English did not. With that genius for accommodation more often seen in women than in men, Jordan took her own measure, made her own peace, avoided threats to that peace: "I hate careless people," she told Nick Carraway. "It takes two to make an accident."

Like Jordan Baker, people with self-respect have the courage of their mistakes. They know the price of things. If they choose to commit adultery, they do not then go running, in an access of bad conscience, to receive absolution from the wronged parties; nor do they complain unduly of the unfairness, the undeserved embarrassment, of being named co-respondent. In brief, people with self-respect exhibit a certain toughness, a kind of moral nerve; they display what was once called *character*, a quality which, although approved in the abstract, sometimes loses ground to other, more instantly negotiable virtues. The measure of its slipping prestige is that one tends to think of it only in connection with homely children and United States senators who have been defeated, preferably in the primary, for reelection. Nonetheless, character— the willingness to accept responsibility for one's own life—is the source from which self-respect springs.

Self-respect is something that our grandparents, whether or not they had it, knew all about. They had instilled in them, young, a certain discipline, the sense that one lives by doing things one does not particularly want to do, by putting fears and doubts to one side, by weighing immediate comforts against the possibility of larger, even intangible, comforts. It seemed to the nineteenth century admirable, but not remarkable, that Chinese Gordon put on a clean white suit and held Khartoum against the Mahdi; it did not seem unjust that the way to free land in California involved death and difficulty and dirt. In a diary kept during the winter of 1846, an emigrating twelve-year-old named Narcissa Cornwall noted coolly: "Father was busy reading and did not notice that the house was being filled with strange Indians until Mother spoke about it." Even lacking any clue as to what Mother said, one can scarcely fail to be impressed by the entire incident: the father reading, the Indians filing in, the mother choosing the words that would not alarm, the child duly recording the event and noting further that those particular Indians were not, "fortunately for us," hostile. Indians were simply part of the *donnée*.

In one guise or another, Indians always are. Again, it is a question of recognizing that anything worth having has its price. People who respect themselves are willing to accept the risk that the Indians will be hostile, that the venture will go bankrupt, that the liaison may not turn out to be one in which *every day is a holiday because you're married to me.* They are willing to invest something of themselves; they may not play at all, but when they do play, they know the odds.

That kind of self-respect is a discipline, a habit of mind that can never 9
be faked but can be developed, trained, coaxed forth. It was once suggested to me that, as an antidote to crying, I put my head in a paper bag. As it happens, there is a sound physiological reason, something to do with oxygen, for doing exactly that, but the psychological effect alone is incalculable: it is difficult in the extreme to continue fancying oneself Cathy in *Wuthering Heights* with one's head in a Food Fair bag. There is a similar case for all the small disciplines, unimportant in themselves; imagine maintaining any kind of swoon, com-miserative or carnal, in a cold shower.

But those small disciplines are valuable only insofar as they represent larger 10
ones. To say that Waterloo was won on the playing fields of Eton is not to say that Napoleon might have been saved by a crash program in cricket; to give formal dinners in the rain forest would be pointless did not the candlelight flicker-ing on the liana call forth deeper, stronger disciplines, values instilled long before. It is a kind of ritual, helping us to remember who and what we are. In order to remember it, one must have known it.

To have that sense of one's intrinsic worth which constitutes self-respect 11
is potentially to have everything: the ability to discriminate, to love and to re-main indifferent. To lack it is to be locked within oneself, paradoxically incapable of either love or indifference. If we do not respect ourselves, we are on the one hand forced to despise those who have so few resources as to consort with us, so little perception as to remain blind to our fatal weaknesses. On the other, we are peculiarly in thrall to everyone we see, curiously determined to live out—since our self-image is untenable—their false notions of us. We flatter ourselves by thinking this compulsion to please others an attractive trait: a gist for im-aginative empathy, evidence of our willingness to give. *Of course* I will play Francesca to your Paolo, Helen Keller to anyone's Annie Sullivan: no expecta-tion is too misplaced, no role too ludicrous. At the mercy of those we cannot but hold in contempt, we play roles doomed to failure before they are begun, each defeat generating fresh despair at the urgency of divining and meeting the next demand made upon us.

It is the phenomenon sometimes called "alienation from self." In its ad- 12
vanced stages, we no longer answer the telephone, because someone might want something; that we could say *no* without drowning in self-reproach is an idea alien to this game. Every encounter demands too much, tears the nerves, drains the will, and the specter of something as small as an unanswered letter arouses such disproportionate guilt that answering it becomes out of the question. To assign unanswered letters their proper weight, to free us from the expectations of others, to give us back to ourselves—there lies the great, the singular power

of self-respect. Without it, one eventually discovers the final turn of the screw: one runs away to find oneself, and finds no one at home.

1961

Purpose and Meaning

1. According to Didion, what is self-respect? Is one born with it, or is it developed later? What are the benefits of having self-respect?

2. In the first two paragraphs, Didion describes a momentous time in her life when her innocence ended. What caused this end of innocence? What was its effect on her? What is its relationship to self-respect?

3. What type of audience is Didion writing for? How do you know?

Language and Style

1. In paragraph 1, Didion uses three images that suggest a somber time in her life: "a dry season"; "stripped of the delusion"; and "particular ashes." How do these images establish the tone of the essay? How do they relate to Didion's concept of self-respect?

2. In paragraph 2, Didion uses three supernatural images: "totem power," "doubtful amulets," and "crucifix at hand." What is the relevance of these images to Didion's thesis? Why are they used as images of the lack of self-respect? In what way do they represent Didion's unique writing style? What other patterns of imagery, simile, and metaphor can you detect in the essay?

3. Study this rather long sentence in paragraph 6: "If they choose to commit adultery, they do not then go running, in an access of bad conscience, to receive absolution from the wronged parties; nor do they complain unduly of the unfairness, the undeserved embarrassment, of being named co-respondent." How many ideas does Didion cover in this sentence? What gives the sentence its complexity? What gives it its strength? How is it representative of other sentences in the essay? Reread the essay to find similar examples of Didion's syntax. What are the similarities between the sample sentence and others?

Strategy and Structure

1. Study the three sections of the essay. Why has Didion divided her essay in this way? What is the relationship of each part to the others?

2. Examine paragraphs 3 and 4. What are the central images of each? How do these central images give the paragraphs their unity?

3. Didion makes some literary and historical references in her essay. What purpose do these references serve? With how many of these were you familiar? Do they contribute to or detract from her argument? Explain.

4. How does Didion develop her extended definition of self-respect in this essay?

Thinking and Writing

1. How does Didion support her thesis: through example; anecdote; facts; personal experience? Make a list of her supporting points, dividing them into appropriate categories. Then write an essay on how the methods she uses to support her argument are appropriate to the subject matter.

2. In paragraph 6, Didion compares self-respect to the concept of character. Write an essay defining and describing the concept of character, employing the same kinds of supports that Didion uses.

3. There are numerous "self-help" books—many of them best-sellers—that claim to offer guidelines to achieve self-respect, self-realization, and personal success. Argue for or against the proposition that one can learn self-respect by following the instructions in a book.

On Morality

As it happens I am in Death Valley, in a room at the Enterprise Motel   1
and Trailer Park, and it is July, and it is hot. In fact it is 119°. I cannot seem
to make the air conditioner work, but there is a small refrigerator, and I can
wrap ice cubes in a towel and hold them against the small of my back. With
the help of the ice cubes I have been trying to think, because *The American
Scholar* asked me to, in some abstract way about "morality," a word I distrust
more every day, but my mind veers inflexibly toward the particular.

Here are some particulars. At midnight last night, on the road in from   2
Las Vegas to Death Valley Junction, a car hit a shoulder and turned over. The
driver, very young and apparently drunk, was killed instantly. His girl was
found alive but bleeding internally, deep in shock. I talked this afternoon to
the nurse who had driven the girl to the nearest doctor, 185 miles across the
floor of the Valley and three ranges of lethal mountain road. The nurse explained
that her husband, a talc miner, had stayed on the highway with the boy's body
until the coroner could get over the mountains from Bishop, at dawn today.
"You can't just leave a body on the highway," she said. "It's immoral."

It was one instance in which I did not distrust the word, because she meant   3
something quite specific. She meant that if a body is left alone for even a few
minutes on the desert, the coyotes close in and eat the flesh. Whether or not
a corpse is torn apart by coyotes may seem only a sentimental consideration,

but of course it is more: one of the promises we make to one another is that we will try to retrieve our casualties, try not to abandon our dead to the coyotes. If we have been taught to keep our promises—if, in the simplest terms, our upbringing is good enough—we stay with the body, or have bad dreams.

I am talking, of course, about the kind of social code that is sometimes   4 called, usually pejoratively, "wagon-train morality." In fact that is precisely what it is. For better or worse, we are what we learned as children: my own childhood was illuminated by graphic litanies of the grief awaiting those who failed in their loyalties to each other. The Donner-Reed Party, starving in the Sierra snows, all the ephemera of civilization gone save that one vestigial taboo, the provision that no one should eat his own blood kin. The Jayhawkers, who quarreled and separated not far from where I am tonight. Some of them died in the Funerals and some of them died down near Badwater and most of the rest of them died in the Panamints. A woman who got through gave the Valley its name. Some might say that the Jayhawkers were killed by the desert summer, and the Donner Party by the mountain winter, by circumstances beyond control; we were taught instead that they had somewhere abdicated their responsibilities, somehow breached their primary loyalties, or they would not have found themselves helpless in the mountain winter or the desert summer, would not have given way to acrimony, would not have deserted one another, would not have *failed*. In brief, we heard such stories as cautionary tales, and they still suggest the only kind of "morality" that seems to me to have any but the most potentially mendacious meaning.

You are quite possibly impatient with me by now; I am talking, you want   5 to say, about a "morality" so primitive that it scarcely deserves the name, a code that has as its point only survival, not the attainment of the ideal good. Exactly. Particularly out here tonight, in this country so ominous and terrible that to live in it is to live with antimatter, it is difficult to believe that "the good" is a knowable quantity. Let me tell you what it is like out here tonight. Stories travel at night on the desert. Someone gets in his pickup and drives a couple of hundred miles for a beer, and he carries news of what is happening, back wherever he came from. Then he drives another hundred miles for another beer, and passes along stories from the last place as well as from the one before; it is a network kept alive by people whose instincts tell them that if they do not keep moving at night on the desert they will lose all reason. Here is a story that is going around the desert tonight: over across the Nevada line, sheriff's deputies are diving in some underground pools, trying to retrieve a couple of bodies known to be in the hole. The widow of one of the drowned boys is over there; she is eighteen, and pregnant, and is said not to leave the hole. The divers go down and come up, and she just stands there and stares into the water. They have been diving for ten days but have found no bottom to the caves, no bodies and no trace of them, only the black 90° water going down and down and down, and a single translucent fish, not classified. The story tonight is that one of the divers has been hauled up incoherent, out of his head, shouting—until they got him out of there so that the widow could not hear—about water that got hotter instead of cooler as he went down, about light flickering through the water, about magma, about underground nuclear testing.

That is the tone stories take out here, and there are quite a few of them tonight. And it is more than the stories alone. Across the road at the Faith Community Church a couple of dozen old people, come here to live in trailers and die in the sun, are holding a prayer sing. I cannot hear them and do not want to. What I can hear are occasional coyotes and a constant chorus of "Baby the Rain Must Fall" from the jukebox in the Snake Room next door, and if I were also to hear those dying voices, those Midwestern voices drawn to this lunar country for some unimaginable atavistic rites, *rock of ages cleft for me,* I think I would lose my own reason. Every now and then I imagine I hear a rattlesnake, but my husband says that it is a faucet, a paper rustling, the wind. Then he stands by a window, and plays a flashlight over the dry wash outside.

What does it mean? It means nothing manageable. There is some sinister hysteria in the air out here tonight, some hint of the monstrous perversion to which any human idea can come. "I followed my own conscience." "I did what I thought was right." How many madmen have said it and meant it? How many murderers? Klaus Fuchs said it, and the men who committed the Mountain Meadows Massacre said it, and Alfred Rosenberg said it. And, as we are rotely and rather presumptuously reminded by those who would say it now, Jesus said it. Maybe we have all said it, and maybe we have been wrong. Except on that most primitive level—our loyalties to those we love—what could be more arrogant than to claim the primacy of personal conscience? ("Tell me," a rabbi asked Daniel Bell when he said, as a child, that he did not believe in God. "Do you think God cares?") At least some of the time, the world appears to me as a painting by Hieronymous Bosch; were I to follow my conscience then, it would lead me out onto the desert with Marion Faye, out to where he stood in *The Deer Park* looking east to Los Alamos and praying, as if for rain, that it would happen: *". . . let it come and clear the rot and the stench and the stink, let it come for all of everywhere, just so it comes and the world stands clear in the white dead dawn."*

Of course you will say that I do not have the right, even if I had the power, to inflict that unreasonable conscience upon you; nor do I want you to inflict your conscience, however reasonable, however enlightened, upon me. ("We must be aware of the dangers which lie in our most generous wishes," Lionel Trilling once wrote. "Some paradox of our nature leads us, when once we have made our fellow men the objects of our enlightened interest, to go on to make them the objects of our pity, then of our wisdom, ultimately of our coercion.") That the ethic of conscience is intrinsically insidious seems scarcely a revelatory point, but it is one raised with increasing infrequency; even those who do raise it tend to *segue* with troubling readiness into the quite contradictory position that the ethic of conscience is dangerous when it is "wrong," and admirable when it is "right."

You see I want to be quite obstinate about insisting that we have no way of knowing—beyond that fundamental loyalty to the social code—what is "right" and what is "wrong," what is "good" and what "evil." I dwell so upon this because the most disturbing aspect of "morality" seems to me to be the frequency with which the word now appears; in the press, on television, in the most perfunctory kinds of conversation. Questions of straightforward power (or survival) politics, questions of quite indifferent public policy, questions of almost anything: they are all assigned these factitious moral burdens. There is something facile going on, some self-indulgence at work. Of course we would all like to "believe" in something, like to assuage our private guilts in public causes, like to lose our tiresome selves; like, perhaps, to transform the white flag of defeat at home into the brave white banner of battle away from home. And of course it is all right to do that; that is how, immemorially, things have gotten done. But I think it is all right only so long as we do not delude ourselves about what we are doing, and why. It is all right only so long as we remember that all the *ad hoc* committees, all the picket lines, all the brave signatures in *The New York Times,* all the tools of agitprop straight across the spectrum, do not confer upon anyone any *ipso facto* virtue. It is all right only so long as we recognize that the end may or may not be expedient, may or may not be a good idea, but in any case has nothing to do with "morality." Because when we start deceiving ourselves into thinking not that we want something or need something, not that it is a pragmatic necessity for us to have it, but that it is a *moral imperative* that we have it, then is when we join the fashionable madmen, and then is when the thin whine of hysteria is heard in the land, and then is when we are in bad trouble. And I suspect we are already there.

1965

Purpose and Meaning

1. According to Didion, what kind of morality is positive and what kind is negative?

2. Toward the end of the last paragraph, Didion mentions certain "agitprop" activities. What is the cultural and historical context of these references? How important is familiarity with them in understanding the cultural and historical significance of the essay?

3. In paragraph 8, Didion states that the "ethic of conscience is intrinsically insidious." What does she mean? How does she support this contention?

Language and Style

1. As in Didion's other essays, this one contains long sentences with complex syntax. What makes the following sentence typical of Didion's style: "Whether or

not a corpse is torn apart by coyotes may seem only a sentimental consideration, but of course it is more: one of the promises we make to one another is
that we will try to retrieve our casualties, try not to abandon our dead to the
coyotes"? What other sentences in the essay bear a syntactic resemblance to this
one? Compare this sentence to those in her other essays. What observations can
you make about her writing style?

2. Paragraph 6 begins, "That is the tone stories take out here." What tone is she
referring to? How does paragraph 5 exemplify this tone?

3. Examine Didion's approach to abstract and concrete language in this essay. What
is the effect on the reader?

4. In what way is Didion's tone a moral one? How seriously does she seem to be
taking the subject she has been asked to write about by *The American Scholar*?
Does her tone contradict her argument?

Strategy and Structure

1. Why has Didion begun her essay with a description of the environment? What
relationship does this description bear to her thesis? Compare the opening of
this essay to those of "Marrying Absurd" and "On Self-Respect." What element
do they have in common? What effect do all three essays have on the reader?

2. Section 2 begins, "You are quite possibly impatient with me by now"; section
3 begins, "Of course you will say that I do not have the right." How does the
use of the pronoun *you* here and elsewhere affect the tone of the essay? How
does it determine the intended relationship between the writer and reader and
the structure of her argument on morality?

3. Section 2 ends with a quotation. Why has Didion chosen this strategy? How
does it contribute to her thesis? How does it contribute to the strength of the
transition between the conclusion to section 2 and the beginning of section 3?

Thinking and Writing

1. Didion is opposed to a *"moral imperative."* What is your understanding of a
moral imperative? Argue against this view by writing an essay supporting the
idea that there are certain issues about which one should adopt a moral imperative.

2. To better understand Didion's argument, review the essay, noting Didion's explicit
and implicit arguments. Then write an essay explaining why Didion is opposed
to an abstract morality.

3. Do you perceive the world as cruel, benevolent, orderly, random, purposeful,
or lacking in purpose? Write a personal essay in which you establish your view
of the world. Support your view with examples. For instance, if the world is
orderly, what particular evidence can you find of this order? If you perceive
the world as cruel, what cruel acts can you present to illustrate your opinion?

Why I Write

Of course I stole the title for this talk, from George Orwell. One reason [1]
I stole it was that I like the sound of the words: *Why I Write*. There you have
three short unambiguous words that share a sound, and the sound they share
is this:

I

I

I

In many ways writing is the act of saying *I*, of imposing oneself upon other [2]
people, of saying *listen to me, see it my way, change your mind.* It's an
aggressive, even a hostile act. You can disguise its aggressiveness all you want
with veils of subordinate clauses and qualifiers and tentative subjunctives, with
ellipses and evasions—with the whole manner of intimating rather than claiming, of alluding rather than stating—but there's no getting around the fact that
setting words on paper is the tactic of a secret bully, an invasion, an imposition
of the writer's sensibility on the reader's most private space.

I stole the title not only because the words sounded right but because they [3]
seemed to sum up, in a no-nonsense way, all I have to tell you. Like many writers
I have only this one "subject," this one "area": the act of writing. I can bring
you no reports from any other front. I may have other interests: I am "interested,"
for example, in marine biology, but I don't flatter myself that you would come
out to hear me talk about it. I am not a scholar. I am not in the least an intellectual, which is not to say that when I hear the word "intellectual" I reach for
my gun, but only to say that I do not think in abstracts. During the years when
I was an undergraduate at Berkeley I tried, with a kind of hopeless late-adolescent
energy, to buy some temporary visa into the world of ideas, to forge for myself
a mind that could deal with the abstract.

In short I tried to think. I failed. My attention veered inexorably back [4]
to the specific, to the tangible, to what was generally considered, by everyone
I knew then and for that matter have known since, the peripheral. I would try
to contemplate the Hegelian dialectic and would find myself concentrating instead on a flowering pear tree outside my window and the particular way the
petals fell on my floor. I would try to read linguistic theory and would find
myself wondering instead if the lights were on in the bevatron up the hill. When

I say that I was wondering if the lights were on in the bevatron you might immediately suspect, if you deal in ideas at all, that I was registering the bevatron as a political symbol, thinking in shorthand about the military-industrial complex and its role in the university community, but you would be wrong. I was only wondering if the lights were on in the bevatron, and how they looked. A physical fact.

I had trouble graduating from Berkeley, not because of this inability to   5
deal with ideas—I was majoring in English, and I could locate the house-and-garden imagery in "The Portrait of a Lady" as well as the next person, "imagery" being by definition the kind of specific that got my attention—but simply because I had neglected to take a course in Milton. For reasons which now sound baroque I needed a degree by the end of that summer, and the English department finally agreed, if I would come down from Sacramento every Friday and talk about the cosmology of "Paradise Lost," to certify me proficient in Milton. I did this. Some Fridays I took the Greyhound bus, other Fridays I caught the Southern Pacific's City of San Francisco on the last leg of its transcontinental trip. I can no longer tell you whether Milton put the sun or the earth at the center of the universe in "Paradise Lost," the central question of at least one century and a topic about which I wrote 10,000 words that summer, but I can still recall the exact rancidity of the butter in the City of San Francisco's dining car, and the way the tinted windows on the Greyhound bus cast the oil refineries around Carquinez Straits into a grayed and obscurely sinister light. In short my attention was always on the periphery, on what I could see and taste and touch, on the butter, and the Greyhound bus. During those years I was traveling on what I knew to be a very shaky passport, forged papers: I knew that I was no legitimate resident in any world of ideas. I knew I couldn't think. All I knew then was what I couldn't do. All I knew then was what I wasn't, and it took me some years to discover what I was.

Which was a writer.   6

By which I mean not a "good" writer or a "bad" writer but simply a writer,   7
a person whose most absorbed and passionate hours are spent arranging words on pieces of paper. Had my credentials been in order I would never have become a writer. Had I been blessed with even limited access to my own mind there would have been no reason to write. I write entirely to find out what I'm thinking, what I'm looking at, what I see and what it means. What I want and what I fear. Why did the oil refineries around Carquinez Straits seem sinister to me in the summer of 1956? Why have the night lights in the bevatron burned in my mind for twenty years? *What is going on in these pictures in my mind?*

When I talk about pictures in my mind I am talking, quite specifically,   8
about images that shimmer around the edges. There used to be an illustration in every elementary psychology book showing a cat drawn by a patient in varying stages of schizophrenia. This cat had a shimmer around it. You could see the molecular structure breaking down at the very edges of the cat: the cat became the background and the background the cat, everything interacting, exchanging ions. People on hallucinogens describe the same perception of objects. I'm

not a schizophrenic, nor do I take hallucinogens, but certain images do shimmer for me. Look hard enough, and you can't miss the shimmer. It's there. You can't think too much about these pictures that shimmer. You just lie low and let them develop. You stay quiet. You don't talk to many people and you keep your nervous system from shorting out and you try to locate the cat in the shimmer, the grammar in the picture.

Just as I meant "shimmer" literally I mean "grammar" literally. Grammar   9
is a piano I play by ear, since I seem to have been out of school the year the rules were mentioned. All I know about grammar is its infinite power. To shift the structure of a sentence alters the meaning of that sentence, as definitely and inflexibly as the position of a camera alters the meaning of the object photographed. Many people know about camera angles now, but not so many know about sentences. The arrangement of the words matters, and the arrangement you want can be found in the picture in your mind. The picture dictates the arrangement. The picture dictates whether this will be a sentence with or without clauses, a sentence that ends hard or a dying-fall sentence, long or short, active or passive. The picture tells you how to arrange the words and the arrangement of the words tells you, or tells me, what's going on in the picture. *Nota bene:*

It tells you.   10

You don't tell it.   11

Let me show you what I mean by pictures in the mind. I began "Play It   12
As It Lays" just as I have begun each of my novels, with no notion of "character" or "plot" or even "incident." I had only two pictures in my mind, more about which later, and a technical intention, which was to write a novel so elliptical and fast that it would be over before you noticed it, a novel so fast that it would scarcely exist on the page at all. About the pictures: the first was of white space. Empty space. This was clearly the picture that dictated the narrative intention of the book—a book in which anything that happened would happen off the page, a "white" book to which the reader would have to bring his or her own bad dreams—and yet this picture told me no "story," suggested no situation. The second picture did. This second picture was of something actually witnessed. A young woman with long hair and a short white halter dress walks through the casino at the Riviera in Las Vegas at one in the morning. She crosses the casino alone and picks up a house telephone. I watch her because I have heard her paged, and recognize her name: she is a minor actress I see around Los Angeles from time to time, in places like Jax and once in a gynecologist's office in the Beverly Hills Clinic, but have never met. I know nothing about her. Who is paging her? Why is she here to be paged? How exactly did she come to this? It was precisely this moment in Las Vegas that made "Play It As It Lays" begin to tell itself to me, but the moment appears in the novel only obliquely, in a chapter which begins:

"Maria made a list of things she would never do. She would never: walk   13
through the Sands or Caesar's alone after midnight. She would never: ball at

a party, do S-M unless she wanted to, borrow furs from Abe Lipsey, deal. She would never: carry a Yorkshire in Beverly Hills."

That is the beginning of the chapter and that is also the end of the chapter, which may suggest what I meant by "white space." 14

I recall having a number of pictures in my mind when I began the novel 15 I just finished, "A Book of Common Prayer." As a matter of fact one of these pictures was of that bevatron I mentioned, although I would be hard put to tell you a story in which nuclear energy figured. Another was a newspaper photograph of a hijacked 707 burning on the desert in the Middle East. Another was the night view from a room in which I once spent a week with paratyphoid, a hotel room on the Colombian coast. My husband and I seemed to be on the Colombian coast representing the United States of America at a film festival (I recall invoking the name "Jack Valenti" a lot, as if its reiteration could make me well), and it was a bad place to have fever, not only because my indisposition offended our hosts but because every night in this hotel the generator failed. The lights went out. The elevator stopped. My husband would go to the event of the evening and make excuses for me and I would stay alone in this hotel room, in the dark. I remember standing at the window trying to call Bogotá (the telephone seemed to work on the same principle as the generator) and watching the night wind come up and wondering what I was doing eleven degrees off the equator with a fever of 103. The view from that window definitely figures in "A Book of Common Prayer," as does the burning 707, and yet none of these pictures told me the story I needed.

The picture that did, the picture that shimmered and made these other 16 images coalesce, was the Panama airport at 6 A.M. I was in this airport only once, on a plane to Bogotá that stopped for an hour to refuel, but the way it looked that morning remained superimposed on everything I saw until the day I finished "A Book of Common Prayer." I lived in that airport for several years. I can still feel the hot air when I step off the plane, can see the heat already rising off the tarmac at 6 A.M. I can feel my skirt damp and wrinkled on my legs. I can feel the asphalt stick to my sandals. I remember the big tail of a Pan American plane floating motionless down at the end of the tarmac. I remember the sound of a slot machine in the waiting room. I could tell you that I remember a particular woman in the airport, an American woman, a *norteamericana*, a thin *norteamericana* about 40 who wore a big square emerald in lieu of a wedding ring, but there was no such woman there.

I put this woman in the airport later. I made this woman up, just as I later 17 made up a country to put the airport in, and a family to run the country. This woman in the airport is neither catching a plane nor meeting one. She is ordering tea in the airport coffee shop. In fact she is not simply "ordering" tea but insisting that the water be boiled, in front of her, for twenty minutes. Why is this woman in this airport? Why is she going nowhere, where has she been? Where did she get that big emerald? What derangement, or disassociation, makes her believe that her will to see the water boiled can possibly prevail?

"She had been going to one airport or another for four months, one could [18] see it, looking at the visas on her passport. All those airports where Charlotte Douglas's passport had been stamped would have looked alike. Sometimes the sign on the tower would say 'Bienvenidos' and sometimes the sign on the tower would say 'Bienvenue,' some places were wet and hot and others dry and hot, but at each of these airports the pastel concrete walls would rust and stain and the swamp off the runway would be littered with the fuselages of cannibalized Fairchild F-227's and the water would need boiling.

"I knew why Charlotte went to the airport even if Victor did not.   [19]

"I knew about airports."   [20]

These lines appear about halfway through "A Book of Common Prayer," [21] but I wrote them during the second week I worked on the book, long before I had any idea where Charlotte Douglas had been or why she went to airports. Until I wrote these lines I had no character called "Victor" in mind: the necessity for mentioning a name, and the name "Victor," occurred to me as I wrote the sentence. *I knew why Charlotte went to the airport* sounded incomplete. *I knew why Charlotte went to the airport even if Victor did not* carried a little more narrative drive. Most important of all, until I wrote these lines I did not know who "I" was, who was telling the story. I had intended until that moment that the "I" be no more than the voice of the author, a 19th-century omniscient narrator. But there it was:

"I knew why Charlotte went to the airport even if Victor did not.   [22]

"I knew about airports."   [23]

This "I" was the voice of no author in my house. This "I" was someone [24] who not only knew why Charlotte went to the airport but also knew someone called "Victor." Who was Victor? Who was this narrator? Why was this narrator telling me this story? Let me tell you one thing about why writers write: had I known the answer to any of these questions I would never have needed to write a novel.

1976

Purpose and Meaning

1. Compare Didion's reasons for writing with those Orwell offers in his "Why I Write" essay. How do their reasons differ? How are they similar?

2. In paragraph 2, Didion likens writing to an aggressive act. In what way is this *particular* essay an example of this? How does this fact influence Didion's attitude toward her audience and her "talk"?

3. What does Didion mean in the final sentence of the essay? How closely does this sentence relate to the reasons for writing she enumerates in paragraph 7?

Language and Style

1. Didion claims to have "stolen" the title from Orwell because it sums up what she has to say about writing—specifically, that writing "is the act of saying I." In what way is the word *I* significant in this essay? What special tone does it give the essay that confirms Didion's statement in paragraph 1 that writing is "an imposition of the writer's sensibility on the reader's most private space"?

2. In paragraph 9, Didion explains how a "picture dictates the arrangement" of a sentence. Taking the types of sentences she specifies in this paragraph, find examples of each in Didion's previous essays. How do the arrangements of the sentences you found determine the "picture" the sentence is describing?

3. In paragraph 14, Didion states that she intends paragraph 13 to serve as an example of her goal to create a "white space." In what way is the example (which she states is one entire chapter from the book) an effective illustration of her goal?

4. Consider the excerpt from *A Book of Common Prayer* that constitutes paragraphs 18 through 20. How does the writer's voice in this excerpt from Didion's fiction resemble or differ from the voice of her nonfiction essays?

Strategy and Structure

1. What is Didion's purpose in graphically illustrating the three *I* sounds in the title "Why I Write"?

2. What is the purpose and effect of paragraphs 10 and 11? How do the paragraphs serve as a transition for the paragraphs that precede and follow them?

3. What is the purpose of repeating the dialogue from *A Book of Common Prayer* in paragraphs 22 and 23? How does this excerpt prepare the reader for the concluding paragraph?

Thinking and Writing

1. In paragraph 4, Didion states that her "attention veered inexorably back to the specific." Are you a person who focuses on physical facts; on ideas and the abstract; or on both? Write an essay entitled "How I Think." What are you doing when you are "thinking," as opposed to daydreaming? Provide personal examples, illustrations, and anecdotes to support your view.

2. Why do *you* write? What kinds of satisfaction do you gain from writing? Write an essay developing this theme. If you hate to write, write an essay with the title, "Why I Don't Write."

3. Using the information Didion provides in paragraph 9 concerning the importance of the arrangement of words in her writing, write an expository essay in

which you discuss the role of Didion's syntax in her writing style. Use the other four essays by Didion in this anthology to gather your examples.

4. Compare and contrast the essays entitled "Why I Write" by Orwell and Didion.

o▬o▬o▬o▬o

Miami

"The general wildness, the eternal labyrinths of waters and marshes, interlocked and apparently never ending; the whole surrounded by interminable swamps. . . . Here I am then in the Floridas, thought I," John James Audubon wrote to the editor of *The Monthly American Journal of Geology and Natural Science* during the course of an 1831 foray in the territory then still called the Floridas. The place came first, and to touch down there is to begin to understand why at least six administrations now have found South Florida so fecund a colony. I never passed through security for a flight to Miami without experiencing a certain weightlessness, the heightened wariness of having left the developed world for a more fluid atmosphere, one in which the native distrust of extreme possibilities that tended to ground the temperate United States in an obeisance to democratic institutions seemed rooted, if at all, only shallowly. At the gate for such flights the preferred language was already Spanish. Delays were explained by weather in Panama. The very names of the scheduled destinations suggested a world in which many evangelical inclinations had historically been accommodated, many yearnings toward empire indulged. The Eastern 5:59 P.M. from New York/Kennedy to Miami and Panama and Santiago and Buenos Aires carried in its magazine racks, along with the usual pristine copies of *Golf* and *Ebony* and *U.S. News & World Report*, a monthly called *South: The Third World Magazine*, edited in London and tending to brisk backgrounders on coup rumors and capital flight.

In Miami itself this kind of news was considerably less peripheral than it might have seemed farther north, since to set foot in South Florida was already to be in a place where coup rumors and capital flight were precisely what put money on the street, and also what took it off. The charts on the wall in a Coral Gables investment office gave the time in Panama, San Salvador, Asunción. A chain of local gun shops advertised, as a "Father's Day Sale," the semiautomatic Intratec TEC-9, with extra ammo clip, case, and flash suppressor, reduced from $347.80 to $249.95 and available on layaway. I recall picking up the *Miami Herald* one morning in July of 1985 to read that the Howard Johnson's hotel near the Miami airport had been offering "guerrilla discounts,"

1

2

rooms at seventeen dollars a day under what an employee, when pressed by the *Herald* reporter, described as "a freedom fighters program" that was "supposed to be under wraps."

As in other parts of the world where the citizens shop for guerrilla discounts and bargains in semiautomatic weapons, there was in Miami an advanced interest in personal security. The security installations in certain residential neighborhoods could have been transplanted intact from Bogotá or San Salvador, and even modest householders had detailed information about perimeter defenses, areas of containment, motion monitors and closed-circuit television surveillance. Decorative grilles on doors and windows turned out to have a defensive intent. Break-ins were referred to by the Metro-Dade Police Department as "home invasions," a locution which tended to suggest a city under systematic siege. A firm specializing in security for the home and automobile offered to install bullet proof windows tested to withstand a 7.62mm NATO round of ammunition, for example one fired by an M60. A ten-page pamphlet found, along with $119,500 in small bills, in the Turnberry Isle apartment of an accused cocaine importer gave these tips for maintaining a secure profile: "Try to imitate an American in all his habits. Mow the lawn, wash the car, etc. . . . Have an occasional barbecue, inviting trusted relatives." The wary citizen could on other occasions, the pamphlet advised, "appear as the butler of the house. To any question, he can answer: the owners are traveling."

This assumption of extralegal needs dominated the advertisements for more expensive residential properties. The Previews brochure for a house on Star Island, built originally as the Miami Beach Yacht Club and converted to residential use in the 1920s by Hetty Green's son, emphasized, in the headline, not the house's twenty-one rooms, not its multiple pools, not even its 255 feet of bay frontage, but its "Unusual Security and Ready Access to the Ocean." Grove Isle, a luxury condominium complex with pieces by Isamu Noguchi and Alexander Calder and Louise Nevelson in its sculpture garden, presented itself as "a bridge away from Coconut Grove," which meant, in the local code, that access was controlled, in this case by one of the "double security" systems favored in new Miami buildings, requiring that the permit acquired at the gate, or "perimeter," be surrendered at the second line of defense, the entrance to the building itself. A bridge, I was told by several people in Miami, was a good thing to have between oneself and the city, because it could be drawn up, or blocked, during times of unrest.

For a city even then being presented, in news reports and in magazine pieces and even in advertising and fashion promotions which had adopted their style from the television show "Miami Vice," as a rich and wicked pastel boomtown, Miami seemed, at the time I began spending time there, rather spectacularly depressed, again on the southern model. There were new condominiums largely unsold. There were new office towers largely unleased. There were certain signs of cutting and running among those investors who had misread the constant cash moving in and out of Miami as the kind of reliable American money they understood, and been left holding the notes. Helmsley-Spear, it was reported, had let an undeveloped piece on Biscayne Bay go into foreclosure, saving itself $3 million a year in taxes. Tishman Speyer had jettisoned plans for an $800-million medical complex in Broward County. WELL-HEELED INVESTORS RETURNING NORTH was a *Herald* headline in June of 1985. COSTLY CONDOS THREATENED WITH MASSIVE FORECLOSURES was a *Herald* headline in August of 1985. FORECLOSURES SOARING IN S. FLORIDA was a *Herald* headline in March of 1986.

The feel was that of a Latin capital, a year or two away from a new government. Space in shopping malls was unrented, or rented to the wrong tenants. There were too many shoe stores for an American city, and video arcades. There were also too many public works projects: a new mass transit system which did not effectively transport anyone, a projected "people mover" around the downtown area which would, it was said, salvage the new mass transit system. On my first visits to Miami the gleaming new Metrorail cars glided empty down to the Dadeland Mall and back, ghost trains above the jammed traffic on the South Dixie Highway. When I returned a few months later service had already been cut back, and the billion-dollar Metrorail ran only until early evening.

A tropical entropy seemed to prevail, defeating grand schemes even as they were realized. Minor drug deals took place beneath the then unfinished people-mover tracks off Biscayne Boulevard, and plans were under way for yet another salvage operation. "Biscayne Centrum," a twenty-eight-acre sports arena and convention hall that could theoretically be reached by either Metrorail or people mover and offered the further advantage, since its projected site lay within the area sealed off during the 1982 Overtown riot, a district of generally apathetic but occasionally volatile poverty, of defoliating at least twenty-eight acres of potential trouble. ARENA FINANCING PLAN RELIES ON HOTEL GUESTS was a *Herald* headline one morning. S. FLORIDA HOTEL ROOMS GET EMPTIER was a *Herald* headline four months later. A business reporter for the *Herald* asked a local real-estate analyst when he thought South Florida would turn around. "Tell me when South America is going to turn around," the analyst said.

Meanwhile the construction cranes still hovered on the famous new skyline, which, floating as it did between a mangrove swamp and a barrier reef, had a kind of perilous attraction, like a mirage. I recall walking one October evening through the marble lobby of what was then the Pavillon Hotel, part of the massive new Miami Center which Pietro Belluschi had designed for a Virginia developer named Theodore Gould. There was in this vast travertine public space that evening one other person, a young Cuban woman in a short black dinner dress who seemed to be in charge of table arrangements for a gala not in evidence. I could hear my heels clicking on the marble. I could hear the young woman in the black taffeta dinner dress drumming her lacquered fingernails on the table at which she sat. It occurred to me that she and I might be the only people in the great empty skyline itself. Later that week control of the

Pavillon, and of Miami Center, passed, the latest chapter in a short dolorous history of hearings and defaults and Chapter 11 filings, from Theodore Gould to the Bank of New York, and it was announced that the Inter-Continental chain would henceforth operate the hotel. The occupancy rate at the Pavillon was, at the time Inter-Continental assumed its management, 7 percent. Theodore Gould was said by the chairman of the Greater Miami Chamber of Commerce to have made "a very unique contribution to downtown Miami."

1988

Purpose and Meaning

1. What does Didion choose to describe or discuss in this essay?
2. What makes this essay different from the typical "guidebook" description of a city? What clues do you gather from the essay "Why I Write" that help elucidate the purpose of the essay?
3. In paragraph 1, Didion states that the destinations listed at the Miami airport suggested "many yearnings toward empire indulged." How does the present Miami seem to reflect this same quality?

Language and Style

1. The essay is full of specific details such as verbatim descriptions of advertisements and headlines. How does such particular attention to detail contribute to our understanding of the city?
2. In creating Miami as an enigmatic place, Didion uses some unusual description. How do the following phrases contribute to the eerie atmosphere of the city: "spectacularly depressed" (paragraph 5); "tropical entropy" (paragraph 7): "a perilous attraction, like a mirage" (paragraph 8)? What is the dominant impression given by such descriptions?
3. In her essay "Why I Write," Didion states, "The arrangement of the words matters" and "The picture dictates the arrangement." In what way is the syntax of the following sentence (paragraph 1) crucial to its meaning: "I never passed through security for a flight to Miami without experiencing a certain weightlessness, the heightened wariness of having left the developed world for a more fluid atmosphere, one in which the native distrust of extreme possibilities that tended to ground the temperate United States in an obeisance to democratic institutions seemed rooted, if at all, only shallowly"?

Strategy and Structure

1. What is the purpose of beginning the essay with the quotation from Audubon? In what sense do his descriptions of the Floridas mirror the Miami Didion describes?

2. What are the major topics discussed in each of the two sections of the essay? Why does the second section follow logically from the first? If you were to give each section a title, what would these titles be?

3. Just as Didion begins the essay with a quotation, she ends it with one. What is the irony of the concluding quotation? How does its grammatical construction add to the irony?

Thinking and Writing

1. Write an essay comparing "Miami" with "Marrying Absurd." Pay particular attention to the way Didion describes the cities of Las Vegas and Miami.

2. Write an essay describing the personality of a city with which you are familiar. Rather than depicting it in a standard "guidebook" way, try to reveal its "underside" through a detailed portrayal of its people, architecture, politics, and geography. It may be helpful to establish a central image of the city to organize your thoughts—for example, by describing the city as a beehive, a battle zone, a sporting event, a corporation, and so forth.

3. Television dramas and soap operas often have the names of cities in their themes—for example, *Miami Vice, Dallas,* and *Santa Barbara.* Select one such show and discuss how the program depicts a particular social, cultural, and economic environment.

JOYCE CAROL OATES

Because she is America's most prolific major writer—the author of more than two dozen novels and short story collections and another dozen volumes of poetry and drama—Joyce Carol Oates's stature as a significant essayist tends to be obscured. Her collections of essays, criticism and reviews include *New Heaven, New Earth* (1974), *Contraries* (1981), *The Profane Art* (1983), *On Boxing* (1987), and *(Woman) Writer* (1988). Together they offer impressive testimony to a wide-ranging critical talent prepared to explore everything from the nature of the creative process to the workings of the Ferrari Testarossa. She is, as her contemporary John Updike has intimated, our foremost woman of letters today.

Oates was born in 1938 and grew up in the country outside Lockport, a small city in western New York. She majored in English at Syracuse University and graduated in 1960, serving as class valedictorian, and earned her master's degree from the University of Wisconsin in 1961. Even before college, Oates's deepest interest was writing; among her earliest awards was first prize in *Mademoiselle*'s college fiction contest in 1959. Although she describes her prodigious literary productivity as laughable, the flood of her publications has earned her high literary acclaim. Beginning with her novel *A Garden of Earthly Delights* (1967), she has been a perennial contender for the National Book Award, which she won for her novel *Them* (1969). Countless short stories by Oates have appeared in the O. Henry Prize Stories collection, and she is the recipient of the O. Henry Special Award for Continuing Achievement. Currently she is the Roger S. Berlind Distinguished Lecturer at Princeton University.

As an essayist, Joyce Carol Oates has been hailed as "perceptive," "provocative," "brilliant." There is a lucidity and ease to even her most demanding nonfiction, as when she examines the motives for criticism in "The Profane Art." Moreover, she is virtually unrivaled in the breadth and diversity of her interests; she is equally at home writing articles for *Art and Antiques, TV Guide, The New York Times*, the *Virginia Quarterly Review*. At all times, whether bemused or astringent, she seeks what she declares in her preface to *Contraries* to be "the spirit of contrariety that lies at the heart of all passionate commitment."

Indeed this spirit of contrariety is personal and pervades both her fiction and nonfiction. "What excites me about writing," she explained in an interview, "is the uses I can make of myself, of various small adventures, errors, miscalculations, stunning discoveries, near-disasters, and occasional reversals of everything." Thus when she writes about boxing, a sport easy to malign, she taps her childhood interest in the contest, first instilled by her father, who took her to Golden Glove matches. She examines boxing in its humorous contraries and reversals—as myth, metaphor, spectacle, pop culture, and psychic watershed between men and women.

If Oates's essays and fiction offer interesting perspectives on men and women, it is because she is a feminist "sympathizer" who loves to confront and attack modern society's "mysogynous bias," as she terms it. Boxing and sleek sports cars are thus twin emblems of the primitive rites that reflect male-dominated culture. She brings to her dissection of gender and other controversies that frame our turbulent era a stylistic power that Edward Hoagland has called "foxfire luminescence," a brilliance of insight permeating every page. Oates herself speaks in *The Profane Art* of the altered state of the writer "overlaid with a peculiar sense of luminosity" as she attempts to dramatize the problems of our age and find ways to transcend them.

The Profane Art

The motives for criticism are even more puzzling than the motives for art. The systematic reflection upon another's creativity; the exploration of the subtleties of a work that lie, in a sense, mute within it; the dialogue with an invisible and perhaps skeptical audience asserting that a work is more resourceful, more astonishing than a casual reading can suggest—all contribute to the critical impulse.

Criticism speaks, as Northrop Frye has observed—and all the arts are silent. Their expression is only *of* themselves and never *for* themselves.

Medusa, that terrible image-bearing goddess of Greek mythology, could not be encountered directly by the hero Perseus, for her power was such that she turned all who gazed upon her into stone. (The "Gorgon" Medusa, formerly a beautiful woman, had been transformed into a winged monster with glaring eyes, tusklike teeth, claws, and—most famously—serpents in place of hair.) Only through indirection, by means of a polished shield, could she be approached in order to be slain. One cannot resist reading the tale as a cautionary parable: the inchoate and undetermined event, the act without structure, without the necessary confinement of the human imagination, is simply too brutal—because too inhuman—to be borne. Perseus, aided by Athene, conquers the barbaric in nature (in his own nature?) by means of reflection. The demonic Medusa is successfully subdued by the godly strategy of restraint, confinement, indirection—in short, by a kind of art; an artfulness that substitutes intellectual caution for the brashness of primitive instinct. So art labors to give meaning to a profusion of meanings; its structures—inevitably "exclusive"— provide a way of seeing with the mind's eye. The journalist's or the historian's hope of gathering in all truths is surrendered in the interest of exploring a single truth. The restraint of art—its subjectivity, its stubborn faith in its own music, an angle of vision, an overriding emotion, an obsession—is its power.

Criticism is, then, the art of reflection upon reflection. It is a distinctly and wonderfully *civilized* venture: the unhurried, systematic, discursive commentary upon another's vision. Its impulses are to synthesize, to abbreviate, to exclaim over origins, analogues, hidden meanings. Like gems turned slowly in the hand, diffracting light in new and startling patterns, all serious works of art yield a multiplicity of meanings. The critic's reflective activity is altogether natural—which is to say "instinctive" and "real"—but this is a naturalness that finds its most comfortable expression in the scrutiny of the artist's interpretation of an image. Not Medusa herself, with her galaxy of possible meanings, but the highly polished shield in which she is framed: the *art* of the shield, in

311

fact; the stratagems of Perseus who is human, and consequently the real object of our fascinated interest. If the greatest works of art sometimes strike us as austere and timeless, self-contained and self-referential, with their own private music, as befits sacred things, criticism is always an entirely human dialogue, a conversation directed toward an audience. It is a conversation between equals, on a subject of acknowledged superiority. Which is why, for many of us, reading it and writing it are such extraordinarily rewarding activities. There is a profoundly satisfying beauty in the very gesture of acquiescence to another's vision—the communal acknowledgment of the greatness and abiding worth of certain works of art. These are, of course, our "sacred things."

Auden has said, "The value of a profane thing lies in what it usefully does, the value of a sacred thing lies in what it *is*." Of course the "sacred thing" may also have a function but that is not its primary role. If art is sacred it is quite reasonable to assume that criticism is profane: it exists not in and for itself; it justifies itself as a service. The artist participates in a sacred rite, the critic in a profane rite. Yet are the two inevitably opposed? Must they be adversaries? There is a chilling truth to Nietzsche's characteristically terse observation that praise is more obtrusive than blame, but both praise and blame are perhaps beside the point in a systematic and reflective criticism. The secular nature of the critical enterprise, its willingness to be secondary, in the service of, *profane* in Auden's sense of the word, gives it a freedom not always available to the artist himself.

Yet there is a tradition of criticism as warfare, defensive or otherwise. The rationalist and combative approach, in which works of art are on trial, to be judged by the critic, insists upon the critic's strength and the artist's passivity. The one represents reason (in its most sinister guise it is presented as "common sense"), the other represents passion, disorder, instability, even madness. Nearly all critics are conservative if only because they cannot presume to judge art by its own standards if those standards are new: even the most well-intentioned critic carries about with him, unacknowledged, his ideas of what a *novel* or a *short story* or a *play* or a *poem* should be, based upon works he has studied. His instinct is to preserve the past because it is *his* past; he has a great deal invested in it. The artist, by contrast, really must follow his instinct into areas not yet mined by others—he cannot even console himself (unless he is Joyce or Stendhal or Flaubert, with a prodigious faith in his own genius) that criticism will someday "catch up" with his innovations. What appears as disorder, instability, and frequent madness to the critic is in fact the creative activity itself: it seeks to blossom in inhospitable climates, break free of its confining species, celebrate the individual and the idiosyncratic, even at the cost of official—that is, "critical"—censure. So it is commonplace to read of the dismaying critical receptions given great works of art, and it is never surprising to discover, in perusing the past, that the best-received works, the *really* successful works, are often by people whose names have long been forgotten.

The history of the critic's distrust of art is hardly felicitous, but it is certainly instructive if one wants to arrive at an understanding of the tacit conservatism of most critics. Consider Plato's *Ion*, for instance, which dramatizes Socrates's surprising hostility toward poets. Why did he so distrust the poetic impulse? Was he not a poet himself? Or was it precisely the poet in himself he feared? Nietzsche has spoken contemptuously of the "Greek superficiality" that sought to supplant an older tragic vision, substituting the bloodless play of logic for the full expression of the emotions, and nowhere is this curious and aggressive hostility more forcefully expressed than in certain of Plato's dialogues. It seems difficult for us to believe, judging Plato by our contemporary standards, as if he *were* a contemporary, that he really believed the poetic impulse was divine, for instance, and *only* divine, and that the poet himself had nothing to do with shaping his art. Yet Socrates speaks clearly: ". . . God takes the mind out of the poets, and uses them as his servants, and so also those who chant oracles, and divine seers; because he wishes us to know that not those we hear, who have no mind in them, are those who say such precious things, but God himself is the speaker, and through them he shows his meaning to us. . . . These beautiful poems are not human, not made by man, but divine and made by God; and the poets are nothing but the gods' interpreters, possessed each by whatever god it may be." *Nothing but!* The murderous sophism, the fallacious logic, that denies individuality to the poet precisely because he *is* a poet, and not (for instance) a blacksmith who follows his predecessors in his trade. One could write a lengthy study of the victimization of both the Poet and Woman, presumed by their judges to embody an impersonal and even supernatural value that nevertheless makes them unfit for most worldly activities, including that of judging. To be *nothing* but possessed by the divine is close to being nothing, in human terms, at all. And the divine may shade horribly into the demonic if the presiding judges decide to revise their judgments.

For despite Socrates's talk of "beauty" and "divinity" we know that the ideal state—the legendary Republic—will not tolerate the presence of poets. Which is to say, in terms of that society, the presence of freethinking individuals, finally ungovernable by external coercion. Of course they must be exiled, under threat of death. Of course they will be killed. For a certain perspective it appears that the sacred rite in which the poet participates is nothing less than the rite of an ineffable freedom of the imagination—in itself paradigmatic of the highest of human experiences.

The ideal criticism, then, aspires to the art of "disinterested" conversation ("disinterested" in Matthew Arnold's sense of the word), a conversation between equals, systematic, unhurried, "profane," reflective. It must take the artist's freedom seriously—it must resist its own conservative and reductive instincts. If only criticism speaks, and all the arts are silent, it is necessary that it speak with both sympathy and rigor; it cannot take its reflective responsibilities lightly.

1983

Purpose and Meaning

1. According to Oates, what distinguishes art from criticism? What distinguishes the artist from the critic?

2. Consider Auden's quote in paragraph 5: "The value of a profane thing lies in what it usefully does, the value of a sacred thing lies in what it *is*." Following the reasoning behind this argument, how can criticism be "the profane art"?

3. What type of audience is Oates writing for in "The Profane Art"? Explain your response.

Language and Style

1. Much of Oates's argument relies on references to literature, myth, and philosophy. How does she introduce these allusions so they are clear for the reader, even if he or she is not familiar with their sources? In paragraph 6, Oates states that the critic must call upon "works he has studied in making judgments." How do Oates's own allusions demonstrate that she has the qualifications of a critic?

2. In paragraph 4, Oates states that criticism "is a conversation between equals." Taking into account Oates's vocabulary and knowledge, who are her implied equals?

3. Like many highly regarded writers, Oates has the ability to create complex sentences that include several distinct ideas, imaginative syntax, and creative use of punctuation. How do the following sentences demonstrate this ability? "The systematic reflection upon another's creativity; the exploration of the subtleties of a work that lie, in a sense, mute within it; the dialogue with an invisible and perhaps skeptical audience asserting that a work is more resourceful, more astonishing than a casual reading can suggest—all contribute to the critical impulse" (paragraph 1). "Not Medusa herself, with her galaxy of possible meanings, but the highly polished shield in which she is framed: the *art* of the shield, in fact; the stratagems of Perseus who is human, and consequently the real object of our fascinated interest" (paragraph 4). What is the effect of these syntactic manipulations?

Strategy and Structure

1. What is the relationship between the topic sentences and their respective paragraphs in this essay? How do they help to make the paragraphs independent and coherent? How do they assist in providing transitions from one topic to another?

2. In paragraph 7, Oates seems to escalate the emotional intensity of her essay. Why and at what point does this occur? How does this contribute to organizing the thrust of her argument?

3. What organizational function does the break serve before the concluding paragraph? In what way can it be related to the concept of disinterestedness in the conclusion?

Thinking and Writing

1. Review Tuchman's description of the artist in "The Historian as Artist." Write an essay summarizing both Oates's description of art and Tuchman's.

2. Is art truly sacred, as Oates maintains in paragraphs 5 and 7? Argue for or against this proposition.

3. Oates claims that "the ideal criticism, then, aspires to the art of 'disinterested' conversation." Select two movie critics from two leading newspapers or magazines, and clip three to five movie critiques by each writer. Compare and contrast the critics in terms of the criteria Oates sets up for ideal criticism.

On Boxing

Why are you a boxer, Irish featherweight champion Barry McGuigan was asked. He said, "I can't be a poet. I can't tell stories. ..."

Each boxing match is a story—a unique and highly condensed drama without words. Even when nothing sensational happens: Then the drama is "merely" psychological. Boxers are there to establish an absolute experience, a public accounting of the outermost limits of their beings; they will know, as few of us can know of ourselves, what physical and psychic power they possess—of how much, or how little, they are capable. To enter the ring near-naked and to risk one's life is to make of one's audience voyeurs of a kind: Boxing is so intimate. It is to ease out of sanity's consciousness and into another, difficult to name. It is to risk, and sometimes to realize, the agony of which *agon* (Greek "contest") is the root.

In the boxing ring there are two principal players, overseen by a shadowy third. The ceremonial ringing of the bell is a summoning to full wakefulness for both boxers and spectators. It sets into motion, too, the authority of Time.

The boxers will bring to the fight everything that is themselves, and everything will be exposed—including secrets about themselves they cannot fully realize. The physical self, the maleness, one might say, underlying the "self." There are boxers possessed of such remarkable intuition, such uncanny prescience, one would think they were somehow recalling their fights, not fighting them as we watch. There are boxers who perform skillfully, but mechanically, who cannot improvise in response to another's alteration of strategy; there are boxers performing at the peak of their talent who come to realize, midfight, that it will not be enough; there are boxers—including great champions—whose careers end abruptly, and irrevocably, as we watch. There has been at least one boxer possessed of an extraordinary and disquieting awareness not only of his opponent's every move and anticipated move but of the audience's keenest shifts in mood as well, for which he seems to have felt personally responsible— Cassius Clay/Muhammad Ali, of course. "The Sweet Science" celebrates the physicality of men even as it dramatizes the limitations, sometimes tragic, more often poignant, of the physical. Though male spectators identify with boxers, no boxer behaves like a "normal" man when he is in the ring and no combination of blows is "natural." All is style.

Every talent must unfold itself in fighting. So Nietzsche speaks of the   4
Hellenic past, the history of the "contest"—athletic and otherwise—by which Greek youths were educated into Greek citizenry. Without the ferocity of competition, without, even, "envy, jealousy, and ambition" in the contest, the Hellenic city, like the Hellenic man, degenerated. If death is a risk, death is also the prize—for the winning athlete.

In the boxing ring, even in our greatly humanized times, death is always   5
a possibility—which is why some of us prefer to watch films or tapes of fights already past, already defined as history. Or, in some instances, art. (Though to prepare for writing this mosaiclike essay I saw tapes of two infamous "death" fights of recent times: the Lupe Pintor–Johnny Owen bantamweight match of 1982, and the Ray Mancini–Deuk Koo Kim lightweight match of the same year. In both instances the boxers died as a consequence of their astonishing resilience and apparent indefatigability—their "heart," as it's known in boxing circles.) Most of the time, however, death in the ring is extremely unlikely; a statistically rare possibility like your possible death tomorrow morning in an automobile accident or in next month's headlined airline disaster or in a freak accident involving a fall on the stairs or in the bathtub, a skull fracture, subarachnoid hemorrhage. Spectators at "death" fights often claim afterward that what happened simply *seemed* to happen—unpredictably, in a sense accidentally. Only in retrospect does death appear to have been inevitable.

If a boxing match is a story it is an always wayward story, one in which   6
anything can happen. And in a matter of seconds. Split seconds! (Muhammad Ali boasted that he could throw a punch faster than the eye could follow, and he may have been right.) In no other sport can so much take place in so brief a period of time, and so irrevocably.

Because a boxing match is a story without words, this doesn't mean that   7
it has no text or no language, that it is somehow "brute," "primitive," "inarticulate," only that the text is improvised in action, the language a dialogue between the boxers of the most refined sort (one might say, as much neurological as psychological: a dialogue of split-second reflexes) in a joint response to the mysterious will of the audience, which is always that the fight be a worthy one so that the crude paraphernalia of the setting—ring, lights, ropes, stained canvas, the staring onlookers themselves—be erased, forgotten. (As in the theater or

the church, settings are erased by way, ideally, of transcendent action.) Ringside announcers give to the wordless spectacle a narrative unity, yet boxing as performance is more clearly akin to dance, or music, than narrative.

To turn from an ordinary preliminary match to a "fight of the century" 8 like those between Joe Louis and Billy Conn, Joe Frazier and Muhammad Ali, Marvin Hagler and Thomas Hearns is to turn from listening or half-listening to a guitar being idly plucked to hearing Bach's *Well-Tempered Clavier* perfectly executed, and that too is part of the story's mystery: So much happens so swiftly and with such heart-stopping subtlety you cannot absorb it except to know that something profound is happening and it is happening in a place beyond words.

1987

Purpose and Meaning

1. Condense all of Oates's descriptions and explanations of boxing and explain how she would ultimately define a boxing match.

2. Oates says that boxing is "an absolute experience." What does this mean?

3. Since Oates is a fiction writer and a literary critic, as well as a woman, one would probably not expect her to know a great deal about boxing. How does her tone suggest that she has the authority to describe the subject?

Language and Style

1. Find examples of metaphor in this selection. What other types of figurative language can you locate? Why does Oates use so much figurative language? What is its overall effect?

2. Is Oates's diction in this essay formal or informal, abstract or concrete? Locate examples to support your position.

3. Oates employs dashes, slashes, italics, words in quotes, and parentheses. Cite examples of these and explain their cumulative stylistic impact.

Strategy and Structure

1. What is the purpose of the epigram at the beginning of the essay? How does it tie in with Oates's contention that a boxing match is a story?

2. How does Oates build her definition of boxing? What rhetorical strategies does she use?

3. The opening sentence states that boxing is a "drama without words." The final sentence of the essay contains the following observation: "You cannot absorb it except to know that something profound is happening and it is happening in

a place beyond words." How does this image of a drama without words provide coherence to the essay? Where else does Oates reiterate the silence of boxing?

4. How many types of boxers does Oates describe in paragraph 3? How does the repetition of the phrase "there are" provide coherence and unity to the paragraph?

Thinking and Writing

1. In paragraph 7, Oates suggests that boxing has its own "language." Select another sport and write an essay in which you describe its language. Consider the hidden communication that goes on among the players, spectators, coaches, and referees.

2. Compare and contrast this essay with Edward Hoagland's "Violence, Violence." What does each author claim is the appeal of boxing? How does each author describe boxing? What does each say about the role of the spectator?

3. Although Oates does not provide an explicit value judgment of boxing, her tone seems to suggest a positive one. Hoagland also seems to enjoy and defend boxing. Argue for or against the idea that boxing is barbaric, violent, and dangerous.

"State-of-the-Art Car": The Ferrari Testarossa

Speak of the Ferrari Testarossa to men who know cars and observe their immediate visceral response: the virtual dilation of their eyes in sudden focused *interest*. The Testarossa!—that domestic rocket of a sports car, sleek, low-slung, aggressively wide; startlingly beautiful even in the eyes of non–car aficionados; so spectacular a presence on the road that—as I can personally testify—heads turn, faces break into childlike smiles in its wake. As one observer has noted, the Testarossa drives "civilians" crazy.

Like a very few special cars, the Ferrari Testarossa is in fact a meta-car, a poetic metaphor or trope: an *object* raised to the level of a near-spiritual *value*. Of course it has a use—as a Steinway concert grand or a Thoroughbred racing horse has a use—but its significance hovers above and around mere use. What can one say about a street car (as opposed to a racing car) capable of traveling 177 effortless miles per hour?—accelerating, as it does, again without effort, from 0 mph to 60 mph in 5 seconds, 107 mph in 13.3 seconds? A car that sells for approximately $104,000—if you can get one? (The current waiting period is twelve months and will probably get longer.) There are said to be no more than 450 Testarossas in private ownership in the United States; only about three hundred models are made by Ferrari yearly. So popular has the model become, due in part to its much-publicized presence in the television series *Miami Vice* (in which, indeed, fast cars provide a sort of subtextual commentary on the men who drive them), that a line of child-sized motorized "Testarossas" is now being marketed—which extravagant toys range in price from $3,500 to $13,000. (Toys bought by parents who don't want to feel guilty, as one Ferrari dealer remarked.)

For all its high-tech styling, its racing-car image, the Ferrari Testarossa is a remarkably easy car to drive: its accelerative powers are first unnerving, then dangerously seductive. You think you are traveling at about 60 miles per hour when in fact you are moving toward 100 miles per hour (with your radar detector—"standard issue for this model"—in operation). In the luxury-leather seats, low, of course, and accommodatingly wide, you have the vertiginous impression of being somehow below the surface of the very pavement, skimming, flying, *rocketing* past vehicles moving at ordinary speeds; as if in a dream, or an "action" film. (Indeed, viewed through the discreetly tinted windshield of a Testarossa, the world, so swiftly passing, looks subtly altered: less assertive in its dimensions, rather more like "background.") Such speeds are heady, intoxicating, clearly addictive: if you are moving at 120 mph so smoothly, why not 130 mph? why not 160 mph? why not the limit—if, indeed, there *is* a limit? "Gusty/Emotions on wet roads on autumn nights" acquire a new significance in a car of such unabashed romance. What godly maniacal power: you have only to depress the accelerator of the Ferrari Testarossa and you're at the horizon. Or beyond.

The mystique of high-performance cars has always intrigued me with its very opacity. Is it lodged sheerly in speed?—mechanical ingenuity?—the "art" of a finely tuned beautifully styled vehicle (as the mere physical fact of a Steinway piano constitutes "art")?—the adrenal thrill of courting death? Has it primarily to do with display (that of male game fowl, for instance)? Or with masculine prowess of a fairly obvious sort? (Power being, as the cultural critic Henry Kissinger once observed, the ultimate aphrodisiac.)

Or is it bound up with the phenomenon of what the American economist Thorstein Veblen so wittily analyzed as "conspicuous consumption" in his classic *Theory of the Leisure Class* (1899)—Veblen's theory being that the consumption of material goods is determined not by the inherent value of goods but by the social standing derived from their consumption. (Veblen noted how in our capitalistic-democratic society there is an endless "dynamics" of style as the wealthiest class ceaselessly strives to distinguish itself from the rest of society and its habits of consumption trickle down to lower levels.)

Men who work with high-performance cars, however, are likely to value them as ends in themselves: they have no time for theory, being so caught up, so mesmerized, in practice. To say that certain cars at certain times determine the "state-of-the-art" is to say that such machinery, on its most refined levels, constitutes a serious and speculative and ever-changing (improving?) art. The Ferrari Testarossa is not a *car* in the generic sense in which, say, a Honda Accord—which my husband and I own—is a *car*. (For one thing, the Accord has about 90 horsepower; the Testarossa 380.) Each Ferrari is more or less unique, possessed of its own mysterious personality; its peculiar ghost-in-the-machine. "It's a good car," I am told, with typical understatement, by a Testarossa owner named Bill Kontes, "—a *good* car." He pauses, and adds, "But not an antique. This is a car you can actually drive."

(Though it's so precious—the lipstick-red model in particular such an   7 attention-getter—that you dare not park it in any marginally public place. Meta-cars arouse emotions at all points of the spectrum.)

Bill Kontes, in partnership with John Melniczuk, owns and operates   8 Checkered Flag Cars in Vineland, New Jersey—a dealership of such choice content (high-performance exotic cars, "vintage" classics, others) as to make it a veritable Phillips Collection amid its larger rivals in the prestige car market. It was by way of their hospitality that I was invited to test-drive the Ferrari Testarossa for *Quality*, though my only qualifications would seem to have been that I knew how to drive a car. (Not known to Mr. Kontes and Mr. Melniczuk was the ambiguous fact that I did once own, in racier days, a sports car of a fairly modest species—a Fiat Spider also in audacious lipstick-red. I recall that it was always stalling. That it gave up, so to speak, along a melancholy stretch of interstate highway in the approximate vicinity of Gary, Indiana, emitting actual flames from its exhaust. That the garage owner to whose garage it was ignominiously towed stared at it and said contemptuously, "A pile of junk!" That we sold it soon afterward and never bought another "sports" car again.)

It was along a semideserted stretch of South Jersey road that Mr. Kontes   9 turned the Ferrari Testarossa over to me, gallantly, and surely bravely: and conscious of the enormity of the undertaking—a sense, very nearly, that the honor of "woman writerhood" might be here at stake, a colossal blunder or actual catastrophe reflecting not only upon the luckless perpetrator but upon an entire generation and gender—I courageously drove the car, and, encouraged by Mr. Kontes, and by the mysterious powers of the radar detector to detect the presence of uniformed and sanctioned enforcers of the law (which law, I fully understand, *is* for our own good and in the best and necessary interests of the commonwealth), I did in fact accelerate through all five gears to a speed rather beyond one I'd anticipated: though not to 120 mph, which was Mr. Kontes's fairly casual speed a few minutes previously. (This particular Testarossa, new to Vineland, had been driven at 160 mph by Mr. Melniczuk the other day, along a predawn stretch of highway presumably sanctioned by the radar detector. To drive behind the Testarossa, as I also did, and watch it—suddenly—ease away toward the horizon is an eerie sight: if you don't look closely you're likely to be startled into asking, Where did it go?)

But the surprise of the Testarossa, *pace Miami Vice* and the hyped-up   10 media image, is that it is an easy, even comfortable car to drive: user-friendly, as the newly coined cliché would have it. It reminded me not at all of the tricky little Spider I'd quite come to hate by the time of our parting but, oddly, of the unnerving but fiercely exhilarating experience of being behind the controls— so to speak—of a two-seater open-cockpit plane. (My father flew sporty airplanes years ago, and my childhood is punctured with images of flight: the wind-ravaged open-cockpit belonged to a former navy bomber recycled for suburban airfield use.) As the Testarossa was accelerated I felt that visceral sense of an irresistibly gathering and somehow condensing power—"speed" being in fact a mere distillation or side effect of power—and, within it, contained by it, an oddly humble sense of human smallness, frailty. One of the perhaps unexamined impulses behind high-speed racing must be not the mere "courting" of death but, on a more primary level, its actual pre-experience; its taste.

But what have such thoughts to do with driving a splendid red Ferrari   11
Testarossa in the environs of Vineland, New Jersey, one near-perfect autumn day, an afternoon shading romantically into dusk? Quite beyond, or apart from, the phenomenal machinery in which Bill Kontes and I were privileged to ride I was acutely conscious of the spectacle we and it presented to others' eyes. Never have I seen so many heads turn!—so much staring!—*smiling!* While the black Testarossa may very well resemble, as one commentator has noted, Darth Vader's personal warship, the lipstick-red model evokes smiles of pleasure, envy, awe—most pointedly in young men, of course, but also in older, even elderly women. Like royalty, the Testarossa seems to bestow a gratuitous benison upon its spectators. Merely to watch it pass is to feel singled out, if, perhaps, rather suddenly drab and anonymous. My thoughts drifted onto the pomp of kings and queens and maharajahs, the legendary excesses of the Gilded Age of Morgan, Carnegie, Rockefeller, Mellon, Armour, McCormick, et al.—Edith Rockefeller McCormick, just to give one small example, served her dinner guests on china consisting of over a thousand pieces containing 11,000 ounces of gold—the Hope Diamond, and Liz Taylor's diamonds, and the vision of Mark Twain, in impeccable dazzling white, strolling on Fifth Avenue while inwardly chafing at his increasing lack of privacy. If one is on public display one is of course obliged not to be conscious of it; driving a $104,000 car means being equal to the car in dignity and style. Otherwise the public aspect of the performance is contaminated: we are left with merely conspicuous consumption, an embarrassment in such times of economic trepidation and worldwide hunger.

Still, it's the one incontrovertible truth about the Ferrari Testarossa: no   12
matter who is behind the wheel people stare, and they stare in admiration. Which might not otherwise be the case.

1985

Purpose and Meaning

1. Is a car a proper subject for an essay? Is it the *treatment* of the subject that gives the essay its authority, or is it a combination of both? What is Oates's purpose here?

2. According to Oates, in what way is our appreciation of the Ferrari Testarossa representative of the sorts of things we appreciate in general in our society?

3. Does the value of a possession increase the value of the possessor? How does Oates answer this question in the essay?

Language and Style

1. How is the opening paragraph structured so that it suggests the speed, uniqueness, and image of the automobile? Consider such things as the word *interest* in italics, the series of descriptions, and the exclamation mark after *Testarossa.*

2. Compare the mood of the essay with that of Oates's "The Profane Art." Do the essays seem to be issuing from the same person? How is Oates's mood in this essay particularly suited to the subject matter, and how does the subject seem to have influenced her mood?

3. Compare the style and tone of the essay with that of "Farewell, My Lovely!" by E. B. White, another essay about a car. How do the "personalities" of the cars help determine the differing tones of the essays?

4. In paragraph 4, Oates uses the dash three times and parentheses twice. Review her use of these punctuation marks here and throughout the essay. How do they provide the essay with a coherent style? You might review Thomas's "Notes on Punctuation" and determine whether Oates is using them according to the prescriptions in the latter essay.

Strategy and Structure

1. What major change in tone and diction corresponds with the end of the first section and the beginning of the second? Why is it integral to the impact of the essay that the first section be first? What would be the effect if the two sections were transposed?

2. Paragraphs 4 and 5 digress somewhat from the car itself. What purpose does this digression serve? How does it contribute to the overall progression and unity of the essay?

3. What extended definitions is Oates trying to establish in this essay?

Thinking and Writing

1. Write a comparative essay about Oates's essay and "Farewell, My Lovely!" by E. B. White.

2. Can you think of a certain model of an object that could be considered the "meta-object" of its particular class? Select the most outstanding example of an object—for example, a boat, a stereo system, or a computer—and describe its properties.

3. Is any subject "worthy" of being written about? The subject of this essay is a car. Argue for or against the proposition that any subject is worth writing about so long as the writer provides an original or interesting perspective on the subject.

MARGARET ATWOOD

Born in Ottawa, Canada, in 1939, Margaret Eleanor Atwood began writing juvenile poems at the age of six and published her first work at the age of eighteen. Today she is a major literary talent, the author of some thirty volumes of poetry, fiction, and essays that have been translated into more than a dozen languages. She lives in Toronto with novelist Graeme Gibson and their daughter, Jess.

Atwood graduated from the University of Toronto in 1961—the same year that she was awarded the E. J. Pratt Medal for her poetry collection *Double Persephone*. In her laconic autobiographical essay "Great Unexpectations," which first appeared in *Ms.* magazine in 1987, Atwood alludes to the force of literature in her life during this period, to the need for literary models, and to her vocation as a writer. After receiving her M.A. degree from Radcliffe College in 1962, Atwood returned to Toronto to teach. At the age of twenty-seven, she received the Governor-General's Award for Poetry for *The Circle Game*. Her major poetry collections are *Selected Poems 1965–1975* and *Selected Poems II: 1976–1986*.

Critics have described the uniqueness of Atwood's writing with such phrases as "violent dualities," "life mostly as wounds," and "distinctly dystopian." She is indeed a serious writer concerned with the struggles of women and men. Still, her writings—particularly those appearing here—are not without humor and joy. Even as Atwood, in her critical study *Survival: A Thematic Guide to Canadian Literature* (1972), speaks of a Canadian national sensibility that is "undeniably somber and negative," she locates subtle, powerful, and complex ways to affirm existence, as she does in the search for personal and national identity in her essay "Travels Back" or in her essay celebrating the feminist poet Adrienne Rich.

Tensions between art and life, the modern and the primitive, Canada and the United States, and most especially women and men are recurring themes in Atwood's work. She is a feminist writer ("Why the hell not!" she once exclaimed), a distinction earned with the publication of her first novel, *The Edible Woman*, in 1970. But her feminism has been generally on such personal terms as to avoid quick and easy categorization. *Surfacing* (1972), *Lady Oracle* (1976), *Life Before Man* (1979), *Bodily Harm* (1982), *The Handmaid's Tale* (1986), and *Cat's Eye* (1989) are her prominent publications containing feminist themes. Perhaps her fiercest and most outwardly feminist work is her dystopian novel *The Handmaid's Tale*, in which the United States bears a likeness to the novel's Republic of Gilead, where women are reduced to slave status and men are their brutal masters.

Atwood's essays and articles, some of them collected in *Second Words* (1982), reflect the essential vision in her work in all genres: the need to hold, to survive in a chaotic age. She brings a tough, resilient phrasing to both her enthusiasm for life's little riches and her abhorrence of contemporary forms of victimization. In her best essays, including those in this collection, she takes the reader on quite personal journeys as she seeks to define her place in the world as a woman and as a Canadian.

Travels Back

Three hours past midnight, Highway 17 between Ottawa and North Bay, November, I'm looking out the Greyhound bus window at the almost nothing I can see. Coffee taste still with me from the Ottawa station, where I was marooned four hours because someone in Toronto mixed up the schedules; I sat writing letters and trying not to watch as the waitresses disposed of a tiny wizened drunk. "I been all over the world, girlie," he told them as they forced his coat on him, "I been places you never seen."

The headlights pick out asphalt, snow-salted road borders, dark trees as we lean round the frequent bends. What I picture is that we'll pass the motel, which they said was on the highway outside Renfrew—but *which* side?—and I'll have to walk, a mile maybe carrying the two suitcases full of my own books I'm lugging around because there may not be any bookstores, who in Toronto knows? A passing truck, Canadian Content squashed all over the road, later the police wondering what I was doing there anyway, as I am myself at this moment. Tomorrow at nine (nine!) I'm supposed to be giving a poetry reading in the Renfrew high school. Have fun in Renfrew, my friends in Toronto said with, I guess, irony before I left.

I'm thinking of summer, a swimming pool in France, an acquaintance of mine floating on his back and explaining why bank managers in Canada shouldn't be allowed to hang Group of Seven pictures on their walls—it's a false image, all nature, no people—while a clutch of assorted Europeans and Americans listen incredulously.

"I mean, *Canada*," one of them drawls. "I think they should give it to the United States, then it would be good. All except Quebec, they should give that to France. You should come and live here. I mean, you don't really live *there* any more."

We get to Renfrew finally and I step off the bus into six inches of early snow. He was wrong, this if anywhere is where I live. Highway 17 was my first highway, I travelled along it six months after I was born, from Ottawa to North Bay and then to Temiskaming, and from there over a one-track dirt road into the bush. After that, twice a year, north when the ice went out, south when the snow came, the time between spent in tents; or in the cabin built by my father on a granite point a mile by water from a Quebec village so remote that the road went in only two years before I was born. The towns I've passed and will pass—Arnprior, Renfrew, Pembroke, Chalk River, Mattawa, the old

gingerbread mansions in each of them built on lumber money and the assumption that the forest would never give out—they were landmarks, way stations.
That was 30 years ago though and they've improved the highway, now there
are motels. To me nothing but the darkness of the trees is familiar.

I didn't spend a full year in school until I was 11. Americans usually find   6
this account of my childhood—woodsy, isolated, nomadic—less surprising than
do Canadians: after all, it's what the glossy magazine ads say Canada is supposed to be like. They're disappointed when they hear I've never lived in an
igloo and my father doesn't say "On, huskies!" like Sergeant Preston on the
defunct (American) radio program, but other than that they find me plausible
enough. It's Canadians who raise eyebrows. Or rather the Torontonians. It's
as though I'm a part of their own past they find disreputable or fake or just
can't believe ever happened.

I've never read at a high school before. At first I'm terrified, I chew Tums   7
while the teacher introduces me, remembering the kinds of things we used to
do to visiting dignitaries when I was in high school: rude whispers, noises, elastic
bands and paper clips if we could get away with it. Surely they've never heard
of me and won't be interested: we had no Canadian poetry in high school and
not much of anything else Canadian. In the first four years we studied the Greeks
and Romans and the Ancient Egyptians and the Kings of England, and in the
fifth we got Canada in a dull blue book that was mostly about wheat. Once
a year a frail old man would turn up and read a poem about a crow; afterward
he would sell his own books (as I'm about to do), autographing them in his
thin spidery handwriting. That was Canadian poetry. I wonder if I look like
him, vulnerable, misplaced and redundant. Isn't the real action—the *real*
action—their football game this afternoon?

Question period: Do you have a message? Is your hair really like that,   8
or do you get it done? Where do you get the ideas? How long does it take?
What does it *mean*? Does it bother you, reading your poems out loud like that?
It would bother me. What is the Canadian identity? Where can I send my poems?
To get them published.

They are all questions with answers, some short, some long. What   9
astonishes me is that they ask them at all, that they want to talk: at my high
school you didn't ask questions. And they *write*, some of them. Inconceivable.
It wasn't like that, I think, feeling very old, in my day.

In Deep River I stay with my second cousin, a scientist with the blue   10
inhuman eyes, craggy domed forehead and hawk nose of my maternal Nova
Scotian relatives. He takes me through the Atomic Research Plant, where he
works; we wear white coats and socks to keep from being contaminated and
watch a metal claw moving innocent-looking lethal items—pencils, a tin can,
a Kleenex—behind a 14-inch leaded glass window. "Three minutes in there,"
he says, "will kill you." The fascination of invisible force.

After that we examine beaver damage on his property and he tells me   11
stories about my grandfather, before there were cars and radios. I like these
stories, I collect them from all my relatives, they give me a link, however tenuous,
with the past and with a culture made up of people and their relationships and
their ancestors rather than objects in a landscape. This trip I learn a new story:
my grandfather's disastrous muskrat farm. It consisted of a fence built carefully
around a swamp, the idea being that it would be easier to gather in the muskrats
that way; though my cousin says he trapped more muskrat outside the fence
than my grandfather ever did inside it. The enterprise failed when a farmer
dumped out some of his apple spray upstream and the muskrats were
extinguished; but the Depression hit and the bottom fell out of the muskrat
market anyway. The fence is still there.

Most of the stories about my grandfather are success stories, but I add   12
this one to my collection: when totems are hard to come by, failure stories have
their place. "Do you know," I say to my cousin, repeating a piece of lore recently
gleaned from my grandmother, "that one of our ancestresses was doused as
a witch?" That was in New England; whether she sank and was innocent or
swam and was guilty isn't recorded.

Out his living-room window, across the Ottawa River, solid trees, is my   13
place. More or less.

Freezing rain overnight; I make it to the next poetry reading pulling my   14
suitcases on a toboggan two miles over thin ice.

I reach North Bay, an hour late because of the sleet. That evening I read   15
at the Oddfellows' Hall, in the basement. The academics who have organized
the reading are nervous, they think no one will come, there's never been a poetry
reading in North Bay before. In a town where everyone's seen the movie, I tell
them, you don't have to worry, and in fact they spent the first fifteen minutes
bringing in extra chairs. These aren't students, there are all kinds of people,
old ones, young ones, a friend of my mother's who used to stay with us in
Quebec, a man whose uncle ran the fishing camp at the end of the lake . . .

In the afternoon I was interviewed for the local TV station by a stiff-spined   16
man in a tight suit. "What's this," he said, dangling one of my books nonchalantly
by the corner to show the viewers that poetry isn't his thing, he's virile really,
"a children's book?" I suggested that if he wanted to know what was inside it
he might try reading it. He became enraged and said he had never been so insulted, and Jack McClelland hadn't been mean like that when *he* was in North
Bay. In place of the interview they ran a feature on green noodles.

Later, 30 poetry readings later. Reading a poem in New York that has   17
an outhouse in it and having to define outhouse (and having the two or three
people come up furtively afterwards and say that they, too, once . . .). Meeting
a man who has never seen a cow; who has never, in fact, been outside the city
of New York. Talking then about whether there is indeed a difference between
Canada and the U.S. (I been places you never seen . . .) Trying to explain, in

Detroit, that in Canada for some strange reason it isn't just other poets who come to poetry readings. ("You mean . . . people like *our mothers* read poetry?") Having someone tell me that maybe what accounts for the "strength" of my work is its fetching "regional" qualities—"you know, like Faulkner . . ."

In London, Ontario, the last poetry reading of the year and perhaps, I'm   18
thinking, for ever, I'm beginning to feel like a phonograph. A lady: "I've never felt less like a Canadian since all this nationalism came along." Another lady, very old, with astonishing sharp eyes: "Do you think in metaphor?" Someone else: "What is the Canadian identity?" That seems to be on people's minds.

How to keep all this together in your head, my head. Because where I   19
live is where everyone lives: it isn't just a place or a region, though it is also that (and I could have put in Vancouver and Montreal, where I lived for a year each, and Edmonton where I lived for two, and Lake Superior and Toronto . . .). It's a space composed of images, experiences, the weather, your own past and your ancestors', what people say and what they look like and how they react to what you're doing, important events and trivial ones, the connections among them not always obvious. The images come from outside, they are *there*, they are the things we live with and must deal with. But the judgements and the connections (what does it *mean?*) have to be made inside your head and they are made with words: good, bad, like, dislike, whether to go, whether to stay, whether to live there any more. For me that's partly what writing is: an exploration of where in reality I live.

I think Canada, more than most countries, is a place you choose to live   20
in. It's easy for us to leave, and many of us have. There's the U.S. and England, we've been taught more about their histories than our own, we can blend in, become permanent tourists. There's been a kind of standing invitation here to refuse authenticity to your actual experience, to think life can be meaningful or important only in "real" places like New York or London or Paris. And it's a temptation: the swimming pool in France is nothing if not detached. The question is always, Why stay? and you have to answer that over and over.

I don't think Canada is "better" than any other place, any more than I   21
think Canadian literature is "better"; I live in one and read the other for a simple reason: they are mine, with all the sense of territory that implies. Refusing to acknowledge where you come from—and that must include the noodle man and his hostilities, the anti-nationalist lady and her doubts—is an act of amputation: you may become free floating, a citizen of the world (and in what other country is that an ambition?) but only at the cost of arms, legs or heart. By discovering your place your discover yourself.

But there's another image, fact, coming from the outside that I have to   22
fit in. This territory, this thing I have called "mine," may not be mine much longer. Part of the much-sought Canadian identity is that few nationals have done a more enthusiastic job of selling their country than have Canadians. Of course there are buyers willing to exploit, as they say, our resources; there always

are. It is our eagerness to sell that needs attention. Exploiting resources and developing potential are two different things: one is done from without by money, the other from within, by something I hesitate only for a moment to call love.

1973

Purpose and Meaning

1. A sense of place is prominent in Atwood's essay. Primarily, the places are Canadian towns and provinces. In paragraph 2, Atwood tells how her friends ironically advise her to "have fun in Renfrew." In paragraph 4, she contrasts France with Canada and quotes a companion who says Canada should be given to the United States. How do these early characterizations of Canada prepare us for Atwood's thesis?

2. What does the interaction between Atwood and the TV station interviewer, in paragraph 16, reveal about the author? What point is she making about cultural attitudes toward women and women writers in particular? How does she want her audience to respond to this incident?

3. Would a reader have to be Canadian to appreciate "Travels Back"? Why or why not? If you are not Canadian, what have you learned about Canada from this essay? What was your previous perception of Canada? Has this essay changed or amplified it?

Language and Style

1. The first sentence of "Travels Back" is a fragment; it contains subjects but no verb. What tone does Atwood create when she uses fragments?

2. How would you characterize Atwood's diction? Is the writing style objective or subjective? Explain.

3. In paragraph 19, Atwood writes that where she lives "isn't just a place. . . . It's a space composed of images, experiences, the weather, your own past and your ancestors', what people say and what they look like and how they react to what you're doing, important events and trivial ones, the connections among them not always obvious." Look over the essay again and note how these items— images in particular—are represented. What is their stylistic effect? What does Atwood mean when she writes that writing is in part "an exploration of where in reality I live"?

Strategy and Structure

1. What connections do you perceive between the beginning and ending paragraphs of this essay?

2. This essay is an exploration of home and how Atwood considers writing itself to be part of that exploration. In what ways is the essay exploratory instead of telling? How does the journal format lend itself to exploration?

3. Many of Atwood's paragraphs begin with references to a change of place: France (paragraph 3); Renfrew (paragraph 4); high school (paragraph 6); Deep River (paragraph 10); and so forth. How do these changes help create a sense of movement, as is reflected in the essay's title?

4. In what way might this essay be considered an extended definition? What is being defined and how is the definition structured?

Thinking and Writing

1. In paragraph 21, Atwood writes, "by discovering your place you discover yourself." Write an essay using Atwood's format in which you explore your home town or neighborhood, or where you live now.

2. Over the next week, keep a log noting all of your travels and changes of place. Characterize each place and reflect upon it in a paragraph or two. At the end of the week, evaluate your writing and see what you have discovered about yourself.

3. Atwood sets up several comparisons of place in her essay. Note the specific elements she compares. Then select two places that you know well, and write a comparative essay on them.

Great Unexpectations

In 1960 I was nineteen years old. I was in third-year college in Toronto, Ontario, which was not then known as People City or The Paris of the Northeast; but as Hogtown, which was not an inaccurate description. I had never eaten an avocado or been on an airplane or encountered a croissant or been south of Vermont. Panty hose had not yet hit the market; neither had the Pill. We were still doing garter belts and repression. Abortion was not a word you said out loud, and lesbians might as well have been mythological hybrids, like Sphinxes; in any case I was quite certain I had never met one. I wanted to be— no, worse—was determined to be, was convinced I was—a writer. I was scared to death.

I was scared to death for a couple of reasons. For one thing, I was Canadian, and the prospects for being a Canadian and a writer, both at the same time, in 1960, were dim. The only writers I had encountered in high school had been dead and English, and in university we barely studied American writers, much less Canadian ones. Canadian writers, it was assumed—by my professors, my contemporaries, and myself—were a freak of nature, like duck-billed platypuses. Logically they ought not to exist, and when they did so anyway, they were just pathetic imitations of the real thing. This estimate was borne out by statistics: for those few who managed, despite the reluctance of publishers, to struggle into print (five novels in English in 1960), two hundred copies of a book of poetry was considered average to good, and a thousand made a novel a Canadian best seller. I would have to emigrate, I concluded gloomily. I faced a future of scrubbing restaurant floors in England—where we colonials could go, then, much more easily than we could to the United States—writing master-pieces in a freezing cold garret at night, and getting T.B., like Keats. Such was my operatic view of my own future.

But it was more complicated than that, because, in addition to being a 3 Canadian, I was also a woman. In some ways this was an advantage. Being a male writer in Canada branded you a sissy, but writing was not quite so un-thinkable for a woman, ranking as it did with flower painting and making roses out of wood. As one friend of my mother's put it, trying to take a cheerful view of my eccentricity, "Well, that's nice dear, because you can do it at home, can't you?" She was right, as it turned out, but at that moment she aroused nothing but loathing in my adolescent soul. Home, hell. It was garret or nothing. What did she think I was, inauthentic? However, most people were so appalled by my determination to be a writer that no one even thought of saying I couldn't because I was a girl. That sort of thing was not said to me until later, by male writers, by which time it was too late.

Strangely, no one was pushing early marriage, not in my case. Canada, 4 being a cultural backwater, had not been swept by the wave of Freudianism that had washed over the United States in the fifties—Canadian women were not yet expected to be fecund and passive in order to fulfill themselves—and there were still some bluestockings around in the educational system, women who warned us not to get silly about boys too soon and throw away our chances. What my elders had in mind for me was more along academic lines. Something, that is to say, with a salary.

But, since gender is prior to nationality, the advantages of being a 5 Canadian woman writer were canceled out by the disadvantages of being a woman writer. I'd read the biographies, which were not encouraging. Jane Austen never married Mr. Darcy. Emily Brontë died young, Charlotte in childbirth. George Eliot never had children and was ostracized for living with a married man. Emily Dickinson flitted; Christina Rossetti looked at life through the wormholes in a shroud. Some had managed to combine writing with what I considered to be a normal life—Mrs. Gaskell, Harriet Beecher Stowe—but everyone knew they were second rate. My choices were between excellence and doom on the one hand, and mediocrity and cosiness on the other. I gritted my teeth, set my face to the wind, gave up double dating, and wore horn-rims and a scowl so I would not be mistaken for a puffball.

It was in this frame of mind that I read Robert Graves's *The White Goddess*, 6 which further terrified me. Graves did not dismiss women. In fact he placed them right at the center of his poetic theory; but they were to be inspirations rather than creators, and a funny sort of inspiration at that. They were to be incarnations of the White Goddess herself, alternately loving and destructive, and men who got involved with them ran the risk of disembowelment or worse. A woman just might—might, mind you—have a chance of becoming a decent poet, but only if she too took on the attributes of the White Goddess and spent her time seducing men and then doing them in. All this sounded a little strenuous, and appeared to rule out domestic bliss. It wasn't my idea of how men and women should get on together—raking up leaves in the backyard, like my mom and dad—but who was I to contradict the experts? There was no one else in view giving me any advice on how to be a writer, though female. Graves was it.

That would be my life, then. To the garret and the T.B. I added the 7 elements of enigma and solitude. I would dress in black. I would learn to smoke cigarettes, although they gave me headaches and made me cough, and drink something romantic and unusually bad for you, such as absinthe. I would live by myself, in a suitably painted attic (black) and have lovers whom I would discard in appropriate ways, though I drew the line at bloodshed. (I was, after all, a nice Canadian girl.) I would never have children. This last bothered me a lot, as before this I had always intended to have some, and it seemed unfair, but White Goddesses did not have time for children, being too taken up with cannibalistic sex, and Art came first. I would never, never own an automatic washer-dryer. Sartre, Samuel Beckett, Kafka, and Ionesco, I was sure, did not have major appliances, and these were the writers I most admired. I had no concrete ideas about how the laundry would get done, but it would only be my own laundry, I thought mournfully—no fuzzy sleepers, no tiny T-shirts— and such details could be worked out later.

I tried out the garrets, which were less glamorous than expected; so was 8 England, and so were the cigarettes, which lasted a mere six months. There wasn't any absinthe to be had, so I tried bad wine, which made me sick. It began to occur to me that maybe Robert Graves didn't have the last word on women writers, and anyway I wanted to be a novelist as well as a poet, so perhaps that would let me off the homicide. Even though Sylvia Plath and Anne Sexton had been setting new, high standards in self-destructiveness for female poets, and people had begun asking me not whether but when I was going to commit suicide (the only authentic woman poet is a dead woman poet?), I was wondering whether it was really all that necessary for a woman writer to be doomed, any more than it was necessary for a male writer to be a drunk. Wasn't all of this just some sort of postromantic collective delusion? If Shakespeare could have kids and avoid suicide, then so could I, dammit. When Betty Friedan and Simone de Beauvoir came my way, like shorebirds heralding land, I read them with much interest. They got a lot right, for me, but there was one thing they got wrong. They were assuring me that I didn't have to get married and have children. But what I wanted was someone to tell me I could.

And so I did. The marriage and the children came in two lots—the marriage with one, child with another—but they did come. This is the part that will sound smug, I suppose, but I also suppose it's not that much smugger than my black-sweatered, garter-belted, black-stockinged, existential pronouncements at the age of nineteen. I now live a life that is pretty close to the leaves-in-the-backyard model I thought would have been out of bounds forever. Instead of rotting my brains with absinthe, I bake (dare I admit it?) chocolate chip cookies, and I find that doing the laundry with the aid of my washer-dryer is one of the more relaxing parts of my week. I worry about things like remembering Parents' Day at my daughter's school and running out of cat food, though I can only afford these emotional luxuries with the aid of some business assistants and a large man who likes kids and cats and food, and has an ego so solid it isn't threatened by mine. This state of affairs was not achieved without struggle, some of it internal—did an addiction to knitting brand me as an inauthentic writer?—but it was reached. The White Goddess still turns up in my life, but mainly as a fantasy projection on the part of certain male book reviewers, who seem to like the idea of my teeth sinking into some cringing male neck. I think of this as fifties nostalgia.

As for writing, yes. You *can* do it at home.

1987

Purpose and Meaning

1. What were the major obstacles to Atwood's becoming a writer? What is her purpose in cataloging these obstacles? What thesis emerges from her inventory of obstacles?

2. Atwood has observed that Canada has a "national inferiority complex." How is this trait reflected in "Great Unexpectations" and also in "Travels Back"?

3. What expectations does the author have of her readers? How do you know?

Language and Style

1. Although Atwood writes about serious problems, her style and tone tend to be breezy, ironic, and humorous. Cite and explain examples of her method.

2. Consider the similes "lesbians might as well have been mythological hybrids, like Sphinxes" (paragraph 1) and "Canadian writers . . . were a freak of nature, like duck-billed platypuses" (paragraph 2). What do these similes have in common? How do they advance Atwood's thesis?

Strategy and Structure

1. Atwood's introductory paragraph offers a striking and graphic overview of the year 1960. What effect do the details have on the reader? In what way do they involve us in the writer's emerging dilemma?

2. What sorts of evidence to support her thesis does Atwood provide in this essay? How does she organize it? How effective is it in supporting her thesis?

3. How does Atwood employ comparison and contrast to advance her essay? What are the major points of comparison?

4. Do you find the one-sentence conclusion to be effective or ineffective? Explain.

Thinking and Writing

1. How do both "Great Unexpectations" and "Travels Back" explore questions of identity, place, and potential loss of self? Write an essay on this topic.

2. Write an autobiographical essay based on Atwood's example in which you describe a specific time in your life when you decided to do something against all odds.

3. Why does Atwood focus so much in the latter part of her essay on the White Goddess? Is the White Goddess metaphor still operative in culture today? Write an argumentative essay on this issue.

Adrienne Rich:
Poems, Selected and New

If you still don't believe in cultural differences between Canada and the United States, you should try comparing poetry readings. You might find the same stanza forms in each country, but you'd probably find very different audiences. Unless the poet is ultra-famous, the U.S. audience would be smaller and would consist largely of students, other poets and assorted literati. In Canada it would be more varied: for some reason, Canadians read more poetry *per capita* than any other country in the English-speaking world. And the difference shows up in the way poets write in the two countries, in their assumptions about their audiences: white male American poets often write as if they think they're talking only to other white male American poets, displaying their professional bags of tricks for other connoisseurs. They have nothing to say to ordinary people, because ordinary people aren't listening. The atmosphere can get fairly rarefied.

The exceptions to this prevailing climate are, of course, the poets from   2
the ethnic minority groups; and women. A sense of grievance, a consciousness of oppression, can often provide a force and a driving power for those who attempt to give them a voice. Such poets are less interested in displaying their verbal virtuosity than in getting something said; urgency replaces ambiguity, all seven types of it.

Adrienne Rich's *Selected Poems* is a perfect demonstration of the evolu-   3
tion from introspective to didactic; it's also a perfect contradiction of those who claim that politics and poetry can't be mixed. Rich is perhaps the best known living woman poet in the United States (although cultural differences of some kind showed up when a leading Canadian book review editor failed to recognize the name). Though she'd published six earlier books, it was *Diving Into the Wreck* (1973) that brought her to her current prominence. It received the National Book Award, which Rich accepted not only for herself but on behalf of the other two women who were nominated but didn't win. The jacket cover proclaims her a radical feminist, with no qualifications.

She's the kind of poet of whom an unwary critic is likely to say, "The   4
strongest voice to emerge from the feminist movement," or some such inaccuracy. For Rich didn't emerge from the feminist movement. She's been publishing books since 1950, that's 25 years, and *Poems Selected And New* is a reminder of that fact. Indeed some of these poems are strangely prophetic, anticipating many of the themes that were later hit on as fresh discoveries by the feminist movement. To read through the book is to feel, often, that others have expanded into whole books what Rich had written in a few lines, ten or fifteen years earlier.

> ...Thus wrote
> a woman, partly brave and partly good,
> who fought with what she partly understood
> hence she was labelled harpy, shrew and whore.

That's Rich on Mary Wollstonecraft in "Snapshots of a Daughter-in-Law,"   5
written, amazingly, in 1958, a poem which also quotes, for Rich's own good purposes, Dr. Johnson's quip about a female preacher being like a dog walking on its hind legs:

> Not that it is done well, but
> that it is done at all? Yes think
> of the odds! or shrug them off forever
> This luxury of the precocious child,
> Time's precious chronic invalid—

> would we, darlings, resign it if we could?
> Our blight has been our sinecure:
> mere talent was enough for us—
> glitter in fragments and rough drafts.

The same poem ends with a prophecy of not the second coming, but the 6
first; the arrival of a woman who will finally take the risks and make the leap,
"be more merciless to herself than history," give up "femininity" for real
achievement.

There's something of self-portraiture here, for this was the line of develop- 7
ment Rich's own poetry took. At the beginning of the book she's just another
young poet learning a craft, a craft whose terms were defined by her male contemporaries. Though her earlier poems already show a certain epigrammatic
terseness of line, a clenched, somewhat unrelenting toughness of intellect, they
are often abstract; it's as if the poet is talking only to herself. Even when the
poems are addressed to a second person, she speaks as if she isn't really sure
she will be heard.

As it develops, Adrienne Rich's poetry moves toward mercilessness, of 8
a desirable kind. Her discovery of her own poetic voice, of what she wants to
say, and of her audience, who she's saying it to, are clearly interdependent.
The early poems skirt emotion or muse upon it; experiences have given rise
to the poems, but we're often not too sure what, exactly, they are. In later ones
emotions are not talked about but expressed or evoked, often with blunt and
sometimes brutal force. The earlier poems are full of "craft"; in the later ones
technique has been so thoroughly assimilated that we don't even notice it.
Language is honed down, decoration trimmed off; the poet has no more use
for frills, no need to demonstrate that she too is an adept. The earlier poems
illustrate; the later ones state.

As the language tightens, the focus narrows and sharpens: Rich's subject 9
becomes the struggle of woman, interpreted on almost every possible level: emotional, political, mythological, symbolic, historical. The poems become at the
same time both personal and more universal: Rich is speaking, not to some
nebulous listener, but to her own deepest self and to the corresponding selves
of other women. For women become the audience: when she says "us," that's
who she means:

> I long to create something
> that can't be used to keep us passive...

When poems are addressed to men, the tone is no longer contemplative. There
are few poets who have been better able to express anger.

The intention and the result, in the last three sections of the book, is nothing 10
less than the creation of a new history and a new mythology. A number of
woman poets have been working along the same lines, but few with such success. Sometimes the poems decline into rhetoric, sometimes they become shrill,

but not often. At their best they are absolutely succinct, absolutely powerful; rooted in the actual, they move into the subterranean levels where myths are alive. "Diving into the Wreck," "From a Survivor," "Trying to Talk with a Man," are Rich at her best.

The long poem at the end of the book, "From an Old House in America," [11] is in some ways Rich's most ambitious, and most definitive poem to date: compact, simple in phrasing, fiercely intellectual, uncompromising, a condensed *Leaves of Grass*, but this time from the woman's point of view:

> Isolation, the dream
> of the frontier woman
>
> levelling her rifle along
> the homestead fence
>
> still snares our pride
> —a suicidal leaf
>
> laid under the burning-glass
> in the sun's eye
>
> Any woman's death diminishes me

This book is clearly a seminal one in the history of women's poetry. It's [12] also an important landmark in the development of a remarkable individual poet. It's a necessary book: necessary for the reader, but also one feels, for the writer. There are few poems that convince you, as the best of Rich's do, that they *had* to be written.

1975

Purpose and Meaning

1. In the opening paragraph of this essay, Atwood remarks that white male American poets "having nothing to say to ordinary people, because ordinary people aren't listening." Who are these ordinary people Atwood identifies, and why aren't they listening to white male poets? How does the statement contribute to her purpose?

2. Atwood contends that in America women and minority poets are "exceptions" in that they are "less interested in displaying verbal virtuosity than in getting something said." What are women and minority poets interested in saying? Does Atwood specify or imply what this interest is?

3. In paragraph 9 Atwood discusses who Rich's audience is, "when she says 'us,'" she means women. Who is Atwood's audience and how does that influence her tone? Does she make certain assumptions based on who she may believe her audience to be?

4. In paragraphs 6 through 8, Atwood makes connections between Rich's growth as a woman and her growth as a poet. How is Rich's personal and poetic development similar to the growth of the women's movement in general?

Language and Style

1. How do Atwood's early reference to male poets and subsequent, repeated allusions and references to women and feminism help to make her thesis clear?

2. Point out examples of the author's use of concrete language. Where is she more abstract? Which type of language tends to predominate and why?

3. Atwood uses colons in interesting ways in this essay. Locate five uses of the colon and explain its function in each example.

Strategy and Structure

1. Atwood's review seems to be as much a study of Rich's poetry as of Rich's place in the world as a woman poet speaking of and for women. How does this make Atwood's piece more than a review? Why might it be considered an argumentative essay?

2. Why doesn't Atwood mention Adrienne Rich until the third paragraph? What is the function of paragraphs 1 and 2?

3. Review Atwood's examples from Rich's poetry. How effective is the order in which Atwood places these examples? How do they reinforce her thesis?

4. Why does Atwood use both comparison and contrast and process analysis as rhetorical strategies? What does she gain from each? Cite examples to support your response.

Thinking and Writing

1. Evaluate the art of the literary review, using Lessing's article on Dinesen and Atwood's essay on Rich as examples.

2. Select a poet you admire and write a review of her or his poetry. Consider the poet's cultural background and how it influences his or her poetry.

3. The issue of politics and poetry and whether the two should ever meet is one that is often debated. Some argue that poetry is and ought to be purely concerned with craft, that the influence of political ideas corrupts that purity. Others believe that politics (issues of power such as race, class, and sex) are in reality *personal* issues. Consequently, they will and must be expressed in a poet's work. Write an essay stating your position in this debate. Feel free to refer to other popular forms such as film and music to support your position.

MAXINE HONG KINGSTON

With the publication of *The Woman Warrior: Memoirs of a Girlhood Among Ghosts* (1976), Maxine Hong Kingston took her place as one of the most distinctive contemporary prose stylists. Kingston's account of growing up female and Chinese-American in California revealed her as a writer not only driven to tell her stories but fascinated with the power of language itself. In his review of *The Woman Warrior*, John Leonard of *The New York Times* wrote that it was "a poem turned into a sword." Throughout her career, Kingston has been preoccupied with words and their unique power—through rhythm, sound, association, and sense—to create, and destroy, worlds.

Kingston's world begins in Stockton, California, where she was born in 1940, the eldest of six children, to Chinese immigrants who operated a laundry. In a 1989 interview, Kingston observed, "We used to run all over Stockton. We were real urchins." With her "pressed duck voice," she did not fit in in high school, a fact amusingly evident in "High School Reunion." The conflict of learning two cultures at once is the dominant theme in *The Woman Warrior* and its sequel *China Men* (1980), which won the American Book Award. Just as her first book examined the lives of Kingston's mother and female relatives (the first section of which is excerpted here), so *China Men* presents the epic Chinese-American story from the viewpoint of her embittered male protagonist. Even outside California, as we see in "The Wild Man of the Green Swamp," racial and gender differences are the foundation of cultural conflict.

Kingston's latest publication, *Tripmaster Monkey: His Fake Book* (1989), is a fictive extension of *China Men* and indeed of Kingston's own life. It is a weave of literary fictions, Chinese and American, revealed in the life of a twenty-three-year-old Chinese-American male named Wittman Ah Sing. Curiously Kingston's hero is very much like herself—a 1960s Berkeley graduate and counterculture rebel addicted to "talk stories." Kingston graduated from the University of California at Berkeley in 1962, returned a year later to obtain a teaching certificate, and subsequently taught high school and college English, largely in Hawaii, where she lived with her husband and son for seventeen years. Today she lives in Oakland, California.

In all her work, Maxine Hong Kingston has the rare ability to make—as the critic Michiko Kakutani declares—a dazzling leap of "imaginative sympathy" in which she projects her life into those of her characters. In her own words, Kingston is interested in "building worlds, inventing selves." She tells her stories with the eye of a child who sees monsters as soon as the lights go out.

No Name Woman

"You must not tell anyone," my mother said, "what I am about to tell 1
you. In China your father had a sister who killed herself. She jumped into the
family well. We say that your father has all brothers because it is as if she had
never been born.

"In 1924 just a few days after our village celebrated seventeen hurry-up 2
weddings—to make sure that every young man who went 'out on the road'
would responsibly come home—your father and his brothers and your grandfather and his brothers and your aunt's new husband sailed for America, the
Gold Mountain. It was your grandfather's last trip. Those lucky enough to get
contracts waved good-bye from the decks. They fed and guarded the stowaways
and helped them off in Cuba, New York, Bali, Hawaii. 'We'll meet in California
next year,' they said. All of them sent money home.

"I remember looking at your aunt one day when she and I were dressing; 3
I had not noticed before that she had such a protruding melon of a stomach.
But I did not think, 'She's pregnant,' until she began to look like other pregnant
women, her shirt pulling and the white tops of her black pants showing. She
could not have been pregnant, you see, because her husband had been gone
for years. No one said anything. We did not discuss it. In early summer she
was ready to have the child, long after the time when it could have been possible.

"The village had also been counting. On the night the baby was to be 4
born the villagers raided our house. Some were crying. Like a great saw, teeth
strung with lights, files of people walked zigzag across our land, tearing the
rice. Their lanterns doubled in the disturbed black water, which drained away
through the broken bunds. As the villagers closed in, we could see that some
of them, probably men and women we knew well, wore white masks. The people
with long hair hung it over their faces. Women with short hair made it stand
up on end. Some had tied white bands around their foreheads, arms, and legs.

"At first they threw mud and rocks at the house. Then they threw eggs 5
and began slaughtering our stock. We could hear the animals scream their
deaths—the roosters, the pigs, a last great roar from the ox. Familiar wild heads
flared in our night windows; the villagers encircled us. Some of the faces stopped
to peer at us, their eyes rushing like searchlights. The hands flattened against
the panes, framed heads, and left red prints.

"The villagers broke in the front and the back doors at the same time, 6
even though we had not locked the doors against them. Their knives dripped
with the blood of our animals. They smeared blood on the doors and walls.

One woman swung a chicken, whose throat she had slit, splattering blood in red arcs about her. We stood together in the middle of our house, in the family hall with the pictures and tables of the ancestors around us, and looked straight ahead.

"At that time the house had only two wings. When the men came back, we would build two more to enclose our courtyard and a third one to begin a second courtyard. The villagers pushed through both wings, even your grand-parents' rooms, to find your aunt's, which was also mine until the men returned. From this room a new wing for one of the younger families would grow. They ripped up her clothes and shoes and broke her combs, grinding them under-foot. They tore her work from the loom. They scattered the cooking fire and rolled the new weaving in it. We could hear them in the kitchen breaking our bowls and banging the pots. They overturned the great waist-high earthenware jugs; duck eggs, pickled fruits, vegetables burst out and mixed in acrid torrents. The old woman from the next field swept a broom through the air and loosed the spirits-of-the-broom over our heads. 'Pig.' 'Ghost.' 'Pig,' they sobbed and scolded while they ruined our house. [7]

"When they left, they took sugar and oranges to bless themselves. They cut pieces from the dead animals. Some of them took bowls that were not broken and clothes that were not torn. Afterward we swept up the rice and sewed it back up into sacks. But the smells from the spilled preserves lasted. Your aunt gave birth in the pigsty that night. The next morning when I went for the water, I found her and the baby plugging up the family well. [8]

"Don't let your father know that I told you. He denies her. Now that you have started to menstruate, what happened to her could happen to you. Don't humiliate us. You wouldn't like to be forgotten as if you had never been born. The villagers are watchful." [9]

Whenever she had to warn us about life, my mother told stories that ran like this one, a story to grow up on. She tested our strength to establish realities. Those in the emigrant generations who could not reassert brute survival died young and far from home. Those of us in the first American generations have had to figure out how the invisible world the emigrants built around our childhoods fits in solid America. [10]

The emigrants confused the gods by diverting their curses, misleading them with crooked streets and false names. They must try to confuse their offspring as well, who, I suppose, threaten them in similar ways—always trying to get things straight, always trying to name the unspeakable. The Chinese I know hide their names; sojourners take new names when their lives change and guard their real names with silence. [11]

Chinese-Americans, when you try to understand what things in you are Chinese, how do you separate what is peculiar to childhood, to poverty, in-sanities, one family, your mother who marked your growing with stories, from what is Chinese? What is Chinese tradition and what is the movies? [12]

If I want to learn what clothes my aunt wore, whether flashy or ordinary, I would have to begin, "Remember Father's drowned-in-the-well sister?" I can- [13]

not ask that. My mother has told me once and for all the useful parts. She will add nothing unless powered by Necessity, a riverbank that guides her life. She plants vegetable gardens rather than lawns; she carries the odd-shaped tomatoes home from the fields and eats food left for the gods.

Whenever we did frivolous things, we used up energy; we flew high kites. We children came up off the ground over the melting cones our parents brought home from work and the American movie on New Year's Day—*Oh, You Beautiful Doll* with Betty Grable one year, and *She Wore a Yellow Ribbon* with John Wayne another year. After the one carnival ride each, we paid in guilt; our tired father counted his change on the dark walk home.

Adultery is extravagance. Could people who hatch their own chicks and eat the embryos and the heads for delicacies and boil the feet in vinegar for party food, leaving only the gravel, eating even the gizzard lining—could such people engender a prodigal aunt? To be a woman, to have a daughter in starvation time was a waste enough. My aunt could not have been the lone romantic who gave up everything for sex. Women in the old China did not choose. Some man had commanded her to lie with him and be his secret evil. I wonder whether he masked himself when he joined the raid on her family.

Perhaps she had encountered him in the fields or on the mountain where the daughters-in-law collected fuel. Or perhaps he first noticed her in the marketplace. He was not a stranger because the village housed no strangers. She had to have dealings with him other than sex. Perhaps he worked an adjoining field, or he sold her the cloth for the dress she sewed and wore. His demand must have surprised, then terrified her. She obeyed him; she always did as she was told.

When the family found a young man in the next village to be her husband, she had stood tractably beside the best rooster, his proxy, and promised before they met that she would be his forever. She was lucky that he was her age and she would be the first wife, an advantage secure now. The night she first saw him, he had sex with her. Then he left for America. She had almost forgotten what he looked like. When she tried to envision him, she only saw the black and white face in the group photograph the men had had taken before leaving.

The other man was not, after all, much different from her husband. They both gave orders: she followed. "If you tell your family, I'll beat you. I'll kill you. Be here again next week." No one talked sex, ever. And she might have separated the rapes from the rest of living if only she did not have to buy her oil from him or gather wood in the same forest. I want her fear to have lasted just as long as rape lasted so that the fear could have been contained. No drawn-out fear. But women at sex hazarded birth and hence lifetimes. The fear did not stop but permeated everywhere. She told the man, "I think I'm pregnant." He organized the raid against her.

On nights when my mother and father talked about their life back home, sometimes they mentioned an "outcast table" whose business they still seemed to be settling, their voices tight. In a commensal tradition, where food is precious, the powerful older people made wrongdoers eat alone. Instead of letting them start separate new lives like the Japanese, who could become samurais and geishas, the Chinese family, faces averted but eyes glowering sideways, hung on to the offenders and fed them leftovers. My aunt must have lived in the same house as my parents and eaten at an outcast table. My mother spoke about the raid as if she had seen it, when she and my aunt, a daughter-in-law to a different household, should not have been living together at all. Daughters-in-law lived with their husbands' parents, not their own; a synonym for marriage in Chinese is "taking a daughter-in-law." Her husband's parents could have sold her, mortgaged her, stoned her. But they had sent her back to her own mother and father, a mysterious act hinting at disgraces not told me. Perhaps they had thrown her out to deflect the avengers.

She was the only daughter; her four brothers went with her father, husband, and uncles "out on the road" and for some years became western men. When the goods were divided among the family, three of the brothers took land, and the youngest, my father, chose an education. After my grandparents gave their daughter away to her husband's family, they had dispensed all the adventure and all the property. They expected her alone to keep the traditional ways, which her brothers, now among the barbarians, could fumble without detection. The heavy, deep-rooted women were to maintain the past against the flood, safe for returning. But the rare urge west had fixed upon our family, and so my aunt crossed boundaries not delineated in space.

The work of preservation demands that the feelings playing about in one's guts not be turned into action. Just watch their passing like cherry blossoms. But perhaps my aunt, my forerunner, caught in a slow life, let dreams grow and fade and after some months or years went toward what persisted. Fear at the enormities of the forbidden kept her desires delicate, wire and bone. She looked at a man because she liked the way the hair was tucked behind his ears, or she liked the question-mark line of a long torso curving at the shoulder and straight at the hip. For warm eyes or a soft voice or a slow walk—that's all—a few hairs, a line, a brightness, a sound, a pace, she gave up family. She offered us up for a charm that vanished with tiredness, a pigtail that didn't toss when the wind died. Why, the wrong lighting could erase the dearest thing about him.

It could very well have been, however, that my aunt did not take subtle enjoyment of her friend, but, a wild woman, kept rollicking company. Imagining her free with sex doesn't fit, though. I don't know any women like that, or men either. Unless I see her life branching into mine, she gives me no ancestral help.

To sustain her being in love, she often worked at herself in the mirror, guessing at the colors and shapes that would interest him, changing them frequently in order to hit on the right combination. She wanted him to look back.

On a farm near the sea, a woman who tended her appearance reaped a reputation for eccentricity. All the married women blunt-cut their hair in flaps about their ears or pulled it back in tight buns. No nonsense. Neither style blew easily into heart-catching tangles. And at their weddings they displayed themselves in their long hair for the last time. "It brushed the backs of my knees," my mother tells me. "It was braided, and even so, it brushed the backs of my knees."

At the mirror my aunt combed individuality into her bob. A bun could 25 have been contrived to escape into black streamers blowing in the wind or in quiet wisps about her face, but only the older women in our picture album wear buns. She brushed her hair back from her forehead, tucking the flaps behind her ears. She looped a piece of thread, knotted into a circle between her index fingers and thumbs, and ran the double strand across her forehead. When she closed her fingers as if she were making a pair of shadow geese bite, the string twisted together catching the little hairs. Then she pulled the thread away from her skin, ripping the hairs out neatly, her eyes watering from the needles of pain. Opening her fingers, she cleaned the thread, then rolled it along her hairline and the tops of her eyebrows. My mother did the same to me and my sisters and herself. I used to believe that the expression "caught by the short hairs" meant a captive held with a depilatory string. It especially hurt at the temples, but my mother said we were lucky we didn't have to have our feet bound when we were seven. Sisters used to sit on their beds and cry together, she said, as their mothers or their slave removed the bandages for a few minutes each night and let the blood gush back into their veins. I hope that the man my aunt loved appreciated a smooth brow, that he wasn't just a tits-and-ass man.

Once my aunt found a freckle on her chin, at a spot that the almanac 26 said predestined her for unhappiness. She dug it out with a hot needle and washed the wound with peroxide.

More attention to her looks than these pullings of hairs and pickings at 27 spots would have caused gossip among the villagers. They owned work clothes and good clothes, and they wore good clothes for feasting the new seasons. But since a woman combing her hair hexes beginnings, my aunt rarely found an occasion to look her best. Women looked like great sea snails—the corded wood, babies, and laundry they carried were the whorls on their backs. The Chinese did not admire a bent back; goddesses and warriors stood straight. Still there must have been a marvelous freeing of beauty when a worker laid down her burden and stretched and arched.

Such commonplace loveliness, however, was not enough for my aunt. 28 She dreamed of a lover for the fifteen days of New Year's, the time for families to exchange visits, money, and food. She plied her secret comb. And sure enough she cursed the year, the family, the village, and herself.

Even as her hair lured her imminent lover, many other men looked at 29 her. Uncles, cousins, nephews, brothers would have looked, too, had they been home between journeys. Perhaps they had already been restraining their curiosity, and they left, fearful that their glances, like a field of nesting birds, might be startled and caught. Poverty hurt, and that was their first reason for leaving. But another, final reason for leaving the crowded house was the never-said.

She may have been unusually beloved, the precious only daughter, spoiled 30 and mirror gazing because of the affection the family lavished on her. When her husband left, they welcomed the chance to take her back from the in-laws; she could live like the little daughter for just a while longer. There are stories that my grandfather was different from other people, "crazy ever since the little Jap bayoneted him in the head." He used to put his naked penis on the dinner table, laughing. And one day he brought home a baby girl, wrapped up inside his brown western-style greatcoat. He had traded one of his sons, probably my father, the youngest, for her. My grandmother made him trade back. When he finally got a daughter of his own, he doted on her. They must have all loved her, except perhaps my father, the only brother who never went back to China, having once been traded for a girl.

Brothers and sisters, newly men and women, had to efface their sexual   31
color and present plain miens. Disturbing hair and eyes, a smile like no other, threatened the ideal of five generations living under one roof. To focus blurs, people shouted face to face and yelled from room to room. The immigrants I know have loud voices, unmodulated to American tones even after years away from the village where they called their friendships out across the fields. I have not been able to stop my mother's screams in public libraries or over telephones. Walking erect (knees straight, toes pointed forward, not pigeon-toed, which is Chinese-feminine) and speaking in an inaudible voice, I have tried to turn myself American-feminine. Chinese communication was loud, public. Only sick people had to whisper. But at the dinner table, where the family members came nearest one another, no one could talk, not the outcasts nor any eaters. Every word that falls from the mouth is a coin lost. Silently they gave and accepted food with both hands. A preoccupied child who took his bowl with one hand got a sideways glare. A complete moment of total attention is due everyone alike. Children and lovers have no singularity here, but my aunt used a secret voice, a separate attentiveness.

She kept the man's name to herself throughout her labor and dying; she   32
did not accuse him that he be punished with her. To save her inseminator's name she gave silent birth.

He may have been somebody in her own household, but intercourse with   33
a man outside the family would have been no less abhorrent. All the village were kinsmen, and the titles shouted in loud country voices never let kinship be forgotten. Any man within visiting distance would have been neutralized as a lover—"brother," "younger brother," "older brother"—one hundred and fifteen relationship titles. Parents researched birth charts probably not so much to assure good fortune as to circumvent incest in a population that has but one hundred surnames. Everybody has eight million relatives. How useless then sexual mannerisms, how dangerous.

As if it came from an atavism deeper than fear, I used to add "brother"   34
silently to boys' names. It hexed the boys, who would or would not ask me to dance and made them less scary and as familiar and deserving of benevolence as girls.

But, of course, I hexed myself also—no dates. I should have stood up, 35
both arms waving, and shouted out across libraries, "Hey, you! Love me back."
I had no idea, though, how to make attraction selective, how to control its direction and magnitude. If I made myself American-pretty so that the five or six
Chinese boys in the class fell in love with me, everyone else—the Caucasian,
Negro, and Japanese boys—would too. Sisterliness, dignified and honorable,
made much more sense.

Attraction eludes control so stubbornly that whole societies designed to 36
organize relationships among people cannot keep order, not even when they
bind people to one another from childhood and raise them together. Among
the very poor and the wealthy, brothers married their adopted sisters, like doves.
Our family allowed some romance, paying adult brides' prices and providing
dowries so that their sons and daughters could marry strangers. Marriage
promises to turn strangers into friendly relatives—a nation of siblings.

In the village structure, spirits shimmered among the live creatures, 37
balanced and held in equilibrium by time and land. But one human being flar-
ing up into violence could open up a black hole, a maelstrom that pulled in
the sky. The frightened villagers, who depended on one another to maintain
the real, went to my aunt to show her a personal, physical representation of
the break she had made in the "roundness." Misallying couples snapped off the
future, which was to be embodied in true offspring. The villagers punished her
for acting as if she could have a private life, secret and apart from them.

If my aunt had betrayed the family at a time of large grain yields and 38
peace, when many boys were born, and wings were being built on many houses,
perhaps she might have escaped such severe punishment. But the men—hungry,
greedy, tired of planting in dry soil—had been forced to leave the village in
order to send food–money home. There were ghost plagues, bandit plagues,
wars with the Japanese, floods. My Chinese brother and sister had died of an
unknown sickness. Adultery, perhaps only a mistake during good times, became
a crime when the village needed food.

The round moon cakes and round doorways, the round tables of graduated 39
size that fit one roundness inside another, round windows and rice bowls—
these talismans had lost their power to warn this family of the law: a family
must be whole, faithfully keeping the descent line by having sons to feed the
old and the dead, who in turn look after the family. The villagers came to show
my aunt and her lover-in-hiding a broken house. The villagers were speeding
up the circling of events because she was too shortsighted to see that her in-
fidelity had already harmed the village, that waves of consequences would return
unpredictably, sometimes in disguise, as now, to hurt her. This roundness had
to be made coin-sized so that she would see its circumference: punish her at
the birth of her baby. Awaken her to the inexorable. People who refused fatalism
because they could invent small resources insisted on culpability. Deny accidents
and wrest fault from the stars.

After the villagers left, their lanterns now scattering in various directions 40 toward home, the family broke their silence and cursed her. "Aiaa, we're going to die. Death is coming. Death is coming. Look what you've done. You've killed us. Ghost! Dead ghost! Ghost! You've never been born." She ran out into the fields, far enough from the house so that she could no longer hear their voices, and pressed herself against the earth, her own land no more. When she felt the birth coming, she thought that she had been hurt. Her body seized together. "They've hurt me too much," she thought. "This is gall, and it will kill me." With forehead and knees against the earth, her body convulsed and then relaxed. She turned on her back, lay on the ground. The black well of sky and stars went out and out and out forever; her body and her complexity seemed to disappear. She was one of the stars, a bright dot in blackness, without home, without a companion, in eternal cold and silence. An agoraphobia rose in her, speeding higher and higher, bigger and bigger; she would not be able to contain it; there would be no end to fear.

Flayed, unprotected against space, she felt pain return, focusing her body. 41 This pain chilled her—a cold, steady kind of surface pain. Inside, spasmodically, the other pain, the pain of the child, heated her. For hours she lay on the ground, alternately body and space. Sometimes a vision of normal comfort obliterated reality: she saw the family in the evening gambling at the dinner table, the young people massaging their elders' backs. She saw them congratulating one another, high joy on the mornings the rice shoots came up. When these pictures burst, the stars drew yet further apart. Black space opened.

She got to her feet to fight better and remembered that old-fashioned 42 women gave birth in their pigsties to fool the jealous, pain-dealing gods, who do not snatch piglets. Before the next spasms could stop her, she ran to the pigsty, each step a rushing out into emptiness. She climbed over the fence and knelt in the dirt. It was good to have a fence enclosing her, a tribal person alone.

Laboring, this woman who had carried her child as a foreign growth that 43 sickened her every day, expelled it at last. She reached down to touch the hot, wet, moving mass, surely smaller than anything human, and could feel that it was human after all—fingers, toes, nails, nose. She pulled it up on to her belly, and it lay curled there, butt in the air, feet precisely tucked one under the other. She opened her loose shirt and buttoned the child inside. After resting, it squirmed and thrashed and she pushed it up to her breast. It turned its head this way and that until it found her nipple. There, it made little snuffling noises. She clenched her teeth at its preciousness, lovely as a young calf, a piglet, a little dog.

She may have gone to the pigsty as a last act of responsibility: she would 44 protect this child as she had protected its father. It would look after her soul, leaving supplies on her grave. But how would this tiny child without family find her grave when there would be no marker for her anywhere, neither in the earth nor the family hall? No one would give her a family hall name. She had taken the child with her into the wastes. At its birth the two of them had felt the same raw pain of separation, a wound that only the family pressing tight could close. A child with no descent line would not soften her life but only trail after her, ghostlike, begging her to give it purpose. At dawn the villagers on their way to the fields would stand around the fence and look.

Full of milk, the little ghost slept. When it awoke, she hardened her breasts against the milk that crying loosens. Toward morning she picked up the baby and walked to the well.   45

Carrying the baby to the well shows loving. Otherwise abandon it. Turn its face into the mud. Mothers who love their children take them along. It was probably a girl; there is some hope of forgiveness for boys.   46

"Don't tell anyone you had an aunt. Your father does not want to hear her name. She has never been born." I have believed that sex was unspeakable and words so strong and fathers so frail that "aunt" would do my father mysterious harm. I have thought that my family, having settled among immigrants who had also been their neighbors in the ancestral land, needed to clean their name, and a wrong word would incite the kinspeople even here. But there is more to this silence: they want me to participate in her punishment. And I have.   47

In the twenty years since I heard this story I have not asked for details nor said my aunt's name; I do not know it. People who can comfort the dead can also chase after them to hurt them further—a reverse ancestor worship. The real punishment was not the raid swiftly inflicted by the villagers, but the family's deliberately forgetting her. Her betrayal so maddened them, they saw to it that she would suffer forever, even after death. Always hungry, always needing, she would have to beg food from other ghosts, snatch and steal it from those whose living descendants give them gifts. She would have to fight the ghosts massed at crossroads for the buns a few thoughtful citizens leave to decoy her away from village and home so that the ancestral spirits could feast unharassed. At peace, they could act like gods, not ghosts, their descent lines providing them with paper suits and dresses, spirit money, paper houses, paper automobiles, chicken, meat, and rice into eternity—essences delivered up in smoke and flames, steam and incense rising from each rice bowl. In an attempt to make the Chinese care for people outside the family, Chairman Mao encourages us now to give our paper replicas to the spirits of outstanding soldiers and workers, no matter whose ancestors they may be. My aunt remains forever hungry. Goods are not distributed evenly among the dead.   48

My aunt haunts me—her ghost drawn to me because now, after fifty years of neglect, I alone devote pages of paper to her, though not origamied into houses and clothes. I do not think she always means me well. I am telling on her, and she was a spite suicide, drowning herself in the drinking water. The Chinese are always very frightened of the drowned one, whose weeping ghost, wet hair hanging and skin bloated, waits silently by the water to pull down a substitute.   49

1976

Purpose and Meaning

1. Some of the themes in Kingston's essay are Chinese-American cultural differences, storytelling, the distortion of facts, male and female positions in Chinese society, and the importance of names and naming. Examine the essay's five opening lines and discuss how many of these themes are foreshadowed. What overarching thesis emerges from these themes?

2. What are some of the differences between Chinese and American culture, as depicted by Kingston, concerning attitudes toward women, sex, and family? What insights does she want to convey to her audience?

3. Read again paragraphs 31 through 33. What are some of the mores that have formed in Chinese society as a result of the tradition of families living together over several generations?

Language and Style

1. Kingston's narrative opens with the shocking revelation that her aunt "jumped into the family well." Following this revelation, she recounts how villagers "threw mud and rocks at the house, . . . began slaughtering [the] stock, . . . smeared blood on the doors and walls." And still later she tells in graphic detail how her aunt gave birth and then committed suicide. What overall effect does this vivid description have on the reader's response to the narrative and perhaps to the writer?

2. Kingston's writing is highly imagistic. Nearly every line contains an image. One could say the images actually tell the story for Kingston. Comb Kingston's story for its images, choose five to ten that particularly strike you, and discuss what each one tells. You may want to refer to the themes mentioned in question 1 under "Purpose and Meaning."

3. Kingston is fond of recurring images or motifs, such as ghosts (see paragraphs 4, 7, 40, 45, 48 and 49) and the unnamed or "unspeakable" (see paragraphs 1, 2, 11, 32, 44, 47, and 48 and the essay's title.) How do these repeated references help to give order to both the form and content of the essay?

Strategy and Structure

1. Kingston begins the essay not in the narrator's voice but in her mother's. How does this approach prepare the reader for certain themes in the essay? How does it shift authority away from the narrator? Why might Kingston wish to shift authority in this way?

2. In paragraphs 15 through 33, Kingston tells several possible versions of her aunt's sexual encounter. It may have been rape, tender love, a passionate affair, an interlude with a relative. Since Kingston cannot know, neither can the reader. How does this uncertainty help to further themes about storytelling, cultural differences, and the distortion of facts?

3. Why does Kingston wait until the final paragraphs to discuss her identity as a writer struggling to tell her family history? Would the story have been strengthened or weakened if she had begun with the focus on her efforts to tell the stories of her ancestry? Why does she include this insight into herself at all, instead of leaving such information to a preface or introduction to the work?

Thinking and Writing

1. Kingston peppers her tale with references to rituals peculiar to Chinese culture, such as the "outcast table" (paragraph 19) and the plucking of hairs (paragraph 25). Describe three American rituals that may sound equally peculiar to people from other cultures.

2. Write about some incident in your family's history that is well known to all family members and has been elevated almost to the point of myth. What does your narrative reveal about your family and your own personal development?

3. Choose one of the following schemas and write three different scenarios for it (as Kingston does when she describes her aunt's sexual encounter):

    (a) A young woman writes poetry in relative secret all her life. After her death, she is recognized as a genius. Explain why she lived in isolation.

    (b) A man is found in his home, a gun in his hand, weeping beside the bed of his fatally shot wife. Describe what happened.

High School Reunion

I just opened an envelope in the mail to find a mimeograph sheet smelling like a school test and announcing the twentieth-year high school reunion. No Host Cocktail Party. Buffet Dinner. Family Picnic, Dancing. In August. Class of '58. Edison High. Stockton. The lurches in my stomach feel like doubt about the strength to stay grown up. 1

I had not gone to the tenth-year reunion; the friends I really wanted to see, I was seeing. But I've been having dreams about the people in high school, and sit up with an urge to talk to them, find out how they turned out. "Did you grow up?" There are emotions connected with those people that I don't feel for friends I've made since. 2

"When I think of you, I remember the hateful look you gave me on the day we signed yearbooks. That face pops into my mind a few times a year for twenty years. Why did you look at me that way?" I'd like to be able to say 3 that at the No Host Cocktail. And to someone else, "I remember you winking at me across the physics lab."

I dreamed that the girl who never talked in all the years of school spoke   4
to me: "Your house has moles living in it." Then my cat said, "I am a cat and not a car. Quit driving me around." High school is a component of the American subconscious.

Another reason I hadn't gone to the tenth was an item in the registration form: 5
"List your publications." (The reunion committee must be the kids who grew up to be personnel officers at universities.) To make a list, it takes more than an article and one poem. Cutthroat competitors in that class. With no snooty questions asked, maybe the people with interesting jail records would come. We were not the class to be jailed for our politics or white-collar crimes but for burglary, armed robbery and crimes of passion. "Reunions are planned by the people who were popular. They want the chance to put us down again," says a friend (Punahou Academy '68), preparing for her tenth.

But surely I am not going to show up this year just because I have a "list."   6
And there is more to the questionnaire: "What's the greatest happiness you've had in the last twenty years?" "What do you regret the most?" it asks. I'm going to write across the paper, "These questions are too hard. Can I come anyway?" No, you can't write, "None of your business." It is their business; these are the special people that formed your growing up.

I have a friend (Roosevelt High '62) who refused to go to his tenth because   7
he had to check "married," "separated," "divorced" or "single." He could not bear to mark "divorced." Family Picnic.

But another divorced friend's reunion (Roosevelt '57) was so much fun   8
that the class decided to have another one the very next weekend—without the spouses, a come-without-spouse party. And my brother (Edison '60) and sister-in-law (Edison '62) went to her class reunion, where they had an Old Flames Dance; you asked a Secret Love to dance. Working out the regrets, people went home with other people's spouses. Fifteen divorces and remarriages by summer's end.

At my husband Earll's (Bishop O'Dowd '56) reunion, there was an uncomfort-   9
ableness whether to call the married priests Father or Mister or what.

What if you can't explain yourself over the dance music? Twenty years   10
of transcendence blown away at the No Host Cocktail. Cocktails—another skill I haven't learned, like the dude in the old cowboy movies who ordered milk or lemonade or sarsaparilla. They'll have disco dancing. Never been to a disco either. Not cool after all these years.

There will be a calling to account. That's why it's hard to go. A judgment   11
by one's real peers. We're going to judge whether The Most Likely to Succeed succeeded.

In high school we did not choose our friends. I ended up with certain   12
people, and then wondered why we went together. If she's the pretty one, then

I must be the homely one. (When I asked my sister, Edison '59, she told me, "Well, when I think of the way you look in the halls, I picture you with your slip hanging." Not well groomed.) We were incomplete, and made complementary friendships, like Don Quixote and Sancho Panza. Or more like the Cisco Kid and Pancho. Friendships among equals is a possibility I have found as an adult.

No, my motive for going would not be because of my "list." I was writing   13
in high school. Writing did not protect me then, and it won't start protecting me now. I came from a school—no, it's not the school—it's the times; we are of a time when people don't read.

There's a race thing too. Suddenly the colored girls would walk up, and   14
my colored girlfriend would talk and move differently. Well, they're athletes, I thought; they go to the same parties. Some years, the only place I ever considered sitting for lunch was the Chinese table. But there were more of us than places at that table. Hurry and get there early, or go late when somebody may have finished and left. Not eat. Who will eat with whom at the Buffet Dinner?

I notice that the chairman of the reunion went to Chinese school, too;   15
maybe seeing her name, the Chinese-Americans will come. I will have people to eat with—unless they're mad at me for having written about them. I keep claiming our mutual material. They will have recognized themselves in the writing, and not like me for it. That people don't read is only my own wishful thinking.

And Earll says he may have to work in August and may not be able to   16
escort me. Alone at the Dance. Again.

One day a popular girl, who had her own car, stamped her foot and   17
shouted to a friend who was walking home with me. "Come here!" she ordered. "We go home with one another." To be seen going home alone was bad. They drove off. "I remember you shouting her away from me," I could say at the reunion, not, I swear, to accuse so much as to get the facts straight. Nobody came out and said that there were groups. I don't even know whether the friendships had a name; they were not called groups or crowds or gangs or cliques or anything. ("Clicks," the kids today say.) "Were there groups?" I could ask at last. "Which one was I in?"

My son, who is a freshman (Class of '81), says he can't make friends outside   18
his group. "My old friends feel iced out, and then they ice me out."

What a test of character the reunion would be. I'm not worried about   19
looks. I and every woman of my age know that we look physically better at thirty-eight than eighteen. I'll have objective proof of the superiority of older women when I see the women who are eighteen in my dreams.

John Gregory Dunne (Portsmouth Priory '50) said to his wife, Joan Didion   20
(McClatchy High '52), "It is your obligation as an American writer to go to your high school reunion." And she went. She said she dreamed about the people for a long time afterward.

I have improved: I don't wear slips anymore; I got tired of hanging around   21 with homely people. It would be nice to go to a reunion where we look at one another and know without explanations how much we all grew in twenty years of living. And know that we ended up at thirty-eight the way we did partly because of one another, pysches and memories intertwining, companions in time for a while, lucky to meet again. I wouldn't miss such a get-together for anything.

1978

Purpose and Meaning

1. Kingston writes that "high school is a component of the American subconscious." In what ways does she consider this to be so?

2. Throughout this essay, Kingston makes references to herself in high school as an outsider. How does this gain the interest and perhaps the sympathy of the reader, as well as further her purpose in writing the piece?

3. As Margaret Atwood does in some of her essays, Kingston refers to herself in this essay and in "No Name Woman" as a writer (see paragraph 15). What do you think is her purpose in such self-referential writing?

Language and Style

1. In this essay, as in "No Name Woman," Kingston often lets images tell her story. What is the significance of opening an essay about a high school with a smell, as opposed to a sight? What effect do smells have on memory?

2. Kingston's essay is very funny at times (note paragraphs 5, 10, 12). How does the humor help to shape the narrator's voice and balance an otherwise serious theme?

3. Kingston makes repeated reference to the invitation items listed in the first paragraph of the essay. She also capitalizes certain phrases such as, Secret Love (paragraph 8); The Most Likely to Succeed (paragraph 11); and Alone at the Dance (paragraph 16). What tone does this device help to create? How might it be considered schoolgirlish to capitalize these words?

Strategy and Structure

1. Kingston begins somewhat unconventionally by listing the items from her high school reunion announcement. In what other ways is this essay like a list or catalog?

2. What does Kingston accomplish in following every reference to a friend or family member with the high school name and year of graduation? How does this device affect the tone and the organization?

3. In the final paragraph, Kingston's tone shifts rather abruptly. Why does she make this shift? What final impression does it leave with the reader?

Thinking and Writing

1. Kingston's writing is similar to Atwood's for her interest in how one's identity is shaped and defined. Write an essay in which you compare and contrast these two writers' approaches to the subject of identity.

2. High school reunions are a conventional topic, but Kingston manages—with her wit and unconventional writing style—to make the essay fresh. Choose one of the following topics and through a fresh approach in tone, perspective, and writing style, develop an original essay on the subject:

   (a.) high school graduation
   (b.) moving away from home
   (c.) first job.

The Wild Man
of the Green Swamp

For eight months in 1975, residents on the edge of Green Swamp, Florida, had been reporting to the police that they had seen a Wild Man. When they stepped toward him, he made strange noises as in a foreign language and ran back into the saw grass. At first, authorities said the Wild Man was a mass hallucination. Man-eating animals lived in the swamp, and a human being could hardly find a place to rest without sinking. Perhaps it was some kind of a bear the children had seen.

In October, a game officer saw a man crouched over a small fire, but as he approached, the figure ran away. It couldn't have been a bear because the Wild Man dragged a burlap bag after him. Also, the fire was obviously man-made.

The fish-and-game wardens and the sheriff's deputies entered the swamp with dogs but did not search for long; no one could live in the swamp. The mosquitoes alone would drive him out.

The Wild Man made forays out of the swamp. Farmers encountered him taking fruit and corn from the turkeys. He broke into a house trailer, but the occupant came back, and the Wild Man escaped out a window. The occupant said that a bad smell came off the Wild Man. Usually, the only evidence of him were his abandoned campsites. At one he left the remains of a four-foot-long alligator, of which he had eaten the feet and tail.

In May a posse made an air and land search; the plane signaled down to the hunters on the ground, who circled the Wild Man. A fish-and-game warden "brought him down with a tackle," according to the news. The Wild Man fought, but they took him to jail. He looked Chinese, so they found a Chinese in town to come translate.

The Wild Man talked a lot to the translator. He told him his name. He said he was thirty-nine years old, the father of seven children, who were in Taiwan. To support them, he had shipped out on a Liberian freighter. He had gotten very homesick and asked everyone if he could leave the ship and go home. But the officers would not let him off. They sent messages to China to find out about him. When the ship landed, they took him to the airport and tried to put him on an airplane to some foreign place. Then, he said, the white demons took him to Tampa Hospital, which is for insane people, but he escaped, just walked out and went into the swamp.

The interpreter asked how he lived in the swamp. He said he ate snakes, turtles, armadillos, and alligators. The captors could tell how he lived when they opened up his bag, which was not burlap but a pair of pants with the legs knotted. Inside, he had carried a pot, a piece of sharpened tin, and a small club, which he had made by sticking a railroad spike into a section of aluminum tubing.

The sheriff found the Liberian freighter that the Wild Man had been on. The ship's officers said that they had not tried to stop him from going home. His shipmates had decided that there was something wrong with his mind. They had bought him a plane ticket and arranged his passport to send him back to China. They had driven him to the airport, but there he began screaming and weeping and would not get on the plane. So they had found him a doctor, who sent him to Tampa Hospital.

Now the doctors at the jail gave him medicine for the mosquito bites, which covered his entire body, and medicine for his stomachache. He was getting better, but after he'd been in jail for three days, the U.S. Border Patrol told him they were sending him back. He became hysterical. That night, he fastened his belt to the bars, wrapped it around his neck, and hung himself.

In the newspaper picture he did not look very wild, being led by the posse out of the swamp. He did not look dirty, either. He wore a checkered shirt unbuttoned at the neck, where his white undershirt showed; his shirt was tucked into his pants; his hair was short. He was surrounded by men in cowboy hats. His fingers stretching open, his wrists pulling apart to the extent of the handcuffs, he lifted his head, his eyes screwed shut, and cried out.

There was a Wild Man in our slough too, only he was a black man. He wore a shirt and no pants, and some mornings when we walked to school, we saw him asleep under the bridge. The police came and took him away. The newspaper said he was crazy; it said the police had been on the lookout for him for a long time, but we had seen him every day.

1980

Purpose and Meaning

1. What expectations does Kingston arouse in the reader with the title of this essay? Would you be more or less interested in the essay if it were titled, "A Chinese Man Confronts American Culture?" How does this writing tactic help to further Kingston's thesis about the Wild Man?

2. In the opening paragraph, Kingston writes, "He made strange noises as in a foreign language . . . and ran back into the saw grass." What does this description suggest about language and culture? If the Wild Man spoke English, would he be considered quite so wild?

3. In paragraph 6, Kingston writes that the Wild Man said, "The white demons took him to Tampa Hospital." Who are the white demons? What does this suggest about cultural perspective and Kingston's relationship to her readers?

Language and Style

1. Why might Kingston choose to capitalize the words "Wild Man" and to use them as a name to refer to the Chinese immigrant? What was your initial response to this term?

2. Time and again, Kingston focuses on extraordinary details: "Man-eating animals lived in the swamp" (paragraph 1); "he left the remains of a four-foot-long alligator" (paragraph 4); "mosquito bites . . . covered his entire body" (paragraph 9). How does this help to make the readers participants in cultural arrogance? What else might it reveal about us and our interests?

3. Kingston seems fond of lists. There are two lists of items in paragraph 7. Sometimes, as in paragraph 10, the sentences are short and read like lists of observations. Since lists contain condensed information, how is this stylistic device representative of Kingston's overall writing style? How is it similar to her use of imagery?

4. Examine Kingston's use of verb tenses. How does she manipulate them to suggest events in time?

Strategy and Structure

1. The first sentence of this essay contains the date, place, and subject. What tone does this journalistic opening create? How does it make us less like readers of an essay and more like participants in an event as it is happening? What pattern do you detect in this narrative sequencing of events?

2. Paragraph 10 contains an image completely contrary to that of the Wild Man depicted earlier. What strategic effect does it have for Kingston to save this information for last?

3. The final paragraph is almost a parable. Analyze it and describe the "moral of the story." Why would Kingston end her essay with such a moral tone?

Thinking and Writing

1. In all three of Kingston's essays, there is a common theme of individuals who are outsiders, as a result of their actions, some physical abnormality, or a relative cultural oddity. Write an essay in which you compare this theme in the three essays.

2. Write an essay describing a way in which you are, or might be considered, out of the ordinary. Use the third-person perspective. In other words, as you describe yourself, pretend that you are someone else and write from his or her point of view.

3. Recall those people with whom you come into frequent contact and consider as "outsiders." Why are they "outsiders"? What "insider" values or behaviors don't they share? Write an essay on the topic.

STEPHEN JAY GOULD

With his wit, clarity, and accessible writing style, Stephen Jay Gould has gained an extraordinary reputation as a popularizer of difficult scientific theories. Over the past twenty-five years of his highly distinguished career as an evolutionary biologist, professor, and writer, he has received dozens of awards and honors—from the American Book Award in science (for *The Panda's Thumb*) to a Distinguished Service Award from the American Geological Institute to a MacArthur Fellowship—as well as more than twenty honorary degrees from colleges and universities.

Gould was born September 10, 1941, in New York City, "not far from Tyranno-saurus," he writes, alluding to the Museum of Natural History and his West Side origins. He received a B.A. degree from Antioch College in 1963, and a doctorate from Columbia University in 1967. He is married with two sons and is currently teaching at Harvard University.

Along with a monthly column called "This View of Life," published in the magazine *Natural History*, Gould has written and collaborated on numerous books and essay collections. *The Panda's Thumb: More Reflections in Natural History* (1980) is perhaps his most widely read work. In this collection of essays, Gould explores his favorite subject: the "miracle" of evolution. What is miraculous about evolution, though, is not the perfect design of a divine creator, but the imperfect evolution of living things as they adjust—or fail to adjust—to their environment. As Gould writes in "Evolution as Fact and Theory," "perfection covers the tracks of history . . . . Evolution lies exposed in the imperfections that record a history of descent." Gould is codeveloper of a theory of evolution called "punctuated equilibrium," which explains these evolutionary "accidents" in a way that Darwinism could not.

Gould has devoted much of his writing to clarifying the arguments that uphold creationism and evolutionary theory, as he does in "Evolution as Fact and Theory." Unlike the stereotypical scientific prose devoid of emotion, Gould's writing often reaches a high emotional pitch, especially when he is writing on the subject of creationism. The misleading claims of creationists infuriate him in his relentless quest for clarity. At the same time, he can reveal his creative, comic, and scientific talents on the subject, as in "A Biological Homage to Mickey Mouse."

What sets Gould apart from much of the scientific community and makes his writings so accessible is in part his insistence that science is culturally embedded. He once said, "Science is not a heartless pursuit of objective information, it is a creative human activity." Time and again—in *Ever Since Darwin* (1977), *Hen's Teeth and Horse's Toes* (1983), *The Flamingo's Smile* (1985) and other books—Gould concerns himself with the abuse and misuse of scientific information. He has written on issues such as sterilization among the mentally ill, and racist and sexist misuse of conclusions falsely drawn from studies of brain size, as in "Women's Brains."

Stephen Jay Gould is a writer whose contributions go beyond the pure pleasure of insightful, humorous, informative reading. He has helped to blur the line between scientist and layperson, science and society. Noted reviewer Ashley Montague puts it nicely: "Stephen Jay Gould is one of the most brilliant of our younger biologists, gifted, among other things, with the ability to write."

Women's Brains

In the prelude to *Middlemarch*, George Eliot lamented the unfulfilled lives   1
of talented women:

> Some have felt that these blundering lives are due to the inconvenient in-
> definiteness with which the Supreme Power has fashioned the natures of women:
> if there were one level of feminine incompetence as strict as the ability to count
> three and no more, the social lot of women might be treated with scientific
> certitude.

Eliot goes on to discount the idea of innate limitation, but while she wrote   2
in 1872, the leaders of European anthropometry were trying to measure "with
scientific certitude" the inferiority of women. Anthropometry, or measurement
of the human body, is not so fashionable a field these days, but it dominated
the human sciences for much of the nineteenth century and remained popular
until intelligence testing replaced skull measurements as a favored device for
making invidious comparisons among races, classes, and sexes. Craniometry,
or measurement of the skull, commanded the most attention and respect. Its
unquestioned leader, Paul Broca (1824–80), professor of clinical surgery at the
Faculty of Medicine in Paris, gathered a school of disciples and imitators around
himself. Their work, so meticulous and apparently irrefutable, exerted great
influence and won high esteem as a jewel of nineteenth-century science.

Broca's work seemed particularly invulnerable to refutation. Had he not   3
measured with the most scrupulous care and accuracy? (Indeed, he had. I have
the greatest respect for Broca's meticulous procedure. His numbers are sound.
But science is an inferential exercise, not a catalog of facts. Numbers, by
themselves, specify nothing. All depends upon what you do with them.) Broca
depicted himself as an apostle of objectivity, a man who bowed before facts
and cast aside superstition and sentimentality. He declared that "there is no faith,
however respectable, no interest, however legitimate, which must not accommodate itself to the progress of human knowledge and bend before truth."
Women, like it or not, had smaller brains than men and, therefore, could not
equal them in intelligence. This fact, Broca argued, may reinforce a common
prejudice in male society, but it is also a scientific truth. L. Manouvrier, a black
sheep in Broca's fold, rejected the inferiority of women and wrote with feeling
about the burden imposed upon them by Broca's numbers:

> Women displayed their talents and their diplomas. They also invoked
> philosophical authorities. But they were opposed by *numbers* unknown to

Condorcet or to John Stuart Mill. These numbers fell upon poor women like a sledge hammer, and they were accompanied by commentaries and sarcasms more ferocious than the most misogynist imprecations of certain church fathers. The theologians had asked if women had a soul. Several centuries later, some scientists were ready to refuse them a human intelligence.

Broca's argument rested upon two sets of data: the larger brains of men   4
in modern societies, and a supposed increase in male superiority through time. His most extensive data came from autopsies performed personally in four Parisian hospitals. For 292 male brains, he calculated an average weight of 1,325 grams; 140 female brains averaged 1,144 grams for a difference of 181 grams, or 14 percent of the male weight. Broca understood, of course, that part of this difference could be attributed to the greater height of males. Yet he made no attempt to measure the effect of size alone and actually stated that it cannot account for the entire difference because we know, a priori, that women are not as intelligent as men (a premise that the data were supposed to test, not rest upon):

> We might ask if the small size of the female brain depends exclusively upon the small size of her body. Tiedemann has proposed this explanation. But we must not forget that women are, on the average, a little less intelligent than men, a difference which we should not exaggerate but which is, nonetheless, real. We are therefore permitted to suppose that the relatively small size of the female brain depends in part upon her physical inferiority and in part upon her intellectual inferiority.

In 1873, the year after Eliot published *Middlemarch,* Broca measured the   5
cranial capacities of prehistoric skulls from L'Homme Mort cave. Here he found a difference of only 99.5 cubic centimeters between males and females, while modern populations range from 129.5 to 220.7. Topinard, Broca's chief disciple, explained the increasing discrepancy through time as a result of differing evolutionary pressures upon dominant men and passive women:

> The man who fights for two or more in the struggle for existence, who has all the responsibility and the cares of tomorrow, who is constantly active in combating the environment and human rivals, needs more brain than the woman whom he must protect and nourish, the sedentary woman, lacking any interior occupations, whose role is to raise children, love, and be passive.

In 1879, Gustave Le Bon, chief misogynist of Broca's school, used these   6
data to publish what must be the most vicious attack upon women in modern scientific literature (no one can top Aristotle). I do not claim his views were representative of Broca's school, but they were published in France's most respected anthropological journal. Le Bon concluded:

> In the most intelligent races, as among the Parisians, there are a large number of women whose brains are closer in size to those of gorillas than to the most

developed male brains. This inferiority is so obvious that no one can contest it for a moment; only its degree is worth discussion. All psychologists who have studied the intelligence of women, as well as poets and novelists, recognize today that they represent the most inferior forms of human evolution and that they are closer to children and savages than to an adult, civilized man. They excel in fickleness, inconstancy, absence of thought and logic, and incapacity to reason. Without doubt there exist some distinguished women, very superior to the average man, but they are as exceptional as the birth of any monstrosity, as, for example, of a gorilla with two heads; consequently, we may neglect them entirely.

Nor did Le Bon shrink from the social implications of his views. He was   7
horrified by the proposal of some American reformers to grant women higher education on the same basis as men:

A desire to give them the same education, and, as a consequence, to propose the same goals for them, is a dangerous chimera. . . . The day when, misunderstanding the inferior occupations which nature has given her, women leave the home and take part in our battles; on this day a social revolution will begin, and everything that maintains the sacred ties of the family will disappear.

Sound familiar?*
I have reexamined Broca's data, the basis for all this derivative pronounce-   8
ment, and I find his numbers sound but his interpretation ill-founded, to say the least. The data supporting his claim for increased difference through time can be easily dismissed. Broca based his contention on the samples from L'Homme Mort alone—only seven male and six female skulls in all. Never have so little data yielded such far ranging conclusions.

In 1888, Topinard published Broca's more extensive data on the Parisian   9
hospitals. Since Broca recorded height and age as well as brain size, we may use modern statistics to remove their effect. Brain weight decreases with age, and Broca's women were, on average, considerably older than his men. Brain weight increases with height, and his average man was almost half a foot taller than his average woman. I used multiple regression, a technique that allowed me to assess simultaneously the influence of height and age upon brain size. In an analysis of the data for women, I found that, at average male height and age, a woman's brain would weigh 1,212 grams. Correction for height and age reduces Broca's measured difference of 181 grams by more than a third, to 113 grams.

I don't know what to make of this remaining difference because I cannot   10
assess other factors known to influence brain size in a major way. Cause of

*When I wrote this essay, I assumed that Le Bon was a marginal, if colorful, figure. I have since learned that he was a leading scientist, one of the founders of social psychology, and best known for a seminal study on crowd behavior, still cited today (La psychologie des foules, 1895), and for his work on unconscious motivation.

death has an important effect: degenerative disease often entails a substantial diminution of brain size. (This effect is separate from the decrease attributed to age alone.) Eugene Schreider, also working with Broca's data, found that men killed in accidents had brains weighing, on average, 60 grams more than men dying of infectious diseases. The best modern data I can find (from American hospitals) records a full 100-gram difference between death by degenerative arteriosclerosis and by violence or accident. Since so many of Broca's subjects were very elderly women, we may assume that lengthy degenerative disease was more common among them than among the men.

More importantly, modern students of brain size still have not agreed on   11
a proper measure for eliminating the powerful effect of body size. Height is partly adequate, but men and women of the same height do not share the same body build. Weight is even worse than height, because most of its variation reflects nutrition rather than intrinsic size—fat versus skinny exerts little influence upon the brain. Manouvrier took up this subject in the 1880s and argued that muscular mass and force should be used. He tried to measure this elusive property in various ways and found a marked difference in favor of men, even in men and women of the same height. When he corrected for what he called "sexual mass," women actually came out slightly ahead in brain size.

Thus, the corrected 113-gram difference is surely too large; the true figure   12
is probably close to zero and may as well favor women as men. And 113 grams, by the way, is exactly the average difference between a 5 foot 4 inch and a 6 foot 4 inch male in Broca's data. We would not (especially us short folks) want to ascribe greater intelligence to tall men. In short, who knows what to do with Broca's data? They certainly don't permit any confident claim that men have bigger brains than women.

To appreciate the social role of Broca and his school, we must recognize   13
that his statements about the brains of women do not reflect an isolated prejudice toward a single disadvantaged group. They must be weighed in the context of a general theory that supported contemporary social distinctions as biologically ordained. Women, blacks, and poor people suffered the same disparagement, but women bore the brunt of Broca's argument because he had easier access to data on women's brains. Women were singularly denigrated but they also stood as surrogates for other disenfranchised groups. As one of Broca's disciples wrote in 1881: "Men of the black races have a brain scarcely heavier than that of white women." This juxtaposition extended into many other realms of anthropological argument, particularly to claims that, anatomically and emotionally, both women and blacks were like white children—and that white children, by the theory of recapitulation, represented an ancestral (primitive) adult stage of human evolution. I do not regard as empty rhetoric the claim that women's battles are for all of us.

Maria Montessori did not confine her activities to educational reform for   14
young children. She lectured on anthropology for several years at the University of Rome, and wrote an influential book entitled *Pedagogical Anthropology*

(English edition, 1913). Montessori was no egalitarian. She supported most of Broca's work and the theory of innate criminality proposed by her compatriot Cesare Lombroso. She measured the circumference of children's heads in her schools and inferred that the best prospects had bigger brains. But she had no use for Broca's conclusions about women. She discussed Manouvrier's work at length and made much of his tentative claim that women, after proper correction of the data, had slightly larger brains than men. Women, she concluded, were intellectually superior, but men had prevailed heretofore by dint of physical force. Since technology has abolished force as an instrument of power, the era of women may soon be upon us: "In such an epoch there will really be superior human beings, there will really be men strong in morality and in sentiment. Perhaps in this way the reign of women is approaching, when the enigma of her anthropological superiority will be deciphered. Woman was always the custodian of human sentiment, morality and honor."

This represents one possible antidote to "scientific" claims for the constitutional inferiority of certain groups. One may affirm the validity of biological distinctions but argue that the data have been misinterpreted by prejudiced men with a stake in the outcome, and that disadvantaged groups are truly superior. In recent years, Elaine Morgan has followed this strategy in her *Descent of Woman*, a speculative reconstruction of human prehistory from the woman's point of view—and as farcical as more famous tall tales by and for men. 15

I prefer another strategy. Montessori and Morgan followed Broca's philosophy to reach a more congenial conclusion. I would rather label the whole enterprise of setting a biological value upon groups for what it is: irrelevant and highly injurious. George Eliot well appreciated the special tragedy that biological labeling imposed upon members of disadvantaged groups. She expressed it for people like herself—women of extraordinary talent. I would apply it more widely—not only to those whose dreams are flouted but also to those who never realize that they may dream—but I cannot match her prose. In conclusion, then, the rest of Eliot's prelude to *Middlemarch:* 16

> The limits of variation are really much wider than anyone would imagine from the sameness of women's coiffure and the favorite love stories in prose and verse. Here and there a cygnet is reared uneasily among the ducklings in the brown pond, and never finds the living stream in fellowship with its own oary-footed kind. Here and there is born a Saint Theresa, foundress of nothing, whose loving heartbeats and sobs after an unattained goodness tremble off and are dispersed among hindrances instead of centering in some long-recognizable deed.

1980

Purpose and Meaning

1. Stephen Jay Gould, a well-respected scientist and writer, establishes his thesis that brain size is irrelevant to intelligence in part by discrediting the opposition.

What does he mean when he argues (paragraph 4) that Paul Broca's premise "women are not as intelligent as men" is "a premise the data were supposed to test, not rest upon?"

2. Gould writes (paragraph 13) that Broca was not singling women out when he argued that they have biologically inferior brains. Does Gould mean that Broca was not motivated by any prejudice against women? What exactly is Gould's purpose here? What is his tone or attitude toward his subject?

3. Discuss how the following statement by Le Bon is similar to arguments put forward today by some conservatives: "The day when . . . women leave the home and take part in our [men's] battles . . . everything that maintains the sacred ties of the family will disappear" (paragraph 7). What counterargument can you make to Le Bon's claim?

Language and Style

1. How does Gould's frequent use of scientific terminology create the tone of his essay? Is such language appropriate to the topic?

2. At times, Gould uses scientific language sarcastically, turning it back on itself: "I have the greatest respect for Broca's meticulous procedure . . . [but] numbers, by themselves, specify nothing" (paragraph 3); "we know, a priori, that women are not as intelligent as men" (paragraph 4); "Gustave Le Bon, chief misogynist . . . ." (paragraph 6). How does this playfulness influence the reader's response and the strength of Gould's argument?

3. Gould does not write in jargon, nor does he simplify his arguments or condescend to his readers. Does this make his essay more or less readable? How? What aspects of style make the essay accessible to readers?

Strategy and Structure

1. Gould's essay is entirely an argument. Outline the steps in his argument. What principle governs his structure?

2. Gould has a point of view that he wants his readers to sympathize and perhaps agree with. Since his topic is women's brains, as the title indicates, of what strategic importance is opening and closing the essay with a quote from a woman, the writer George Eliot?

3. Gould roots his argument in history. How does he present chronology and narrative to strengthen his major and minor propositions?

4. What techniques of refutation does Gould employ? How effective are they?

5. What is the effect of the extended quotations in this essay? How does Gould make them an organic part of the essay's structure?

Thinking and Writing

1. Write an essay in which you elaborate on Gould's statement that "women's battles are for all of us" (paragraph 13).

2. Reread and analyze George Eliot's prelude to *Middlemarch*, quoted in two parts at the beginning and end of Gould's essay. Relate Eliot's lament to Gould's argument.

3. In the essay, Gould alludes to the " 'scientific' claims for the constitutional inferiority of certain groups." Think of instances when false or misapplied science has led to controversy and crisis in recent history. Write an essay on the topic.

o⚫━o⚫━o⚫━o⚫━o⚫━o⚫━o⚫━o⚫━o⚫━o⚫━o⚫━o⚫o

A Biological Homage
to Mickey Mouse

Age often turns fire to placidity. Lytton Strachey, in his incisive portrait   1
of Florence Nightingale, writes of her declining years:

> Destiny, having waited very patiently, played a queer trick on Miss Nightingale.
> The benevolence and public spirit of that long life had only been equalled by
> its acerbity. Her virtue had dwelt in hardness.... And now the sarcastic years
> brought the proud woman her punishment. She was not to die as she had lived.
> The sting was to be taken out of her; she was to be made soft; she was to be
> reduced to compliance and complacency.

I was therefore not surprised—although the analogy may strike some   2
people as sacrilegious—to discover that the creature who gave his name as a
synonym for insipidity had a gutsier youth. Mickey Mouse turned a respectable fifty last year. To mark the occasion, many theaters replayed his debut
performance in *Steamboat Willie* (1928). The original Mickey was a rambunctious, even slightly sadistic fellow. In a remarkable sequence, exploiting the exciting new development of sound, Mickey and Minnie pummel, squeeze, and
twist the animals on board to produce a rousing chorus of "Turkey in the Straw."
They honk a duck with a tight embrace, crank a goat's tail, tweak a pig's nipples,
bang a cow's teeth as a stand-in xylophone, and play bagpipe on her udder.
Christopher Finch, in his semiofficial pictorial history of Disney's work,   3
comments: "The Mickey Mouse who hit the movie houses in the late twenties

Stage 1   Stage 2   Stage 3

Mickey's evolution during 50 years (left to right). As Mickey became increasingly well behaved over the years, his appearance became more youthful. Measurements of three stages in his development revealed a larger relative head size, larger eyes, and an enlarged cranium—all traits of juvenility.

was not quite the well-behaved character most of us are familiar with today. He was mischievous, to say the least, and even displayed a streak of cruelty." But Mickey soon cleaned up his act, leaving to gossip and speculation only his unresolved relationship with Minnie and the status of Morty and Ferdie. Finch continues: "Mickey...had become virtually a national symbol, and as such he was expected to behave properly at all times. If he occasionally stepped out of line, any number of letters would arrive at the Studio from citizens and organizations who felt that the nation's moral well-being was in their hands....Eventually he would be pressured into the role of straight man."

As Mickey's personality softened, his appearance changed. Many Disney fans are aware of this transformation through time, but few (I suspect) have recognized the coordinating theme behind all the alterations—in fact, I am not sure that the Disney artists themselves explicitly realized what they were doing, since the changes appeared in such a halting and piecemeal fashion. In short, the blander and inoffensive Mickey became progressively more juvenile in appearance. (Since Mickey's chronological age never altered—like most cartoon characters he stands impervious to the ravages of time—this change in appearance at a constant age is a true evolutionary transformation. Progressive juvenilization as an evolutionary phenomenon is called neoteny. More on this later.)

The characteristic changes of form during human growth have inspired a substantial biological literature. Since the head-end of an embryo differentiates first and grows more rapidly in utero than the foot-end (an antero-posterior gradient, in technical language), a newborn child possesses a relatively large head attached to a medium-sized body with diminutive legs and feet. This gradient is reversed through growth as legs and feet overtake the front end. Heads continue to grow but so much more slowly than the rest of the body that relative head size decreases.

In addition, a suite of changes pervades the head itself during human 6 growth. The brain grows very slowly after age three, and the bulbous cranium of a young child gives way to the more slanted, lower-browed configuration of adulthood. The eyes scarcely grow at all and relative eye size declines precipitously. But the jaw gets bigger and bigger. Children, compared with adults, have larger heads and eyes, smaller jaws, a more prominent, bulging cranium, and smaller, pudgier legs and feet. Adult heads are altogether more apish, I'm sorry to say.

Mickey, however, has traveled this ontogenetic pathway in reverse dur- 7 ing his fifty years among us. He has assumed an ever more childlike appearance as the ratty character of *Steamboat Willie* became the cute and inoffensive host to a magic kingdom. By 1940, the former tweaker of pig's nipples gets a kick in the ass for insubordination (as the *Sorcerer's Apprentice* in *Fantasia*). By 1953, his last cartoon, he has gone fishing and cannot even subdue a squirming clam.

The Disney artists transformed Mickey in clever silence, often using sug- 8 gestive devices that mimic nature's own changes by different routes. To give him the shorter and pudgier legs of youth, they lowered his pants line and covered his spindly legs with a baggy outfit. (His arms and legs also thickened substantially—and acquired joints for a floppier appearance.) His head grew relatively larger and its features more youthful. The length of Mickey's snout has not altered, but decreasing protrusion is more subtly suggested by a pronounced thickening. Mickey's eye has grown in two modes: first, by a major, discontinuous evolutionary shift as the entire eye of ancestral Mickey became the pupil of his descendants, and second, by gradual increase thereafter.

Mickey's improvement in cranial bulging followed an interesting path since 9 his evolution has always been constrained by the unaltered convention of representing his head as a circle with appended ears and an oblong snout. The circle's form could not be altered to provide a bulging cranium directly. Instead, Mickey's ears moved back, increasing the distance between nose and ears, and giving him a rounded, rather than a sloping, forehead.

To give these observations the cachet of quantitative science, I applied 10 my best pair of dial calipers to three stages of the official phylogeny—the thin-nosed, ears-forward figure of the early 1930s (stage 1), the later-day Jack of Mickey and the Beanstalk (1947, stage 2), and the modern mouse (stage 3). I measured three signs of Mickey's creeping juvenility: increasing eye size (maximum height) as a percentage of head length (base of the nose to top of rear ear); increasing head length as a percentage of body length; and increasing cranial vault size measured by rearward displacement of the front ear (base of the nose to top of front ear as a percentage of base of the nose to top of rear ear).

All three percentages increased steadily—eye size from 27 to 42 percent 11 of head length; head length from 42.7 to 48.1 percent of body length; and nose to front ear from 71.7 to a whopping 95.6 percent of nose to rear ear. For comparison, I measured Mickey's young "nephew" Morty Mouse. In each case,

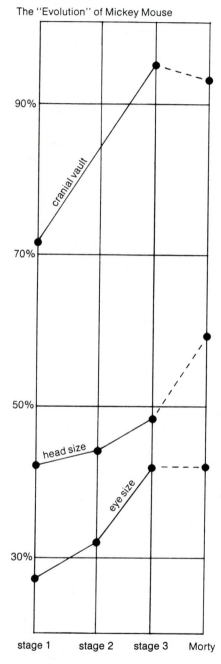

The "Evolution" of Mickey Mouse

At an early stage in his evolution, Mickey had a smaller head, cranial vault, and eyes. He evolved toward the characteristics of his young nephew Morty.

Mickey has clearly been evolving toward youthful stages of his stock, although he still has a way to go for head length.

You may, indeed, now ask what an at least marginally respectable scientist has been doing with a mouse like that. In part, fiddling around and having fun, of course. (I still prefer *Pinocchio* to *Citizen Kane*.) But I do have a serious point—two, in fact—to make. We must first ask why Disney chose to change his most famous character so gradually and persistently in the same direction? National symbols are not altered capriciously and market researchers (for the doll industry in particular) have spent a good deal of time and practical effort learning what features appeal to people as cute and friendly. Biologists also have spent a great deal of time studying a similar subject in a wide range of animals.

In one of his most famous articles, Konrad Lorenz argues that humans use the characteristic differences in form between babies and adults as important behavioral cues. He believes that features of juvenility trigger "innate releasing mechanisms" for affection and nurturing in adult humans. When we see a living creature with babyish features, we feel an automatic surge of disarming tenderness. The adaptive value of this response can scarcely be questioned, for we must nurture our babies. Lorenz, by the way, lists among his releasers the very features of babyhood that Disney affixed progressively to Mickey: "a relatively large head, predominance of the brain capsule, large and low-lying eyes, bulging cheek region, short and thick extremities, a springy elastic consistency, and clumsy movements." (I propose to leave aside for this article the contentious issue of whether or not our affectionate response to babyish features is truly innate and inherited directly from ancestral primates—as Lorenz argues—or whether it is simply learned from our immediate experience with babies and grafted upon an evolutionary predisposition for attaching ties of affection to certain learned signals. My argument works equally well in either case for I only claim that babyish fearures tend to elicit strong feelings of affection in adult humans, whether the biological basis be direct programming or the capacity to learn and fix upon signals. I also treat as collateral to my point the major thesis of Lorenz's article—that we respond not to the totality or *Gestalt*, but to a set of specific features acting as releasers. This argument is important to Lorenz because he wants to argue for evolutionary identity in modes of behavior between other vertebrates and humans, and we know that many birds, for example, often respond to abstract features rather than *Gestalten*. Lorenz's article, published in 1950, bears the title *Ganzheit und Teil in der tierischen und menschlichen Gemeinschaft*—"Entirety and part in animal and human society." Disney's piecemeal change of Mickey's appearance does make sense in this context—he operated in sequential fashion upon Lorenz's primary releasers.)

Lorenz emphasizes the power that juvenile features hold over us, and the abstract quality of their influence, by pointing out that we judge other animals by the same criteria—although the judgment may be utterly inappropriate in an evolutionary context. We are, in short, fooled by an evolved response to our own babies, and we transfer our reaction to the same set of features in other animals.

Many animals, for reasons having nothing to do with the inspiration of   15
affection in humans, possess some features also shared by human babies but
not by human adults—large eyes and a bulging forehead with retreating chin,
in particular. We are drawn to them, we cultivate them as pets, we stop and
admire them in the wild—while we reject their small-eyed, long-snouted relatives
who might make more affectionate companions or objects of admiration. Lorenz
points out that the German names of many animals with features mimicking
human babies end in the diminutive suffix *chen*, even though the animals are
often larger than close relatives without such features—*Rotkehlchen* (robin),
Eichhörnchen (squirrel), and *Kaninchen* (rabbit), for example.

In a fascinating section, Lorenz then enlarges upon our capacity for   16
biologically inappropriate response to other animals, or even to inanimate objects that mimic human features. "The most amazing objects can acquire
remarkable, highly specific emotional values by 'experiential attachment' of
human properties. . . . Steeply rising, somewhat overhanging cliff faces or dark
storm-clouds piling up have the same, immediate display value as a human being who is standing at full height and leaning slightly forwards"—that is,
threatening.

We cannot help regarding a camel as aloof and unfriendly because it   17
mimics, quite unwittingly and for other reasons, the "gesture of haughty rejection" common to so many human cultures. In this gesture, we raise our heads,
placing our nose above our eyes. We then half-close our eyes and blow out
through our nose—the "harumph" of the stereotyped upperclass Englishman
or his well-trained servant. "All this," Lorenz argues quite cogently, "symbolizes
resistance against all sensory modalities emanating from the disdained counterpart." But the poor camel cannot help carrying its nose above its elongate eyes,

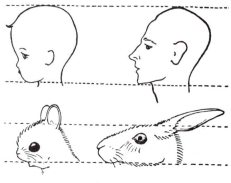

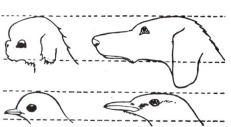

Humans feel affection for animals
with juvenile features: large eyes,
bulging craniums, retreating chins
(left column). Small-eyed, long-
snouted animals (right column) do
not elicit the same response. From
*Studies in Animal and Human
Behavior*, vol. II, by Konrad Lorenz,
1971. Methuen & Co. Ltd.

with mouth drawn down. As Lorenz reminds us, if you wish to know whether a camel will eat out of your hand or spit, look at its ears, not the rest of its face.

In his important book *Expression of the Emotions in Man and Animals*, [18] published in 1872, Charles Darwin traced the evolutionary basis of many common gestures to originally adaptive actions in animals later internalized as symbols in humans. Thus, he argued for evolutionary continuity of emotion, not only of form. We snarl and raise our upper lip in fierce anger—to expose our nonexistent fighting canine tooth. Our gesture of disgust repeats the facial actions associated with the highly adaptive act of vomiting in necessary circumstances. Darwin concluded, much to the distress of many Victorian contemporaries: "With mankind some expressions, such as the bristling of the hair under the influence of extreme terror, or the uncovering of the teeth under that of furious rage, can hardly be understood, except on the belief that man once existed in a much lower and animal-like condition."

In any case, the abstract features of human childhood elicit powerful emo- [19] tional responses in us, even when they occur in other animals. I submit that Mickey Mouse's evolutionary road down the course of his own growth in reverse reflects the unconscious discovery of this biological principle by Disney and his artists. In fact, the emotional status of most Disney characters rests on the same set of distinctions. To this extent, the magic kingdom trades on a biological illusion—our ability to abstract and our propensity to transfer inappropriately to other animals the fitting responses we make to changing form in the growth of our own bodies.

Donald Duck also adopts more juvenile features through time. His [20] elongated beak recedes and his eyes enlarge; he converges on Huey, Louie, and Dewey as surely as Mickey approaches Morty. But Donald, having inherited the mantle of Mickey's original misbehavior, remains more adult in form with his projecting beak and more sloping forehead.

Mouse villains or sharpies, contrasted with Mickey, are always more adult [21] in appearance, although they often share Mickey's chronological age. In 1936, for example, Disney made a short entitled *Mickey's Rival*. Mortimer, a dandy in a yellow sports car, intrudes upon Mickey and Minnie's quiet country picnic. The thoroughly disreputable Mortimer has a head only 29 percent of body length, to Mickey's 45, and a snout 80 percent of head length, compared with Mickey's 49. (Nonetheless, and was it ever different, Minnie transfers her affection until an obliging bull from a neighboring field dispatches Mickey's rival.) Consider also the exaggerated adult features of other Disney characters—the swaggering bully Peg-leg Pete or the simple, if lovable, dolt Goofy.

As a second, serious biological comment on Mickey's odyssey in form, [22] I note that his path to eternal youth repeats, in epitome, our own evolutionary story. For humans are neotenic. We have evolved by retaining to adulthood the originally juvenile features of our ancestors. Our australopithecine forebears, like Mickey in *Steamboat Willie*, had projecting jaws and low vaulted craniums.

Our embryonic skulls scarcely differ from those of chimpanzees. And we [23] follow the same path of changing form through growth: relative decrease of

Dandified, disreputable Mortimer (here stealing Minnie's affections) has strikingly more adult features than Mickey. His head is smaller in proportion to body length; his nose is a full 80 percent of head length.

the cranial vault since brains grow so much more slowly than bodies after birth, and continuous relative increase of the jaw. But while chimps accentuate these changes, producing an adult strikingly different in form from a baby, we proceed much more slowly down the same path and never get nearly so far. Thus, as adults, we retain juvenile features. To be sure, we change enough to produce a notable difference between baby and adult, but our alteration is far smaller than that experienced by chimps and other primates.

A marked slowdown of developmental rates has triggered our neoteny.   24
Primates are slow developers among mammals, but we have accentuated the trend to a degree matched by no other mammal. We have very long periods of gestation, markedly extended childhoods, and the longest life span of any mammal. The morphological features of eternal youth have served us well. Our enlarged brain is, at least in part, a result of extending rapid prenatal growth rates to later ages. (In all mammals, the brain grows rapidly in utero but often very little after birth. We have extended this fetal phase into postnatal life.)

But the changes in timing themselves have been just as important. We   25
are preeminently learning animals, and our extended childhood permits the transference of culture by education. Many animals display flexibility and play in childhood but follow rigidly programmed patterns as adults. Lorenz writes, in the same article cited above: "The characteristic which is so vital for the human peculiarity of the true man—that of always remaining in a state of development—is quite certainly a gift which we owe to the neotenous nature of mankind."

In short, we, like Mickey, never grow up although we, alas, do grow old.   26
Best wishes to you, Mickey, for your next half-century. May we stay as young as you, but grow a bit wiser.

1980

Cartoon villains are not the only Disney characters with exaggerated adult features. Goofy, like Mortimer, has a small head relative to body length and a prominent snout.

©Walt Disney Productions

Purpose and Meaning

1. Explain the opening sentence of Gould's essay: "Age often turns fire to placidity."

2. Gould observes that he wrote this essay in part to have fun (paragraph 12). Is Gould strictly "having fun"? Is this his only purpose? What, for example, are some of the social implications of his thesis that Mickey Mouse became gradually more youthful because that's what Americans wanted him to be? Why would they want him that way?

3. Gould begins philosophically and ends with an affectionate tribute to his subject, Mickey Mouse. In what way does this "humanize" the writer and endear him to his readers?

Language and Style

1. Gould's opening line is philosophical, as is the quote from Lytton Strachey, in which he uses abstract language such as "age," "destiny," and "spirit." In the very next paragraph, however, we find these lines: "They honk a duck with a tight embrace, crank a goat's tail, tweak a pig's nipples, bang a cow's teeth . . . ." How does this contrast in language set the tone and theme of the essay?

2. Gould, being a scientist, also introduces a bit of scientific terminology, such as "evolutionary transformation" (paragraph 4); "neoteny" (paragraph 4); and "antero-posterior gradient" (paragrah 5). Define these terms. Does Gould abuse his use of such jargon, or does he speak in those terms only when necessary? How does this increase his authority with readers?

3. In paragraph 13, Gould takes a long detour to carefully consider a possible point of contention. How is this characteristic of a scientist, as well as of a strong argument?

Strategy and Structure

1. The title of this essay contains an interesting conflict of tone: We don't ordinarily expect to find "biological" and "Mickey Mouse" in the same sentence, since Mickey Mouse is a fictional character and not a real character. How does this combination foreshadow Gould's thesis and his presentation of it?

2. As he does in "Women's Brains," Gould opens with a quote from someone he admires. He also quotes other authorities (Christopher Finch, paragraph 3; and Konrad Lorenz, paragraph 13). In what way does this allow readers to trust Gould's assertions, as well as to relate to him on a more personal level?

3. Gould speaks of Mickey's "transformation through time" (paragraph 4). What rhetorical strategy does this prompt Gould to apply? How does he develop this strategy?

4. Where does Gould employ classification? What is the effect?

5. Gould includes two charts in his essay: one to map Mickey's "evolution," and one to detail the profiles to which most Americans respond affectionately. Is this rather scientific method appropriate for an essay about Mickey Mouse? Why or why not?

Thinking and Writing

1. Gould asserts that juvenile features—big eyes, small nose and chin—arouse an affectionate response in most Americans. Write an analytical essay in which you discuss how standards for beauty in women may also be shown to be juvenile.

2. Choose a popular cartoon character and, in an essay, discuss what social needs that character fulfills.

3. Research how cartoon characters have changed over the past decade or two, focusing on three or four of the most popular, and write an extended essay on what social factors have influenced the changes.

Evolution as Fact
and Theory

Kirtley Mather, who died last year at age ninety, was a pillar of both science 1
and Christian religion in America and one of my dearest friends. The difference
of a half-century in our ages evaporated before our common interests. The most
curious thing we shared was a battle we each fought at the same age. For Kirtley
had gone to Tennessee with Clarence Darrow to testify for evolution at the
Scopes trial of 1925. When I think that we are enmeshed again in the same
struggle for one of the best documented, most compelling and exciting concepts
in all of science, I don't know whether to laugh or cry.

According to idealized principles of scientific discourse, the arousal of dor- 2
mant issues should reflect fresh data that give renewed life to abandoned notions. Those outside the current debate may therefore be excused for suspecting that creationists have come up with something new, or that evolutionists
have generated some serious internal trouble. But nothing has changed; the creationists have presented not a single new fact or argument. Darrow and Bryan
were at least more entertaining than we lesser antagonists today. The rise of
creationism is politics, pure and simple; it represents one issue (and by no means
the major concern) of the resurgent evangelical right. Arguments that seemed
kooky just a decade ago have reentered the mainstream.

The basic attack of modern creationists falls apart on two general counts 3
before we even reach the supposed factual details of their assault against evolution. First, they play upon a vernacular misunderstanding of the word "theory"
to convey the false impression that we evolutionists are covering up the rotten
core of our edifice. Second, they misuse a popular philosophy of science to argue
that they are behaving scientifically in attacking evolution. Yet the same
philosophy demonstrates that their own belief is not science, and that "scientific creationism" is a meaningless and self-contradictory phrase, an example
of what Orwell called "newspeak."

In the American vernacular, "theory" often means "imperfect fact"—part 4
of a hierarchy of confidence running downhill from fact to theory to hypothesis
to guess. Thus, creationists can (and do) argue: evolution is "only" a theory,
and intense debate now rages about many aspects of the theory. If evolution
is less than a fact, and scientists can't even make up their minds about the theory,
then what confidence can we have in it? Indeed, President Reagan echoed this
argument before an evangelical group in Dallas when he said (in what I devoutly

hope was campaign rhetoric): "Well, it is a theory. It is a scientific theory only, and it has in recent years been challenged in the world of science—that is, not believed in the scientific community to be as infallible as it once was."

Well, evolution *is* a theory. It is also a fact. And facts and theories are different things, not rungs in a hierarchy of increasing certainty. Facts are the world's data. Theories are structures of ideas that explain and interpret facts. Facts do not go away while scientists debate rival theories for explaining them. Einstein's theory of gravitation replaced Newton's, but apples did not suspend themselves in mid-air pending the outcome. And human beings evolved from apelike ancestors whether they did so by Darwin's proposed mechanism or by some other, yet to be discovered.

Moreover, "fact" does not mean "absolute certainty." The final proofs of logic and mathematics flow deductively from stated premises and achieve certainty only because they are *not* about the empirical world. Evolutionists make no claim for perpetual truth, though creationists often do (and then attack us for a style of argument that they themselves favor). In science, "fact" can only mean "confirmed to such a degree that it would be perverse to withhold provisional assent." I suppose that apples might start to rise tomorrow, but the possibility does not merit equal time in physics classrooms.

Evolutionists have been clear about this distinction between fact and theory from the very beginning, if only because we have always acknowledged how far we are from completely understanding the mechanisms (theory) by which evolution (fact) occurred. Darwin continually emphasized the difference between his two great and separate accomplishments: establishing the fact of evolution, and proposing a theory—natural selection—to explain the mechanism of evolution. He wrote in *The Descent of Man:* "I had two distinct objects in view; firstly, to show that species had not been separately created, and secondly, that natural selection had been the chief agent of change . . . Hence if I have erred in . . . having exaggerated its [natural selection's] power . . . I have at least, as I hope, done good service in aiding to overthrow the dogma of separate creations."

Thus Darwin acknowledged the provisional nature of natural selection while affirming the fact of evolution. The fruitful theoretical debate that Darwin initiated has never ceased. From the 1940s through the 1960s, Darwin's own theory of natural selection did achieve a temporary hegemony that it never enjoyed in his lifetime. But renewed debate characterizes our decade, and, while no biologist questions the importance of natural selection, many now doubt its ubiquity. In particular, many evolutionists argue that substantial amounts of genetic change may not be subject to natural selection and may spread through populations at random. Others are challenging Darwin's linking of natural selection with gradual, imperceptible change through all intermediary degrees; they are arguing that most evolutionary events may occur far more rapidly than Darwin envisioned.

Scientists regard debates on fundamental issues of theory as a sign of intellectual health and a source of excitement. Science is—and how else can I say it?—most fun when it plays with interesting ideas, examines their implications, and recognizes that old information may be explained in surprisingly new ways. Evolutionary theory is now enjoying this uncommon vigor. Yet amidst all this turmoil no biologist has been led to doubt the fact that evolution occurred; we are debating *how* it happened. We are all trying to explain the same thing: the tree of evolutionary descent linking all organisms by ties of genealogy. Creationists pervert and caricature this debate by conveniently neglecting the common conviction that underlies it, and by falsely suggesting that we now doubt the very phenomenon we are struggling to understand.

Secondly, creationists claim that "the dogma of separate creations," as   10
Darwin characterized it a century ago, is a scientific theory meriting equal time with evolution in high school biology curricula. But a popular viewpoint among philosophers of science belies this creationist argument. Philosopher Karl Popper has argued for decades that the primary criterion of science is the falsifiability of its theories. We can never prove absolutely, but we can falsify. A set of ideas that cannot, in principle, be falsified is not science.

The entire creationist program includes little more than a rhetorical attempt   11
to falsify evolution by presenting supposed contradictions among its supporters. Their brand of creationism, they claim, is "scientific" because it follows the Popperian model in trying to demolish evolution. Yet Popper's argument must apply in both directions. One does not become a scientist by the simple act of trying to falsify a rival and truly scientific system; one has to present an alternative system that also meets Popper's criterion—it too must be falsifiable in principle.

"Scientific creationism" is a self-contradictory, nonsense phrase precisely   12
because it cannot be falsified. I can envision observations and experiments that would disprove any evolutionary theory I know, but I cannot imagine what potential data could lead creationists to abandon their beliefs. Unbeatable systems are dogma, not science. Lest I seem harsh or rhetorical, I quote creationism's leading intellectual, Duane Gish, Ph.D., from his recent (1978) book, *Evolution? The Fossils Say No!* "By creation we mean the bringing into being by a supernatural Creator of the basic kinds of plants and animals by the process of sudden, or fiat, creation. We do not know how the Creator created, what processes He used, *for He used processes which are not now operating anywhere in the natural universe* [Gish's italics]. This is why we refer to creation as special creation. We cannot discover by scientific investigations anything about the creative processes used by the Creator." Pray tell, Dr. Gish, in the light of your last sentence, what then is "scientific" creationism?

Our confidence that evolution occurred centers upon three general   13
arguments. First, we have abundant, direct, observational evidence of evolution in action, from both field and laboratory. This evidence ranges from countless experiments on change in nearly everything about fruit flies subjected to artificial selection in the laboratory to the famous populations of British moths that became black when industrial soot darkened the trees upon which the moths

rest. (Moths gain protection from sharp-sighted bird predators by blending into the background.) Creationists do not deny these observations; how could they? Creationists have tightened their act. They now argue that God only created "basic kinds," and allowed for limited evolutionary meandering within them. Thus toy poodles and Great Danes come from the dog kind and moths can change color, but nature cannot convert a dog to a cat or a monkey to a man.

The second and third arguments for evolution—the case for major   14
changes—do not involve direct observation of evolution in action. They rest upon inference, but are no less secure for that reason. Major evolutionary change requires too much time for direct observation on the scale of recorded human history. All historical sciences rest upon inference, and evolution is no different from geology, cosmology, or human history in this respect. In principle, we cannot observe processes that operated in the past. We must infer them from results that still surround us: living and fossil organisms for evolution, documents and artifacts for human history, strata and topography for geology.

The second argument—that the imperfection of nature reveals   15
evolution—strikes many people as ironic, for they feel that evolution should be most elegantly displayed in the nearly perfect adaptation expressed by some organisms—the camber of a gull's wing, or butterflies that cannot be seen in ground litter because they mimic leaves so precisely. But perfection could be imposed by a wise creator or evolved by natural selection. Perfection covers the tracks of past history. And past history—the evidence of descent—is the mark of evolution.

Evolution lies exposed in the *imperfections* that record a history of descent.   16
Why should a rat run, a bat fly, a porpoise swim, and I type this essay with structures built of the same bones unless we all inherited them from a common ancestor? An engineer, starting from scratch, could design better limbs in each case. Why should all the large native mammals of Australia be marsupials, unless they descended from a common ancestor isolated on this island continent? Marsupials are not "better," or ideally suited for Australia; many have been wiped out by placental mammals imported by man from other continents. This principle of imperfection extends to all historical sciences. When we recognize the etymology of September, October, November, and December (seventh, eighth, ninth, and tenth), we know that the year once started in March, or that two additional months must have been added to an original calendar of ten months.

The third argument is more direct: transitions are often found in the fossil   17
record. Preserved transitions are not common—and should not be, according to our understanding of evolution (see next section)—but they are not entirely wanting, as creationists often claim. The lower jaw of reptiles contains several bones, that of mammals only one. The non-mammalian jawbones are reduced, step by step, in mammalian ancestors until they become tiny nubbins located at the back of the jaw. The "hammer" and "anvil" bones of the mammalian ear are descendants of these nubbins. How could such a transition be accomplished? the creationists ask. Surely a bone is either entirely in the jaw or in

the ear. Yet paleontologists have discovered two transitional lineages of therapsids (the so-called mammal-like reptiles) with a double jaw joint—one composed of the old quadrate and articular bones (soon to become the hammer and anvil), the other of the squamosal and dentary bones (as in modern mammals). For that matter, what better transitional form could we expect to find than the oldest human, *Australopithecus afarensis*, with its apelike palate, its human upright stance, and a cranial capacity larger than any ape's of the same body size but a full 1,000 cubic centimeters below ours? If God made each of the half-dozen human species discovered in ancient rocks, why did he create in an unbroken temporal sequence of progressively more modern features— increasing cranial capacity, reduced face and teeth, larger body size? Did he create to mimic evolution and test our faith thereby?

Faced with these facts of evolution and the philosophical bankruptcy of their own position, creationists rely upon distortion and innuendo to buttress their rhetorical claim. If I sound sharp or bitter, indeed I am—for I have become a major target of these practices. [18]

I count myself among the evolutionists who argue for a jerky, or episodic, rather than a smoothly gradual, pace of change. In 1972 my colleague Niles Eldredge and I developed the theory of punctuated equilibrium. We argued that two outstanding facts of the fossil record—geologically "sudden" origin of new species and failure to change thereafter (stasis)—reflect the predictions of evolutionary theory, not the imperfections of the fossil record. In most theories, small isolated populations are the source of new species, and the process of speciation takes thousands or tens of thousands of years. This amount of time, so long when measured against our lives, is a geological microsecond. It represents much less than 1 per cent of the average lifespan for a fossil invertebrate species—more than ten million years. Large, widespread, and well established species, on the other hand, are not expected to change very much. We believe that the inertia of large populations explains the stasis of most fossil species over millions of years. [19]

We proposed the theory of punctuated equilibrium largely to provide a different explanation for pervasive trends in the fossil record. Trends, we argued, cannot be attributed to gradual transformation within lineages, but must arise from the differential success of certain kinds of species. A trend, we argued, is more like climbing a flight of stairs (punctuations and stasis) than rolling up an inclined plane. [20]

Since we proposed punctuated equilibria to explain trends, it is infuriating to be quoted again and again by creationists—whether through design or stupidity, I do not know—as admitting that the fossil record includes no transitional forms. Transitional forms are generally lacking at the species level, but they are abundant between larger groups. Yet a pamphlet entitled "Harvard Scientists Agree Evolution Is a Hoax" states: "The facts of punctuated equilibrium which Gould and Eldredge . . . are forcing Darwinists to swallow fit the picture that Bryan insisted on, and which God has revealed to us in the Bible." [21]

Continuing the distortion, several creationists have equated the theory 22
of punctuated equilibrium with a caricature of the beliefs of Richard
Goldschmidt, a great early geneticist. Goldschmidt argued, in a famous book
published in 1940, that new groups can arise all at once through major muta-
tions. He referred to these suddenly transformed creatures as "hopeful monsters."
(I am attracted to some aspects of the non-caricatured version, but Goldschmidt's
theory still has nothing to do with punctuated equilibrium—see essays in section 3 and my explicit essay on Goldschmidt in *The Panda's Thumb*.) Creationist Luther Sunderland talks of the "punctuated equilibrium hopeful monster
theory" and tells his hopeful readers that "it amounts to tacit admission that
anti-evolutionists are correct in asserting there is no fossil evidence supporting
the theory that all life is connected to a common ancestor." Duane Gish writes,
"According to Goldschmidt, and now apparently according to Gould, a reptile
laid an egg from which the first bird, feathers and all, was produced." Any evolu-
tionist who believed such nonsense would rightly be laughed off the intellectual stage; yet the only theory that could ever envision such a scenario for the
origin of birds is creationism—with God acting in the egg.

I am both angry at and amused by the creationists; but mostly I am deeply 23
sad. Sad for many reasons. Sad because so many people who respond to creationist appeals are troubled for the right reason, but venting their anger at the
wrong target. It is true that scientists have often been dogmatic and elitist. It
is true that we have often allowed the white-coated, advertising image to
represent us—"Scientists say that Brand X cures bunions ten times faster than . . ."
We have not fought it adequately because we derive benefits from appearing
as a new priesthood. It is also true that faceless and bureaucratic state power
intrudes more and more into our lives and removes choices that should belong
to individuals and communities. I can understand that school curricula, imposed
from above and without local input, might be seen as one more insult on all
these grounds. But the culprit is not, and cannot be, evolution or any other
fact of the natural world. Identify and fight your legitimate enemies by all means,
but we are not among them.

I am sad because the practical result of this brouhaha will not be expanded 24
coverage to include creationism (that would also make me sad), but the reduction or excision of evolution from high school curricula. Evolution is one of
the half dozen "great ideas" developed by science. It speaks to the profound
issues of genealogy that fascinate all of us—the "roots" phenomenon writ large.
Where did we come from? Where did life arise? How did it develop? How are
organisms related? It forces us to think, ponder, and wonder. Shall we deprive
millions of this knowledge and once again teach biology as a set of dull and
unconnected facts, without the thread that weaves diverse material into a supple
unity?

But most of all I am saddened by a trend I am just beginning to discern 25
among my colleagues. I sense that some now wish to mute the healthy debate
about theory that has brought new life to evolutionary biology. It provides
grist for creationist mills, they say, even if only by distortion. Perhaps we should

lie low and rally round the flag of strict Darwinism, at least for the moment—a kind of old-time religion on our part.

But we should borrow another metaphor and recognize that we too have   26 to tread a straight and narrow path, surrounded by roads to perdition. For if we ever begin to suppress our search to understand nature, to quench our own intellectual excitement in a misguided effort to present a united front where it does not and should not exist, then we are truly lost.

1981

Purpose and Meaning

1. In this essay, Gould takes up the case of evolution versus creationism as an explanation of how our world came to be. His title asserts that evolution is both fact and theory. Reread paragraphs 3 through 8, and explain the significance of this assertion. Why is creationism theory but not fact? To what group of readers would this thesis appeal? Why?

2. In paragraph 12, Gould writes that "unbeatable systems are dogma." What does he mean by this? Why is it necessary for a theory to be "falsifiable"? If a theory cannot be shown to be wrong, does that mean it is necessarily true? If I assert that there are Martians living in my bedroom, but I won't allow anyone in to check, does that mean that Martians are indeed living in my bedroom?

3. What does Gould mean when he writes that "evolution lies exposed in the *imperfections*" (paragraph 16)? If we could not trace the gradual "perfecting" of a species, by studying its previous imperfections, could we determine whether any evolution had occurred?

4. What is Gould's theory of "punctuated equilibrium" (paragraph 19), and how have creationists caricatured this theory?

Language and Style

1. In paragraph 3, Gould writes that creationists "play upon a vernacular misunderstanding of the word 'theory.' " He calls this distortion of meaning "newspeak," a term coined by George Orwell in his famous novel *1984*. How is Gould's use of language distinctly *not* newspeak? Does he write in ways that seem to distort or clarify ideas?

2. In paragraph 9, Gould sounds almost as though he is straining to set the record straight on what evolutionists believe. Why does he take such a serious stylistic approach to this issue?

3. At times Gould maintains his humor; indeed, his wit becomes a weapon: "The only theory that could ever envision such a scenario for the origin of birds is creationism—with God acting in the egg" (paragraph 22). But here, and throughout the essay, an angry tone prevails. Indeed, Gould writes "I am both

angry at and amused by the creationists" (paragraph 23). Does this high level of emotion ever overtake or undercut Gould's argument? Explain.

Strategy and Structure

1. Gould opens with a reference to a person he admires, someone who is also well respected and admired in society. In this case, the person is Kirtley Mather, "a pillar of both science and Christian religion." What is the significance of this description?

2. Gould immediately places in his corner of the intellectual arena Mather, Clarence Darrow, and Charles Darwin. How does this give him an advantage in the debate? How does he exploit this advantage in terms of the essay's structure?

3. This is a rigorously organized argument. Cite examples of formal organizing principles used by Gould to carry the reader through the main points of the debate.

4. Gould strikes a high moral tone in the final paragraph: "We too have to tread a straight and narrow path, surrounded by roads to perdition...." Considering who the opposition is and who many of his readers may be, what is the significance of these words? Why do they constitute a fitting conclusion to the essay?

Thinking and Writing

1. Write an essay in which you take a position in this debate. Do you believe in evolutionary theory or creationism? (You may need to go to the library and gather more information on the creationist's point of view.)

2. Many Christians who believe in the Bible's teachings have rejected the creationist point of view as outdated. Make a case for why this could be so.

3. Compare the "scientific" style of Gould and that of either Selzer or Thomas in this book.

RICHARD RODRIGUEZ

"I am a journalist," declares Richard Rodriguez modestly, for he is also a fine prose stylist. Rodriguez was born July 31, 1944, in San Francisco, California. He was educated at Stanford, Columbia, and the University of California at Berkeley, receiving a Fulbright fellowship in 1972 to study in London. Rodriguez is a writer by profession, primarily of essays and journalistic pieces. His major work is an autobiography, published in 1982, entitled *Hunger of Memory; The Education of Richard Rodriguez*, and a more recent book, *Mexico's Children* (1990).

In *Hunger of Memory*, from which "Complexion" is taken, Rodriguez writes about his upbringing as the son of Mexican-American immigrants. He vividly recounts his education in the United States school system and explores the issues of bilingual education and assimilation. He attacks bilingual education for failing to help children assimilate, and instead causing painful identity confusion between the "public" individual and the "private" individual. One's own family language, he contends, gives one a sense of belonging. When one loses that language to the public language, one's identity is lost as well. Rodriguez's straightforward and at times angry prose gives his account a raw emotional power. In the early stages of the memoir, he writes, "This is what matters to me: the story of the scholarship boy who returns home one summer from college to discover bewildering silence, facing his parents." His advanced education and studies of English Renaissance literature as a Fulbright scholar left him feeling like an "anthropologist in the family kitchen." The loss of his private self through the gradual linguistic drift from Spanish to English caused this terrible separation between himself and his family. That is why he writes, "This autobiography . . . is a book about language."

Since publishing *Hunger of Memory*, Rodriguez has worked primarily as a journalist and specialist in Hispanic affairs. He has published numerous articles on such subjects as emigration in "Across the Borders of History" and cultural assimilation in "Children of a Marriage." He writes for magazines as diverse as *Time, Mother Jones, Harper's,* and *Reader's Digest.* In an interview, Rodriguez once remarked that as a journalist he is concerned with "separating the prosaic world from the poetic world." But his writing is not only about language; it is about the world as well: "I try to write about everyday concerns—an educational issue say, or the problems of the unemployed—but to write them as powerfully, as richly, as well as I can."

Rodriguez's own loss of ethnicity as recorded in *Hunger of Memory* is evident also in his essays and articles on Hispanic-American culture. His personal experience of assimilation and conflicts of language and culture, combined with a keen ear for the poetry and power of language, often move his writing beyond reportage into the realm of excellent prose.

Complexion

Complexion. My first conscious experience of sexual excitement concerns my complexion. One summer weekend, when I was around seven years old, I was at a public swimming pool with the whole family. I remember sitting on the damp pavement next to the pool and seeing my mother, in the spectators' bleachers, holding my younger sister on her lap. My mother, I noticed, was watching my father as he stood on a diving board, waving to her. I watched her wave back. Then saw her radiant, bashful, astonishing smile. In that second I sensed that my mother and father had a relationship I knew nothing about. A nervous excitement encircled my stomach as I saw my mother's eyes follow my father's figure curving into the water. A second or two later, he emerged. I heard him call out. Smiling, his voice sounded, buoyant, calling me to swim to him. But turning to see him, I caught my mother's eye. I heard her shout over to me. In Spanish she called through the crowd: 'Put a towel on over your shoulders.' In public, she didn't want to say why. I knew.

That incident anticipates the shame and sexual inferiority I was to feel in later years because of my dark complexion. I was to grow up an ugly child. Or one who thought himself ugly. (*Feo.*) One night when I was eleven or twelve years old, I locked myself in the bathroom and carefully regarded my reflection in the mirror over the sink. Without any pleasure I studied my skin. I turned on the faucet. (In my mind I heard the swirling voices of aunts, and even my mother's voice, whispering, whispering incessantly about lemon juice solutions and dark, *feo* children.) With a bar of soap, I fashioned a thick ball of lather. I began soaping my arms. I took my father's straight razor out of the medicine cabinet. Slowly, with steady deliberateness, I put the blade against my flesh, pressed it as close as I could without cutting, and moved it up and down across my skin to see if I could get out, somehow lessen, the dark. All I succeeded in doing, however, was in shaving my arms bare of their hair. For as I noted with disappointment, the dark would not come out. It remained. Trapped. Deep in the cells of my skin.

Throughout adolescence, I felt myself mysteriously marked. Nothing else about my appearance would concern me so much as the fact that my complexion was dark. My mother would say how sorry she was that there was not money enough to get braces to straighten my teeth. But I never bothered about my teeth. In three-way mirrors at department stores, I'd see my profile dramatically defined by a long nose, but it was really only the color of my skin that caught my attention.

I wasn't afraid that I would become a menial laborer because of my skin. 4
Nor did my complexion make me feel especially vulnerable to racial abuse. (I
didn't really consider my dark skin to be a racial characteristic. I would have
been only too happy to look as Mexican as my light-skinned older brother.)
Simply, I judged myself ugly. And, since the women in my family had been
the ones who discussed it in such worried tones, I felt my dark skin made me
unattractive to women.

Thirteen years old. Fourteen. In a grammar school art class, when the 5
assignment was to draw a self-portrait, I tried and tried but could not bring
myself to shade in the face on the paper to anything like my actual tone. With
disgust then I would come face to face with myself in mirrors. With disappointment I located myself in class photographs—my dark face undefined by the
camera which had clearly described the white faces of classmates. Or I'd see
my dark wrist against my long-sleeved white shirt.

I grew divorced from my body. Insecure, overweight, listless. On hot 6
summer days when my rubber-soled shoes soaked up the heat from the sidewalk,
I kept my head down. Or walked in the shade. My mother didn't need anymore
to tell me to watch out for the sun. I denied myself a sensational life. The normal, extraordinary, animal excitement of feeling my body alive—riding shirtless
on a bicycle in the warm wind created by furious self-propelled motion—the
sensations that first had excited in me a sense of my maleness, I denied. I was
too ashamed of my body. I wanted to forget that I had a body because I had
a brown body. I was grateful that none of my classmates ever mentioned the fact.

I continued to see the *braceros,* those men I resembled in one way and, 7
in another way, didn't resemble at all. On the watery horizon of a Valley afternoon, I'd see them. And though I feared looking like them, it was with silent
envy that I regarded them still. I envied them their physical lives, their freedom
to violate the taboo of the sun. Closer to home I would notice the shirtless construction workers, the roofers, the sweating men tarring the street in front of
the house. And I'd see the Mexican gardeners. I was unwilling to admit the attraction of their lives. I tried to deny it by looking away. But what was denied
became strongly desired.

In high school physical education classes, I withdrew, in the regular com- 8
pany of five or six classmates, to a distant corner of a football field where we
smoked and talked. Our company was composed of bodies too short or too
tall, all graceless and all—except mine—pale. Our conversation was usually
witty. (In fact we were intelligent.) If we referred to the athletic contests around
us, it was with sarcasm. With savage scorn I'd refer to the 'animals' playing
football or baseball. It would have been important for me to have joined them.
Or for me to have taken off my shirt, to have let the sun burn dark on my skin,
and to have run barefoot on the warm wet grass. It would have been very important. Too important. It would have been too telling a gesture—to admit
the desire for sensation, the body, my body.

Fifteen, sixteen. I was a teenager shy in the presence of girls. Never dated. 9
Barely could talk to a girl without stammering. In high school I went to several
dances, but I never managed to ask a girl to dance. So I stopped going. I cannot
remember high school years now with the parade of typical images: bright drive-
ins or gliding blue shadows of a Junior Prom. At home most weekend nights,
I would pass evenings reading. Like those hidden, precocious adolescents who
have no real-life sexual experiences, I read a great deal of romantic fiction. 'You
won't find it in your books,' my brother would playfully taunt me as he prepared
to go to a party by freezing the crest of the wave in his hair with sticky pomade.
Through my reading, however, I developed a fabulous and sophisticated sexual
imagination. At seventeen, I may not have known how to engage a girl in small
talk, but I had read *Lady Chatterley's Lover.*

It annoyed me to hear my father's teasing: that I would never know what 'real 10
work' is; that my hands were so soft. I think I knew it was his way of admitting
pleasure and pride in my academic success. But I didn't smile. My mother said
she was glad her children were getting their educations and would not be pushed
around like *los pobres.* I heard the remark ironically as a reminder of my separation from *los braceros.* At such times I suspected that education was making
me effeminate. The odd thing, however, was that I did not judge my classmates
so harshly. Nor did I consider my male teachers in high school effeminate. It
was only myself I judged against some shadowy, mythical Mexican laborer—
dark like me, yet very different.

Language was crucial. I knew that I had violated the ideal of the *macho* 11
by becoming such a dedicated student of language and literature. *Machismo*
was a word never exactly defined by the persons who used it. (It was best
described in the 'proper' behavior of men.) Women at home, nevertheless, would
repeat the old Mexican dictum that a man should be *feo, fuerte, y formal.* 'The
three F's,' my mother called them, smiling slyly. *Feo* I took to mean not literally
ugly so much as ruggedly handsome. (When my mother and her sisters spent
a loud, laughing afternoon determining ideal male good looks, they finally settled
on the actor Gilbert Roland, who was neither too pretty nor ugly but had looks
'like a man.') *Fuerte,* 'strong,' seemed to mean not physical strength as much
as inner strength, character. A dependable man is *fuerte. Fuerte* for that reason
was a characteristic subsumed by the last of the three qualities, and the one
I most often considered—*formal.* To be *formal* is to be steady. A man of responsibility, a good provider. Someone *formal* is also constant. A person to be relied
upon in adversity. A sober man, a man of high seriousness.

I learned a great deal about being *formal* just by listening to the way my 12
father and other male relatives of his generation spoke. A man was not silent
necessarily. Nor was he limited in the tones he could sound. For example, he
could tell a long, involved, humorous story and laugh at his own humor with
high-pitched giggling. But a man was not talkative the way a woman could

be. It was permitted a woman to be gossipy and chatty. (When one heard many voices in a room, it was usually women who were talking.) Men spoke much less rapidly. And often men spoke in monologues. (When one voice sounded in a crowded room, it was most often a man's voice one heard.) More important than any of this was the fact that a man never verbally revealed his emotions. Men did not speak about their unease in moments of crisis or danger. It was the woman who worried aloud when her husband got laid off from work. At times of illness or death in the family, a man was usually quiet, even silent. Women spoke up to voice prayers. In distress, women always sounded quick ejaculations to God or the Virgin; women prayed in clearly audible voices at a wake held in a funeral parlor. And on the subject of love, a woman was verbally expansive. She spoke of her yearning and delight. A married man, if he spoke publicly about love, usually did so with playful, mischievous irony. Younger, unmarried men more often were quiet. (The *macho* is a silent suitor. *Formal.*)

At home I was quiet, so perhaps I seemed *formal* to my relations and other   13
Spanish-speaking visitors to the house. But outside the house—my God!—I talked. Particularly in class or alone with my teachers, I chattered. (Talking seemed to make teachers think I was bright.) I often was proud of my way with words. Though, on other occasions, for example, when I would hear my mother busily speaking to women, it would occur to me that my attachment to words made me like her. Her son. Not *formal* like my father. At such times I even suspected that my nostalgia for sounds—the noisy, intimate Spanish sounds of my past—was nothing more than effeminate yearning.

High school English teachers encouraged me to describe very personal   14
feelings in words. Poems and short stories I wrote, expressing sorrow and loneliness, were awarded high grades. In my bedroom were books by poets and novelists—books that I loved—in which male writers published feelings the men in my family never revealed or acknowledged in words. And it seemed to me that there was something unmanly about my attachment to literature. Even today, when so much about the myth of the *macho* no longer concerns me, I cannot altogether evade such notions. Writing these pages, admitting my embarrassment or my guilt, admitting my sexual anxieties and my physical insecurity, I have not been able to forget that I am not being *formal.*

So be it.   15

1982

Purpose and Meaning

1. From one incident in his childhood—when his mother told him to cover his shoulders with a towel—Richard Rodriguez unfolds all of his teen years up to adulthood. "That incident," he writes, "anticipates the shame and sexual inferiority I was to feel in later years because of my dark complexion" (paragraph 1).

What does this suggest about the power of a mother's words? About the fragility of one's psyche? About society's attitudes toward skin color?

2. What is Rodriguez's purpose in devoting most of the last half of this essay to a discussion of the male ideal in Hispanic society? How did the three *F*s of masculinity conflict with Rodriguez's interests in words, both written and spoken?

3. Is the thesis of this essay stated or implied? Explain.

Language and Style

1. *Complexion* is the first word, and the first sentence, of Rodriguez's essay. How does this one-word beginning characterize Rodriguez's direct writing style? Are his sentences generally long or short? Is his word order complex or simple? Explain. Does he use many words with which you are not familiar? What relationship does this help to establish between writer and reader?

2. Although this essay suggests a great deal about cultural attitudes toward skin color and about male and female roles, Rodriguez does not spell out what those attitudes are. He, like many of the writers in this collection, allows the images he creates to do the telling. What does this dual image tell about men, women, and power: "When one heard many voices in a room, it was usually women who were talking.... When one voice sounded in a crowded room, it was most often a man's voice one heard." How is this method more effective than direct commentary? How does it involve the reader?

3. Throughout the essay, Rodriguez uses Spanish terminology. What are some *stylistic* reasons he might do this? What are some *personal* reasons he, as a Hispanic—might do this?

Strategy and Structure

1. Rodriguez repeats the one-word paragraph beginnings in paragraphs 5 and 9. Each time he does so, he marks his age. How does this give this essay a "linear" shape? Is a linear approach a logical one to take? Explain.

2. In the early part of the essay, Rodriguez describes himself—his insecurities, his "abnormality," his failure to "fit in." In paragraphs 7 and 8 he contrasts himself with *los braceros.* Is this comparison effective? In what way does it caricature both Rodriguez and the *braceros* and consequently make both look ridiculous?

3. Because of Rodriguez's linear approach, and in part because of actual circumstances, readers are left seeing his talents as a writer emerging almost directly from his dark skin. In what ways does Rodriguez employ definition to explore his development as a Hispanic American and a writer?

Thinking and Writing

1. Write an autobiography of your life from the age of 6 to 16 in which you focus on some particular development, such as a talent, career interest, or personal

quality. Detail the events or influences—in society as well as at home—that led to this development.

2. Teen-agers often are pressured by their peers to fit in—to wear the right clothes, say the right things, have the right look. However, many creative people in the arts and sciences were in fact "outcasts" in their teens. In an essay, analyze what social and personal factors may influence this phenomenon.

3. Compare and contrast concepts of masculinity or feminity in American culture and one other culture that you are familiar with.

Across the Borders
of History

Palm Sunday. I am sitting in a parking lot at the edge of California. I have heard there is a city, invisible from here, a Third World capital like Calcutta or Cairo, a great, sore Lazarus sprawled at our gate. In the parking lot there is only silence and the scent of suntan lotion. There is a turnstile.   1

Through which American tourists enter as at a state fair. Mexicans pass with the cardboard boxes they are using as suitcases. Some men are putting up palm trees. A fluttering white banner overhead heralds the Señorita Mexico pageant. An old Mexican woman proffers sno-cones that look like bulbs of blood. She is wearing Gloria Vanderbilt jeans and jogging shoes. A billboard in sixteen languages implores: "Welcome to Mexico."   2

I am thinking of my first trip across: the late 1950s. My family was on its way to visit relatives in Ensenada. We had driven all day from Sacramento in the blue DeSoto and we reached the border around midnight. I remember waking in the back seat. A fat Mexican in a brown uniform is making beckoning gestures in the light from our headlamps. This isn't Mexico, this isn't Mexico, my mother keeps saying. Clucking, smoothing. Tijuana is just a border town; you see the worst here. You'll see. I remember my father hunched forward at the wheel. The DeSoto was acting up. It was too late to drive any more. I remember the main street, full of scuffle and shadow: naked lights, persons stumbling, jeering. We found a motel by the bus station. We all slept on a double bed with a green velvet cover. We kept our clothes on. The air was heavy. Wet. I listened to faraway music. American music. Mexico!   3

The Tijuana that Americans grew up with was a city they thought they had created. The Tijuana that has grown up is a city that will recreate us.   4

Tijuana has a million, perhaps two million people. Tijuana will double   5
itself in twelve years. Tijuana is the new Pacific city. Tijuana is already larger
than Vancouver or Seattle or San Francisco. Tijuana is larger than San Diego.

In its official census of 1980, the Mexican government entered Tijuana's   6
population as 500,000. Mexico might have chosen to bid modestly as a way
of dissuading attention from the swell along its northern border.

What is intriguing is the exhilarated rate of swelling. What intrigues us   7
is that we cannot know. There is an uncountable *poblacion flotante*. How does
one number fluid shadows passing back and forth over the border and whose
business it is to elude any count?

Tijuana is several million lifetimes posing as one street, a metropolis   8
crouched behind a hootchy-kootch curtain. Most Americans head for the tourist
street called Avenida Revolución. From the border you can share a cab for five
bucks a head or you can walk along the dirty Tijuana River, where you will
see broken bottles and young men asleep on the grass. It is more fun, perhaps,
to approach Revolución with adolescent preconceptions of lurid possibility.
Marrakesh, Shanghai. For this you will need a cab. In the first place, where
is he taking me? In the second place cabdrivers still offer male passengers
cualquier cosa as a matter of form.

For all that, you are deposited safely when the driver announces with a   9
distracted wave of his hand, "El Main Street." El Main Street is what you'd expect of the region's fifth tourist attraction, after the San Diego Zoo, Sea World,
and some others. A Mexico ride.

Most tourists come for the afternoon. Most tourists stay three or four   10
hours, just between meals. After the shops, after the scolding sighs, after the
bottled drinks, there is nothing to do but head back.

Consider Tijuana from Mexico's point of view. Tijuana is farther away   11
from Mexico City than any other city in Mexico. In Mexico City you will waste
an afternoon if you go to bookstores looking for books about Tijuana. The
clerk will scarcely conceal his amusement. (And what would be in a book about
Tijuana?) People in Mexico City will tell you, if they have anything at all to
say about Tijuana, that Tijuana is a city without history; a city without
architecture; that it is, in fact, an American city.

San Diego may worry about Mexican hordes crawling over the border.   12
Mexico City worries about a cultural spill from the United States.

From pre-history, the north has been the problem. Mexico City (*la*   13
Capital), the watered heart of Mexico, has been the platform from which all
provincialism is gauged. From the north came marauding tribes, iconoclasts,
destroyers of high Indian civilization. During the Spanish colonial era, the north
was settled, even garrisoned, but scarcely civilized. In the nineteenth century,
Mexico's northernmost territories were too far from the center to be defended
against the western migration of Americans. Mexico City lost what is now the
gringo Southwest.

The new American cliché about border towns is that they represent some 14
blending of cultures. But beyond all the ribbon-cutting palaver about good
neighbors, there is the awesome distance of time. Tijuana and San Diego are
not in the same historical time zone. Tijuana is at the beginning of an industrial
age, a Dickensian city with palm trees. San Diego is a post-industrial city of
high-impact plastic and despair diets. And palm trees.

San Diego faces west, looks resolutely out to sea. Tijuana stares north, 15
as toward the future. San Diego is the future, secular, soulless. San Diego is
the past, guarding its quality of life. Tijuana is the future. On the Mexican side
there is flux, a vast migration, a camp of siege. On the Mexican side is youth,
with bad skin or bad teeth, but with a supple naiveté appropriate to youth.

On the American side are English-language amendments; the Ku Klux 16
Klan; racist groups posing as environmental groups blaming illegal immigration
for freeway congestion. And late at night, on the radio call-in shows, hysterical,
reasonable American voices say they have had enough. Of this or that. Of
waiting in line or crowded buses, or real or imagined rudeness, or welfare.

Whereas San Diego remains provincial and retiring, the intrusion of the 17
United States galvanizes Tijuana to cosmopolitanism. There are seven
newspapers in Tijuana; there is American television—everything we see they
see. Central American refugees and California *turistas* cross paths in Tijuana.
There are new ideas. Most worrisome to Mexico City has been the emergence
of a right-wing idea—a pro-American politics to challenge the one-party system
that has governed Mexico for most of this century.

Because the United States is the richer country, the more powerful broad- 18
caster, Mexicans know more about us than we care to know about them.
Mexicans speak of America as "the other side," saying they are going to *el otro
lado* when they cross the border for work, legal or illegal. The border is real
enough; it is guarded by men with guns. But Mexicans incline to view the border
without reverence, referring to the American side as *el otro cachete*, the other
buttock.

Traditionally, Mexican cities are centered by a town square, or *zócalo*, 19
on either side of which stand city hall and cathedral, counterweights to balance
the secular with the eternal. Tijuana has a town square a few blocks from
Avenida Revolución. But like other California cities, Tijuana is drawing away
from its old downtown.

The new commercial district of Tijuana, three miles east of downtown, 20
is called the Zona del Río. For several blocks within the Zona del Río, on grass
islands in the middle of the Paseo de los Heroes, stand monuments to various
of Mexico's heroes. There is one American (Abraham Lincoln) in a line that
otherwise connects the conquered Aztec emperor Cuauhtemoc with the victorious Mexican general Zaragoza. With a Kremlin-like dullness, these
monuments were set down upon the city like paperweights upon a map. They
are gifts from the capital, meant as reminders.

Prominent along the Paseo de los Heroes is Tijuana's Cultural Center,   21
Mexico City's most insistent token of troth. Tijuana might better have done
with sewers or streetlights, but in 1982 the Mexican government built Tijuana
a cultural center, an orange concrete *bomba* in the brutal architectural idioms
of the 1970s. The main building is a museum, very clean and empty during my
visit except for a janitor, who trails me with a vacuum cleaner. Together we
tread a ramp past fairly uninteresting displays of Mayan pottery, past folk crafts,
past reproductions of political documents and pictures of Mexico's military
heroes. The lesson to Tijuana is apparent. She belongs to Mexico.

As the exhibits travel in time, south to north, the umbilical approach   22
narrows to gossamer. We reach a display devoted to Tijuana's own history.
We find a collection of picture postcards from the twenties, some with the perfer-
vidly daubed sunsets of paradise and emblazoned in English with "Greetings
from Mexico."

One sympathizes with the curator's dilemma. How does one depict the   23
history of an unmonumental city, a city occasioned by defeat and submission
to the enemy's will?

Tijuana came into being by an accident of war, after Mexico lost Califor-   24
nia to the gringo in 1848. The treaty ending the Mexican-American war granted
Mexico access to the Pacific across the northern mainland. Tijuana was that
point of access. For decades thereafter, Tijuana remained vacant land at the
edge of the sea, an arid little clause dangling from Mexico's disgraced nineteenth
century.

No one in town is able to fix for me the derivation of the name of the   25
place. Some think it is an Indian word. Others think the town was named for
a woman who lived in a shack in the late nineteenth century, a Mexican Ma
Kettle known in the region as Tia Juana.

Mexico City tried to get rid of the name in 1925. By an act of Mexico's   26
congress, Tijuana was proclaimed to be Ciudad Zaragoza. A good name. A
monumental name. A patriot's name. The resolution languished in a statute
book on a shelf in Mexico City.

Monday of Holy Week. On the side streets of the Zona Norte, by the   27
bus station, Mexican men loiter outside the doors of open bars; from within
come stale blasts of American rock. Is this all that is left of the passé fleshpots
of T.J.?

We are a generation removed from that other city, the city generations   28
of American men mispronounced as "Tee-ah-wanna," by which they named
the alter ego American city that would take them about as far as they wanted
to go. At the turn of the century, when boxing was illegal in San Diego, there
was blood sport in Tijuana. There were whores and there was gambling and
there was drink.

Citizens of today's Tijuana will tell you that the Tijuana of memory was   29
always more American than Mexican. A teen-age policeman with bad acne says:

"The gringos find our downtown so ugly? They were the ones who made it."
Which is true enough, though the lustier truth is that Mexico laid down and
the gringo paid in the morning.

At its best and worst, Mexico is tolerant. Spanish Catholicism has be-   30
queathed to Mexico the assumption of original sin. Much in life is failure or
compromise. The knowledge has made Mexico patient as a desert, and it has
left Mexico tolerant of corruptions that have played upon its surface. Public
officials tread a path to corruption, just as men need their whores. *No importa.*
Mexico manages to live.

The intimate life, especially the family—abundant and eternal—is Mexico's   31
consolation. *Mamasita,* sainted mama, tends her daughter's purity, which is
a votive ruby betokening the family's virtue. A woman of Tijuana, the daughter
of wealth, tells me that, as a *señorita,* she was never permitted within one block
of Avenida Revolución. She tells me young ladies of Tijuana required *dueñas*
long after Mexico City had discontinued the habit.

In the afternoon, I am chaperoned through the city by an official from   32
the Comite de Turismo. Her English is about as bad as my Spanish. We walk
along Avenida Revolución, recently beautified—wider sidewalks, new blighted
trees.

There, says my hostess, where the Woolworth's now stands (where   33
disinterested hag beggars squat, palms extended over their heads), used to be
the longest bar in the world. And over there, beyond the blue tourist bus (which
is being decanted by a smiling guide with a very wide tie), is the restaurant where
two Italian brothers named Cardini created the Caesar salad back in the twenties.

In Tijuana, as in Las Vegas, another city constructed on sand, and almost   34
as old, history is a matter of matchbook covers and cocktail napkins.

It was during reformist America's Prohibition that cynical Tijuana flour-   35
ished. Tijuana used to be very glamorous, promises my companion from the
Comite de Turismo. We are considering a building (a trade school) that used
to be the Casino de Agua Caliente. She thinks. She herself is from Guadalajara.
Anyway, all the famous movie stars used to come down.

Among the however many million volumes in the library at the University   36
of California at San Diego there is one green book about Tijuana, not thick,
a history written by John Price, an American professor. It includes photographs
of the Casino de Agua Caliente in the twenties—whitewashed Mission architecture, shadows of palm trees, black limos, silver sky.

There survives from that era (in the same green book) a photo of Sheilah   37
Graham, she on a mule, Tijuana sombrero, hilarious. Her attendant Joseph is
none other than the great tarnished priest of the twenties, F. Scott Fitzgerald.
Both look foolish in ways they hadn't intended.

San Diego changed first. By the 1940s, Prohibition was over, and Tijuana   38
had lost some of its glamorous utility. During the war, Tijuana was relegated
to the sailor's rest. Since the war years a Venusberg lore has passed from fathers

to sons, together with prescriptions against infection. A night-town mirage advances on the squeal of a wet horn: a blinking neon cactus; a two-quart margarita; and any of several more lurid images, like the demoiselles who can pick quarters off the table without using their hands.

Tijuana is off-limits now to the Navy between eight at night and dawn. The press officer at the San Diego Naval Station tells me that our boys have been harassed by the Tijuana police.   39

If you want pornography, go to San Diego, the Mexicans say. You won't see people selling drugs on the street in Tijuana. When the woman wants an abortion, she crosses the border, the Mexicans say.   40

There is the father in Tijuana who worries that his teen-age son is living under the radiant cloud of American pop culture—its drugs, its disrespect, its despair. On the other side, San Diego's morning paper quotes officials in Washington concerning the corruption of the Mexican government and the unchecked northern flow of drugs. Washington officials do not say that it is America's hunger for drugs that has raised drug lords south of the border.   41

Mexico does not deny any of it—well, some—but the Mexican has a more graceful sense of universal corruption. What Mexico comprehends is a balance between supply and demand. The Mexican comprehends public morality as a balance—the ethereal parts of any balanced thing rise by virtue of the regrettable ballast. The border, for instance. For Mexico the border is not that rigid Puritan thing, a line; straight lines are unknown in Mexico. The border, like everything else, is subject to supply and demand. The border is a revolving door.   42

Tijuana proudly bills itself "the most visited city in the world." U.S. immigration officials counted 34 million people entering the United States at the San Ysidro border crossing last year. (The U.S. government bills the San Ysidro border crossing "the busiest in the world.") Mexico, assuming a two-way street, reverses the numbers. So: Tijuana had 34 million visitors last year. It becomes, in a way, Mexico's joke on the gringo's paranoia, his penchant for numbers, his fear of invasion or contamination.   43

America imagines itself clean, ingenuous, virgin. Aliens are carriers of chaos as well as pigment. Mexicans are obviously carriers of chaos—their backs are broken with bundles of it: gray air, brown water, papacy, leprosy, crime, white powders, and a language full of newts and cicadas.   44

Mexico does not say it publicly but Mexico perceives America as sterile, as sterilizing, as barren as the nose of a missile. "Don't drink the water in Los Angeles, it will clean you out like a scalpel," goes the joke. Because Americans are barren by choice, they are perceived by Mexico as having relinquished gravity. Within the porticos of the great churches of Mexico, Mexico posts signs reminding visitors to dress modestly and to behave with dignity. The signs are in English.   45

Seasoned visitors from southern California pass right on through Tijuana, into the vacant depths of Baja—California's newest, unofficial national park.   46

Just as earlier generations used Tijuana to refresh their virtue, so, once again, Californians use Mexico as an opposite planet. As pollution settles over Orange County, Baja California is prized for its pristine desert, its abiding austerity.

Gingerly, I am steered through the inedible city by my hostess from the   47
Comite de Turismo. Street vendors offer unclean enchantments, whirling platters of melon and pineapple, translucent candies, syrups, charcoaled meats, black and red. I begin to feel myself a Jamesian naif who puzzles and perspires and will not dare.

"The usual visit, then, three or four hours?"   48

I notice my hostess from the Comite is surreptitiously consulting her   49
wristwatch. I'm spending the week. Then I admit to her that I am visiting Tijuana by day, sleeping in San Diego at night. Ah.

We stop at a café where she offers me something to drink. A soft drink?   50
No, I say. ¿Cerveza? Not really? But suddenly I fear giving offense. I notice the apothecary jars full of improbably colored juices. Just some jugo, please. Offense to whom? That I fear drinking Mexico? A waiter appears from stage left with a tall glass of canary yellow. Ah. We are all very pleased. It's lovely today. I put the glass to my lips. But I do not drink.

Tuesday of Holy Week. A noisy artificial waterfall outside my window   51
at the Inter-Continental Hotel in San Diego is supposed to drown out the noise of traffic. The traffic report on the radio posts a thirty-minute delay at the San Ysidro border crossing. The children of upper-class Tijuana are traveling in car pools into San Diego for school. Mexicans with green cards are crossing to work. From this side, there are Americans—technicians, engineers, supervisors—heading for jobs in Tijuana.

It was in the nineteenth century that American entrepreneurs began   52
reaching into Mexico for cheap labor to build California. Many of these lodestar Mexican laborers passed through Tijuana. Some stayed, living in Tijuana, working in America.

In good times the United States approved the arrangement, hard work   53
for low wages. But when the American economy dipped in the 1930s, Mexicans in California slid down the board—were deported. They bumpered up in Tijuana. In the 1940s, America again siphoned Mexico to replace Americans who had gone off to war. In the late 1950s, the *bracero* guest worker program was discontinued. Mexicans were again sent home and Tijuana took many.

Leo Chavez, an anthropologist in San Diego, tells me that there is nothing   54
inexplicable about illegal immigration. America lured the Mexican worker; America established the financial dependency that today America relegates to realms of tragedy. Sons following fathers north: it has become a Mexican rite of passage—"like going to college," says Chavez. Tijuana is crowded today with such families. The males cross over into the twentieth century; mama raises her children at the end of the nineteenth century.

Tijuana is not Mayhew's London. There are none of the Gothic brick fac-   55
tories, no dark naves of Victorian mills. You see billowing smoke on the horizon,

it turns out to be a bonfire in a vacant lot. That this is a viable city is apparent mainly in the congested traffic.

One sees few pedestrians. (Few sidewalks.) Occasional children. Dogs roam dusty lots. In Colonia Libertad some teen-agers gather about a car without wheels. If the car had wheels they wouldn't be there.

All the adages about California's cities—suburbs in search of a center, no there there—describe Tijuana also, Tijuana ranging across the hills to the south and, more evenly, to the east. Tijuana is a *municipio*, something like an American county. Tijuana extends about twenty-five miles south and east from the central city to include surrounding townships. All are united by one mayor, and a single ambition. The ambition of Tijuana is American money.

In the lobby of the Lucerna Hotel I see the sort of family one sees in only two or three hotels in Mexico City. Father with a preoccupied look and thin watch; mother elegant, glacially indulgent of her three children, who squirm under the watchful eye, the iron grasp, of an Indian nanny.

The word signifying money in Tijuana today is *maquiladora*. Twenty years ago, the Mexican government established a duty-free zone, permitting American companies to transport parts and raw materials across the border for assembly in Mexico, after which the products are returned to America. The Mexican assembly plant is called a *maquiladora* or, when paired with a manufacturing plant on the American side, a twin plant.

For their labor, Mexicans are paid Mexican wages. (Mexico's daily minimum wage is roughly America's hourly wage.) Some such deal involving cheap labor has doubtless brought papa to meet his American counterpart in the lobby of the Lucerna Hotel.

Most of the twin-plant operations in Tijuana are in new, quietly marked buildings on the east side of town wherein thousands of doomed Señorita Mexicos spin out soft-focus dreams of love and idleness even as their nimble fingers assemble the detritus of a waning Western civilization—flashbulbs, electric plugs, stuffed toys.

Ciudad Juárez, which borders El Paso, has the greatest number of *maquiladoras*, but Tijuana and San Diego share advantages over other *maquiladora* regions. On both sides of the border there is land on which to build, and there is access to the sea. The land is called Otay Mesa or Mesa de Otay, depending. San Diego expects 3,800 American acres to be developed, creating 77,000 new American jobs. On the Mexican side, 1,000 *maquiladoras* are projected, employing 200,000 Mexicans.

There is complicity between businessmen, hands across the border, and shared optimism. On the American side, particularly, businessmen anticipate "mutual benefit," by which is meant profit from the proximity of technology and despair. Who needs Hong Kong or Taiwan? Tijuana is right here, on the American border, at the rim of the sea.

What American capitalism has in mind for Tijuana depends on the availability of great numbers of the Mexican poor; on the willing acceptance of Third World wages by the Mexican poor; on the poor remaining poor.

Mexico acquiesces. Mexico complies.   65

A new border crossing has been completed at Otay Mesa in anticipation   66 of the coming panoply of corporate pennants. In my rented car I slowly traverse the rust-colored fields. I look to left and to right, trying to imagine the industrial Camelot.

I am convinced it is not going to work. Yes, the factories will rise. Yes,   67 freighted trucks will pass emptied trucks back and forth across the border. Yes, there will be profit, just as in the past when America imported cheap Mexican labor. But this time we will not be able to get rid of Mexico once we have done with the poor. The anticipatory, desperate city massing beyond the cyclone fence is not going to dissipate into ether at the sound of the five o'clock whistle.

The poor can live on far less than justice. But the poor have a half-life   68 to outlast radium.

Back at the Inter-Continental Hotel, Twelfth Night is in progress.   69 Businessmen in baggy swimsuits sit around the noisy waterfall reading about Japan. A woman of profoundly indeterminate age lopes by, leotards, sunglasses, earphones. An aging kiddo in a bikini stands on his head, just as a gold Frisbee divides the air, slices up to catch the fading light of California.

Spy Wednesday. Mexico would rather schedule a sucker-appointment than   70 seem to deny a journalist's request. I phone a city official in Tijuana. His secretary is at my service (*a sus órdenes*): she will call me right back; no one calls back. I rush in for a 10:30 appointment with *Señor* B. or *Licenciado* R. His secretary is desolated to have to tell me that *Señor* B. or *Licenciado* R. is at a "mixer" in San Diego.

Information in an authoritarian society is power. In Mexico, power accu-   71 mulates as information is withheld.

Or else I get an interview with a Mexican official and find that even the   72 most innocuous rag of fact is off the record, *por favor*. The professor from the Collegio de la Frontera stops in midsentence to crane his neck across the table whenever my pen touches paper.

I sit on an oversize sofa in the outer office of a Mexican big shot, studying   73 his air-brushed photograph on the wall. I wait thirty minutes, an hour, before I pad back to the secretary's desk. *Señor* B. was called away to Mexicali by the governor of Baja California two days ago. Everything is so upset. Then the radiant smile, the dawning of an explanation: This is Easter week, *señor*.

Holy Thursday. I am going to La Casa de los Pobres, a kitchen for the   74 poor run by Franciscan nuns, and evidently well known. The taxi driver doesn't ask for directions.

I have seen worse neighborhoods than the ones we drive through. Detroit   75 is worse. East London. But this is Mexico. Perhaps because Mexico is brown and I am brown, I fear being lost in Mexico. I don't have the easy names for things. As I sit in the back seat of the taxi, lulled by pleasant sensations of peram-bulation, distance, I nevertheless attempt to memorize the route.

I get out of the cab and I am in a crowd; I am forced by the crowd into   76
a courtyard the color of yellow cake. I can smell coffee, cinnamon, eggs, *frijoles.*
Within the courtyard the crowd dissolves into reassuring presences, old men,
women, children, dogs. This is Mexico.

There are a number of Americans helping at La Casa this Easter week.   77
I look around for Tom Lucas, a Jesuit priest from Berkeley who invited me here.
Tom is in the kitchen drinking coffee with three Mexican nuns.

All that I know about Tom Lucas I have heard from him over lunch at   78
Chez Panisse. The man I see drinking coffee in Mexico is speaking Spanish.
He walks me through the buildings, tells me that at eleven o'clock groceries
are going to be handed out.

The nuns are in control. The poor form a line; everyone in line holds a   79
number. What a relief it seems to me, after days of dream-walking, invisible,
through an inedible city, to feel myself actually doing something, picking up
something to hand to someone. Thus Mexico's poor pass through my hands.
Most women bring their own plastic bags. The bags are warm and smell of
sweat as I fill them with four potatoes, two loaves of bread, two onions, a cup
of pinto beans, a block of orange cheese. I thank each of the Mexicans. This
baffles them, but they nod.

In the afternoon, Father Lucas takes me with him to the Colonia Flores   80
Magon, a poor section of Tijuana, but not the poorest, considering the hills
are green and there is a fresh wind blowing.

Even before our pickup comes to a full stop, doors have started to open.   81
First one woman comes out of a house, then several more women come out
of their houses, then more women are descending from the hillsides.

"*Padrecito,*" the call is tossed among the women playfully. Most of these   82
women are in their late twenties; most have several children. Would it be possible, Father, for you to bless my house? In the seminary Father Lucas may have
imagined an activist, perhaps even a revolutionary, ministry. With a smile, he
discourages the women from kissing his hand. Yes, he says, yes he will bless
houses.

Some houses are solidly built of concrete blocks. Some houses resemble   83
California suburban houses of the 1960s. Some houses have dirt floors and walls
of tin, papered with the *Los Angeles Times.* In front of many houses are tubs
of soapy water.

No announcement of a mass has been made. People have heard there is   84
a priest. Together we walk toward a neighborhood park—*padrecito,* the
children, the barking dogs. We find that a crowd has gathered, an altar is already
up. There are carnations in coffee cans, white light bulbs are strung in the olive
trees. This is Holy Thursday, the commemoration of the Last Supper and of
the institution of the Eucharist. Twelve teenage boys have been rounded up
by their mothers to slouch at the altar, dressed in sheets and bathrobes to represent the twelve Apostles. They grin stupidly at each other as Father Lucas washes
their feet according to the ancient rite of divine humility.

A yellow fog is coming in over the hills behind us. Overhead a jetliner 85
is pushing up from Tijuana International, slowly turning left, south, toward
Guadalajara and Mexico City. Some people in the crowd seemed bored, grow
restless; other faces are stern.

In the back of our pickup are cartons of day-old junk pastries from a San 86
Diego bakery. My job is to distribute these to the children after mass. When
I hear my cue from the altar—in the name of the Father and of the Son and
of the Holy Spirit—I climb over the tailgate and wait there with my arms folded,
my legs apart, like a temple guardian. Parents are instructed to bring their *niños*
to the truck for a special treat.

Five or six children come forward. All goes well for less than a minute. 87
The crowd has slowly turned away from the altar; the crowd advances zombie-
like against the truck. I fear children will be crushed. Silent faces regard me
with incomprehension. *Cuidado*, damn it! An old hag with chicken skin on
her arms grabs for my legs—extravagant swipes, lobster-like, or as if she were
plucking a harp—trying to reach the boxes behind me.

I throw the pastries over the outstretched hands to the edge of the crowd. 88
I fling package after package until there are no more. The carrion crowd hesitates,
draws back.

I sit in the truck for an hour waiting for Father Lucas to finish with them. 89
Some bratty children hang around the truck, trying to get my attention. I watch
instead some old men as they stretch their hands toward a bonfire.

Around seven o'clock, Father Lucas puts the unused consecrated wafers 90
inside the glove compartment. The truck bounces on the dusty roads. There
are few streetlights, no street names. After several dead ends, we are lost.

Down one road we come upon a pack of snarling dogs. Backing up, we 91
come near to backing off a cliff. Once more we drive up the hill. Then Tom
recognizes a house. A right turn, a left. The road takes on gravel. At the base
of a canyon we see the highway leading to Ensenada. In the distance, to the
right, I can see the lights of downtown Tijuana, and beyond, the glamorous
lights that cradle San Diego Bay. It is a sight I never expected to see with Mexican
eyes.

Good Friday. A gray afternoon in Chula Vista, a few miles north of the 92
border. I make several notes. The U.S. Border Patrol station is Spanish colonial
in style. The receptionist is Mexican-American. On the wall of the press office
is a replica of an Aztec stone calendar. There is a press office.

I get introduced to Officer Robert Martinez, my guide to the night. He 93
is about my age and of about my accent, about my build. We drive out. Almost
immediately Martinez stops his truck on a cliff. He hands me his binoculars.
In the foreground are the last two miles of the United States, scrub canyon;
and beyond, Tijuana—the oldest neighborhood, Colonia Libertad; and beyond,
the new commercial skyline; and beyond, the sovereign hills of Mexico, which
are none of our business.

Somewhere up in those Mexican hills Father Lucas is leading a Good Fri-   94
day service. The Crucifixion will be reenacted. There will be a procession. The
man elected to play Christ will drag a pine cross up a gravel path. At the top
of the hill the Christ-elect will be strapped to his cross, the cross will be hoisted.
Cristo will stand on a pedestal on the upraised cross for about half an hour.
He will hear only the wind in his ears as, below him, the crowd prays.

I have elected to spend the afternoon among the chariots and the   95
charioteers. I raise the binoculars of Officer Martinez to my eyes. Throughout
the canyon are people, men, in twos and threes. Down below, perhaps three
miles away, is a level plain called the soccer field—because men who will cross
the border often pass the time before dark playing soccer. A Brueghel-like wintry
haze attends the setting of the sun. There are pale fires: women from Tijuana
cooking chickens to sell. About ten yards below the Otay Mesa, where our truck
is parked, a man, a boy, sits cross-legged by a fire, reading from a book. He
looks up to us, but seems not to be aware of us. His lips move. He looks down
to his book. He is memorizing. "It's almost always a learn-English book," says
Martinez.

Around six o'clock the wind comes up, the sky begins to flap like a tent.   96
I can see the lights of rush-hour traffic at the San Ysidro border crossing. By
now we are cruising a ragged cyclone fence. Some Mexican kids peek through;
they are smiling. "Sometimes people throw rocks," says Martinez.

Again we are on the mesa. It is dark. I hear hoofs of horses; American   97
patrolmen, says Martinez. I can hear the voices of men speaking English. I hear
helicopters.

The copters pour down blades of light that rake through the canyons,   98
rendering crooked straight and the rough places plain. Officer Martinez con-
fides he is using a code on his radio to alert his fellows that he carries press.
Even as I quicken to the chase, I realize my tour will remain pretty much *son
et lumière.* An officer we meet obliges me with his night-vision telescope, from
which I am encouraged to take a random sample of the night.

The night is alive. The night is green as pond water, literally crawling   99
with advancing lines of light.

A VIP shuttle van speeds down a hill stateside, comes to a stop twenty   100
feet beyond our truck. A side door slides open; five men in suits emerge. We
stand together on a bluff, silent, grave as Roman senators in a Victor Mature
movie.

We drive away. Martinez has not turned on his headlamps in order that,   101
at intervals, we may surprise with our flashlights: the post of a fence, a boulder,
a tree…"Nothing."

Ten minutes later we are about a mile from the border at a Burger King,   102
where Martinez says his job is more frustrating than dangerous. He wears a
gun. The danger, he says, is for the people, the Mexicans, in the dark. People
get killed running across freeways. And the dark becomes a gypsy pass; there

are Mexican robbers who prey upon *pollos*—travelers, in Tijuana slang. Women have been raped. Throats slit. Peasants have been robbed. Nearly 26 percent of all those arrested for burglary in San Diego, something like 12 percent of all those arrested on felony charges, are illegal aliens, probably the highwaymen among them.

Around eleven o'clock we see two teen-agers walking along the side of the highway. Their eyes slide into panic as they peer through the window I have rolled down. Martinez gets out of the truck. In Spanish they tell Officer Martinez that they are Americans on their way home from a high school dance. Flashlight. No identification. Chat. Yes, they live in Chula Vista. Just up there. Yes, they had a good time at the dance. Yes, many girls. But what did you say was the name of your high school . . . ? Martinez has decided the game is over. "Get in," he shouts in Spanish.   103

Chula Vista. The streets are quiet. Officer Martinez has his eye on the taxi idling near the phone booth behind the 7-Eleven. ("They call for a taxi to take them into L.A. Anywhere from fifty bucks.") Ignition. Lights. As we hurl forward, the taxi tears away. In front of the phone booth a solitary Mexican man about fifty years old makes one complete turn in our spotlight. He wears a Dodgers cap to make himself invisible. His hands are extended toward us in a clownish gesture of resignation. He smiles as Officer Martinez gets out of the truck, then he bows his head and delivers over his spirit.   104

Most people arrested are docile. They know the rules favor them. They will be taken to a detention center, which is a room full of Mexicans watching Johnny Carson, where they will waive their right to a trial; in the cool of the morning, they will be driven back to the border.   105

Holy Saturday. "Show me Tijuana, what you think I should see." Four times during the week, with four different guides, I am given more or less the identical tour. Downtown *muy rápido.* Then leisurely south to Rosarito Beach, where the gringos have built condos ("like illegal aliens," according to native wit). Then backtrack to Rodriquez Dam. The gray international airport, the smoked-glass twin towers of the Fiesta Americana Hotel, then a slow sweep around the Tijuana Country Club and golf course, climbing toward the grandest houses.   106

Architectural styles derive less from Spanish colonial memory, scarce in Tijuana, than from international eclecticism—Cinderella château, California Bauhaus. One is not rebuffed by the tall gates characteristic of the colonial high style of Mexico; one is rewarded, rather, with picture windows. This is a section of Tijuana known as Chapultepec. The name pays homage to a fancy part of Mexico City. But these houses are constructed to face the United States.   107

Shall we stop the car? Get out for a look?   108

The view from the hills of Tijuana must stand as the modern vision of California. In an earlier generation, California was seen from the east. Think of the Joad family's first view of the paradisical Central Valley. Then think, many generations before the Joads, of Spanish galleons sailing up the Pacific   109 coast. California was first seen by the Spanish—as through Asian eyes—from the sea, west to east.

Show me Tijuana. My final tour of the city ends as an afterthought (because my host wants to buy some liquor for Easter) at the Río Plaza, an American-style shopping mall. Walking through the parking lot in front of Sears, I think I might be in Stockton. But once inside the mall, I realize I have stumbled upon the true zócalo of Tijuana. And it is pagan. 110

Overfragranced crowds of Mexican teen-agers are making their *paseo* between the record shop and the four-theater *cine*-complex. I pause to get my bearings and to measure the proportions of this city within a city. I am reminded of the model of an Aztec metropolis in a Mexico City museum; fancy leads me further to seek the *templo mayor.* I turn around, intending to amuse my host with a lame conceit, and there I see it, belching incense and idolatry, and pulling like a magnet, the great temple of middle-class desire, a supermarket called Comercial Mexicana. More than an American Safeway; Comercial is bigger, more crowded—happier—more prodigiously stocked than any supermarket I have seen. The meat counter ranges from beef intestines to translucent, delicate, slimy fish. To snake. To lung. To snout. To hoof. Boxes of detergent and bags of metallic-looking candies and packages of toilet paper come in gigantic Mexican "family" sizes never seen in America. There are luxuries, conveniences, necessities—everything. Everything! The only souvenir of the New World I decide to bring back with me are five bottles of Liquid Paper correction fluid because I can't believe the price. 111

Easter Sunday. Father Lucas phones me before I check out of my hotel in San Diego. The chubby Mexican who played Jesus in the Good Friday passion refused, when the time came, to take off his shirt, so they had to hoist him up like Christ the King in a gold sweat shirt. In the end he relented, the shirt came off. Somehow it all worked and Tom wishes I had been there. I should have heard the sound the cross made as it was dragged across the gravel. I should have seen the devout old ladies, the awestruck children, the overexcited children. Jesus brought along some cronies to chat with him while he was on the cross, "the way it must have been in Jerusalem—a curious mixture of mood." 112

Tom spent most of Saturday looking for a coffin for a baby. The parents were too poor to afford more than a shoe box. "Even the children here know about death. Brother lifts baby sister up so she can peek into the coffin." For once, says Tom, for his own sake, he was glad of the book—the proscribed magisterium, the consolation of liturgy. 113

Tom says he is going back to the Colonia Flores Magon to celebrate Easter mass in the soccer field. Do I want to come along? 114

I do not. I have only a couple of hours left for one last visit to Tijuana. I do not tell him that I have made plans to meet friends in La Jolla for brunch. I put down the receiver and not for the first time I am glad of the complacencies of the Inter-Continental Hotel. 115

The theme of city life is the theme of difference. People living separately, 116 simultaneously. In all the great cities of the world, as in all the great novels, one senses this. The village mourns in unison, rejoices as one. But in the city . . . in Athens once, I remember sitting in an outdoor café, amid sun and cheese and flies, when a hearse with a picture window slid by, caught in rush-hour traffic and separated from its recognizing mourners—an intersecting narrative line, which, nevertheless, did not make mourners of us, of the café.

Taken together as one, Tijuana and San Diego form perhaps the most fascinating new city in the world, a city of metropolitan disparity, worthy of world-class irony. Within thirty minutes from the lobby of the Inter-Continental, I am once more on Avenida Revolución, where the shopkeepers are sweeping sidewalks, awaiting the onslaught of *turistas*.   117

Inside Tijuana's aquamarine cathedral I sit behind a family of four—a father, a mother, a boy, a girl. They have thick hair. At the elevation of the host, each holds up a tiny homemade cross of stapled palm leaves.   118

Less than an hour later I am in La Jolla.   119

Where friends want to know what I think of Tijuana. I shrug. I imagine the dead baby packed away in orchids. It is there, I say.   120

But what I want to say is that Tijuana is here. It has arrived. Silent as a Trojan horse, larger than a flotilla of scabrous boat people, more confounding in its innocence, in its power of proclamation, than Spielberg's most pious vision of a flying saucer.   121

Later in the afternoon, in a cold wind, we walk around Louis Kahn's brilliant concrete Salk Institute, admiring the way California wanted to imagine its future. We walk on toward the beach. The sky has filled with hang gliders, drifting, silently drifting, like wondrous red- and blue-winged angels, over the sea.   122

1988

Purpose and Meaning

1. In this essay, Rodriguez compares the Mexican city of Tijuana to nearby San Diego, California. In her essay "Travels Back," Margaret Atwood makes comparisons between Canadian and American culture. What similarities exist between Atwood's and Rodriguez's profiles of the United States? Where do they stand in relation to their audience?

2. Rodriguez notes that "Mexico City worries about a cultural spill from the U.S." What aspects of American culture might be perceived as a threat to Mexico? Why?

3. In paragraph 46, Rodriguez writes, "Just as earlier generations used Tijuana to refresh their virtue, so, once again, Californians use Mexico as an opposite planet." In what ways is the U.S. the "user" and Tijuana the "used"? What does Rodriguez mean by "an opposite planet"?

4. Cultural perspective is important in Rodriguez's writing. What does he mean when he writes in paragraph 91, "I can see the lights of downtown Tijuana, and beyond, the glamorous lights that cradle San Diego Bay. It is a sight I never expected to see with Mexican eyes"?

Language and Style

1. At the end of paragraph 1 and the beginning of paragraph 2 are two halves of one sentence. What is the significance of this "broken" sentence? What is on either side of the turnstile?

2. Rodriguez begins countless sentences and paragraphs with the word *Tijuana.* In fact, every sentence in paragraph 5 begins this way. Rodriguez is clearly analyzing the relationship between Tijuana and San Diego, yet San Diego is not named nearly as often. What effect does this refrain of *Tijuana* have on the reader's focus?

3. Rodriguez creates a number of metaphors for the relationship between Mexico and the United States. Analyze the following two metaphors and discuss their effectiveness: "Tijuana is several million lifetimes posing as one street, a metropolis crouched behind a hootchy-kootch curtain" (paragraph 8); "Mexico laid down and the gringo paid in the morning" (paragraph 29). Locate other metaphors and similes and explain their significance.

Strategy and Structure

1. As with his approach in "Complexion," Rodriguez follows a linear progression of time marked at intervals by phrases in the beginning of paragraphs. Locate all of those phrases. What do they denote? What is the overall significance as a "map" for an essay on Mexico and the United States?

2. Rodriguez "shows" us Tijuana and San Diego from several perspectives. In paragraph 3, we see Mexico through the writer's eyes as a child. We see Tijuana "from Mexico's point of view" (in paragraph 11 and following); as American men once saw it (in paragraph 28); and as the University of California library sees it (in paragraph 36). Likewise, we see San Diego and the United States through a Mexican father's eyes (in paragraph 41) and from "Mexico's" point of view (in paragraph 45). How does this varying of perspectives make the essay more interesting as well as sharpen and broaden our view of the cities? How does Rodriguez achieve a unified comparative effect?

Thinking and Writing

1. Compare two cities where you have lived. If you have lived in another country, compare a city in that country to a U.S. city. Or compare the area in your own city where you live with another area in your city where you would not want to live. What are the differences? Does your image of this other area "refresh your virtue"?

2. Take a day trip to a small nearby city or town. Ask locals about the place, read about its history in the library, and write a short sketch of it. Try to capture what makes the city or town unique.

3. Contrast Rodriguez's style with that of Joan Didion or Joyce Carol Oates.

Children of a Marriage

What is culture?   1

The immigrant shrugs. Latin American immigrants come to the United   2
States with only the things they need in mind—not abstractions like culture.
Money. They need dollars. They need food. Maybe they need to get out of
the way of bullets.

Most of us who concern ourselves with Hispanic-American culture, as   3
painters, musicians, writers—or as sons and daughters—are the children of immigrants. We have grown up on this side of the border, in the land of Elvis
Presley and Thomas Edison; our lives are prescribed by the mall, by the DMV
and the Chinese restaurant. Our imaginations yet vascillate between an Edenic
Latin America (the blue door)—which nevertheless betrayed our parents—and
the repellent plate glass of a real American city—which has been good to us.

Hispanic-American culture is where the past meets the future. Hispanic-   4
American culture is not an Hispanic milestone only, not simply a celebration
at the crossroads. America transforms into pleasure what America cannot avoid.
Is it any coincidence that at a time when Americans are troubled by the encroachment of the Mexican desert, Americans discover a chic in cactus, in the
decorator colors of the Southwest? In sand?

Hispanic-American culture of the sort that is now showing (the teen movie,   5
the rock song) may exist in an hourglass; may in fact be irrelevant to the epic.
The U.S. Border Patrol works through the night to arrest the flow of illegal
immigrants over the border, even as Americans wait in line to get into "La
Bamba." Even as Americans vote to declare, once and for all, that English shall
be the official language of the United States, Madonna starts recording in
Spanish.

But then so is Bill Cosby's show irrelevant to the 10 o'clock news, where   6
families huddle together in fear on porches, pointing at the body of the slain
boy bagged in tarpoline. Which is not to say that Bill Cosby or Michael Jackson
are irrelevant to the future or without neo-Platonic influence. Like players within
the play, they prefigure, they resolve. They make black and white audiences
aware of a bond that may not yet exist.

Before a national TV audience, Rita Moreno tells Geraldo Rivera that her   7
dream as an actress is to play a character rather like herself: "I speak English
perfectly well...I'm not dying from poverty...I want to play *that* kind of
Hispanic woman, which is to say, an American citizen." This is an actress talking, these are show-biz pieties. But Moreno expresses as well the general Hispanic-
American predicament. Hispanics want to belong to America without betray-
ing the past.

Hispanics fear losing ground in any negotiation with the American city.   8
We come from an expansive, an intimate culture that has been judged second-
rate by the United States of America. For reasons of pride, therefore, as much
as of affection, we are reluctant to give up our past. Hispanics often express
a fear of "losing" culture. Our fame in the United States has been our resistance
to assimilation.

The symbol of Hispanic culture has been the tongue of flame—Spanish.   9
But the remarkable legacy Hispanics carry from Latin America is not language—
an inflatable skin—but breath itself, capacity of soul, an inclination to live.
The genius of Latin America is the habit of synthesis.

We assimilate. Just over the border there is the example of Mexico, the   10
country from which the majority of U.S. Hispanics come. Mexico is mestizo—
Indian and Spanish. Within a single family, Mexicans are light-skinned and dark.
It is impossible for the Mexican to say, in the scheme of things, where the Indian
begins and the Spaniard surrenders.

In culture as in blood, Latin America was formed by a rape that became   11
a marriage. Due to the absorbing generosity of the Indian, European culture
took on new soil. What Latin America knows is that people create one another
as they marry. In the music of Latin America you will hear the litany of
bloodlines—the African drum, the German accordian, the cry from the minaret.

The United States stands as the opposing New World experiment. In North   12
America the Indian and the European stood apace. Whereas Latin America was
formed by a medieval Catholic dream of one world—of meltdown conversion—
the United States was built up from Protestant individualism. The American
melting pot washes away only embarrassment; it is the necessary initiation into
public life. The American faith is that our national strength derives from
separateness, from "diversity." The glamour of the United States is a carnival
promise: You can lose weight, get rich as Rockefeller, tough up your roots,
get a divorce.

Immigrants still come for the promise. But the United States wavers in   13
its faith. As long as there was space enough, sky enough, as long as economic
success validated individualism, loneliness was not too high a price to pay. (The
cabin on the prairie or the Sony Walkman.)

As we near the end of the American century, two alternative cultures   14
beckon the American imagination—both highly communal cultures—the Asian
and the Latin American. The United States is a literal culture. Americans devour
what we might otherwise fear to become. Sushi will make us corporate warriors.
Combination Plate #3, smothered in mestizo gravy, will burn a hole in our hearts.

Latin America offers passion. Latin America has a life—I mean *life*—big   15
clouds, unambiguous themes, death, birth, faith, that the United States, for
all its quality of life, seems without now. Latin America offers communal riches:
an undistressed leisure, a kitchen table, even a full sorrow. Such is the solitude
of America, such is the urgency of American need, Americans reach right past
a fledgling, homegrown Hispanic-American culture for the real thing—the darker
bottle of Mexican beer; the denser novel of a Latin American master.

For a long time, Hispanics in the United States withheld from the United   16
States our Latin American gift. We denied the value of assimilation. But as our
presence is judged less foreign in America, we will produce a more generous
art, less timid, less parochial. Carlos Santana, Luis Valdez, Linda Ronstadt—
Hispanic Americans do not have a "pure" Latin American art to offer. Expect
bastard themes, expect ironies, comic conclusions. For we live on this side of
the border, where Kraft manufactures bricks of "Mexican style" Velveeta, and
where Jack in the Box serves "Fajita Pita."

The flame-red Chevy floats a song down the Pan American Highway: 17
From a rolled-down window, the grizzled voice of Willie Nelson rises in dis-
embodied harmony with the voice of Julio Iglesias. Gabby Hayes and Cisco
are thus resolved.

Expect marriage. We will change America even as we will be changed.   18
We will disappear with you into a new miscegenation.

Along the border, real conflicts remain. But the ancient tear separating   19
Europe from itself—the Catholic Mediterranean from the Protestant north—
may yet heal itself in the New World. For generations, Latin America has been
the place—the bed—of a confluence of so many races and cultures that Protestant North America shuddered to imagine it.

Imagine it.   20

1988

Purpose and Meaning

1. What aspects of "Across the Borders of History" may have made you a better
   audience for the thesis of this essay?

2. In "Across the Borders of History" one dominant theme was that of immigrants
   seeking refuge in the United States—primarily for jobs, to pursue dreams, to
   partake of the "land of plenty." In this essay, however, Rodriguez reverses those
   roles somewhat. What does he say Hispanics have to give to the United States?

3. Analyze the last line of this essay. What does Rodriguez want imagined? Who
   does he want to imagine it, and why?

Language and Style

1. While Rodriguez's language is largely concrete in "Complexion" and "Across
   the Borders," this essay alternates between concrete imagery and abstract reflections. Locate examples of this procedure. How effective is the contrast? What
   tone does the more abstract, reflective language create?

2. Other contrasts are at work in this essay as well, such as in this sentence from
   paragraph 5: "The U.S. Border Patrol works through the night to arrest the flow
   of illegal immigrants over the border, even as Americans stand patiently in line

for *La Bamba*." This is a contrast of a different kind however. What is its purpose? What point is Rodriguez making about the two cultures when he juxtaposes them syntactically in this way?

3. In "Across the Borders of History," Rodriguez sometimes attributed human characteristics to Tijuana. He uses this same approach in "Children of Marriage" when he writes about the "genius of Latin America" (paragraph 9) and when he writes that "Latin America knows . . . people create one another" (paragraph 11). How does this personification strengthen Rodriguez's characterizations?

4. Adjectives abound in this essay. Latin America, for example, has "passion," a "full sorrow," "darker" beer, and "denser" novels. How do these emphatic words help Rodriguez to make his point? What culture suffers from the depravity of no passion, lighter beer, thinner novels?

Strategy and Structure

1. Rodriguez begins his essay with a giant question. Does he expect an absolute answer? Why does he provoke the reader with such an abstraction? How does the very difficulty of answering such a question help to support his thesis and lead into his extended definition?

2. Throughout this essay Rodriguez develops a series of contrasts. What are they and where do they occur? What principle holds them together?

3. How might this essay be considered an argumentative one? What is Rodriguez's main proposition? What are his key supporting reasons?

4. Why does Rodriguez end his essay with a one-sentence paragraph? What is the effect? Does it end his argument?

Thinking and Writing

1. Characterize U.S. culture today. Is our "culture" the same in every part of the United States? Write your essay as a presentation to a group of visitors from various countries around the world.

2. Evaluate Rodriguez's evolving vision of United States and Hispanic culture in these three essays. What, ultimately, would he wish for these two cultures in terms of the American experience?

ALICE WALKER

Alice Walker's fiction, poetry, and essays have earned her a reputation as a clear and provocative voice for African Americans, particularly black American women. Her book *The Color Purple* (1982) received both the Pulitzer Prize and the American Book Award. Widely read and debated, it was made into a feature film in 1985 that received several Academy Award nominations. The panorama of characters in the novel are almost archetypal in the way they define the African-American experience.

Walker was born February 9, 1944, in Eatonton, Georgia, into a sharecropping family. She studied at Spellman and Sarah Lawrence colleges, and upon graduation became active in the civil rights movement. Walker married a civil rights lawyer in 1967 and was divorced from him in 1976. She has one child, a daughter, Rebecca Grant.

Walker often remembers her mother, as well as her father and her childhood, in her writing. One of her earliest volumes of poetry, *Goodnight, Willie Lee, I'll See You in the Morning* (1979), contains her father's name in the title, and one essay presented here, "Father," deals with him. The essay "In Search of Our Mothers' Gardens" is essentially a tribute to her mother. But it is through her own past that Walker speaks of the collective past of black Americans. She does not, nor do her characters, live in isolation from historical and societal influences. For this reason, her novels—*The Color Purple*, *Meridian* (1976), and her most recent work, *The Temple of My Familiar* (1989)—are in many ways regarded as historical records. Of *Meridian*, Gloria Steinem has remarked that it "is often cited as the best novel of the civil rights movement, and it is taught as part of some American history as well as literature courses."

In her early writings, Walker's particular concern was black women in America. In 1973, she published a collection of short stories called *In Love and Trouble: Stories of Black Women*. This focus continues in her novels and a second collection of short stories entitled *You Can't Keep a Good Woman Down* (1981). However, in later writings, such as the collection *Living by the Word: Selected Writings* (1973–1987), Walker's concerns are universalized to include the suffering and survival of humanity as a whole. She considers issues as diverse as racism in China, Native Americans, and the nuclear arms threat. In essays like "Am I Blue?" she writes eloquently and with metaphorical subtlety about animal nature and its human implications. Always she seeks to expose faults in the American landscape. "I was brought up to try to see what was wrong, and right it. Since I am a writer, writing is how I right it." Walker once described the characters in *The Color Purple* as "all parts of myself, composites and memories and reconstructions" for which she created a "place where they could be free." She is haunted by these yearning, loving spirits. This sense of the characters and writings of Alice Walker coming from a wellspring of memory released into the present is what makes her work so richly alive and deeply rooted in history.

In Search
of Our Mothers' Gardens

I described her own nature and temperament. Told how
they needed a larger life for their expression....I pointed
out that in lieu of proper channels, her emotions had
overflowed into paths that dissipated them. I talked,
beautifully I thought, about an art that would be born, an
art that would open the way for women the likes of her.
I asked her to hope, and build up an inner life against the
coming of that day....I sang, with a strange quiver in my
voice, a promise song.

Jean Toomer, "Avey,"
CANE

The poet speaking to a prostitute who falls asleep while he's talking— 1

When the poet Jean Toomer walked through the South in the early twenties, 2
he discovered a curious thing: black women whose spirituality was so intense,
so deep, so *unconscious*, that they were themselves unaware of the richness
they held. They stumbled blindly through their lives: creatures so abused and
mutilated in body, so dimmed and confused by pain, that they considered
themselves unworthy even of hope. In the selfless abstractions their bodies
became to the men who used them, they became more than "sexual objects,"
more even than mere women: they became "Saints." Instead of being perceived
as whole persons, their bodies became shrines: what was thought to be their
minds became temples suitable for worship. These crazy Saints stared out at
the world, wildly, like lunatics—or quietly, like suicides; and the "God" that
was in their gaze was as mute as a great stone.

Who were these Saints? These crazy, loony, pitiful women? 3

Some of them, without a doubt, were our mothers and grandmothers. 4

In the still heat of the post-Reconstruction South, this is how they seemed 5
to Jean Toomer: exquisite butterflies trapped in an evil honey, toiling away their
lives in an era, a century, that did not acknowledge them, except as "the *mule*
of the world." They dreamed dreams that no one knew—not even themselves,
in any coherent fashion—and saw visions no one could understand. They
wandered or sat about the countryside crooning lullabies to ghosts, and drawing the mother of Christ in charcoal on courthouse walls.

417

They forced their minds to desert their bodies and their striving spirits   6
sought to rise, like frail whirlwinds from the hard red clay. And when those
frail whirlwinds fell, in scattered particles, upon the ground, no one mourned.
Instead, men lit candles to celebrate the emptiness that remained, as people do
who enter a beautiful but vacant space to resurrect a God.

Our mothers and grandmothers, some of them: moving to music not yet   7
written. And they waited.

They waited for a day when the unknown thing that was in them would   8
be made known; but guessed, somehow in their darkness, that on the day of
their revelation they would be long dead. Therefore to Toomer they walked,
and even ran, in slow motion. For they were going nowhere immediate, and
the future was not yet within their grasp. And men took our mothers and grandmothers, "but got no pleasure from it." So complex was their passion and their
calm.

To Toomer, they lay vacant and fallow as autumn fields, with harvest   9
time never in sight: and he saw them enter loveless marriages, without joy; and
become prostitutes, without resistance; and become mothers of children, without
fulfillment.

For these grandmothers and mothers of ours were not Saints, but Artists;   10
driven to a numb and bleeding madness by the springs of creativity in them
for which there was no release. They were Creators, who lived lives of spiritual
waste, because they were so rich in spirituality—which is the basis of Art—
that the strain of enduring their unused and unwanted talent drove them insane.
Throwing away this spirituality was their pathetic attempt to lighten the soul
to a weight their work-worn, sexually abused bodies could bear.

What did it mean for a black woman to be an artist in our grandmothers'   11
time? In our great-grandmothers' day? It is a question with an answer cruel
enough to stop the blood.

Did you have a genius of a great-great-grandmother who died under some   12
ignorant and depraved white overseer's lash? Or was she required to bake biscuits
for a lazy backwater tramp, when she cried out in her soul to paint watercolors
of sunsets, or the rain falling on the green and peaceful pasturelands? Or was
her body broken and forced to bear children (who were more often than not
sold away from her)—eight, ten, fifteen, twenty children—when her one joy
was the thought of modeling heroic figures of rebellion, in stone or clay?

How was the creativity of the black woman kept alive, year after year   13
and century after century, when for most of the years black people have been
in America, it was a punishable crime for a black person to read or write? And
the freedom to paint, to sculpt, to expand the mind with action did not exist.
Consider, if you can bear to imagine it, what might have been the result if singing, too, had been forbidden by law. Listen to the voices of Bessie Smith, Billie
Holiday, Nina Simone, Roberta Flack, and Aretha Franklin, among others, and
imagine those voices muzzled for life. Then you may begin to comprehend the
lives of our "crazy," "Sainted" mothers and grandmothers. The agony of the

lives of women who might have been Poets, Novelists, Essayists, and Short-Story Writers (over a period of centuries), who died with their real gifts stifled within them.

And, if this were the end of the story, we would have cause to cry out   14
in my paraphrase of Okot p'Bitek's great poem:

> O, my clanswomen
> Let us all cry together!
> Come,
> Let us mourn the death of our mother,
> The death of a Queen
> The ash that was produced
> By a great fire!
> O, this homestead is utterly dead
> Close the gates
> With *lacari* thorns,
> For our mother
> The creator of the Stool is lost!
> And all the young women
> Have perished in the wilderness!

But this is not the end of the story, for all the young women—our mothers   15
and grandmothers, *ourselves*—have not perished in the wilderness. And if we ask ourselves why, and search for and find the answer, we will know beyond all efforts to erase it from our minds, just exactly who, and of what, we black American women are.

One example, perhaps the most pathetic, most misunderstood one, can   16
provide a backdrop for our mothers' work: Phillis Wheatley, a slave in the 1700s.

Virginia Woolf, in her book *A Room of One's Own*, wrote that in order   17
for a woman to write fiction she must have two things, certainly: a room of her own (with key and lock) and enough money to support herself.

What then are we to make of Phillis Wheatley, a slave, who owned not   18
even herself? This sickly, frail black girl who required a servant of her own at times—her health was so precarious—and who, had she been white, would have been easily considered the intellectual superior of all the women and most of the men in the society of her day.

Virginia Woolf wrote further, speaking of course not of our Phillis, that   19
"any woman born with a great gift in the sixteenth century [insert "eighteenth century," insert "black woman," insert "born or made a slave"] would certainly have gone crazed, shot herself, or ended her days in some lonely cottage outside the village, half witch, half wizard [insert "Saint"], feared and mocked at. For it needs little skill and psychology to be sure that a highly gifted girl who had tried to use her gift for poetry would have been so thwarted and hindered by contrary instincts [add "chains, guns, the lash, the ownership of one's body by someone else, submission to an alien religion"], that she must have lost her health and sanity to a certainty."

The key words, as they relate to Phillis, are "contrary instincts." For when 20
we read the poetry of Phillis Wheatley—as when we read the novels of Nella
Larsen or the oddly false-sounding autobiography of that freest of all black
women writers, Zora Hurston—evidence of "contrary instincts" is everywhere.
Her loyalties were completely divided, as was, without question, her mind.

But how could this be otherwise? Captured at seven, a slave of wealthy, 21
doting whites who instilled in her the "savagery" of the Africa they "rescued"
her from...one wonders if she was even able to remember her homeland as
she had known it, or as it really was.

Yet, because she did try to use her gift for poetry in a world that made 22
her a slave, she was "so thwarted and hindered by...contrary instincts, that
she...lost her health...." In the last years of her brief life, burdened not only
with the need to express her gift but also with a penniless, friendless "freedom"
and several small children for whom she was forced to do strenuous work to
feed, she lost her health, certainly. Suffering from malnutrition and neglect and
who knows what mental agonies, Phillis Wheatley died.

So torn by "contrary instincts" was black, kidnapped, enslaved Phillis 23
that her description of "the Goddess"—as she poetically called the Liberty she
did not have—is ironically, cruelly humorous. And, in fact, has held Phillis
up to ridicule for more than a century. It is usually read prior to hanging Phillis's
memory as that of a fool. She wrote:

> The Goddess comes, she moves divinely fair,
> Olive and laurel binds her *golden* hair.
> Wherever shines this native of the skies,
> Unnumber'd charms and recent graces rise. [My italics]

It is obvious that Phillis, the slave, combed the "Goddess's" hair every 24
morning; prior, perhaps, to bringing in the milk, or fixing her mistress's lunch.
She took her imagery from the one thing she saw elevated above all others.

With the benefit of hindsight we ask, "How could she?" 25

But at last, Phillis, we understand. No more snickering when your stiff, 26
struggling, ambivalent lines are forced on us. We know now that you were not
an idiot or a traitor; only a sickly little black girl, snatched from your home
and country and made a slave; a woman who still struggled to sing the song
that was your gift, although in a land of barbarians who praised you for your
bewildered tongue. It is not so much what you sang, as that you kept alive,
in so many of our ancestors, *the notion of song.*

Black women are called, in the folklore that so aptly identifies one's status in 27
society, "the *mule* of the world," because we have been handed the burdens
that everyone else—*everyone* else—refused to carry. We have also been called
"Matriarchs," "Superwomen," and "Mean and Evil Bitches." Not to mention
"Castraters" and "Sapphire's Mama." When we have pleaded for understanding,

our character has been distorted; when we have asked for simple caring, we have been handed empty inspirational appellations, then stuck in the farthest corner. When we have asked for love, we have been given children. In short, even our plainer gifts, our labors of fidelity and love, have been knocked down our throats. To be an artist and a black woman, even today, lowers our status in many respects, rather than raises it: and yet, artists we will be.

Therefore we must fearlessly pull out of ourselves and look at and identify   28
with our lives the living creativity some of our great-grandmothers were not allowed to know. I stress *some* of them because it is well known that the majority of our great-grandmothers knew, even without "knowing" it, the reality of their spirituality, even if they didn't recognize it beyond what happened in the singing at church—and they never had any intention of giving it up.

How they did it—those millions of black women who were not Phillis Wheatley,   29
or Lucy Terry or Frances Harper or Zora Hurston or Nella Larsen or Bessie Smith; or Elizabeth Catlett, or Katherine Dunham, either—brings me to the title of this essay, "In Search of Our Mothers' Gardens," which is a personal account that is yet shared, in its theme and its meaning, by all of us. I found, while thinking about the far-reaching world of the creative black woman, that often the truest answer to a question that really matters can be found very close.

In the late 1920s my mother ran away from home to marry my father. Mar-   30
riage, if not running away, was expected of seventeen-year-old girls. By the time she was twenty, she had two children and was pregnant with a third. Five children later, I was born. And this is how I came to know my mother: she seemed a large, soft, loving-eyed woman who was rarely impatient in our home. Her quick, violent temper was on view only a few times a year, when she battled with the white landlord who had the misfortune to suggest to her that her children did not need to go to school.

She made all the clothes we wore, even my brothers' overalls. She made   31
all the towels and sheets we used. She spent the summers canning vegetables and fruits. She spent the winter evenings making quilts enough to cover all our beds.

During the "working" day, she labored beside—not behind—my father   32
in the fields. Her day began before sunup, and did not end until late at night. There was never a moment for her to sit down, undisturbed, to unravel her own private thoughts; never a time free from interruption—by work or the noisy inquiries of her many children. And yet, it is to my mother—and all our mothers who were not famous—that I went in search of the secret of what has fed that muzzled and often mutilated, but vibrant, creative spirit that the black woman has inherited, and that pops out in wild and unlikely places to this day.

But when, you will ask, did my overworked mother have time to know   33
or care about feeding the creative spirit?

The answer is so simple that many of us have spent years discovering it.   34
We have constantly looked high, when we should have looked high—and low.

For example: in the Smithsonian Institution in Washington, D.C., there   35
hangs a quilt unlike any other in the world. In fanciful, inspired, and yet simple
and identifiable figures, it portrays the story of the Crucifixion. It is considered
rare, beyond price. Though it follows no known pattern of quilt-making, and
though it is made of bits and pieces of worthless rags, it is obviously the work
of a person of powerful imagination and deep spiritual feeling. Below this quilt
I saw a note that says it was made by "an anonymous Black woman in Alabama,
a hundred years ago."

If we could locate this "anonymous" black woman from Alabama, she   36
would turn out to be one of our grandmothers—an artist who left her mark
in the only materials she could afford, and in the only medium her position
in society allowed her to use.

As Virginia Woolf wrote further, in *A Room of One's Own*:   37

Yet genius of a sort must have existed among women as it must have existed
among the working class. [Change this to "slaves" and "the wives and daughters
of sharecroppers."] Now and again an Emily Brontë or a Robert Burns [change
this to "a Zora Hurston or a Richard Wright"] blazes out and proves its presence.
But certainly it never got itself on to paper. When, however, one reads of a witch
being ducked, of a woman possessed by devils [or "Sainthood"], of a wise woman
selling herbs [our root workers], or even a very remarkable man who had a
mother, then I think we are on the track of a lost novelist, a suppressed poet,
of some mute and inglorious Jane Austen.... Indeed, I would venture to guess
that Anon, who wrote so many poems without signing them, was often a
woman....

And so our mothers and grandmothers have, more often than not   38
anonymously, handed on the creative spark, the seed of the flower they
themselves never hoped to see: or like a sealed letter they could not plainly read.

And so it is, certainly, with my own mother. Unlike "Ma" Rainey's songs,   39
which retained their creator's name even while blasting forth from Bessie Smith's
mouth, no song or poem will bear my mother's name. Yet so many of the stories
that I write, that we all write, are my mother's stories. Only recently did I fully
realize this: that through years of listening to my mother's stories of her life,
I have absorbed not only the stories themselves, but something of the manner
in which she spoke, something of the urgency that involves the knowledge that
her stories—like her life—must be recorded. It is probably for this reason that
so much of what I have written is about characters whose counterparts in real
life are so much older than I am.

But the telling of these stories, which came from my mother's lips as   40
naturally as breathing, was not the only way my mother showed herself as an
artist. For stories, too, were subject to being distracted, to dying without conclusion. Dinners must be started, and cotton must be gathered before the big

rains. The artist that was and is my mother showed itself to me only after many years. This is what I finally noticed:

Like Mem, a character in *The Third Life of Grange Copeland*, my mother [41] adorned with flowers whatever shabby house we were forced to live in. And not just your typical straggly country stand of zinnias, either. She planted ambitious gardens—and still does—with over fifty different varieties of plants that bloom profusely from early March until late November. Before she left home for the fields, she watered her flowers, chopped up the grass, and laid out new beds. When she returned from the fields she might divide clumps of bulbs, dig a cold pit, uproot and replant roses, or prune branches from her taller bushes or trees—until night came and it was too dark to see.

Whatever she planted grew as if by magic, and her fame as a grower of [42] flowers spread over three counties. Because of her creativity with her flowers, even my memories of poverty are seen through a screen of blooms—sunflowers, petunias, roses, dahlias, forsythia, spirea, delphiniums, verbena...and on and on.

And I remember people coming to my mother's yard to be given cuttings [43] from her flowers; I hear again the praise showered on her because whatever rocky soil she landed on, she turned into a garden. A garden so brilliant with colors, so original in its design, so magnificent with life and creativity, that to this day people drive by our house in Georgia—perfect strangers and imperfect strangers—and ask to stand or walk among my mother's art.

I notice that it is only when my mother is working in her flowers that [44] she is radiant, almost to the point of being invisible—except as Creator: hand and eye. She is involved in work her soul must have. Ordering the universe in the image of her personal conception of Beauty.

Her face, as she prepares the Art that is her gift, is a legacy of respect [45] she leaves to me, for all that illuminates and cherishes life. She has handed down respect for the possibilities—and the will to grasp them.

For her, so hindered and intruded upon in so many ways, being an artist [46] has still been a daily part of her life. This ability to hold on, even in very simple ways, is work black women have done for a very long time.

This poem is not enough, but it is something, for the woman who literal- [47] ly covered the holes in our walls with sunflowers:

> They were women then
> My mama's generation
> Husky of voice—Stout of
> Step
> With fists as well as
> Hands
> How they battered down
> Doors
> And ironed

Starched white
Shirts
How they led
Armies
Headragged Generals
Across mined
Fields
Booby-trapped
Kitchens
To discover books
Desks
A place for us
How they knew what we
Must know
Without knowing a page
Of it
Themselves.

Guided by my heritage of a love of beauty and a respect for strength—in   48
search of my mother's garden, I found my own.

And perhaps in Africa over two hundred years ago, there was just such   49
a mother; perhaps she painted vivid and daring decorations in oranges and
yellows and greens on the walls of her hut; perhaps she sang—in a voice like
Roberta Flack's—*sweetly* over the compounds of her village; perhaps she wove
the most stunning mats or told the most ingenious stories of all the village
storytellers. Perhaps she was herself a poet—though only her daughter's name
is signed to the poems that we know.

Perhaps Phillis Wheatley's mother was also an artist.   50

Perhaps in more than Phillis Wheatley's biological life is her mother's   51
signature made clear.

1974

Purpose and Meaning

1. In the title of this essay, Alice Walker uses the possessive pronoun *our*. To whom
   does *our* refer? What is her purpose in writing the essay? Later in the essay, she
   writes of her own mother's garden. What do the gardens symbolize?

2. Why do the women Walker writes of force "their minds to desert their bodies"
   (paragraph 6)? How are their bodies "shrines" (paragraph 2)? What is the effect
   on a human being when she is made into a shrine or temple?

3. Compare George Eliot's prelude, quoted in Stephen Jay Gould's essay "Women's
   Brains," with these words from paragraph 10: "For these grandmothers and
   mothers of ours were not Saints, but Artists; driven to a numb and bleeding
   madness by the springs of creativity in them for which there was no release."

Language and Style

1. Strongly emotional language characterizes Walker's style early in the essay—for example, "exquisite butterflies trapped in evil honey" (paragraph 5); "they dreamed dreams no one knew" (paragraph 5); "their striving spirits sought to rise" (paragraph 6). Locate other instances of emotional language. What effect does such language have on the reader? Why does she write in such a lyrical, emotional voice?

2. Beginning in paragraph 13, Walker's voice becomes somewhat less lyrical and more biting. Paragraphs 19 and 37 in particular have no talk of souls or dreams or butterflies. Instead she takes a piece from Virginia Woolf, already sharp in tone, and sharpens it further with her own insertions. What effect might this have on white male readers? What effect might an essay expressive of such anger have on black women? Who is Walker probably writing for?

3. Walker uses many names to describe the black American woman: saint, "the mule of the world," artist, creator. She also lists what they might have been: poets, novelists, essayists (paragraph 13). Why does she capitalize all the names? In paragraph 27, she lists yet more names. What is their significance? What power do names have in language? Recall Maxine Hong Kingston's "No Name Woman." Do Walker's women have individual, given names? Why not?

Strategy and Structure

1. Why does Walker begin by quoting Jean Toomer? How does this quote relate to her later quote from Virginia Woolf? How do these quotes help to universalize Walker's thesis? What common experiences do black women share with other women? Are hidden or uncultivated gardens unique to black women? What is the essence of Walker's argument?

2. Identify the key examples that Walker uses to organize her essay. Which two examples are more extended than the others?

3. Why does Walker wait until nearly the end of this essay to introduce her own mother? Does she want this to be an essay only about her personal search?

Thinking and Writing

1. Walker paraphrases a poem in paragraph 14 as well as one of her own poems in paragraph 47. Analyze the meaning and effectiveness of these poems. How do they add to, or detract from, the essay?

2. Interview your mother, grandmother, or others close to you. Ask them whether they have ever had a "garden," a talent they would like to have cultivated had their lives been different. Ask whether they did cultivate their talents and what advantages they had if they did; or ask what inhibited them if they did not. Take notes on your conversations and compile these notes into an organized form. Give your work a title.

3. Write your own extended definition of what it means to be a woman in American society. How does that definition change when you ask what it means to be a black woman in society?

o—●—o—●—o—●—o—●—o—●—o—●—o

Am I Blue?

"Ain't these tears in these eyes tellin' you?"

For about three years my companion and I rented a small house in the country that stood on the edge of a large meadow that appeared to run from the end of our deck straight into the mountains. The mountains, however, were quite far away, and between us and them there was, in fact, a town. It was one of the many pleasant aspects of the house that you never really were aware of this.

It was a house of many windows, low, wide, nearly floor to ceiling in the living room, which faced the meadow, and it was from one of these that I first saw our closest neighbor, a large white horse, cropping grass, flipping its mane, and ambling about—not over the entire meadow, which stretched well out of sight of the house, but over the five or so fenced-in acres that were next to the twenty-odd that we had rented. I soon learned that the horse, whose name was Blue, belonged to a man who lived in another town, but was boarded by our neighbors next door. Occasionally, one of the children, usually a stocky teen-ager, but sometimes a much younger girl or boy, could be seen riding Blue. They would appear in the meadow, climb up on his back, ride furiously for ten or fifteen minutes, then get off, slap Blue on the flanks, and not be seen again for a month or more.

There were many apple trees in our yard, and one by the fence that Blue could almost reach. We were soon in the habit of feeding him apples, which he relished, especially because by the middle of summer the meadow grasses—so green and succulent since January—had dried out from lack of rain, and Blue stumbled about munching the dried stalks half-heartedly. Sometimes he would stand very still just by the apple tree, and when one of us came out he would whinny, snort loudly, or stamp the ground. This meant, of course: I want an apple.

It was quite wonderful to pick a few apples, or collect those that had fallen to the ground overnight, and patiently hold them, one by one, up to his large, toothy mouth. I remained as thrilled as a child by his flexible dark lips, huge, cubelike teeth that crunched the apples, core and all, with such finality, and his high broad-breasted *enormity;* beside which, I felt small indeed. When I was a child, I used to ride horses, and was especially friendly with one named Nan until the day I was riding and my brother deliberately spooked her and I was thrown, head first, against the trunk of a tree. When I came to, I was in bed and my mother was bending worriedly over me; we silently agreed that perhaps horseback riding was not the safest sport for me. Since then I have walked, and prefer walking to horseback riding—but I had forgotten the depth of feeling one could see in horses' eyes.

I was therefore unprepared for the expression in Blue's. Blue was lonely.   5
Blue was horribly lonely and bored. I was not shocked that this should be the case; five acres to tramp by yourself, endlessly, even in the most beautiful of meadows—and his was—cannot provide many interesting events, and once rainy season turned to dry that was about it. No, I was shocked that I had forgotten that human animals and nonhuman animals can communicate quite well; if we are brought up around animals as children we take this for granted. By the time we are adults we no longer remember. However, the animals have not changed. They are in fact *completed* creations (at least they seem to be, so much more than we) who are not likely *to* change; it is their nature to express themselves. What else are they going to express? And they do. And, generally speaking, they are ignored.

After giving Blue the apples, I would wander back to the house, aware   6
that he was observing me. Were more apples not forthcoming then? Was that to be his sole entertainment for the day? My partner's small son had decided he wanted to learn how to piece a quilt; we worked in silence on our respective squares as I thought . . .

Well, about slavery: about white children, who were raised by black peo-   7
ple, who knew their first all-accepting love from black women, and then, when they were twelve or so, were told they must "forget" the deep levels of communication between themselves and "mammy" that they knew. Later they would be able to relate quite calmly, "My old mammy was sold to another good family." "My old mammy was ——— ———." Fill in the blank. Many more years later a white woman would say: "I can't understand these Negroes, these blacks. What do they want? They're so different from us."

And about the Indians, considered to be "like animals" by the "settlers"   8
(a very benign euphemism for what they actually were), who did not understand their description as a compliment.

And about the thousands of American men who marry Japanese, Korean,   9
Filipina, and other non-English-speaking women and of how happy they report they are, *"blissfully,"* until their brides learn to speak English, at which point the marriages tend to fall apart. What then did the men see, when they looked into the eyes of the women they married, before they could speak English? Apparently only their own reflections.

I thought of society's impatience with the young. "Why are they playing   10
the music so loud?" Perhaps the children have listened to much of the music

of oppressed people their parents danced to before they were born, with its passionate but soft cries for acceptance and love, and they have wondered why their parents failed to hear.

I do not know how long Blue had inhabited his five beautiful, boring acres before we moved into our house; a year after we had arrived—and had also traveled to other valleys, other cities, other worlds—he was still there. 11

But then, in our second year at the house, something happened in Blue's life. One morning, looking out the window at the fog that lay like a ribbon over the meadow, I saw another horse, a brown one, at the other end of Blue's field. Blue appeared to be afraid of it, and for several days made no attempt to go near. We went away for a week. When we returned, Blue had decided to make friends and the two horses ambled or galloped along together, and Blue did not come nearly as often to the fence underneath the apple tree. 12

When he did, bringing his new friend with him, there was a different look in his eyes. A look of independence, of self-possession, of inalienable *horse*ness. His friend eventually became pregnant. For months and months there was, it seemed to me, a mutual feeling between me and the horses of justice, of peace. I fed apples to them both. The look in Blue's eyes was one of unabashed, "this is *it*ness." 13

It did not, however, last forever. One day, after a visit to the city, I went out to give Blue some apples. He stood waiting, or so I thought, though not beneath the tree. When I shook the tree and jumped back from the shower of apples, he made no move. I carried some over to him. He managed to half-crunch one. The rest he let fall to the ground. I dreaded looking into his eyes—because I had of course noticed that Brown, his partner, had gone—but I did look. If I had been born into slavery, and my partner had been sold or killed, my eyes would have looked like that. The children next door explained that Blue's partner had been "put with him" (the same expression that old people used, I had noticed, when speaking of an ancestor during slavery who had been impregnated by her owner) so that they could mate and she conceive. Since that was accomplished, she had been taken back by her owner, who lived somewhere else. 14

Will she be back? I asked. 15

They didn't know. 16

Blue was like a crazed person. Blue *was*, to me, a crazed person. He galloped furiously, as if he were being ridden, around and around his five beautiful acres. He whinnied until he couldn't. He tore at the ground with his hooves. He butted himself against his single shade tree. He looked always and always toward the road down which his partner had gone. And then, occasionally, when he came up for apples, or I took apples to him, he looked at me. It was a look so piercing, so full of grief, a look so *human*, I almost laughed (I felt too sad to cry) to think there are people who do not know that animals suffer. People like me who have forgotten, and daily forget, all that animals try to tell us. "Everything you do to us will happen to you; we are your teachers, 17 as you are ours. We are one lesson" is essentially it, I think. There are those who never once have even considered animals' rights: those who have been taught that animals acutally want to be used and abused by us, as small children "love" to be frightened, or women "love" to be mutilated and raped. . . . They are the great-grandchildren of those who honestly thought, because someone taught them this: "Women can't think," and "niggers can't faint." But most disturbing of all, in Blue's large brown eyes was a new look, more painful than the look of despair: the look of disgust with human beings, with life, the look of hatred. And it was odd what the look of hatred did. It gave him, for the first time, the look of a beast. And what that meant was that he had put up a barrier within to protect himself from further violence; all the apples in the world wouldn't change that fact.

And so Blue remained, a beautiful part of our landscape, very peaceful   18
to look at from the window, white against the grass. Once a friend came to visit and said, looking out on the soothing view: "And it *would* have to be a *white* horse; the very image of freedom." And I thought, yes, the animals are forced to become for us merely "images" of what they once so beautifully expressed. And we are used to drinking milk from containers showing "contented" cows, whose real lives we want to hear nothing about, eating eggs and drumsticks from "happy" hens, and munching hamburgers advertised by bulls of integrity who seem to command their fate.

As we talked of freedom and justice one day for all, we sat down to steaks.   19
I am eating misery, I thought, as I took the first bite. And spit it out.

1986

Purpose and Meaning

1. If this essay were simply a description of a horse in a meadow, would it have been as interesting? Does it have a meaning beyond pure description? What comment is Walker making on societal attitudes toward animals (paragraph 5), young people (paragraph 10), and people of other cultures (paragraphs 8 and 9)?

2. Walker writes that some people "have been taught that animals actually want to be used and abused by us, as small children 'love' to be frightened, or women 'love' to be mutilated and raped." What happens to Blue that leads Walker to say this? What is the connection between this isolated incident and Walker's more general condemnation? Is she justified in making this generalization? How does she expect her audience to respond to this assumption?

Language and Style

1. The first sentence in paragraph 2 extends for six lines. Many of the sentences are long series of dependent clauses that ramble along. How is this similar to

speech? Would a formal structure have been more effective? What relationship does this establish between writer and reader?

2. The first several paragraphs of this essay are descriptive. Here, Walker writes in a rather gentle manner. How does this voice compare to the opening of "In Search of Our Mothers' Gardens?" How is the language plainer and less dramatic?

3. By paragraph 5, language with a moral message enters the essay—a prominent characteristic seen also in "In Search of Our Mothers' Gardens." Walker discusses the ability of animals to communicate and the ability of human beings to ignore their communications. Would her essay have been more or less effective without this commentary? Would you have discerned the same message about human beings and animals without Walker's explications?

Strategy and Structure

1. Why does Walker delay getting to her commentary until later in the essay? If she had begun with a statement about how human beings fail to learn from other species, would the reader have stayed interested? In what ways is it more effective to have the essay's focus on a particular horse?

2. As in many of the essays in this collection, the author begins by establishing the reader's perspective. Walker describes the setting and gives us a sense of place. How does this make the reader feel and why?

3. Walker takes great care to describe Blue: how he stomped for an apple (paragraph 3); how he crunched the apples she fed to him (paragraph 6); the expression in his eyes (paragraph 5); and how he observed her walking away from him (paragraph 6). In what way does this help us to "identify" with Blue? What effect does our identification with him have on our feelings toward him? How does it prepare us for the disturbing climax in paragraph 17?

Thinking and Writing

1. In the final paragraphs of this essay, Walker raises an important issue about human beings and our conflicting attitudes toward animals. On the one hand, we love our pets and we admire animals in zoos and the wilderness. On the other hand, many people condescend to them, hunt them for sport, and kill them for food. Write an essay stating your opinion on this issue. Are we inconsistent in our treatment of other species, or are we not? Do we have a natural right to use animals as we please? Do we have an obligation—moral or otherwise—to treat them with respect and care?

2. Argue for or against one of these practices: (a) hunting; (b) eating meat; (c) keeping animals in zoos.

Father

Though it is more difficult to write about my father than about my mother, since I spent less time with him and knew him less well, it is equally as liberating. Partly this is because writing about people helps us to understand them, and understanding them helps us to accept them as part of ourselves. Since I share so many of my father's characteristics, physical and otherwise, coming to terms with what he has meant to my life is crucial to a full acceptance and love of myself.

I'm positive my father never understood why I wrote. I wonder sometimes if the appearance, in 1968, of my first book, *Once*, poems largely about my experiences in the Civil Rights movement and in other countries, notably African and Eastern European, surprised him. It is frustrating that, because he is now dead, I will never know.

In fact, what I regret most about my relationship with my father is that it did not improve until after his death. For a long time I felt so shut off from him that we were unable to talk. I hadn't the experience, as a younger woman, to ask the questions I would ask now. These days I feel we are on good terms, spiritually (my dreams of him are deeply loving and comforting ones), and that we both understand our relationship was a casualty of exhaustion and circumstances. My birth, the eighth child, unplanned, must have elicited more anxiety than joy. It hurts me to think that for both my parents, poor people, my arrival represented many more years of backbreaking and spirit-crushing toil.

I grew up to marry someone very unlike my father, as I knew him—though I feel sure he had these qualities himself as a younger man—someone warm, openly and spontaneously affectionate, who loved to talk to me about everything, including my work. I now share my life with another man who has these qualities. But I would give a lot to be able to talk grownup to grownup with Daddy. I'd like to tell him how hard I am working to understand. And about the humor and solace I occasionally find (while writing *The Color Purple*, for instance, in which some of his early life is imagined) in the work.

> My father
> (back blistered)
> beat me
> because I
> could not
> stop crying.

> He'd had
> enough "fuss"
> he said
> for one damn
> voting day.

In my heart, I have never wanted to be at odds with my father, but I have   5
felt, over the years, especially when I was younger, that he gave me no choice.
Perhaps if I could have relaxed and been content to be his favorite, there would
have been a chance for closeness, but because a sister whom I loved was clearly
not favorite material I did not want to be either. When I look back over my
life, I see a pattern in my relationships going back to this, and in my love relationships I have refused men who loved me (at least for a time) if they in turn
were loved by another woman but did not love her in return. I am the kind
of woman who could positively forbid a married lover to leave his wife.

The poem above is one of my earliest as an adult, written after an abor-   6
tion of which my father would not have approved, in which I felt that visceral
understanding of a situation that for a poet can mean a poem. My father far
away in the South, me in college in the North—how far away from each other!
Yet in the pain of the moment and the illumination of some of what was wrong
between us, how close. If he ever read the poem, I wonder what he thought.
We never discussed my work, though I thought he tended to become more like
some of my worst characters the older he got. I remember going home once
and being told by my mother of some of the curses he was capable of, and hardly
believing her, since the most I'd ever heard my father say was "God damn!"
and I could count the number of times on toes and fingers. (In fact, his favorite
curse, when a nail refused to go in straight or he dropped the hammer on his
sore corn was "God damn the goddam luck to the devil!" which always sounded
rather ineffectual and humorous to me, and which, thinking of it, I hear him
say and see his perspiring dark face.)

Did he actually beat me on voting day? Probably not. I suppose the illegal   7
abortion caused me to understand what living under other people's politics can
force us to do. The only time I remember his beating me was one day after he'd
come home tired and hungry from the dairy (where he and my brothers milked
a large herd of cows morning and afternoon), and my brother Bobby, three
years older than me and a lover of chaos, and I were fighting. He had started
it, of course. My mother, sick of our noise, spoke to my father about it, and
without asking questions he took off his belt and flailed away, indiscriminate-
ly, at the two of us.

Why do certain things stick in the mind? I recall a scene, much earlier,   8
when I was only three or so, in which my father questioned me about a fruit
jar I had accidentally broken. I felt he knew I had broken it; at the same time,
I couldn't be sure. Apparently breaking it was, in any event, the wrong thing
to have done. I could say, Yes, I broke the jar, and risk a whipping for breaking

something valuable, or, No, I did not break it, and perhaps bluff my way through.

I've never forgotten my feeling that he really wanted me to tell the truth. 9 And because he seemed to desire it—and the moments during which he waited for my reply seemed quite out of time, so much so I can still feel them, and, as I said, I was only three, if that—I confessed. I broke the jar, I said. I think he hugged me. He probably didn't, but I still feel as if he did, so embraced did I feel by the happy relief I noted on his face and by the fact that he didn't punish me at all, but seemed, instead, pleased with me. I think it was at that moment that I resolved to take my chances with the truth, although as the years rolled on I was to break more serious things in his scheme of things than fruit jars.

It was the unfairness of the beating that keeps it fresh in my mind. (And 10 this was thirty-seven years ago!) And my disappointment at the deterioration of my father's ethics. And yet, since I am never happy in my heart when estranged from my father, any more than I would be happy shut off from sunlight, in writing this particular poem I tried to see my father's behavior in a context larger than our personal relationship.

Actually, my father was two fathers. 11

To the first four of his children he was one kind of father, to the second 12 set of four he was another kind. Whenever I talk to the elder set I am astonished at the picture they draw, for the man they describe bears little resemblance to the man I knew. For one thing, the man they knew was physically healthy, whereas the man I knew was almost always sick; not sick enough to be in bed, or perhaps he was but with so many children to feed he couldn't afford to lie down, but "dragging-around" sick, in the manner of the very poor. Overweight, high blood pressure, diabetes, or, as it was called, "sugar," rotten teeth. There are certain *facts*, however, that identify our father as the same man; one of which is that, in the 1930s, my father was one of the first black men to vote in Eatonton, Georgia, among a group of men like himself he helped organize, mainly poor sharecroppers with large families, totally at the mercy of the white landlords. He voted for Roosevelt. He was one of the leading supporters of the local one-room black school, and according to everyone who knew him then, including my older brothers and sister, believed in education above all else. Years later, when I knew him, he seemed fearful of both education and politics and disappointed and resentful as well.

And why not? Though he risked his life and livelihood to vote more than 13 once, nothing much changed in his world. Cotton prices continued low. Dairying was hard. White men and women continued to run things, badly. In his whole life my father never had a vacation. (Of course my mother had less of one: she could not even get in the car and drive off to town, as he could.) Education merely seemed to make his children more critical of him. When I went south in the mix-sixties to help register voters, I stopped by our house to say hello but never told either of my parents what I planned to do. I didn't want them to worry about my safety, and it never occurred to me that they cared much about the vote. My father was visibly ill, paranoid, complaining the whole time of my mother's religious activities (she had become a Jehovah's Witness). Then, for no apparent reason, he would come out with one of those startlingly intelligent comments about world affairs or some absolutely clear insight into the deficiencies of national leaders, and I would be reminded of the father I didn't know.

For years I have held on to another early memory of my life between the   14
ages of two and four. Every afternoon a tired but jolly very black man came up to me with arms outstretched. I flew into them to be carried, to be hugged, to be kissed. For years I thought this black man was my father. But no. He was my oldest brother, Fred, whose memories of my father are, surprisingly, as painful as *my* memories of him, because as my father's first child, and a son, he was subjected to my father's very confused notions of what constituted behavior suitable for a male. And of course my father himself didn't really know. He was in his late teens, a child himself, when he married. His mother had been murdered, by a man who claimed to love her, when he was eleven. His father, to put it very politely, drank, and terrorized his children.

My father was so confused that when my sister Ruth appeared in the world   15
and physically resembled his mother, and sounded like his mother, and had similar expressions, he rejected her and missed no opportunity that I ever saw to put her down. I, of course, took the side of my sister, forfeiting my chance to be my father's favorite among the second set of children, as my oldest sister, Mamie, was favorite among the first. In her case the favoritism seemed outwardly caused by her very light color, and of course she was remarkably intelligent as well. In my case, my father seemed partial to me because of my "smartness" and forthrightness, but more obviously because of my hair, which was the longest and "best" in the family.

And yet, my father taught me two things that have been important to   16
me: he taught me not to bother telling lies, because the listener might be delighted with the truth, and he told me never to cut my hair. Though I have tried not to lie, the sister he rejected and I loved became a beautician, and one of the first things she did—partly in defiance of him—was to cut my shoulder-blade-length hair. I did not regret it so much while in high school and college (everyone kept their hair short, it seemed), but years later, after I married, I grew it long again, almost as long as it had been when I was growing up. I'd had it relaxed to feathers. When I walked up to my father, as he was talking to a neighbor, I stooped a little and placed his hand on my head. I though he'd be pleased. "A woman's hair is her glory," he'd always said. He paid little attention. When the black power movement arrived, with its emphasis on cropped natural hair, I did the job myself, filling the face bowl and bathroom floor with hair and shocking my husband when he arrived home.

Only recently have I come to believe he was right in wanting me to keep   17
my hair. After years of short hair, of cutting my hair back each time it raised its head, so to speak, I have begun to feel each time as if I am mutilating my

antennae (which is how Rastafarians, among others, think of hair) and attenuating my power. It seems imperative not to cut my hair anymore.

I didn't listen to my father because I assumed he meant that in the eyes   18
of a *man*, in his eyes, a woman's hair is her glory (unfortunately, he wore his own head absolutely clean-shaven all his life); and that is probably what he did mean. But now I begin to sense something else, that there is power (would an ancient translation of glory *be* power?) in uncut hair itself. The power (and glory) perhaps of the untamed, the undomesticated; in short, the wild. A wildness about the head, as the Rastas have discovered, places us somehow in the loose and spacious freedom of Jah's universe. Hippies, of course, knew this, too.

As I write, my own hair reaches just below my ears. It is at the dangerous   19
stage at which I usually butt my forehead against the mirror and in resignation over not knowing "what to do with it" cut it off. But this time I have thought ahead and have encased it in braids made of someone else's hair. I expect to wear them, braces for the hair, so to speak, until my own hair replaces them. Eventually I will be able, as I was when a child, to tie my hair under my chin. But mostly I would like to set it free.

My father would have loved Jesse Jackson. On the night Jesse addressed   20
the Democratic convention I stayed close to my radio. In my backwoods cabin, linked to the world only by radio, I felt something like my father must have, since he lived most of his life before television and far from towns. He would have appreciated Jesse's oratorical gift, and, unlike some newscasters who seemed to think of it primarily as technique, he would have felt, as I did, the transformation of the spirit of the man implicit in the words he chose to say. He would have felt, as I did, that in asking for forgiveness as well as votes and for patience as well as commitment to the Democratic party, Jackson lost nothing and won almost everything: a cleared conscience and peace of mind.

My father was never able to vote for a black candidate for any national   21
or local political office. By the time black people were running for office and occasionally winning elections, in the late sixties and early seventies, he was too sick to respond with the exhilaration he must have felt. On the night of Jackson's speech, I felt it for him; along with the grief that in neither of our lifetimes is the United States likely to choose the best leadership offered to it. This is the kind of leader, the kind of ever-growing, ever-expanding spirit *you* might have been, Daddy, I thought—and damn it, I love you for what you might have been. And thinking of you now, merging the two fathers that you were, remembering how tightly I hugged you as a small child returning home after two long months at a favorite aunt's, and with what apparent joy you lifted me beside your cheek; knowing now, at forty, what it takes out of body and spirit to go and how much more to stay, and having learned, too, by now, some of the pitiful confusions in behavior caused by ignorance and pain, I love you no less for what you were.

1984

Purpose and Meaning

1. Walker writes in the opening paragraph that "writing about people helps us to understand them." How is this so? She goes on to write that "understanding them helps us to accept them as a part of ourselves." How is this similar to Margaret Atwood's thesis in "Travels Back"? What, specifically, is Walker's thesis?

2. Recall Richard Rodriguez's account of when his mother told him to cover his dark skin with a towel. Rodriguez associates that incident with his growth as an individual and as a writer. Walker tells of an incident that was just as significant in her development. She breaks a fruit jar and subsequently tells her father the truth about it, anticipating his delight with her honesty (paragraphs 8 and 9). How does this incident affect her as an individual? How does her need to tell the truth come through in her writing?

3. In paragraph 12, as Walker struggles to describe her and her siblings' father, she writes, "There are certain *facts*, however, that identify our father as the same man." What is the difference between the "facts" and the rest of her description? How much, if anything, can we know of other people that is pure fact?

Language and Style

1. In this essay there is very little imagery or metaphor. Walker's language is direct and unembellished. Is the absence of metaphor notable? How does it affect the style and the reader's response?

2. In what ways is Walker's writing in this essay more conversational than in many of the other essays in this collection?

Strategy and Structure

1. At the beginning of the essay, Walker simply announces that she is writing about her father in an effort to understand him. Is this opening effective? What reason could she have for avoiding a more leisurely or more poetic introduction?

2. This essay is obviously not fiction. But neither is it purely autobiographical. It is closer to journal writing than anything else. What makes this writing journal-like? Why would this be an appropriate approach for Walker's subject?

3. Walker alternates between discussion of herself as a child and as an adult. How does this juxtaposition aid the reader in understanding both Walker and her father? If we were limited to insights about her early relationship with him, would our understanding be as deep? Of whom do we have a better, more rounded understanding—Walker or her father? Why?

4. Beginning in paragraph 14, Walker takes a long diversion about hair and its social and political power. Is this an appropriate diversion? Why or why not?

Thinking and Writing

1. Adopting Walker's journal-like method of writing, explore your relationship with your father. As she did, make reference to both your past and present, and give your readers factual information about your father.

2. Examine the relationship between style, subject matter, and the reader's response in "Father."

3. Compare Walker's writing in this essay with Maxine Hong Kingston's in "No Name Woman." Consider writing styles, such as the use of figurative language and directness of speech. Also consider issues of content, such as cultural backgrounds and attitudes toward telling the truth.

ANNIE DILLARD

Annie Dillard was born April 30, 1945, in Pittsburgh, Pennsylvania. She received a B.A. from Hollins College in 1967 and an M.A. the following year. In 1974, she published a collection of poetry, *Tickets for a Prayer Wheel,* and a collection of essays, *Pilgrim at Tinker Creek,* for which she received a Pulitzer Prize for nonfiction. Since then, Dillard has published several books, including the essay collection *Teaching a Stone to Talk* (1982); a memoir, *An American Childhood* (1987); and *A Writing Life* (1989). Dillard is a writer of major stature whose fascination with the natural world and its mystery has led some to compare her writing with that of Thoreau and his famous pastoral meditation, *Walden.*

Echoes of Thoreau's vow to "live life to the bone" and "suck out all its marrow" can be heard in Dillard's urging in "Push It" for young writers to "write as if you were dying. . . . Examine all things intensely and relentlessly." And so she does in her own writing, examining with an intense, relentless eye, whether the subject is an old snakeskin, a total eclipse, or her mother's curious sense of humor. Interwoven with Dillard's observations of the natural world is her fascination with mystery as the manifestation of God. Typically, in essays like "Singing with the Fundamentalists," Dillard finds that everything in life is holy. One critic has written that "Dillard brings to her work an artist's eye, a scientist's curiosity, a metaphysician's mind, all woven together in what might be called, essentially, a theologian's quest." Dillard herself admits, "I am a wanderer with a background in theology and a penchant for quirky facts."

Not only does Dillard work as a writer and teach writing, but much of her recent work has been about the writing process. In an interview, she lamented the mistaken impression some readers have that "you just sit on a tree stump and take dictation from some little chipmunk!" Instead, writing is "hard, conscious, terribly frustrating work!" The rich, poetic journey into nature, its mystery and wonder, that Dillard takes in *Pilgrim at Tinker Creek,* was written over an eight-month period at the pace of fifteen to sixteen hours a day, seven days a week—in a library, not in the wilderness. She is also a voracious reader and researcher of all that she writes about and has some fifty volumes of notes from her readings. Presently, she is living in Washington State where she is working on a novel about Puget Sound during frontier times, a book she has described as a story about "two men and a gun."

"Writing is work" is one message that is clear from Dillard's ambitious publications. She is a painstaking writer and reviser. But there is also present in her writing the unmistakable mark of inspiration.

Untying the Knot

Yesterday I set out to catch the new season, and instead I found an old snakeskin. I was in a sunny February woods by the quarry; the snakeskin was lying in a heap of leaves right next to an aquarium someone had thrown away. I don't know why that someone hauled the aquarium deep into the woods to get rid of it; it had only one broken glass side. The snake found it handy, I imagine; snakes like to rub against something rigid to help them out of their skins, and the broken aquarium looked like the nearest likely object. Together the snakeskin and the aquarium made an interesting scene on the forest floor. It looked like an exhibit at a trial—circumstantial evidence—of a wild scene, as though a snake had burst through the broken aquarium, burst through his ugly old skin, and disappeared, perhaps straight up in the air, in a rush of freedom and beauty. [1]

The snakeskin had unkeeled scales, so it belonged to a non-poisonous snake. It was roughly five feet long by the yardstick, but I'm not sure because it was very wrinkled and dry, and every time I tried to stretch it flat it broke. I ended up with seven or eight pieces of it all over the kitchen table in a fine film of forest dust. [2]

The point I want to make about the snakeskin is that, when I found it, it was whole and tied in a knot. Now there have been stories told, even by reputable scientists, of snakes that have deliberately tied themselves in a knot to prevent larger snakes from trying to swallow them—but I couldn't imagine any way that throwing itself into a half hitch would help a snake trying to escape its skin. Still, ever cautious, I figured that one of the neighborhood boys could possibly have tied it in a knot in the fall, for some whimsical boyish reason, and left it there, where it dried and gathered dust. So I carried the skin along thoughtlessly as I walked, snagging it sure enough on a low branch and ripping it in two for the first of many times. I saw that thick ice still lay on the quarry pond and that the skunk cabbage was already out in the clearings, and then I came home and looked at the skin and its knot. [3]

The knot had no beginning. Idly I turned it around in my hand, searching for a place to untie; I came to with a start when I realized I must have turned the thing around fully ten times. Intently, then, I traced the knot's lump around with a finger: it was continuous. I couldn't untie it any more than I could untie a doughnut; it was a loop without beginning or end. These snakes *are* magic, I thought for a second, and then of course I reasoned what must have happened. The skin had been pulled inside-out like a peeled sock for several inches; then [4] an inch or so of the inside-out part—a piece whose length was coincidentally equal to the diameter of the skin—had somehow been turned right-side out again, making a thick lump whose edges were lost in wrinkles, looking exactly like a knot.

So. I have been thinking about the change of seasons. I don't want to miss 5 spring this year. I want to distinguish the last winter frost from the out-of-season one, the frost of spring. I want to be there on the spot the moment the grass turns green. I always miss this radical revolution; I see it the next day from a window, the yard so suddenly green and lush I could envy Nebuchadnezzar down on all fours eating grass. This year I want to stick a net into time and say "now," as men plant flags on the ice and snow and say, "here." But it occurred to me that I could no more catch spring by the tip of the tail than I could untie the apparent knot in the snakeskin; there are no edges to grasp. Both are continuous loops.

I wonder how long it would take you to notice the regular recurrence of 6 the seasons if you were the first man on earth. What would it be like to live in open-ended time broken only by days and nights? You could say, "it's cold again; it was cold before," but you couldn't make the key connection and say, "it was cold this time last year," because the notion of "year" is precisely the one you lack. Assuming that you hadn't yet noticed any orderly progression of heavenly bodies, how long would you have to live on earth before you could feel with any assurance that any one particular long period of cold would, in fact, end? "While the earth remaineth, seedtime and harvest, and cold and heat, and summer and winter, and day and night shall not cease": God makes this guarantee very early in Genesis to a people whose fears on this point had perhaps not been completely allayed.

It must have been fantastically important, at the real beginnings of human 7 culture, to conserve and relay this vital seasonal information, so that the people could anticipate dry or cold seasons, and not huddle on some November rock hoping pathetically that spring was just around the corner. We still very much stress the simple fact of four seasons to schoolchildren; even the most modern of modern new teachers, who don't seem to care if their charges can read or write or name two products of Peru, will still muster some seasonal chitchat and set the kids to making paper pumpkins, or tulips, for the walls. "The people," wrote Van Gogh in a letter, "are very sensitive to the changing seasons." That we are "very sensitive to the changing seasons" is, incidentally, one of the few good reasons to shun travel. If I stay at home I preserve the illusion that what is happening on Tinker Creek is the very newest thing, that I'm at the very vanguard and cutting edge of each new season. I don't want the same season twice in a row; I don't want to know I'm getting last week's weather, used weather, weather broadcast up and down the coast, old-hat weather.

But there's always unseasonable weather. What we think of the weather 8 and behavior of life on the planet at any given season is really all a matter of statistical probabilities; at any given point, anything might happen. There is a bit of every season in each season. Green plants—deciduous green leaves—grow everywhere, all winter long, and small shoots come up pale and new in every season. Leaves die on the tree in May, turn brown, and fall into the creek. The calendar, the weather, and the behavior of wild creatures have the slimmest of connections. Everything overlaps smoothly for only a few weeks each season, and then it all tangles up again. The temperature, of course, lags far behind the calendar seasons, since the earth absorbs and releases heat slowly, like a leviathan breathing. Migrating birds head south in what appears to be dire panic, leaving mild weather and fields full of insects and seeds; they reappear as if in all eagerness in January, and poke about morosely in the snow. Several years ago our October woods would have made a dismal colored photograph for a sadist's calendar: a killing frost came before the leaves had even begun to brown; they drooped from every tree like crepe, blackened and limp. It's all a chancy, jumbled affair at best, as things seem to be below the stars.

Time is the continuous loop, the snakeskin with scales endlessly overlapping without beginning or end, or time is an ascending spiral if you will, like a child's toy Slinky. Of course we have no idea which arc on the loop is our time, let alone where the loop itself is, so to speak, or down whose lofty flight of stairs the Slinky so uncannily walks.   9

The power we seek, too, seems to be a continuous loop. I have always   10 been sympathetic with the early notion of a divine power that exists in a particular place, or that travels about over the face of the earth as a man might wander—and when he is "there" he is surely not here. You can shake the hand of a man you meet in the woods; but the spirit seems to roll along like the mythical hoop snake with its tail in its mouth. There are no hands to shake or edges to untie. It rolls along the mountain ridges like a fireball, shooting off a spray of sparks at random, and will not be trapped, slowed, grasped, fetched, peeled, or aimed. "As for the wheels, it was cried unto them in my hearing, O wheel." This is the hoop of flame that shoots the rapids in the creek or spins across the dizzy meadows: this is the arsonist of the sunny woods: catch it if you can.

1974

Purpose and Meaning

1. Annie Dillard is fascinated with mystery. What knot, or knots, does her title refer to? Is she referring only to the snakeskin? Interpret this statement from paragraph 10: "The power we seek, too, seems to be a continuous loop."

2. Why does Dillard write at length about the weather in paragraphs 7 and 8? What is the significance of her claim that "the calendar, the weather, and the behavior of wild creatures have the slimmest of connections" (paragraph 8)?

3. Dillard refers to God, the Bible, and the spirit. In light of these religious over-tones, interpret this statement from paragraph 8: "It's all a chancy, jumbled af-fair at best, as things seem to be below the stars." How might this statement appeal to a diverse audience?

Language and Style

1. Dillard has a knack for contrast. Consider these sentences: "Yesterday I set out to catch the new season, and instead I found an old snakeskin" (paragraph 1); "Migrating birds head south in what appears to be dire panic, leaving mild weather and fields full of insects and seeds; they reappear . . . in January, and poke about morosely in the snow" (paragraph 8); "the arsonist of the sunny woods" (paragraph 10). Locate other examples of this stylistic method. How does set-ting up contrasts in this way help the writer to avoid overstatement? Why is this advantageous?

2. Dillard also plays with contrasting sounds. There are many instances of hard *k* sounds with long vowel sounds, as in "old snakeskin" (paragraph 1); "the snakeskin and the aquarium . . . on the forest floor" (paragraph 1); "the quarry pond and . . . the skunk cabbage" (paragraph 3). Find other instances in para-graphs 4, 5, 7, and 8. How does such contrasting tighten the sentences and sharpen the sound? Why is sound important to good writing? How does this attention to sound make Dillard's writing poetic?

3. There are aspects other than those mentioned in questions 1 and 2 that help to tighten Dillard's language. What are they? Does Dillard's language tend to be abstract or concrete?

4. Dillard often uses a metaphor that takes us away from the subject being described: "Together the snakeskin and the aquarium . . . looked like an exhibit at a trial—circumstantial evidence" (paragraph 1); "time is an ascending spiral if you will, like a child's toy Slinky" (paragraph 9). Why is a metaphor most effective when its two parts are most different?

Strategy and Structure

1. Dillard begins her essay with a concrete account. She then uses this account—finding the knotted snakeskin—as a metaphor for a more abstract discussion on time, life's mysteries, and the "power we seek" (10). Why does she begin this way? Why is a discussion about something abstract best put into concrete terms?

2. Dillard refers to the loop in the snakeskin again and again. Spring and the knot "are continuous loops" (paragraph 5); in nature "everything overlaps smoothly . . . then it all tangles up again" (paragraph 8); "Time is the continuous loop" (paragraph 9). Does Dillard succeed in keeping the image fresh? Why or why not?

3. Every once in a while, Dillard drops an informative tidbit into her writing: "Snakes like to rub against something rigid to help them out of their skins" (paragraph 1);

"the snakeskin had unkeeled scales, so it belonged to a non-poisonous snake" (paragraph 2); "there have been stories. . .of snakes that have deliberately tied themselves up in a knot to prevent larger snakes from trying to swallow them" (paragraph 3); "there is a bit of every season in each season. Green plants. . .grow everywhere, all winter long. . . .Leaves die on the tree in May" (paragraph 8). How does such evidence help to capture the reader's attention? How do these details add to Dillard's authority and secure the reader's trust?

Thinking and Writing

1. Analyze the vivid, often surprising language that Dillard uses in "Untying the Knot." Explain the message that such language is intended to convey.

2. Over the next week, keep a daily journal of events you observe in nature. (Remember, even in the city there are seasonal and weather changes, trees, birds, squirrels, spiderwebs, cockroaches—and human beings!) In your writing, make connections between what you see, hear, and smell, and ideas you have about life.

An American Childhood

One Sunday afternoon Mother wandered through our kitchen, where Father was making a sandwich and listening to the ball game. The Pirates were playing the New York Giants at Forbes Field. In those days, the Giants had a utility infielder named Wayne Terwilliger. Just as Mother passed through, the radio announcer cried—with undue drama—"Terwilliger bunts one!" 1

"Terwilliger bunts one?" Mother cried back, stopped short. She turned. "Is that English?" 2

"The player's name is Terwilliger," Father said. "He bunted." 3

"That's marvelous," Mother said. " 'Terwilliger bunts one.' No wonder you listen to baseball. 'Terwilliger bunts one.' " 4

For the next seven or eight years, Mother made this surprising string of syllables her own. Testing a microphone, she repeated, "Terwilliger bunts one"; testing a pen or a typewriter, she wrote it. If, as happened surprisingly often in the course of various improvised gags, she pretended to whisper something else in my ear, she actually whispered, "Terwilliger bunts one." Whenever someone used a French phrase, or a Latin one, she answered solemnly, "Terwilliger bunts one." If Mother had had, like Andrew Carnegie, the opportunity to cook up a motto for a coat of arms, hers would have read simply and tellingly, "Terwilliger bunts one." (Carnegie's was "Death to Privilege.") 5

She served us with other words and phrases. On a Florida trip, she repeated 6
tremulously, "That...is a royal poinciana." I don't remember the tree; I
remember the thrill in her voice. She pronounced it carefully, and spelled it.
She also liked to say "portulaca."

The drama of the words "Tamiami Trail" stirred her, we learned on the 7
same Florida trip. People built Tampa on one coast, and they built Miami on
another. Then—the height of visionary ambition and folly—they piled a slow,
tremendous road through the terrible Everglades to connect them. To build the
road, men stood sunk in muck to their armpits. They fought off cottonmouth
moccasins and six-foot alligators. They slept in boats, wet. They blasted muck
with dynamite, cut jungle with machetes; they laid logs, dragged drilling
machines, hauled dredges, heaped limestone. The road took fourteen years to
build up by the shovelful, a Panama Canal in reverse, and cost hundreds of
lives from tropical, mosquito-carried diseases. Then, capping it all, some genius
thought of the word Tamiami: they called the road from Tampa to Miami, this
very road under our spinning wheels, the Tamiami Trail. Some called it Alligator
Alley. Anyone could drive over this road without a thought.

Hearing this, moved, I thought all the suffering of road building was worth 8
it (it wasn't my suffering), now that we had this new thing to hang these new
words on—Alligator Alley for those who liked things cute, and, for connoisseurs
like Mother, for lovers of the human drama in all its boldness and terror, the
Tamiami Trail.

Back home, Mother cut clips from reels of talk, as it were, and played 9
them back at leisure. She noticed that many Pittsburghers confuse "leave" and
"let." One kind relative brightened our morning by mentioning why she'd
brought her son to visit: "He wanted to come with me, so I left him." Mother
filled in Amy and me on locutions we missed. "I can't do it on Friday," her
pretty sister told a crowded dinner party, "because Friday's the day I lay in the
stores."

(All unconsciously, though, we ourselves used some pure Pittsburghisms. 10
We said "tele pole," pronounced "telly pole," for that splintery sidewalk post
I loved to climb. We said "slippy"—the sidewalks are "slippy." We said, "That's
all the farther I could go." And we said, as Pittsburghers do say, "This glass
needs washed," or "The dog needs walked"—a usage our father eschewed; he
knew it was not standard English, nor even comprehensible English, but he never
let on.)

"Spell 'poinsettia,'" Mother would throw out at me, smiling with pleasure. 11
"Spell 'sherbet.'" The idea was not to make us whizzes, but, quite the contrary,
to remind us—and I, especially, needed reminding—that we didn't know it all
just yet.

"There's a deer standing in the front hall," she told me one quiet evening 12
in the country.

"Really?" 13

"No. I just wanted to tell you something once without your saying, 'I 14
know.'"

Supermarkets in the middle 1950s began luring, or bothering, customers   15
by giving out Top Value Stamps or Green Stamps. When, shopping with
Mother, we got to the head of the checkout line, the checker, always a young
man, asked, "Save stamps?"

"No," Mother replied genially, week after week, "I build model airplanes."   16
I believe she originated this line. It took me years to determine where the joke lay.

Anyone who met her verbal challenges she adored. She had surgery on   17
one of her eyes. On the operating table, just before she conked out, she appealed
feelingly to the surgeon, saying, as she had been planning to say for weeks,
"Will I be able to play the piano?" "Not on me," the surgeon said. "You won't
pull that old one on me."

It was, indeed, an old one. The surgeon was supposed to answer, "Yes,   18
my dear, brave woman, you will be able to play the piano after this operation," to which Mother intended to reply, "Oh, good, I've always wanted to
play the piano." This pat scenario bored her; she loved having it interrupted.
It must have galled her that usually her acquaintances were so predictably
unalert; it must have galled her that, for the length of her life, she could surprise everyone so continually, so easily, when she had been the same all along.
At any rate, she loved anyone who, as she put it, saw it coming, and called
her on it.

She regarded the instructions on bureaucratic forms as straight lines. "Do   19
you advocate the overthrow of the United States government by force or
violence?" After some thought she wrote, "Force." She regarded children, even
babies, as straight men. When Molly learned to crawl, Mother delighted in buy-
ing her gowns with drawstrings at the bottom, like Swee'pea's, because, as she
explained energetically, you could easily step on the drawstring without the
baby's noticing, so that she crawled and crawled and crawled and never got
anywhere except into a small ball at the gown's top.

When we children were young, she mothered us tenderly and dependably;   20
as we got older, she resumed her career of anarchism. She collared us into her
gags. If she answered the phone on a wrong number, she told the caller, "Just
a minute," and dragged the receiver to Amy or me, saying, "Here, take this,
your name is Cecile," or, worse, just, "It's for you." You had to think on your
feet. But did you want to perform well as Cecile, or did you want to take pity
on the wretched caller?

During a family trip to the Highland Park Zoo, Mother and I were alone   21
for a minute. She approached a young couple holding hands on a bench by
the seals, and addressed the young man in dripping tones: "Where have you
been? Still got those baby-blue eyes; always did slay me. And this"—a swift
nod at the dumbstruck young woman, who had removed her hand from the
man's—"must be the one you were telling me about. She's not so bad, really,
as you used to make out. But listen, you know how I miss you, you know where
to reach me, same old place. And there's Ann over there—see how she's grown?
See the blue eyes?"

And off she sashayed, taking me firmly by the hand, and leading us around 22
briskly past the monkey house and away. She cocked an ear back, and both
of us heard the desperate man begin, in a high-pitched wail, "I swear, I never
saw her before in my life. . . ."

On a long, sloping beach by the ocean, she lay stretched out sunning with 23
Father and friends, until the conversation gradually grew tedious, when without
forethought she gave a little push with her heel and rolled away. People were
stunned. She rolled deadpan and apparently effortlessly, arms and legs extended
and tidy, down the beach to the distant water's edge, where she lay at ease just
as she had been, but half in the surf, and well out of earshot.

She dearly loved to fluster people by throwing out a game's rules at 24
whim—when she was getting bored, losing in a dull sort of way, and when
everybody else was taking it too seriously. If you turned your back, she moved
the checkers around on the board. When you got them all straightened out,
she denied she'd touched them; the next time you turned your back, she lined
them up on the rug or hid them under your chair. In a betting rummy game
called Michigan, she routinely played out of turn, or called out a card she didn't
hold, or counted backward, simply to amuse herself by causing an uproar and
watching the rest of us do double takes and have fits. (Much later, when serious
suitors came to call, Mother subjected them to this fast card game as a trial
by ordeal; she used it as an intelligence test and a measure of spirit. If the poor
man could stay a round without breaking down or running out, he got to marry
one of us, if he still wanted to.)

She excelled at bridge, playing fast and boldly, but when the stakes were 25
low and the hands dull, she bid slams for the devilment of it, or raised her
opponents' suit to bug them, or showed her hand, or tossed her cards in a handful
behind her back in a characteristic swift motion accompanied by a vibrantly
innocent look. It drove our stolid father crazy. The hand was over before it
began, and the guests were appalled. How do you score it, who deals now,
what do you do with a crazy person who is having so much fun? Or they were
down seven, and the guests were appalled. "Pam!" "Dammit, Pam!" He groaned.
What ails such people? What on earth possesses them? He rubbed his face.

She was an unstoppable force; she never let go. When we moved across 26
town, she persuaded the U.S. Post Office to let her keep her old address—
forever—because she'd had stationery printed. I don't know how she did it.
Every new post office worker, over decades, needed to learn that although the
Doaks' mail is addressed to here, it is delivered to there.

Mother's energy and intelligence suited her for a greater role in a larger 27
arena—mayor of New York, say—than the one she had. She followed American
politics closely; she had been known to vote for Democrats. She saw how things
should be run, but she had nothing to run but our household. Even there, small
minds bugged her; she was smarter than the people who designed the things
she had to use all day for the length of her life.

"Look," she said. "Whoever designed this corkscrew never used one. Why   28
would anyone sell it without trying it out?" So she invented a better one. She
showed me a drawing of it. The spirit of American enterprise never faded in
Mother. If capitalizing and tooling up had been as interesting as theorizing and
thinking up, she would have fired up a new factory every week, and chaired
several hundred corporations.

"It grieves me," she would say, "it grieves my heart," that the company   29
that made one superior product packaged it poorly, or took the wrong tack
in its advertising. She knew, as she held the thing mournfully in her two hands,
that she'd never find another. She was right. We children wholly sympathized,
and so did Father; what could she do, what could anyone do, about it? She
was Samson in chains. She paced.

She didn't like the taste of stamps so she didn't lick stamps; she licked   30
the corner of the envelope instead. She glued sandpaper to the sides of kitchen
drawers, and under kitchen cabinets, so she always had a handy place to strike
a match. She designed, and hounded workmen to build against all norms, doubly
wide kitchen counters and elevated bathroom sinks. To splint a finger, she stuck
it in a lightweight cigar tube. Conversely, to protect a pack of cigarettes, she
carried it in a Band-Aid box. She drew plans for an over-the-finger toothbrush
for babies, an oven rack that slid up and down, and—the family favorite—
Lendalarm. Lendalarm was a beeper you attached to books (or tools) you loaned
friends. After ten days, the beeper sounded. Only the rightful owner could silence
it.

She repeatedly reminded us of P. T. Barnum's dictum: You could sell   31
anything to anybody if you marketed it right. The adman who thought of making Americans believe they needed underarm deodorant was a visionary. So,
too, was the hero who made a success of a new product, Ivory soap. The execu-
tives were horrified, Mother told me, that a cake of this stuff floated. Soap wasn't
supposed to float. Anyone would be able to tell it was mostly whipped-up air.
Then some inspired adman made a leap: Advertise that it floats. Flaunt it. The
rest is history.

She respected the rare few who broke through to new ways. "Look," she'd   32
say, "here's an intelligent apron." She called upon us to admire intelligent control
knobs and intelligent pan handles, intelligent andirons and picture frames and
knife sharpeners. She questioned everything, every pair of scissors, every knitting
needle, gardening glove, tape dispenser. Hers was a restless mental vigor that
just about ignited the dumb household objects with its force.

Torpid conformity was a kind of sin; it was stupidity itself, the mighty   33
stream against which Mother would never cease to struggle. If you held no
minority opinions, or if you failed to risk total ostracism for them daily, the
world would be a better place without you.

Always I heard Mother's emotional voice asking Amy and me the same   34
few questions: "Is that your own idea? Or somebody's else's?" "*Giant* is a good

movie," I pronounced to the family at dinner. "Oh, really?" Mother warmed to these occasions. She all but rolled up her sleeves. She knew I hadn't seen it. "Is that your considered opinion?"

She herself held many unpopular, even fantastic, positions. She was scathingly sarcastic about the McCarthy hearings while they took place, right on our living-room television; she frantically opposed Father's wait-and-see calm. "We don't know enough about it," he said. "I do," she said. "I know all I need to know." 35

She asserted, against all opposition, that people who lived in trailer parks were not bad but simply poor, and had as much right to settle on beautiful land, such as rural Ligonier, Pennsylvania, as did the oldest of families in the finest of hidden houses. Therefore, the people who owned trailer parks, and sought zoning changes to permit trailer parks, needed our help. Her profound belief that the country-club pool sweeper was a person, and that the department-store saleslady, the bus driver, telephone operator, and house-painter were people, and even in groups the steelworkers who carried pickets and the Christmas shoppers who clogged intersections were people—this was a conviction common enough in democratic Pittsburgh, but not altogether common among our friends' parents, or even, perhaps, among our parents' friends. 36

Opposition emboldened Mother, and she would take on anybody on any issue—the chairman of the board, at a cocktail party, on the current strike; she would fly at him in a flurry of passion, as a songbird selflessly attacks a big hawk. 37

"Eisenhower's going to win," I announced after school. She lowered her magazine and looked me in the eyes: "How do you know?" I was doomed. It was fatal to say, "Everyone says so." We all knew well what happened. "Do you consult this Everyone before you make your decisions? What if Everyone decided to round up all the Jews?" Mother knew there was no danger of cowing me. She simply tried to keep us all awake. And in fact it was always clear to Amy and me, and to Molly when she grew old enough to listen, that if our classmates came to cruelty, just as much as if the neighborhood or the nation came to madness, we were expected to take, and would be each separately capable of taking, a stand. 38

1987

Purpose and Meaning

1. What does learning about Annie Dillard's mother tell us about Annie Dillard? What influences can you detect in Dillard's writing that may have come from her mother's curious sense of humor and excellent ear?

2. In paragraph 2, Dillard recounts how her mother repeated the phrase "Terwilliger bunts one" for years after she first heard it, and at the most outrageous moments.

In paragraphs 7 and 8, she discusses the names of a road and the effect they had on her and others. In paragraph 9, she writes about various "Pittsburghisms." How do these examples characterize the power of language to amuse, place, and even separate people? How is this essay in some ways more about language than about Dillard's mother?

3. What is the thesis of this essay?

Language and Style

1. What is phonetically appealing about "Terwilliger bunts one"; "royal poinciana" (paragraph 6); "Tamiami Trail" (paragraph 7)? Read the phrases out loud as you consider sound here and also in "Untying the Knot."

2. Note the powerful mixing of nouns and verbs in this series of sentences: "men stood sunk in muck to their armpits. . . . They blasted muck with dynamite, cut jungle with machetes; they laid logs, dragged drilling machines, hauled dredges, heaped limestone" (paragraph 7). How does the mixing of contrasting sounds, hard images, active verbs, and one- or two-syllable words invigorate the writing? Find other examples of this stylistic method.

3. Another feature of Dillard's writing is its specificity. The men weren't using an explosive; they used *dynamite*. The machines were *drilling* machines. The rock was *limestone*. Choose any paragraph in the essay and notice how specific her references are. Why is Dillard so careful to be specific?

4. What stylistic devices does Dillard employ to create a humorous tone in this essay?

Strategy and Structure

1. While Dillard is interested in characterizing her mother, her subject is an American childhood, *her* childhood. Still, she focuses on her mother for many pages. We learn indirectly about Dillard's interest in language, her "know-it-all" attitude, her conditioning toward intellectual rigor and a questioning mind, as well as some of her politics. How effective is this approach? Why is her mother such a good model for Dillard's self-revelations?

2. Why doesn't Dillard ever tell us her mother's name? Is she failing to see her mother as an individual? What effect does it have on the readers' point of view?

3. Dillard separates her essay into segments through spatial breaks. How many are there? What is in each segment? How do the segments finally cohere?

4. It is often said the people tend to remember best what comes first or last—in a poem, a movie, or a story. Since Dillard ends her essay with an account of her mother's insistence on a questioning, think-for-yourself kind of mind, she probably wants her readers particularly to remember this. Why? What is its significance to Dillard the writer?

Thinking and Writing

1. Analyze the literary influences Dillard may have gained from her mother. Consider content as well as style.

2. Adopt Dillard's approach and write an essay about your own mother, or about someone you considered as a mother. Focus on those qualities and occurrences that most strongly affected you.

3. Pretend you are a child again and from that perspective describe an incident, or two or three related incidents, that involved your mother. Use the first person.

Singing with the Fundamentalists

It is early spring. I have a temporary office at a state university on the West Coast. The office is on the third floor. It looks down on the Square, the enormous open courtyard at the center of the campus. From my desk I see hundreds of people moving between classes. There is a large circular fountain in the Square's center.

Early one morning, on the first day of spring quarter, I hear singing. A pack of students has gathered at the fountain. They are singing something which, at this distance, and through the heavy window, sounds good.

I know who these singing students are: they are the Fundamentalists. This campus has a lot of them. Mornings they sing on the Square; it is their only perceptible activity. What are they singing? Whatever it is, I want to join them, for I like to sing; whatever it is, I want to take my stand with them, for I am drawn to their very absurdity, their innocent indifference to what people think. My colleagues and students here, and my friends everywhere, dislike and fear Christian fundamentalists. You may never have met such people, but you've heard what they do: they pile up money, vote in blocs, and elect right-wing crazies; they censor books; they carry handguns; they fight fluoride in the drinking water and evolution in the schools; probably they would lynch people if they could get away with it. I'm not sure my friends are correct. I close my pen and join the singers on the Square.

There is a clapping song in progress. I have to concentrate to follow it:

> Come on, rejoice,
> And let your heart sing,
> Come on rejoice,
> Give praise to the king.

Singing alleluia—
He is the king of kings;
Singing alleluia—
He is the king of kings.

Two song leaders are standing on the broad rim of the fountain; the water is splashing just behind them. The boy is short, hardfaced, with a moustache. He bangs his guitar with the backs of his fingers. The blonde girl, who leads the clapping, is bouncy; she wears a bit of makeup. Both are wearing blue jeans.

The students beside me are wearing blue jeans too—and athletic jerseys, parkas, football jackets, turtlenecks, and hiking shoes or jogging shoes. They all have canvas or nylon book bags. They look like any random batch of seventy or eighty students at this university. They are grubby or scrubbed, mostly scrubbed; they are tall, fair, or red-headed in large proportions. Their parents are white-collar workers, blue-collar workers, farmers, loggers, orchardists, merchants, fishermen; their names are, I'll bet, Olsen, Jensen, Seversen, Hansen, Klokker, Sigurdsen.

Despite the vigor of the clapping song, no one seems to be giving it much effort. And no one looks at anyone else; there are no sentimental glances and smiles, no glances even of recognition. These kids don't seem to know each other. We stand at the fountain's side, out on the broad, bricked Square in front of the science building, and sing the clapping song through three times.

It is quarter to nine in the morning. Hundreds of people are crossing the Square. These passersby—faculty, staff, students—pay very little attention to us; this morning singing has gone on for years. Most of them look at us directly, then ignore us, for there is nothing to see; no animal sacrifices, no lynchings, no collection plate for Jesse Helms, no seizures, snake handling, healing, or glossolalia. There is barely anything to hear. I suspect the people glance at us to learn if we are really singing: How could so many people make so little sound? My fellow singers, who ignore each other, certainly ignore passersby as well. Within a week, most of them will have their eyes closed anyway.

We move directly to another song, a slower one.

He is my peace
Who has broken down every wall;
He is my peace,
He is my peace.

Cast all your cares on him,
For he careth for you—oo—oo
He is my peace,
He is my peace.

I am paying strict attention to the song leaders, for I am singing at the top of my lungs and I've never heard any of these songs before. They are not the old American low-church Protestant hymns; they are not the old European high-church Protestant hymns. These hymns seem to have been written just yesterday, apparently by the same people who put out lyrical Christian greeting cards and bookmarks.

"Where do these songs come from?" I ask a girl standing next to me. She   10
seems appalled to be addressed at all, and startled by the question. "They're from the praise albums!" she explains, and moves away.

The songs' melodies run dominant, subdominant, dominant, tonic, domi-   11
nant. The pace is slow, about the pace of "Tell Laura I Love Her," and with that song's quavering, long notes. The lyrics are simple and repetitive; there are very few of them to which a devout Jew or Mohammedan could not give wholehearted assent. These songs are similar to the things Catholics sing in church these days. I don't know if any studies have been done to correlate the introduction of contemporary songs into Catholic churches with those churches' decline in membership, or with the phenomenon of Catholic converts' applying to enter cloistered monasteries directly, without passing through parish churches.

> I'm set free to worship,
> I'm set free to praise him,
> I'm set free to dance before the Lord . . .

At nine o'clock sharp we quit and scatter. I hear a few quiet "see you"s.   12
Mostly the students leave quickly, as if they didn't want to be seen. The Square empties.

The next day we show up again, at twenty to nine. The same two leaders   13
stand on the fountain's rim; the fountain is pouring down behind them.

After the first song, the boy with the moustache hollers, "Move on up!   14
Some of you guys aren't paying attention back there! You're talking to each other. I want you to concentrate!" The students laugh, embarrassed for him. He sounds like a teacher. No one moves. The girl breaks into the next song, which we join at once:

> In my life, Lord,
> Be glorified, be glorified, be glorified;
> In my life, Lord.
> Be glorified, be glorified, today.

At the end of this singularly monotonous verse, which is straining my tolerance for singing virtually anything, the boy with the moustache startles me by shouting, "Classes!"

At once, without skipping a beat, we sing, "In my classes, Lord, be   15
glorified, be glorified . . ." I give fleet thought to the class I'm teaching this afternoon. We're reading a little "Talk of the Town" piece called "Eggbag," about

a cat in a magic store on Eighth Avenue. "Relationships!" the boy calls. The students seem to sing "In my relationships, Lord," more easily than they sang "classes." They seemed embarrassed by "classes." In fact, to my fascination, they seemed embarrassed by almost everything. Why are they here? I will sing with the Fundamentalists every weekday morning all spring; I will decide, tentatively, that they come pretty much for the same reasons I do: Each has a private relationship with "the Lord" and will put up with a lot of junk for it.

I have taught some Fundamentalist students here, and know a bit of what [16] they think. They are college students above all, worried about their love lives, their grades, and finding jobs. Some support moderate Democrats; some support moderate Republicans. Like their classmates, most support nuclear freeze, ERA, and an end to the draft. I believe they are divided on abortion and busing. They are not particularly political. They read *Christianity Today* and *Campus Life* and *Eternity*—moderate, sensible magazines, I think; they read a lot of C. S. Lewis. (One such student, who seemed perfectly tolerant of me and my shoddy Christianity, introduced me to C. S. Lewis's critical book on Charles Williams.) They read the Bible. I think they all "believe in" organic evolution. The main thing about them is this: There isn't any "them." Their views vary. They don't know each other.

Their common Christianity puts them, if anywhere, to the left of their [17] classmates. I believe they also tend to be more able than their classmates to think well in the abstract, and also to recognize the complexity of moral issues. But I may be wrong.

In 1980, the media were certainly wrong about television evangelists. [18] Printed estimates of Jerry Falwell's television audience ranged from 18 million to 30 million people. In fact, according to Arbitron's actual counts, fewer than 1.5 million people were watching Falwell. And, according to an Emory University study, those who did watch television evangelists didn't necessarily vote with them. Emory University sociologist G. Melton Mobley reports, "When that message turns political, they cut it off." Analysis of the 1982 off-year election turned up no Fundamentalist bloc voting. The media were wrong, but no one printed retractions.

The media were wrong, too, in a tendency to identify all fundamentalist [19] Christians with Falwell and his ilk, and to attribute to them, across the board, conservative views.

Someone has sent me two recent issues of *Eternity: The Evangelical* [20] *Monthly*. One lead article criticizes a television preacher for saying that the United States had never used military might to take land from another nation. The same article censures Newspeak, saying that government rhetoric would have us believe in a "clean bomb," would have us believe that we "defend" America by invading foreign soil, and would have us believe that the dictatorships we support are "democracies." "When the President of the United States says that one reason to support defense spending is because it creates jobs," this lead article says, "a little bit of *1984* begins to surface." Another article criticizes a "heavy-handed" opinion of Jerry Falwell Ministries—in this case a broadside attack on artificial insemination, surrogate motherhood, and lesbian motherhood. Browsing through *Eternity*, I find a double crosstic. I find an intelligent, analytical, and enthusiastic review of the new London Philharmonic recording of Mahler's second symphony—a review which stresses the "glorious truth" of the Jewish composer's magnificent work, and cites its recent perform-ance in Jerusalem to celebrate the recapture of the Western Wall following the Six Day War. Surely, the evangelical Christians who read this magazine are not bookburners. If by chance they vote with the magazine's editors, then it looks to me as if they vote with the American Civil Liberties Union and Americans for Democratic Action.

21   Every few years some bold and sincere Christian student at this universi-ty disagrees with a professor in class—usually about the professor's out-of-hand dismissal of Christianity. Members of the faculty, outraged, repeat the stories of these rare and uneven encounters for years on end, as if to prove that the crazies are everywhere, and gaining ground. The notion is, apparently, that these kids can't think for themselves. Or they wouldn't disagree.

22   Now again the moustached leader asks us to move up. There is no harangue, so we move up. (This will be a theme all spring. The leaders want us closer together. Our instinct is to stand alone.) From behind the tall fountain comes a wind; on several gusts we get sprayed. No one seems to notice.

23   We have time for one more song. The leader, perhaps sensing that no one likes him, blunders on. "I want you to pray this one through," he says. "We have a lot of people here from a lot of different fellowships, but we're all one body. Amen?" They don't like it. He gets a few polite Amens. We sing:

> Bind us together, Lord,
> With a bond that can't be broken;
> Bind us together, Lord,
> With love.

Everyone seems to be in a remarkably foul mood today. We don't like this song. There is no one here under seventeen, and, I think, no one here who believes that love is a bond that can't be broken. We sing the song through three times; then it is time to go.

24   The leader calls after our retreating backs, "Hey, have a good day! Praise Him all day!" The kids around me roll up their eyes privately. Some groan; all flee.

25   The next morning is very cold. I am here early. Two girls are talking on the fountain's rim; one is part Italian. She says, "I've got the Old Testament, but I can't get the New. I screw up the New." She takes a breath and rattles

off a long list, ending with "Jonah, Micah, Nahum, Habakkuk, Zephaniah, Haggai, Zechariah, Malachi." The other girl produces a slow, sarcastic applause. I ask one of the girls to help me with the words to a song. She is agreeable, but says, "I'm sorry, I can't. I just became a Christian this year, so I don't know all the words yet."

The others are coming; we stand and separate. The boy with the moustache [26] is gone, replaced by a big, serious fellow in a green down jacket. The bouncy girl is back with her guitar; she's wearing a skirt and wool knee socks. We begin, without any preamble, by singing a song that has so few words that we actually stretch one syllable over eleven separate notes. Then we sing a song in which the men sing one phrase and the women echo it. Everyone seems to know just what to do. In the context of our vapid songs, the lyrics of this one are extraordinary:

> I was nothing before you found me.
> Heartache! Broken people! Ruined lives
> Is why you died on Calvary.

The last line rises in a regular series of half-notes. Now at last some people are actually singing; they throw some breath into the business. There is a seriousness and urgency to it: "Heartache! Broken people! Ruined lives...I was nothing."

We don't look like nothing. We look like a bunch of students of every [27] stripe, ill-shaven or well-shaven, dressed up or down, but dressed warmly against the cold: jeans and parkas, jeans and heavy sweaters, jeans and scarves and blow-dried hair. We look ordinary. But I think, quite on my own, that we are here because we know this business of nothingness, brokenness, and ruination. We sing this song over and over.

Something catches my eye. Behind us, up in the science building, pro- [28] fessors are standing alone at opened windows.

The long brick science building has three upper floors of faculty offices, [29] thirty-two windows. At one window stands a bearded man, about forty; his opening his window is what caught my eye. He stands full in the open window, his hands on his hips, his head cocked down toward the fountain. He is drawn to look, as I was drawn to come. Up on the building's top floor, at the far right window, there is another: An Asian-American professor, wearing a white shirt, is sitting with one hip on his desk, looking out and down. In the middle of the row of windows, another one, an old professor in a checked shirt, stands sideways to the open window, stands stock-still, his long, old ear to the air. Now another window cranks open, another professor—or maybe a graduate student—leans out, his hands on the sill.

We are all singing, and I am watching these five still men, my colleagues, [30] whose office doors are surely shut—for that is the custom here: five of them alone in their office in the science building who have opened their windows on this very cold morning, who motionless hear the Fundamentalists sing, utterly unknown to each other.

We sing another four songs, including the clapping song, and one which   31
repeats, "This is the day which the Lord hath made; rejoice and be glad in it."
All the professors but one stay by their opened windows, figures in a frieze.
When after ten minutes we break off and scatter, each cranks his window shut.
Maybe they have nine o'clock classes too.

I miss a few sessions. One morning of the following week, I rejoin the   32
Fundamentalists on the Square. The wind is blowing from the north; it is sunny and cold. There are several new developments.

Someone has blown up rubber gloves and floated them in the fountain.   33
I saw them yesterday afternoon from my high office window, and couldn't quite
make them out: I seemed to see hands in the fountain waving from side to side,
like those hands wagging on springs which people stick in the back windows
of their cars. I saw these many years ago in Quito and Guayaquil, where they
were a great fad long before they showed up here. The cardboard hands said,
on their palms, HOLA GENTE, hello people. Some of them just said HOLA, hello,
with a little wave to the universe at large, in case anybody happened to be looking. It is like sending radio signals to planets in other galaxies: HOLA, if anyone
is listening. Jolly folk, these Ecuadorians, I thought.

Now, waiting by the fountain for the singing, I see that these particular   34
hands are long surgical gloves, yellow and white, ten of them tied off at the
cuff. They float upright and they wave, *hola, hola, hola;* they mill around like
a crowd, bobbing under the fountain's spray and back again to the pool's rim,
hola. It is a good prank. It is far too cold for the university's maintenance crew
to retrieve them without turning off the fountain and putting on rubber boots.

From all around the Square, people are gathering for the singing. There   35
is no way I can guess which kids, from among the masses crossing the Square,
will veer off to the fountain. When they get here, I never recognize anybody
except the leaders.

The singing begins without ado as usual, but there is something different   36
about it. The students are growing prayerful, and they show it this morning
with a peculiar gesture. I'm glad they weren't like this when I first joined them,
or I never would have stayed.

Last night there was an educational television special, part of "Mid-   37
dletown." It was a segment called "Community of Praise," and I watched it
because it was about Fundamentalists. It showed a Jesus-loving family in the
Midwest; the treatment was good and complex. This family attended the prayer
meetings, healing sessions, and church services of an unnamed sect—a very
low-church sect, whose doctrine and culture were much more low-church than
those of the kids I sing with. When the members of this set prayed, they held
their arms over their heads and raised their palms, as if to feel or receive a blessing or energy from above.

Now today on the Square there is a new serious mood. The leaders are   38
singing with their eyes shut. I am impressed that they can bang their guitars,

keep their balance, and not fall into the pool. It is the same bouncy girl and earnest boy. Their eyeballs are rolled back a bit. I look around and see that almost everyone in this crowd of eighty or so has his eyes shut and is apparently praying the words of this song or praying some other prayer.

Now as the chorus rises, as it gets louder and higher and simpler in 39 melody—

> I exalt thee,
> I exalt thee,
> I exalt thee,
> Thou art the Lord—

then, at this moment, hands start rising. All around me, hands are going up— that tall girl, that blond boy with his head back, the red-headed boy up front, the girl with the MacDonald's jacket. Their arms rise as if pulled on strings. Some few of them have raised their arms very high over their heads and are tilting back their palms. Many, many more of them, as inconspicuously as possible, have raised their hands to the level of their chins.

What is going on? Why are these students today raising their palms in 40 this gesture, when nobody did it last week? Is it because the leaders have set a prayerful tone this morning? Is it because this gesture always accompanies this song, just as clapping accompanies other songs? Or is it, as I suspect, that these kids watched the widely publicized documentary last night just as I did, and are adopting, or trying out, the gesture?

It is a sunny morning, and the sun is rising behind the leaders and the 41 fountain, so those students have their heads tilted, eyes closed, and palms upraised toward the sun. I glance up at the science building and think my own prayer: Thank God no one is watching this.

The leaders cannot move around much on the fountain's rim. The girl 42 has her eyes shut; the boy opens his eyes from time to time, glances at the neck of his guitar, and closes his eyes again.

When the song is over, the hands go down, and there is some desultory 43 chatting in the crowd, as usual: Can I borrow your library card? And, as usual nobody looks at anybody.

All our songs today are serious. There is a feudal theme to them, or a 44 feudal analogue:

> I will eat from abundance of your household.
> I will dream beside your streams of righteousness.

> You are my king.

> Enter his gates
> with thanksgiving in your heart;
> come before his courts with praise.

He is the king of kings.

Thou art the Lord.

All around me, eyes are closed and hands are raised. There is no social   45
pressure to do this, or anything else. I've never known any group to be less
cohesive, imposing fewer controls. Since no one looks at anyone, and since
passersby no longer look, everyone out here is inconspicuous and free. Perhaps
the palm-raising has begun because the kids realize by now that they are not
on display; they're praying in their closets, right out here on the Square. Over
the course of the next weeks, I will learn that the palm-raising is here to stay.

The sun is rising higher. We are singing our last song. We are praying.   46
We are alone together.

He is my peace
Who has broken down every wall . . .

When the song is over, the hands go down. The heads lower, the eyes   47
open and blink. We stay still a second before we break up. We have been standing
in a broad current; now we have stepped aside. We have dismantled the radar
cups; we have closed the telescope's vault. Students gather their book bags and
go. The two leaders step down from the fountain's rim and pack away their
guitars. Everyone scatters. I am in no hurry, so I stay after everyone is gone.
It is after nine o'clock, and the Square is deserted. The fountain is playing to
an empty house. In the pool the cheerful hands are waving over the water,
bobbing under the fountain's veil and out again in the current, *hola.*

1984

Purpose and Meaning

1. In this essay, Dillard considers prejudicial opinions about fundamentalist Christians. How do her actions support her opinion that we should take a closer look at people before we judge them? What expectations does she have of her audience? To what things does she respond besides these fundamentalist views?

2. In paragraph 16, Dillard writes that the fundamentalist singers are "college students above all" and that "they are not particularly political." What point is she making in this paragraph? Why is this point important to our overall understanding of the essay and Dillard's experience?

3. How does Dillard anticipate and deal with her audience's possible objection to her position?

Language and Style

1. The sentences in this essay tend to be short and to begin with the basic subject-verb pattern. How does the language differ from the first two Dillard essays? What tone does this style create?

2. Generally, the language in this essay is plainer than in Dillard's other work. Still, she employs imagery and resonating sounds to inform her subject. Lists are a common feature: "athletic jerseys, parkas, football jackets, turtlenecks..." (paragraph 5); "white-collar workers, blue-collar workers, farmers, loggers, orchardists...Olsen, Jensen, Seversen, Hansen, Klokker...." (paragraph 5). Find other examples. What do lists add to a piece of writing?

3. Considering Dillard's subject and its potential for controversy, what reason could she have for writing in a plain, unaffected style?

4. What is unusual about Dillard's point of view in this essay?

Strategy and Structure

1. Dillard begins her essay with a view of the Christian singers from a distance, from her third-floor office window. Why might she begin this way? How does Dillard involve the reader in getting to know the singers?

2. How does Dillard organize the body of her essay? Is she consistent in her rhetorical approach? Explain.

3. How does Dillard's writing contrast with the quoted lyrics of the fundamentalist songs? Why would she want to create this contrast?

4. When Dillard decided to write an essay about her experience with the fundamentalist singers, she had the choice to begin and end her account at any point. Why do you suppose she chose to end after the description of the morning when students had begun to raise their arms to the sky in emulation of some evangelicals in a television documentary? That day, she writes, all the songs were "serious." What effect is this final image likely to have on the readers' evaluation of the group and Dillard's experience?

Thinking and Writing

1. Although metaphorical language is rare in this essay, several metaphors occur in the final paragraph. Dillard writes: "We have been standing in a broad current; now we have stepped aside. We have dismantled the radar cups; we have closed the telescope's vault." Analyze the meaning of these metaphors and explain their relation to the essay.

2. Write about a religious or spiritual experience you have had or have observed. Following Dillard's lead, write effectively but don't sensationalize.

Push It

People love pretty much the same things best. A writer looking for subjects inquires not after what he loves best, but after what he alone loves at all. Strange seizures beset us. Frank Conroy loves his yo-yo tricks, Emily Dickinson her slant of light; Richard Selzer loves the glistening peritoneum, Faulkner the muddy bottom of a little girl's drawers visible when she's up a pear tree. "Each student of the ferns," I once read, "will have his own list of plants that for some reason or another stir his emotions."

Why do you never find anything written about that idiosyncratic thought you advert to, about your fascination with something no one else understands? Because it is up to you. There is something you find interesting, for a reason hard to explain. It is hard to explain because you have never read it on any page; there you begin. You were made and set here to give voice to this, your own astonishment.

Write as if you were dying. At the same time, assume you write for an audience consisting solely of terminal patients. That is, after all, the case. What would you begin writing if you knew you would die soon? What could you say to a dying person that would not enrage by its triviality?

Write about winter in the summer. Describe Norway as Ibsen did, from a desk in Italy; describe Dublin as James Joyce did, from a desk in Paris. Willa Cather wrote her prairie novels in New York City; Mark Twain wrote "Huckleberry Finn" in Hartford. Recently scholars learned that Walt Whitman rarely left his room.

The writer studies literature, not the world. She lives in the world; she cannot miss it. If she has ever bought a hamburger, or taken a commercial airplane flight, she spares her readers a report of her experience. She is careful of what she reads, for that is what she will write. She is careful of what she learns, because that is what she will know.

The writer knows her field—what has been done, what could be done, the limits—the way a tennis player knows the court. And like that expert, she, too, plays the edges. That is where the exhilaration is. She hits up the line. In writing, she can push the edges. Beyond this limit, here, the reader must recoil. Reason balks, poetry snaps; some madness enters, or strain. Now gingerly, can she enlarge it, can she nudge the bounds? And enclose what wild power?

A well-known writer got collared by a university student who asked, "Do you think I could be a writer?"

"Well," the writer said, "I don't know....Do you like sentences?"

The writer could see the student's amazement. Sentences? Do I like 9 sentences? I am 20 years old and do I like sentences? If he had liked sentences, of course, he could begin, like a joyful painter I knew. I asked him how he came to be a painter. He said, "I liked the smell of the paint."

Hemingway studied, as models, the novels of Knut Hamsun and Ivan 10 Turgenev. Isaac Bashevis Singer, as it happened, also chose Hamsun and Turgenev as models. Ralph Ellison studied Hemingway and Gertrude Stein. Thoreau loved Homer; Eudora Welty loved Chekhov. Faulkner described his debt to Sherwood Anderson and Joyce; E. M. Forster, his debt to Jane Austen and Proust. By contrast, if you ask a 21-year-old poet whose poetry he likes, he might say, unblushing, "Nobody's." He has not yet understood that poets like poetry, and novelists like novels; he himself likes only the role, the thought of himself in a hat. Rembrandt and Shakespeare, Bohr and Gauguin, possessed powerful hearts, not powerful wills. They loved the range of materials they used. The work's possibilities excited them; the field's complexities fired their imaginations. The caring suggested the tasks; the tasks suggested the schedules. They learned their fields and then loved them. They worked, respectfully, out of their love and knowledge, and they produced complex bodies of work that endure. Then, and only then, the world harassed them with some sort of wretched hat, which, if they were still living, they knocked away as well as they could, to keep at their tasks.

It makes more sense to write one big book—a novel or nonfiction 11 narrative—than to write many stories or essays. Into a long, ambitious project you can fit or pour all you possess and learn. A project that takes five years will accumulate those years' inventions and richnesses. Much of those years' reading will feed the work. Further, writing sentences is difficult whatever their subject. It is no less difficult to write sentences in a recipe than sentences in "Moby Dick." So you might as well write "Moby Dick." Similarly, since every original work requires a unique form, it is more prudent to struggle with the outcome of only one form—that of a long work—than to struggle with the many forms of a collection.

Every book has an intrinsic impossibility, which its writer discovers as 12 soon as his first excitement dwindles. The problem is structural; it is insoluble; it is why no one can ever write this book. Complex stories, essays and poems have this problem, too—the prohibitive structural defect the writer wishes he had never noticed. He writes it in spite of that. He finds ways to minimize the difficulty; he strengthens other virtues; he cantilevers the whole narrative out into thin air and it holds.

Why are we reading, if not in hope of beauty laid bare, life heightened 13 and its deepest mystery probed? Can the writer isolate and vivify all in experience that most deeply engages our intellects and our hearts? Can the writer renew our hopes for literary forms? Why are we reading, if not in hope that the writer will magnify and dramatize our days, will illuminate and inspire us with wisdom, courage and the hope of meaningfulness, and press upon our minds the deepest mysteries, so we may feel again their majesty and power? What do we ever know that is higher than that power which, from time to time, seizes our lives, and which reveals us startlingly to ourselves as creatures set down here bewildered? Why does death so catch us by surprise, and why love? We still and always want waking. If we are reading for these things, why would anyone read books with advertising slogans and brand names in them? Why would anyone write such books? We should mass half-dressed in long lines like tribesmen and shake gourds at each other, to wake up; instead we watch television and miss the show.

No manipulation is possible in a work of art, but every miracle is. Those 14 artists who dabble in eternity, or who aim never to manipulate but only to lay out hard truths, grow accustomed to miracles. Their sureness is hard won. "Given a large canvas," said Veronese, "I enriched it as I saw fit."

The sensation of writing a book is the sensation of spinning, blinded by 15 love and daring. It is the sensation of a stunt pilot's turning barrel rolls, or an inchworm's blind rearing from a stem in search of a route. At its worst, it feels like alligator wrestling, at the level of the sentence.

At its best, the sensation of writing is that of any unmerited grace. It is 16 handed to you, but only if you look for it. You search, you break your fists, your back, your brain, and then—and only then—it is handed to you. From the corner of your eye you see motion. Something is moving through the air and headed your way. It is a parcel bound in ribbons and bows; it has two white wings. It flies directly at you; you can read your name on it. If it were a baseball, you would hit it out of the park. It is that one pitch in a thousand you see in slow motion; its wings beat slowly as a hawk's.

One line of a poem, the poet said—only one line, but thank God for that 17 one line—drops from the ceiling. Thornton Wilder cited this unnamed writer of sonnets: one line of a sonnet falls from the ceiling, and you tap in the others around it with a jeweler's hammer. Nobody whispers it in your ear. It is like something you memorized once and forgot. Now it comes back and rips away your breath. You find and finger a phrase at a time, you lay it down as if with tongs, restraining your strength, and wait suspended and fierce until the next one finds you: yes, this; and yes, praise be, then this.

Einstein likened the generation of a new idea to a chicken's laying an egg: 18 "Kieks—auf einmal ist es da." Cheep—and all at once there it is. Of course, Einstein was not above playing to the crowd.

Push it. Examine all things intensely and relentlessly. Probe and search 19 each object in a piece of art; do not leave it, do not course over it, as if it were understood, but instead follow it down until you see it in the mystery of its own specificity and strength. Giacometti's drawings and paintings show his bewilderment and persistence. If he had not acknowledged his bewilderment, he would not have persisted. A master of drawing, Rico Lebrun, discovered that "the draftsman must aggress; only by persistent assault will the live image capitulate and give up its secret to an unrelenting line." Who but an artist fierce to know—not fierce to seem to know—would suppose that a live image possessed a secret? The artist is willing to give all his or her strength and life to probing with blunt instruments those same secrets no one can describe any way but with the instruments' faint tracks.

Admire the world for never ending on you as you would admire an 20 opponent, without taking your eyes off him, or walking away.

One of the few things I know about writing is this: spend it all, shoot 21 it, play it, lose it, all, right away, every time. Do not hoard what seems good for a later place in the book, or for another book; give it, give it all, give it now. The impulse to save something good for a better place later is the signal to spend it now. Something more will arise for later, something better. These things fill from behind, from beneath, like well water. Similarly, the impulse to keep to yourself what you have learned is not only shameful, it is destructive. Anything you do not give freely and abundantly becomes lost to you. You open your safe and find ashes.

After Michelangelo died, someone found in his studio a piece of paper 22 on which he had written a note to his apprentice, in the handwriting of his old age: "Draw, Antonio, draw, Antonio, draw and do not waste time."

1989

Purpose and Meaning

1. What is Dillard's purpose in writing this essay? What assumptions does she make about her audience?

2. In paragraph 2, Dillard writes, "The writer studies literature, not the world. She lives in the world; she cannot miss it." What do you think Dillard means by this, specifically? Do you agree with her? Does everyone "living in the world" really experience it?

3. Dillard seems to be writing to her audience in several "voices." Identify these multiple voices and explain their effect.

Language and Style

1. Dillard begins her essay using the pronoun *he* to refer to the writer. The next time she refers to the writer, in paragraph 5, she uses *she*. Why does she alternate her usage and why does she continue with the altered usage? What reasons could she have—both ideological and stylistic—for this usage?

2. Commands appear frequently in this essay: "Write as if you were dying" (paragraph 3); "Write about winter in summer" (paragraph 4); "Examine all things intensely and relentlessly" (paragraph 9); "Probe and search each object" (paragraph 11); "Admire the world for never ending on you" (paragraph 20). What tone is generated by these commands?

3. Some of Dillard's sentences are exceedingly compact, reminiscent of an Emily Dickinson poem: "Strange seizures beset us" (paragraph 1); "Reason balks, poetry snaps; some madness enters, or strain" (paragraph 6). What is poetic about such language?

4. Many of the metaphors Dillard has chosen liken writing to a physical experience—for instance, "The writer knows her field . . . the way a tennis player knows the court" (paragraph 6). Cite additional examples of this technique. What effect do these metaphors produce? In what way are they more effective than a nonfigurative explanation of writing? Why does she choose such physical imagery?

Strategy and Structure

1. For the first twelve paragraphs, Dillard's approach is direct. In paragraph 13, she becomes questioning. Why does she shift her tone at this point?

2. Beginning in paragraph 15, Dillard shifts her approach again and becomes rather lyrical. Why is a lyric tone appropriate now? What shift has occurred in the discussion?

3. For most of the essay, Dillard has been writing as an authority. She is a widely read, Pulitzer Prize–winning author who knows her subject well. However, at the end of the essay, she begins paragraph 21 by saying, "One of the few things I know about writing is this. . . ." Why does she affect modesty at this point? Is it effective, or does it sound false?

Thinking and Writing

1. In paragraph 16, Dillard writes: "You search, you break your fists, your back, your brain, and then—and only then—it is handed to you. From the corner of your eye you see motion. Something is moving through the air and headed your way. It is a parcel bound in ribbons and bows; it has two white wings. It flies directly at you; you can read your name on it. If it were a baseball, you would hit it out of the park. It is that one pitch in a thousand you see in slow motion; its wings beat slowly as a hawk's." Analyze this passage for meaning and effectiveness. Evaluate those features that are characteristic of Dillard's writing in all four essays—both in style and content.

2. Choose an activity you know well and write an essay instructing your readers on how to do it best. Try to imitate some of Dillard's techniques.

3. Write an extended essay on the role and mission of writers and artists in modern times, drawing on relevant essays and essayists in this anthology. Consult, for example, Orwell's "Why I Write" and Didion's essay by the same title; Hoagland's "What I Think, What I Am"; Baldwin's "Autobiographical Notes"; and Selzer's "The Pen and the Scalpel."

Acknowledgements

Margaret Atwood, "Adrienne Rich: Poems, Selected and New" from *Second Words* by Margaret Atwood. Copyright © 1982 by O. W. Toad, Ltd. Reprinted by permission of Beacon Press and Stoddart Publishing Company Limited. "Great Unexpectations." Originally published in *Ms. Magazine*, July/August 1987. Reprinted by permission of the author. Copyright © 1987 by Margaret Atwood. "Travels Back" from *Second Words* by Margaret Atwood. Copyright © 1982 by O. W. Toad, Ltd. Reprinted by permission of Beacon Press and Stoddart Publishing Company Limited.

Russell Baker, "The Flag" from *So This Is Depravity*. Copyright © 1982 by Russell Baker. Reprinted by arrangement with Contemporary Books, Inc. "Growing Up" from *Growing Up*. Copyright © 1982 by Russell Baker. Reprinted by arrangement with Contemporary Books, Inc. "Let Them Play Guitars." Copyright © 1989 by The New York Times Company. Reprinted by permission.

James Baldwin, "Autobiographical Notes" from *Notes of a Native Son* by James Baldwin. Copyright © 1955, renewed 1983 by James Baldwin. Reprinted by permission of Beacon Press. "The Discovery of What it Means to Be an American" from *The New York Times Book Review*, January 25, 1958. Copyright © 1959 by James Baldwin, © 1989 by Gloria Karefa-Smart. Used by arrangement with the James Baldwin Estate. "Fifth Avenue Uptown: A Letter From Harlem." © 1960 by James Baldwin; © 1988 by Gloria Karefa-Smart. Used by arrangement with the James Baldwin Estate. "If Black English Isn't A Language, Then Tell Me, What Is?" from *The New York Times*, July 29, 1979 (op-ed). Copyright © 1979 by The New York Times Company. Reprinted by permission.

Joan Didion, "Marrying Absurd" from *Slouching Towards Bethlehem*. Copyright © 1961, 1965, 1967, 1968 by Joan Didion. Reprinted by permission of Farrar, Straus & Giroux, Inc. "Miami." Copyright © 1987 by Joan Didion. Reprinted by permission of Simon & Schuster, Inc. "On Morality," and "On Self Respect" from *Slouching Towards Bethlehem*. Copyright © 1961, 1965, 1967, 1968 by Joan Didion. Reprinted by permission of Farrar, Straus & Giroux, Inc. "Why I Write." Reprinted by permission of the Wallace Literary Agency, Inc. Copyright © 1976 by Joan Didion. First appeared in *The New York Times Book Review*, December 5, 1976.

Annie Dillard, "An American Childhood" from *An American Childhood*. Copyright © 1987 by Annie Dillard. Reprinted by permission of Harper & Row, Publishers, Inc. "Push It" from *The Writing Life*. Copyright © 1989 by Annie Dillard. Reprinted by permission of Harper & Row, Publishers, Inc. "Singing With the Fundamentalists," © 1984 by Annie Dillard. Reprinted by permission of the author and her agent, Blanche C. Gregory, Inc. "Untying the Knot" from *Pilgrim at Tinker Creek*. Copyright © 1974 by Annie Dillard. Reprinted by permission of Harper & Row, Publishers, Inc.

Isak Dinesen, "Old Knudsen," "The Oxen," and "Some African Birds" from *Out of Africa*. Copyright © 1937 by Random House, Inc., and renewed 1965 by The Rungstedlund Foundation. Reprinted by permission of Random House, Inc., and The Rungstedlund Foundation of Denmark.

Stephen Jay Gould, "A Biological Homage to Mickey Mouse" is reprinted from *The Panda's Thumb: More Reflections in Natural History*, by permission of W. W. Norton & Company, Inc. Copyright © 1980 by Stephen Jay Gould. "Evolution as Fact and Theory" is reprinted from *Hen's Teeth and Horse's Toes*, by permission of W. W. Norton & Company, Inc. Copyright © 1983 by Stephen

467

Richard Selzer, "Bald!" Copyright © 1974, 1975, 1976 by Richard Selzer. Reprinted by permission of Simon & Schuster, Inc. "Lessons from the Art." Copyright © 1974, 1975, 1976 by Richard Selzer. Reprinted by permission of Simon & Schuster, Inc. "A Mask on the Face of Death." Reprinted by permission of Georges Borchardt, Inc. for the author. Copyright © 1987 by Richard Selzer. "The Pen and the Scalpel." Copyright © 1988 by The New York Times Company. Reprinted by permission.

Lewis Thomas, "Computers" and "The Iks" from *The Lives of a Cell: Notes of a Biology Watcher.* Copyright © 1974 by Lewis Thomas. Originally published in the *New England Journal of Medicine.* Reprinted by permission of Viking Penguin, Inc. "Late Night Thoughts on Listening to Mahler's Ninth Symphony." from *Late Night Thoughts on Mahler's Ninth Symphony.* Copyright © 1982 by Lewis Thomas. Reprinted by permission of Viking Penguin, Inc. "Notes on Punctuation" from *The Medusa and the Snail.* Copyright © 1979 by Lewis Thomas. Reprinted by permission of Viking Penguin Inc.

Barbara Tuchman, "The Historian as Artist," "Mankind's Better Moments," and "On Our Birthday—America As Idea." Reprinted by permission of Russell & Volkening as agents for the author. Copyright © 1981 by Barbara Tuchman.

Alice Walker, "Am I Blue?" from *Living By the Word,* copyright © 1986 by Alice Walker, reprinted by permission of Harcourt Brace Jovanovich, Inc. "Father" from *Living By the Word,* copyright © 1985 by Alice Walker, reprinted by permission of Harcourt Brace Jovanovich, Inc. (This essay includes "The Democratic Order, Such Things in Twenty Years I Understood" from *Once,* copyright © 1968 by Alice Walker, reprinted by permission of Harcourt Brace Jovanovich, Inc.) "In Search of Our Mothers' Gardens" from *In Search of Our Mothers' Gardens,* copyright © 1974 by Alice Walker, reprinted by permission of Harcourt Brace Jovanovich, Inc. (This essay includes "Women" from *Revolutionary Petunias & Other Poems,* copyright © 1970 by Alice Walker, reprinted by permission of Harcourt Brace Jovanovich, Inc.)

E. B. White, "Education" from *One Man's Meat.* Copyright 1944 by E. B. White. Reprinted by permission of Harper & Row, Publishers, Inc. "Farewell, My Lovely!" from *Essays of E. B. White* (Harper & Row); © 1936, 1964 The New Yorker Magazine, Inc. Originally published in *The New Yorker* in 1936 over the pseudonym "Lee Strout White." Richard L. Strout had submitted a manuscript on the Ford, and White, with his collaboration, rewrote it. "Once More to the Lake," "The Ring of Time," and "The Sea and the Wind That Blows," from *Essays of E. B. White.* Copyright © 1977 by E. B. White. Reprinted by permission of Harper & Row, Publishers, Inc.

Virginia Woolf, "The Death of the Moth," Middlebrow," and "Professions for Women" from *The Death of the Moth and Other Essays,* copyright 1942 by Harcourt Brace Jovanovich, Inc. and renewed 1970 by Marjorie T. Parsons, Executrix, reprinted by permission of the publisher, the Executors of the Virginia Woolf Estate, and The Hogarth Press.

Photo Credits

Virginia Woolf, AP/Wide World Photos; Isak Dinesen, The Bettmann Archive; E. B. White, Jill Krementz; George Orwell, AP/Wide World Photos; Barbara Tuchman, UPI/Bettmann Newsphotos; Lewis Thomas, Nancy Crampton; Doris Lessing, Jill Krementz; Richard Selzer, Carl L. Howard; Martin Luther King, Jr., Library of Congress; Edward Hoagland, Nancy Crampton; Joan Didion, Jill Krementz; Joyce Carol Oates, Nancy Crampton; James Baldwin, UPI/Bettmann Newsphotos; Russell Baker, UPI/Bettmann Newsphotos; Margaret Atwood, AP/Wide World Photos; Maxine Hong Kingston, Nancy Crampton; Stephen J. Gould, Harvard University News Office, Cambridge, MA; Alice Walker, AP/Wide World Photos; Richard Rodriguez, David R. Godine; Annie Dillard, Photo from Harper & Row Publishers, Inc.

Rhetorical Index

ANALOGY

VIRGINIA WOOLF   *The Death of the Moth*   9
ISAK DINESEN   *The Oxen*   22
ISAK DINESEN   *Some African Birds*   24
E. B. WHITE   *The Ring of Time*   50
GEORGE ORWELL   *Politics and the English Language*   80
LEWIS THOMAS   *Computers*   131
LEWIS THOMAS   *The Iks*   134
RUSSELL BAKER   *Let Them Play Guitars*   205
RICHARD SELZER   *The Pen and the Scalpel*   233
MARTIN LUTHER KING, JR.   *I Have a Dream*   242
JOYCE CAROL OATES   *On Boxing*   315
ALICE WALKER   *Am I Blue?*   426
ANNIE DILLARD   *Untying the Knot*   441

ARGUMENT AND PERSUASION

VIRGINIA WOOLF   *Middlebrow*   12
E. B. WHITE   *Education*   50
GEORGE ORWELL   *A Hanging*   69
GEORGE ORWELL   *Politics and the English Language*   80
BARBARA TUCHMAN   *The Historian as Artist*   105
BARBARA TUCHMAN   *On Our Birthday—America as Idea*   110
LEWIS THOMAS   *Computers*   131
LEWIS THOMAS   *The Iks*   134
DORIS LESSING   *A Deep Darkness: A Review of* Out of Africa   158
JAMES BALDWIN   *Fifth Avenue, Uptown*   173
JAMES BALDWIN   *The Discovery of What It Means to Be an American*   181

JAMES BALDWIN   *If Black English Isn't a Language, Then Tell Me, What Is?*   187

RUSSELL BAKER   *The Flag*   193

MARTIN LUTHER KING, JR.   *I Have a Dream*   242

MARTIN LUTHER KING, JR.   *Letter from Birmingham City Jail*   246

MARTIN LUTHER KING, JR.   *Where Do We Go from Here: Chaos or Community?*   260

JOYCE CAROL OATES   *The Profane Art*   311

STEPHEN JAY GOULD   *Women's Brains*   363

STEPHEN JAY GOULD   *Evolution as Fact and Theory*   379

RICHARD RODRIGUEZ   *Children of a Marriage*   410

ALICE WALKER   *In Search of Our Mothers' Gardens*   417

ANNIE DILLARD   *Push It*   462

CAUSE AND EFFECT

VIRGINIA WOOLF   *Professions for Women*   4

E. B. WHITE   *Once More to the Lake*   44

E. B. WHITE   *The Sea and the Wind that Blows*   61

GEORGE ORWELL   *Politics and the English Language*   80

GEORGE ORWELL   *Why I Write*   95

BARBARA TUCHMAN   *On Our Birthday—America as Idea*   110

LEWIS THOMAS   *Late Night Thoughts on Listening to Mahler's Ninth Symphony*   141

DORIS LESSING   *Being Prohibited*   147

DORIS LESSING   *My Father*   151

JAMES BALDWIN   *Autobiographical Notes*   168

JAMES BALDWIN   *If Black English Isn't a Language, Then Tell Me, What Is?*   187

RICHARD SELZER   *Bald!*   218

EDWARD HOAGLAND   *Violence, Violence*   275

JOAN DIDION   *Marrying Absurd*   285

JOAN DIDION   *Why I Write*   298

MARGARET ATWOOD   *Travels Back*   327

MAXINE HONG KINGSTON   *No Name Woman*   343

MAXINE HONG KINGSTON   *High School Reunion*   353

STEPHEN JAY GOULD   *Women's Brains*   363

RICHARD RODRIGUEZ   *Complexion*   389

RICHARD RODRIGUEZ   *Children of a Marriage*   410

CLASSIFICATION

VIRGINIA WOOLF   *Middlebrow*   12
GEORGE ORWELL   *Politics and the English Language*   80
GEORGE ORWELL   *Why I Write*   95
LEWIS THOMAS   *Notes on Punctuation*   137
STEPHEN JAY GOULD   *A Biological Homage to Mickey Mouse*   369

COMPARISON AND CONTRAST

VIRGINIA WOOLF   *Middlebrow*   12
E. B. WHITE   *Once More to the Lake*   44
E. B. WHITE   *Education*   50
LEWIS THOMAS   *Computers*   131
LEWIS THOMAS   *The Iks*   134
JAMES BALDWIN   *Fifth Avenue, Uptown*   173
JAMES BALDWIN   *The Discovery of What It Means to Be an American*   181
JAMES BALDWIN   *If Black English Isn't a Language, Then Tell Me, What Is?*   187
RUSSELL BAKER   *The Flag*   193
RUSSELL BAKER   *Let Them Play Guitars*   205
RICHARD SELZER   *Bald!*   218
RICHARD SELZER   *The Pen and the Scalpel*   213
MARTIN LUTHER KING, JR.   *I Have A Dream*   242
MARTIN LUTHER KING, JR.   *Letter from Birmingham City Jail*   246
MARTIN LUTHER KING, JR.   *Where Do We Go from Here: Chaos or Community?*   260
EDWARD HOAGLAND   *What I Think, What I Am*   278
MARGARET ATWOOD   *Great Unexpectations*   332
STEPHEN JAY GOULD   *A Biological Homage to Mickey Mouse*   369
RICHARD RODRIGUEZ   *Complexion*   389
RICHARD RODRIGUEZ   *Across the Borders of History*   394
RICHARD RODRIGUEZ   *Children of a Marriage*   410

DEFINITION

VIRGINIA WOOLF   *Middlebrow*   12
GEORGE ORWELL   *Politics and the English Language*   80

BARBARA TUCHMAN   *The Historian as Artist*   105

BARBARA TUCHMAN   *On Our Birthday—America as Idea*   110

JAMES BALDWIN   *If Black English Isn't a Language, Then Tell Me,
                    What Is?*   187

RUSSELL BAKER   *The Flag*   193

RICHARD SELZER   *Bald!*   218

RICHARD SELZER   *The Pen and the Scalpel*   233

EDWARD HOAGLAND   *What I Think, What I Am*   278

JOAN DIDION   *On Self-Respect*   288

JOAN DIDION   *On Morality*   293

JOYCE CAROL OATES   *The Profane Art*   311

JOYCE CAROL OATES   *On Boxing*   315

JOYCE CAROL OATES   *"State-of-the-Art Car": The Ferrari
                        Testarossa*   318

MARGARET ATWOOD   *Travels Back*   327

MAXINE HONG KINGSTON   *The Wild Man of the Green Swamp*   357

RICHARD RODRIGUEZ   *Complexion*   389

DESCRIPTION

VIRGINIA WOOLF   *The Death of the Moth*   9

ISAK DINESEN   *The Oxen*   22

ISAK DINESEN   *Some African Birds*   24

E. B. WHITE   *Once More to the Lake*   44

E. B. WHITE   *The Ring of Time*   50

GEORGE ORWELL   *A Hanging*   69

GEORGE ORWELL   *Shooting an Elephant*   73

GEORGE ORWELL   *"The Moon Under Water"*   91

LEWIS THOMAS   *The Iks*   134

DORIS LESSING   *My Father*   151

JAMES BALDWIN   *Fifth Avenue, Uptown*   173

RICHARD SELZER   *Lessons from the Art*   211

RICHARD SELZER   *A Mask On the Face of Death*   222

EDWARD HOAGLAND   *The Courage of Turtles*   269

JOAN DIDION   *On Morality*   293

JOAN DIDION   *Miami*   304

JOYCE CAROL OATES   *"State-of-the-Art Car": The Ferrari
                        Testarossa*   318

MARGARET ATWOOD   *Travels Back*   327

ALICE WALKER   *Am I Blue?*   426

ALICE WALKER   *Father*   431

ANNIE DILLARD   *Untying the Knot*   441

ANNIE DILLARD   *Singing With the Fundamentalists*   452

HUMOR, IRONY, SATIRE

VIRGINIA WOOLF   *Middlebrow*   12

E. B. WHITE   *Farewell, My Lovely!*   38

E. B. WHITE   *Education*   50

GEORGE ORWELL   *Shooting an Elephant*   73

LEWIS THOMAS   *Notes on Punctuation*   137

RUSSELL BAKER   *The Flag*   193

RUSSELL BAKER   *Growing Up*   198

RUSSELL BAKER   *Let Them Play Guitars*   205

RICHARD SELZER   *Bald!*   218

JOAN DIDION   *Marrying Absurd*   285

MARGARET ATWOOD   *Great Unexpectations*   332

MAXINE HONG KINGSTON   *No Name Woman*   343

MAXINE HONG KINGSTON   *High School Reunion*   353

STEPHEN JAY GOULD   *Women's Brains*   363

STEPHEN JAY GOULD   *A Biological Homage to Mickey Mouse*   369

ANNIE DILLARD   *An American Childhood*   445

ILLUSTRATION

VIRGINIA WOOLF   *Professions for Women*   4

ISAK DINESEN   *Some African Birds*   24

E. B. WHITE   *Farewell, My Lovely!*   38

GEORGE ORWELL   *Politics and the English Language*   80

GEORGE ORWELL   *Why I Write*   95

BARBARA TUCHMAN   *The Historian as Artist*   105

BARBARA TUCHMAN   *Humanity's Better Moments*   113

LEWIS THOMAS   *Notes on Punctuation*   137

DORIS LESSING   *A Deep Darkness: A Review of* Out of Africa   158

JAMES BALDWIN   *If Black English Isn't a Language, Then Tell Me, What Is?*   187

RUSSELL BAKER   *Let Them Play Guitars*   205

RICHARD SELZER   *Lessons from the Art*   211

RICHARD SELZER   *A Mask on the Face of Death*   222

MARTIN LUTHER KING, JR.   *Letter from Birmingham City Jail*   246

EDWARD HOAGLAND   *The Courage of Turtles*   269

JOAN DIDION   *Marrying Absurd*   285

JOYCE CAROL OATES   *The Profane Art*   311

MARGARET ATWOOD   *Adrienne Rich: Poems, Selected and New*   336

MAXINE HONG KINGSTON   *No Name Woman*   343

STEPHEN JAY GOULD   *Women's Brains*   363

STEPHEN JAY GOULD   *A Biological Homage to Mickey Mouse*   369

ALICE WALKER   *In Search of Our Mothers' Gardens*   417

ANNIE DILLARD   *Push It*   462

NARRATION

VIRGINIA WOOLF   *The Death of the Moth*   9

ISAK DINESEN   *The Oxen*   22

ISAK DINESEN   *Old Knudsen*   28

E. B. WHITE   *Once More to the Lake*   44

GEORGE ORWELL   *A Hanging*   69

GEORGE ORWELL   *Shooting an Elephant*   73

BARBARA TUCHMAN   *Humanity's Better Moments*   113

DORIS LESSING   *Being Prohibited*   147

DORIS LESSING   *My Father*   151

JAMES BALDWIN   *Autobiographical Notes*   168

JAMES BALDWIN   *The Discovery of What It Means to Be an American*   181

RUSSELL BAKER   *Growing Up*   198

RICHARD SELZER   *Lessons from the Art*   211

RICHARD SELZER   *A Mask on the Face of Death*   222

EDWARD HOAGLAND   *The Courage of Turtles*   269

JOAN DIDION   *Why I Write*   298

MARGARET ATWOOD   *Travels Back*   327

MAXINE HONG KINGSTON   *No Name Woman*   343

MAXINE HONG KINGSTON   *The Wild Man of the Green Swamp*   357

RICHARD RODRIGUEZ   *Complexion*   389

RICHARD RODRIGUEZ   *Across the Borders of History*   394

ALICE WALKER   *Am I Blue?*   426
ALICE WALKER   *Father*   431
ANNIE DILLARD   *An American Childhood*   445
ANNIE DILLARD   *Singing With the Fundamentalists*   452

PROCESS ANALYSIS

VIRGINIA WOOLF   *The Death of the Moth*   9
E. B. WHITE   *Farewell, My Lovely!*   28
RICHARD SELZER   *Lessons from the Art*   211
RICHARD SELZER   *Bald!*   218
RICHARD SELZER   *A Mask on the Face of Death*   222
JOAN DIDION   *Why I Write*   298
MARGARET ATWOOD   *Adrienne Rich: Poems, Selected and New*   336
STEPHEN JAY GOULD   *A Biological Homage to Mickey Mouse*   369